MANCHESTER UNITED
THE FORGOTTEN
FIXTURES

MANCHESTER UNITED
THE FORGOTTEN
FIXTURES

IAIN McCARTNEY   **FOREWORD BY PAT CRERAND**

breedon **books**
PUBLISHING

First published in Great Britain in 2009 by
The Breedon Books Publishing Company Limited
Breedon House, 3 The Parker Centre,
Derby, DE21 4SZ.

British Library Cataloguing in Publication Data

A catalogue record for this book is available from the British Library.

ISBN 978-1-85983-702-3

Printed and bound by TJ International Ltd, Padstow, Cornwall.

Contents

Acknowledgements

I would like to thank all of the following for their time and help in supplying the odd piece of statistical information that I was missing, or recalling their travels in following the Red Army. To a greater extent I would like to thank those who delved into their collections to supply scans of programmes, tickets and photographs: Frank Gray, Dave Boult, John Hewitt, Mark Wylie, John Tuckett, Eifion Evans, James Davidson, James Thomas, John Mason, Kevin Donald, Peter Molyneux, Mick Groom, Ray Adler, Keith Wales, Simon Rumsey, Peter Rourke and Leslie Millman.

Dedication

This book is dedicated to the memory of the late Mike Dobbin, Manchester United supporter extraordinaire. I had the privilege of knowing Mike for over 30 years and he was going to contribute a few of his tales from following his beloved United over the years. However, sadly, circumstances prevented him from doing so and he passed away as I was putting the finishing touches to the book.

Born in Manchester, but having moved to London, Mike was the Travel Secretary of the London Fan Club and he held the most remarkable attendance record for following United. He was a well-known and highly respected supporter within the ranks of the travelling Red Army and it is safe to say that no matter where the United first-team were playing, you could guarantee that the ginger haired and bearded figure of Mike Dobbin would be there, armed with his customary carrier bag for the match programmes.

On the domestic front, I believe that the match at Old Trafford against Everton on 31 January (48 hours after his untimely death) would have been his 1,000th consecutive competitive fixture.

As for friendlies, he had only missed the second fixture in South Africa in the summer of 2008, necessary if he was to tick Nigeria off his countries visited to watch the shirts, since 1988. During that summer, however, Mike flew from South Africa to London, then drove to Oxford to watch a United reserve-team friendly, before heading back to Heathrow and flying back to Nigeria. Obviously, his 'record' does not take into consideration when United played two fixtures on the same day. Not even Mike Dobbin could manage that. He would, of course, have looked into it, just in case it was possible.

A number of years ago, Mike admitted that his plan regarding following United was to continue until he died, but he did acknowledge that there was always the possibility of other distractions coming between him and the club.

'You never know, I might meet a lady tomorrow. But then, United produce fewer complications than women and, of course, I'm sure I wouldn't get away with it if I was married!'

So, the Red Army is now one foot-soldier less. The 'Gypsy King' of Manchester United followers will wander the world no more. He will, however, never be forgotten.

No one could match Mike's record, not even Sir Alex Ferguson, and I can safely say that nobody ever will.

Mike Dobbin Supporter Supreme. RIP.

Author's Notes

From around 1990, the statistical details change slightly. Not in the actual layout, which remains the same throughout the book, but in the way the team is written. No longer did wearing the number-five shirt mean that the player concerned played in a central defensive role. It was simply a form of identification for the match programme or team sheet.

In season 1990–91, for example, you would get a team listing beginning: Sealey, Irwin, Donaghy, Bruce, Phelan, Pallister, with the player's shirt numbers reading one through to six. Although Mike Phelan wore the number five shirt, he played in midfield, with Bruce (number four) and Pallister (number six), the two central defenders.

Why then did I not write out the team as it played, for example, with a back four? That could have been done, but in later years would simply have led to confusion, for both myself and the reader, due to team formations altering on a match-by-match basis.

I therefore decided to keep the line ups from 1990 onwards as printed in the *Manchester United Official Yearbook*.

Foreword

For many, friendly fixtures are a meaningless 90 minutes of football, often played in a light-hearted manner, since the actual outcome is of little or no significance. It must, however, be said that they can form an important part of the fixture list, despite at times being considered little more than an inconvenience to players and supporters alike.

Pre-season, they can form the platform for the months ahead, easing the players back into the swing of things following their summer break, while at the same time they go a long way into helping new signings get to know their teammates.

From a personal point of view, one friendly in particular stands out in the memory and that was my Manchester United debut in Cork against Bolton Wanderers, way back in February 1963. If I am honest, I should actually have made that two friendlies, but the other was one that I always try to forget, as it was my return to the east end of Glasgow in 1966, a game at Celtic Park that saw us beaten 4–1.

More than me have made their United debuts in a friendly, as I share that distinction with the likes of Eric Cantona and Sir Bobby Charlton, among others.

In my role as a pundit with *MUTV*, I have the opportunity to travel the world with United, taking in most, if not all, of their friendlies, and it never ceases to amaze me the interest that there is in the club around the globe. The dedication of a small band of supporters who always turn up wherever there is a game, no matter where the fixture is being played, always surprises me.

Those non-competitive games, be they challenge matches, floodlight openings, testimonials or whatever, while playing a part in the United's seasonal fixture list, are rarely documented in detail or given any real coverage in the Manchester United histories that appear on the bookshelves. Here, however, in Iain McCartney's aptly named *Manchester United: The Forgotten Fixtures*, every post-war friendly played by United is covered in full, with a summary of the game, statistical details and numerous interesting tales surrounding many of those obscure 90 minutes of football.

With this publication, the post-war history of Manchester United is now complete.

Pat Crerand

MARCH 2009

Introduction

It used to be said, 'Join the navy and see the world'. Today, however, that particular saying could quite easily be rewritten to read 'follow a football team and see the world'. This is certainly true if you are a member of Manchester United's travelling 'Red Army'.

Thanks to United's continuing on-field success, European football is practically guaranteed each season, enabling trips to many, if not most, of Europe's most beautiful and historical cities. At the same time, United's global appeal sees pre-season tours offering exotic locations in which to watch the team play.

United's travels have always taken them from the top venues in European and, indeed, world football, to the smaller, more nondescript, venues, with many of the locations, such as Clyde's Shawfield Stadium and Real Madrid's Bernabeu, being simply incomparable.

The League Championship and domestic Cup triumphs and failures, along with those in the European competitions, have been well documented in the past, but here, for the first time, is the book that completes the Manchester United history in words and statistics. It takes you the length and breadth of Britain and beyond, from Mallorca to Melbourne and Israel to Iran, detailing often meaningless games of football at obscure, out-of-the-way places, while also looking back at the non-competitive fixtures played at Old Trafford.

Within *Manchester United: The Forgotten Fixtures* there are some 400-odd games. The testimonials, ground openings and everything in between from 1946 to the present day, bring Manchester United's statistical history up to date. Also included are the many strange events from these often briefly documented 90 minutes of football, and some unfamiliar names crop up in the United team line ups. The history of Manchester United Football Club is now complete.

The 1940s

A return to footballing normality was still a few months away in the aftermath of World War Two and Old Trafford was in a state of disrepair, with the club not only homeless but managerless. It was not until 19 February 1945 that Manchester United's managerial vacancy was officially filled, when Company Sergeant-Major Instructor Matt Busby, considered by many to be something of an average wing-half, who had played for Liverpool and Manchester City, as well as gaining international recognition with the Scottish national side, was named as the new man at the helm. Along with Welshman Jimmy Murphy, whom he appointed as his assistant, Busby proceeded to transform the club from an average First Division side into one capable of challenging for the top domestic honours.

The War League system had kept the majority of Manchester United players, most of whom were in the armed forces, ticking over fitness-wise. They often guested for a club near to where they were stationed, all the while achieving the minimum of success. However, despite this and despite finishing in the rather average mid-table League position of 14th at the end of season 1938–39, upon their return to the First Division in that last full pre-war campaign before the hostilities, United were the club that the FA invited to travel to Germany to play a British Army on the Rhine (BAOR) team in Hamburg on 20 March 1946.

As things turned out, it was a fixture fraught with problems from start to finish, and it must have made the Manchester United directors more than a little apprehensive about accepting similar invitations in the future.

It was originally planned for the United party to fly from Manchester's Ringway airport on the Monday prior to the game, but those plans were cancelled at the last minute, as the plane they were to travel on had not had its planned overhaul, and departure was scheduled for the following day.

As fate would have it, the Tuesday flight also encountered problems, being forced to land at Celle, about 70 miles from Hamburg, due to poor flying conditions. The two motor lorries that had been arranged to take the passengers to their intended destination then broke down, forcing the United players and directors to spend the night at an RAF station at Celle.

Wednesday morning saw alternative transport arrangements made – an RAF three-ton lorry – and it was a rather tired and fed up United team that arrived in Hamburg a mere two hours prior to the intended kick-off time. On their arrival, they were informed that they would have to make their return journey to England by rail and sea, as no planes were available as had been originally agreed.

It is little wonder then that Matt Busby's team failed to get the better of their Rhine Army opponents in a rather uninspired match, which was played before a crowd of around 25,000 servicemen inside the stadium and a considerable number of interested Germans, who claimed various vantage points overlooking the ground.

As the events on the field progressed, high-ranking army officers tried unsuccessfully to charter a special plane to take the United players and officials back to England. As it was, they had to travel to Badenhausen by road and then catch a train to Calais, using a special duty train normally reserved for brigadiers and colonels.

Matt Busby told Tom Jackson of the *Manchester Evening News*, 'I spoke to a major-general after the game and told him that plans for our flight back to England had

Players lining up prior to the BAOR game.

broken down. He was very concerned and said he would get in touch with Rhine Army Headquarters and try and arrange a Stirling Bomber to take us back. However, he was not able to do this and we must return by the longer route.

'League clubs have fixtures to fulfil at home and it is very unfair and very unsatisfactory that we shall get back only a few hours before we are due at Bradford on Saturday.'

The United manager did add, however, that the army arrangements for the visit were very good, but that it was an unfortunate series of events that had marred the trip.

Due to the change in arrangements, there was indeed every possibility that the United party would not manage to reach Bradford in time for their Saturday afternoon fixture. The Football League were duly informed, with secretary Fred Howarth saying, 'The responsibility so far as we are concerned rests with Manchester United. If the match is postponed, then United will have to pay compensation to Bradford. Clubs will probably think twice about going to play matches on the Continent if they meet difficulties like this.'

However, luck was finally on United's side as they arrived at London's Victoria Station on Friday afternoon after a long rail and sea trip. The party was rushed across the city in special transport to Euston, where they caught the 1pm train to Manchester, arriving back at the familiar London Road Station at around 6pm.

One wonders whether the above events had any echoes 10 years later, when the Football League were very much against United's participation in the European Cup?

The programme for the game versus BAOR, 20 March 1946.

ASSOCIATION FOOTBALL

MANCHESTER UNITED

versus

BAOR Combined Services
(Germany)

played at

Bahrenfeld Stadium, Hamburg

on

Wednesday, 20 March 1946

KICK-OFF 1415 hrs.

20 March 1946	**BAOR at Bahrenfeld Stadium, Hamburg**

Attendance: 25,000.

Lost: 2–1.

Scorer: Wrigglesworth.

Team: Tapken, Whalley, Walton, Carey, Chilton, Cockburn, Delaney, Smith, Hanlon, Pearson, Wrigglesworth.

With football, and indeed the country as a whole, still regaining its feet following World War Two, friendlies were not considered an important inclusion on many clubs' fixture lists. There were more pressing matters to hand, namely the rebuilding work on both stadium and team. Much can be said of Matt Busby's influence on the latter, as the three immediate post-war seasons saw his team finish runners-up in the First Division, a vast improvement on that 14th-place finish in season 1938–39.

While the League Championship was just outside Busby's grasp, early post-war success was achieved with a 4–2 FA Cup Final triumph against Lancashire rivals Blackpool in April 1948, which today is still considered one of the best ever witnessed beneath Wembley's twin towers.

Following their Cup victory and 11 days after their final League fixture of the season, a 4–1 home victory over Blackburn Rovers, Busby took his team to Ireland for a three-match, seven-day mini-tour, where they faced Bohemians, Shelbourne and Linfield.

The opening fixture, against a Bohemians Select XI at Dublin's Dalymount Park, attracted a crowd officially given as 37,500, but this was nothing more than an estimate, as many 'hundreds' according to eyewitnesses, pushed past police or scaled the walls of the ground to gain free admission. Those who did pay were certainly given good value for their money, with the FA Cup holders facing a testing 90 minutes, rather than the leisurely exhibition-style game that they perhaps anticipated. This was mainly due to the Bohemians side being augmented by six guest players, four coming from Blackpool, three of whom, Shimwell, Johnston and Hayward, were members of the Seasiders XI defeated at Wembley just over two weeks previously.

On a hard and bumpy playing surface, the *Manchester Evening Chronicle's* United correspondent, Alf Clarke, thought that United, who fielded eight of their Cup-winning side, had 'taken things too much for granted', as they struggled at times to contain their guest-enhanced opponents.

Captain Johnny Carey was back in his home city and was given a hero's welcome, before proceeding to turn in a superb performance, seldom putting a foot wrong. The crowd quickly warmed to the quality of football on offer and it was certainly fair that United took the lead in the 32nd minute. A through pass from Warner split the home defence, allowing Mitten the opportunity to shoot past MacAlinden, the guesting Coleraine goalkeeper. It was a lead that was short-lived, however, as seven minutes later O'Kelly grabbed an equaliser.

An injury to Delaney upset the rhythm of the visitors and, to a certain extent, the flow of the game, as did the home side's persistence in adapting offside tactics, which United failed to counter. At one point it looked as though the game was going to finish with the honours even, but then the O'Flanagan brothers crafted the winner. Arsenal's Kevin got the better of the United defence before passing to Michael to score the deciding goal.

12 May 1948	**Bohemians Select XI at Dalymount Park, Dublin.**

Attendance: 37,500.

Lost 2–1.

Scorer: Mitten.

Team: Crompton, Carey, McGlen, Anderson, Chilton, Warner, Delaney, Morris, Burke, Rowley, Mitten.

Substitutes: Hanlon for Delaney.

United returned to Dalymount Park four days later, this time to face what was classed as a Shelbourne Select XI, whose line up included seven Football League players.

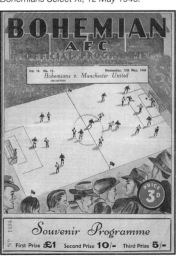

The programme for the match versus Bohemians Select XI, 12 May 1948.

Refreshed from their days of leisure in the Emerald Isle, United overcame the opposition, who were obviously unfamiliar with each other, by four goals to three in an entertaining 90 minutes for the 25,000 crowd, who paid gate receipts of £1,650.

The Shelbourne XI were caught cold as United began the game at a whirlwind speed, scoring twice in the opening 11 minutes, with goals from Buckle and Anderson. However, the frantic opening soon gave way to a more relaxed pace and in United's case it was slightly too relaxed, as they allowed their hosts back into the game, with Broome of Derby County reducing the advantage just before the interval.

Broome was again on target soon after the restart to level the score, but Eddie Buckle, United's most promising forward, restored the two-goal advantage with a terrific drive, as United once again took command of the game. Their lead was again increased in the 77th minute, thanks to an own-goal by Leuty of Derby County as he attempted to keep out Rowley.

Rowley showed moments of brilliance, while Mitten came to the fore in the last 20 minutes with some fine wing play, giving Manchester City's Sproston some anxious moments. In defence, Carey was his usual unflappable self in front of an appreciative 'home' crowd, while Warner, Chilton and McGlen were also in fine form, Warner in particular, as he had to contend with the irrepressible Peter Doherty.

Ten minutes from the end, Broome's third goal gave Shelbourne a slight glimmer of hope that they could perhaps snatch a draw, but the United defence held firm and managed to subdue any attacks that came their way, with the score remaining 4–3 in United's favour, as another 'goal' from Rowley, described by the *Cork Examiner* as 'the best of the match', was disallowed as offside.

16 May 1948 **Shelbourne Select XI at Dalymount Park, Dublin.**

Attendance: 25,000.

Won: 4–3.

Scorers: Buckle 2, Anderson, opp. own-goal.

Team: Crompton, Carey, Ball, Warner, Chilton, McGlen, Hanlon, Anderson, Rowley, Buckle, Mitten.

The third and final match of the close-season tour took United to Northern Ireland and to Windsor Park, Belfast, where they came up against Linfield, who had also felt the need to add guest players to their side.

Whether it was a tactical plan by the United manager, or simply the way the opening minutes of the game unfolded is uncertain, but United once again stormed into an early lead, with three goals in the opening 11 minutes. However, if the tactics were to score two or three early goals and then simply contain their opponents with some less strenuous play, then the strategy backfired.

With United easing off perhaps a little too much, Linfield stormed back into the game, with Burrell and McMorran reducing the arrears prior to the interval and setting up an interesting second half.

Sadly for those present, the second half fell a little flat compared to the first, with no further scoring, although there was some fine play from both sides. The inexperienced Ball, Lowrie and Lynn gave a good account of themselves.

19 May 1948	**Linfield at Windsor Park, Belfast.**

Attendance: 30,000.

Won: 3–2.

Scorers: Morris, Buckle, Rowley.

Team: Crompton, Carey, Ball, Warner, Lynn, Lowrie, Hanlon, Morris, Rowley, Buckle, Mitten.

The end-of-season break in Ireland must have been to the liking of Matt Busby and his players as they returned 12 months later, but this time they played only two games, against Shamrock Rovers and a Bohemians Select XI.

Months before the return trip, with season 1948–49 still in its infancy, United travelled north to Edinburgh to face Hibernian in a benefit match for the family of former Hibs manager William McCartney, who had recently died.

Inviting the FA Cup holders to Easter Road created considerable interest in and around the Scottish capital, as the 45,000 attendance shows, but there was more to the selection of United to participate in this fund-raising fixture than meets the eye.

Matt Busby had played under McCartney while guesting for the Scottish side during World War Two, commenting in the match programme: 'My association with Mr McCartney, "the boss", was indeed a very happy one and he did try to help me at all times while I was with his club. I am delighted to be able to make a little return for his many kindnesses and I do hope the visit of Manchester United will be a most successful one.'

William McCartney also had family ties with United, as his father, John McCartney, (whom he had succeeded as manager of Hearts in 1919), had played for and captained Newton Heath way back in 1894. (Adding to the trivia aspect, John McCartney was also my grandfather's cousin).

As for the match itself, which had the early evening kick-off time of 6pm, forcing many to leave work early, United enjoyed a 1–0 victory. Many considered the result to be slightly flattering to the visitors, as the home side had the bulk of the play, with Crompton keeping the Hibs forwards at bay on numerous occasions.

It was not until the referee requested a white ball to be brought on as the light began to fade that United began to look threatening. The white ball idea was something of a novelty, with Jimmy Delaney giving it a close examination at the first opportunity. It had been the idea of the Hibs trainer, who had painted two of the ordinary brown balls with gloss paint and arranged with the referee beforehand to use them.

Having survived a Hibs attack, Crompton managing to get a hand to a Reilly shot, United moved forward, with Buckle scoring what was to be the only goal of the game as he hit a rising shot from around 20 yards out, which Kerr in the Hibs goal could do little about.

As it was, the result mattered little and in the boardroom following the game, Mr H.S. Swan, the Hibs chairman, thanked everyone for the contribution to the fund, with the end total expected to be between £5,500 and £6,000 and the gross drawings from the game amounting to £4,021 and seven shillings.

After the match there was a dinner in the North British Station Hotel, with an invitation extended to Hibs by the Manchester United directors to visit Old Trafford for a return fixture. Following the meal and the various speeches came the highlight of the evening, with the players of both teams entertaining those in attendance with their 'party piece' songs. Johnny Carey and Jack Warner received rapturous applause for their renderings in Italian and Welsh respectively. The United players also received tartan travel rugs.

The programme for the match versus Hibernian, 22 September 1948.

22 September 1948	Hibernian at Easter Road, Edinburgh.

Attendance: 30,225.

Won: 1—0.

Scorer: Buckle.

Team: Crompton, Ball, Carey, Anderson, Chilton, McGlen, Delaney, Buckle, Rowley, Pearson, Mitten.

Back across the Irish Sea, the first of the two end-of-season fixtures took United to Glenmalure Park, Dublin, on 29 May, to face Shamrock Rovers. By the end of half-time they found themselves two goals down, and by the end of the game, having managed to get back on level terms, they had squandered enough scoring opportunities to win both of their scheduled fixtures.

As in the previous season's fixtures, the host club had strengthened their side with guest players, Middlesbrough's Hardwick, Walsh of West Bromwich Albion and Everton's Farrell and Eglington bolstering the Rovers line up, but not exactly boosting the crowd, although heavy rain prior to kick-off got the blame for the poor attendance of 18,000 (paying £960).

All the 'guests' played a part in Shamrock achieving their two-goal lead, but it was Eglington on the left wing, reportedly 'always to be at his best when opposed to Carey', whose good work set up Coad to score after only five minutes.

Play moved from end to end, but failed to produce the further goals that the crowd craved, with the United forward duo of Rowley and Mitten coming closest to scoring for the visitors. However, it was not until immediately prior to the interval that the second goal was scored. A long clearance out of defence by Rovers centre-half Daly saw Chilton and Walsh tussle for possession, but in his efforts to head the ball back to Jack Crompton, the big United centre-half could only watch as the ball floated over his goalkeeper's hands and into the net.

Twelve minutes after half-time United pulled a goal back, a Jack Rowley 'special', leaving Godwin helpless as the ball flew past him from 30 yards, high into the roof of the net. Slowly they began to gain the upper hand and Downie missed two easy opportunities to give United the lead. The first was a simple header from a few yards out, after he had hit the crossbar. The second saw him shoot directly at Godwin, with only the 'keeper to beat.

United continued to press and it did not come as a surprise when they equalised. Good work between Mitten and Pearson resulted in the latter scoring with an excellent effort.

29 May 1949	Shamrock Rovers at Glenmalure Park, Dublin.

Attendance: 18,000.

Draw: 2—2.

Scorers: Rowley, Pearson.

Team: Crompton, Carey, Aston, Lowrie, Chilton, Cockburn, Delaney, Downie, Rowley, Pearson, Mitten.

The second of the two fixtures, on 1 June, took United back to the familiar surroundings of Dalymount Park, with a Bohemians XI once again the opposition.

It took United only two minutes to open the scoring. A Delaney free-kick was headed against the Bohemians crossbar by Downie, only for Rowley to snatch the rebound and hit it home.

Unfortunately for Downie, he was injured amid the goalmouth scramble and was forced to leave the field, being replaced by 17-year-old Frank Clempson. Downie's injury was later diagnosed as a fractured ankle and was something of a blow to both club and player, as he had only signed for United in March from Bradford Park Avenue for a fee of £18,000. For his replacement there were to be no teenage heroics or headlines, as he only lasted 15 minutes before an injury forced him to leave the field as well. United played for the remainder of the first half with only 10 men, but after the interval they were back at full strength, another 17-year-old, Brian Birch, filling the vacancy in the United forward line.

Despite his obvious nerves on what was his United debut, Birch quickly settled into the flow of things and to a passing observer would have come across as a seasoned professional, such was his passing and all-round contribution to the game in general. He was perhaps unfortunate not to mark his debut with a goal, but he just failed to connect with a pass from his idol Stan Pearson.

Bohemians, strengthened with five players from Blackpool and one each from Arsenal, Preston North End, Shelbourne and Drumcondra, were no match for an on-song United. They were particularly poor in attack, with Blackpool's Mortensen the only real threat, as full-backs Ball and Aston kept wingers Jackson and Henderson under strict control.

It was not until the 62nd minute that United scored their second goal. Rowley once again showed his alertness in front of goal, winning a goalmouth scramble to drive the ball home after a shot from Birch had hit the crossbar. Pearson added a third eight minutes later, effectively bringing the game to an end, although Mortensen did score a consolation effort for the home side five minutes later.

---

1 June 1949   **Bohemians Select XI at Dalymount Park, Dublin.**

Attendance: 22,000.

Won: 3–1.

Scorers: Rowley 2, Pearson.

Team: Crompton, Ball, Aston, Anderson, Lynn, Cockburn, Delaney, Downie, Rowley, Pearson, Mitten.

Substitutes: Clempson for Downie, Birch for Clempson.

The following day's *Manchester Evening Chronicle* carried the headline 'United Find a New Star', with the article serving as something of an introduction of the practically unknown Salford-born Birch to the newspapers' readership.

Alf Clarke's brief article mentioned that Birch had been with United since he was 14, having joined the club from St Ambrose School, and having represented the Association of Boys' Clubs and Salford Boys. Sadly, his last line prediction failed to come true. 'I consider that he will be an England proposition in five years' wrote the United scribe. It was season 1950–51 before Birch appeared in the United side with any regularity, having made his League debut against West Bromwich in August 1949, and in 1952, after a mere 15 appearances and five goals, he moved to Wolverhampton Wanderers.

The 1950s

Much can be made of United's style of football in the early 1950s from the fact that, despite not being among the game's honours, they were much in demand to participate in friendly fixtures at home and abroad, with approaches being made to the directors from European clubs, all of which were politely declined in favour of the aforementioned trips across the Irish Sea. However, when an invitation to play a series of games in Canada and the United States of America popped through the Old Trafford letterbox, it was eagerly accepted. Had the directors been aware of what was in store they would probably have opted for their usual haunts nearer to home.

No sooner had the 1949–50 season drawn to a close than the United players and directors were heading for Southampton to board the *Queen Mary* for the journey across the Atlantic to Canada. Today such a journey would be made in a matter of hours, rather than days, but the United party were certainly not bored on their Atlantic crossing.

Each morning they were up at 7.30am for training in the ship's fully equipped gymnasium, working out on the various rowing machines, dumb-bells and punch bags, but there was also plenty of time for less strenuous activities, such as table tennis and darts, with the United players taking on members of the ship's crew.

When it came to the darts, it was the crew members who came out on top 6–3, but the rolling and pitching of the ship did little to prevent United coming out on top in the table-tennis, with goalkeeper Jack Crompton winning a cigarette case, having beaten Stan Pearson in the semi-final and Johnny Carey in the Final.

In those somewhat distant days, neither the *Manchester Evening News* nor the *Evening Chronicle* sent reporters with the United party, relying instead on 'a special correspondent' from wherever United happened to be playing to relay the reports and any other snippets of news back to England. With football not something that those chosen journalists might normally cover, and Manchester United as familiar to most Americans as black pudding, the reports wired from the States often provided interesting reading.

In the *Evening Chronicle* for 8 May the correspondent wrote: 'Welcoming the players and officials when they disembarked from the *Queen Mary* were Mr James McGuire, president of the American Soccer League, and other sporting officials', but he failed to identify Matt Busby, as he continued, 'Dr William MacLean, United's manager, said that his players were fit for the ordeal ahead, but expressed the hope that they might avoid the heat waves he had heard about. "We are here for a vacation, but also to show you our brand of first-class English soccer. Above all we have come with the interests of goodwill between our peoples".'

The *Evening News* appeared to have retained the better of the local press corps, as their man on the spot identified Dr MacLean as merely a director.

The United headquarters were at the Paramount Hotel on West 46th Street, which had put up a large banner in the lobby saying 'Welcome to the great Manchester United soccer team', and, following a good night's sleep, the players had a training session at the Trilborough Stadium before leaving for their first fixture of the tour.

The first game in the 12-match tour took United to Toronto on 10 May, where they faced the National League All-Stars in front of 14,000 enthusiastic spectators, twice as many as a professional baseball game being played at a nearby stadium attracted.

Despite the time spent on the high seas, United need little time to show that they were not there for a leisurely holiday and, although the Chicago side contained eight former Scottish professionals, they were no match for the visitors, with Jack Crompton in the United goal only handling the ball on three occasions, with one of them being when he picked the ball from the back of his net following an offside 'goal' early in the game.

Henry Cockburn opened the scoring for United in the ninth minute when his header into the home goalmouth bounced through the hands of goalkeeper Arends, who appeared to have it well covered, and into the net. The second goal came six minutes later, although there seems to have been a little confusion between Bill Entwhistle, reporting for the *Evening News,* and McKenzie Porter, the *Evening Chronicle*'s man at the match, as the former states that 'the second came from a Mitten corner, which Delaney transferred to Pearson and Stanley rapped home', while the latter wrote, 'Downie got his first six minutes later and that was all the scoring until the 33rd minute.' A local Toronto paper goes along with the second version, stating 'Johnny Downie booted home the second goal when he converted a fine pass from Delaney.'

Confusion reigns further, as the *Evening News* goes on to report the third goal as 'Rowley rattled in with a daisy cutter from 30 yards, which Arends watched creep inside the upright', while those who purchased the *Chronicle* read that following Downie's goal 'that was all the scoring until after 30 minutes when a shot along the carpet from Pearson found the corner of the net.' Once again the Toronto-based paper agreed with the latter: 'The best goal was Stanley Pearson's tally, third for the winners. Pearson, kicking left-footed, shot from 25 yards out and grazed the upright with a rapier-like try which gave Arends no chance.'

In any case, it was now 3–0 to United, but while both the Manchester papers agreed that it was Downie who had headed home, two minutes prior to half-time, to make it four, back in Toronto Ed Waring wrote: 'Just before the interval, Rowley made the count 4–0 with a hard shot.' And there were still a further 11 games to play!

Local Toronto reporter Ed Waring (whether he was familiar with the game or not is not recorded) did not seem too impressed by the first half of the evening's entertainment, writing: 'Although four goals were scored in the initial stanza, it certainly wasn't a fair reflection of the play. At least two of the counters were on the shady side, while another could have been averted had the Stars' defence been on its toes.'

In the second half, which saw United enjoy the novelty of playing under floodlights and with a white ball, a goal from Jack Rowley, crashing home a pass from Delaney, was all the crowd had to savour, despite some excellent play by Man of the Match Jimmy Delaney, whom the crowd christened 'The Rumba Man'. However, despite his elementary mistake for United's first goal, the All-Stars goalkeeper Arends kept the score down with a number of fine saves.

Commenting on the game, Johnny Carey thought the standard of the opposition, which had been made up mainly of players of Scottish descent, was similar to that of a Football League Third Division side, and he noted that they had been allowed to bring on three substitutes during the second half.

---

10 May 1950 **National League All-Stars at CNE Stadium Toronto.**

Attendance: 12,049.

Won: 5–0.

Scorers: Downie 2, Cockburn, Pearson, Rowley, or Rowley 2, Cockburn, Downie, Pearson.

Team: Crompton, Carey, Ball, Warner, Chilton, Cockburn, Delaney, Pearson, Rowley, Downie, Mitten.

Following this opening fixture the local Canadian press filled a few column inches with slightly more than the details of United's emphatic victory, as much was made of the fact that the Ontario government had decided to tax any game in which an English touring team played. This came as something of a blow to the six Toronto-based and two Hamilton-based teams from which United's opponents had been drawn.

The attendance was given as 'just under 10,000', despite some sources giving it as 14,000. Receipts were $13,720 and of this, the government claimed $1,783, ground rent soaked up a further $2,948, the Dominion Football Association took a four per cent cut – a further $477.44 – and the American Soccer League, the tour sponsors, came in for a guarantee of 80 per cent of the gate after taxes, which amounted to $4,000. That left between $2,000 and $3,000 to pay all the other expenses, including advertising, leaving the eight clubs whose players took part with around $100 each if they were lucky.

There was also some furore just prior to the game itself, with the National League officials becoming involved in a confrontation with the union as, in a bid to cut expenses, they had decided to drop the brass band. However, they required *God Save the King* to be played, but the union governing the power facilities said 'No union music, no union power'. The band played, receiving between $100 and $200, probably more than United's opponents!

Returning to New York, Matt Busby prepared his players to face a New York All-Stars side at Randalls Island's Trilborough Stadium.

Rather surprisingly, Eamon Dunphy, in his book *A Strange Kind of Glory – Sir Matt Busby and Manchester United*, wrote, 'Soon after they docked in New York, though, the glamour [enjoyed on the crossing of the Atlantic] began to pale. Results were poor, the travelling, mostly by train, soon wore them out.' If the performance against the American Soccer League was when they were tired, a resounding 9–2 victory, one wonders what sort of performance they would have turned in otherwise? United once again thrilled the predominantly novice American crowd with another display of attacking football, notching up nine goals in the 11-goal exhibition.

Within five minutes of the kick-off, the visitors were in front, Mitten setting up Downie for the first of a quartet of goals. Ten minutes later Pearson added a second, slamming the ball home after Mitten's cross had been blocked by a defender.

Much to United's surprise, and the crowd's delight, the home side pulled a goal back in the 20th minute, Maca scoring from Gaetjen's pass, but their joy was short-lived, as Downie put United 3–1 in front minutes later. Three minutes prior to the interval, however, the Americans scored a second through Gaetjen after Crompton failed to hold a shot at goal.

After the interval there was to be no spirited fightback, as United took command of the second half. Mitten scored from the penalty spot after Watman

The programme for the match versus National League All-Stars, 10 May 1950.

handled. Nine minutes later United were 6–2 in front, Downie notching both goals with headers.

Despite their unassailable advantage, United continued to push forward at every opportunity and added to their tally in the 83rd minute through Pearson from Mitten's centre and again in the 86th and 87th minutes with a Bogan header and a 20-yard drive from Rowley.

The United States of America 1950 Tour Pennant for Manchester United.

14 May 1950	New York All-Stars at New York.

Attendance: 12,000.

Won: 9–2.

Scorers: Downie 4, Pearson 2, Mitten (pen.), Bogan, Rowley.

Team: Crompton, Carey, Ball, Lowrie, Chilton, Cockburn, Bogan, Pearson, Rowley, Downie, Mitten.

If United had found their opening two games a leisurely stroll, they were given something of a wake-up call in the third fixture of the tour when they came up against the New England All-Stars at Fall River, Massachusetts. Here they had to put up a spirited second half performance in order to achieve their victory.

As they had done in their previous two fixtures, United took an early lead, Bogan's cross being converted by Rowley as goalkeeper Romanowicz was caught out of position. This time, however, United failed to capitalise on the opportunities created by their obviously superior playing strength, as it was not until five minutes prior to half-time that they managed to score a second; Downie netting from a Pearson pass.

Programme and line ups for the match versus New York All-Stars, 14 May 1950.

After the interval United were seldom in the game as the All-Stars kept them tightly under control, with teenage local boy Costa enjoying a particularly good game against Charlie Mitten.

In the 77th minute, the home side had an opportunity to pull a goal back when a penalty was awarded against Chilton (or Pearson, depending on which 'special correspondent' you care to believe). American international Eddie Souza, however, hit the spot kick against the post. Had it gone in, United could have had their backs to the wall for the remainder of the game, with some of the play being rather physical, but there was little in the way of goalmouth action and the game fizzled out.

17 May 1950	New England All-Stars at Fall River, Massachusetts.

Attendance: 3,704.

Won: 2–0.

Scorers: Rowley, Downie.

Team: Crompton, McNulty, Ball, Lowrie, Chilton, Cockburn, Bogan, Pearson, Rowley, Downie, Mitten.

News filtering home from America was not all about how the tour was progressing, as rumours appeared regarding approaches being made to United players with offers of big money moves to certain South American clubs. Stoke City's Neil Franklin and George Mountford had already hit the headlines when they had admitted that they had signed two-year contracts for Bogotá's Santa Fe club, a move that was in breach of FA rule 23, which stated that no player was allowed to join with or against any club not a member of one of the associations affiliated to FIFA. The Santa Fe club was not a member.

Programme and line ups for the Kearny-Philadelphia Select Match on 21 May 1950. News reads 'Manchester United acclaimed by all after powerful display in debut, after last Sunday's 9–2 victory over the New York ASL team'.

American League Soccer News welcomes Besiktas Istanbul and reads 'Famed Turkish team to write new chapter in tours history', 21 May 1950.

On Friday 19 May, in a transatlantic telephone call with Matt Busby, the *Manchester Evening Chronicle*'s Harry Mitchell reported that no United players had received offers to join any South American team. 'Neither I nor any of the team has yet been contacted by Mr Percy Wynn, reported to be in New York on behalf of the Bogotá team. We have not seen this chap, nor heard anything from him. In any case, from the club's point of view, I should have no truck with him,' the United manager said. He did, however, add, 'But I could not prevent him talking to the players if he did contact them.'

Four days after the Fall River fixture, United returned to New York, (or 'Gadget Town' as Johnny Carey christened it, due to the fact that 'everywhere you go, there are machines to put in a nickel and get something out'), where they faced a Kearny-Philadelphia Select side. They began this match as they had finished their previous one, struggling to string their passes together, with the hosts more than capable of causing a few problems.

McPhail in the home goal pulled off a series of notable saves, but could do little to prevent Rowley scoring after nine minutes following a goalmouth scramble. It was a lead that lasted a mere two minutes, when Campbell equalised and from then on the Americans seemed to go from strength to strength, their defence withstanding almost every United attack.

Eight minutes after half-time, Sheppell put the Americans in front. Accepting a pass from Campbell, he prodded the ball past a badly positioned Crompton and United found themselves behind for the first time on the tour.

A foul on Mitten inside the area in the 61st minute should have seen United draw level, but after picking himself, the United inside-forward failed to convert the penalty, with McPhail in the Kearny goal pulling off a fine save.

The Select side's defensive play allowed United more into the game and, as they looked for the equaliser, Matt Busby pushed full-back John Aston forward into the attack. It proved to be an inspired move, as it was the United defender, who had only joined up with his teammates a couple of days previously following England international duty, who scored the equaliser 10 minutes from time.

21 May 1950	Kearny-Philadelphia Select at Randalls Island.
Attendance: 13,147.
Drew: 2–2.
Scorers: Rowley, Aston.
Team: Crompton, Ball, Aston, Warner, Lynn, Cockburn, Delaney, Pearson, Rowley, Downie, Mitten.

Those who thought that United were beginning to feel the effects of their protracted season following that rather fortunate 2–2 draw were to be proven wrong, as Johnny Downie regained his scoring form, notching up a hat-trick in the 5–0 victory over the Simpkins Club in St Louis.

Downie's hat-trick, in a game manager Matt Busby described as one which saw his team play their best football of the tour, was overshadowed by the tussle between Colombo, the United States international centre-half, and Jack Rowley, with the United man only getting the better of his opponent 12 minutes from the end when he scored the goal of the match. Out-pacing his marker, Rowley drew the goalkeeper out and slipped the ball into the corner of the net just before all three collided.

25 May 1950	Simpkins Club at Public School Stadium, St Louis.

Attendance: 7,700.

Won: 5–0.

Scorers: Downie 3, Rowley, Pearson.

Team: Crompton, Carey, Aston, Lowrie, Chilton, Cockburn, Delaney, Downie, Rowley, Pearson, Mitten.

The programme for the match versus Simpkins Club, 25 May 1950.

Leaving New York behind them, the United party headed for the brighter lights of Los Angeles, where they continued their goalscoring form, overwhelming an LA Select XI 7–1, in a game which was more a one-half match than a one-sided one, with six of their seven goals being scored during the first 45 minutes.

Rowley, Pearson and Delaney were outstanding in a sublime attacking performance which saw United entertain the Californian public with an exhibition of ball control, short passing and movement, to which their hosts had little answer.

The reports which filtered back to Manchester told little of the United goals, simply naming the scorers: Delaney, with a couple, Jack Rowley, the unfamiliar Tommy Lowrie, Charlie Mitten, another unknown, Brian Birch, and Johnny Downie. Slightly more was made of the solitary LA goal, which materialised following a defensive mix-up between Johnny Carey and Jack Crompton, allowing Carruthers, a former Scottish schoolboy international, to lob the ball over the goalkeeper's head.

31 May 1950	Los Angeles Select in Los Angeles.

Attendance: 18,000.

Won: 7–1.

Scorers: Delaney 2, Rowley, Lowrie, Mitten, Birch, Downie.

Team: Crompton, Carey, Aston, Lowrie, Chilton, Warner, Delaney, Downie, Rowley, Birch, Mitten.

Remaining in Los Angeles, United came up against their strongest opponents thus far, a side described by Frank Percy, the *Manchester Evening News* 'special correspondent', as 'the damndest combination of speed, guts and tenacity I have ever encountered in any sport.' The game against the Atlas Club of Mexico produced something of a goal feast for those fortunate enough to be in attendance. Captain Johnny Carey had his own thoughts on the game, considering it to be 'like playing for the championship of the world.'

Not for the first time on the tour, United surprised their opponents, with whom they had enjoyed a pre-match breakfast, by taking an early lead, Tommy Lowrie scoring after only three minutes with a low 30-yard drive, and for the following 20 minutes they continued to press forward.

Atlas had their moments, playing a short passing game with Cubero at the hub of things, often causing full-backs Carey and Aston concern, but it was their final touch and weak finishing which let them down time and again.

As the game progressed, play swung from end to end, with both sides matching

The team on the United States of America Tour at Los Angeles Airport in 1950.

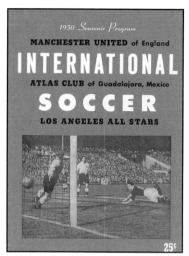

The programme for the match versus Atlas,
4 June 1950.

each other goal for goal. When United eased in front at 6–5 through Mitten's penalty, it looked as though the goal-fest was complete. However, when Carey handled inside the area, up stepped Man of the Match Cubero to once again level the scores, with what proved to be the final goal of a thoroughly entertaining game.

After the match there was a farewell dinner at which all the members of the United touring party received a special trophy, along with the trophy which had been put up for the game itself, for their 10 corners against the Mexicans' three.

4 June 1950	**Atlas Club Mexico at Los Angeles.**

Attendance: 15,000.

Draw: 6–6.

Scorers: Mitten 2 (1 pen.), Pearson, Delaney, Rowley, Lowrie.

Team: Crompton, Carey, Aston, Lowrie, Chilton, Cockburn, Delaney, Downie, Rowley, Pearson, Mitten.

Despite football being something of a low-profile sport in the United States, Manchester United had created quite a stir in the short period of time that they had been there. Their arrival in Los Angeles was heralded by a number of Hollywood stars, the British and Mexican Consul-Generals and a 16-strong band of Scottish pipers. The President of Mexico even sent a special message to the Manchester United party via Senor Peon, the president of the Mexican Football League.

Manager Matt Busby, Johnny Carey, John Aston, Stan Pearson, Jack Crompton and Johnny Downie were all thrown further into the spotlight with television and radio interviews, while there were also a number of functions to be attended. One such event was a garden party at the Encino home of Walter Tetley, a well-known voice actor, whose home included 'a shaded area, a dancing barn, a nice bar, a corral full of horses and a dandy swimming pool.'

The programme for the match versus
Montreal All Stars, 7 June 1950.

The latter seemed to hold the attention of the United players and a relay race was soon underway, with Mitten, Pearson, Cockburn and Bogan in one team and McNulty, Carey, Downie and Crompton in the other. Apparently all went well 'until a couple of sweet-looking Hollywood sirens slipped into the pool and ruined what was left of the competition.'

United returned to Canada and the city of Montreal to face a Select XI, in a game which saw a narrow victory rather than the goal avalanche that had become something of the norm.

Being held to 1–1 at the interval, it would have been expected that United would step up a gear or two in the second half, but, despite a few promising attacks, their second goal contained an element of luck. Jimmy Delaney's right wing cross-cum-shot hit full-back Gammon on the head and went in off the post to give United a 2–1 victory.

7 June 1950	**Montreal Select at Delorimier Stadium, Montreal.**

Attendance: Unknown

Won: 2–1.

Scorers: Downie, own-goal.

Team: Crompton, Carey, Aston, Lowrie, Lynn, Cockburn, Delaney, Bogan, Rowley, Downie, Mitten.

The Polo Grounds in New York, home of the local 'Giants' baseball team, hosted United's international-style fixture against Swedish side Jonkopping. Under the floodlights United managed to get back to their stylish winning ways with a 4–0 victory, although it must be acknowledged that this was the Swedish team's first fixture in the unfamiliar American surroundings.

It was also a game which brought about a situation that no United team had ever before found itself in, as the match was actually played over two days! Kicking-off at 10.15pm on 7 June, it ended at 12.05am on 8 June, a strange experience for all concerned.

'The game was actually a double-header', recalled United captain Johnny Carey, 'and as we travelled in private cars through Harlem, we were filled with an air of expectancy. When we got there, we were thrilled with the wonderful sight. The vast stadium was an incandescent arena, lit by 640 lamps.

'Seated around the field were thousands of onlookers, husbands with their wives and children and their mothers too. Whole families came as a party to enjoy the fun. They gave the whole affair a homely aspect.

'When we arrived, the first game was in progress. As we watched from a veranda outside the players' entrance we were impressed, not only by the colourful scene, but by the play itself. It seemed faster, much faster, than in broad daylight.

'When our turn came, we enjoyed the whole 90 minutes. It was not the novelty of the thing that appealed, because we were almost accustomed to it by that time. Nearly all our games in America and Canada were played by artificial light.

'It was the atmosphere, the friendliness and the spectacular nature of the game that got hold of the United players. But I must make the exception here [for] our winger.

'Just as he was about to take a corner-kick during the closing stages of our game – the time was then five minutes past midnight – he was heard to mutter something about games that start on a certain day should at least finish on the same day.

'It may have been rather late – or should I say very early – for football, but there is no doubt the customers were delighted. They left for home happy, having spent an entertaining evening with their families and friends.'

Under those perfect conditions, United immediately took the game to their opponents, with the effervescent Mitten forcing the goalkeeper into two early saves. It was Mitten, too, who gave United the lead from the penalty spot in the 10th minute after Bogan was tripped by Sjostrand just as he was about to shoot.

Three minutes later Bogan, this time dribbling through the Swedish defence unhindered, added a second, with Stan Pearson securing a third just before the interval, after Downie had beaten three defenders to progress down the touchline. Beating another defender, he drew the goalkeeper from his goal before slipping the ball to his unmarked teammate to score.

United coasted through the second half, although Jonkopping did mount a couple of attacks, only to find Jack Crompton in fine form when they managed to get shots in on the United goal.

In the 73rd minute Pearson had a goal disallowed as offside, but two minutes later United scored their fourth when Delaney was tripped inside the area. Mitten once again scored from the spot.

The programme for the match versus Jonkopping, 9 June 1950.

Attendance: 16,000.

Won: 4–0.

Scorers: Mitten 2 (pen.), Bogan, Pearson.

Team: Crompton, Carey, Ball, Lowrie, Chilton, Cockburn, Delaney, Downie, Bogan, Pearson, Mitten.

The match against Turkish side Besiktas was part of a double-header at the Kearny High School Stadium, with Swedish side Jonkopping facing a Kearny Select. In the build-up to the game, the *Newark Evening News* reporter wrote 'Manchester United, England's "wonder team" of the post-war era, has made a tremendous hit with American fans by its superb play and sportsmanship over here. No other club, with the possibility of Liverpool, has been more popular with local fans.'

In front of a capacity 10,000 crowd, United took the lead after nine minutes, with the *Newark Evening News* correspondent describing the goal as follows: 'United got off to a lead in the first nine minutes of play. Jack Warner shook Jack Rowley loose with a "give and go" pass up the right wing and the speedy Manchester center [sic] raced away from full-back Vedii into clear territory and slipped the leather out of the reach of goalie Feyzi.'

United increased their lead in the 35th minute through Cockburn, with the diminutive half-back scoring from 15 yards out after accepting a pass from Mitten. Besiktas, who were undefeated in their previous half-dozen tour outings, showed some fine touches towards the end of the first half, forcing three corners as they took the game to United. They were, however, to suffer a setback when Sukru was injured in a goalmouth incident, although he refused to leave the field for further attention.

Sukru did leave the field shortly after the second half began, but was soon to return to the fray, with United once again playing the better football and forcing the Besiktas goalkeeper into making a number of fine saves.

As the second half moved towards its conclusion, with a mere 30 seconds remaining and United failing to create much in the way of clear-cut scoring opportunities, while at the same time managing to contain any attacks by the Turkish side, 'a penalty-kick was blown against Carey for a foul in the forbidden area, allowing Sukru, who had been a constant menace to the United defence, to score from the spot.'

As it was, the *Newark Evening News* got it wrong, as it was Chilton whose arm the ball had struck and Sukru's well-placed shot beat Crompton.

The programme for the match versus Besiktas, 11 June 1950.

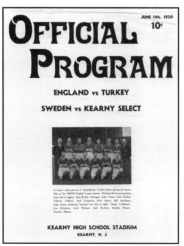

Attendance: 10,000.

Won: 2–1.

Scorers: Rowley, Cockburn.

Team: Crompton, Carey, Aston, Warner, Chilton, Cockburn, Delaney, Downie, Rowley, Pearson, Mitten.

Substitutes: Bogan for Downie.

Prior to the fixture against the FA Touring XI in Toronto, the United party received some bad news from home when they were told of the death of long-time Old Trafford stalwart Louis Rocca. Aged 67, he had filled countless roles at the club since making his first venture to Clayton many years previously. The news cast a cloud over the remainder of the tour.

Perhaps the standard of football that United had come up against so far on their tour was reflected in the result of their next fixture, which brought their first reversal in fortunes in a 4–2 defeat.

Played at Toronto's Lakeside Exhibition Stadium in front of almost 25,000 spectators (a record for any sport, even in Canada), paying around £10,000, both the local-based reporters, Noel Greenwood and Bill Entwhistle, were in agreement that the game was the best seen in Toronto. In the *Evening Chronicle* Entwhistle wrote of 'the finest exhibition of football ever staged on the North American Continent. The fans will be talking about it for months to come.' The *News* correspondent commented 'The game showed the Canadians how soccer should be played – the passing and precision-like accuracy, heading and dribbling, was something the Canadians had never seen in Toronto before and will not forget for some time.'

For a change it was not United who took an early lead, but their opponents, with Sheffield United's Jimmy Hagan heading home an accurate cross from the feet of Stanley Matthews after only five minutes. Caught on the hop, United looked rather ordinary for a few minutes, but they soon got themselves organised and not only levelled the scoring, but also took the lead.

In the 10th minute Rowley leaped high to head home a Mitten corner and this was followed two minutes later by another as Mitten dribbled past Jackie Milburn before hitting a low drive past Hanson.

United then began to dominate play, with their defence well on top, particularly early in the second half, and they looked to be the most likely winners. A goal from the Touring XI in the 62nd minute, Stoke City's Frank Bowyer converting an easy opportunity after Hagan had dribbled past three United defenders, however, changed the course of the game.

Slowly United found themselves wrongfooted, with their familiar opponents gradually taking command. Johnny Hancocks of Wolves scored a third, with the United defence shouting for offside. The same player netted a fourth with only six minutes remaining, putting the game beyond even United's grasp.

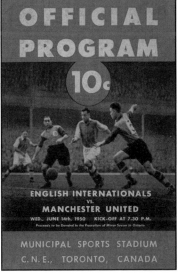

The programme for the match versus the English Internationals, 14 June 1950.

14 June 1950	**FA XI at Municipal Sports Stadium, Toronto.**
Attendance: 24,809.	
Lost: 4–2.	
Scorers: Rowley, Mitten.	
Team: Crompton, Ball, Aston, Warner, Chilton, Cockburn, Delaney, Bogan, Rowley, Pearson, Mitten.	

Before the United party left Canada they took on the Ontario Cricket Club, where the players showed themselves to be more than adaptable when changing their red shirts for cricket whites. Having dismissed the host side for 151 runs, with Jack Rowley taking five for 32, United then proceeded to take their turn at the wicket.

However, having lost Crompton and Mitten before reaching 30, they then saw Rowley dismissed before Stan Pearson rallied the side with an innings of 74. This gave United 142 with the last two players, Tom McNulty and Johnny Ball, out at the stumps.

In typical English fashion, a thunderstorm broke over the ground and, with the pitch beginning to flood and the prospect of things becoming somewhat farcical, the game was declared a draw.

And so United moved into the final game of their tour, with the players, according to captain Johnny Carey in his *Evening Chronicle* updates, 'getting a little homesick', although they had no complaints, despite travelling over 4,000 miles to play four games in eight days on bone hard grounds and finding the weather 'too hot to be bothered with juicy steaks.'

The tour was brought to a close in the Windy City of Chicago, with a 3–1 victory over the Swedish amateurs of Jonkopping, in what was, according to Jack Johnstone of the *Chicago Tribune*, the 'first ever floodlit match played between two European teams.'

Having already defeated the Swedes, United were out to do the double over their less experienced opponents, while also wishing to conclude their tour with a victory. They came close to opening the scoring after only seven minutes when Downie burst through the centre, only for Stahl in the Jonkopping goal to save. The Swedish custodian pulled off a couple of notable saves in this opening period, with Svensson also bringing the crowd to its feet as he shot narrowly over.

Rather surprisingly, the first 45 minutes failed to produce any goals, but with only three minutes of the second period played, the Swedes soon took the lead. Anderson rounded Carey, cut inside and hit the ball high into the roof of the net, well out of Jack Crompton's reach.

United appeared to step up a gear after this setback, coming close to equalising when Downie fired over from close range and as they maintained the pressure they finally managed to breach the Swedes' defence. Mitten took the ball down the touchline and his cross was met by Downie, who shot past Stahl from 15 yards.

Three minutes later Jonkopping regained the lead. Ball attempted to clear the ball by kicking it against the oncoming Svensson, who was left with an easy scoring opportunity.

United pushed for an equaliser, but they found it difficult to break down the resolute Swedish defence. With only three minutes remaining the game was put beyond United's reach when Svenson beat Crompton with an angular shot, earning his side revenge for their earlier 4–0 defeat by United.

21 June 1950	**Jonkopping at Chicago.**

Attendance: 8,000.

Lost: 3–1.

Scorer: Downie.

Team: Crompton, Carey, Ball, Warner, Chilton, Lowrie, Delaney, Downie, Rowley, Pearson, Mitten.

United's tour had now drawn to a close, but there was still some further drama to materialise Stateside before thoughts of returning home became a reality.

Earlier reports of approaches from Bogotá for the services of United players had came to nothing, but while his teammates were packing their cases, or shopping for family presents, Charlie Mitten had other thoughts on his mind.

In the *Manchester Evening Chronicle* Rodney Campbell reported from New York: 'Hatless and clutching a small suitcase, Charlie Mitten, Manchester United's star outside-left, ran up the gangway of flight 606 at La Guardia airport today and joined the British footballers' Bogotá trail.

'Less than an hour earlier, he had slipped from his room at the Paramount hotel in the first move of a prearranged secret departure plan.

'But he almost left it too late. After a mad midnight dash through the half-lit streets of New York, Mitten arrived at the airport with three-quarters of an hour to spare.

'He was the last person to board the plane, and the engines were already revving as he tore across the tarmac with his well-known Cup tie turn of speed.

'He didn't have time to sign out of his hotel. He didn't have time to insure his flight. He only just had time to check his ticket against the counterfoil paid for by the wealthy Santa Fe club of Bogotá.'

Mitten had, however, told his teammates and manager, Matt Busby, what he intended to do and while speaking to Rodney Campbell, prior to his departure, had said, 'I am only going down to Bogotá to see how things are. There is no contract. I want to see the grounds, see what playing conditions are like and see what the place is like.'

Charlie Mitten must have liked what he saw, as the following day the *Manchester Evening Chronicle*'s sports pages headline proclaimed: 'Mitten Joins Santa Fe for £40 a week'. It was to be a move which was to see him suspended by the Football Association for six months and fined £250 when he returned home in June 1951, somewhat disillusioned by things in South America.

Strangely enough, United did not return from the States a player short due to Mitten's defection, as they had made arrangements to sign Eddie McIlvenny, whom they had come up against when they were held to a 2–2 draw by the Kearny-Philadelphia select side early in the tour.

McIlvenny, born in Greenock, had served his home-town club Morton before joining Wrexham in March 1947. It was from the Welsh side that he had moved Stateside, signing for Fairhill Club Inc before joining the Philadelphia Nationals.

He was not, however, able to travel back across the Atlantic with his new teammates, as he had more pressing business, captaining the United States in the 1950 World Cup. He led his adopted country to a memorable, not to say sensational, 1–0 victory over England at Belo Horizonte.

As a matter of note, McIlvenny's United career spanned some three years, but the record books show only two first-team performances – the opening two fixtures of season 1950–51.

Back in familiar surroundings and with season 1950–51 underway, Matt Busby continued his policy of fitting friendlies into United's fixture list whenever possible, and towards the end of September 1950 he took his United side north to Aberdeen for a mid-week challenge match, having seen a 2–1 win at Middlesbrough three days previously take his side to second place in the First Division.

Having made three changes to the team that had defeated Boro, Busby could only watch as his championship hopefuls were run ragged at Pittodrie in the opening 10 minutes.

Within five minutes of the game kicking off Hamilton beat Reg Allen after McGlen had missed the ball. Yorkston made it 2–0 two minutes later after Baird had beaten McIlvenny and Hamilton had headed the ball on. Regaining possession from the restart, Aberdeen again pushed forward, Hather collecting Yorkston's through ball before slamming it home via the post for a third.

Many in the 10,000 crowd must have begun to wonder how United had gained the reputation for being one of the top sides south of the border, but it was a question that they would certainly know the answer to by the end of the evening.

Three goals behind, and with the game still in its infancy, Busby decided to make changes to his selected team formation. Aston was pushed forward into an attacking role, with Carey moving to centre-half. These two decisions would change the course of the game.

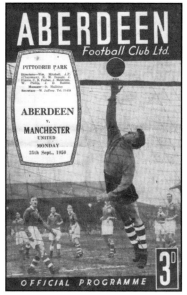

The programme for the match versus Aberdeen, 25 September 1950.

In the 31st minute McGlen reduced the Dons' advantage and a minute later a Bogan cross was blocked and McShane scrambled home.

The second half was only 14 minutes old when United drew level. Bruce attempted a pass back, but mishit the ball. The ever-alert McShane quickly nipped in and, with Aberdeen goalkeeper Martin stranded off his line, the winger calmly lobbed the ball into the empty net.

Ten minutes later United were in front through Bogan and, with seven minutes remaining, the United centre-forward slipped the ball through to Pearson to score a fifth. It is little wonder that the visiting players left the field to rapturous applause from the home crowd.

It is interesting to note that, less than two months later, Jimmy Delaney joined Aberdeen, having impressed their manager, David Halliday, in the above friendly, while in March 1951 another of the United stars that night, Tommy Bogan, also moved from Manchester to the Granite City.

26 September 1950	Aberdeen at Pittodrie.

Attendance: 10,000.

Won: 5–3.

Scorers: McShane 2, McGlen, Bogan, Pearson.

Team: Allen, Carey, Aston, McIlvenny, McGlen, Gibson, Delaney, Downie, Bogan, Pearson, McShane.

On the evening of 25 January 1951, a sprinkling of dyed-in-the-wool United supporters and inquisitive neighbours made their way to the Cliff training ground in Lower Broughton, Salford. The reason for venturing to United's spartan training ground on a cold winter's evening was to watch a nondescript friendly, a mere kick-about really, between two teams made up of United's junior players. There was, however, a bit more to it than that, as the match was something of an experiment and was labelled by George Follows of the *News Chronicle* as 'probably the most important football match seen in the north since the war.' The reason for this was that the game was played under floodlights.

Although the *News Chronicle* correspondent mentioned that there was a crowd of around 100 present, his fellow scribe from the *Manchester Guardian* called it 'a private practice match'. Either way, it was a friendly and certainly worthy of inclusion among the more glamorous fixtures.

The floodlights were primitive, even by today's non-League standards, and consisted of eight poles, evenly spaced on each side of the ground about 20 feet clear of the touchline. Each pole carried two 1,500 watt lights. The running cost was four shillings, with the electricity measured at one old penny per unit.

The idea of installing the lights had come from manager Matt Busby, following the club's American tour, on which such facilities were common. They were to enable his youngsters to play mid week fixtures, as many of them were employed elsewhere during the weekday afternoons. At this time, Football League fixtures could only be played under floodlights by special permission of the Football Association, something which was very seldom (if ever) granted.

Kicking off at 6.30pm, the white ball made following play 'easier than on an average Saturday afternoon', with the game itself made even more interesting by the inclusion of manager Matt Busby and his assistant Jimmy Murphy in the teams, lining up alongside the likes of Byrne, Foulkes, Viollet and Bent.

The result? Who knows! It was not even mentioned in the reports.

25 April 1951 also saw United play two friendlies, although only one, played at Reading's Elm Park, was a first-team fixture. The other saw the up-and-coming juniors make the short journey to Glebelands Road, for the second year in succession, to take on Sale. The game was organised as part of the Festival of Britain celebrations and a United line up of Wood, Lomas, Killin, Evans, Cope, Bent, Bradley, Clempson, Ritchie, Lewis and Bond was held to a 2–2 draw by the locals.

The visitors were two goals in front within the first five minutes, through Ritchie and Bradley, but as the game progressed the play deteriorated, especially after the interval, by which time Sale had drawn level.

While there was only a sprinkling of spectators lining the grassy knolls of the Sale Gas Social Club ground, there were 13,268 at Elm Park to watch a much stronger and more familiar United XI take on Reading.

Two members of the United side who travelled to Berkshire, Roger Byrne and Dennis Viollet, could quite easily have been playing in the more familiar environs of Cheshire, but instead they were lining up at left-back and outside-right respectively to make their Manchester United first-team debuts.

The game in Berkshire was a joint testimonial match for Reading duo Freddie Fisher and Jeff Gulliver, but unfortunately for the former he was unable to play on such a memorable occasion, as he had broken his leg at the start of the season. He did, however, make a brief appearance on the pitch, kicking-off.

In what was an entertaining and quite even opening 45 minutes, United had the home side on the defensive early on, but the Third Division (South) club were equal to anything that their illustrious visitors put their way.

It was not long before the initiative was with Reading and Blackman was only thwarted in front of goal by the combined efforts of Byrne, Chilton and Allen. Soon afterwards, a right-wing cross saw Brooks bring the best out of Reg Allen, with the United 'keeper producing an equally fine save moments later, fingertipping a Blackman header round the post.

With half an hour gone, Reading almost broke the deadlock when a Wicks lob into the United goalmouth caught the defence by surprise and Allen off his line. The ball bounced over the goalkeeper's head and, with Blackman moving in on goal, Byrne just managed to nip in and clear the ball as it moved close to the vacant goal. Two minutes later, however, United's luck ran out when Reading opened the scoring with a well-deserved goal. Outside-left Amor, who had been keeping Carey on his toes, sent over an inviting cross and Blackman headed past the helpless Allen.

The goal relaxed Reading a little bit too much, as United equalised almost immediately. Aston, playing in the slightly unfamiliar centre-forward position, took the ball from Brice and found the unmarked Rowley wide on the left. The winger's cross-cum-shot went across the face of the goal rather invitingly, but no connection was made.

Ten minutes before the interval United equalised. Aston, who had been left unmarked, took his time to pick his spot and calmly slotted the ball past McBride in the Reading goal. Seven minutes later the United number nine added a second, controlling a centre from Viollet before scoring with a low drive.

Festival of Britain 1004

LOCAL CELEBRATIONS

Grand Football Match

A MANCHESTER UNITED TEAM

v.

A SALE TEAM

at Stretford Gas Social Club Ground, Glebelands Road, Sale.

Wednesday, April 25th, 1951

KICK-OFF 6·30 p.m.

Admission by SOUVENIR PROGRAMME (with Autographs of M c United players)

ONE SHILLING

The programme for the match versus Sale, 25 April 1951.

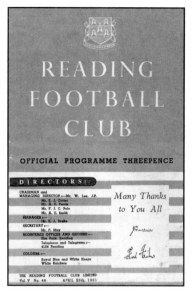

The programme for the match against Reading Football Club, 25 April 1951.

Anyone who had left the action early for the interval would have returned to the stand disappointed, as a minute after Aston's second Reading equalised, Brooks finding Allen out of position following a corner and scoring before the 'keeper had a chance to recover.

Within five minutes of the restart Gulliver blotted his copybook, and probably spoiled his evening, when he brought down Viollet inside the area and could only stand and watch as Carey restored United's lead. Pearson almost increased this as McBride fumbled his shot, but managed to hold it at a second attempt with the ball agonisingly close to crossing the goalline. United were now well on top and it came as no surprise when they increased their lead, Pearson scoring after Aston had created the opening.

However, Reading were not going to be pushovers and two goals from Edelston, the second five minutes from the end, gave the home side a well-deserved draw.

Following the match the teams enjoyed a meal together, with the Reading chairman, Mr William Lee, thanking Manchester United for making the evening, which brought in receipts of just over £1,255, a success. He also recalled Matt Busby's contribution to Reading's wartime campaign as a guest player.

During the evening prizes were presented to the winners of the pre-match golf tournament between the two sets of players, with Matt Busby receiving a tankard for his net score of 73.

25 April 1951	**Reading at Elm Park.**

Attendance: 13,268.

Drew: 4–4.

Scorers: Aston 2, Carey (pen.), Pearson.

Team: Allen, Carey, Byrne, Gibson, Chilton, McGlen, Viollet, Pearson, Aston, Downie, Rowley.

Despite Hibs having an open invitation to visit Old Trafford, it was one of the Scottish side's domestic rivals, Aberdeen, who became the first Scottish side to visit Manchester in the immediate post-war period.

Although it was just over seven months since the two sides had met north of the border, United's first post-war Old Trafford friendly could be perceived as a sign of things to come, with Aberdeen making the journey from the north-east of Scotland to Lancashire for the 'second leg' of the 'Auld Enemy' challenge.

Having lost 5–3 at Pittodrie, the Dons had considerable ground to make up and, as the resulting 90 minutes showed, there was, as there still is today, a clear gulf between the domestic leagues of Scotland and England.

Admittedly, Aberdeen held their own in the opening half, passing the ball around confidently, but even Jimmy Delaney, back on his old stomping ground and receiving a warm welcome from the 17,000 crowd, could do little to keep United at bay. After changing ends the contrasting styles began to become more noticeable.

A defence-splitting move between Downie and Pearson presented Aston with an easy opportunity to open the scoring in the 25th minute, but it was to take Aberdeen only four minutes to draw level, Rodgers heading past Reg Allen.

As the second half progressed, Pearson, Aston, Downie and Rowley kept the visitors' defence on their toes and the inevitable goals came from Pearson and Rowley.

| **2 May 1951** | **Aberdeen at Old Trafford.** |

Attendance: 17,000.

Won: 3–1.

Scorers: Aston, Pearson, Rowley.

Team: Allen, Carey, Redman, Cockburn, Chilton, McGlen, McShane, Pearson, Aston, Downie, Rowley.

The programme for the match versus Aberdeen, 2 May 1951.

Ten days after the visit of Aberdeen to Old Trafford, Manchester's footballing public were given the opportunity to watch yet another unfamiliar side. Although not all the Aberdeen players had been totally alien, those who made their way to Old Trafford on 12 May knew virtually nothing about the visiting Yugoslav side Red Star Belgrade.

This fixture had been arranged, as indeed had many others around the country, as part of the Festival of Britain celebrations, and it presented the First Division runners-up with a sterling test.

With quite a few of the 41,743 crowd still making their way into the ground, the Yugoslavians took the lead in the third minute, with what was their first goal attempt. Centre-forward Zicanovick, the goalscorer, along with teammates Mitic and Zlatkovic, caused the United defence numerous problems. Only Chilton and Redman showed any sign of being able to cope with their undoubted skill.

In attack United struggled, with Downie missing through injury and his replacement Birch rarely in the game. Aston, playing at centre-forward, received little in the way of support, although it was he who played a part in the equaliser. With eight minutes remaining he chased a loose ball into the Red Star penalty area, only to be brought down. Rowley scored from the resulting spot-kick to give United a draw that few present thought United deserved.

| **12 May 1951** | **Red Star Belgrade at Old Trafford.** |

Attendance: 41,743.

Drew: 1–1.

Scorer: Rowley (pen.).

Team: Allen, McNulty, Redman, Cockburn, Chilton, McGlen, McShane, Pearson, Aston, Birch, Rowley.

Substitute: McIlvenny for McGlen.

Ticket for the match versus Red Star at Old Trafford, 12 May 1951.

The programme for the match versus Red Star at Old Trafford, 12 May 1951.

For those United players who had made the journey across the Atlantic Ocean the previous year, the 1951 end-of-season tour to Denmark was a very different affair – much more relaxed – which, rather surprisingly, showed in the performances of the team out on the pitch.

Certainly, the results did not really matter and the players had just completed a long and taxing campaign. However, with the Danes knowing all about English football as their Government used Football League matches for their Football Pools fixtures during their close season, they would have expected considerably more from their renowned visitors.

The five-game tour got underway in Copenhagen, where United came up against a local amateur XI in a game which many considered that United would have won, had they not played in such a relaxed fashion.

On a dry, uneven surface the home side opened the scoring through outside-right Roenvang, but United equalised in the 34th minute when Rowley ghosted past three defenders before scoring with a powerful shot.

Four minutes into the second half the Copenhagen side once again took the lead. A free-kick was awarded against United goalkeeper Reg Allen for taking too many steps while holding the ball; following the resulting kick, Dahlfelts shot through a number of United players.

Rowley, one of the few 'name' players on show, displayed the form which had brought him international recognition, hitting the post on two occasions, while Downie and Pearson both missed easy scoring opportunities. United were also denied a penalty when the opposition centre-half handled the ball.

United did, however, eventually secure an equaliser when a move, started by Cockburn, was finished by Aston as a couple of defenders closed in on him.

---

22 May 1951   **Copenhagen XI.**

Attendance: 14,700.

Drew: 2–2.

Scorers: Rowley, Aston.

Team: Allen, Carey, Byrne, Cockburn, Chilton, McGlen, McShane, Pearson, Aston, Downie, Rowley.

Two days later United again faced a Copenhagen XI and, with the exception of inside-left Bjerregaard, it was an entirely different team that attempted to get the better of their more illustrious visitors.

The United players had difficulty in coming to terms with a ball much lighter than they were used to, but *Manchester Evening News* correspondent Alf Clarke, who was with the United party, thought differently, writing: 'I blame the players. They discarded the type of play which has endeared them to their supporters. They failed to keep the ball moving from man to man and their long haphazard kicking was more in keeping with Third Division standards.'

As it was, United opened the scoring just after the half hour, Aston back-heeling to Rowley, who cut the ball back from the goalline into the path of Birkett, who scored with a cross-shot.

Three minutes after the interval, with the Danish defence looking for an offside decision which was not to materialise, Aston scored from close range, but within a minute the home side had pulled a goal back, Oennesen scoring with a low drive after a corner had been headed out by the United defence.

---

25 May 1951   **Copenhagen XI.**

Attendance: 9,700.

Won: 2–1.

Scorers: Birkett, Aston.

Team: Allen, Carey, Byrne, Cockburn, Chilton, McGlen, Birkett, Pearson, Aston, Downie, Rowley.

Moving on to Odense, United faced a combination side made up of players from the three local League clubs, where Henry Cockburn's performance was widely acclaimed by the locals in the 4–1 United victory.

Heavy rain prior to kick-off softened the ground, making it more favourable to United. They were rather surprised when the locals took the lead, with the United defence caught in a similar situation to their Copenhagen counterparts in the previous fixture, looking for an offside decision which never came.

If the Danes thought that they were going to achieve something of a surprise result, they were quickly proved wrong as United scored four, through Pearson, Downie and a Cassidy double, to claim their second victory of the tour.

The only downside of the game was an injury to goalkeeper Reg Allen, who received a cut head in a first half collision with an Odense forward and had to leave the field to receive stitches. His place between the sticks was taken by young centre-half Mark Jones.

---

27 May 1951   **Odense XI.**

Attendance: 2,800.

Won: 4–1.

Scorers: Cassidy 2, Pearson, Downie.

Team: Allen, McNulty, McGlen, Gibson, Chilton, Cockburn, Birkett, Pearson, Cassidy, Downie, Rowley.

Substitute: Jones for Allen.

It was not all work and no play for the United party as, following the game in Odense, they enjoyed a post-match banquet followed by a leisurely day which took them north of Copenhagen to Kronberg Castle, made famous by Shakespeare's *Hamlet*, and to Fredensborg, home of the Danish king and queen. The day was rounded off by what Alf Clarke described as 'the most sumptuous meal that any of the United party has had since pre-war days.'

Back in the action, or perhaps the lack of it, United stuttered to a rather surprising 1–0 defeat at the hands of the amateur side Aalborg, becoming the first senior English side to lose there.

'United Disappoint in First Reverse' was the headline above the Sports Editor of the *Berlingske Tidende*'s report for the *Manchester Evening News*, while their rival publication, the *Evening Chronicle,* preceded Alf Clarke's report with 'Soccer Lesson for United'. Either way, it was a poor display against the local combination side.

United were without captain Johnny Carey, who had returned home to link up with the Republic of Ireland side, and their play at times was described as 'sluggish', especially in the goalless first half.

After the interval the game immediately sprang to life, with Chilton giving away a penalty in the opening minute of that second period, but to the big defender's relief the spot-kick was slammed against the crossbar by Larsen.

With the crowd solidly behind them, the Aalborg players raised their game and their determination paid off on the hour, when Terkelsen headed a centre from his left-wing partner, Hansen, past Reg Allen for what was to be the only goal of the game.

Rowley moved from the wing into the centre, but there was to be no change in fortune for United. The crowd did, however, get a few moments of action which brought them to their feet in the closing minutes, when Brian Birch was sent off for allegedly slapping the Aalborg outside-right. The general feeling, particularly in the United camp, was that the referee should have turned a blind eye to the incident, but at the end of the day, rules are rules.

---

29 May 1951   **Aalborg.**

Attendance: 7,000.

Lost: 1–0.

Team: Allen, McNulty, Chilton, Whitefoot, Jones, McGlen, McShane, Pearson, Cassidy, Birch, Rowley.

Following this surprising defeat, Eric Thornton, of the *Manchester Evening News,* asked 'Are these tours worth the candle?', writing: 'United's unexpected reverse at Aalborg swings discussion around the old question whether these tours are of any particular value. It might be argued that they do at least provide the players and officials with pleasant holidays.

'Agreed. But surely that point alone is a dangerous one on which to lay foundations of fixtures with overseas clubs.

'Let us approach these tours in a more serious manner if it is intended they should continue in future years. Don't let there be any risk of flop which labelled most of the Festival games.

'It is becoming the same with these close season tours abroad. The cash is dropping simultaneously with prestige lost with defeats. At the same time, the list of injured is slowly mounting. And on top of all that, the players will be returning tired and listless with the new season not far away'.

Strong words indeed for the *Evening News* correspondent and, strangely enough, manager Matt Busby issued strong words of his own to his players prior to the final match of the five-game tour against Aarhus.

Busby's pre-match dressing room pep talk seemed to have some effect on the United players, as their 3–0 victory was considered by those in attendance to be their best performance of the five fixtures.

Jack Rowley was once again considered to be the most outstanding United player on view, claiming two of the goals, the other being a Frandsen own-goal. United, however, were guilty of missing numerous scoring opportunities, while at the opposite end Reg Allen had a relatively quiet 90 minutes, having to make only a couple of saves as Aarhus rallied back following United's first goal.

31 May 1951	**Aarhus.**

Attendance: 5,600.

Won: 3–0.

Scorers: Rowley 2, opp. own-goal.

Team: Allen, Aston, McGlen, Whitefoot, Chilton, Cockburn, Birkett, Pearson, Rowley, Downie, McShane.

Menu from a dinner in honour of Hapoel FC, held at the Grand Hotel, Manchester, 26 September 1951.

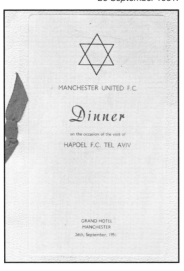

MANCHESTER UNITED F.C.

Dinner

on the occasion of the visit of

HAPOEL F.C. TEL AVIV

GRAND HOTEL
MANCHESTER
28th, September, 195.

The decision by the Manchester United board of directors to appoint Matt Busby as the club's manager had been a brave one. He had no track record in a similar role and, with the club needing to regain their footing when domestic football resumed again after the war, it was an appointment which could quite easily have proved fatal. Busby, however, proved to the directors that their judgement had indeed been correct and, having won the FA Cup in 1948 and made more than a token challenge in the First Division title race, it was felt that the championship itself would soon find its way to Old Trafford.

Busby not only wanted his team to be the best in the country, but he also wanted them to be capable of overcoming opponents from outside England's top flight, hence his increasing involvement with friendly fixtures. Not only did many of those fixtures present a challenge for his team, but they also provided a challenge to the players as individuals. Those players, however, who had helped the manager, and also the club, through the difficult immediate post-war period, now had to look over their shoulders as new names began to find their way onto the team sheets.

On the afternoon of 26 September many work places around Trafford Park and in Manchester suffered earlier than normal clocking-off times from members of their workforce, as the visit of Tel Aviv amateur side Hapoel to Old Trafford kicked-off at the unusual time of 5.25pm, due to the lack of floodlights at the ground.

The 12,000 present were treated to a somewhat one-sided, but nevertheless entertaining, 90 minutes, with United hitting six without reply. It was not until the second half, however, that United got into their stride and the supporters were given something to shout about.

The visitors, unperturbed by their opponents or their surroundings, began prominently, with their goalkeeper Chodorov making several fine saves. However, there was no penetrative punch in their attack to bring them the necessary goals to trouble United.

As the game progressed a 35-minute period saw United simply overwhelm the Israeli side, who had no answer to the powerful running, distribution and overall play of the red-shirted home side.

Although they conceded six goals, they were not disgraced, as stronger teams of better ability would also have struggled to contain Busby's side.

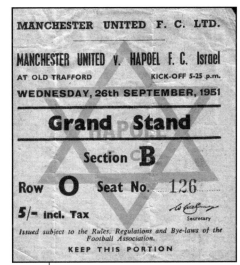

Ticket for the game versus Hapoel FC, 26 September 1951.

26 September 1951	Hapoel at Old Trafford.

Attendance: 12,000.

Won: 6–0.

Scorers: Rowley 2, Pearson 2, Walton, Aston.

Team: Allen, Carey, Redman, Gibson, Chilton, Cockburn, Berry, Walton, Aston, Pearson, Rowley.

With an early FA Cup exit at the hands of Hull City, whose 2–0 victory at Old Trafford shocked many up and down the country, there were now a few vacant Saturdays on the United fixture list. With Championship success certainly a possibility, Busby wanted his players to maintain their momentum and filled two of the 'free' Saturday afternoons with friendlies.

On 23 February, when the preferred fixture would have been an FA Cup fifth-round tie, United had to be content with winning some local pride by entertaining neighbours Manchester City at Old Trafford.

The game allowed both sides the opportunity to experiment, something that Matt Busby took full advantage of by giving 17-year-old John Scott, who had recently signed professional terms, his first-team debut.

Prior to kick-off, Manchester University students entertained the crowd, but once the referee's whistle got the game underway it was United who took over the role of entertainers, coming close on a few occasions in the opening minutes.

These opening exchanges were not the usual fare for a friendly fixture, with Rigby and Hannaway both requiring treatment, although City stood up to their hosts and received a boost when they opened the scoring through Clarke on the half-hour.

Moments later United should have been level. Aston collected a throw-in on the right, broke through on goal and, from 15 yards, unleashed a shot which Trautmann in the City goal somehow managed to divert over the bar while on his knees. It was a save described by Alf Clarke of the *Manchester Evening Chronicle* as 'the best save we have seen at Old Trafford for years. I can remember nothing like it.'

The programme for the match versus Hapoel FC, 26 September 1951.

The programme for the match versus Manchester City, 23 February 1952.

Play moved from end to end, with the United forwards failing to make the most of their opportunities, but their task was made somewhat easier when Rigby failed to reappear for the second half and City were forced to continue with only 10 men.

With this advantage it took United only three minutes of the second half to draw level. Aston rounded City captain Paul before turning the ball to Clempson, who drove the ball left-footed high into the City net.

Two minutes later United were in front. A clearance by Byrne was headed on by Pearson and Aston outpaced Paul before beating Trautmann.

Much to the crowd's surprise, City returned to full strength, bringing on a substitute after 55 minutes. However, this failed to make any real difference to the game as a whole, as United were now well in control, although it took them a further 20 minutes or so to score a third, Pearson prodding the ball home after it had hit the crossbar.

The game was now all but over, although two goals, one for either side in the 82nd and 84th minutes, from Broadis, an 18-yard drive, and Pearson deflecting an Aston cross past Trautmann, kept the majority of the crowd interested until the final whistle.

23 February 1952	**Manchester City at Old Trafford.**

Attendance: 25,002.

Won: 4–2.

Scorers: Pearson 2, Aston, Clempson.

Team: Crompton, McNulty, Byrne, Carey, Chilton, Whitefoot, Scott, Clempson, Aston, Pearson, Bond.

With United contemplating yet another blank Saturday due to the FA Cup, Matt Busby again decided to keep his first-team players on their toes with a friendly against Hibernian, who had recently played a similar fixture at Maine Road, defeating City 4–1. On this occasion they were to find the red-shirted Manchester side a much more difficult team to get the better of than those in the light blue.

With only seven League fixtures remaining and United still in pole position in the First Division (although only ahead of Arsenal on goal difference), Busby decided to experiment slightly by playing his regular full-back Roger Byrne at outside-left. Although he had filled this position in the reserves, it was his first senior outing on the wing.

Amid a driving snowstorm United took the lead after only 30 seconds. A miskick by Smith gave United possession and the defensive clearance found Rowley, who pushed the ball between Paterson and Buchanan towards the on-running Byrne and Clempson to give United a surprise lead. Minutes later it could have been two, but Berry put his shot over the bar.

Hibs, with their 'Famous Five' forward line of Smith, Johnstone, Reilly, Turnbull and Ormond, soon found their feet, playing some fine football, but United were able to match them move for move. It was thanks mainly to the Hibs goalkeeper that United failed to increase their lead, as he pulled off a number of fine saves.

Half-time in the 1952 match versus Hibernian.

Five minutes before the interval the Edinburgh side equalised. Mark Jones failed to clear a centre and the ball fell to the feet of Turnbull, whose shot beat Crompton with considerable power.

United substituted Ernie Bond for the injured Cockburn at half-time, as the snow swirled around Old Trafford, and in the opening minutes of the second half Hibs took up where they left off, but the United defence stood firm. Play moved from end to end, with an offside decision robbing Clempson of an opportunity, while a clearance by McNulty kept the visitors out. As the snow showers eased so did the momentum of the game and both teams were seemingly content to share the spoils.

The programme for the match versus Hibernian, 29 March 1952.

29 March 1952	Hibs at Old Trafford.

Attendance: 20,098.

Drew: 1–1.

Scorer: Clempson.

Team: Crompton, McNulty, Aston, Carey, Jones, Cockburn, Berry, Clempson, Rowley, Pearson, Byrne.

Substitute: Bond for Cockburn.

Matt Busby took his team back to the United States and Canada at the end of what was their first post-war Championship-winning season, having claimed the crown with a sublime performance, defeating nearest challengers Arsenal 6–1 at Old Trafford.

The title success had prompted the head baker aboard the *Queen Elizabeth*, Alex Brewer, to create a 'championship cake', which took pride of place at the Championship dinner on board the liner. The cake, described by Johnny Carey as 'a masterpiece of confectionary, iced in red and white and made to represent a football field', even had a sugar sign behind one of the goals which read 'United 6 Arsenal 1'.

As with the previous transatlantic sailing, the United party found plenty to occupy them, taking the honours 10–4 in a darts tournament against the crew, who were the reigning North Atlantic champions. At an entertainment evening, the 'United Choir' treated their fellow passengers to 'The Sunshine of Your Smile', which was apparently the team's favourite.

The welcome Stateside was just as warm as it had been two years previously. Matt Busby received the keys of Newark on behalf of the club and the team settled into the same New York hotel that they had occupied on their first visit, although one or two of the players who had not been present to enjoy the experience of the first trip found the Big Apple more than a little daunting.

'Manchester Best England Can Offer' proclaimed the headline on the sports pages of the *Newark Evening News* of 8 May, where United were to open their lengthy tour, 12 games and some 6,000 miles, against a Select XI at the Kearny High School Stadium the following evening.

Despite United's domestic success, they were obviously still relatively unknown away from their native shores and Tom Connell, the Newark correspondent who penned United's welcome, had certainly not done his homework on the visiting playing squad. In more modern times a club media guide would have given both the reporter and the locals all the information that they would have required about the players and the club as a whole. However, through his newspaper, the readers, if they were interested in the first place, were told a few untruths within his lengthy introduction.

Introducing the United players, Connell wrote about 'goalkeeper Reggy Allen' and that 'John Aston was a "versatile kicker"', but he was to make a mistake, in a piece on Johnny Carey when he wrote 'two other sons of Erin in the Manchester line up are Tom McNulty and Rodger [sic] Byrne, a pair of 21-year-old youngsters who rate as the most promising young stars in the game. Each has an individual $50,000 sale value.' Obviously the scribe felt that the names were not 'English' enough.

Included in the United squad were one or two names that would be unfamiliar to a few football lovers back in Britain, never mind on the other side of the Atlantic, as Matt Busby was giving the rather inexperienced Jackie Blanchflower, Jeff Whitefoot and Mark Jones a taste of the big time.

Blanchflower had made his first-team debut along with Roger Byrne at Anfield on 24 November 1951, but while the latter had cemented his place in the first team, moving from full-back to outside-left and scoring seven important goals in the Championship run, the young Irishman had to be content with reserve-team football.

Jeff Whitefoot had secured himself a place in the record books by becoming the youngest player to represent the club in the Football League when he made his debut against Portsmouth in April 1950 aged 16 years and 105 days. Since then his appearances had been limited, with only a further five before this tour.

Yorkshireman and former England Schoolboy international Mark Jones had made his first-team debut against Sheffield Wednesday in October 1950 and, like the aforementioned Whitefoot, had only managed a handful of appearances prior to his American adventure. In one of his regular tour updates for the *Manchester Evening Chronicle* Johnny Carey wrote that 'Jeff Whitefoot, Mark Jones and Jackie Blanchflower spent a couple of hours on top of the Empire State Building. Mark explained he was trying to get used to heights because we have a lot of flying to do and he has never been in a plane.' For all three it would be a trip to remember.

United were soon in action, with the first of their scheduled 12 fixtures against a New Jersey XI in Kearny. Their opponents, a mixture of Scots and Portuguese, were no real match for United and no sooner had the Mayor of Kearny, Joseph Healy, kicked-off, than the home goal found itself under pressure.

It took United 14 minutes to open the scoring, Johnny Carey firing home a free-kick. Six minutes later Roger Byrne had made it two. Considered by many to be the best individual on the pitch, he then gave United a three-goal advantage by the half-hour mark.

Encouraged by the home support, the Select XI did not give up, forcing five corners during the opening 45 minutes, but those were well dealt with by full-backs McNulty and Aston.

Strangely, United failed to increase their lead until 12 minutes from time, when Rowley set up Johnny Berry to score the fourth, although they had played some excellent football, with one shot from Clempson almost breaking the crossbar, such was its ferocity.

A series of late attacks from the locals kept the United defence on their toes, but they proved equal to anything that came their way.

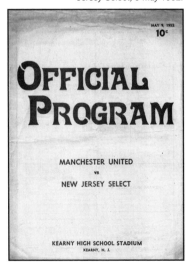

The programme for the match versus New Jersey Select, 9 May 1952.

9 May 1952	New Jersey XI at Kearny High School Stadium, Kearny.

Attendance: 9,000.

Won: 4–0.

Scorers: Byrne 2, Berry, Carey.

Team: Allen, McNulty, Aston, Carey, Jones, Cockburn, Berry, Clempson, Rowley, Downie, Byrne.

Moving on to the Lighthouse Field in Philadelphia, where their opponents were made up of members of the Philadelphia Americans (the current American League champions) and the Philadelphia Nationals (who had won the title for the three previous years), with the latter having a couple of American internationals who had recently played against Scotland at Hampden, United found themselves under quite a bit of pressure during the first 45 minutes, with Reg Allen having to make a number of fine saves.

Despite play being considered by the local correspondent as 'about even', United took the lead on the half-hour when Jack Rowley drove the ball home for what was the only goal of the opening half.

Five minutes after the break Roger Byrne, taking a pass from Clempson five yards from goal, added a second, with Clempson himself scoring the third three minutes later.

In the Philadelphia goal Yingling saved his team on a number of occasions, while Gormley also gave a good account of himself. However, neither could prevent United from adding a fourth, with Rowley latching on to a corner for his second goal of the game.

The programme for the match versus Philadelphia All-Stars, 11 May 1952.

11 May 1952	Philadelphia All-Stars at Lighthouse Field, Philadelphia.

Attendance: 5,000.

Won: 4–0.

Scorers: Rowley 2, Clempson, Byrne.

Team: Allen, McNulty, Aston, Gibson, Carey, Whitefoot, Berry, Clempson, Rowley, Downie, Byrne.

Crossing the border into Canada, United completely outclassed the Montreal All-Stars in the local baseball stadium 10–0, with an outstanding display of short passing and shooting, the likes of which had never been seen in Eastern Canada before. 'They ran us into the ground' was all that Montreal manager Alex Samson could say at full-time.

The onslaught got underway rather slowly, with United only scoring on three occasions in the first half after Montreal had put Jack Crompton under some pressure, forcing the 'keeper into a couple of good saves.

One of the Montreal attempts on goal earned a corner and McKenna's kick was cleared, but only as far as Gummer. The full-back failed to control the ball, allowing Byrne the opportunity to latch onto the ball and release Rowley, who moved in to open the scoring.

Rowley added a second two minutes later with a low drive, while McShane scored a third, a 25-yard shot, with the ball cannoning off goalkeeper Sandrin and into the net.

The second half was one-way traffic, with the former Italian and Hungarian professionals in the Montreal side having no answer to United's free-flowing football. The seven goals in this final half produced something of an argument for ownership of the match ball at full-time, with three United players claiming hat-tricks. Jack Rowley added to his first-half strike with two further goals, only to be matched with three each from teammates Johnny Downie and Frank Clempson.

Downie's first came when he reacted quickly as the ball rebounded off the post, and his second was a fine solo effort a minute later, but these were completely overshadowed by Clempson's trio. The first two were well-taken following passes from teammates, and the third involved a run down the touchline leaving defenders in his wake before shooting past the helpless goalkeeper.

The Manchester United 1952 Tour Pennant.

The programme for the match versus Montreal All Stars, 13 May 1952.

---

13 May 1952   **Montreal All-Stars at Montreal.**

Attendance: 6,400.

Won: 10–0.

Scorers: Rowley 3, Downie 3, Clempson 3, McShane.

Team: Crompton, McNulty, Aston, Gibson, Carey, Whitefoot, McShane, Clempson, Rowley, Downie, Byrne.

The fourth match of the tour saw United increase their goals for tally to 23, although it also allowed Frank Monteigo the distinction of becoming the first player to score against the tourists in a 5–1 victory against an American League XI at New York's Trilborough Stadium.

Frank Clempson put United on the road to victory in the 25th minute, crashing a low shot past the 'keeper following a headed centre from Roger Byrne before adding a second, eight minutes later. This time Downie was the provider. Downie himself got his name on the score sheet in the 38th minute with a 30-yard drive, increasing the lead to 3–0.

United's defence let themselves down when the home side pulled a goal back midway through the second half. Reg Allen pushed the ball round the post and from the resulting corner-kick Monteigo, on as a substitute and amid a goalmouth scramble, managed to force the ball through the outstretched arms of the United goalkeeper. Going by one of the local match reports the goal did have an element of luck about it. It was described as follows: 'It must be chronicled, however, that the goal was made principally because there was no one near the British nets, Reggie Allen, the visitors' goal tender, was flat on his stomach at the time. Thus because of a futile dive on the corner kick, Monteiga found it a simple manoeuvre to send the ball home.'

Any thoughts the Select side had of staging a fightback quickly evaporated a minute later. With the celebrations still in full swing Jack Rowley made it 4–1, moving on to a loose ball to score from around 20 yards out.

Johnny Berry added a fifth in the 73rd minute, running in from the wing before shooting into the far corner of the goal and rounding off the scoring.

---

18 May 1952   **American League XI at Randalls Island, New York.**

Attendance: 7,150.

Won: 5–1.

Scorers: Clempson 2, Bery, Rowley, Downie.

Team: Allen, McNulty, Aston, Gibson Carey, Whitefoot, Berry, Clempson, Rowley, Downie, Byrne.

The games were proving to be little more than practice outings for United, with the 23 goals for tally increasing to a slightly embarrassing 34 in Massachusetts three days later when Fall River were defeated 11–1. The semi-professional club, members of the American Soccer League, New England Division, had no answer to United's play and Jack Rowley's seven-goal performance in particular.

The meagre 3,102 crowd was a disappointment and one of the smallest that a United team have ever played before. However, those who were present certainly obtained value for money and were appreciative of United's play, while Joe Kitchen in the Fall River goal produced a number of fine saves that kept the goal tally from being doubled.

The programme for the match versus American League XI, 18 May 1952.

The game was won and lost in the opening 20 minutes, when Jack Rowley claimed his first hat-trick of the evening. Although the hosts pulled a goal back, having been awarded a somewhat dubious penalty for handball against Tom McNulty, they were never likely to cause United any concern.

Johnny Downie got into the scoring frame with a further three goals, before Rowley netted four on the trot, three of those in an eight-minute second-half spell. United's 11th and final goal was an own-goal from full-back Martin, who deflected McShane's cross into his own net as he attempted to clear.

---

21 May 1952　　　　**Fall River All-Stars at Fall River, Mass.**

Attendance: 3,102.

Won: 11–1.

Scorers: Rowley 7, Downie 3, opp. own-goal.

Team: Allen, McNulty, Aston, Carey, Jones, Blanchflower, Berry, Downie, Rowley, McShane, Byrne.

Moving on to New York, United found themselves up against sterner opponents than they had previously experienced. The Stuttgart Kickers were enjoying the backing of the crowd, making sure that they were not going to be defeated without a fight.

The first half was an evenly fought contest, with United giving as good as they got on the rain-sodden pitch and the Scottish referee keeping firm control of the game, which at times threatened to get out of hand.

It was United who broke the deadlock as early as the fourth minute when Roger Byrne moved in from the touchline to beat the goalkeeper with a firm shot. In their previous fixtures an early goal had heralded an onslaught, but on this occasion United found themselves pegged back, with Kronenbitter equalising after picking up a loose ball.

A corner from Byrne gave Clempson the opportunity to put United back in front, but just before the half-hour mark the Germans equalised again, Jackstell converting a cross from the ever dangerous Pflum.

Just prior to the interval United scored their third, with a little confusion between those covering the game as to the name of the actual scorer, just as there is with the fourth. In the *Evening Chronicle* Rodney Campbell's account of the game states: 'United settled down again, and Downie, who has scored several surprise goals from long range in the tour so far, smashed in a left foot shot which went in under the bar to give them a 3–2 interval lead.'

In the *Evening News*, however, Jim Kelly pens a different story: 'The Manchester boys were having much the better of the play, and a fine individual effort by Jack Rowley gave his team the lead just before half-time.'

As the second half got underway United began putting pressure on the German defence and this paid off in the 59th minute when they increased their lead as Downie, from a Rowley pass, scored from 30 yards out. That was according to the *Evening News*. If your choice of reading matter was the *Chronicle* then 'Byrne put United on to a 4–2 lead.' Both, however, were in agreement that Rowley added a fifth four minutes later to round off the scoring.

25 May 1952   **Stuttgart at Randalls Island, New York.**

Attendance: 5,874.

Won: 5–2.

Scorers: Rowley 2, Clempson, Downie, Byrne, or Byrne 2, Clempson, Rowley, Downie.

Team: Allen, McNulty, Aston, Carey, Jones, Whitefoot, Berry, Clempson, Rowley, Downie, Byrne.

Substitute: Gibson for McNulty.

For the second successive fixture United found themselves playing in conditions which seemed more like Manchester than America, the rain once again keeping the attendance down to a few thousand less than had been originally expected to see United take on the Chicago All-Stars.

More than a few of the 3,564 crowd were still finding their seats in the Shewbridge Field Stadium when the home side opened the scoring with a totally unexpected goal. Vantimilla's 20-second strike certainly jolted United into action, and by the half-time whistle they had managed 19 shots on target compared to the home side's three, but only two had beaten the competent Carlos Mottes in the Chicago goal. Jack Rowley put United level within five minutes, scoring from 15 yards, with John Aston scoring a second, 20 minutes later, with a hard, low shot.

After the interval the goals did come regularly, United scoring four without reply. Rowley notched his second from five yards out in the 53rd minute. Clempson also scored from close in, connecting with a Berry pass, five minutes later. Rowley claimed his hat-trick eight minutes later and Downie rounded off the scoring two minutes from time, having been put through by Clempson.

27 May 1952   **Chicago All-Stars at Shewbridge Field, Chicago.**

Attendance: 3,564.

Won: 6–1.

Scorers: Rowley 3, Downie 2, Aston.

Team: Allen, Carey, Aston, Gibson, Jones, Whitefoot, Berry, Clempson, Rowley, Downie, Byrne.

The programme for the match versus Chicago All-Stars, 27 May 1952.

If the United players had enjoyed both this and the previous tour as something like an end-of-season break, then they were about to be given a rude awakening in the East Los Angeles Stadium, where they came up against Atlas FC of Guadalajara, Mexico.

'United in "free-for-all", but win 2–0', 'Free-fight fiasco as United win', 'Fists Fly as Manchester Beats Atlas' and 'Near riot for United: Referee hit', were just a few of the headlines that appeared in the after-match calm.

In the local *Los Angeles Times* Don Snyder wrote: 'In a sizzling game of soccer, fraught with flying fists, rabid rhubarbs and all the pent-up emotion that created a near riot at its end'… 'It was 90-minutes of hectic head-and-toe play, accentuated by three pugilistic eruptions that came midway through the final half and immediately following the game.'

The *Manchester Evening News* report began: 'After a sensational chapter of incidents in which the referee was knocked to the ground and play held up for 15 minutes as spectators joined in a general mêlée, Manchester United beat the fiery Atlas FC, of Guadalajara, Mexico by 2–0 in a "rough house" match here at East Los Angeles Stadium.' Its Manchester rival, the *Chronicle*, began its match summary:

'The fiery Atlas Soccer Club of Guadalajara, Mexico – a near international team – lost to Manchester United in Los Angeles after causing a near riot on the ground last night.'

Both teams had met without incident during the previous tour, playing their part in a thoroughly entertaining 90 minutes of football, which had ended 6–6. This time around, however, the early stages of the game did little to prepare those present for what was to follow.

The Mexican side displayed signs of brilliance in the early stages of the game, but they were to find both Johnny Carey and Reg Allen in fine form. However, it was United who enjoyed most of the play, with Pearson coming close to scoring and his effort just going narrowly past the post.

On the half-hour United did take the lead through Stan Pearson, who had only joined up with his teammates the previous day, having been on international duty in Zurich. Collecting a pass from Johnny Berry he turned the ball into the net, leaving Cordova in the Atlas goal helpless.

The game now had the makings of a thrilling spectacle, but what followed after the interval was certainly not what the crowd had expected.

Roger Byrne, playing in his now familiar outside-left position, took the ball into the Atlas penalty area, only to be brought down by Juan Gomez. Glasgow-born referee Al Thompson immediately pointed to the penalty spot and all hell broke loose.

An Atlas player swung a punch at the referee, while their right-half, Varrillo, charged at the official, knocking him to the ground. This action could only have one outcome and, upon regaining his feet, the referee ordered Varrillo off the pitch. As he did so, further confusion erupted.

The Mexican substitutes and coaching staff all ran onto the pitch, making a beeline for the official, who was soon under attack. For some 16 minutes chaos reigned, with one or two of the estimated 1,000 Mexican supporters in the crowd encroaching onto the pitch and joining in the attack on the unfortunate Scot. Sheriff officers now had to come to the referee's aid, with five of them required to drag one spectator off the man in black.

Roger Byrne gave the 'keeper no chance, giving United a 2–0 lead. However, as the game continued the Atlas players turned what had looked in the opening minutes of the game like a thrilling encounter into something of a rough house.

The final whistle also prompted a further pitch invasion from a number of the Mexican supporters, with the sheriff's officers again having to restrain one of the supporters who managed to reach the referee. They were, however, left with no other option than to release him, as around 200 of his fellow countrymen surrounded the arresting officers.

Would things have cooled down by the time the two sides met again in seven days time?

1 June 1952	Atlas Club of Mexico at Los Angeles.

Attendance: Unknown

Won: 2–0.

Scorers: Pearson, Byrne (pen.).

Team: Allen, McNulty, Aston, Carey, Chilton, Whitefoot, Berry, Downie, Rowley, Pearson, Byrne.

It was reported that manager Matt Busby had wanted to call the second meeting between Atlas and United off, as he did not wish to witness similar scenes, even though no United players had been involved in any of the incidents in the previous encounter. The United players, however, had apparently told their manager that it was not a Cup Final and that they were more than able to look after themselves.

So the game went ahead as planned and much to the relief of everyone concerned (perhaps not the crowd), the game passed without any major incidents.

Following the troubles of the previous encounter this meeting was described by one correspondent 'as the finest game ever seen on the Pacific coast', as play moved from end to end, with both sets of forwards attacking strongly.

Stan Pearson was in fine form, well supported by Byrne, Rowley, Berry and Carey, while Atlas outside-left Cubero kept the United defence on its toes at the opposite end.

United opened the scoring through Pearson after some fine work from Carey and Byrne, and it was United's long passing and skilful dribbling that produced the second goal for Byrne, who scored with a terrific drive following a pass from Rowley.

The game was now being played mainly in the Atlas half of the field, but thanks mainly to goalkeeper Gonzalez, who made a number of fine saves, it still hung in the balance. The ever-dangerous Cubero broke away but his shot was stopped by Allen, only for it to find its way into the United net following a goalmouth mêlée.

There was to be no immediate fightback, however, as United took command of the second half. A lobbed corner from Berry found Pearson for a third goal, while minutes later the same player claimed his hat-trick following an excellent passing movement which began in midfield.

At 4–1 it looked like game, set and match to United, but to their credit the Mexicans rallied. Cubero scored from a seemingly impossible angle to make it 4–2, creating a third for his inside-left, while, with the game moving towards a close, an equaliser was only prevented by John Aston, who cleared off the line after Reg Allen had missed the ball. It was a clearance which secured the Helms Foundation Trophy for United, although it was widely felt that a draw would have been a fair result.

8 June 1952 — **Atlas Club of Mexico at Los Angeles.**
Attendance: 12,000.
Won: 4–3.
Scorers: Pearson 3, Byrne.
Team: Allen, McNulty, Aston, Carey, Chilton, Whitefoot, Berry, Downie, Rowley, Pearson, Byrne.
Substitute: McShane for Byrne.

So Anglo/South American relations had been restored. However, back in Manchester some of the reports filtering through painted an entirely different picture, with stories circulating about further disruptions during the game and two United players being sent off. It was not until Johnny Carey's latest 'Letter from America' appeared in the *Manchester Evening Chronicle* over a week later that the truth surrounding the second United versus Atlas encounter emerged. Or did it?

'There have been many things said about Manchester United's match against the Atlas Club of Mexico, particularly the second game, but here are the true facts.

'First there is absolutely no truth in the report that the referee, or anyone else, sent Jack Rowley or Roger Byrne off the field. The "Gunner" never left the field of play and he gave no cause for anyone to suggest such a step to be taken.

'I myself brought Harry McShane on for Roger Byrne midway through the second half, because the Mexicans didn't like the way Roger was skating past them and Roger didn't like the methods they were using to stop him.

'As we had the game nicely in hand I decided to prevent trouble before it started and made the change which later Mr Busby and Roger himself agreed was the best thing to do'.

A local journalist, however, painted a rather different picture, with Don Hyland writing: 'Indeed, their [United's] great international captain, John Carey, sent two of his men, Roger Byrne and John Rowley, off before they could create real "incidents". Both were rough beyond reason.

'Rowley had been somewhat whacky from midway in the first 45 minute half when his teammate John Downie sent a high shot from a corner to the centre of the field. Rowley headed it perfectly to Stan Pearson and the Manchester ace scored the first goal of the game. Making that shot, Rowley hurt his neck but got it into his head that a Mexican had clipped him. From then on he made war until Carey removed him from the game.'

However, in his book *Soccer at the Top*, Sir Matt Busby wrote: 'Atlas were a rough, tough lot. Seeing how things were going, I told Johnny Carey to instruct the team to keep their heads, keep together and keep calm. He did this, but Roger defied him and was sent off. I was annoyed about this. I did not like Manchester United players being sent off. I especially did not like my players to be sent off abroad, where club and national reputations suffer more than an individual player's reputation. Nor did I like my instructions or my captain's instructions to be forgotten, even allowing for provocation, of which there was plenty.

'So I had to make my point once more. I was the boss. We would do it my way. I told Roger that he must apologise to Johnny Carey or I would send him home the next day. I would give him two hours to do it in. No more than 15 minutes later Johnny Carey came to see me to say, "Roger has been to apologise".'

So, what indeed did go on against the Mexicans? Sadly, we will probably never know, but I myself believe that the Johnny Carey version is the true one.

United left Los Angeles for the city of Detroit and a less confrontational fixture against the Champions of Canada, Toronto Ulster, in the University Stadium. A crowd of around 10,000, including many British-born residents, had gathered to see United gain their 10th consecutive tour victory. This attendance, however, was considered ridiculously small, as the population of the immediate Detroit area was around two million.

The fixture, originally scheduled for 24 hours earlier, gave the United players an extra day of rest and it looked to have been beneficial as United took an early lead. There were signs of tiredness, however, particularly in the latter stages of the first half when the Canadians matched their visitors, holding them to 2–2 at the interval.

United opened the scoring after only 30 seconds, Frank Clempson managing to find some space to squeeze the ball home after Aston had headed the ball through. Five minutes later Aston himself scored the second, accepting a long-range pass from Pearson, and his long-range effort going in off the post.

The two-goal lead was to last for only 10 minutes, as an angled shot from Jack Long reduced the leeway. The same player levelled the score with a 30-yard free-kick three minutes later, after Mark Jones had been pulled up for pushing. Crompton seemed to misjudge the free-kick, allowing it to beat him just under the crossbar.

Despite their determination, Toronto were no match for United in the second half. Downie put United back in front following a move involving both Whitefoot and Byrne. Four minutes from the end, the result was put beyond doubt when Pearson headed home a Byrne cross after the latter had collected an attempted clearance by Gifford.

12 June 1952 Toronto Ulster United at University of Detroit Stadium.

Attendance: 10,000.

Won: 4–2.

Scorers: Clempson, Aston, Downie, Pearson.

Team: Crompton, McNulty, Carey, Gibson, Jones, Cockburn, McShane, Clempson, Aston, Pearson, Byrne.

Substitute: Rowley for Gibson, Downie for Clempson.

The programme for the match versus Toronto Ulster United FC, 12 June 1952.

OFFICIAL PROGRAM

INTERNATIONAL SOCCER GAME

1951-52 English League Champions

Manchester United

vs.

1952 Dominion of Canada Champions

Ulster United F. C.

June 12, 1952 — U. of D. Stadium

Junior Game 6:30 Kickoff
TRAILBLAZERS vs. COMPLEX

25c

There were a few familiar faces awaiting United when they took the field at the Yankee Stadium, New York, for what was the penultimate game of the tour, as the opposition for this, and for the final fixture, were First Division rivals Tottenham Hotspur, who had finished just behind United in the previous season's title chase.

Interest on both sides of the Atlantic was high, despite the match being a friendly, with the outcome of the first of the double-header all-English confrontation producing something of a shock result.

'King "Fitba" Reigns Brightens Blue Bowl With Old Land Color' proclaimed the headline in the *Toronto Telegram* and underneath staff reporter Gerry Pratt had written: 'It wasn't Varsity Stadium this afternoon as 26,000 Toronto soccer fans turned out to watch Manchester United and Tottenham Hotspur, two of the world's top 11s, tangle in a soccer classic.

'To one old country fan, it was White City Stadium alongside the Thames as his idols of the English first division trotted onto the field.

'To another, it was Wembley Stadium with the great open gap at one end where so many of the football classics that have made England the home of soccer were played.

'But there were still hot dogs, Toronto streetcars speeding by, and fans who were not from the old country to remind those who sat in the stands dreaming of English soccer days that this game was being played in Toronto'.

Headlines in the British press were slightly more hard-hitting, especially for United supporters, with the likes of the now defunct *Empire News* proclaiming 'Manchester United Are Thrashed By Spurs', following the White Hart Lane side's 5–0 victory.

Played in a temperature of around 80 degrees Fahrenheit, an opening-minute goal by Bennett set the pattern for the game, with Tottenham's defence equal to anything that the United forwards produced. For once on the tour the players were severely stretched.

Following that early goal, with Ditchburn in the Tottenham goal called upon to make a couple of fine saves, there was no further scoring until two minutes prior to the interval. A quick through ball down the middle caught the United defence out of position and, upon collecting the ball, Duquemin left Reg Allen helpless with a strong, low shot.

Berry came close when his run down the wing was followed by a powerful shot from 15 yards, but Ditchburn once again proved equal to this by pulling off a fine save.

A long pass from the Spurs defence saw Bailey outpace both Aston and McNulty before lobbing the ball over Allen for the third, while Medley scored a fourth, heading the ball into the net after Allen had managed to stop his initial effort. Two minutes later it was five; Walters prodding the ball over the line amid a goalmouth scramble.

There was a great deal of shock at United's poor performance and numerous calls were made for manager Matt Busby to go on radio to explain the reasons for the result.

The programme for the match versus Tottenham Hotspur, 14 June 1952.

---

14 June 1952   **Tottenham Hotspur at Varsity Stadium, Toronto.**

Attendance: 25,321.

Lost: 5–0.

Team: Allen, McNulty, Aston, Carey, Chilton, Whitefoot, Berry, Downie, Rowley, Pearson, Byrne.

'"One and a half million dollars" worth of prime British booting beef on hook at the Yankee Stadium today' read one of the pre-match headlines, amid scenes of white-hatted hawkers selling Spurs and United favours for the equivalent of three shillings and six pence outside the gates. Beer salesmen were doing a roaring trade, as special police were called out to handle the crowds for what was to be the biggest gate in United States soccer history.

However, if Matt Busby had some explaining to do following his team's embarrassing 5–0 defeat in Toronto, he had even more to do the following day when Tottenham completed the double over United in an equally convincing fashion, this time hitting seven goals with United managing only one in reply.

As the final 90 minutes of the tour kicked-off, revenge was at the forefront of United's mind. It looked as though it might be achieved when Jack Rowley gave them the lead after 13 minutes with a left-foot drive, which Ditchburn had little hope of saving. Those thoughts, however, were short-lived, as Bennett equalised within 60 seconds following a centre from Medley and five minutes later the same player beat Allen again to give Spurs the lead.

A misunderstanding in the United defence led to Duquemin scoring a third, with a cross from Medley giving the same player the opportunity to notch up a fourth.

Ticket and badge from the game versus Tottenham Hotspur, 15 June 1952.

United began the second half strongly. Downie and Rowley each forced Ditchburn into producing fine saves as the thermometer moved over 85 degrees, while Tottenham also kept the heat on the United defence, scoring a further three goals.

McLellan made it five before Duquemin took his tally to four, with the ground announcer adding to United's embarrassment by keeping up a running commentary throughout.

15 June 1952	**Tottenham Hotspur at Yankee Stadium, New York.**

Attendance: 24,582.

Lost: 7–1.

Scorer: Rowley.

Team: Allen, McNulty, Aston, Carey, Chilton, Cockburn, Berry, Downie, Rowley, Pearson, McShane.

A few weeks later the *Picture Post* magazine added to United's New York embarrassment by carrying a four page feature under the heading 'The Mangling of the Mancs', which was followed by a brief write-up of the game, accompanied by a number of photographs. None of these, rather surprisingly, showed any of the seven goals.

However, the embarrassment of conceding seven goals was less than it might have been, as the fixture was not played in Manchester and there would only have been a handful of United supporters present to witness the humiliation, if any at all. The regular Old Trafford attendees would, however, read all about the crushing defeat by Hibs in the newspapers the following day.

The game was not simply a friendly between old friends, but a testimonial for Hibs stalwart Gordon Smith. The Scottish League champions outmatched United in all departments, especially during the second half.

'Dirt cheap at two bob for the game of the century' was the verdict of the 30,000-odd crowd, who maintained a crescendo of noise throughout the 90 minutes, even booing referee Jack Mouwat when he awarded two penalty-kicks against United. These awards were to alter the course of the whole game.

It was United who set the pace of the match, playing fast, accurate football, with 16-year-old debutant John Scott cleverly beating the more experienced John Hewie with ease, before hitting a strong shot at McCracken, who was grateful to see the ball go wide.

Reilly forced Wood into making a fine save with a first-time effort, while at the opposite end Rowley almost broke the crossbar with a 25-yard drive that the Hibs goalkeeper never even saw. However, it was the home side that broke the deadlock in the 16th minute when Turnbull scored from 20 yards, the ball taking a slight deflection off Johnny Carey.

Within six minutes United were level. Carey and Gibson avoided gifting Hibs a second goal by getting out of a defensive mix-up on the edge of the 18-yard box and, three passes later, the ball was nestling in the back of the Hibs net. Rowley calmly flicked the ball over the head of centre-half Paterson, before moving round him and volleying the ball home before it had touched the ground from 25 yards out.

On the half-hour an Aston free-kick, following a foul on Pearson by Gallacher, was headed towards goal by Downie. McCracken in the Hibs goal could only push the ball out and Pearson nipped in to tap the ball into the empty net.

Three minutes later came the first of a trio of penalty decisions. A long ball into the United penalty area was chased by Chilton and Reilly and the latter went down as the pair challenged for the ball. Many were surprised when the referee pointed to the spot. Eddie Turnbull's kick was brilliantly saved by Ray Wood, but the United 'keeper could not hold the ball and Turnbull hooked the ball into the net for the equaliser.

For the spectator, it was everything a football match should be when, in the 37th minute, United once again took the lead. Pearson beat Johnstone for possession some 20 yards from goal and his subsequent shot beat the Hibs 'keeper just inside the post.

The cheers and applause that had greeted every goal and skilful play were to be replaced with boos, with only seconds remaining before the interval. Rowley, who had already been spoken to by referee Mowat, showed dissent when a free-kick was awarded against him and to everyone's surprise the official took his name. That did not go down at all well with the crowd.

There was widespread belief that the second half would conjure up football more in keeping with what the Edinburgh public were accustomed to. They were, however, very much mistaken, as the second period outshone the first, producing a further five goals, one disallowed and a missed penalty.

Playing down their favoured slope, Hibs opened strongly and in the first few minutes Wood was forced into three notable saves, from Gordon Smith twice and Bobby Johnstone. At the opposite end, McCracken in the Hibs goal breathed a sigh of relief when Carey stopped two scoring opportunities and a Rowley 'goal', after a Berry, Scott and Pearson move, with the latter beating three men in a cross-field run, was disallowed as offside.

Ormond equalised in the 62nd minute from a Reilly pass and five minutes later the Hibs goal provider was brought down by McNulty inside the penalty area, Turnbull giving the home side a 4–3 lead from what was considered by some to be a harsh penalty award.

Scott and Berry switched wings as Hibs upped the pressure on their guests. Rowley was unlucky not to score, having beaten McCracken, but Hewie was on the line to clear. From the resulting corner Rowley headed against the crossbar, with Pearson netting the rebound. Unfortunately for United, the referee had spotted a defender handle the ball before it entered the net and awarded a penalty-kick. Carey, however, put the spot kick wide.

Hibs slowly took over the running of the game as United began to tire and, to the delight of the appreciative crowd, added a further three goals from Lawrie Reilly with two and Gordon Smith.

Despite the taxman taking almost half the evening's takings, (although one report stated that many supporters who had attended the game had sent postal orders to Smith, to supplement his benefit fund, as they considered the game worthy of a little extra payment), Gordon Smith reckoned that he would still earn around £1,500 and was more than grateful to United for providing the opposition for his benefit match: 'Matt Busby taught me how to play, when he assisted Hibs during the war. I shall never forget him, and neither will I forget such a wonderful match. A draw would have best represented the game.'

Similar sentiments were echoed by others. Mr Harry Swan, the Hibernian chairman, said, 'Best game at Easter Road for 30 years', while Dr W. MacLean, a United director, called it 'a match to be remembered'. Matt Busby acclaimed the 90 minutes as 'classical soccer and methodical soccer rolled into one. There was more shooting in this game than in a dozen ordinary matches.'

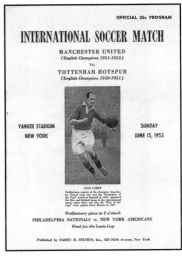

The programme for the match versus Tottenham Hotspur, 15 June 1952.

GORDON SMITH'S TESTIMONIAL
MATCH

Pictorial Souvenir Programme

HIBERNIAN V MANCHESTER UNITED

Scottish Champions 1951-52   English Champions 1951-52

Easter Road, Edinburgh, Monday, 15th September, 1952, at 6.25 p.m.

The Proceeds of the Game and Revenue from the Programme
will be devoted to Gordon Smith's Testimonial Fund.   *PRICE* 1'-

*The programme for the match versus
Hibernian, 15 September 1952.*

15 September 1952   **Hibs at Easter Road.**

Attendance: 30,500.

Lost: 7–3.

Scorers: Pearson 2, Rowley.

Team: Wood, McNulty, Aston, Carey, Chilton, Gibson, Scott, Downie, Rowley, Pearson, Berry.

Away friendlies on foreign fields were normally close-season affairs, but on 10 November 1952 a party of 13 players and club officials travelled to Northolt in Middlesex where they boarded a flight for Antwerp, their destination a fixture against Austria Vienna.

Missing from the United ranks were the injured trio of Jack Rowley and Johnny Berry, who had both travelled with the party, and Allenby Chilton, who had remained in Manchester, forcing Matt Busby into some pre-match juggling. Henry Cockburn made his first senior appearance in two months and Johnny Carey took on the role of centre-half. The Austrians, on the other hand, fielded a strong side consisting of eight internationals.

Amid brilliant sunshine and backed by a party of British soldiers garrisoned in Antwerp, United had come close on three or four occasions before they opened the scoring. Pearson had shot just wide, with another effort brilliantly saved by Andreiska. Aston came close with both a header and a shot, while the Austrian goalkeeper made a further excellent save from a Downie pile-driver. At the opposite end Crompton had to make one notable save from Huber, but it was the Austrian half of the field which saw most of the action.

It was no surprise then when United scored, the goal coming in the 18th minute from Stan Pearson, who fastened onto a pass through the centre from Harry McShane, driving the ball wide of the Austrian goalkeeper.

United continued to force the pace, Aston, Clempson and McShane all bringing gasps from the crowd with close efforts, while Carey in the centre of the United defence kept close tabs on the roving Austrian centre-forward Huber.

'This was soccer at its best' proclaimed Alf Clarke, with the Austrians' interposing play causing United problems, especially in the second half. John Aston, playing at centre-forward, led the line well and kept centre-half Ocwirk, who had shone in a recent international against England, on his toes. On one occasion Aston broke clean through and with only the goalkeeper to beat, six yards from goal, had his legs pulled from under him by right-back Stotz. Rather surprisingly, the referee failed to award a penalty.

In the second half the Austrians attempted a reshuffle, while also making one substitution, and gave United a few anxious moments. Melchior forced a corner off Byrne, while Huber had a goal-bound shot well saved by Crompton. Carey was also caught out when Kaminek whipped the ball off his toe before crashing a shot just wide. McShane was caught up in a minor scene with full-back Stotz and was frequently booed by the crowd for the remainder of the game. Pearson and Clempson also got themselves involved in tussles as the Austrians chased the game and the referee began to penalise United for every tackle. Even the fairest of shoulder charges was pulled up and the United players deserved credit for controlling their tempers when things could quite easily have got out of hand.

Twelve minutes from time Berry replaced Clempson and, despite the close attention of the Austrian defence and being brought down on three occasions, he almost increased United's lead, but his shot was turned against the bar by a defender.

Hanging on to their slender 1–0 lead, United returned to Manchester with the Austrians eagerly requesting a return fixture in the very near future. They had been presented with a trophy awarded in the memory of John Langenus, a famous Belgian referee who had recently died.

Menu from the dinner to celebrate the match against Austria Wien, 11 November 1952. This menu was formerly the property of Henry Cockburn.

11 November 1952	Austria Wien at Antwerp.

Attendance: 50,000.

Won: 1–0.

Scorer: Pearson.

Team: Crompton, McNulty, Byrne, Cockburn, Carey, Gibson, Clempson, Downie, Aston, Pearson, McShane.

Substitute: Berry for Clempson.

Upon returning home, Matt Busby said that he was 'very proud indeed' and that he believed that 'this success has put English soccer back on the map on the continent.' It also prompted officials of Dutch teams to enquire whether United would be prepared to visit Holland at the end of the season, but it was an invitation that the directors had to decline, as arrangements had already been made to play in the Coronation Cup, which was to be held in Scotland.

In more recent times there is a distinct possibility that a friendly fixture will receive little or no coverage in the national press, but back on Thursday 4 December 1953 the *Manchester Guardian* (as it was then known) carried a long, detailed report of a match between United and the famed amateur side Northern Nomads, played under floodlights at the Cliff training ground in Lower Broughton.

Readers of this particular newspaper might have been surprised to find such a report among the other football and sports news, and they would have been equally surprised when their eyes fell on the heading at the top of the report: 'Northern Nomads Victory', with the scoreline below proclaiming 'Manchester United XI 3 Northern Nomads 4'.

The 'Manchester United XI' was in reality a junior side, augmented with the experience of Johnny Carey and Jack Rowley, and allowing many their first glimpse of a promising young player by the name of Duncan Edwards.

Ticket for the match versus Austria Wien, 11 November 1952.

The *Manchester Guardian* correspondent wrote: 'Carey and Rowley did sufficient to suggest that they may both be fit for the Football League match at Old Trafford on Saturday. But one expected the occasional masterly touch from them and of course was not disappointed. The most encouraging thing about the game was that it showed a player of real promise in Edwards, aged 16, and two other likely youngsters in Mooney and Doherty. Edwards is remarkably strong for his years, is fast, and tackled well, but best of all shot with real power with either foot. Even Rowley would not have criticised several of Edwards's drives for strength and direction.'

Of the game there was certainly nothing for the observer to be critical about, as the Nomads matched United stride for stride on a surface that was 'so hard and rather slippery, for the white ball leaped and spun from it like a live thing, making control and passing very awkward.'

Perhaps through being more familiar with the ground, it could be assumed that it would have taken the visitors time to adapt to the conditions, but it was the Nomads who took the lead through Fairclough, although they could only hold it for a minute before Mooney equalised.

Fairclough missed an open goal, while at the opposite end Edwards shot narrowly wide, but by the interval the visitors were 3–1 in front, although few of the 2,000-odd crowd could complain about the football being played.

After the restart, with Edwards moved from half-back to an attacking position, United attempted to get back into the game and pulled a goal back through the

The programme for the match versus Northern Nomads, 3 December 1952.

Floodlit Football Match at The Cliff, Broughton

FRIENDLY MATCH

Manchester United XI v. Northern Nomads
WEDNESDAY, 3rd DECEMBER, 1952   Kick Off 7-15 p.m.

MANCHESTER UNITED XI
RED SHIRTS AND WHITE SHORTS

1
CLAYTON

2   3
FULTON   KENNEDY

4   5   6
CAREY   JONES   EDWARDS

7   8   9   10   11
HAMPSON   McFARLANE   MOONEY   DOHERTY   ROWLEY

Referee: *Linesmen:* J. S. ORCHARD
S. WOODWARD   R. HARDING

11   10   9   8   7
GOALEN   BROMILOW   FAIRCLOUGH   WALTON   BIGLEY

6   5   4
WADE   LANGFORD   MURRAY

3   2
BOOTH   CHILDS

1
SHERRIFF

NORTHERN NOMADS
AMBER SHIRTS AND WHITE SHORTS

TO READ—HOLD PROGRAMME TO LIGHT   ★   Price 1d.

lively Mooney, as he latched onto a ball that rebounded off the crossbar following a shot by Rowley.

There was, however, to be no spirited fightback as the Nomads scored a fourth and, although Mooney claimed his hat-trick by heading home a Carey free-kick and Rowley hit the bar, it was the amateur side who celebrated victory.

---

9 February 1953   Northern Nomads at Cliff training ground, Lower Broughton.

Attendance: Unknown

Lost: 4–3.

Scorer: Mooney 3.

Team: Clayton, Fulton, Kennedy, Carey, Jones, Edwards, Hampson, McFarlane, Mooney, Doherty, Rowley.

There are fixtures that are not so much 'forgotten' as more or less completely unknown to the vast majority of supporters.

One such fixture occurred towards the end of March 1953, when in front of the vast empty terracing and seating of Old Trafford and a handful of onlookers, United defeated England 1–0.

The game, a 30 minutes each-way affair, was arranged in order for Walter Winterbottom's England to have some practice playing together prior to a home international fixture against Scotland at Hampden Park.

England, with the likes of Tom Finney, Ivor Broadis, Billy Wright and United's Roger Byrne in their ranks, found a United team, which included four reserves, more than a handful behind the locked Old Trafford gates. However, it proved to be a worthwhile exercise, as a few days later, in front of a fanatical 134,000 Hampden crowd, England recorded a 4–2 victory.

On 10 January United had travelled to south London for a third-round FA Cup tie against Millwall, winning a closely fought encounter 1–0, with a Stan Pearson goal taking them into round four. However, having been knocked out in the fifth round by Everton, they were involved in 90 minutes of football in Cold Blow Lane, rather than the twin-towered stadium in north London, playing Millwall in a friendly.

While Stanley Matthews was keeping the Wembley crowds on the edge of their seats as he strove towards that elusive FA Cup-winners' medal in the Final on 2 May, a crowd of just under 15,000 was being equally thrilled and entertained as Millwall and United shared eight goals between them.

There was not the same fire that was present when the two sides had met in the FA Cup and, in the more relaxed atmosphere, the crowd were treated to some excellent football. Millwall took the lead as early as the fourth minute, when Morgan beat Jack Crompton with a low drive.

Finlayson in the Millwall goal was forced into three excellent saves in quick succession from Downie, Pearson and Taylor, the latter recently signed for £29,999 from Barnsley, ably leading the United front line, but the equally quick passing movements of the home side, with Neary and Byrne enjoying some rare tussles, gave them an equal share of the play.

Goals from Pearson (United), Neary (Millwall), Downie (United), Pearson (United) and Jardine from the penalty spot for Millwall made it 3–3 at half-time.

Perhaps the quantity of goals was not to be surpassed in the second half, but the quality certainly was, with the best goal of the game coming after only five minutes of the restart from Tommy Taylor, who ran half the length of the field, beating two men, before finishing with a shot into the corner of the net.

The programme for the match versus Millwall, 2 May 1953.

The former Barnsley player was always a threat to the Millwall defence, as were Downie and Berry, but they failed when it came to increasing United's lead, as did Roger Byrne with a penalty-kick. As so often happens, the opposition sneaked in to grab a goal, Chilton being caught out by the home centre-forward Shepherd, who scored the last goal of an interesting encounter.

2 May 1953	**Millwall at The Den.**

Attendance: 14,127.

Drew: 4–4.

Scorers: Pearson 2, Downie, Taylor.

Team: Crompton, Aston, Byrne, Carey, Chilton, Whitefoot, Berry, Downie, Taylor, Pearson, Rowley.

To coincide with the coronation of Queen Elizabeth II, an eight-club tournament was organised, which was to be played in Glasgow and would involve Rangers, Celtic, Hibs, Aberdeen, Tottenham, Newcastle, Arsenal and United, using Hampden and Ibrox as the venues. Due to United's involvement in this, the board had decided to forgo a close-season tour, which had become the norm.

Matt Busby took his players north a week before they were due to face Rangers in their first-round tie, basing them at Troon on the Ayrshire coast. Provisional arrangements were made to remain there until 20 May, the date of the Final.

The game against Scottish League and Cup winners Rangers was expected to attract more than 100,000 fans to the vast Hampden Park arena, but in the end there were only 75,546 to see United win 2–1. It was a result that restored some credibility to English football, while also preventing a Scottish treble, following the defeats of Arsenal and Tottenham Hotspur by Celtic and Hibs respectively.

United's victory was thoroughly deserved and the winning margin could easily have been considerably bigger, as the team played open, attractive football, while the loss of a first-half goal did little to upset their momentum.

United began briskly and tried to break the Rangers defence down with methodical football, but it proved to be to no avail, as Niven in the Rangers goal was a mere spectator as his opposite number found himself the busiest man on the park.

It was therefore no real surprise when Rangers took the lead in the 11th minute, McMillan heading home a Hubbard cross from 10 yards out. As the first half progressed it was to be the 20th minute before United had their first real goalscoring opportunity, Rowley heading past Niven in the Rangers goal. Unfortunately for the United forward, Young was well positioned on the goalline to head clear.

Play was now beginning to hot up, with both defences coming under pressure. A Rangers attack caught the United re</br>rearguard off balance and it was left to Crompton to make a fine save from Prentice after Hubbard had headed the ball down to his feet. Seconds later, Simpson headed a Hubbard corner narrowly over.

United did have their chances, with the nearest to a goal coming from Pryde, the Rangers number six, who, running back to cover, almost hit the ball past his own goalkeeper from six yards out. Niven made an excellent save to prevent the blushes of his teammate. Soon afterwards Woodburn, the Rangers centre-half, stumbled, allowing Rowley the opportunity to run at goal. Instead of shooting himself, Rowley quite unselfishly passed to Downie, who had nothing else to do but place the ball into an empty net. However, from only 10 yards out, he put the ball wide of the post.

In the second half United took control of the game, scoring twice in the opening 10 minutes. A misjudged pass by Woodburn was pounced upon by Byrne, who quickly slipped the ball inside to Pearson to put United on level terms. Two minutes later, Rangers were to find themselves behind.

Byrne, proving to be a real handful for the Rangers defence, was again involved, with his cross finding Pearson, who in turn tapped the ball back into the path of Jack Rowley. Taking two steps, the United centre-forward lined up his shot and beat Niven with a powerful left-footed drive from 12 yards.

Despite play swinging from end to end and there being no further goals, at times United simply overwhelmed their opponents and it was widely believed that whoever defeated Matt Busby's side would win the competition.

The programme for the match versus Rangers, 3 May 1953.

3 May 1953	Rangers at Hampden Park, Glasgow.

Attendance: 75,546.

Won: 2–1.

Scorers: Rowley, Pearson.

Team: Crompton, Carey, Aston, Gibson, Chilton, Cockburn, Viollet, Downie, Rowley, Pearson, Byrne.

The United party enjoyed the relaxing atmosphere of Troon, with training sessions held at Kilmarnock's Rugby Park, but it was on the local championship golf course that the players found most enjoyment.

Before the semi-final tie with Celtic, the tournament organisers found themselves with a problem, as the Players' Union of both England and Scotland protested that those taking part were only to receive £10 per game. The Cup Committee quickly organised a meeting in order to discuss the problem, having originally ignored the protests, and they eventually decided to raise the scale of payment to the players, although the increased figure was not divulged.

Returning to Hampden three days after their victory over one half of the 'Old Firm', United looked to complete the double, but they were to find semi-final opponents Celtic much sterner opposition.

Having won many plaudits for their performance against Rangers, United were disappointing against the green and white-hooped Celtic, never really finding their rhythm, with their final pass often letting them down. Perhaps having being forced into making changes to the side was the issue, with Henry Cockburn being forced out with an ankle injury and Matt Busby having to push Johnny Carey forward to right-half, shifting Don Gibson over to left-half, and Tom McNulty coming in at full-back.

The Celtic defence were seldom troubled in the opening half, thereby relieving their forwards from having to trail back to assist, giving them more opportunities to put the United defence under serious pressure. As it turned out, they failed to make the most of their opportunities, scoring only once: Tully rolled the ball into the path of Peacock, who crashed the ball past the helpless Crompton.

With the second half less than a minute old, United almost snatched the equaliser when a Pearson/Rowley move ended with the former missing an ideal opportunity while practically under the Celtic crossbar.

That close call seemed to do Celtic more good than it did United, as they were soon two goals to the good, Tully lifting the ball over the head of Chilton for the on-running Mochan to beat Crompton at the foot of the post.

The programme for the match versus Celtic, 16 May 1953.

Even with the strong wind behind them in the second half, United seldom threatened and, as the game progressed, Busby tried to improve matters by moving Aston from full-back to centre-forward, Rowley to outside-left and Byrne back into defence.

However, this failed to make any improvement, although the lackadaisical United side did manage to pull one goal back when Rowley scored 15 minutes from time. There was to be no equaliser though, despite the prompting and inspired play from Don Gibson, which on the whole went unrewarded.

United calls for a penalty were ignored and Collins hit the crossbar at the opposite end, just as the supporters on the open terracing covered their heads with newspapers and handkerchiefs while the rain poured down.

With 13 minutes to go Carey hooked the ball towards the Celtic goal, which Pearson back-headed towards Rowley, who smashed the ball past a helpless Bonnar in the Celtic goal, bringing the game back to life. Many thought that United might now snatch an equaliser, but Celtic held on to go into the Final and eventually lifted the trophy itself.

16 May 1953	**Celtic at Hampden Park, Glasgow.**

Attendance: 73,436.

Lost: 2–1.

Scorer: Rowley.

Team: Crompton, McNulty, Aston, Carey, Chilton, Gibson, Viollet, Downie, Rowley, Pearson, Byrne.

The game against Celtic marked the end of the career of one of United's greatest-ever players. Johnny Carey announced his retirement a week later. The 34-year-old United captain had crossed the Irish Sea as a fresh-faced youngster in 1936, joining the club from St James's Gate, a Dublin junior club, for a fee of £250.

It was certainly money well spent, as Carey went on to give United sterling service in a number of positions (including goalkeeper), leading them to League and FA Cup success and representing both Northern and the Republic of Ireland, as well as captaining the Rest of Europe.

On 8 September 1953 the United youngsters played a friendly charity match in aid of the World Jewish Sports Festival in Israel, at the Cliff training ground at Lower Broughton, against the unusually named Fourth Maccabiah XI. It was possibly the most unusually named side that a Manchester United team has ever faced.

Included in the 'United XI' were a few names who, in a short period of time, would become familiar to United followers. Taking part in this 3–1 victory were the likes of Bill Foulkes, Billy Redman, Bobby Harrop, Ian Greaves and Liam Whelan, with the former going on to carve out one of the most illustrious careers in United history.

Twelve months previously, United had visited Edinburgh to face the familiar opposition of Hibernian and found themselves on the receiving end of a 7–3 defeat. An invitation was left at Easter Road for the Scottish League side to make the journey to Manchester for a return match, but it was not purely in the hope of obtaining some form of revenge, as the game was billed as a benefit match for United's trainer, Tom Curry.

Despite fielding something of an under-strength team, with Chilton, Berry, Rowley and Pearson all missing, United pushed their visitors to the limit and were only robbed of victory in the dying seconds of the game.

United took the game to Hibs, playing some fine attacking football, and fully deserved their two-goal interval lead. Tommy Taylor headed the first in the 23rd minute, with Aston, again with a header, adding the second four minutes later.

Colin Webster, making his first-team debut at outside-right and Jackie Blanchflower, in the somewhat unfamiliar position of centre-forward, both distributed the ball well as United pushed forward, but at times the build-up play as a whole was just that little bit too slow to be effective.

There was, however, a scare for United as the first half moved to a close, when Reilly, playing his first game of the season, displayed some rustiness by missing an open goal from a mere five yards out.

The second half conjured up an entirely different 45 minutes, not only for Reilly, but for the visiting team as well. Their play was more fluent as they switched from defence to attack, with McFarlane, Coombe and Howie keeping a tight grip on the United forwards. Their task was made easier as the game progressed and legs became weaker.

Johnstone and Smith were always troublesome to the United defence and the home side were soon struggling even more after Reilly pulled a goal back with a well-hit left-footed shot. Despite Hibs having most of the second-half play, it did look as though United were going to hold out and win the game, but, in the final minute, Reilly pounced once again to score the equaliser.

The programme for the match versus Hibs, 30 September 1953.

30 September 1953	**Hibs at Old Trafford.**

Attendance: 8,441.

Draw: 2–2.

Scorers: Aston, Taylor.

Team: Wood, Foulkes, Byrne, Carey, Jones, Cockburn, Webster, Aston, Blanchflower, Taylor, McShane.

United returned to Millwall only a matter of months after being held to an entertaining 4–4 draw, with the Londoners giving United a return invitation in order to celebrate the switching on of their floodlights.

This fixture was a far cry from the previous meeting and was described by one newspaper correspondent as 'the most unfriendly friendly match I can remember', while another wrote 'I doubt if the word "friendly" should be applied at all, for the atmosphere throughout was more like a bitter Cup tie with everything at stake.' Possibly the hurt from the previous season's FA Cup defeat was still there, but it was certainly to turn into a bruising encounter.

Into the United side came 18-year-old Noel McFarlane, a Dubliner, making his first senior outing and stepping into the team at outside-right as part of an experimental forward line, which had Tommy Taylor moving to centre-forward, Jack Rowley to inside-left and Johnny Aston, as he had done against Hibs, lining up at inside-right.

Right from the kick-off Millwall would not let United settle on the ball, with centre-forward Frank Neary leading the line with much more than enthusiasm, giving Allenby Chilton a difficult time. His 'enthusiasm' was most explicit when he waved away his trainer and a stretcher as blood poured from his right cheek following a clash with Jeff Whitefoot.

There was little to suggest a difference in divisions between the two sides and it was Millwall who went in front in the 10th minute, with a penalty from Jardine after Foulkes had handled in the area. From that moment on Millwall never looked back and, even though it was something of a short-lived lead, as United equalised eight minutes later when Taylor headed home, the crowd sensed that here was a creditable scrap for the taking.

United did show moments of class, with Taylor and Rowley both prominent. However, what the Third Division side lacked in that department they certainly made up for in spirit and endeavour, egged on by a fiercely partisan crowd.

Their grit and determination brought apt rewards, as through Neary they snatched a 73rd-minute equaliser. The centre-forward jumped with an unsighted Ray Wood as a curling Monkhouse corner came towards the United goal. Ball and goalkeeper finished up in the back of the net to give Millwall a memorable and creditable 2–1 victory.

---

5 October 1953   **Millwall at The Den.**

Attendance: 20,092.

Lost: 2–1.

Scorer: Taylor.

Team: Wood, Foulkes, Byrne, Whitefoot, Chilton, Blanchflower, McFarlane, Aston, Taylor, Rowley, McShane.

As has been mentioned previously, friendly fixtures are rarely documented in any official history of Manchester United, but of the few scattered throughout the various publications that have appeared over the years, there is one which always rates a mention.

Matt Busby, having created a League Championship and FA Cup-winning side during his seven years as manager of United, knew that the players who remained from that initial trophy win in 1948, the likes of Chilton, Cockburn, Pearson and Rowley, were all reaching the end of their careers in the top flight and sooner, rather than later, he would have to make the decision to replace them and create a new Manchester United.

He had already sown the seeds of this 'new' team, with Johnny Berry and Roger Byrne having won championship medals in 1952 and the likes of Tommy Taylor, a rare dip into the transfer market, and Ray Wood establishing themselves in the first team.

On 24 October 1953 United had beaten Aston Villa 1–0 at Old Trafford in what was widely considered to be a rather poor 90 minutes. One correspondent actually began his match report by writing: 'How can football sink so low as in this game at Old Trafford? You expect £15- a-week players to serve up something better than this, which was the season's worst at the ground.' He brought his report to a close with: 'Drastic United changes might be expected, and while the players are having a week's holiday at Troon, Scotland, this week, manager Matt Busby will, no doubt, be giving serious thought to the reason why the United forward line is not blending.' It was to be the friendly against Kilmarnock at Rugby Park that would provide him with the ideal platform to try out a few ideas.

Out from the side that had under-performed against Aston Villa went Stan Pearson and Jack Rowley, while an injury midway through the first half forced Henry Cockburn from the field. Into the forward line came Jackie Blanchflower and Dennis Viollet, while Cockburn's injury worked very much in Busby's favour, as it saw the introduction of a replacement whose arrival on the pitch was acknowledged by 'Waverley' in the *Daily Record* by no more than 'Cockburn then received an injury and was taken off. Ten minutes later a substitute took his place at left-half'. That man was Duncan Edwards.

The fixture, arranged to mark the opening of the Rugby Park floodlights, was a far cry from the mediocre fare dished up at Old Trafford four days previously, with the 16,000 crowd treated to an action-packed evening with football of the highest quality.

United opened the scoring after only three minutes, with Cockburn lobbing the ball towards the Kilmarnock goal from 20 yards. It was clearly the goalkeeper's ball, but the unfortunate Brown slipped and fell as the ball came towards him and he could only look on as it dropped under the bar and into the net.

Although not as fast as their visitors, Kilmarnock stuck to their task and, just before Cockburn's exit from the field, Crompton had to produce a save at his right-hand post from Henaughan. However, following the introduction of Edwards, United gradually established their superiority, although their finishing still left a little to be desired.

Ten minutes prior to the interval, United scored a second. Blanchflower crossed the ball beyond a Kilmarnock defender, allowing Taylor to run through, and the United centre was able to wrong-foot the goalkeeper before walking the ball into the vacant net. Faced with a similar opportunity shortly afterwards, Taylor placed the ball wide of an open goal from eight yards out.

After the interval it looked as though United would swamp the home side, but good saves from Brown and the continued poor finishing kept the score at 2–0. McNulty and Chilton both headed off the line, while Crompton pulled off two excellent saves, from Harvey and Murray, as Kilmarnock pushed forward in search of some consolation. However, it was United who found the back of the net, Viollet scoring against the run of play with only five minutes remaining.

---

28 October 1953   **Kilmarnock at Rugby Park.**

Attendance: 16,000.

Won: 3–0.

Scorers: Cockburn, Viollet, Taylor.

Team: Crompton, McNulty, Byrne, Gibson, Chilton, Cockburn, Berry, Blanchflower, Taylor, Viollet, McShane.

Substitutes: Edwards for Cockburn.

The name Western Command will mean little to many of today's football followers; it is also a team that will fail to appear in any club histories, as it was made up of serving soldiers and played only friendly fixtures. They do, however, turn up in opposition to United on a number of occasions in the mid-1950s.

The first encounter between the two teams occurred on Wednesday 9 December at Wrexham's Racecourse Ground. It must be noted that, although they were serving soldiers, the Western Command side were also seasoned professional footballers. Names in the opposition line up who will be familiar to those readers who had an interest in football in the late 1950s to the early 1960s were the likes of Private Hopkins of Tottenham Hotspur, Lieutenant Corporal Meadows of Manchester City, Gunner Clayton of Blackburn Rovers and Corporal Deeley of Wolverhampton Wanderers. The latter two caused United goalkeeper Jack Crompton a couple of anxious moments in his muddy goalmouth.

Matt Busby did not select any of those players who had been involved against Sheffield United in a Football League First Division fixture the previous Saturday, but did include nine players with First Division experience. Two youngsters who made the journey to north Wales, Salford-born full-back Geoff Bent and inside-forward Liam Whelan from Dublin, were making what could be considered their first-team debuts. It would be another year before Bent made his League debut and Whelan was not to grace the First Division stage until March 1955.

United's somewhat unfamiliar side certainly gave a good account of themselves, despite going behind to a goal by Pattison of Barnsley. They soon took command of the game and made the contest a rather unmatched confrontation.

Stan Pearson levelled the scoring before the interval and in the second half, when the army side found the going just that little bit too much and the defensive trio of Aston, Jones and Bent too hard to break down, United scored a further three goals through an Eddie Lewis double and another from Pearson.

---

9 December 1953   Western Command at Racecourse Ground, Wrexham.

Attendance: Unknown

Won: 4–1.

Scorers: Lewis 2, Pearson 2.

Team: Crompton, Aston, Bent, Gibson, Jones, Cockburn, Scott, Whelan, Lewis, Pearson, Pegg.

Despite achieving FA Cup success in season 1947–48 and reaching the semi-finals the following year, the competition produced little in the way of note in the early and mid-1950s. Season 1951–52 had seen defeat at the hands of Hull City in the third round, while the following season United took two attempts to overcome Walthamstow Avenue.

Another third-round exit in 1953–54, this time at the hands of fellow First Division side Burnley, produced a number of blank Saturdays on the United fixture list and, on the day of the fourth-round ties, a friendly was arranged against Second Division Bristol Rovers at Eastville.

The home side welcomed the opportunity to flex their muscles against the much classier opposition, but were certainly not overawed by their presence and, had it been a Cup tie rather than a somewhat meaningless friendly, United might have found themselves on the end of yet another embarrassing FA Cup exit.

Rovers pressed forward straight from the kick-off and forced a corner in the first minute, with the ball remaining in and around the United goalmouth for a few minutes before Roger Byrne finally managed to head it clear.

United slowly came into the game and Rowley had both an accurate centre and an in-swinging corner dramatically cleared by a Bristol defender. Eddie Lewis also came close to opening the scoring but he shot too quickly, putting his effort wide of the post.

The home side were certainly not content just to sit back and allow United to run the show and responded by creating chances of their own. Sykes tested Ray Wood from 25 yards with a powerful drive, while the United goal had an even more fortunate escape when outside-right Biggs sent over a high centre that forced Wood into making a fine save. Shortly afterwards, Hale did beat the United 'keeper, but his shot went over the bar when he should have done much better.

It was United, though, who took the lead a minute from half-time. McFarlane got away on the right and from around 25 yards out hit a searing shot which rattled off the Bristol Rovers crossbar. The ball rebounded to the feet of Lewis, who grasped the opportunity to tap the ball into the almost empty net.

In the second half Rovers pushed United to the limits coming close to scoring on several occasions. Biggs could only watch his effort slip past the post by a matter of inches, and Hale then forced another good save out of Wood. Watling also brought the best out of the United goalkeeper, with Wood diving to push the outside-left's shot round the post.

United did have their moments in the second half, with Rowley as the main danger man. However, with the home side enjoying most of the play, the visitors did well to win to hold on to their lead.

30 January 1954	**Bristol Rovers at Eastville.**

Attendance: 10,898.

Won: 1–0.

Scorer: Lewis.

Team: Wood, Foulkes, Byrne, Whitefoot, Chilton, Cockburn, McFarlane, Blanchflower, Lewis, Viollet, Rowley.

The programme for the match versus Bristol Rovers, 30 January 1954.

Having lost 3–1 against Arsenal at Highbury on Saturday 27 March, Matt Busby's team retuned to London two days later to face Queen's Park Rangers in a testimonial match for former United and QPR goalkeeper Reg Allen.

Allen had joined the Loftus Road club in May 1938, but his playing career had been put on temporary hold during World War Two, when he served in the Commandoes and spent three years as a prisoner of war after being captured in North Africa. He had joined United in June 1950 and made 80 appearances, winning a League Championship medal in 1952, before being forced to retire the following year.

Matt Busby had hoped to call on the services of former United favourite Stan Pearson, now with Bury and a former teammate of Allen's, to line up as a guest, but an injury received in the Shakers' Second Division match with Birmingham ruled him out. Busby was also forced to make the journey south without Duncan Edwards, who was required for United's FA Youth Cup semi-final tie with West Bromwich Albion on the Wednesday. He was also aware that Tommy Taylor and Roger Byrne might also pull out of his squad upon arrival if they had been named that afternoon in the England team for their match against Scotland on the forthcoming Saturday. As it turned out, only the latter was required, although Taylor was omitted due to an ankle injury.

Under the Loftus Road floodlights a decent crowd turned out to honour the popular goalkeeper and they were treated to five goals, although the quality of defending was, at times, not of the highest standard, as three of the goals were scored by defenders against their own side.

The scoring began when the home defender Peter Angell headed a free-kick past his own 'keeper. Jack Rowley put United two up with Queen's Park Rangers captain Jim Taylor giving the visitors a rather flattering 3–0 half-time lead.

In the second half Queen's Park Rangers put United under periods of pressure with United more than a little grateful to have the gifted own-goals and the Rowley strike in their favour. There must, however, have been something of an 'own-goal bug' at one end of the Loftus Road pitch, with United's Geoff Bent catching it as he put the ball past Jack Crompton in the 73rd minute. The home forwards had struggled to do the same.

There was some debate, however, relating to United's fourth goal in the final minute: Viollet and Lewis are both credited with this.

The programme for the match versus Queen's Park Rangers, 29 March 1954.

29 March 1954   **Queen's Park Rangers at Loftus Road.**

Attendance: 15,529.

Won: 4–1.

Scorers: Rowley, Lewis, 2 opp. own-goals, or Rowley, Viollet, 2 opp. own-goals.

Team: Crompton, Foulkes, Bent, Whitefoot, Chilton, Cockburn, Berry, Aston, Lewis, Viollet, Rowley.

Despite the intensity of the First Division programme, United lined up for their seventh friendly of the season against neighbours Manchester City in a charity match for Henshaw's Institute of the Blind. Once again manager Matt Busby was restricted in his choice of team personnel, as Henry Cockburn, Tommy Taylor, Roger Byrne, Dennis Viollet and Duncan Edwards had all been selected for an England versus Young England match at Highbury three days later, while Jeff Whitefoot had been called up to represent the RAF.

The crowd of just over 10,000, who raised the sum of £779 19s for the evening's benefactors, were treated to an entertaining match, with United establishing a two-goal lead through Blanchflower and Aston.

City's chances of clawing back some local respectability seemed remote when their centre-half Dave Ewing was led off the pitch after 23 minutes following a collision with his teammate McTavish, which resulted in a cut eye that required two stitches.

After the interval, however, City, without Ewing and also Hart, who injured a knee, turned the game around, with substitutes Whitfield and Hayes playing a prominent part in the fightback, which saw three goals in the space of seven minutes, leaving United stunned. Clarke, McAdams and Meadows scored those City goals and there could easily have been a fourth had Jones not headed a Meadows effort off the line just before the end.

The only consolation for the United players was the gift of specially knitted pullovers by the employees of the Institute.

The programme for the match versus Manchester City, 28 April 1954.

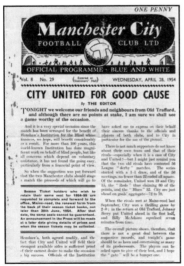

28 April 1954   **Manchester City at Maine Road.**

Attendance: 10,261.

Lost: 3–2.

Scorers: Aston, Blanchflower.

Team: Crompton, Foulkes, Bent, Gibson, Jones, Chilton, Bery, Aston, Rowley, Blanchflower, Pegg.

United went from the familiar to the unfamiliar in a matter of days with an excursion to Carrow Road to take on Norwich City for the right to own the Norfolk and Norwich Charities Cup for 12 months.

It was perhaps appropriate, therefore, that in the jubilee year of the competition the trophy would remain on home territory, with the Second Division side, backed by an enthusiastic following, playing somewhat above themselves to defeat a strong United side.

Faster to the ball, while at the same time displaying more verve and imagination than their more notable opponents, Norwich could, if it had not been for one or two glaring goalmouth misses, have won even more convincingly.

United's attack was disappointing, despite its trio of England internationals. The Norwich defenders Foulkes and Lewis were in outstanding form, with the visiting defence kept on its toes by Woan, the scorer of both the Norwich goals, and the lively Brennan. In the 25th minute Gordon began a cross-field move on the left involving Woan, Gavin and Carberry, which saw the former beating Crompton from close range. With the deadlock broken the crowd anticipated the game evolving into a goalscoring free-for-all.

However, they were to be disappointed, as there was to be no more scoring until five minutes from time when the home side added a second. A through pass from Brennan was picked up by Johnston, who squared the ball to the waiting Woan, who calmly picked his spot to put the game beyond United's reach.

United were, however, to snatch a consolation effort in the final minute, when an injudicious back pass left Viollet with only the 'keeper to beat, which he did with ease.

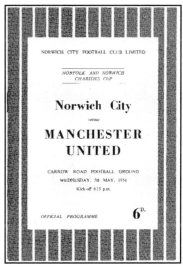

The programme for the match versus Norwich City, 5 May 1954.

5 May 1954 — Norwich City at Carrow Road.

Attendance: 9,000.

Lost: 2–1.

Scorer: Viollet.

Team: Crompton, Foulkes, Aston, Gibson, Chilton, Cockburn, Berry, Whelan, Taylor, Viollet, Rowley.

The name of Clyde does not conjure up the same visions as that of Rangers, Celtic, Hibs or Hearts, but in the mid to late 1950s, the team from Glasgow's south side were something of a force to be reckoned with, lifting the Scottish Cup in 1955 and 1958 and the Second Division championship in 1957.

As they approached those halcyon days in their history, Clyde entertained United on a couple of occasions, with the first meeting seeing a very strong United side being taken by surprise at the spartan south Glasgow stadium, which was also used for greyhound racing.

United travelled north minus Ray Wood, Bill Foulkes, Roger Byrne and Jackie Blanchflower, who were all required for the Northern Ireland v England international fixture three days later. However, it was still a strong squad that Matt Busby had available for selection and in the early stages of the game the quartet were not missed, as United were faster to the ball than their opponents.

A four-man move created an ideal scoring opportunity for the usually dependable Tommy Taylor, but the Yorkshireman shot weakly past the post and this miss seemed to galvanise the home side into action. A desperate lunge by Greaves at Ring prevented a certain goal, while the United full-back almost undid his good work minutes later when he misdirected a pass back to Crompton and could only watch open-mouthed as the ball hit a post and rebounded to safety. The United goal had another narrow escape when a 20-yard shot from Laing was only gathered by Crompton at the second attempt.

Despite the prolonged Clyde pressure, it was United who took the lead in the 22nd minute, mounting a counter-attack which caught the home defence out of position. Kennedy, having stopped a Clyde attack, promptly cleared the ball upfield towards Taylor and, although closely marked by centre-half Anderson, the United centre-forward dummied his marker before shooting past Hewkins with a shot that the goalkeeper got only a glimpse of.

United continued to press, with Berry in fine form, forcing Hewkins into making three excellent saves. However, to their credit Clyde got their game together and equalised in the 34th minute through Buchanan, who headed home from a corner. Shortly afterwards they were unlucky not to take the lead when a Ring shot cannoned off the crossbar.

Early in the second half Jack Rowley brought the best out of Hewkins, who did well to gather the United forward's shot at head height. However, United were knocked off their stride when, in the 15th minute, Jones upended Ring inside the penalty area as the Clyde man moved in on goal. From the spot-kick Robertson gave Crompton little chance.

Buchanan was slow to react to a teammate's back-heeler with the goalmouth beckoning, but a third goal soon materialised. Robertson was again the scorer, finishing off a good move with an unexpected shot from 25 yards out.

This goal seemed to demoralise the visitors, and even Busby's reorganisation of the forward line failed to inject any new rhythm or method into their play. It was really no surprise when Clyde added a fourth goal. A high lob from Ring into the United area was met by Hill, whose shot beat Crompton at his left-hand post. The 'keeper then managed to collect the ball, but turned towards the net, prompting many of those on the terracing behind and the Clyde players nearby to shout 'goal'. Much to their dismay, the referee said 'no goal' and Clyde had to be content with their highly creditable 4–1 victory.

29 September 1954 **Clyde at Shawfield.**

Attendance: 11,000.
Lost: 4–1.
Scorer: Taylor.
Team: Crompton, Greaves, Kennedy, Gibson, Jones, Edwards, Berry, Viollet, Taylor, Pegg, Rowley.

Just over a fortnight later Matt Busby took his team back over Hadrian's Wall and, under the familiar shadow of the towering Arthur's Seat, they managed to overcome Hibs for the first time since 1948.

Despite the fast running of Johnny Berry, tormenting the Hibs defence at every opportunity, it was Ray Wood who was the busier of the two goalkeepers in the opening half, making brilliant saves against Reilly, Smith and Ormond. He had little chance, however, with an excellent Reilly header from a Smith centre, which gave the home side an 18-minute lead.

United could have considered themselves fortunate to be only one goal behind at the interval, but after the turnaround their attack seemed to show more power as they slowly clawed themselves into the game. Tommy Taylor, although well held by 17-year-old centre-half Plenderleith, who was playing only his third first-team game, pounced on a chance to score a deserved equaliser 12 minutes after the restart.

Albert Scanlon put United in front, but the United goal soon found itself under intense pressure, with Wood fumbling a tremendous shot from Moran amid cries of 'goal' from the green and white-shirted players and the home support behind the goal.

During the final quarter of an hour play revolved around Wood's goal, but the home side just could not make the necessary breakthrough and, much to their dismay, a quick throw-in found Blanchflower, who made United's third.

15 November 1954	Hibs at Easter Road.

Attendance: 25,500.

Won: 3–1.

Scorers: Taylor, Scanlon, Blanchflower.

Team: Wood, Foulkes, Byrne, Gibson, Chilton, Goodwin, Berry, Blanchflower, Taylor, Viollet, Scanlon.

Having been dumped out of the FA Cup by local rivals Manchester City 2–0 in the fourth round at the end of January, United had a free weekend on the day of the sixth round, which ironically saw Notts County and York City face each other. Therefore, in order to keep up the fitness level of his players, Busby arranged to play a friendly against the unfamiliar opposition of Lincoln City.

The Second Division side were certainly not overawed by United, with Ray Wood called into the action early on and producing two fine saves from Gibson and Hails. Gibson continued to be something of a threat, forcing Wood into making a further two good saves.

Lincoln centre-half Emery did well to clear from Scanlon, as United rallied with some stylish play, but the outside-left should have perhaps passed to the better-placed Webster. Goalkeeper Downie saved a stinging shot from Taylor as United pushed for the equaliser.

The early goal had failed to settle Lincoln, whose play at times was erratic, with passes going astray with too much regularity, while United, on the other hand, had now begun to play with their accustomed flowing style. A Whitefoot pass split the Lincoln defence, but Scanlon had wandered too far forward and was flagged offside.

Very much against the run of play, Lincoln scored a second on the half-hour through Munro. Receiving the ball from Neal, he raced through on his own before shooting low into the goalmouth as Byrne and Foulkes unsuccessfully attempted to clear the ball.

By half-time, however, United were level. Colin Webster scored both, in the 42nd and 43rd minutes. The first saw Berry's right-wing centre cause three Lincoln defenders to hesitate in an 'after you, no after you' fashion, with Webster taking advantage of their failure to make up their minds to prod the ball over the line. The second came straight from the kick-off as United regained possession and another ball from the wing found Webster moving in on goal, with his header beating Downie.

Play in the second half was rather subdued and it took a goal from Scanlon in the 57th minute to bring the game back to life. This was only fleeting, as the game once again fizzled out as the interest from both sides slowly disappeared.

12 March 1955	Lincoln City at Sincil Bank.

Attendance: 7,844.

Won: 3–2.

Scorers: Webster 2, Scanlon.

Team: Wood, Foulkes, Byrne, Gibson, Jones, Whitefoot, Berry, Taylor, Webster, Whelan, Scanlon.

United returned to Scandinavia for their second close-season tour and following a smooth but tiring journey from Copenhagen, the United party docked very early in the morning at Aarhus, their first port of call, where they played a Jutland Select XI in the first of their four games.

The programme for the match versus Lincoln City, 12 March 1955.

Made up of players from the top four Jutland clubs, seven of whom were full Danish internationals, the first match of the tour marked the 10th anniversary of Denmark's liberation from German occupation during World War Two.

United set Jackie Blanchflower playing at centre-forward, in a move which caused the Danish defence numerous problems as the big Irishman combined well with inside partner Tommy Taylor. However, it was winger Johnny Berry who took the Man of the Match award, with some outstanding play on the wing earning him the tag 'little Matthews' from the appreciative home crowd.

Mark Jones and Roger Byrne were well in command at the back, with goalkeeper Ray Wood also turning in a fine display, but the 1–0 victory was considered something of a disappointing result as a few of the United players seemed to be playing at half pace. Even with only 10 men, following Berry's departure with an injury in the 85th minute, they were never under threat of losing their advantage.

The only goal of the game came three minutes before the interval and was scored by Tommy Taylor with a fierce drive. The England international also came close on three other occasions with powerful headers.

---

3 May 1955   **Jutland XI at Aarhus Stadium.**

Attendance: 5,900.

Won: 1–0.

Scorer: Taylor.

Team: Wood, Foulkes, Byrne, Gibson, Jones, Whitefoot, Berry, Taylor, Blanchflower, Viollet, Scanlon.

As in the first game of the tour, it was the United defence which stood out in the fixture against a Copenhagen Select XI, Jones and Byrne once again playing brilliantly. Had the visiting forwards been of the same high standard then United would certainly have won the game by more than the solitary goal.

Despite their determination and attitude, the Danish team were outclassed by their opponents and were more than grateful to escape with the single, well-taken Blanchflower goal against them.

---

6 May 1955   **Copenhagen XI.**

Attendance: 15,600.

Won: 1–0.

Scorer: Blanchflower.

Team: Wood, Foulkes, Byrne, Whitefoot, Jones, Edwards, Webster, Taylor, Blanchflower, Viollet, Pegg.

Against a team made up of players from the five Copenhagen clubs, United maintained a 100 per cent tour record with a fine 3–1 win against what was listed as a Copenhagen Combination XI. They treated the crowd to a display of exhibition football at its best.

For the third consecutive game the plaudits went to defenders Mark Jones and Roger Byrne, but the crowd were disappointed when it was announced that Johnny Berry would not be playing due to a back injury. They were, however, compensated by the inclusion of Duncan Edwards for his first appearance of the tour. The 18-year-old Dudley youngster was the player everyone wanted to meet and the number one target for the numerous autograph hunters who besieged the players at every opportunity.

Berry's replacement, Colin Webster, missed a couple of chances which the former would probably have put away, but the young Welshman did have a hand in two of United's goals. The first, in the 24th minute, saw his corner headed forward by Tommy Taylor and into the path of Viollet, who tapped it home from close range.

Viollet also scored United's second in the 58th minute, running onto a pass from Blanchflower to hit a rising drive past a helpless goalkeeper from 20 yards out. Ten minutes later it was 3–0. Webster turned the ball into the goalmouth for Blanchflower to head through with ease.

Busby was forced into a substitution 15 minutes from the end after Taylor pulled a muscle. However, before Eddie Lewis could come on as his replacement, Roger Byrne blotted his copybook by giving away a penalty when he handled inside the penalty area. Henning Jensen scored from the spot.

8 May 1955	**Copenhagen Combination.**

Attendance: 11,500.
Won: 3–1.
Scorers: Viollet 2, Blanchflower.
Team: Wood, Foulkes, Byrne, Whitefoot, Jones, Edwards, Webster, Taylor, Blanchflower, Viollet, Pegg.
Substitute: Lewis for Taylor.

It was a somewhat depleted United side that finished the tour against the Gothenburg Alliance, with Tommy Taylor out due to a pulled muscle and Roger Byrne and Duncan Edwards having to leave for London to meet up with the England squad. Despite these setbacks, Matt Busby's selection still proved too strong for the local 11 and their guest players.

Johnny Berry, acting as captain, finished the tour as he began, as the star attraction in the United line up, thrilling the crowd with his skills while scoring two of United's four goals, in a display which was more akin to the football played by Continental sides, than those of the English First Division.

United opened strongly, but it was half an hour before they opened the scoring. Berry ended a mazy dribble by beating the goalkeeper with ease. He also scored the second 12 minutes later, heading a Blanchflower cross into the net.

In the second half the hard-tackling Swedes mounted something of a fightback and scored in the 71st minute through their outside-right Olsson, but United increased their lead 60 seconds later when Whitefoot scored from 25 yards out. United's lead was once again pegged back when Jacobsson collected the ball in a clear offside position, but he was allowed to run on by the sympathetic officials and beat the helpless Crompton in the United goal.

Six minutes from time United restored their two-goal advantage with a fine strike by Whelan.

At the official reception following the match Jackie Blanchflower led the United players in entertaining their hosts with a variety of songs in an enjoyable evening of food and drink before a further two-day break in Copenhagen. They took in some of the sights in a 60-mile coastal trip, including a visit to the King's Summer Palace at Fridensburg and the legendary home of Hamlet at Elsinore.

The programme for the match versus Gothenburg Alliance, 10 May 1955.

Ticket for the match versus Gothenburg Alliance, 10 May 1955.

The programme for the match versus Hibernian, 19 September 1955.

10 May 1955   **Gothenburg Alliance at Ullevi Sports Stadium.**

Attendance: 15,473.

Won: 4–2.

Scorers: Berry 2, Whitefoot, Whelan.

Team: Crompton, Foulkes, Bent, Gibson, Jones, Whitefoot, Berry, Whelan, Blanchflower, Viollet, Scanlon.

Season 1955–56 saw old adversaries Hibernian make something of a giant step for British football when they took part in the inaugural European Cup competition. The following season would see United take a similar path, but for now they had to be content with a friendly against a team who were now a 'name' in European football. Fortunately it was only a friendly, as Hibs really turned on the style, defeating what was an under-strength United side 5–0. Had it been in the European Cup, even United would have stood little chance of overturning such a reversal.

United began the game well. However, it was Hibs who put the ball in the back of the net when a Younger clearance was headed forward to Reilly by Mulkerrin. The centre-forward pushed the ball out to Ormond, who beat Ray Wood with a rising left-footed shot. Five minutes later it was 2–0, an unmarked Reilly scoring from 20 yards out. Blanchflower almost pulled a goal back, but Younger won the appreciation of the crowd with a fine save and, as the game progressed, Hibs began to dictate the play with the United defence being made to look slow and cumbersome. Hibs made it three in the 24th minute when Mulkerrin finished off a fine passing move, beating Wood with an unstoppable shot.

A four-minute spell either side of the interval finished the game from a goalscoring point of view, with the fourth Hibs goal coming three minutes before half-time. Following a foul on Mulkerrin, out near to touchline, Ormond's free-kick was only partly cleared and Reilly quickly snatched the opportunity to beat Wood. A minute after the restart, Thomson passed to McFarlane, who launched the ball forward towards Mulkerrin, who headed it down to the feet of Turnbull and from six yards out the Hibs inside-forward made no mistake.

United rarely got within shooting distance of the Hibs goal and on the odd occasion that they did, the finishing was rather erratic. Even when the home side eased up, United failed to make any leeway on what was a disappointing night in the Scottish capital.

28 September 1955   **Hibs at Easter Road.**

Attendance: 22,500.

Lost: 5–0.

Team: Wood, Foulkes, Bent, Whitefoot, Jones, Goodwin, Scott, Blanchflower, Lewis, Doherty, Pegg.

Friendly fixtures are often ignored by supporters, who consider the majority of such games to be little more than glorified training sessions, with many of the players on show simply going through the motions and the eventual outcome at the end of the 90 minutes of no consequence whatsoever. There are, however, plus points to attending some of those friendlies and that is the satisfaction of being able to say that 'I was there', when a young, previously unknown player makes his initial senior appearance, going on to enjoy a long aand fruitful career in the game.

On one late autumn evening in 1955, less than 9,000 people visited Gigg Lane in Bury to watch something of a local derby, unaware that they were about to witness the first tentative steps on the rungs of the professional football ladder by a Northumberland teenager by the name of Bobby Charlton.

On the day of the game, the following appeared in the local *Evening News*: 'Manchester United completely reshuffle their inside-forward positions and give 17-year-old Bobby Charlton his big chance in tonight's floodlit match with Bury at Gigg Lane.

'Charlton, who comes from the North-East, has been in great form for the reserves. He has scored nine times in nine Central League appearances.'

The game provided the crowd with value for money, conjuring up six goals. Although three of United's five came in the first half, the second 45 minutes lacked much of the entertainment value that the first had created.

Bury opened brightly, putting the United goal under some pressure, but such attacks were to prove fruitless and three goals in the space of 20 minutes, from John Doherty, Colin Webster and debutant Bobby Charlton, knocked them off their stride.

An early second-half goal from Doherty finished the game as a contest and, despite Daniel pulling one back for the home side with arguably the best goal of the game, there was little hope of Bury rallying to thrill their supporters with a valiant fightback.

Berry and Webster caused the Bury defence considerable problems, with the former scoring a fifth for United, signalling for many that there was little point in remaining until the final whistle.

Rather surprisingly, Bobby Charlton fails to mention the game in his recently penned autobiography.

4 October 1955	**Bury at Gigg Lane.**

Attendance: 8,817.

Won: 5–1.

Scorers: Doherty 2, Berry, Webster, Charlton.

Team: Wood, Byrne, Bent, Whitefoot, Jones, Goodwin, Berry, Doherty, Webster, Charlton, Pegg.

The next friendly is another which you can not find in any of the record books, as it was played behind closed doors at Old Trafford, with the England B team in opposition. It was perhaps fortunate for the international hopefuls that the game was only 25 minutes each way, as who knows what the score would have been if the game had gone the full 90 minutes?

There was no fluke about the 6–0 scoreline, with the England selectors left with something of a headache before the B international against Yugoslavia at Maine Road the following evening. Obviously, none of the England players would have wanted to pick up an injury, but at the same time they wanted to create a favourable impression. As it was, they did receive a couple of injuries, with centre-half Kennedy and inside-forward Perry both picking up knocks.

From the kick-off United controlled the game and they were three goals in front by half-time, with the international attack more than disappointing. With United's goals coming from the England trio of Tommy Taylor, with three, Bobby Charlton claiming a double and Johnny Berry, the selectors should perhaps have made some additions to their squad.

The programme for the match versus Bury, 4 October 1955.

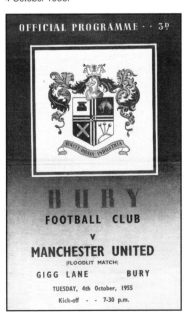

The heavy defeat, by the way, served as something of a wake-up call to the England players, as they went out and defeated the Yugoslavs 5–1 at Maine Road.

---

18 October 1955   **England B at Old Trafford.**

Won: 6–0.

Scorers: Taylor 3, Charlton 2, Berry.

Team: Crompton, Greaves, Bent, Whitefoot, Jones, Edwards, Berry, Doherty, Taylor, Charlton, Pegg.

Substitutes: McGuinness for Edwards, Blanchflower for Charlton.

Just over 24 hours later, an almost identical United side lined up against Clyde at Shawfield, something that would certainly not occur today, at least not in early or mid-season.

On a rain-soaked Glasgow evening, United's mixture of reserve and first-team players came unstuck against a determined Clyde team. They were eager to maintain the dominance of Scottish League sides over their English counterparts during the current season, when only one club from south of the border had managed to defeat a Scottish 11.

Despite the conditions, which saw the ball skid around the sodden playing surface, United managed to maintain their passing game while bombarding the Clyde goal from a variety of angles, and they looked on course for a notable victory north of Hadrian's Wall. Their supremacy, however, did not count, as they could not turn it into goals.

In the eighth minute Taylor had an 18-yard effort tipped over the bar by Clyde goalkeeper Wilson. A 25-yard drive, 17 minutes later, rebounded off the underside of the crossbar before being scrambled away by goalkeeper Wilson. In between those two efforts, a left-footed thunderbolt from Duncan Edwards also came close, but cannoned off the bottom of the post. Wilson also made a couple of outstanding saves, punching the ball clear while under pressure.

Tommy Taylor continued the one-man crusade on the Clyde goal as the second half got underway and it seemed only a matter of time before United took the lead. A goal did finally appear, in the 67th minute, but it was scored by Lennox of Clyde, who out-jumped the United defence to head home a McHard cross in a move begun by the effervescent Divers.

The goal upset the United momentum and they were dealt a second blow seven minutes later when Divers created space for Gallacher, who passed to McHard, who in turn crossed for Lennox to head his second.

Four minutes from the end United did manage to score, but it was through the bad luck of Clyde defender Gallacher rather than their own creativity, as the unfortunate bully wee player slipped as he was about to clear and the ball rolled to Blanchflower, who gratefully accepted the gift.

---

19 October 1955   **Clyde at Shawfield.**

Attendance: 12,000.

Lost: 2–1.

Scorer: Blanchflower.

Team: Crompton, Greaves, Bent, Whitefoot, Jones, Edwards, Berry, Blanchflower, Taylor, Doherty, Pegg.

On 7 January 1956 United travelled to Eastville for what was, on paper at least, a straightforward third-round FA Cup tie against Second Division Bristol Rovers. It was to be the only Cup tie of a season which saw United lift the First Division championship, as the underdogs recorded a memorable 4–0 victory.

So, on the afternoon of the FA Cup fourth-round ties, United were forced to look for an alternative fixture and this was found across the Pennines against Leeds United at Elland Road.

Matt Busby was forced into making a couple of changes to his preferred line up, with Greaves and Goodwin deputising for Foulkes and Colman, who were on army duty, but the return of centre-forward Tommy Taylor bolstered the attack.

It was an ideal fixture to keep things ticking over, as Leeds were challenging for promotion from the Second Division and were eager to test themselves against their Lancastrian visitors. However, it was United who made most of the early running.

The majority of those early attacks materialised down the left, where Pegg was in excellent form, ably assisted by Byrne, who came closest to scoring with an angled drive that went narrowly past the post.

It was not all one-way traffic, however, as Leeds eased their way into the game and were soon dictating the play. Scott, on the United right, was robbed of the ball and Overfield came close after getting the better of Greaves. Another couple of opportunities went astray when a free-kick in a good position was wasted and Charles shot well wide of the United goal from around 22 yards out. Thankfully for United, Mark Jones was in good form, breaking down several attacks, with Edwards alongside him also doing his fair share of defensive work.

Halfway through the first half United almost broke the deadlock, when Leeds United goalkeeper Scott dropped the ball following a Pegg centre. This led to a scramble in the goalmouth, which saw Whelan gain possession and push the ball towards the empty net. Fortunately for Leeds, Jones had dropped back and was able to clear the ball off the line.

Play swung from end to end, with both goals having narrow escapes, but it was United who opened the scoring in the 35th minute, when Duncan Edwards beat the Leeds 'keeper with an opportunist effort from around 12 yards out, after both Scott and Blanchflower had come close with headers.

Leeds immediately retaliated, with both D. Jones and Brooks coming close, but they were caught on the hop when, three minutes prior to the interval, John Scott added a second for United.

The second half saw United control the game, showing the gulf between the two sides. They added a third just as the floodlights came on, Taylor putting the ball beyond goalkeeper Scott, while Edwards added a fourth, his second of the game, with the home side gaining a consolation goal for their afternoon's endeavours.

28 January 1956	Leeds United at Elland Road.

Attendance: 13,000.

Won: 4–1.

Scorers: Edwards 2, Scott, Taylor.

Team: Wood, Greaves, Byrne, Goodwin, Jones, Edwards, Scott, Whelan, Taylor, Blanchflower, Pegg.

Friendlies against the Western Command were now something of a regular feature on the calendar, with the next meeting between the two sides scheduled for 21

The programme for the match versus Leeds United, 28 January 1956.

FLOODLIT FOOTBALL

MANCHESTER
UNITED

versus

WESTERN
COMMAND

BELLE VUE GROUND, RHYL
TUESDAY, FEBRUARY 21, 1956
Kick-off 7.15

SOUVENIR PROGRAMME SIXPENCE

The programme for the match versus
Western Command, 21 February 1956.

February at Rhyl. This game, however, was actually postponed and played a month later on 20 March. It is not classed as a United first-team fixture.

It is worth noting, however, that among the listed Western Command players were the likes of Jimmy Armfield of Blackpool, Don Howe of West Bromwich Albion, United reserve goalkeeper Gordon Clayton and England's and United's regular number six, Duncan Edwards.

Despite Matt Busby fielding something of a reserve side, United were simply too strong for their opponents and dictated the play for the complete 90 minutes, with the 4–0 score line failing to fully justify the pressure that the Western Command side found themselves under. The quartet of goals, however, could well have been doubled, had it not been for the heroics of United's reserve team 'keeper Gordon Clayton facing his teammates in the home side's goal.

The danger of centre-forward Colin Webster was subdued somewhat by Wolves defender Walmsley, but it was winger Albert Scanlon who caused most of the problems, moving at ease from one side of the pitch to the other across the United front line.

A Bobby Charlton double in the seventh and 40th minutes put United well on the road to victory, with Noel McFarlane and Colin Webster adding the other two goals.

On Saturday 7 April 1956 United defeated Blackpool 2–1 at Old Trafford, with goals from Tommy Taylor and Johnny Berry, to secure the First Division Championship, with two games remaining, for the first time since 1952. Like many of the 62,277 ecstatic supporters who attended the game, the players celebrated long into the night, rounding off the evening with a 2am meal of steak and chips. Sleep, however, was restricted to a few hours, as, hangovers or not, the majority of the players had to be up bright and early to catch a 9.30am train for Scotland.

Up until now, United's sojourns north of the border had taken them no further than the Firth's of Clyde and Forth, but they were now to venture slightly further afield to Dundee, a city that had provided Newton Heath with the likes of Fred and Harry Erentz, Frank Barrett and James Brown many years previously.

Without the services of his England international trio of Byrne, Edwards and Taylor, who were due to face Scotland at Hampden, Matt Busby was forced into making a few changes to his title-winning side and once again introduced Bobby Charlton into the first-team set-up.

'Champions fall at Dundee' proclaimed the *News Chronicle* and *Daily Despatch* in bold black letters, above the scoreline 'Dundee 5 Manchester United 1', but in between the two 'Ray Wood Injured in Friendly Game' revealed the real reason behind the shock defeat for the newly crowned title-winners.

Playing with a strong breeze at their backs, Dundee, who were fighting against relegation in an on-going season, fielded six reserves in their line up. They started briskly and soon found themselves 3–0 in front, with goals from Merchant, Cousins (who later added a second) and O'Hara. The absence of Byrne and Edwards was as much of a factor behind the defence being breached as the weather.

In the 18th minute, with the score 2–0, goalkeeper Ray Wood injured his right ankle in a clash with Dundee's left-winger Ritchie and was forced to leave the pitch. A visit to the local hospital for an X-ray revealed that no bones were broken, but United's defence was further unsettled.

Fortunately, the use of substitutes had been agreed. Liam Whelan came on to take United back to full strength, with full-back Paddy Kennedy taking over between the sticks, but the introduction of the talented 21-year-old Irishman did little to enhance the visitors.

Berry, the best forward on show, toiled to no avail and was frequently ignored by his teammates when in a good position. Greaves managed to keep Ritchie under control, but Mark Jones had a difficult evening up against the somewhat unorthodox Merchant, who claimed his second goal, Dundee's last of the evening, in the 55th minute.

Despite the wind on their backs, United failed to take any advantage, with the defenders frequently over-kicking the ball to their forwards, who themselves often lost possession. It was not until the final minute of the game that Webster grabbed a consolation goal, converting a Berry cross.

---

9 April 1956   **Dundee at Dens Park.**

Attendance: 11,000.

Lost: 5–1.

Scorer: Webster.

Team: Wood, Greaves, Kennedy, Goodwin, Jones, McGuinness, Berry, Viollet, Webster, Charlton, Pegg.

Substitute: Whelan for Wood.

Seven days later, United were back in Scotland. This time they were in Glasgow, where they were up against Celtic, playing a charity match in aid of the Mission for the Relief of Suffering, founded by Group Captain Leonard Cheshire VC DSO DFC. Having lost to Celtic in the semi-final of the Coronation Cup some three years previously, the new generation of United players would have gained some satisfaction from a victory over their green and white-hooped opponents, but, as it turned out, it was not to be.

Considered by Robert Russell of the *Scottish Daily Express* 'not a very exciting game', the crowd (given in the *Express* as '20,000', but only 'about 15,000' in the *Glasgow Herald*) had plenty to shout about, although heavy rain fell throughout the game, dampening their spirits a little.

Celtic had one eye on their forthcoming Scottish Cup Final date against Hearts and were slightly taken aback by United's rather robust approach to the game; Duncan Edwards and Roger Byrne were both spoken to by the referee for overzealous tackles. To their credit though, the visitors did play some attractive football, while also having a physical superiority.

United's cross-field play was usually comfortably dealt with by centre-half Evans and full-backs Haughney and Meechan, but as early as the sixth minute the Celtic defence was put under pressure when Scanlon crossed the ball into the goalmouth and Beattie rose to collect it. The ball squirmed out of his hands just as Tommy Taylor charged in and, although it crossed the line, the referee awarded a free-kick. Beattie suffered a shoulder injury following this incident and was forced to leave the field in the 24th minute, being replaced by Bonnar.

In the 20th minute Celtic should have taken the lead as Sharkey headed the ball down to Higgins, but the Celtic right-winger, just five yards from goal, put the ball wide. Five minutes later the United defence had another narrow escape when Fernie turned the ball back from the byline to Sharkey, who completely missed in front of goal.

The crowd had to wait until the third minute of the second half for the first goal, which was claimed by the home side. A Haughney free-kick was headed out by Colman, but only as far as Neil Mochan, who hit the ball as it dropped and watched as it hit the post before bouncing over the line behind Ray Wood.

The programme for the match versus Celtic, 16 April 1956.

Two minutes later it should have been 2–0; Mochan turned the ball back to Higgins, who hit the ball against Wood. Fernie was ideally placed for the rebound, but he failed to make the most of the opportunity.

Celtic were clearly holding back in the hope of avoiding injury, due to their scheduled Cup Final appearance, but in the 55th minute they did go 2–0 in front. Roger Byrne was penalised for a tackle on Mochan and Haughney crashed the spot-kick high into the United net.

This reversal saw Matt Busby make a tactical change, pushing Duncan Edwards, considered by the *Glasgow Herald* correspondent as 'far and away the most outstanding player afield, apart from his breach of etiquette', up into the attack, in the hope that his constant presence in heart of the Celtic defence would pay dividends. It turned out to have the required effect, but it was not the United strongman who got his name on the score sheet.

Ten minutes after Celtic's second goal, United pulled one back. Albert Scanlon headed home a cross from Colman and then, in the 72nd minute, the comeback was complete. Tommy Taylor, constantly moving out to the wing in an effort to drag Evans away from the centre, crossed from the right, but Doherty could only head the ball against the post. As the ball rolled towards the line, Albert Scanlon prodded the ball into the net once again.

16 April 1956	Celtic at Celtic Park.

Attendance: 14,000.

Draw: 2–2.

Scorer: Scanlon 2.

Team: Wood, Greaves, Byrne, Colman, Jones, Edwards, Scanlon, Doherty, Taylor, Viollet, Pegg.

The tour of the Champions continued at Dublin's Dalymount Park and, despite being augmented by players from Fulham, Everton, Bolton and Wolves, with United missing Byrne, Colman and Taylor, Home Farm were still no match for United. Clever positional play and accurate passing gave United complete control of the game, which they won without really exerting themselves.

Nat Lofthouse, the Bolton centre-forward, did produce a couple of scoring opportunities, but Ray Wood was at his best, producing two excellent saves to keep the goal intact. The Everton pair of Republic of Ireland players, Eglington and Farrell, however, were disappointing, but another Republican, United's Liam Whelan, did his international chances no harm whatsoever with a fine display which he capped with a goal.

It was Whelan's goal that opened the scoring in the 14th minute, after Blanchflower had headed against the crossbar, and despite enjoying most of the play, United could not add to their goal tally until after the interval.

Blanchflower added a second following a free-kick from Berry shortly after the restart, with the same two players scoring United's third and fourth to complete the scoring.

The programme for the match versus Home Farm, 23 April 1956.

23 April 1956	Home Farm at Dalymount Park, Dublin.

Attendance: 23,000.

Won: 4–0.

Scorers: Blanchflower 2, Whelan, Berry.

Team: Wood, Greaves, Bent, Whitefoot, Jones, Edwards, Berry, Whelan, Blanchflower, Viollet, Pegg.

Prestwich-born John Aston had joined Manchester United as an amateur in January 1938, turning professional 11 months later. He went on to enjoy a career which saw him play 282 games for the club, mainly as a full-back, scoring 30 goals and winning League Championship and FA Cup-winners' medals, along with 17 England caps.

Unfortunately, his career came to a sudden end in 1954 when, following a visit to his doctor, he was diagnosed with TB and had to spend around 17 months in an Abergele sanatorium belonging to Manchester Corporation. As his contract did not end until June 1956, and as a tribute to his services to the club, the directors voted to keep him on full wages, something he was not keen to accept. He eventually agreed to this proposal, but only if his £14 per week was reduced to £9.

Due to these unfortunate circumstances, it was also decided to award him a testimonial match, with United taking on an All Star XI shortly after being crowned First Division champions for the fourth time.

The visiting line up of Swift, Walton, Eckersley, Docherty, Carey, Cockburn, Finney, Morris, Lofthouse, Pearson and Rowley was almost an United old boys XI, and, had they taken their chances following some excellent build-up play, then they would certainly have run out winners.

As it was, two early goals from the League Champions, the first from David Pegg after 15 minutes, pouncing on an effort from Doherty that had been punched out by Swift, and the second when Blanchflower side-footed a Pegg centre into the net, gave United a lead that they managed to hold onto for the rest of the game.

Holding on was certainly the best way to describe most of the remaining 90 minutes, as the often-stretched United defence was severely tested by the scheming Stan Pearson and the perfect wing-half play of Preston's Tommy Docherty.

Amid heavy rain and falling darkness the All-Stars certainly entertained the crowd, despite losing Jack Rowley with an ankle injury (he was replaced by Albert Scanlon), with Lofthouse coming close to scoring on two occasions and Wood denying him on another. The burly Bolton centre-forward did eventually manage to get the better of the United defence, pulling a goal back in the 74th minute, but there was to be no dramatic fightback by the All-Stars.

From his testimonial match John Aston received £4,285, from receipts of £6,243, considered at that time to be a record benefit for any Football League player. The figure included £204 in donations, while entertainment tax took £1,220.

25 April 1956	All Star XI at Old Trafford.

Attendance: 40,350.

Won: 2–1.

Scorers: Pegg, Blanchflower.

Team: Wood, Greaves, Bent, Whitefoot, Jones, Goodwin, Berry, Doherty, Blanchflower, Viollet, Pegg.

While the supporters put away their rattles and scarves for the summer, their red-shirted favourites were not able to get into the holiday mood, at least for a couple of weeks as they had to head for Scandinavia for a quartet of fixtures. Within 24 hours of arriving in the Swedish capital of Gothenburg they were running out to face a team made up of the three local sides, a combination that included six full internationals. However, there was no sign of any tiredness, as United ran out easy winners, scoring four without reply.

Ticket for the game versus an All Star XI, 25 April 1956

JOHNNY ASTON TESTIMONIAL MATCH
On the Ground of Manchester United F. C. Ltd.
(By kind permission of the Directors)

STAND **B**

ROW **R**

SEAT 15

WED. 25th APRIL 1956

Kick-off 7 p.m.

Admission 6/6 (inc. Tax)

MANCHESTER UNITED versus **AN ALL STAR XI**
KEEP THIS PORTION

It was to take United most of the first half to find their feet and to convert their chances into goals. However, inspired by Tommy Taylor, who failed to get his name on the score sheet but had a hand in three of the four goals, the visitors eventually took command, with a Pegg – Berry – Taylor move creating the opening in the 31st minute for Whelan to score.

Two minutes after the interval Taylor was again the provider, laying on a chance for Dennis Viollet, which he gratefully accepted to make it 2–0. The same player should have made it 3–0 shortly afterwards after Taylor had once again carved out an opening, but the opportunity went astray.

United's play in the second half utterly demoralised the home side, who, at times, were made to look third rate. There was a distinct lack of goals until almost the end of the game, when the visitors had all but given up hope of obtaining anything from the fixture. Eight minutes from time, Taylor's handiwork was whipped home by Berry to make three, and four followed minutes later, with Whelan on the spot to accept an easy scoring opportunity.

1 May 1956	**Gothenburg Alliance at Ullevi Stadium.**

Attendance: 17,700.

Won: 4–0.

Scorers: Whelan 2, Viollet, Berry.

Team: Wood, Greaves, Byrne, Colman, Jones, Edwards, Berry, Whelan, Taylor, Viollet, Pegg.

Despite the 3–1 scoreline, United had to fight hard for their victory against a Copenhagen XI in the second game of their Scandinavian tour. However, even without the services of Tommy Taylor, Duncan Edwards and Roger Byrne, who had all returned home for training with the England team for a forthcoming clash with Brazil, it looked as if they would record a runaway win, especially when John Doherty finished off a David Pegg – Jackie Blanchflower left-wing move, with a well-taken goal in the 21st minute.

As the game progressed they appeared to be a little uncertain in front of goal instead of their usual positive selves and, despite going that goal behind, the Danes equalised through Torstenson 11 minutes later and began to come more into the game.

One minute after the interval, Jackie Blanchflower headed United's second, but still the Danish side, which included nine internationals, showed that they were going to be no pushovers, forcing Ray Wood into making a couple of brilliant saves.

In the end, though, it was Johnny Berry who guaranteed United victory, evading his markers to score a third near the end.

5 May 1956	**Copenhagen XI at Idraets Park.**

Attendance: 9,800.

Won: 3–1.

Scorers: Berry, Doherty, Blanchflower.

Team: Wood, Greaves, Bent, Colman, Jones, Whitefoot, Berry, Doherty, Blanchflower, Viollet, Pegg.

The third game of the tour, against a Copenhagen XI, was generally considered to be the one that would provide United with their sternest test, but as the 90 minutes unfolded it turned out to be the exact opposite, with United notching up six goals without reply. It was a scoreline which actually did not do justice to their performance, as they simply ran rings round their opponents.

Within four minutes of the kick-off Webster, scoring from a Scanlon cross, and Scanlon himself, heading home a Pegg centre, had given United a two-goal lead, but rather surprisingly, given the final outcome, there were to be no further goals in the opening half, despite some excellent football.

In the second half, however, the internationally-studded Copenhagen side had no answer to their visitors' outstanding play. Viollet, from a defence-splitting Whelan pass in the 55th minute, Scanlon three minutes later, Pegg on the hour and Whelan in the 71st minute added further goals, giving all five forwards a share of the spoils.

6 May 1956	**Copenhagen XI.**

Attendance: 11,800.

Won: 6–0.

Scorers: Scanlon 2, Whelan, Webster, Viollet, Pegg.

Team: Wood, Foulkes, Bent, Whitefoot, Jones, Blanchflower, Scanlon, Whelan, Webster, Viollet, Pegg.

For anyone who has moved a few lines down the page to the statistical details for this particular match, the United line up does not contain an error, as Jackie Blanchflower did actually play in goal. With Ray Wood, the only 'keeper on the tour, having been called up by the Football Association for training prior to a continental tour, Matt Busby decided against bringing Jack Crompton over to Sweden just for one game and opted for Blanchflower instead.

Although he had played at centre-forward and left-half already on the tour, and shown his versatility in the Football League in other positions, Blanchflower had never played between the sticks before, although he had shown a liking for the goalkeeping role in training sessions.

The switching around allowed reserve-team player Ronnie Cope to step into the limelight and he did well in the wet conditions which did little to prevent United from once again producing some excellent football and earning a standing ovation from the Helsingborg crowd at the end of the game.

Once again, it could well have been double figures had United taken all their chances, mainly created by Dennis Viollet, but instead they had to be content with five. It was actually the local side who took the lead, in the 17th minute, and Matt Busby's decision to play Blanchflower in goal looked to have backfired.

A left-wing centre floated into the United penalty area and Blanchflower and Geoff Bent left the ball for each other. This allowed the Swedish outside-right to nip in and push the ball into the vacant net.

The lead was short-lived, however, as Pegg equalised four minutes later. Doherty added a second in the 31st minute, while Viollet made it 3–1 a minute after the interval.

Blanchflower redeemed himself for his earlier error shortly afterwards, running from his goal to smother a shot at the edge of his area. Had it not been for his actions, the Swedes could well have been encouraged to mount something of a fightback.

Busby had his forwards switching positions with some regularity, a ploy which the Helsingborg side could not cope with, especially when Viollet was pushed onto the wing. It came as no surprise when Webster, with a spectacular header in the 69th minute and Doherty again, four minutes from the end, scored to give United a 5–1 win.

8 May 1956	Helsingborg.

Attendance: 8,606.

Won: 5–1.

Scorers: Doherty 2, Webster, Viollet.

Team: Blanchflower, Greaves, Bent, Cope, Jones, Whitefoot, Scanlon, Doherty, Webster, Viollet, Pegg.

There were to be no first-team friendlies before or during season 1956–57, but, following another Championship-winning First Division season, United made it three in a row, as they once again made an end-of-season trip to Scandinavia, this time playing only a couple of fixtures in Copenhagen.

A surprise inclusion among the party of 15 who travelled across the North Sea was goalkeeper Ray Wood, whose cheekbone had been fractured in four places following the Wembley Cup Final collision with Aston Villa's Peter McParland. The 'keeper still bore the scars of a recent operation and was certainly not fit to take part in any of the games, despite their 'friendly' tag, so it was a step up for 21-year-old reserve-team custodian Gordon Clayton to the senior ranks.

For the opening fixture, the kick-off time was changed to allow spectators time to get home so that they could watch a gala reception for a visit by Queen Elizabeth and Prince Philip on television, but with the popularity of Manchester United in the Danish capital there would have been only one winner had the two gone head-to-head.

Matt Busby decided to play Roger Byrne at outside-left, but the move failed to have the same effect as it did in the final games of season 1951–52, when the Gorton-born defender's goals had helped United towards the Championship. This time he failed to finish the game due to blistered feet, which had forced him to turn out in 'training pumps'. Byrne, to his credit, had only volunteered to play at the last minute, when Albert Scanlon was ruled out with a foot injury received in training, but the hard pitch proved to be a severe handicap.

For once United found their Copenhagen opposition no mere pushovers and in a rather uninspiring game they were to struggle at times, while the Danes created numerous openings and often caught out the United defence with their speed.

However, it was United who took the lead in the 11th minute when Taylor snapped up a Whelan pass to open the scoring with a shot from 18 yards out. It was a lead that lasted until a minute before half-time, when centre-forward Dideriksen equalised after Larsen had created the opening.

The appearance of Viollet in place of the ineffectual Byrne after the restart injected some life into the United front line and in the 54th minute Tommy Taylor added the finishing touches to a Viollet – Whitefoot – Webster move to put United in front. However, nine minutes later the Danes were again on level terms; this time Petersen was the scorer.

This was probably the toughest test United had faced in all their Scandinavian games and, as the minutes ticked away, there was little between the two teams, with either capable of snatching the winner.

In the end, it was the grit and determination of the visitors which brought the decisive goal, Taylor laying on the chance for substitute Viollet to score three minutes from time.

---

21 May 1957   Copenhagen XI.

Attendance: 10,104.

Won: 3–2.

Scorers: Taylor 2, Viollet.

Team: Clayton, Foulkes, Greaves, Colman, Blanchflower, Whitefoot, Berry, Whelan, Taylor, Webster, Byrne.

Substitute: Viollet for Byrne.

Back in 1950 United's tour of America had gone slightly off the rails when a successful move was made to prise Charlie Mitten away from Manchester to the big money of South America. This time the target was England centre-forward Tommy Taylor, with an agent from Inter Milan, a Mr Lajos Cseisler, sent to make the neccessary arrangements.

The Hungarian had been authorised to try and negotiate a deal, which was believed to be around £65,000 (£55,000 to United, £10,000 to the player), but was given a short and straight to the point reply from manager Matt Busby: 'United had no intention of parting with Taylor or any other player'.

Rather surprisingly, the Danish newspaper *Politiken* reported that Tommy Taylor was 'deeply disappointed' that the club were unwilling to release him, while at the same time the *Manchester Evening News* quoted Taylor as saying, 'It's a lot of money to be offering, but it makes no difference to me.' These off-field goings-on had little effect on Taylor, as he was by far the best player on the pitch; time and time again he brought applause from the terracing for his display, even though he was hampered by an ankle injury.

The first half of the game against Stævnet ended on level terms, Whelan scoring for United, but a Webster goal, one minute after the interval, once again put United in front. However, instead of moving up a gear and killing the game off, the game swung from end to end with the Danes matching United goal for goal, and it was not until Billy Whelan completed his hat-trick that United could claim victory.

It was a result that should never have been in any doubt, as the referee had disallowed two perfectly good United goals as offside.

---

23 May 1957   Stævnet at Copenhagen.

Attendance: 10,800.

Won: 4–3.

Scorers: Whelan 3, Webster.

Team: Clayton, Foulkes, Greaves, Whitefoot, Jones, Blanchflower, Berry, Whelan, Taylor, Webster, Byrne.

United's pre-and post-season friendly sojourns to Scandinavia and beyond had stood them in good stead in their inaugural European Cup campaign, with only the might of Real Madrid preventing them from reaching the Final and perhaps even winning the coveted trophy. Even being crowned Football League champions for the second season in succession did not prevent manager Matt Busby from continuing his search for improvement, with non-competitive fixtures against foreign opposition still high on the agenda.

So in mid-August 1957 the United players went to Germany to further their European education, with the performances over the two fixtures indicating that they were a match for anyone.

Ticket for the game in Berlin, 14 August 1957.

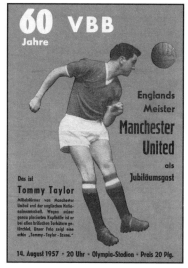

Programme for the Berlin match, which features Tommy Taylor, 14 August 1957.

The first of the German fixtures took United to Berlin, where they came up against a side called Berliner Stadtelf made up of the city's five senior clubs. In a stadium built by Hitler, they gave the 1,400 or so British servicemen in the strictly partisan crowd much to shout about as they overpowered their opponents with an excellent performance.

The noisy home crowd had very little to celebrate in the opening quarter of an hour as United put the rugged German defence under severe pressure, forcing a dozen corners and prompting goalkeeper Mehlmann to make some outstanding saves.

Any frustration that was beginning to show thawed in the 16th minute when Billy Whelan threaded a pass through a crowded defence. A couple of well-timed strides took Dennis Viollet clear and he drew the goalkeeper out before ramming the ball home. Amid the cheers of the khaki-clad British supporters, a sigh of relief was emitted from the United bench, as they had struggled for goals in the final games of the previous season. There were, however, derisive whistles and cat-calls from the home support when the referee disallowed a Berlin goal soon afterwards. By half-time United were two in front, with Tommy Taylor snatching a half chance after the 'keeper had punched out a shot from Whelan.

After the interval, which, very strangely, had seen the floodlights being turned off and the crowd asked to light matches to create something of a display of dancing glow-worms, United continued the unrelenting pressure on their hosts with Whelan displaying a wide array of skills, Duncan Edwards bombarding the German goal with shots from various areas of the field, and Taylor keeping the Germans on their toes as he busied himself around the penalty area.

It was Dennis Viollet, however, who was to score the third and what was to be final goal. Johnny Berry, having collected the ball, passed to his inside partner and, from a seemingly impossible angle, Viollet managed to beat the 'keeper.

14 August 1957	**Berliner Stadtelf at Olympic Stadium, Berlin.**

Attendance: 60,000.

Won: 3–0.

Scorers: Viollet 2, Taylor.

Team: Wood, Foulkes, Byrne, Colman, Blanchflower, Edwards, Berry, Whelan, Taylor, Viollet, Pegg.

For the second of the two fixtures, three days later, United travelled to Hanover, where there was little sign of any pre-season rustiness or even tiredness from the previous 90 minutes, as they once again treated the sprinkling of British supporters in the crowd, many kitted out in red and white, to another notable display of slick ball-playing skills.

Rated much more highly than the previous Berlin opposition, the green-shirted Saxony side were made to look third-rate, but this was only after United had been kick-started by a German goal in the 16th minute.

Play had begun at exhibition-game pace, but when Bruske raced through the middle to beat Ray Wood for the opening goal, the United players shook away the cobwebs and began to set about the task in hand in devastating fashion, scoring three times in nine minutes.

Almost straight from the restart they were on level terms, Tommy Taylor launching himself into mid-air to head home a Berry corner. This was followed two minutes later by a second when Dennis Viollet dribbled past three defenders before flicking the ball to David Pegg. Continuing with his run, he accepted the return pass to score with ease. A minute later Taylor added a third, again leaping to head home, this time from a Pegg centre.

By half-time it was 4–1, Dennis Viollet notching up his second by finishing off another series of defence-splitting passes.

The half-time whistle came as something of a relief for the Germans, as did United's more relaxed approach to the second half, which allowed them to settle into some form of rhythm. It also led to a second goal in the 84th minute as centre-forward Meyer burst through the middle alongside Schicks and headed past Wood. By then, however, the game was over as a contest, with the scoreline flattering the Saxony players.

17 August 1957	Lower Saxony XI at Hanover.

Attendance: 30,000.

Won: 4–2.

Scorers: Viollet 2, Taylor 2.

Team: Wood, Foulkes, Byrne, Colman, Blanchflower, Edwards, Berry, Whelan, Taylor, Viollet, Pegg.

Following the two performances in Germany, the pressmen who had followed United on their trip were unanimous in their belief that you could put your money on them equalling Huddersfield Town and Arsenal's feat of winning the First Division title three seasons in succession, as well as mounting a notable challenge in the European Cup. Little did they know what lay ahead.

As things turned out, there was to be no League Championship treble, no European triumph – just tears, as Matt Busby's years of painstaking work building up a team capable of challenging the best at home and abroad were torn to shreds on a Munich runway on 6 February 1958. Many of the players who had captured the hearts and minds of countless supporters across the globe were dead. Busby himself was very unwell, but Manchester United had to go on and under the watchful eye of assistant manager Jimmy Murphy a new team was to rise from the ashes.

With Matt Busby seriously ill in the Recht's der Isar hospital in Munich, Murphy had the unenviable position of having to find a team, never mind select one, for the FA Cup fifth-round tie against Sheffield Wednesday.

On Tuesday 11 February Murphy arranged a game which fails to appear in the record books, in order to assess who was available and had a place to play in the weeks and months ahead.

Under the supervision of assistant trainer Bill Inglis, a mixture of reserve professionals and unknown and untried youngsters made their way to the White City greyhound stadium. They were a motley collection of 22 players, a few looking no older than schoolboys, who listened to Inglis as he told them 'remember you are the new Manchester United. We have got to get going and all of us do our very best.'

Inglis divided his charges into two teams (injuries prevented Wilf McGuinness and Gordon Clayton from playing): Gaskell, Greaves, Peter Jones, Goodwin, Cope, Bratt, Webster, Harrop, Dawson, Pearson and Hunter; and Spiers, Smith, Shiels, English, Holland, Carolan, Stiles, Giles, Mooney, Brennan and Elms.

Ticket for the game versus Lower Saxony, 17 August 1957.

The game resembled little more than a playground kick-about, as youthful enthusiasm abounded and a handful of spectators looked on. Manchester United were back in action.

Whether Manchester United would have won the European Cup in that traumatic 1957–58 season is something that will never be known, but an invitation was sent to Old Trafford asking them to participate in the 1958–59 competition. It was an invite which was warmly applauded by everyone. Everyone that is except the Football authorities, who rather callously refused to give the club permission to compete.

Following their weekly board meeting, United released the following statement: 'Manchester United, while accepting the decision of the Football Association Consultative Committee feel they must in justification of their attitude and actions state the following facts:-

'The FA, in their letter of 5 July, stated that they had no objection to Manchester United entering the European Cup this season.

'The Football League wrote to the club that they could not give their consent to the club to enter. The club appealed to the League's board of Appeal and this appeal was upheld.

'The decision of the Board of Appeal is, by the rules of the Football League, FINAL.

'Therefore, the club were allowed by the FA to enter the competition. By the decision of the Board of Appeal, which is FINAL, the Football League were prevented from interfering with our entry.

'In these circumstances there was no reason why the dates we submitted to the Football Association should not be approved, nor why the FA should depart from the terms of their letter of 5 July in which they stated, as before mentioned "The Football Association have no objection to your taking part."'

After issuing the statement United revealed that they had asked the FA for permission to play their two Cup fixtures with Berne Young Boys as friendly matches.

Prior to the start of season 1958–59 the United players and staff made a poignant return to Munich to take on a combined Bayern Munich and Munich 1860 side. It was obvious that flying to the German city was out of the question, so they travelled by train to the south of England and across the channel to Ostend. From there a special coach was added to the Corinthian night express train for the long journey to Munich. Arriving at their destination, they were warmly greeted by a host of photographers, autograph hunters and civic officials. Matt Busby got down from the train to rapturous applause and walked proudly down the platform to be met by Munich officials, who presented him with a large bouquet of red and white carnations, while each member of the party was presented with a small silver monk – the symbol of the city.

The crowds flocking towards the stadium prior to kick-off caused traffic jams the like of which had never been seen before, with many latecomers finding the gates locked with a capacity crowd inside. Despite scoring three times against the combined Munich XI, it was the Germans' domination of the opening 45 minutes that secured them victory, as they clicked practically from the kick-off and at times ran rings around the United defence. This was despite the attempts of Foulkes to keep the United back line as steady as possible and some magnificent saves from Harry Gregg.

Early mistakes led to the home side scoring four before the interval, having taken the lead with only five minutes gone. Freddie Goodwin passed the ball direct to the Munich inside-right Hahn, who accepted the gift and scored with ease from outside the penalty area. It was a lead, however, which was to last only seven minutes, as Charlton rounded off a fine dribble with an equaliser. But with the congratulations of his teammates still ringing in his ears, the stadium erupted into a wall of noise following the select side's second in the 15th minute, scored by Albert, direct from a corner. To their credit United responded well, drawing level almost immediately through Ernie Taylor.

Slowly, the Germans took command of the game and, after coming close to adding further goals on several occasions, Harry Gregg, who had been playing well up until that point, blotted his copy book in the 26th minute when he hit a clearance from about 15 yards directly to the feet of Kolbl, who could not believe his luck. A fourth Munich goal was to follow before the half-time whistle sounded.

As individuals, United were the better team, but in their team play, the Munich players were more direct and effective. However, the dominance in overall play in the second half swung in United's favour, but their failings were in their tendency to dribble or pass when a shot on goal might have been more productive. Scanlon, in particular, was guilty of holding onto the ball for too long, causing several promising moves to stutter to a premature halt.

Substitute goalkeeper Bechtold kept United at bay, with fine saves from Viollet and Taylor in quick succession, the latter also having a goal-bound shot blocked on the line by a Munich defender. Charlton alone had three efforts stopped on the line.

A penalty for hand ball against a German defender who fisted off the goalline five minutes from the end was converted by Taylor at the second attempt, the German 'keeper getting his hands to it, but failing to hold. By then it was too late for any dramatic fightback. Had Dennis Viollet converted his two good scoring chances, and had the positional play of Ian Greaves been better, then United might at the very least, have come away with a draw.

After the match, another of the Munich survivors, Albert Scanlon, was more than relieved to have got the game over with: 'I'm glad it is over. I felt terrible. I felt very nervous and strange playing in my first proper match since the crash.'

While Scanlon was relieved the ordeal was over, Matt Busby was far from happy. 'Something will have to be done', he said, 'I am not satisfied.'

13 August 1958	**Munich XI at Grünwalder Stadium, Munich.**

Attendance: 32,000.

Lost: 4–3.

Scorers: Taylor 2, Charlton.

Team: Gregg, Foulkes, Greaves, Goodwin, Cope, Crowther, Morgans, Taylor, Viollet, Charlton, Scanlon.

Three days later United made the 10-hour journey to Hamburg, where they fared little better against the previous season's runners-up in the German Federal Association Championship, losing 2–0 in the superb 78,000 capacity Volkspark Stadium.

Despite the 2–0 defeat on a night of heavy rain, United certainly played better than in the previous match, showing a bit of style, especially in the second

The programme for the match versus Hamburg SV, 16 August 1958.

half. However, they were slightly hampered by injuries to outside-right Webster and centre-half Cope, the former having to go to hospital for treatment to a gash on his left calf. This prompted reshuffling within the United ranks, with Alex Dawson and Shay Brennan coming on as replacements.

Uwe Seeler gave the Germans the lead in the 13th minute, with Wulf adding a second 24 minutes into the second half, but for long periods United enjoyed most of the play, failing, however, to get the better of the compact home defence.

Certainly, in the final 20 minutes United dominated the game, but through bad luck, fine goalkeeping by Schnoor and the post preventing Charlton from scoring with a long-range effort, the German goal remained intact.

16 August 1958	**Hamburg SV at Volkspark Stadium.**

Attendance: 50,000.

Lost: 2–0.

Team: Gregg, Foulkes, Harrop, Goodwin, Cope, McGuinness, Webster, Taylor, Viollet, Charlton, Morgans.

Substitutes: Dawson for Webster, Pearson for Cope.

As United had lost their bid to take part in the 1958–59 European Cup competition, Berne Young Boys were therefore given a bye into the second round. United did, however, receive permission to play against the Swiss club at home and away in friendlies. This gave United the opportunity to continue team building, testing themselves, as they had done in previous years against opposition away from the domestic game.

So, in what should have been the first leg tie of the European Cup first round, United lost 2–0, despite a superb display from the club's latest acquisition, Albert Quixall. Having been signed only a few days previously for a British-record fee of £45,000, he had made his debut the previous Saturday against Tottenham but, away from the spotlight, the 90 minutes in Switzerland gave Quixall some additional time to get to know his new teammates.

United began strongly, stretching the Swiss defence, but the attack, with Dawson leading the line in place of tonsillitis victim Viollet, faded, allowing the home side into the game.

Berne took advantage of their visitors' poor play and opened the scoring in the 20th minute, the unmarked Schneiter receiving the ball and beating Gregg from 25 yards with a firm drive. At the opposite end Dawson went close on a couple of occasions, with headers which went narrowly over.

Three minutes before half-time Berne's lead was almost increased when inside-right Wechselberger fired a hard shot at Gregg, but to United's good fortune, although not that of the unfortunate 'keeper, the ball hit him full in the face, knocking him out for a couple of minutes.

The second half practically belonged to Berne, who attacked strongly and were rewarded with a second goal from centre-forward Meier, with a third almost following when a mis-hit was fortunately stopped on the line by Gregg.

For United, Ernie Taylor gave another cool and calm exhibition of a midfield general, with Ian Greaves the most improved player in the team. Alex Dawson and Kenny Morgans did little to impress, with the latter still failing to show any of his pre-Munich form, while Dawson looked tired.

The crowds, the atmosphere and even the style of play were all different on the Continent and the new look United side certainly found it difficult to adjust to the change. Since Munich they had played four games abroad and lost them all. The need for such friendlies was never more in evidence.

24 September 1958	**Berne Young Boys at Wankdorf Stadium.**

Attendance: 20,000.

Lost: 2—0.

Team: Gregg, Foulks, Greaves, Goodwin, Cope, Crowther, Webster, Quixall, Dawson, E. Taylor, Morgans.

The programme for the match versus Berne Young Boys, 24 September 1958.

Having lost the unofficial first leg in Berne there was a considerable amount of United's self respect at stake when the two teams met again under the Old Trafford lights. The 30,000 souls who braved the wet weather were rewarded with a sterling display of football from the bedraggled, white-shirted United players, who certainly gave the crowd value for money, not only by clawing back the two-goal deficit, but also by scoring a third to give them what would have been an aggregate win.

The attendance might have been much lower, not only because of the dreadful weather, but also because of the possibility of the game being televised. Under a new arrangement, if a club wanted a game televised then it had to make the initial approach to a television company rather than the game's governing body, but it was a move that United did not make as they prepared to overturn their 2–0 defeat of the week before.

Pouring rain made the pitch very slippery and, apart from a 10-minute spell early in the game, when the visiting forwards caused the home defence a few problems, the Swiss champions were rarely given the opportunity to shine, as United played much better than they had done in the previous encounter.

Webster and Viollet interchanged frequently, a tactic which the Swiss found hard to handle and, had it not been for their goalkeeper Eich, who was tested by Quixall, Crowther and Viollet, then they would have found themselves in considerable trouble. In a rare break, however, Allemann also missed a good scoring chance when he passed instead of shooting.

United should have gone in front after 15 minutes, when Webster threaded an excellent pass through to Quixall, but his shot was blocked by the advancing 'keeper. Seconds later, however, United had scored, Viollet notching up his first goal of the season.

A Scanlon volley was blocked on the goalline, with another great effort from a Quixall cross going just wide. A third attempt with a header also went wide as a cross from the United winger flew untouched across the Swiss goalmouth.

Whistles of disappointment filled the air on more than one occasion as narrow offside decisions went against United, with the cries of disapproval growing even louder after the up ending of Quixall in the penalty area resulted in nothing more than a goal-kick.

For what was only a friendly, some of the play, particularly in the second half and on Quixall, was quite physical and the longer the game went on, the worse it became, with the referee receiving much abuse from the crowd for his handling of the game. It reached a crescendo when he booked Crowther and 10 minutes from the end sent off Webster for allegedly kicking an opponent after he had been fouled.

Much to the baying crowd's surprise, as the dejected Webster walked off the field Dawson ran on, but his presence soon brought strong complaints from the Swiss and he was asked by the referee to leave the pitch.

The programme for the match versus Berne Young Boys, 1 October 1958.

W.R. Taylor, who reported on the game for the *Guardian* wrote: 'It was a good thing it was only a friendly match instead of a European Cup tie; [the] imagination boggles about what might have happened otherwise. The description "friendly match" was as laughable as calling the Berne players "Young Boys", for they have certainly nothing to learn. It was a thousand pities that the game deteriorated as it did, for some most entertaining play was most forthcoming before half-time'.

For most of the second half Harry Gregg was a mere spectator, while his opposite number seemed to be unbeatable as he withstood what seemed to be a constant bombardment of his goal. However, with 12 minutes remaining Eich was finally beaten for a second time. Pearson's pass to Viollet was put past the 'keeper from a narrow angle.

Meier, in a rare Berne attack, almost beat Gregg, but with seconds to go Quixall was brought down once too often in the penalty area for the rather lenient referee and the blond-headed forward took pleasure in converting the kick to give United a 3–0 win and what would have been a passage into the second round of the competition had it been a Cup tie, rather than a victory in a meaningless friendly.

1 October 1958	Berne Young Boys at Old Trafford.

Attendance: 30,000.

Won: 3–0.

Scorers: E. Taylor, Viollet, Quixall (pen.).

Team: Gregg, Foulkes, Greaves, Goodwin, Harrop, Crowther, Viollet, Quixall, Webster, E. Taylor, Scanlon.

Substitute: Pearson for E. Taylor.

As had occurred on more than one occasion in the previous decade, United found themselves without a fixture due to their early exit in the FA Cup. This time it was a defeat at Carrow Road against Norwich City that had found United missing from the list of clubs competing in the fourth round of the competition on 24 January 1959.

Matt Busby had thus to look elsewhere for a game, as a postponed fixture at Blackburn the previous Saturday saw his charges requiring 90 minutes to keep their fitness levels up. His search took him to Wales for a game against Swansea Town, at that time a mid-table side in the Second Division.

The game started at a lively pace, with Charlton releasing Scanlon down the left, but the winger's cross was too far from his teammates to cause any problems, while at the opposite end Gregg had to be alert to prevent Charles from opening the scoring.

Swansea took the lead after five minutes, former United man and captain for the day Colin Webster nipping in to push the ball past Gregg from close range.

It took United only seven minutes to draw level and this time a Charlton-Scanlon move did prove productive, with the outside-left crossing to the feet of Viollet, whose shot went in off the crossbar. Soon afterwards they should have been in front, with Swansea rather fortunate not to have

Signatures on a dinner menu from the match against Berne Young Boys, 1 October 1958.

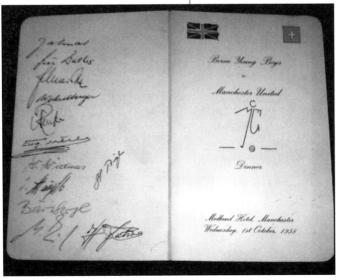

conceded a penalty. Scanlon was brought down inside the area but, amid howls of protest from the United players, the referee awarded a free-kick outside the box.

As luck would have it, it was Swansea who took the lead in the 21st minute, with what was undoubtedly the best goal of the game. Charles got the better of Carolan on the right before cutting inside and scoring with ease.

There was, however, little time for Swansea to rest on their laurels, as straight from the kick-off United went upfield and again equalised, Charlton gratefully accepting a misplaced ball from Johns before shooting past King in the Swansea goal.

Determined not to be outdone by their more illustrious opponents, Swansea once again took the lead with Charles once more the scorer. This time he latched on to a through ball from Davies before hammering home an unstoppable shot from the edge of the penalty area.

Shortly before the interval Ronnie Cope was hurt in a tackle and was forced to leave the field, his place being taken by Irish youngster Johnny Giles, making his Manchester United debut. However, this alteration did little to affect United's play, as in the final two minutes of the half they not only drew level again, but also took the lead. In the 43rd minute Scanlon shot past the unsuspecting 'keeper, while sixty seconds later Quixall scored the seventh goal of an eventful first half. A free-flowing movement by the United forward line had ended with Quixall shooting past King, the ball being helped into the net by the head of Griffiths.

After the goal spree of the opening 45 minutes it was not surprising that there would be some let up in play after the interval, but United still endeavoured to put as much into the game as possible. Quixall hit the post and then headed a Bradley centre wide, while Bradley and Giles both came close amid a goalmouth scramble.

It was not until the 70th minute that the crowd had another goal to savour, with Bobby Charlton unleashing what was by now becoming something of a trademark, a soaring drive from the edge of the area. It was a goal which should have effectively put the game beyond the Welsh side, but to their credit they did reduce the leeway when Davies headed past Gregg to make it 5–4.

No one in the packed ground thought about leaving early and they were certainly correct in their decision, as a 10th goal materialised two minutes from the end, with Charlton finishing off a flashing cross-field move.

As the final whistle blew, dozens of schoolboys invaded the pitch to engulf the players as the rest of the crowd headed for the exits, more than happy with their afternoon's entertainment.

24 January 1959 — **Swansea Town at Vetch Field.**

Attendance: 23,624.

Won: 6–4.

Scorers: Charlton 3, Viollet, Scanlon, Quixall.

Team: Gregg, Foulkes, Carolan, Goodwin, Cope, McGuinness, Bradley, Quixall, Viollet, Charlton, Scanlon.

Substitute: Giles for Cope.

Continuing their quest for knowledge of European football, Austrian side Wiener Sports Club arrived in Manchester to accept the invitation to play a floodlit friendly fixture. For most people today, the name of the visitors will mean virtually nothing, but in 1959 the Austrians arrived with an excellent reputation, having mastered the likes of Dukla Prague and Juventus in that season's European Cup, with a quarter-final tie against Real Madrid looming on the horizon.

The programme for the match versus Wiener Sport Club, 11 February 1959.

So Wiener's visit to Old Trafford was to conjure up something of a test for United, and it was one that they passed, although it must be added that Wiener had not played a competitive match for a number of weeks prior to this fixture. Despite this, they displayed remarkable pace, while also causing the United players some concern with their shirt numbering, as they bore no relation to the positions occupied.

It was United who made most of the early running, Szanwald saving from Bradley and Viollet, but in the 15th minute he could not prevent the home side from taking the lead. A shot from Scanlon was only parried and Viollet, following up, banged the ball into the inviting net.

Jaros got his body in the way of a McGuinness drive which knocked him off his feet as Wiener began to turn things around, but it was only momentarily as back came United, with the action around the Wiener goalmouth frantic to say the least. McGuinness and Goodwin both had good scoring efforts kept out by the agile Szanwald, while a goal-bound effort from Scanlon was headed off the line by Oslansky.

Play in the second half rebounded from end to end. Charlton hit the post with a fierce drive that the 'keeper never saw, while in the United goalmouth Gregg and his fellow defenders stood transfixed as a centre from Horak trickled slowly across the goalmouth before Greaves stepped in to clear. The Wiener outside-right constantly prompted his fellow forwards, but to no avail.

United's inter-passing movements kept the Austrians on their toes and the confrontation between the two was ideal entertainment for the appreciative crowd, who along with the United players applauded the Wiener players off the pitch at the end.

11 February 1959	**Wiener Sports Club at Old Trafford.**

Attendance: 37,834.

Won: 1–0.

Scorer: Viollet.

Team: Gregg, Greaves, Carolan, Goodwin, Cope, McGuinness, Bradley, Quixall, Viollet, Charlton, Scanlon.

Three days after season 1958–59 drew to a close with a 2–1 defeat at Filbert Street, Leicester, United headed to a new location to advance their European pedigree, making the short Channel crossing to Rotterdam in Holland to take on the local Feijenoord club. It was a trip organised by the directors to show their appreciation to the players for their efforts over the course of the previous season.

For the likes of Matt Busby and Bill Foulkes, the short, 70-minute flight was particularly nerve-wracking, as it was the first time since Munich that either of them had flown. The other survivors, Harry Gregg, Dennis Viollet, Bobby Charlton and Albert Scanlon had all taken their tentative first flight on a previous occasion. When asked if he had considered sending the team to Holland on different flights,

Busby replied, 'We are a team when we are playing and when we are travelling I do not want to split the team up.'

In front of a passionate crowd of around 55,000, which included around 1,000 British servicemen, the home side played some good football, but local comment around the ground following the game suggested that they had played above themselves in scoring their three goals.

Alex Dawson, 'looking bigger and sharper', according to one reporter, made a return to the first team, having been out through injury since scoring twice in the 6–3 defeat at Bolton way back in November. He celebrated his re-appearance by notching up a hat-trick and leaving a few bruises on the legs of the Feijenoord defenders. United's other two goals came from Dennis Viollet.

Away from the tensions brought about by First Division football, United looked totally relaxed and, despite losing the services of Wilf McGuinness after 20 minutes, with Shay Brennan taking his place, their momentum was not affected. Over the 90 minutes of play they once again showed that they were ready to compete in Europe on a regular basis.

Following the game, every member of the United party was presented with a box of Dutch cheese.

28 April 1959	**Feijenoord at Feijenoord Stadion.**

Attendance: 55,000.
Won: 5–3.
Scorers: Dawson 3, Viollet 2.
Team: Gregg, Cope, Carolan, Goodwin, Foulkes, McGuinness, Dawson, Quixall, Viollet, Charlton, Scanlon.
Substitute: Brennan for McGuinness.

The pre-season for season 1959–60 saw Manchester United return to Germany, now the favoured destination, with the fixtures against the German sides being much more competitive. After the opening fixture against Bayern Munich, however, Matt Busby might have been wishing he had taken the team elsewhere.

The first half of the match was played at a rather leisurely pace, amid something of a serene, garden party atmosphere. Play was relatively even, with neither side being able to claim the upper hand, but it was United who managed to break the deadlock through Dennis Viollet, the United forward getting the better of Titz, Mai and Launderer before beating goalkeeper Fazekas with a low shot into the far corner.

Within four seconds of the start of the second half, United were 2–0 in front, the quick-thinking Albert Quixall catching the Germans flat-footed. 'I noticed that Fazekas, the Bayern 'keeper, often wandered right to the edge of the penalty area,' said the blond-headed forward, 'so I asked Dennis Viollet for a short pass and then managed to catch the 'keeper napping with my shot.' Five minutes later the Germans had the opportunity to pull a goal back from the penalty spot, but Zsamboki blasted it wide.

A second spot kick should have been awarded to the home side 15 minutes later, when Foulkes appeared to bring down Zsamboki, but the referee waved play on, much to the Germans' disgust, and as play continued the match suddenly spiralled out of control.

With 25 minutes remaining, the aggrieved and perhaps frustrated Zsamboki clashed with Bobby Charlton and moments later fouled Joe Carolan. The United left-back, not as mild mannered as his teammate, immediately retaliated, catching the German a glancing blow on the back of the neck. The action was enough to warrant a sending off and the referee immediately pointed towards the tunnel. Seconds later it looked as if Zsamboki was to follow Carolan to the dressing rooms, but the referee appeared to change his mind and simply issued a warning. 'The outside-right had been niggling us all the game, but it was silly of me to lose my head', said Carolan later.

The United man's dismissal did not throw cold water on the proceedings, as two minutes later all hell broke loose. Quixall and Zsamboki were involved in a touchline scuffle, resulting in a cameraman, who was sitting close to the action, rushing onto the pitch gesticulating at the linesman and the United inside-forward. So heated were his protests that the linesman frantically waved his flag to attract the referee's attention and, following a brief discussion between the two officials and the cameraman, Quixall was ordered off.

Bayern officials, to their credit, attempted in vain to persuade the referee to change his mind, as United trainer Jack Crompton threw his towel to the ground in disgust. He quickly retrieved the towel and, without the permission of either Matt Busby or Jimmy Murphy, who were sitting in the stand, sent Jimmy Shiels on as a substitute for the departed Quixall!

Several minutes then elapsed before the linesman once again began waving his flag frantically, having noticed that United had 10 men on the field instead of nine. Upon checking the number of red shirts, referee Fischer attempted to make Bill Foulkes leave the pitch, but it was down to captain Dennis Viollet to restore some order and ask Shiels to leave, giving the youngster one of the shortest first-team debuts on record.

Thankfully the game reverted back to some sort of normality, with the nine-man United team managing to hold out until the last minute, when substitute Huber beat Harry Gregg.

After the game Matt Busby said, 'I thought the decision in respect of Quixall was absolutely outrageous, while Carolan hardly did enough to warrant a sending off in a match of this nature. Neither player has been sent off or had his name taken before.

'I found it hard to understand the referee's actions throughout. He blew for fouls which I did not see and ignored some which should certainly have been awarded.

'We owe so much to the people of this city and I wanted the game to go off smoothly. The Bayern officials were particularly upset about the harsh decisions. We do not feel – and neither do Bayern – that our friendship has suffered in any way. It is my opinion, and theirs, that neither of these boys should have been sent off, though they may take some blame.'

As for the referee, all he would say was 'no comment'.

8 August 1959	**Bayern Munich at Grünwalder Stadium.**

Attendance: 32,000.

Lost: 4–3.

Scorers: Taylor 2, Charlton.

Team: Gregg, Foulkes, Greaves, Goodwin, Cope, Crowther, Morgans, Taylor, Viollet, Charlton, Scanlon.

If the first of United's two pre-season warm up games in Germany gave Matt Busby food for thought, the second did the same, as hosts Hamburg recorded a 3–1 victory, much to the delight of their fanatical partisan crowd. The main cause of this completely unwarranted reversal was one man, Uwe Seeler, the German World Cup centre-forward and a player rated as arguably the best in his position in Europe, who hit a sparkling hat-trick.

The United defence looked cumbersome during the first 45 minutes, as Seeler and his fellow forwards pushed forward with rapier-like thrusts, with Foulkes struggling to hold down Seeler and teammates Cope and McGuinness also looking rather shaky. With Viollet missing through a calf injury, United struggled to penetrate the home defence.

Obeying Matt Busby's orders to 'keep their cool' following the previous encounter, and with the referee a much better official, the game was played in a sporting manner, although some of the free-kicks given against United were slightly harsh.

The crowd were still settling down to enjoy the game when the opening goal was scored, but it could quite as easily have come at the opposite end 90 seconds after the kick-off. Bradley and Dawson broke away down the right with a neat inter-passing movement, which resulted in the latter driving the ball against the foot of the far post from the edge of the box. As it rebounded, Scanlon dallied, the ball was cleared and Hamburg launched a counter-attack. Beckmann raced down the deserted right wing and from 20 yards out hit a powerful shot which Gregg failed to hold, allowing the alert Seeler to score.

Dawson soon realised that it was just not going to be his night. A second effort hit the post in the seventh minute and another was thwarted by Schnoor in the Hamburg goal seven minutes later.

With 19 minutes gone Seeler made it 2–0. Cope allowed Neisner to cut inside and the left-winger squared the ball across the face of the United goal to the waiting Seeler, who beat the helpless Gregg with power and ease from close range.

To their credit United, hampered at times by the overly officious referee, fought back and reduced the Germans' lead in the 31st minute through Charlton, who fired a rare United free-kick past a five-man wall from around 22 yards out after the ever dangerous Dawson had been fouled. Gregg did well to keep the score down, while Scanlon was spoken to by the referee for a foul on Seeler. After the break Charlton almost notched up a second with a 35-yard blockbuster, which the 'keeper was fortunate to fumble for a corner.

Seven minutes after the restart Seeler, jumping for the ball with Foulkes, headed past the post, but as Gregg prepared to take the goal-kick, everyone was surprised to see Herr Imkamp, the referee, point to the penalty spot. Despite United's fervent protests, the decision stood, with the official indicating that a German player had been tripped. Justice was done, however, when Surmer's shot hit the top of the crossbar and went over.

The programme for the match versus Hamburg SV, 12 August 1959.

The 'unofficial' programme for the match versus Hamburg SV, 12 August 1959.

Ticket for the match versus Hamburg SV, 12 August 1959.

The programme for the match versus Hamburg SV, 12 August 1959.

Slowly United began to claw their way back into the game. Dawson was frustrated by Schooner on more than one occasion, while the German B international 'keeper also kept out Charlton. However, with only a couple of minutes remaining, any hopes of snatching a draw disintegrated when Seeler rose to head home his hat-trick.

12 August 1959	**Hamburg SV at Volkspark Stadium.**

Attendance: 40,000.

Lost: 3–1.

Scorer: Charlton.

Team: Gregg, Cope, Carolan, Goodwin, Foulkes, McGuinness, Bradley, Quixall, Dawson, Charlton, Scanlon.

The two pre-season defeats in Germany had clearly shown that United were still some way from the form that was required to challenge Europe's best, a position that they had certainly been in prior to the Munich disaster. If they needed a benchmark then the visit of Real Madrid to Old Trafford would certainly create one, but the fixture, which earned a five-star rating throughout the national press, saw United dealt a footballing lesson.

With the likes of Santamaria, Didi, Gento, Di Stefano and Puskas in the all-white attire of the visitors, United were swept aside in something akin to a snowstorm as the Spanish side rattled home six goals in a devastating display. Sam Leitch of the *Daily Herald* proclaimed the performance as 'Football From Outer Space', which saw the visitors warmly applauded off the pitch at full-time.

United had begun well and were certainly aiming to make their visitors work for their £50 win bonus. Charlton came close with two excellent efforts in the first 15 minutes, as the crowd anticipated a display from their favourites which might have surprised their guests and created a memorable Old Trafford evening. Memorable it certainly was to be, but not for the reasons they had hoped.

The Brazilian star Didi supplied Puskas with a delightful through ball for the first goal in the seventh minute, the Hungarian allowing Gregg to commit himself before slipping the ball outside his reach. Magyar struck again in the 25th minute, beating Gregg with a swerving shot after having accepted a pass from Gento.

Five minutes later it was 3–0. Didi again made a knife-thrust of a pass from 30 yards to the on-running Di Stefano, who scored without much difficulty. Four minutes prior to the interval came the fourth. Di Stefano, standing by a goalpost, trapped the ball, turned and flicked it, seemingly all in one movement.

United were relieved to enjoy a 10-minute break from the onslaught and it was certainly advantageous, as they pulled a goal back within five minutes of the restart. Charlton sliced open the Madrid defence, allowing Bradley to run through from the halfway line and score from a tight angle. This goal should really have been United's second of the half, as Scanlon had missed a good opportunity earlier on.

There was to be no spirited fightback, however, as in the 63rd minute a poor clearance was snapped up by Didi and pushed forward to Puskas, before being crossed to the unmarked Pepillo to score number five. Another defensive error in the 78th minute gave the Spaniards their sixth, with Gento almost lifting the net from its pegs.

Even the United players applauded the world's number-one side from the pitch, while in his weekly *Manchester Evening News* column captain Dennis Viollet wrote, 'It seems odd to lose 6–1 and yet enjoy a match so much! But I think I speak for the whole team when I say we all thoroughly enjoyed the hiding Real Madrid gave us.'

Attendance: 63,500.

Lost: 6–1.

Scorer: Bradley.

Team: Gregg, Foulkes, Carolan, Goodwin, Cope, McGuinness, Bradley, Quixall, Viollet, Charlton, Scanlon.

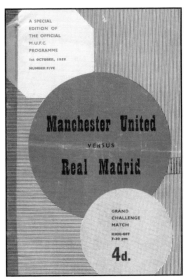

The programme for the match versus Real Madrid, 1 October 1959.

A fixture as far removed from the glamorous encounter against Real Madrid as you could probably get saw a United side travel to North Wales a fortnight later, to face Rhyl, a Cheshire County League side supplemented by a handful of guest players, at their Belle Vue ground. The strange pairing for a mid week friendly came about because of the transfer from Rhyl to United of winger Ken McDowell.

McDowell was initially rejected by United following a spell spent training with the juniors and had been around a few clubs before moving to North Wales. Having been transferred to United, he was able to line up against his former Rhyl teammates as part of a team that was basically United's central league side. His reappearance at Rhyl, however, was short-lived, as he had to go off with an injury just before the interval.

Everton's Dave Hickson, Tranmere's Tommy Eglington and Peter Farrell, Dennis Wilson of Stoke, Wrexham's Grenville Jones and former Manchester United favourite, Stan Pearson, now manager of Chester, added some punch to the home side, although it was United who opened the scoring.

On the half-hour Brennan gave United the initial advantage, but they went in at half-time all square following a goal from Hickson two minutes prior to the break. Any hopes of a second-half revival by Rhyl soon evaporated when United took a 3–1 lead with two goals inside a minute, 15 minutes after the restart, but further goals from Elms (on as a substitute for the unfortunate McDowell who had to leave the field injured on what was not only his return to his old stomping ground, but also his United second-team debut), Lawton and Morgans put the outcome of the match beyond any doubt.

Two minutes from time Hickson scored a second for the home side with what was arguably the best goal of the night on a memorable occasion for the Welsh League side. The evening brought Rhyl £500 in gate money and a cheque for a further £1,000 from United for the signature of Ken McDowell. It also brought a couple of comments from 'W.H.P.' of the *Rhyl Journal* that could quite easily have soured the occasion. He wrote: 'The Rhyl club must, however, look at their stewarding arrangements for such occasions in future. There were far too many youngsters swarming virtually unchecked all over the place – and the top of the cover on the "popular" side is not a safe "grandstand" for the "spectators" on top or those standing underneath.'

As a matter of interest, the United team for the above match was: Clayton, Holland, Heron, Harrop, Smith, Bratt, Morgans, Brennan, Lawton and McDowell (sub. Elms).

Some five weeks after being literally 'hit for six' at Old Trafford, a party of Manchester United players and officials left Manchester's Ringway airport on a flight bound for Madrid, for what could be termed the 'second leg' of their head-to-head against the Spanish champions.

United would have required five goals just to draw level, had the game been of a competitive nature, and they rocked Real Madrid and the 80,000 crowd by doing just that. Unfortunately the Spanish masters were again in top form, once again hitting United for six.

The programme for the match versus Rhyl, 14 October 1959.

A signed menu from a Madrid dinner, 11 November 1959.

It was, however, almost a triumphant reversal for United, as they were twice in front with a two-goal advantage in an outstanding first 45 minutes. They strolled into an audacious 2–0 lead, with goals in the 12th and 13th minutes from Quixall and Bradley.

The first came from the penalty spot after Charlton was brought down inside the area by Santamaria. Goalkeeper Dominguez saved the shot, but was unable to prevent Quixall from lashing home the rebound. Sixty seconds later Scanlon got the better of Marquitos and his long ball to the opposite flank was picked up by Bradley, who raced past Pachin to beat the goalkeeper with a right-footed drive, which took a deflection off Santamaria.

At the opposite end Harry Gregg was warmly applauded for two tremendous saves from Mateos and Di Stefano, but in the 21st minute the referee decided to play his part in allowing the home side back into the game, by awarding a penalty when the ball bounced against the arm of Bill Foulkes as he challenged Di Stefano for the ball. The United protests were to no avail and Di Stefano blasted the ball home off the crossbar.

The referee could do little to prevent United from once again taking a two-goal lead. An excellent four-man move in the 33rd minute, between Goodwin, Charlton, Scanlon and Viollet, saw the latter prod the ball home from only five yards out.

Much to their frustration, the Spaniards continued to find Gregg in inspired form and it once again took a rather dubious decision to pull the home side back into the game. Mateos looked suspiciously offside as he sprinted away to score two minutes before half-time.

Five minutes after the break the Spaniards were level, Bueno scoring after being put through by Di Stefano, but once again United were frustrated by the bizarre decisions of the French referee, who awarded Madrid a 54th-minute penalty for a rather innocuous tackle by Goodwin on Mateos. In fact Di Stefano, after having a word with the United players, waved his hands rather imperiously before hammering the spot-kick well over the bar for a deliberate miss.

Two minutes later United were again in front, Scanlon putting Charlton through, and his shot going in off the post. However, with 24 minutes still to play, the odds on the visitors holding on to their lead would not have been taken up by many, and any thoughts that United had of conjuring up a shock victory in the Spanish capital soon evaporated, with three goals, in the 62nd, 76th and 80th minutes, all scored by outside-left Bueno.

To their great credit, United kept plodding away and pulled the scoreline back to 6–5 when Dawson, on as substitute, scored with a drive after cutting in from the left. It was, however, too late to scavenge for that greatly deserved equaliser.

11 November 1959	**Real Madrid at Bernabeu Stadium.**

Attendance: 80,000.

Lost: 6–5.

Scorers: Quixall, Bradley, Viollet, Charlton, Dawson.

Team: Gregg, Foulkes, Carolan, Goodwin, Cope, McGuinness, Bradley, Quixall, Viollet, Charlton, Scanlon.

Substitute: Dawson for Scanlon.

The 1960s

A 1–0 fifth-round defeat in the 1959–60 FA Cup competition against Sheffield Wednesday at Old Trafford on 20 February 1960 produced a blank Saturday on the fixture list, as their opponents on the day of the sixth round were none other than the side who had just unceremoniously despatched them from the competition. So instead of twiddling their thumbs at home, the Saturday afternoon was taken over with a friendly against neighbours Manchester City at Maine Road.

The friendly was perhaps more advantageous to City than it was to United, as the Maine Road club were situated perilously on the edge of the relegation zone, four from the bottom, with 27 points from their 32 games. This was only four more than bottom-placed Luton Town.

For United, it gave Matt Busby the opportunity to give reserve-team centre-half Frank Haydock a taste of first-team football, with Tommy Heron, another reserve-team player, making only his second senior appearance.

United set the pace of the game and should actually have gone in front after only six minutes when Dennis Viollet, a mere six yards out and right in front of the City goal, uncharacteristically blasted the ball over the crossbar. A second effort also fell to the usually reliable forward, but this time Trautmann saved.

The action continued to be mostly around the City goalmouth, with Quixall coming close, a Brennan cross evading everyone, Sear doing well to stop Giles in full flight and Charlton, after evading Leivers, hitting the ball wide of the post.

Suddenly, as if awoken from a spell, City took command and United found themselves on the defensive. Foulkes collided with Sambrook in the area, but the referee had little interest in the shouts for a penalty, with the same City player forcing Gregg into a fine save on the line. Barlow wasted a good opportunity, but it was Leivers who should have opened the scoring for the home side. Brennan brought down Fagan inside the area and this time the referee had no hesitation in awarding a penalty, but Leivers hit the spot kick wide.

United were reduced to 10 men on the half-hour when Quixall went off injured. Following his return, just before the interval, the deadlock was broken, with Viollet scoring from eight yards out.

City, revitalised by the half-time break, quickly put the United defence under pressure, but Sambrook was gaining little leeway against Foulkes. Both Fagan and Barlow came close to equalising, but it was at the opposite end that the second goal of the afternoon came in the 61st minute. Brennan and Quixall opened up the City defence and Charlton squared the ball into the centre to the waiting Viollet, who made no mistake from close range.

Seven minutes later City pulled a goal back when Barlow cut in from the wing before letting fly from around 18 yards out, beating Gregg for power more than anything else.

Any hopes that City had of securing something from the game following this goal were soon extinguished, as Charlton scored a third for United in the 72nd minute. Running on to a long through ball from Giles, he hit a 15-yard drive into the far bottom corner.

Despite a late City rally, the game was beyond them, with their disgruntled supporters leaving the ground criticising manager Les McDowell, who had arrived at the ground prior to the match to find 'Get out, McDowell' and 'Down With Les' painted on the walls of the ground.

The programme for the match versus Manchester City, 12 March 1960.

12 March 1960	**Manchester City at Maine Road.**

Attendance: 29,476.

Won: 3–1.

Scorers: Viollet 2, Charlton.

Team: Gregg, Foulkes, Heron, Setters, Haydock, Brennan, Giles, Quixall, Viollet, Pearson, Charlton.

With little interest in the destination of the League title, or indeed the FA Cup, United were able to squeeze in a mid week fixture in Edinburgh against old rivals Hibs. Honours had been fairly evenly split in their meetings over the years, but on this occasion there was only ever going to be one winner. Despite the 4–0 scoreline in United's favour, it was certainly not a one-sided game, with Hibs coming close to scoring on several occasions. Baker and Johnstone, in particular, caused the United defence problems, the latter even missing a penalty after Cope handled a certain Baker 'goal' on the line.

Inspired by the recently signed Maurice Setters, who gave United much-needed power and direction, it was the burly figure of Alex Dawson who scored three of United's quartet of goals, while making the other for Viollet towards the end.

21 March 1960	**Hibs at Easter Road.**

Attendance: 15,000.

Won: 4–0.

Scorers: Dawson 3, Viollet.

Team: Gregg, Foulkes, Carolan, Setters, Cope, Brennan, Giles, Viollet, Dawson, Pearson, Charlton.

Despite its close proximity to the British mainland, as well as it being only a relatively short journey from Manchester, Ireland had, rather surprisingly, failed to feature as a regular destination for United in their pursuit of friendly fixtures. It therefore came as something of a surprise when United announced that they were to play a friendly against old European Cup opponents Shamrock Rovers in Dublin a few weeks prior to the end of the season.

Against the League of Ireland champions, something of an under-strength United commanded the first half, outpacing and indeed outclassing their opponents, but failing to produce the goals that would have reflected their superiority.

Even with a trio of debutants in their ranks, in the form of Stiles, Spratt and Moir, United should still have been able to overcome the determined Shamrock team with a voracious crowd behind them. However, despite leading 2–1 at half-time, through goals from Scanlon and Dawson, they found themselves struggling in the second period, allowing their hosts to score twice. Hamilton, a former United player, equalised 12 minutes after the interval, with Hennessy scoring what was to be the winner from the penalty spot 15 minutes from time, to record a memorable 3–2 victory.

Nobby Stiles and Ian Moir both came through their debuts with much acclaim, the former standing out as a replacement for Maurice Setters while Moir, a Scottish-born winger, showed some fine touches. Giles and Foulkes also stood out for United, but despite this there were too many wasted opportunities, allowing Shamrock Rovers to mount that second-half fightback.

The programme for the match versus Hibernian, 21 March 1960.

5 April 1960	Shamrock Rovers at Dalymount Park, Dublin.

Attendance: 10,000.

Lost: 3–2.

Scorers: Scanlon, Dawson.

Team: Gaskell, Foulkes, Carolan, Stiles, Cope, Brennan, Moir, Giles, Dawson, Spratt, Scanlon.

The programme for the match versus Shamrock Rovers, 5 April 1960.

It had been eight years since a Manchester United side had ventured across the Atlantic Ocean and, although they were scheduled to play only 10 games compared to the 12 of the 1950 and 1952 tours, it was still a hectic programme. It was also to be made with something of a depleted squad, due to the England call-ups for Maurice Setters, Bobby Charlton and Dennis Viollet, which forced them to miss the early games of the tour, coupled with the fact that Matt Busby only took 14 players, two of whom were goalkeepers. He had considered bringing in a couple of youngsters to bolster the squad, but decided against this, allowing them to go to Switzerland for the Blue Stars youth tournament.

Following a visit to Niagara Falls, the opening fixture took United to Toronto, where there was to be no easy start to the tour, with Hearts eager to put one over on their opponents and claim a victory in what could be considered an England–Scotland encounter as much as anything.

The game, however, turned out to be a rather dull, lacklustre affair, with both teams guilty of missing scoring opportunities, although the crowd showed a little enthusiasm as play swung from end to end in the early stages.

Hearts tried to push the ball down the United left at every opportunity, testing full-back Tommy Heron, who was making a rare first-team appearance following a training-ground injury to Joe Carolan. They did manage to get the ball past Harry Gregg after 23 minutes, but Blackwood's effort was disallowed for offside, much to the disapproval of some of the crowd. However, it was at the opposite end of the ground that the opening goal of the game was to come, with United catching Hearts on the hop.

Alex Dawson gave United the lead towards the end of the first half, as a slip by Hearts defender Thomson gave 'Dreadnought' the space and time he required to score. This, unfortunately, was followed by another injury setback, when Ronnie Cope took a knock on the thigh and had to go off. He was replaced by Nobby Lawton, who had only made his United debut a couple of weeks previously.

Within minutes of the second half getting under way Bauld should have equalised, but instead he sliced his kick. Hearts were soon level, however, through Thomson on the penalty spot, following a rather harsh decision against Haydock.

To their credit, United kept their heads up and, with around 15 minutes remaining, fine play from Quixall saw him thread the ball through to Giles, who restored United's lead and the hope that they had done enough to win the game.

It was, however, a lead which was to be rather short-lived, as two minutes later, much to the delight of the vast Scottish support in the ground, Bauld once again put Hearts on level terms. Blackwood drew Gregg from his goal and out of position before passing to teammate Bauld to score with ease.

This was the goal which brought an end to the scoring, leaving both teams content with the draw and hoping for improvement in the three other meetings between the two sides that were to follow.

The programme for the match versus Hearts, 14 May 1960.

14 May 1960 **Hearts at Varsity Stadium, Toronto.**

Attendance: 17,874.

Drew: 2–2.

Scorers: Dawson, Giles.

Team: Gregg, Foulkes, Heron, Cope, Haydock, Brennan, Giles, Quixall, Dawson, Pearson, Scanlon.

Substitute: Lawton for Cope.

The early days of the tour were not much of a holiday for the United party, as they left Canada almost immediately after the Hearts game due to the fact that they had two games to play within 24 hours, with the second fixture in New York. Trainer Jack Crompton described things as 'Fairyland in technicolour as you fly over this breathtaking skyscraper land with its millions of twinkling lights – a sight I will never forget', although he was quick to add that they did not arrive at their hotel until 2am, with their fixture against the German/American League All-Stars scheduled for that afternoon.

The state of the playing surface at the New York stadium left a lot to be desired, Crompton describing it as looking like a 'tank training ground'. Such conditions obviously prevented good, passing football from being played and, along with the heat and the travel tiredness, it could be considered rather surprising that United managed to win against what was a strong and capable side.

United went a goal behind in the opening 45 minutes as they attempted to shake off the cobwebs, the sometimes robust German-American XI breaking down the left and the cross into the centre being hammered home by their outside-right.

The second half saw something of what was expected during the tour from United as they turned the game around. Shay Brennan equalised 10 minutes after the restart, forcing the ball home following a free-kick on the edge of the penalty area, while Alex Dawson scored the winner with a great left-footed drive 10 minutes from the end.

15 May 1960 German/US League All-Stars at Trilborough Stadium, New York.

Attendance: 14,600.

Won: 2–1.

Scorers: Brennan, Dawson.

Team: Gregg, Foulkes, Heron, Lawton, Haydock, Brennan, Giles, Quixall, Dawson, Pearson, Scanlon.

Played under floodlights on the rock hard New York Polo Grounds, United lost the first game of their tour against the strong German side Munich 1860. It wasn't, however, until the second half that the game was lost, as an Albert Scanlon goal, from a Pearson centre, saw United go in at half-time on level pegging at 1–1, the Germans having opened the scoring in the third minute.

Within 15 minutes of the second half getting underway, United found themselves 3–1 behind, but a Quixall penalty did give them hope of snatching something from the game. These hopes were soon dashed, with a penalty decision against them, which was initially saved by Harry Gregg but had to be retaken by a different player, this time getting the better of the 'keeper.

18 May 1960	Munich 1860 at Polo Grounds, New York.

Attendance: 7,500.

Lost: 4–2.

Scorers: Scanlon, Quixall (pen.).

Team: Gregg, Foulkes, Heron, Lawton, Haydock, Brennan, Giles, Quixall, Dawson, Pearson, Scanlon.

The programme for the match versus Munich 1860, 18 May 1960.

Round two of the United–Hearts, Scotland–England confrontation continued back at New York's Trilborough Stadium, with its wooden-sided long-jump pit, which had come in for so much criticism when United had played there previously. This time, knowing what to expect, United were prepared and lived up to their billing in the *American Soccer News* bulletin as 'The world's most glamorous team' by defeating Hearts 3–0.

United had the crowd on the edge of their seats as early as 90 seconds after the kick-off, when Mark Pearson dribbled round a defender before giving Gordon Marshall in the Hearts goal no chance with an unstoppable shot.

By the fifth minute it was 2–0, a centre by Giles on the right finding Dawson, who was certainly not going to waste the opportunity.

In the second half Hearts pressed hard, but they were to find Harry Gregg, who was well-supported by his defenders, in fine form and as United continued to press, the game was wrapped up three minutes from time when Giles slipped the ball through to Dawson, who scored from 15 yards.

22 May 1960	Hearts at Trilborough Stadium, New York.

Attendance: 10,411.

Won: 3–0.

Scorers: Dawson 2, Pearson.

Team: Gregg, Foulkes, Carolan, Lawton, Haydock, Brennan, Giles, Quixall, Dawson, Pearson, Heron

With the United tour party now strengthened by the arrival of Setters, Charlton and Viollet, fresh from England duty, it would be something like the real Manchester United who were entertaining the American audience, and the trio of international stars did not disappoint against the Catholic Youth XI.

25 May 1960	Catholic Youth XI at Public Schools Stadium, St Louis.

Attendance: 6,000.

Won: 4–0.

Scorers: Quixall 2 (1 pen.), Viollet, Dawson.

Team: Gregg, Foulkes, Carolan, Setters, Haydock, Brennan, Giles, Quixall, Dawson, Viollet, Charlton.

It was an own-goal by Bobby Kirk of Hearts which decided this penultimate encounter between the two touring sides and it was something of a cruel blow to the Scottish First Division side, as they had bravely fought back from being two goals behind at half-time to level the match.

With their two-goal advantage United were the better team in the first half and again in the closing stages, when they had two goal-bound efforts cleared off the line, with Hearts goalkeeper Gordon Marshall caught out of position.

Alex Dawson gave United the lead in the ninth minute, running some 15 yards on goal following a Dennis Viollet pass. Twelve minutes later Johnny Giles made it 2–0, beating a defender before shooting under Marshall, who dived too late. Dennis Viollet was again the provider.

Hearts opened the second half strongly and pulled one goal back after eight minutes, when Bobby Blackwood drew Gregg from his goal before scoring from 10 yards out. Six minutes later they drew level when Johnny Hamilton ran down the left and passed to Crawford, who caught the United defence on the wrong foot before volleying home.

The game then opened up, with some excellent exhibition football, and it was an error by Bobby Kirk that decided the outcome. Some 12 yards from goal, with Dawson behind him, the Hearts defender tried to pass back to his goalkeeper, but somehow managed to put it past him, a goal that was enough to give United victory.

28 May 1960　　　　　**Hearts at Empire Stadium, Vancouver.**

Attendance: 18,600.

Won: 3–2.

Scorers: Dawson, Giles, opp. own-goal.

Team: Gregg, Foulkes, Carolan, Setters, Haydock, Brennan, Giles, Quixall, Dawson, Viollet, Charlton.

United's meeting with Hearts found its way on to the front page of the *Los Angeles Examiner*, but it was certainly not a headline-making performance from United, as they lost 4–0 in their fourth meeting against their fellow pioneers.

Hearts, having failed to get the better of United in any of the previous three meetings, were certainly out for revenge, but on a foggy evening they could consider themselves rather fortunate to have taken the lead three minutes prior to the interval following a rather dubious hand ball decision against Maurice Setters, with George Thomson scoring from the spot.

There was certainly nothing untoward about the second Hearts goal, scored by Bauld straight from the restart, with the Hearts forward blasting home a Smith cross. It did, however, knock United off their stride, as the Scottish side gained further encouragement from the goal and proceeded to take the game to their opponents.

Harry Gregg saved United on numerous occasions, but was helpless against the third Hearts goal. The ball once again found its way to Bauld, but the Hearts forward was this time denied by Gregg. The United 'keeper, however, could only block the ball and with his defenders slow to react Crawford fired home, while Gregg was helpless on the ground.

The direct game and the long passing of the Scottish side seemed to trouble the United defence and it came as no surprise when Hearts added a fourth three minutes before the end, Bauld again the scorer.

The programme for the match versus Hearts, 1 June 1960.

1 June 1960　　　　　**Hearts at Wrigley Fields, Los Angeles.**

Attendance: 11,000.

Lost: 4–0.

Team: Gregg, Foulkes, Carolan, Setters, Haydock, Brennan, Giles, Quixall, Dawson, Viollet, Charlton.

It took United only four minutes to open the scoring against the Pacific Coast All-Stars. That opening goal came courtesy of Albert Scanlon in the fourth minute, who scored with a penalty-kick. Soon afterwards Johnny Giles added a second with a 25-yard drive into the corner of the net, and it looked as though there would be something of a deluge of goals from United.

To their credit, the All-Stars plodded away and, with a brisk breeze behind them, soon earned their reward. Sixteen minutes before the interval a cross from Wellisch found its way through to Paton, one of the many Scots in the home side, who beat Gaskell from close range and then, with the half drawing to a close, Wellisch, to the delight of the crowd, blasted the ball past a helpless Gaskell from 30 yards out to level the scoring.

Scanlon, displaying the form of his pre-Munich days, restored United's lead shortly after the restart, beating Ottoboni with an unstoppable shot. Quixall was introduced into the fray for the second half and supplied an easy fourth for Viollet, having drawn Ottoboni from his goal and presenting his teammate with an empty net.

Only once in the second half did the All-Stars threaten the United goal and that was from Doherty, but his header towards the top corner of the goal was superbly saved by Gaskell. Ultimately, United maintained command of the game as they besieged the All-Stars goal in the closing minutes.

The programme for the match versus Pacific Coast All-Stars, 5 June 1960.

5 June 1960 Pacific Coast All-Stars at Balboa Soccer Stadium, San Francisco.

Attendance: 8,500.

Won: 4–2.

Scorers: Scanlon 2 (1 pen.), Giles, Viollet.

Team: Gaskell, Foulkes, Carolan, Setters, Haydock, Brennan, Giles, Lawton, Dawson, Pearson, Scanlon.

Substitutes: Heron for Carolan, Quixall for Lawton, Viollet for Pearson.

Fall River, about 200 miles north of New York, was home to a vast number of English immigrants, many of them from Lancashire, giving United strong support for their game against the New England All-Stars. Unfortunately, the visit of United did not conjure up a creditable attendance, as a sparse crowd of around 1,800 turned up to see United record a free-scoring 7–0 victory.

On a rough pitch, United proved to be too fast and skilful for their opponents, scoring three times prior to the interval. Quixall opened the scoring in the sixth minute from the penalty spot, Viollet claimed the second with a fine drive after 25 minutes, and Dawson scored a third five minutes before half-time.

In the second half Dawson captured the headlines, scoring twice, in the 68th and 76th minutes. The second of the two was an eye-opening dribble which took him the length of the field, before he calmly took the ball round the 'keeper to score.

Pearson and Quixall completed the scoring for United, with the All-Stars more than grateful to hear the final whistle.

8 June 1960 New England All-Stars at Fall River Stadium, Massachusetts.

Attendance: 1,800.

Won: 7–0.

Scorers: Dawson 3, Quixall 2 (1 pen.), Viollet, Pearson.

Team: Gregg, Foulkes, Heron, Lawton, Cope, Setters, Giles, Quixall, Dawson, Viollet, Scanlon.

Substitute: Pearson for Viollet.

With a four-day break before the final match of the long and tiring tour, there was plenty to keep the United players and staff occupied. Coney Island's beach turned out to be one of the most popular attractions, with a number of the players competing for the best tan as they relaxed in the sunshine.

There was, however, still one game to play, with United rounding off their 10-game tour with a superb display of exhibition football against the Ukrainian National XI, but it was not until the second half that they turned on the style.

After the restart, with the score at 1–1, any hopes that the home support had of their favourites pulling off some kind of turnaround quickly evaporated and they settled down to enjoy United's slick, short passing game, which saw them score five times in the opening 17 minutes of the half.

Already without their United States National Championship top scorer Noha, who had suffered a broken leg, and top player Campo, who was also injured, the Ukrainians did have some excuse for what was a rather humiliating defeat. The display from United would have been good enough to get the better of almost any team and salt was rubbed into the Ukrainians' wounds when Harry Gregg left his goal unattended to slot home a penalty.

---

12 June 1960   Ukranian National XI at Edison High Field, Philadelphia.

Attendance: 5,000.

Won: 10–1.

Scorers: Viollet 3, Quixall 2, Dawson 2, Charlton 2, Gregg (pen.).

Team: Gregg, Foulkes, Carolan, Setters, Haydock, Brennan, Giles, Quixall, Dawson, Viollet, Scanlon.

As always, the name Real Madrid attracted a favourable attendance to Old Trafford, with not only the regulars attending, but also countless locals of different persuasions eager to see the Spanish giants in action. At the end of a highly entertaining 90 minutes, the neutrals in the 50,000 crowd would have been equally impressed by United as by Real Madrid.

United were certainly not overawed by their opponents and must have considered themselves rather unfortunate to go a goal behind in the 19th minute, although there could be no complaints about the quality of the goal. A perfect cross from Puskas found Di Stefano and the centre-forward beat Gregg from close range.

Further attacks by the Spaniards were broken down by the United defence, while at the opposite end Vincente made a magnificent save from Charlton before the home side equalised on the half-hour. A corner from Charlton was headed out, but Quixall first-timed the ball back into the goalmouth and Pearson flicked the ball past Vincente with his head. Many had thought that the Spaniards would have had things their own way, but United had certainly held their own as the interval approached.

Charlton once again came close to scoring, his shot beating the 'keeper but hitting the side netting. At the same time Real began to threaten the United goal, with both Puskas and Gento causing problems for the home defence. With seven minutes to the break, the visitors gained the initiative, Vidal driving the ball past Gregg from 25 yards out. Moments later they were almost further in front, but Gregg did well to save from Puskas.

Three substitutes after the interval gave Real Madrid fresh legs, while United, who had not felt the need to make any changes, were forced into making one 15 minutes after the restart when Brennan was carried off after falling heavily as he

The programme for the Ukrainian National XI, 12 June 1960.

attempted to tackle Gento. He was replaced by 18-year-old former Shelbourne youngster Tony Dunne on his Manchester United debut.

For a player who was to go on to enjoy a fruitful 13-year career with United, making over 520 appearances for the club, making his debut against such notable opponents was perhaps fate, but any early nerves that were shown soon subsided and he was cheered loudly by the crowd whenever he touched the ball.

The change in personnel had little effect on United's play, as they continued to entertain, but despite this, many felt that the play could easily swing to the opposite end of the Old Trafford pitch with dire consequences.

In the 74th minute those thoughts became reality when Puskas sent Gento scurrying down the wing. A Di Stefano effort, which looked likely to bring a fourth Madrid goal, was blocked by a defender as United were constantly pushed back.

If it was felt that United simply required a small amount of good fortune in an effort to turn the game, it came in the 75th minute when Puskas went off injured, but it was not until two minutes from time that they managed to make any breakthrough. Charlton was again heavily involved, breaking down the left, and after two United shots had been blocked the ball broke to Nicholson, who let fly from 30 yards with the ball flashing past Vincente and into the far corner of the net.

The United players warmly applauded the Real Madrid players from the pitch, while they too left the arena to the cheers of the crowd. It was an acknowledgement of the entertaining 90 minutes and a more pleasant sound than those that had greeted the full-time whistle at recent First Division fixtures.

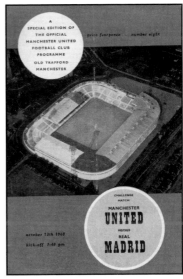

The programme for the match versus Real Madrid, 13 October 1960.

13 October 1960	**Real Madrid at Old Trafford.**

Attendance: 51,506.

Lost: 3–2.

Scorers: Pearson, Nicholson.

Team: Gregg, Setters, Brennan, Stiles, Foulkes, Nicholson, Quixall, Giles, Viollet, Pearson, Charlton.

Substitute: Dunne for Brennan.

An ingoing and an outgoing transfer, either side of the visit of Bayern Munich to Old Trafford, captured the back-page headlines just as much as the game itself. On the day prior to the match, manager Matt Busby had paid out a fee of £20,000 to bring in the Republic of Ireland full-back Noel Cantwell from West Ham United, while a fee of £15,000 was agreed between the United officials and former Old Trafford favourite Charlie Mitten, now manager of Newcastle United, to take Albert Scanlon to Tyneside.

Scanlon certainly gave the watching Newcastle officials the impression that they were going to get value for money, turning in a superb display and laying on two of Alex Dawson's three goals.

Cantwell also gave the impression of being an excellent acquisition, playing a typically polished game and almost scoring with a fierce left-footed drive in the second half.

United certainly deserved their victory and, had it not been for some fine goalkeeping from Fazekas, it would certainly have been by more. However, the night belonged to Alex Dawson, scorer of all three United goals. His first two came from Scanlon centres in the 22nd and 74th minutes, while his third came one minute from the end following good work from Viollet.

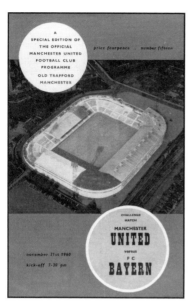

The programme for the match versus Bayern Munich, 21 November 1960.

Bayern's only goal came in the 83rd minute, following a defensive mistake by Brennan.

21 November 1960	**Bayern Munich at Old Trafford.**

Attendance: 15,769.

Won: 3–1.

Scorer: Dawson 3.

Team: Gregg, Brennan, Cantwell, Setters, Foulkes, Nicholson, Bradley, Quixall, Dawson, Viollet, Scanlon.

The next game for United was something of a 'bargain basement' encounter: a visit to Chester. In the build up to the game it was suggested by many that United would not send their first 11 for the initial friendly fixture under floodlights at The Stadium. However, with a certain Stan Pearson, the former United inside-forward, in charge at Chester, it was a strong Manchester United side that ran out to entertain the crowd with a devastating display of football.

Pearson himself had been tempted to take part in the game, but later confessed, 'I think they would have been too fast for me.' One of the Chester directors told Jimmy Murphy, acting manager on the night, 'You can take the gate money but leave us a couple of players.'

During the first 45 minutes the home side were in little need of any assistance from their First Division visitors, holding their own admirably with goalkeeper Brown dealing efficiently with the variety of efforts that came his way.

Although United led 1–0 at the interval, Moir, who had had an excellent game, heading home a Charlton cross in the 25th minute, Chester had come close to scoring, with an effort from Croft in the second minute being deflected past by Foulkes, with Gregg caught out of position.

If Chester thought that they had an opportunity to treat their support to a memorable night, by achieving a draw or, even better, a morale-boosting victory against their illustrious opponents, their hopes were dashed within 10 minutes of the second half getting underway when United scored their second goal.

Charlton, who had received a tremendous ovation from the crowd at the start of the game, swung yet another ball into the Chester penalty box, where the lurking Quixall shot home. The same player notched up a second shortly afterwards, this time from the penalty spot after Watson had brought down Moir.

Alex Dawson soon made it four and that seemed to be that, but with the game slowly dwindling away, Bobby Charlton satisfied his adoring public by scoring twice in the final three minutes to give United a 6–0 victory.

1 March 1961	**Chester at The Stadium, Sealand Road.**

Attendance: 8,673.

Won: 6–0.

Scorers: Quixall 2 (1 pen.), Charlton 2, Dawson, Moir.

Team: Gregg, Brennan, Cantwell, Setters, Foulkes, Stiles, Moir, Quixall, Dawson, Giles, Charlton.

There were to be three ports of call at the end of season 1960–61, with the United directors treating the players to some Mediterranean sunshine. The only downside was that they also had to play three friendlies, although they would be spread over a 12-day period, leaving plenty of time for relaxation.

First up was a fixture against Torino, which left the Italians stunned as United turned round a half-time one-goal deficit to win 2–1.

Six minutes prior to the interval Ferrini, the Torino inside-left, had given the home side the lead, but in the second half United came back strongly. Maurice Setters equalised in the 53rd minute and, following a corner, Dennis Viollet added another.

Among the interested spectators were a delegation from Inter Milan, who were reportedly keen on taking Bobby Charlton to Italy. It was an interest which would certainly have been maintained following a fine display against the Italians, as he was behind the majority of United's best moves.

Despite bringing on four second-half substitutes, Torino still could not get the better of United and the visitors managed to hold on to their slender lead, earning a very creditable victory.

The menu for the match versus Torino, 2 May 1961.

2 May 1961   **Torino at Stadio Comunale, Turin.**

Attendance: 25,000.

Won: 2–1.

Scorers: Setters, Viollet.

Team: Gaskell, Dunne, Brennan, Setters, Cope, Stiles, Moir, Quixall, Viollet, Pearson, Charlton.

The second of the tour fixtures saw the United players booed off the pitch at the end of the game, but it was any underhand tactics, robust play or ungentlemanly conduct that the locals took exception to. It was simply because the United players had shouted for the ball during the game instead of clapping their hands, as was the custom in that part of the world.

Not only did the shouting for the ball upset the crowd, it was also disapproved of by the referee, who awarded four free-kicks against United because of it, with one of those also leading to the booking of Albert Quixall.

Despite this 'handicap' United played well, especially Cope and Cantwell, but their poor shooting, along with their tendency to play too square, cost them the victory. United could argue, however, that they should have been awarded two first-half penalties when both Viollet and Charlton were upended in the area. The referee thought otherwise.

The crowd were vocal in their disapproval when Stiles and Viollet tackled just a little too hard for their liking, creating a similar wall of noise when the home team scored their three goals, Selmosson in the 18th minute and a Manfredini double in the 40th and 63rd minutes.

The best goal of the evening, which did bring a ripple of approval, came from Ian Moir, who wriggled past two defenders before unleashing a superb drive from well out.

10 May 1961   **Roma at Stadio Olympico.**

Attendance: 8,000.

Lost: 3–2.

Scorers: Moir, Viollet.

Team: Gaskell, Brennan, Cantwell, Setters, Cope, Stiles, Giles, Quixall, Viollet, Pearson, Moir.

'Welcome to Malta' proclaimed the headlines on page four of the Maltese *Sporting Star* on Monday 8 May, prior to United's four-day visit to the George Cross island for a fixture against a Malta League XI.

United's arrival from Rome, at the island's Luqa Airport, was greeted by hundreds of Maltese United supporters and among the party, led by Chairman Harold Hardman, was a certain Tommy Doherty. Why 'the Doc' was present, the *Sporting Star* does not mention.

A reception party at the Anglo-Maltese League Club at Valletta preceded the match and, in his speech, the president of the four-year-old Malta Branch of the Supporters' Club mentioned that during correspondence with manager Matt Busby the United manager had promised to bring his team to Malta should his team ever be anywhere near the island.

So, with Italy only a short flight from Malta, Matt Busby kept his promise and on a hard, sandy pitch the much-fêted visitors, although not comfortable with their surroundings, managed a 2–0 victory. This was thanks mainly to their defence, who had at times to adopt something of a 'route one' way to goal.

In the opening 45 minutes United were seldom out of their own half of the field, with David Gaskell performing heroics in goal, ably supported by Cantwell and Cope. However, in a rare foray upfield they took the lead in the 30th minute. A foul on Stiles by Borg saw Quixall's free-kick fly low into the penalty area, where Noel Cantwell hooked the ball into the net.

An injury to Theobald slightly unsettled the League XI, as United pushed forward, happy to play an offside game, and they continued to take the game to the home side as the second half got underway, playing some attractive football at times.

United's effectiveness was blunted by an injury to Setters, which saw him exchange places with Dennis Viollet, but despite the knock the move paid off, with the United wing-half revelling in his new position. However, it was not all one-way traffic and in a rare breakaway Zammit had the ball in the United net with a fine effort, but was to be disappointed when the referee ruled him offside.

Back on the attack, Quixall hit the post and in the 70th minute a Moir corner was headed home by Setters. The goal ended any hopes the League XI had of squeezing anything out of the game.

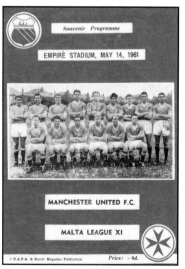

The programme for the match versus Malta League XI, 14 May 1961.

14 May 1961	Malta League XI at Empire Stadium, Valletta.

Attendance: 18,000.

Won: 2–0.

Scorers: Setters, Cantwell.

Team: Gaskell, Brennan, Cantwell, Setters, Cope, Stiles, Giles, Quixall, Dawson, Viollet, Moir.

Pre-season 1961 saw United travel to Germany and Austria as part of their build-up programme, with the fixture in Germany against Bayern Munich offering the Germans the opportunity of revenge, for United's 3–1 victory at Old Trafford the previous November. However, it was to be United who triumphed once again, thanks to two goals from David Herd.

The former Arsenal centre-forward was a real thorn in the side of the Germans, ensuring that their defenders never had a minute's peace during the entire 90 minutes. After a quarter of an hour his right-footed effort was headed over by Tietz. Moments later he shot wide, with the ball knocking over an unassuming ball-boy, who sat on the ground for a couple of minutes shaking his head.

The first half remained goalless, but seven minutes after the interval United took the lead. As Mark Pearson moved forward with the ball, Herd slowly manoeuvred himself into a wider position ready to accept a pass, but to the surprise of the German defenders Pearson took the opportunity himself, clipping the ball just under the crossbar.

Herd once again caused the Bayern defence problems, launching a powerful right-footed drive goalwards. Not having learned from the incident with the ball-boy, left-back Olk got his head to the ball, but almost instantly collapsed on the line. As the defender wondered where he was, the ball ricocheted onto the inside of the post and back into play.

Immediately christened 'Die Bombe' by the German journalists, it was perhaps only fitting that United's second goal should be scored by the Scot in the 72nd minute. A pass from Moir set him off on a 20-yard run and after beating two defenders he calmly slotted the ball into the net.

The Germans lost a little of their fluency following an injury to Gieseman, just after United's opening goal, but in the final 10 minutes of the game they produced some of their best football. Peschen and Froelich both hit the post, with Harry Gregg in the United goal also making a number of fine saves.

There was no way back for them, however, and it would be a number of years before Bayern would be able to claim the upper hand against a United side.

9 August 1961	**Bayern Munich at Grünwald Stadium.**

Attendance: 15,000.

Won: 2—0.

Scorers: Pearson, Herd.

Team: Gregg, Brennan, Cantwell, Stiles, Foulkes, Setters, Giles, Violet, Herd, Pearson, Moir.

Arriving on the banks of the Danube, the United party were hit with a 90-degree heatwave and on the evening prior to the match against First Vienna, they struggled to sleep in their hotel rooms. If that was not enough to contend with, they found themselves up against a match official who was to appal the United officials and players with some of his decisions.

Despite being forced to play Cantwell and Giles with slight injuries, United still dominated the game, and they have to be applauded for keeping their cool in the face of severe provocation. Giles was grabbed by the neck by goalkeeper Schmidt, while Herd should have won a penalty when he was crudely brought down. On another occasion the ball was at one end of the pitch while a squabble was taking place at the other.

United took the lead through Viollet in the eighth minute, but they were denied victory by the referee when he penalised Harry Gregg for exceeding the four steps. The resulting free-kick cannoned off a defender's shin and into the net in the only opportunity that the Vienna side would get.

11 August 1961	**First Vienna at Hohe Warte Stadium.**

Attendance: 15,000.

Drew: 1—1.

Scorer: Viollet.

Team: Gregg, Brennan, Cantwell, Stiles, Foulkes, Setters, Giles, Viollet, Herd, Pearson, Moir.

Die Blaue

SPORTSCHAU

9. August 1961

38. Jahrg. 20 Pfg

Der Bergschuh mit Pfiff

Lowa-Spezial-Bergschuh
in der Eiger-Nordwand
und vielen Expeditionen bewährt

TIP TOP Vulkanisier-Material für Auto und Rad

Manchester United
traditioneller Münchner Gast

Möbel kauft bei Strobl

MÜNCHENS MÖBEL-SPEZIALKAUFHAUS
BAYERSTRASSE 83

Denkwürdige Spiele

hat Manchester United auf Münchner Boden ausgetragen: am 13. August 1958 mit 4:3 für die Münchner Kombination Bayern/1860 und am 8. August 1959 mit 2:1 für Manchester United gegen den FC Bayern. Und heute also, wie es der Zufall will, zum dritten Mal wieder im selben „englischen Monat" August. Das 1960 in England ausgetragene Rückspiel gewann Manchester United gegen den FC Bayern vor 40 000 Zuschauern mit 3:1.

Eine große Kapitalsanlage

machte Manchester United mit der Verpflichtung des schußgefürchteten Mittelstürmers David Herd, der nach deutschem Geld für 500 000 Mark von Arsenal London erworben wurde. Herd ist 28 Jahre alt und kam 1954 von Stockport zu Arsenal. Er führte drei Jahre lang die Torschützenliste der „Kanoniere" an und spielte oftmals in der schottischen Nationalmannschaft. Matt Busby, Manager von Manchester United, der den berühmten Schotten für zwei Jahre engagierte, sagte: Herd

ist der derzeit beste Mittelstürmer in Großbritannien, mit ihm haben wir Titelchancen. Er absolviert in München sein erstes Spiel für Manchester United!

FOTO-FACHMANN

RUMFORDSTRASSE 8
RUF N: 227224

ELGAS

Von München nach Wien

Nach dem Spiel reist die Manchesterexpedition nach Wien weiter. United wird dort am 12. August auf der Hohen Warte gegen die Vienna antreten.

Heute 17 Uhr 30 Säbener Platz

Schiedsrichter Bayern Lombos
Hausberger Fischl
Streitle Brennauer Wengenmayer II
Füßl Schmid Wengenmayer I Procher Kurz

Auswechselspieler: Bordo, Struff, Ott

Schiedsrichter München Sing
Baumann Dischl
Kellner Forster Kronschnabel
Heppner Bobkiewicz Heiß Priesnitz Hübner

Spielleiter: Heinrich Tischler

Wie der Augsburger Kritiker der dortigen „Allgemeinen" die Bayernmannschaft sah

Herausragender Stürmer war der Neuzugang Thimm, der einen Mordsschuß besitzt. Der beste Mannschaftsteil der Bayern: die Verteidigung. Auch die Läuferreihe hat durchaus Format. Ohne die zwei, im wesentlichen doch typischen Haller-einzelaktionen entspringenden Tore seines Nationalspielers, hätte der BCA vermutlich Schwierigkeiten gegen diese starke Deckung gehabt. Kosar ist ein guter Hüter. Der Mann des Tages jedoch war trotz Haller der Augsburger Neuzugang vom 1. FC Nürnberg, Mittelstürmer Herbert Ammer (22), dessen kluge, genau an den Mann adressierten Pässe jede Hintermannschaft aufreißen können. Der BCA hat mit Ammer einen großen Fang getan.

POLSTERMÖBELFABRIK

Segmüller

Das Spezialhaus für anspruchsvolle Kunden

MÜNCHEN 15
Sonnenstraße 19 im Sonnenblock

Liebe Blaue!

Für Ihren Bericht in der Blauen über die Schirigruppe des FC Bayern möchte ich Ihnen im Namen unseres Obmannes Franz Xaver Wengenmayer senior und aller SR-Kameraden des FC Bayern herzlichst danken. Sie haben damit wieder einen Beweis mehr an sportlicher Aufgeschlossenheit und Liebe zum runden Leder geliefert. Mit Bayerngrüßen Ihr ergebener Toni Procher, München 9, Chiemgaustraße 46.

The programme for the match versus Bayern Munich, 9 August 1961.

With United struggling around the foot of the First Division, few would have thought they could defeat Spanish giants Real Madrid under the Old Trafford lights, especially with the likes of Santamaria, Di Stefano and Gento still wearing the famous all-white strip.

It was most definitely not the Real Madrid side of old, and the above trio were all substituted in the second half. However, away from the rigours of League football United were more relaxed and perhaps caught their visitors out by playing some excellent football, with 19-year-old Phil Chisnall, playing in only his third senior game, named as Man of the Match.

With only 14 minutes gone United took the lead following a short corner by Chisnall. Passing to Giles, the ball was quickly returned to the youngster and he calmly hit a low shot past Araquistain in the Madrid goal.

Undeterred by this setback, Madrid pushed forward time and time again, but found the United defence standing firm. It was not until three minutes before the interval that they managed to make any breakthrough. Up until then Foulkes had kept Di Stefano under close control, but the Madrid centre, for once, had evaded his marker, seizing upon a loose ball and sending a virtually unstoppable shot past Gaskell from around 25 yards.

Rather surprisingly, United regained their lead almost immediately after the restart. Nicholson sent a precise pass through to Herd, who beat the Madrid 'keeper without too much of a problem.

United continued where they had left off as the second half got underway, despite Madrid making a trio of changes. Herd had a goal disallowed, as did Ruiz, while a Giles shot was cleared off the line by Pachin but, try as they might, they could not find a way through the resilient Madrid defence to increase their lead.

With 10 minutes remaining Quixall replaced the injured Giles and it was the substitute who managed to finally prise open the visitors' defence. Passing to Herd, the United number nine powered the ball past Araquistain, whose desperate dive was to no avail.

It was a notable victory for United and one that they certainly achieved on merit.

13 December 1961	Real Madrid at Old Trafford.

Attendance: 43,000.

Won: 3–1.

Scorers: Herd 2, Chisnall.

Team: Gaskell, Brennan, Dunne, Setters, Foulkes, Nicholson, Chisnall, Giles, Herd, Lawton, Charlton.

Substitute: Quixall for Giles.

In the close season of 1961–62 United journeyed to destinations quite different from those they had travelled to before.

The first port of call took the United party to Palma, Majorca, where in the first match of a three-game tour they defeated Italian First Division side Mantova 3–0. It was a fixture that they never looked like losing and they were cheered on by a small number of British tourists.

The Italians did well to go in at half-time without conceding a goal, but after the interval they were no match for a United side the *Daily Express* soccer reporter wrote as having 'touched the peak of destructive perfection.' A local radio commentator was also lavish in his praise for Matt Busby's team, saying they were 'the best visiting team we've seen and their style is typically British and their speed was surprising.'

The programme for the match versus Real Madrid, 13 December 1961.

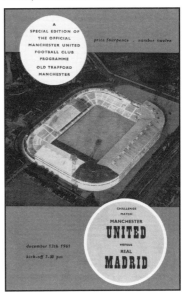

Just after the restart David Herd put them in front following some fine play between Mark Pearson and Sammy McMillan, with McMillan adding a second. The third was scored by the other player involved in that first goal, Mark Pearson, who capped a fine display with a brilliant run to complete the scoring.

15 May 1962	Mantova at Palma.

Attendance: 20,000.

Won: 3–0.

Scorers: Herd, McMillan, Pearson.

Team: Gaskell, Brennan, Dunne, Stiles, Foulkes, Setters, Giles, Quixall, Herd, Pearson, McMillan.

The second of the trio of games saw United up against the hosts Majorca and, as they had recently defeated Mantova 5–1, United would have expected to face a much harder 90 minutes. As it turned out, their expectations proved correct, with the Spanish First Division side holding firm to register a 1–0 victory.

Not for the first time, and certainly not for the last, United failed to record a victory due to bad luck and poor finishing. They should have been a goal in front after 18 minutes, but instead David Herd hit the post and shortly afterwards Johnny Giles shot wide with the Spanish 'keeper beaten.

United once again played some good football and Giles, along with Sammy McMillan and David Herd, was a constant danger, but Mark Pearson and the out-of-position Noel Cantwell, playing at inside-right, failed to support their teammates when it mattered.

The defence was resolute and impressive, although they had one lapse in the second half which allowed Majorca to snatch the only goal of the game. Outside-right Mir managed to pass through between two defenders before finding Oviedo, his teammate on the opposite flank, who beat Gaskell with a left-footed drive.

Three minutes from the end, with United still pressing for an equaliser, captain Maurice Setters was sent off following a tackle, a decision which meant both teams had to play with only 10 men, as Majorca's centre-half Balao had been dismissed earlier for a similar challenge.

The sending off, while not creating much of a stir at the time, certainly did once the next day's newspapers appeared, as the guilty man was named by the Spanish correspondents covering the game as Bill Foulkes. This mistake apparently occurred due to the fact that the match programme (which I believe no collector has ever seen) carried the teams with the Continental form of numbering, with the centre-half as number three and the right-half as number five.

16 May 1962	Majorca at Palma.

Attendance: 20,000.

Lost: 1–0.

Team: Gaskell, Brennan, Dunne, Setters, Foulkes, Nicholson, Giles, Cantwell, Herd, Pearson, McMillan.

Moving on to mainland Spain, United came up against tougher opposition in the form of Valencia, a team they would face in European competitions. In that first encounter United were hit with two early goals and never really recovered.

Playing fast, skilful football, Valencia were in command for long periods, with their defence breaking down United's attacks with ease. Their two goals, in the 14th and 27th minutes, both scored by Nunez, gave them an advantage that they were never likely to relinquish.

Four minutes before the interval Maurice Setters reduced the arrears with a shot from 25 yards, which gave Ginesta no chance, but 10 minutes after the restart Nunez completed his hat-trick. A second Valencia penalty was converted by Chicao in the 74th minute, while Sammy McMillan scored twice, his second a long-range spectacular, to keep the contest open. However, just when it was felt that Valencia might crack under the pressure, Waldo scored Valencia's fifth nine minutes from the end to round off the scoring. The United players complained that the ball had gone out of play prior to the cross which led to the goal being scored, but the referee showed no interest in their complaints.

Despite the defeat, United earned praise for their fitness levels and the spirit they showed but, as had been the case in the previous match, their finishing proved weak. On the other hand, had it not been for David Gaskell, who made a number of fine saves, the margin between the two sides could have certainly been greater.

---

20 May 1962   **Valencia at Mestalla Stadium.**

Attendance: 55,000.

Lost: 5–3.

Scorers: McMillan 2, Setters.

Team: Gaskell, Brennan, Dunne, Stiles, Foulkes, Setters, Giles, Quixall, Herd, Pearson, McMillan.

Today, any announcement that United are undertaking a close or pre-season tour is greeted with considerable delight from members of the club's worldwide support.

In the 1960s it was different, with travel nothing like as economical as it is today, but this particular end-of-season jaunt would have been well attended by the Red Army as few would have been able to resist a few days of sand and sun and a trip to Amsterdam thrown in for good measure.

Having lost two of the three Spanish fixtures, the United party headed for home, stopping off in Holland to take on an Amsterdam XI in the Dutch capital and rounding off the tour with a well-earned victory.

With the Dutch used to a more refined style of football, the 10,000-strong crowd were slightly surprised by United's rather robust tackling, although they were quick to admit that the visitors were certainly the better team when it came to both individual play and tactical awareness.

Following a goalless first half, United went ahead six minutes after the restart, when Eire international Johnny Giles, the outstanding success of the tour, finished off a fine solo run by giving the Dutch goalkeeper, Hoogerman, no chance with a powerful left-footed drive.

Bill Foulkes and David Gaskell were both in outstanding form in the United defence, but the latter could do little to prevent Amsterdam winger Keizer equalising from the penalty spot after Shay Brennan had handled.

Up front, David Herd was far from his best, displaying little in the way of his usual skill and speed, while Mark Pearson showed some sparkling form under the floodlights. However, it was his fellow forward Johnny Giles, the star of the show, who secured the victory for United in the 75th minute, when he hammered home a free-kick from just outside the penalty area.

23 May 1962	Amsterdam XI at Olympic Stadium.

Attendance: 10,000.

Won: 2—1.

Scorers: Giles 2.

Team: Gaskell, Brennan, Cantwell, Stiles, Foulkes, Setters, Giles, Quixall, Herd, Pearson, McMillan.

The vast oval bowl-like arena of Hampden Park in the southern suburbs of Glasgow was one of football's great stadiums, regularly squeezing over 100,000 onto its sloping cinder terraces. This was a venue which, when packed with vociferous Scots, was certainly not for the faint-hearted. The 'Hampden Roar', however, was stunned into silence on the evening of 8 August 1962 by a superb Manchester United display, orchestrated by Caledonia's favourite son, Denis Law, making his debut in a red shirt following his £115,000 transfer.

The programme for the match versus Amsterdam XI, 23 May 1962.

23 mei 1962   Prijs 15 cent

STADION NIEUWS

Amsterdam

tegen

Manchester United

Nadat in de laatste jaren het District Amsterdam van de K.N.V.B. zulk een doorslaand succes boekte met het engageren van de Europese topclubs, was het moeilijk thans een tegenstander van groot formaat bereid te vinden hier het beste Britse profvoetbal te vertonen. Manchester United lijkt ons daartoe in staat. De club, opgericht in 1885 door employees van de spoorwegen, had een moeilijke start totdat de groot-industrieel Mr. J. H. Davies met raad en daad voor de United op de bres sprong. Toen steeg de club met sprongen en in 1908 werd de eredivisie bereikt en in 1909 de cup. Er volgden slechte en goede seizoenen. Na de oorlog steeg de ster der roodhemden en werd in '52, '56 en '57 het kampioenschap behaald.

Tot de vliegtuigramp bij München op de terugreis van Belgrado (waar de halve eindstrijd voor de Europa-cup werd gewonnen) Manchester United de grootste slag toebracht die ooit een Europese topclub overkwam. Behalve de secretaris Walter Crickmer, trainer Tom Curry en coach Bert Whally verloren toen het leven de spelers Roger Byrne (captain), Geoff Bent, Eddy Colman, Duncan Edwards, Mark Jones, David Pegg, Tommy Taylor en Billy Whelen.

In Nederland heeft men toen intens meegeleefd met de slag die het noodlot Manchester United toebracht. De club heeft zich onder de eminente leiding van Mr. Busby prachtig hersteld; ze presenteert thans het Amsterdamse publiek een ploeg die in Engeland als een van de beste representanten van het Britse profvoetbal mag worden beschouwd.

De geschiedenis van het Amsterdams elftal van vóór de oorlog hier te releveren zou te ver voeren. De huidige generatie stelt echter wèl belang in de gebeurtenissen op voetbalgebied na de oorlog. We volstaan met deze te vermelden. Het zijn er 24 in totaal:

4-8-'45 Amsterdam—Brussel 1—2, 15-5-'46 Amsterdam—Stockholm 3—1, 6-5-'47 Kopenhagen—Amsterdam 3—3, 8-5-'47 Stockholm—Amsterdam 4—0, 3-9-'47 Amsterdam—Kopenhagen 2—3, 8-6-'49 Amsterdam—Wiener S.K. 1—1, 5-11-'49 Amsterdam—Brussel 1—4, 15-4-'50 Brussel—Amsterdam 2—3, 10-11-'50 Amsterdam—Brussel 1—4, 14-4-'51 Brussel—Amsterdam 1—1, 24-11-'51 Amsterdam—Brussel 0—1, 5-4-'52 Brussel—Amsterdam 5—0, 18-10-'52 Brussel—Amsterdam 1—2, 18-4-'53 Amsterdam—Brussel 1—0, 24-10-'53 Amsterdam—Brussel 2—2, 20-1-'54 Amsterdam—Independento 1—3, 14-5-'54 Amsterdam—Boedapest 1—4, 27-4-'55 Amsterdam—Berlijn 0—0, 19-5-'55 Duisburg—Amsterdam 3—0, 20-5-'56 Berlijn—Amsterdam 3—1, 29-5-'58 Amsterdam—Wenen 1—2, 30-6-'59 Amsterdam—Real Madrid 1—4, 25-8-'60 Amsterdam—Barcelona 3—4, 17-5-'61 Amsterdam—Tottenham Hotspur 0—3.

Against what was in reality the Scottish international side, playing under the guise of the Glasgow Select, United stunned their white-shirted hosts in a frantic 14-minute period, to record a notable 4—2 victory.

It was the predominately Rangers and Celtic Select who broke the deadlock in the 23rd minute, as Davy Wilson crossed from the left, finding Hughes, whose shot was blocked by Gaskell. The United 'keeper failed to hold the ball and as it rolled from his grasp, Divers stepped forward to prod the ball home. This was the second occasion that the Glasgow side had put the ball in the net, but a 17th-minute shot from Hughes had been disallowed for offside.

United, however, had come close to opening the scoring as early as the first minute. Law expertly wrong-footed a defender before sending a perfect pass towards Herd, but the centre-forward had decided to move to his left, away from the ball, and the opportunity was lost. Just after the Select's offside 'goal' Moir had been foiled by Niven, with Law once again at the forefront, eagerly supported by Setters.

Play flowed from end to end, keeping the crowd on its toes. Caldow broke up a Herd–Law move that many felt was going to produce the equaliser, while Divers headed a Henderson cross towards the corner of the United net, only to see Gaskell spring across his goal to push the ball round the post for a corner.

Two minutes from the interval United finally drew level. George Niven in the Select goal failed to clear a simple Herd header and as the ball broke to Moir, the Aberdonian youngster drove the ball into the top corner with a brilliant right-footed shot.

Almost immediately after the restart United came close to taking the lead, but MacKay was on hand to clear a Setters rocket off the line. It was the Glasgow Select side who were to go in front as Ian McMillan restored their lead in the 59th minute, running on to a through ball from Crerand before beating Gaskell.

With only a quarter of an hour remaining the game looked as if it might be about to slip away from United. Referee Wharton then awarded the Select a penalty after Henderson was brought down in the box. The ever-dependable Caldow stepped forward and, true to form, blasted the ball past Gaskell.

The referee's whistle was faint above the noise from the terraces, but it had been blown, with the official ordering the kick to be re-taken due to trainer Willie Gibson being on the pitch attending to Jim Baxter.

This time, however, Caldow was out of luck, as Gaskell pulled off a brilliant save from his spot-kick.

This miss, or indeed Gaskell's save, seemed to give United inspiration and, with the light fading, Denis Law showed just why Matt Busby had invested so much money into securing his signature. Beating three men he raced across the pitch before passing to Setters, and the United wing-half did not shun the opportunity, driving the ball home from around 25 yards out to level the scoring.

Ten minutes from time United took the lead for the first time when Herd rose to head home a Moir corner. With only two minutes remaining it was Moir himself who put the game beyond the reach of the home side, as the Scottish Schoolboy international scored his second of the night and United's fourth.

8 August 1962	**Glasgow Select at Hampden Park.**

Attendance: 80,000.

Won: 4–2.

Scorers: Moir 2, Setters, Herd.

Team: Gaskell, Brennan, Dunne, Stiles, Foulkes, Setters, Giles, Quixall, Herd, Law, Moir.

Despite the victory in Glasgow, Manchester United's 1962–63 campaign did not get off to the best of starts as they struggled to put together any form of consistency. A 1–0 defeat at newly promoted Leyton Orient on 8 September was perhaps the biggest embarrassment.

Their League form, however, was thrown out the window when they travelled to Madrid for yet another friendly against the Spanish giants. Relations between the two clubs had certainly blossomed since the European Cup semi-final of 1957, which perhaps in itself was rather surprising, as the Old Trafford second leg had seen some physical tussles on the pitch and the Spaniards' coach bombarded by an assortment of missiles as it left the ground.

However, the hand of friendship had certainly been grasped by United, with Matt Busby more than happy to take on Madrid whenever possible in order to judge the progress of his team rebuilding. This latest encounter, a testimonial for Zarraga, conjured up something of a surprise in its final outcome.

Real Madrid were certainly not the team they once were, though they could still boast players of the calibre of Di Stefano, Santamaria and Gento, although their best days were behind them. This time it was the turn of United, in front of around 80,000 spectators, to achieve a memorable victory and become the first English club to win there.

There was no luck involved in United's 2–0 victory. Di Stefano rallied his teammates time and time again, but the United defence stood firm. The Spaniards used four substitutes, but none could turn the game in their favour. It was United's night.

The opening 45 minutes produced chances for both teams and Herd could have scored in the 23rd minute when Santamaria floundered. Nobby Stiles outfoxed Di Stefano, while the constant threat of Denis Law kept the Madrid defence on its toes. But there was still little to separate the two sides as the half-time whistle blew.

Three minutes after the restart, however, the game quickly swung in United's favour. A loose ball was collected by Mark Pearson on the edge of the Madrid penalty area and he shot left-footed, hard, fast and low towards goal. Goalkeeper Vincente dived and stopped the ball, but, to the surprise and indignation of the home support, allowed it to roll out of his hands and into the net.

Twelve minutes later, with the majority of the crowd still voicing their disapproval, United struck again, momentarily silencing the baying mob, although they sportingly acknowledged a goal of class. Denis Law, once again the thorn in Madrid's side, sent the perfect ball forward to Giles. The Irishman took a couple of steps forward before crossing perfectly to the unmarked David Herd, who headed the ball into the roof of the net.

'I doubt if Madrid have ever had such treatment from their own crowd,' wrote Derek Hodgson of the *Daily Express*, as, for the second time in the game, they voiced their disapproval, with many heading for the exits, shaking their fists at the pitch as they went.

Those that remained missed a flurry of activity in the final minutes, with a fusillade of free-kicks and the United rearguard of Brennan, Foulkes and Dunne standing firm against any Madrid threat. The home crowd also sportingly stood to acclaim the victors at the final whistle, acknowledging a memorable United performance.

19 September 1962	**Real Madrid at Bernabeu Stadium.**

Attendance: 80,000.

Won: 2–0.

Scorers: Herd, Pearson.

Team: Gaskell, Brennan, Dunne, Stiles, Foulkes, Lawton, Giles, Law, Herd, Pearson, Moir.

Even louder in their acclaim were a small pocket of red and white-scarfed supporters from Manchester. One of those who made the trip to Spain was Kevin Burthem from Warrington, then 17 years old, who had been watching United since before Munich. He remembers: 'During the 1960s, I hardly missed a home game and went to many of the aways. The trip to Madrid, however, was my first abroad and certainly one to remember.

'Together with around 100 other United supporters, I left Manchester's Ringway airport at around 11am the day before the game, arriving at the ultra-modern Madrid airport some four hours later. From the airport, we were driven by coach to the Hotel Emperatrig.

'After unpacking, we discovered that United would probably be training that evening at the Bernabeu, and, minutes later, we were on a bus heading in the direction of the ground and upon arrival we were allowed in to watch the session.

'Having put the players through their paces, Matt Busby came over and invited a few of us to the players' hotel for a drink. There were a few surprised looks on the faces of United players' as we clambered aboard their coach, but as we drove through the streets of the Spanish capital, the players chatted happily with us. Denis Law, I remember, was particularly surprised to learn that we had travelled so far just to watch the game, as he had thought that we were just on holiday in Madrid.

'The following morning, the day of the match, we went sight-seeing around the capital. During the afternoon who should we meet but Tony Dunne, Phil Chisnall, Ian Moir and Jimmy Nicholson, who were also strolling around the city taking in the sights. Obligingly, the players posed for photographs.

'At around 7pm, our coach left the hotel for the match, which was scheduled to kick-off at 9pm. Our tickets, which we had received earlier from the trip organiser, cost around 18 shillings.

'After the match, while celebrating United's victory, some of the Real supporters that we had met showed their appreciation by buying us drinks.'

Having won comfortably against Real Madrid, United had the opportunity to clinch a unique double when Old Trafford welcomed the current European Cup holders, Benfica. The glamour friendly not only promised a superb evening's entertainment, but threw together two of the world's greatest football talents in Denis Law and Eusebio.

The Mozambique forward, valued at around £250,000, carved holes in the United defence, giving full-backs Tony Dunne and Shay Brennan a difficult time, while centre-half Bill Foulkes did his best to contain the danger from what seemed like every attack.

Sadly, the game failed to live up to its billing, but in common with almost any European night at Old Trafford, a huge wave of emotion engulfed the ground, more so when the ball found its way through to either the fair-haired Law or the dark-skinned Eusebio.

Just after the half-hour mark, it was the genius of Law that conjured up the opening goal. Albert Quixall, enjoying something of a deep-lying centre-forward role, sent Lawton scurrying down the wing. When it looked as though the United wing-half was going to run the ball out of play, he suddenly turned the ball inside and into the path of the oncoming Law, whose left-footed shot was too hard for Barroca to stop from entering the net.

Eusebio, not wishing to be upstaged by the Scot, took only 90 seconds to level the scores. A mix-up between Lawton and Brennan left the latter exposed and the Benfica talisman was past him in a flash. An attempted challenge by Foulkes was shrugged off, before he drew Harry Gregg from his goal and slipped a left-footed shot past him.

The game was now bubbling away nicely and, with only one minute remaining before the interval, United regained their lead with Law once again involved. Quixall sent the ball into the Benfica area and, under pressure from Law, Humberto handled. From the spot-kick Quixall blasted the ball past the helpless 'keeper.

Ten minutes into the second half United almost increased their lead when Sammy McMillan came close, but despite some fine play a third goal failed to materialise. Benfica, having made one substitution at the interval, were certainly not performing like European champions, with many of their shots failing to trouble Harry Gregg, who was playing his first game in 10 months following a shoulder injury.

The programme for the match versus Benfica, 25 September 1962.

With 13 minutes remaining, the Portuguese brought on the towering Torres in place of Aguas and it was to prove a deciding factor in the outcome of the game. One minute after taking to the field, he headed the ball down to the feet of Eusebio. In a flash the ball was in the back of the net for the equaliser.

It was disappointing to lose a late goal, but, overall, it was a creditable performance against the European Cup holders, proving that the earlier victories over the Glasgow Select and Real Madrid were not simply a flash in the pan. It also revealed that United were capable of playing much better than they had been doing in their recent Football League fixtures.

25 September 1962	**Benfica at Old Trafford.**

Attendance: 47,532.

Drew: 2–2.

Scorers: Law, Quixall.

Team: Gregg, Brennan, Dunne, Stiles, Foulkes, Lawton, Giles, Law, Quixall, Chisnall, McMillan.

Substitute: Moir for Chisnall.

Having faced two of Europe's top sides in the past few weeks, Matt Busby perhaps felt that his team's next opponents should be of a standard a few steps down the ladder from Real Madrid and Benfica. The Old Trafford faithful, however, were not impressed by the class of opposition due to grace the famous stadium, showing their lack of interest by remaining at home, with just over 15,000 clicking through the turnstiles to watch First Vienna. Another reason for the poor attendance could have been the weather, with the rain pouring down as the match kicked off. Either way, the lack of support came as a surprise to the United directors, with the receipts falling way below the guaranteed expenditure. Most who did attend were in agreement that, as a spectacle, the game fell short of being a memorable encounter.

However, the game did begin promisingly, with United a goal in front within five minutes. Albert Quixall weaved through a rather crowded defence before providing Bobby Charlton with his first goal of the season.

As the game progressed, it continued to be all United, with full-backs Brennan and Cantwell supporting their forwards at every opportunity. It was 25 minutes before David Gaskell had a save to make, getting his body behind a 20-yard drive from the Vienna inside-right Pichler.

There should certainly have been no lack of goals, but United's lead was only increased prior to the interval by an own-goal from the First Vienna captain Koller, who found himself under pressure from Law and appeared to be bundled into the net by the on-rushing Scot.

After the break, the standard of play deteriorated considerably, with no one prepared to put their foot on the ball and slow the game down. United were forced into playing Tony Dunne in the unfamiliar role of outside-left when Bobby Charlton was forced to leave the field with an ankle injury.

Stiles and Setters in midfield made their presence known with some forceful tackles, but their final ball was often wasted. One tackle from Stiles in the 51st minute, however, was perhaps just a little too strong in the referee's opinion, as he pointed to the penalty spot without any hesitation, Koller slotting the ball home.

With seven minutes remaining, the game as a contest came to an end with United's third goal, the best of the evening, scored by David Herd. A ball from the wing floated through the Manchester drizzle and, as it dropped out of the night sky, Herd met it on the volley with his right foot, propelling the ball past a helpless Schmied from 18 yards.

29 October 1962	**First Vienna at Old Trafford.**

Attendance: 15,035.

Won: 3–1.

Scorers: Charlton, Herd, opp. own-goal.

Team: Gaskell, Brennan, Cantwell, Stiles, Foulkes, Setters, Giles, Quixall, Herd, Law, Charlton.

Substitute: Dunne for Charlton.

League form continued to be inconsistent. Eight goals were conceded in consecutive fixtures against Manchester City and Burnley, both at Old Trafford, while a 5–1 home victory against Nottingham Forest on 8 December was followed seven days later by a 3–0 defeat at West Bromwich Albion.

Attendances had also dropped significantly, with the visit of Forest only attracting 27,946. This was quite a considerable difference compared to the 63,437 that had passed through the turnstiles for the second home fixture of the season against Everton.

A 1–0 Boxing Day win over Fulham at Craven Cottage followed the West Bromwich reversal, but United then found a most welcome ally in the form of the weather, which could have played a major part in not only saving United's 1962–63 season, but also preventing a drop into the Second Division. Heavy snow covered most of the British Isles, causing major disruptions, with the sporting calendar wiped out for weeks on end. United did not play a League fixture between the Boxing Day visit to London and when they entertained Blackpool on 23 February at Old Trafford. The odd postponement is acceptable, but when it became obvious that it would be some time before the League and Cup programme would get back to normal, something had to be done, particularly in United's case, as they were in a rather precarious position in the First Division.

Thus, in a bid to keep his charges ticking over, Matt Busby managed to arrange a trio of fixtures in Ireland, where the weather had not been as severe as on the mainland.

So it was to Glenmalure Park, the home of Shamrock Rovers, that United went in search of some much-needed match fitness, with Second Division promotion hopefuls Coventry City providing the opposition. However, if Busby and his players thought that they were in for a problem-free afternoon, they were soon to be proved wrong.

The Milltown pitch looked worse than the one United had left behind at Old Trafford; it was heavily frozen with deep ruts, forcing the local referee in charge of the game, Mr J. Meighan, to admit that had it been a normal Irish League fixture he would never have considered allowing the game to take place. An icy Arctic wind did little to help either, but it did not prevent a healthy crowd of around 18,000 from turning out to witness the first Saturday fixture in Dublin for a number of years.

Most of the shivering mass on the terracing had come to see United and their star performers, but it was Jimmy Hill's Coventry, unbeaten in their previous 14 outings, who adjusted best to the conditions and warmed the hearts of their Irish

The programme for the match versus First Vienna, 29 October 1962.

hosts. Law was subdued, while home-grown favourites Noel Cantwell and Johnny Giles were both disappointing for United. Sillett and Kearns, Coventry's full-backs, were able to keep a tight rein on United's wingers, with goalkeeper Wesson saving well on a couple of occasions from Charlton.

It was United, however, who took the lead in the 26th minute through Albert Quixall, the forward collecting a pass from Law before racing some 30 yards to score. It was to be a short-lived lead, however, as Coventry drew level within minutes, Sillett lobbing the ball through to Farmer, who hooked it over the advancing Harry Gregg.

Clearly inspired by their equaliser, Coventry more than held their own as the second half got underway, showing more movement than their considered superior opponents, and it came as no surprise when they took the lead. A centre from Humphries was headed past Gregg by Whitehouse two minutes prior to the interval.

United did manage to come more into the game, but still they could not penetrate the Coventry defence. When they did so, Herd prodding the ball over the line, a linesman's flag ended the celebrations with an offside decision.

As the late afternoon air chilled the bones, and with Coventry hanging onto their one-goal advantage for what would have been a confidence-boosting victory, Bobby Charlton ran onto a loose ball in the 80th minute to blast an unstoppable shot past Wesson for the equaliser. It was a goal that was to spare any further embarrassment for United.

2 February 1963	**Coventry City at Glenmalure Park, Dublin.**

Attendance: 18,000.
Drew: 2–2.
Scorers: Quixall, Charlton.
Team: Gregg, Brennan, Cantwell, Crerand, Foulkes, Setters, Giles, Quixall, Herd, Law, Charlton.

The cold spell continued and so did United's search for 90 minutes of football. Having faced near farcical conditions in Dublin, many thought that the risk of injury was not worth the gamble for meaningless fixtures. They did provide the players with much-needed match fitness, but if an individual was injured due to the state of the pitch and missed more important domestic fixtures then it really was a pointless exercise.

Once again, though, the conditions at Flowers Lodge in Cork were such that had this fixture, against Lancastrian neighbours Bolton Wanderers, been a normal League match, then it would have been abandoned at half-time, if indeed it had started at all. Rain had poured continuously prior to the match and continued to do so during it, with the only cover alongside the pitch being a stand with no seating, leaving manager Matt Busby and his fellow directors open to the elements. The rain also reduced the crowd dramatically, from the expected 20,000 to a mere 6,000.

The squelching mud of the Cork ground was not ideal conditions for any of the players and Pat Crerand, making his United debut following his recent £55,000 transfer from Celtic, would certainly have preferred a better playing surface on which to make his first appearance in a United shirt.

However, Crerand and his fellow United debutant Dennis Walker, a product of the United youth team, were forced to take something of a back seat as Bolton dictated the early play, with their teenage wingers, Francis Lee and Denis Butler, causing the United defence a few nervous moments. Thus it was Bolton who took the lead in the 15th minute, having seen a Wyn Davies effort in the opening five minutes crash off the United crossbar.

Law, back in the unfamiliar territory of the United defence, fouled Butler on the edge of the penalty area. The winger took the resulting free-kick himself, with the ball drifting over the head of Harry Gregg before becoming lodged in the ankle-deep mud. The on-rushing Lee skipped past the stranded 'keeper and bundled the ball over the line.

Despite the conditions, Crerand began to make an impression on the game, and it was his 36th minute 25-yard drive which brought United's equaliser. Only a fine save by Hopkinson, diving to turn the ball round the post, prevented him from adding a second.

United did score a second 10 minutes after the restart, when Quixall netted from the penalty spot after Edwards had handled. As the second half progressed, Bolton's enthusiastic play and early pressure on United was rarely in evidence.

Law put United 3–1 in front with the goal of the game on the hour mark. Accepting a pass from Walker, he wrong-footed not one, but three defenders, before slipping past Hartle and firing an unstoppable shot past Hopkinson from 18 yards.

Bolton, despite being grossly outplayed, clawed their way back into the game with a Lee penalty 10 minutes from time after Crerand had upended Hill. However, before the Wanderers winger could take the kick, the referee had to step out 12 paces from the centre of the United goal in order to estimate the whereabouts of the obliterated penalty spot. As it turned out, the goal was to have little effect on the outcome of the farcical 90 minutes, as three minutes later a cheeky lob over the head of Hopkinson from Johnny Giles gave United a fourth.

'It was a great day for me' said Pat Crerand after the game. 'I am delighted we won, but I have never seen mud like this before and I never expect to have to play in anything like it again.'

13 February 1963	**Bolton Wanderers at Flowers Lodge, Cork.**

Attendance: 6,000.

Won: 4–2.

Scorers: Crerand, Quixall (pen.), Law, Giles.

Team: Gregg, Brennan, Cantwell, Crerand, Foulkes, Setters, Giles, Quixall, Herd, Law, Charlton.

Despite having endured the paddy field conditions of Cork and the Arctic-like weather of Dublin, United flew out of Ringway airport en route for Ireland for a third time, returning to the Southern Ireland capital to face a Select XI.

Six days previously, the United players and their Bolton opposite numbers had been applauded off the pitch following their creditable display in Cork, but this time they were to leave amid a crescendo of boos, following what was at times a rather explosive 90 minutes.

Against the Bohemians/Shamrock Rovers Select, the game got under way with little hint of what was to come, but a tackle by Noel Cantwell on Frank O'Neill in the 20th minute, which resulted in Shamrock Rovers' £3,000 purchase from Arsenal having to leave the field to go to hospital for stitches, lit the blue touch paper.

The programme for the match versus Bolton Wanderers, 13 February 1963.

The team who played against Bolton Wanderers at Cork, 13 February 1963.

For the remainder of the game, Cantwell was booed whenever he touched the ball, and tempers were frayed further when Maurice Setters and Pat Crerand were booked for fouls and another tackle saw Bohemians amateur winger Mick Dalton carried from the field.

'The booing did not upset me at all', said Cantwell after the game. 'The tackle on O'Neill was just one of those things. These are not just friendly games to us. We treat them as League games.

'The Irish players cannot be expected to be allowed to tip and tap the ball around the place and get away with it. The tackle was purely an accident, although the crowd did not seem to think so.'

The boos had little effect on Cantwell's teammates either, as the majority of the game was played out in the Select's half and Harry Gregg, in an attempt to beat the cold caused by long periods of inactivity, pulled on an additional sweater at half-time.

Rather surprisingly, the first half produced only one goal, David Herd beating Denis Law to the ball amid a goalmouth scramble to force it over the line in the 34th minute. The second goal, in the 63rd minute, was the exact opposite, with Herd's goalmouth shot being helped over the line by Law.

Herd did claim a second, two minutes later, after accepting an easy chance from Law. Charlton made it four with an in-swinging left-footed drive six minutes from the end.

The part-time Dubliners had fought hard to gain some credibility against the more experienced professionals, but had presented United with scoring opportunities that they were certainly not going to refuse, despite the status of the fixture. The 90 minutes, however, had provided Matt Busby's team with a good workout and those who had been in attendance had enough talking points to debate over the forthcoming weeks.

19 February 1963   **Dublin XI at Dublin.**

Attendance: 20,000.

Won: 4–0.

Scorers: Herd 2, Law, Charlton.

Team: Gregg, Brennan, Cantwell, Crerand, Foulkes, Setters, Giles, Quixall, Herd, Law, Charlton.

Four days after the visit to Dublin United finally played a competitive fixture, a First Division match against Blackpool at Old Trafford, their first since their Boxing Day victory over Fulham. The new addition to the squad, Pat Crerand, had fitted into the team more than adequately and, despite the continuous struggle at League level, a 1–1 draw against Manchester City at Maine Road and a 3–2 victory over the already-relegated Leyton Orient at Old Trafford ensured that First Division status remained intact, for another season at least.

Crerand, of whom it was later said 'if he played well, then United played well', went on to make almost 400 appearances for the club, with one of his most outstanding 90 minutes in the red shirt coming at Wembley in May 1963, when United defeated Leicester City 3–1 to lift the FA Cup.

That Wembley success gave Matt Busby another tilt at competitive European football, his first since that fateful campaign of 1957–58. Preparation for this latest sojourn abroad began a matter of days after Noel Cantwell had lifted the FA Cup, when United travelled to Italy for a trio of fixtures, although there was also some time for relaxation following what had been a strenuous yet rewarding season.

Having finished their domestic season as runners-up, Juventus were certainly ideal opponents for a pre-European Cup-Winners' Cup campaign warm-up, although as it came a mere four days after their Wembley success the United players could have been forgiven if there was something of a relaxed manner in their play. As it was, against a team well versed in defensive play, with a rapier-like thrust on the counter-attack, United stunned the crowd by securing a notable victory.

Away legs in European competitions more often than not demand a somewhat cautious approach, often bordering on complete negativity, but if Matt Busby treated this particular fixture as something of a dress rehearsal for what lay ahead, then there was little chance of those in attendance at United's away fixtures of going home feeling short-changed.

Juventus opened the game with the intention of catching United cold, grabbing a couple of early goals and then simply sitting back and soaking up anything that came their way. United, however, were prepared for the initial onslaught and so weathered the storm and soon adjusted to the pace of the game.

Frustrated by their initial lack of penetration against a resolute United defence, Juventus were forced to reconsider their tactics and adapted a long-ball game, which brought an equal lack of success, with Harry Gregg having only one save of any significance to make in the opening 45 minutes, foiling centre-forward Miranda.

A 20-minute rainstorm, either side of the interval, was more to United's liking than their hosts and, within four minutes of the second half getting underway, they were in front. Phil Chisnall sent Sammy McMillan away on the left and the reserve-team winger, who had come close to scoring twice in the first half, shrugged off a double-headed challenge from Salvadore and Emoli before calmly slotting the ball past goalkeeper Anzolin.

Within a minute Juventus were almost level. A 25-yard drive from right-half Salvadore slipped from Gregg's grasp and rolled antagonisingly towards the goalline before Gregg captured the ball at a second attempt.

Del Sol caused the United defence numerous problems, but Foulkes and Crerand stood firm, with the latter giving a repeat showing of his notable Wembley display. Denis Law also contributed to Matt Busby's defensive plans, but the former Turin forward was constantly booed throughout the game, with one tackle on Del Sol bringing cries for a penalty.

United held on to their solitary goal advantage and the measure of their victory could be heard in the prolonged booing that accompanied the final whistle, the Italians having been outfoxed.

29 May 1963	**Juventus at Stadio Communale, Turin.**

Attendance: 20,000.

Won: 1—0.

Scorer: McMillan.

Team: Gregg, Dunne, Cantwell, Crerand, Foulkes, Setters, Giles, Chisnall, Herd, Law, McMillan.

The second leg of the post FA Cup-winning season saw United up against another Italian side who would feature in competitive European Cup football in later years. The meeting with Roma, in front of a mainly Italian crowd, was to see United claim a victory in Rome.

On a warm Italian evening, United continued to play the confident, self-assured football that had overwhelmed Leicester at Wembley and had claimed the scalp of Juventus.

It took United a mere three minutes to open the scoring through Johnny Giles, his effort being helped into the net by goalkeeper Matteucci, who had made a dramatic first-minute save from the same United player. Sadly, it was to be the diminutive winger's only contribution to the game, as he failed to make the most of the excellent service he received from Setters and McMillan.

United's advantage lasted only a matter of minutes, as Roma, led by Welsh legend John Charles, responded strongly, Argelillo equalising before the visitors had the opportunity to regroup. Rather surprisingly, instead of pressing forward in search of further goals, Roma were content to sit back and soak up any attacks that the dominant midfielders Crerand and Setters could mount, and the score remained level until the interval.

After the restart the most outstanding team in the Italian League in recent weeks found themselves up against it, falling behind for the second time in the 69th minute when outside-left Sammy McMillan, who up until now had failed to shine, moved inside the full-back to score.

Once again, however, United failed to hold on to their advantage. John Charles led the Italian front line with purpose, keeping the United defence at full stretch and setting up a second equalising goal, this time for Manfredini.

With tempers often near breaking point, United were often stretched by the Italians. Foulkes brought down Charles in full flight, resulting in a mêlée, which saw Setters spoken to by the referee. However, they endured whatever their hosts threw at them and on a familiar stage Denis Law moved onto a cross from fellow Scot David Herd to hammer the ball into the net for what was to prove the winner, eight minutes from time.

1 June 1963	**Roma at Flamino Stadium, Rome.**

Attendance: 20,000.

Won: 3—2.

Scorers: Giles, McMillan, Law.

Team: Gregg, Dunne, Cantwell, Crerand, Foulkes, Setters, Giles, Chisnall, Herd, Law, McMillan.

Having faced first-class opposition in the opening two fixtures, it was something of a relief for the United players to be up against a lesser side in the form of Leghorn, a local Livorno amateur side, in the third.

A thunderstorm an hour prior to kick-off reduced the crowd by half, but United, despite playing at a casual pace at times, with Harry Gregg a virtual spectator, still treated the crowd to some fine football.

Seven minutes after the interval McMillan broke away, passing the ball to Giles, who turned it inside to Chisnall to score with ease. The deadlock was broken. Three minutes later Bobby Charlton, who had flown in from Switzerland following international duty with England, set up an opportunity for Herd, but this was disallowed for offside against the Scot.

It was only a minor setback for Herd, as within two minutes he had put United 2–0 in front. Racing from the halfway line, with full-back Lessi in close pursuit and a linesman frantically waving his flag once again for offside, he gave goalkeeper Bellinelli no chance with a searing drive.

Referee Angelini incurred the wrath of the crowd for ignoring his linesman's flag waving on the touchline and came in for further verbal abuse shortly afterwards when he disallowed what appeared to everyone else as a perfectly good goal by Colombo.

The amateurs, despite fine showings from the likes of Balestra, Lessi and Bellinelli, were completely overshadowed and perhaps overwhelmed by United, who at times were rather poor with their finishing, but it was a result that stood Matt Busby and his team in good stead for the new season.

6 June 1963	**Leghorn, Livorno.**

Attendance: 15,000.

Won: 2–0

Scorers: Herd, Chisnall.

Team: Gregg, Dunne, Cantwell, Stiles, Foulkes, Lawton, Giles, Chisnall, Herd, Charlton, McMillan.

Having won the FA Cup at Wembley the previous May and brushed away the relegation cobwebs with the creditable victories against Roma and Juventus, not forgetting the victory in Madrid almost 12 months earlier, United were in a confident mood for not only the domestic campaign ahead, but also the return to the competitive European stage in the Cup-Winners' Cup.

Pre-season brought a return invitation to Glasgow to once again play a Glasgow Select side for the Glasgow Charity Cup at Hampden Park. Having won the corresponding fixture last season, hopes were high for a repeat performance, with this initial pre-season friendly providing a strong base on which to build the campaign ahead. As it turned out, United received something of a jolt, conceding two goals in a four-minute second-half spell and thus having to leave the trophy behind in Glasgow.

The attendance was some 30,000 less than the previous season, due to public disapproval of the under-strength team the home side had selected, as well as the dull evening. United were quick off the mark, with Law only stopped from breaking through by a strong tackle from Greig. Seconds later, however, United were a goal in front. Quickly regaining possession, Charlton accepted a pass from Setters before outfoxing a bewildered McGillivary and hammering the ball past a helpless Niven.

The United outside-left seemed to thrive in the vast stadium, something that his teammates were well aware of, as, whenever possible, they pushed the ball in his direction. On the opposite flank Giles was also in fine form during the early stages, giving Partick Thistle's Brown a hectic evening.

A glint of sunshine through the dark, overcast sky seemed to awaken the home side, giving them some encouragement, with Brand coming close, his shot cannoning off a defender for a corner. Chalmers also tormented the United defence, with Greig prompting from midfield and the Rangers pairing of Brand and Wilson a constant danger. Hughes also missed the chance of an equaliser, wasting a golden opportunity following excellent work by Brand.

However, it was United who looked the more likely to score, the Law-Charlton duo keeping the Glasgow defence on their toes, with the Aberdonian hitting the bar and creating something of a panic in the goalmouth before the ball was eventually cleared. Herd and Quixall both missed inviting opportunities to increase the United lead, with Niven on two occasions enjoying the good fortune of goal-bound shots hitting his post and rebounding into his arms.

Despite being in his home city and playing in front of many who had cheered him as a Celtic player, Pat Crerand was loudly booed on a couple of occasions following rather robust tackles on Brand, actions which also caused the crowd to get more behind the home side. As the first half drew to a close, there was a notable improvement in the play of the Select XI and, had it not been for a rather inept display from Hughes, they could well have gone in at the break on level terms.

Law returned for the second half with a bandage round his thigh, taking up the outside-right position, making the United attacking threat a little subdued, while at the same time giving the Glasgow side something of a boost. They were given further encouragement 15 minutes after the restart when Law was forced to leave the field due to his injury, reducing United to only 10 men for the remainder of the game.

This setback prompted the home side into all-out attack in search for the equaliser, Gaskell making fine saves from Hughes, Chalmers and Wilson, but it was not until the 72nd minute that the United defence was finally breached. A scramble in the United goalmouth saw the ball frantically cleared twice, but the second of the two, following a point-blank save by Gaskell from a Henderson shot, saw the ball go only as far as Chalmers, who blasted the ball past the helpless United 'keeper.

With the bit firmly between their teeth, it was now an all-out attack on the United goal and two minutes later the Select side were in front. A Wilson cross, which carried little danger, was back-headed over the advancing Gaskell by Maurice Setters.

Ticket for the match versus Glasgow XI, 7 August 1963.

7 August 1963	**Glasgow Select at Hampden Park.**

Attendance: 48,576.

Lost: 2–1.

Scorer: Charlton.

Team: Gaskell, Dunne, Cantwell, Crerand, Foulkes, Setters, Giles, Quixall, Herd, Law, Charlton.

Continuing their pre-season preparations, United travelled to Germany six days later to face Eintracht Frankfurt, where their plans were once thrown into disarray. The Germans faced something of a subdued United side, one which seemed lacking in the attacking flair that had played a major part in their previous season's Cup success, with David Gaskell keeping them in the game with a number of notable saves.

With play rather scrappy, considering the array of talent on show, tempers also became frayed early in the game, resulting in a backdrop of booing and whistling from the crowd. Tackling, while on par with that of a typical Football League fixture, could have been considered slightly more robust than what is normally acceptable on the Continent and, despite several early warnings from the referee, United continued to take risks in their efforts to win the ball.

Five minutes prior to the interval the game eventually bubbled over. Noel Cantwell robbed Frankfurt's outside-right Kress of the ball out on the touchline to then be confronted by the German's inside partner, Trimhold. A rather untidy scuffle for the ball, which eventually ran out of play, saw both players gesture angrily at each other, with Kress also getting involved by shaking his fist in the United captain's face.

Referee Handwerker was quickly involved and awarded a free-kick to Eintracht before sending off Cantwell, to the delight of the home crowd and the surprise and protests of the United players. With Cantwell unwilling at first to leave the field, it was a couple of minutes before order was restored.

'He made an example out of me,' the United captain was later to say. 'I had not committed a single foul in the game, although he had warned me for a normal charge earlier. One of the German players was screening me and I had to try and kick the ball with him in between.'

Surprisingly, it was a view shared by the German official, who said after the match, 'The Manchester player did not lay a finger on the Germans. He did not kick them. But he was willing – and that is the same.'

The incident, no worse than any of those previously ignored by the referee, including a rather vigorous tackle by Setters which resulted in only a lecture, saw United reduced to 10 men for the second consecutive fixture, but following a 'calm down' warning from Matt Busby at half-time, United surprised Eintracht by taking the lead three minutes after the restart. It was something of a gift goal, as 'keeper Loy dropped a shot from Herd and the lurking Crerand prodded the ball home from close range.

It was, however, a short-lived lead, with the equaliser coming within four minutes, Lothar Schamer beating Gaskell from 15 yards out, prompting a volley of rockets to soar into the night sky from the terraces. It was an unfortunate moment for the United 'keeper, as he was by far the man of the match, having produced a number of excellent saves.

Following the Frankfurt goal the 10-man United team battled on bravely, with Setters having moved to full-back and Chisnall into the half-back line. They did well to keep the Germans out, but there were still few opportunities created in the German half of the field.

13 August 1963	**Eintracht Frankfurt at Waldstadion, Frankfurt.**

Attendance: 15,000.

Drew: 1–1.

Scorer: Crerand.

Team: Gaskell, Dunne, Cantwell, Crerand, Foulkes, Setters, Giles, Quixall, Herd, Chisnall, Charlton.

So it was a disappointing result for United, but there was to be further dismay upon the return of players and staff to their dressing room at full-time, when they found that a number of them had been the victims of a pickpocket. The light-fingered intruder had made off with the sum of £145 and two gold watches. That may seem like loose change by today's standards, but not so in the early 1960s.

Trainer Jack Crompton lost £15 in British money and £9 in German; Pat Crerand lost £24 in British money and £4 in German; Nobby Stiles £50; Bill Foulkes £6 and his car keys; while David Gaskell lost a gold watch and signet ring, which were tied together in his handkerchief, along with what he described as 'all my money'. Albert Quixall also lost a gold watch, along with £19 in British currency and almost £5 in German. Maurice Setters, Johnny Giles and Shay Brennan lost £2, £10 and £1 respectively, while Tony Dunne had his trousers torn, in what he put down to the intruder's haste to get away, rather than their disappointment in not finding anything of value in his pockets. Apparently, the dressing room doors had been locked during the game, so it was a mystery to both United and their embarrassed hosts how the robbery had occurred.

With United's involvement in the European Cup-Winners' Cup, which saw them reach the quarter-final stages before being eliminated by Sporting Lisbon 6–4 on aggregate (this was after winning the first leg at Old Trafford 4–1), coupled with a run through to the semi-final of the FA Cup, where they lost 3–1 to West Ham at Hillsborough, there were few mid week dates available to Matt Busby for arranging friendlies. It was 7 May, therefore, before such a fixture took place. This time there was a short jaunt across Manchester to Moss Side to face Manchester City in a fixture arranged by the Variety Club of Great Britain for the Duke of Edinburgh trophy.

Disappointed by their failure in both the Cup competitions, coupled with Liverpool snatching the League title from their grasp by a solitary point, for United the Maine Road meeting conjured up an atmosphere akin to an FA Cup Final in a no-holds-barred end of season finale. The Manchester Senior Cup was also at stake, along with local pride, producing a tasty cocktail for those in attendance.

With the Duke of Edinburgh, a life member of the Variety Club, watching from the flower-bedecked directors' box, it was perhaps fitting that the 'king' of Old Trafford stole the show, with the mercurial Denis Law rising to the occasion on his old stomping ground.

It was City, however, who took the lead as early as the fifth minute. Neil Young caught Harry Gregg unawares with a rather spectacular left-footed drive from 25 yards, but it was to be something of a short-lived advantage, as within two minutes United had not only equalised, but were also in front.

United's first goal came courtesy of an error by City defender Kennedy, whose attempted pass back to his goalkeeper Ogley, from a free-kick, was badly misjudged, with the ever-alert Law nipping in to beat the advancing City 'keeper from the edge of the penalty area. The blond-headed Scot also claimed the second, rising above a rather static City defence to head home a Moir corner.

A minute before the interval United, or rather Denis Law, scored a third. Once again the Scot's lightning quick reflexes got the better of the home defence, as he headed home Connelly's right-wing corner, following Ogley's excellent tip over the bar from a Moore drive.

Half-time not only brought a few minutes respite for City, but also a cloudburst, torrential even by Manchester standards, which soaked the United

States Air Force band, who were providing the entertainment. Seventeen minutes after the restart Herd made it 4–1, following good work from the Aberdonian duo of Law and Moir.

However, it was not all United and City showed great resilience and fought back. Gray put Pardoe through to make it 4–2 in the 70th minute, while a brilliant individual goal by Oakes, getting the better of two defenders in an overcrowded penalty area before beating Gregg from 10 yards, made it 4–3 two minutes later.

A further downpour had reduced the centre of the pitch to little more than a quagmire, while the players, some of whom were barely recognisable due to their head to foot covering of mud, continued to treat the match seriously, one side trying to continue their revival and snatch a dramatic equaliser, the other pushing forward in the hope of stretching the advantage even further in their favour. With six minutes remaining, David Herd put the game beyond City's reach, converting Moir's centre for United's fifth.

Thus United lifted both the trophies. The under-privileged children, the recipients of the evenings gate money, were better off by around £20,000. There were also smiles all round at the after-match banquet, held at the Midland Hotel, which was attended by the Duke of Edinburgh, players and officials of both teams and showbusiness personalities.

---

7 May 1964   **Manchester City at Maine Road.**

Attendance: 36,434.

Won: 5–3.

Scorers: Law 3, Herd 2.

Team: Gregg, Brennan, Dunne, Crerand, Foulkes, Stiles, Connelly, Moore, Herd, Law, Moir.

Today pre-season fixtures in the Far East are considered the norm and are organised purely for financial reasons and to increase the ever-growing fan base. It might then come as something of a surprise to learn that in May 1964 United had planned to undertake a tour of the Far East.

FIFA President Sir Stanley Rous, who had watched the Merdeka Cup Tournament in Malaysia the previous season, was heavily involved in the organising of the tour and was very disappointed when negotiations broke down, due to the fact that Malaysia was the only one of the Far East countries that was prepared to meet the £1,000 per match guarantee for United's visit.

As it was, United headed to Bilbao at the end of May to play a local select 11, drawn from five different clubs, in a fixture organised to help celebrate the 50th anniversary of Bilbao Province.

If the 20,000 crowd who had braved the rather severe weather conditions had expected something of an enthralling 90 minutes, given United's highly thought of reputation across Europe over the past few years, especially their previous visit to the city in January 1957, when they won the first leg of the European Cup quarter-final tie 5–3, then they were in for a big disappointment.

The programme for the match versus Manchester City, 7 May 1964.

Starting off at half pace, United continued to stroll through the 90 minutes, shunning countless scoring opportunities, with Denis Law, according to the *Daily Express* correspondent at the match, 'hardly raising a gallop – instead he wandered, mostly aimlessly, in the centre of the field in an exhibition that didn't help his reputation before the 20,000 crowd.'

United certainly had the chances to win the game in the first half, when the underfoot conditions were more on the firm side, as they sliced through the local defence. Crerand put Moir through in the 20th minute, but the United inside-forward swept his shot wide of the post. He was to miss a second opportunity shortly afterwards, when Herd set up the chance. This time he shot straight at the 'keeper. Herd and Graham Moore both squandered fine opportunities on three other occasions.

Slowly, as if they had been initially overawed by their visitors, Bilbao began to realise that they could perhaps win the game. On the half-hour inside-right Arzae tested Gaskell from 20 yards and had the United 'keeper leaping across his goal to keep the ball out.

When the heavens opened United began to lose their grip on the game, as both Foulkes and Stiles, who had stood firm in the opening stages, began to wilt under the Bilbao pressure. Busby brought on Cantwell and Setters to try to reaffirm United's grip on the game, but it made little difference, as the home side continued to dominate and Gaskell had to dive around his goalmouth to keep out numerous shots and headers.

Despite United's rather lacklustre performance, and Bilbao's constant pressure, it was not until nine minutes from time that the home side finally managed to score. It was a goal that not only secured victory for the Select XI, but also brought some form of revenge for the scorer, Jesus Garay, who beat Gaskell direct from a free-kick some 20 yards out.

The 32-year-old Garay, now a Barcelona player, had been a member of the Bilbao side beaten by United back in 1957 and had returned to his former club especially for the game. Although that European Cup defeat had been some seven years previously, a smile of satisfaction must have been very noticeable across the face of the 6ft 4in wing-half when the ball flew past the helpless Gaskell.

At full-time the United players trooped off to polite but half-hearted applause from the Spanish crowd. However, it was applause that they certainly did not deserve for such a poor display.

28 May 1964	**Bilbao XI at Estadio San Mames, Bilbao.**
Attendance: 20,000.	
Lost: 1—0.	
Team: Gaskell, Brennan, Dunne, Crerand, Foulkes, Stiles, Connelly, Moore, Herd, Law, Best.	
Substitutes: Cantwell for Dunne, Setters for Crerand, Dunne for Brennan	

An invitation to visit Glasgow for a third consecutive season to play in the Charity Cup fixture was declined by the United management in favour of a two-match tour of Germany. However, as things turned out the 16 August fixture against Bayern Munich was cancelled, with a short trip to Dublin to face Shamrock Rovers fitted into the pre-season schedule as a replacement.

Matt Busby, having ignored press speculation regarding the future of Denis Law, who was reportedly haggling over a new contract, then flew out to Germany with his players for some serious pre-season work.

Opponents Hamburg were certainly not unfamiliar opposition and, as they had been unbeaten on their home ground during the previous season, they would provide a testing run-out for United's first fixture on the eve of a new campaign.

The game kicked off in steady drizzle, but Matt Busby and his assistant, Jimmy Murphy, barely had time to readjust the towels they had wrapped around their heads to keep them dry before United were ahead. With a mere 90 seconds played, centre-forward David Herd moved wide to the right and slipped past centre-half Giesemann before crossing the ball to the waiting John Connelly, who calmly side-footed the ball past the Hamburg goalkeeper for the simplest of goals on his United debut.

Connelly had been signed from Burnley at the end of the previous season for a fee of £60,000, having gained a reputation with the Turf Moor side as a notable goal-scoring winger, while helping the Lancastrian side to the First Division title in 1960 and a Cup Final appearance two years later. Many within the game were of the opinion that he might now be past his best, but he proved them wrong with this debut performance.

Having lost twice to the Germans in the past six years, United knew that they faced a difficult game, but the early goal certainly settled them and they soon had the Germans at sixes and sevens with creative, accurate football. However, to their credit, Hamburg managed to keep United at bay and fought back to snatch an equaliser in the 33rd minute, when the United defence allowed Kurth to move in from the byline and present his fellow inside-forward Mate with the opportunity to beat Gaskell from close range.

Shortly after drawing level, the familiar Seeler saw a firmly hit drive bounce off Gaskell's chest, as the home side pushed forward. However, two minutes prior to the interval United's more adventurous and skilful play saw Connelly restore their lead.

Midway through the second half, the ever-dangerous Seeler hit the post with Gaskell beaten as the Germans sought the equaliser but, to their disappointment, Man of the Match Connelly, who had his name taken for a fairly inoffensive tackle on Mate, once again proved his worth when he found Herd with a well-timed pass and the centre-forward scored United's third, nine minutes from the end.

Although it was little more than a pre-season warm up game, United's performance brought much acclaim from the Germans, who went as far as to say that they were the best club team ever to have visited the country. The newspaper *Sport* rated the performance of Bill Foulkes as 'outstanding', while it regarded Law, Charlton, Connelly and Best as 'players of a calibre rarely seen in Germany.'

Praise also came from Sergeant James Doyle, stationed in Germany with the fifth Royal Tank regiment, who had watched United beaten by Hamburg five years before. With the British soldiers taking much pre-match stick from their German neighbours, he wrote to the *Manchester Evening News* saying: 'It was a shocker of a day yesterday, but a crowd of us from the regiment and also parties from other regiments, travelled to Hamburg to see United well and truly rub the faces of the German team in the mud.

'United played very well, the defence in particular. Foulkes had Seeler in his pocket, and Charlton, Law, Best, Crerand and Stiles moved around the Volkspark stadium as if they owned it, which they did for that night anyway.

'But I will fault them on one point; apart from Charlton they will not have a go until they are inside the box.

'Charlton played a blinder, his shrug of the shoulders was vintage Eddie Colman, he sent three Germans the wrong way at one time.

'The passing by United was the best I have seen by them for a very long time. Law's distribution was masterful, his cross-field passes were beautiful to watch and the long ball out of defence to wee Best on the wing was one of the features of this match.

'If they can find that killer instinct United can go places this season.'

12 August 1964	Hamburg at Volkspark Stadium.

Attendance: 40,000.

Won: 3–1.

Scorers: Connelly 2, Herd.

Team: Gaskell, Brennan, Dunne, Crerand, Foulkes, Setters, Connelly, Herd, Charlton, Law, Best.

Instead of remaining in Germany for a few days longer, as originally planned, United flew back to England before crossing the Irish Sea to face Shamrock Rovers, in what, on paper at least, would not be quite as testing a 90 minutes as they had faced in Hamburg.

As it was, they almost found themselves a goal behind after only two minutes, when the Rovers inside-left Mulligan drove a hard shot at Gaskell, the 'keeper doing well to hold onto the ball. However, the tide was soon to turn, as by the 10th minute United were in front. Best's centre was touched on by Law to Charlton, who scored with a low drive.

A Best centre also brought United a second goal in the 36th minute, Herd jumping to head the ball past Henderson to establish a firm 2–0 half-time lead.

Several positional changes at the interval saw Shamrock begin the second half strongly and for a while United found themselves under pressure. Mooney, having moved from inside to centre-forward, saw one shot bounce off the top of the United bar and, as the Irishmen fought hard to pull at least one goal back, Tony Dunne was rather unceremoniously bundled over the touchline.

United, having endured the brief attacking foray from their hosts, suddenly stepped up a gear and had soon doubled their lead, scoring twice in a four-minute spell. David Herd made it 3–0 in the 65th minute, pouncing on a Charlton free-kick which rebounded off the post, while Best added a fourth, taking the ball across the front of the Shamrock goal.

With the game more or less won, United eased up considerably, allowing Shamrock the opportunity to once again get back into the game and take advantage of some slack defending. Mooney scored twice, in the 76th and 86th minutes, to add some respectability to the scoreline.

The programme for the match versus Shamrock Rovers, 14 August 1964.

14 August 1964	Shamrock Rovers at Glenmalure Park, Dublin.

Attendance: 20,000.

Won: 4–2.

Scorers: Herd 2, Best, Charlton.

Team: P. Dunne, Brennan, T. Dunne, Crerand, Foulkes, Setters, Connelly, Charlton, Herd, Law, Best.

Substitute: Setters for Law.

Winning the League Championship in season 1964–65 was something of a personal triumph for Matt Busby, who had rebuilt his shattered side following the disaster at Munich some six years previously. He had also taken them from a relegation-threatened side to a Championship-winning one in two years.

Preparations for the retention of the League title took United back to this popular haunt of Germany, for two fixtures against Hanover and Nuremburg. Both games ended in 2–0 defeats, which was certainly not the ideal outcome for the season ahead.

In the first of the two fixtures, against Hanover, the Germans hammered home a message to the League Champions, who were poor throughout the 90 minutes. Bobby Charlton could only watch in vain as one effort rolled along the goalline, while Denis Law was robbed by the bounce of the ball when in a good scoring position.

Despite the chances at either end, the first half ended goalless, but within 10 minutes of the restart the Germans were in front, centre-forward Radekamp quickly moving on to the ball to beat Pat Dunne. Five minutes later it was 2–0, Tony Dunne blocking an opponent and giving away a penalty.

Some of the German tackling left a lot to be desired, with United becoming rather unsettled by the scything and sometimes overzealous collisions, but in the end they were well outplayed.

8 August 1965	Hanover at Lower Saxony Stadium.

Attendance: 40,000.

Lost: 2–0.

Team: P. Dunne, Brennan, T. Dunne, Crerand, Foulkes, Stiles, Connelly, Charlton, Herd, Law, Best.

The second fixture took United to Nuremburg, where once again they came face to face with a hard and aggressive side who certainly did not treat the game as the friendly it was billed as.

Right from the first whistle the Germans' tackling left a lot to be desired, and it was rather ironic that the German press were quick to criticise Nobby Stiles, while Stefan Reisch was, at times, just as hard on Bobby Charlton. Poor refereeing also did little to protect the United players from the rather physical Germans during 90 minutes.

As it was, United conceded two goals without reply and therefore had to go into their season with two defeats and little of note to show for 180 minutes of football.

10 August 1965	Nuremburg at Zeppelin Park.

Attendance: 38,000.

Lost: 2–0.

Team: P. Dunne, Brennan, T. Dunne, Crerand, Foulkes, Stiles, Sadler, Charlton, Herd, Law, Best.

The euphoria which swept England following the World Cup Final on 30 July did not stretch any further north than Hadrian's Wall and United's visit to Glasgow's East End, with World Cup winners Bobby Charlton and Nobby Stiles in their ranks, was treated as much as a Scotland-England affair as it was an inter-club friendly.

The programme for the match versus Hanover, 7 August 1965.

The programme for the match versus Nuremburg, 10 August 1965.

United were no match for the fast-flowing football played by the Celtic team and, by all accounts, they were fortunate to finish the game only three goals in arrears.

Any latecomers into the Parkhead cauldron could well have missed three of the afternoon's five goals. Indeed, if they were 15 minutes late in squeezing onto the packed terracing then they would have missed four.

Celtic wasted little time, with Bobby Lennox opening the scoring after only eight minutes. A cross from Auld was collected by Chalmers and almost immediately whipped into the goalmouth, where the lightning-quick anticipation of Lennox outfoxed the United defence as the Celtic forward blasted the ball past Gregg.

Three minutes later it was 2–0. Chalmers, again in the thick of the action, pushed the ball out to the right towards McBride, but a neat dummy saw the ball roll to Johnstone, whose inviting centre was thundered home by the advancing Murdoch.

Before the jubilant cheers of the Celtic support had died down, United had pulled a goal back. Straight from the restart Charlton passed to Sadler, who in turn pushed the ball back to Crerand. The former Celtic favourite squared the ball to Law. A long pass through the green and white-hooped defence allowed Sadler to volley the ball into the roof of Simpson's goal.

This goal brought the home support and their team back down to earth with a bang, but the setback was only momentary, as within three minutes the two-goal advantage was restored. A 25-yard drive from McBride found its way into the corner of Gregg's net.

The partisan home crowd were soon back in full cry, taunting the United team' and Stiles in particular, with chants of 'Go home!' and 'Ea-sy, Ea-sy'.

The second 45 minutes failed to live up to the first in terms of both goals and excitement, but United certainly did their best to reduce the two-goal deficit, with Sadler hitting the bar and Ronnie Simpson pulling off a trio of superb saves from Denis Law. At the opposite end Harry Gregg made four crucial saves, three from Lennox and the other from Chalmers, to keep United in with a shout of salvaging some pride.

As it was, Celtic added a fourth in the 63rd minute, or perhaps to be more exact, an own-goal from Bill Foulkes gave the home side a three-goal advantage. As McBride charged into the United penalty area, Stiles attempted to clear and, to the delight of the baying crowd, the ball cannoned off Foulkes and past a totally surprised Gregg.

That was that, and United failed to produce anything that might have created panic in the Celtic defence, with their only real goalmouth action coming in their own area when Stiles and Gregg were involved in a rare old argument.

6 August 1966	Celtic at Celtic Park.

Attendance: 60,000.

Lost: 4–1.

Scorer: Sadler.

Team: Gregg, Dunne, Brennan, Crerand, Foulkes, Stiles, Best, Law, Charlton, Sadler, Connelly.

Substitute: Cantwell for Sadler.

Still rather shell-shocked by their defeat in Glasgow, United travelled to Germany to face the West German Cup holders Bayern Munich four days later. They ended the game struggling to find some form of inspiration following a 4—1 defeat at the hands of the Germans.

There was little to encourage the United management, with only brief flashes of skill from Denis Law and odd moments of true form from the likes of Crerand, Best and Stiles. On the whole it seemed an evening that most would simply like to forget, with the forward line showing little punch and the likes of Stiles and Brennan frequently moving up to try to bolster the attack.

In defence, where Harry Gregg was at fault for two of the four goals, and with Bill Foulkes in somewhat hesitant form, there was a great need to tighten things up, while the forwards showed a distinct lack of enthusiasm, with scoring opportunities in rather short supply.

The Germans were inspired by the stylish Franz Beckenbauer, who had won much praise during the World Cup, with United attempting to man-mark him. It was a ploy which only occasionally worked, as he opened the scoring for the Munich side in the 36th minute, taking a return pass from Muller before driving the ball low past Gregg.

Rather surprisingly, Bayern's second did not come until the 61st minute, Muller heading home Nafziger's free-kick. This acted like a wake-up call to United, as it was immediately following this that the visitors enjoyed their best spell of the game.

It took a last-ditch tackle from Beckenbauer to prevent Shay Brennan from scoring a rare goal, but he could do little to prevent David Herd from pulling one back in the 70th minute, scoring with a powerful left-footed shot after two efforts from George Best had been blocked.

Momentarily it looked as though United might indeed salvage something from the game, but it was only a matter of minutes before Gregg found his goal under siege, with Muller eventually making it 3–1.

Five minutes later it was 4–1 and the contest was over. A rather feeble shot from Bayern left-back Oik was fumbled by Gregg and the ball rolled towards Brenninger, who gratefully accepted the simplest of chances.

10 August 1966	**Bayern Munich at Grünwallder Stadium.**

Attendance: 20,000.

Lost: 4–1.

Scorer: Herd.

Team: Gregg, Brennan, Dunne, Crerand, Foulkes, Stiles, Best, Law, Charlton, Herd, Connelly.

In his report on the Bayern Munich match the *Sportsmail* reporter noted, 'unless their [United's] defence is tightened considerably and the attack becomes a lot busier and sharper, a similar fate probably awaits them in their third pre-season game, against FK Austria in Vienna on Friday.' The correspondent was 100 per cent correct in his prediction, as United did indeed suffer their third pre-season defeat in succession, with FK Austria going one better than Celtic and Bayern by scoring five.

As if a third defeat was not enough of a problem for Matt Busby, the match produced yet another headache for the United manager with the dismissal of Nobby Stiles. The tough-tackling defender was already walking something of a disciplinary tightrope as the Football Association had received a letter from FIFA following England's World Cup tie with France, a game in which Nobby had been booked, which said that if the United player was reported to them again, then they would take 'serious action.'

The flashpoint had come in the 80th minute, with United heading for defeat and Nobby having already had the disappointment of scoring an own-goal, as well as being booed throughout the game. Denis Law had rather needlessly pulled down Sara midway inside the United half and, as the Austrians jostled around the fiery Scot, Stiles stepped into the fray in an attempt to defend his captain. Moving to the edge of the pushing and shoving mêlée, closely followed by Austrian winger Kodat, Nobby appeared to be struck by his opponent, but when the referee stepped in to try and restore some sort of order, it was the United player who was sent off.

Amid a backdrop of whistles and boos, United trainer Jack Crompton and reserve goalkeeper David Gaskell ran on to the field to escort the dejected Stiles, who had earlier been involved in an incident with outside-right Parits, away from the throng of players on the pitch and towards the safety of the dressing rooms.

Harry Gregg, who had raced 60 yards from his goal to become involved in the pushing and shoving, had been at fault for the Austrians' opening goal in the third minute but, despite their early advantage, it was not until the deflected Stiles own-goal, 14 minutes after half-time, that they scored their second.

Rather surprisingly, two David Herd goals levelled the score, but Parits made it 3–2 in the 74th minute, with Binder and Heisl adding a fourth and a fifth after the Stiles sending off.

12 August 1966   **FK Austria at Horr Stadion, Vienna.**

Attendance: 20,000.

Lost: 5–2.

Scorer: Herd 2.

Team: Gregg, Brennan, Dunne, Fitzpatrick, Cantwell, Stiles, Ryan, Law, Charlton, Herd, Best.

With the season barely underway, Matt Busby rather surprisingly took his team to Italy for a one-off fixture against Fiorentina, in a match organised as part of the 'British Week' celebrations.

Although competitive, the game lacked any real enthusiasm, which was reflected in the 0–0 half-time scoreline. However, after the interval United took the initiative and goals from Charlton and Best were enough to give United victory and a boost for the long hard season ahead.

12 October 1966   **Fiorentina at Stadio Comunale, Florence.**

Attendance: 15,000.

Won: 2–1.

Scorers: Charlton, Best.

Team: Stepney, Dunne, Noble, Crerand, Cantwell, Stiles, Herd, Law, Sadler, Charlton, Best.

Saturday 13 May 1967 saw the United players, accompanied by manager Matt Busby, triumphantly stroll around Old Trafford with the First Division Championship trophy, accepting the plaudits of the 61,071 crowd, following a 0–0 draw with Stoke City. The title had been secured some seven days previously, with a 6–1 hammering of West Ham United at Upton Park.

Four days later the United players found themselves in much more luxurious surroundings than Trafford Park, having flown across the Atlantic to Los Angeles for the first leg of their close-season tour, a gruelling 42-day adventure which was to take them across two continents to play 12 fixtures.

Having endured a long and, at times, tiring season, the United party were looking forward to a relaxing few weeks away. They were certainly not expecting anything like the tumultuous opening fixture against Benfica.

Having demoralised Benfica 5–1 in Lisbon the previous March, in that memorable George Best-inspired European Cup tie, the Portuguese were looking to secure some sort of revenge, despite this particular fixture being as far removed from a European Cup tie as was possible. As it was, with only 11 minutes gone, Eusebio rose unchallenged to head a Garca cross past Stepney to open the scoring.

For the remainder of the first half, play moved from end to end, both sides creating chances but failing to convert them into goals.

With 12 minutes of the second half gone, United equalised when Sadler, accepting a pass from Aston, slipped the ball past Perreira. The goal was considered by many, both on and off the pitch, to have been offside.

Minutes later Eusebio, forever a danger to the United defence and having endured a rough ride throughout the evening, broke through on goal, but was tripped by Stepney and fell to the ground in apparent pain. Still aggrieved by the decision to allow United's equaliser, a handful of spectators managed to get on to the pitch and made for the cluster of players who were by now in heated conversation about the foul on the Mozambique-born forward. One spectator made to confront two United players, but suddenly found himself under assault from another pitch invader and it took the two originally targeted players to keep the hotheads apart. The on-field trouble soon spread to the terracing and it took 25 police officers to quell the fighting that broke out among the spectators.

Tempers eventually cooled and some sort of normality was restored. Shortly afterwards things threatened to flare up again, but the referee had a clear view of Crerand handling the ball in the penalty area and awarded the spot-kick without hesitation. Eusebio calmly notched up his second of the night.

With five minutes remaining, Calado broke through to make it 3–1 and round off the scoring, beating Stepney from 18 yards.

In *The Guardian* the following day, the United correspondent Eric Todd wrote: 'It is sad to think that what was advertised as an exhibition match turned out to be an exhibition of crowd misbehaviour which has brought an increasing blight on the game in recent years. It was doubly unfortunate that it should have happened in the United States, where Association football is being cultivated no less assiduously than baseball.

'No information is forthcoming as to who started the fighting off the field. The inhabitants of the Stretford Road end of United's ground at Old Trafford have earned themselves a mixed reputation – not all of it wholly justified – for doubtful conduct, but I cannot believe that any of them have the money to accompany United on tour. In this instance at least, the Stretford Road-enders surely are above suspicion? It may be nearer the truth, unpalatable though it be, to suggest that in America, no less than anywhere else, there are professional trouble makers for whom the enjoyment of the majority is theirs to ruin.'

In his report in the Los Angeles *Daily Pilot* Glenn White wrote: 'A throng of 20,380 was witness to what was unquestionably the top soccer match ever played in the Southlands as both sides treated fans to aggressive play, fast action and superb performance.' He went on to mention that Matt Busby 'refused to comment on rough play', but added, 'however, the visitors were not the least bit reluctant to offer their opinion on the goings-on which triggered a near-fight between fans who had worked their way on to the field of play.

'Full-back Cavem of Benfica told the *Daily Pilot*, "the English played a very rough brand of ball. There was too much tripping. However, if you think they were bad tonight, you should see them when they are at home!"'

17 May 1967	**Benfica at Memorial Coliseum, Los Angeles.**

Attendance: 22,380.

Lost: 3–1.

Scorer: Sadler.

Team: Stepney, Brennan, Dunne, Crerand, Foulkes, Stiles, Ryan, Best, Sadler, Charlton, Aston.

Thankfully there was almost a week to recover from that unwelcome opening to the tour, but the second of the two fixtures on the American leg of the end-of-season jaunt, against Dundee in San Francisco, failed to produce anything better result-wise.

United took an unsurprising 16-minute lead through Charlton, but for some unknown reason completely fell apart soon afterwards. Goals from Wilson, Bryce and Campbell stunned United and although Brian Kidd, making his United debut and on as a second-half substitute for the injured Denis Law, scored a second for United from the penalty spot, they were soundly beaten for the second successive game.

23 May 1967	**Dundee at San Francisco.**

Attendance: 9,787.

Lost: 4–2.

Scorers: Charlton, Kidd (pen.).

Team: Stepney, Brennan, Dunne, Crerand, Foulkes, Stiles, Best, Law, Sadler, Charlton, Aston.

Substitutes: Kidd for Law, Fitzpatrick for Foulkes.

Despite the defeat, the game served as an ideal early present for Brian Kidd, who was to celebrate his 18th birthday six days later. It was a rather meteoric rise to fame as he had signed for United as an associate schoolboy in December 1963 and only signed his professional forms in June 1966, but, having shown excellent form in the previous season's Central League side, he was rewarded with a place in the tour party.

He went on to make over 250 appearances for United, celebrating his 19th birthday in rather more spectacular fashion by scoring in the European Cup Final. He was later to return to the club as assistant to Alex Ferguson.

The tour now took on a more relaxed pace as the team travelled to the southern hemisphere, arriving in New Zealand, where the opposition were of a lower standard and the results finally went United's way.

First stop was Auckland, where an enthusiastic crowd were treated to a deluge of goals, with five coming in a breathtaking first half.

The home side were considered to be one of the strongest in New Zealand footballing circles, but they had no answer to their more superior opponents. They began brightly but, following John Aston's opener in the 14th minute, they soon found themselves playing nothing more than a supporting role.

The programme for the match versus Dundee, 23 May 1967.

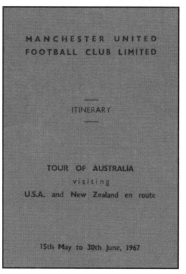

A booklet detailing the itinerary for the tour at Australia dating from 15 May to 30 June 1967.

Aston's goal, a low and hard shot from outside the penalty area, was followed eight minutes later by a second from Noel Cantwell. Playing in the rather unfamiliar position of centre-forward, the former United captain gratefully accepted a pass from George Best, who completely outfoxed the Auckland defenders with a brilliant run. Best himself added a third, while further goals from Cantwell and Aston gave United a 5–0 interval lead.

In the second half United eased off slightly and it was not until the final 15 minutes that there were any further goals. Rather surprisingly, when a goal did materialise, it fell to the hosts, Lamont lifting the ball coolly past Stepney for what was to prove little more than a consolation, as Aston went on to score two more, with Kidd making it eight with a penalty after Best was brought down.

28 May 1967	Auckland.

Attendance: 26,000.

Won: 8–1.

Scorers: Aston 4, Cantwell 2, Best, Kidd (pen.).

Team: Stepney, Dunne, Burns, Crerand, Sadler, Stiles, Best, Charlton, Cantwell, Kidd, Aston.

Substitute: Fitzpatrick for Crerand.

The programme for the match versus Auckland, 28 May 1967.

Three days later, in Christchurch, United took their tally to 19 goals in two games when they defeated a local side 11–0.

This time around the first half produced only four goals, but the final 20-odd minutes produced five, creating something of a dispute about who could claim the match ball, as both Bobby Charlton and Noel Cantwell, once again leading the attack, notched up three goals.

George Best chipped in with two goals, while Aston and Kidd kept up their fine scoring form with one apiece. The other goal was put past his own goalkeeper by centre-half McNab.

31 May 1967	Christchurch.

Attendance: 12,000.

Won: 11–0.

Scorers: Charlton 3, Cantwell 3, Best 2, Kidd, Aston, opp. own-goal.

Team: Stepney, Brennan, Dunne, Crerand, Sadler, Stiles, Best, Charlton, Cantwell, Kidd, Aston.

Substitutes: Rimmer for Stepney, Fitzpatrick for Crerand.

The programme for the match versus Christchurch, 31 May 1967.

Moving on to Australia, the first port of call was Brisbane, where the goals continued to flow against an unfortunate Queensland side, as United scored seven without reply in an outstanding display of football. The appreciative home crowd were kept riveted by the action, as United displayed an array of skills and attacked and defended in numbers, allowing the home side little time to settle.

With both Charlton and Best in commanding form, United were three goals in front at half-time, a total that could have been at least doubled had it not been for the top-class goalkeeping of Kelly in the Queensland goal. Noel Cantwell opened the scoring with a header in the eighth minute, while some fine work by the stand-in number nine produced a second for John Aston. George Best rounded off the first half trio of goals with a left-footed shot in the 37th minute.

To their credit, Queensland showed a little more enterprise in the second half and came close on a couple of occasions, but any hopes of a spirited comeback were soon forgotten about when Charlton added a fourth, sweeping home Aston's pass. The crowd rose to their feet to salute the same individual's second goal two minutes later, when he thundered the ball past a helpless 'keeper from 25 yards out.

Despite their superior play and advantage, United did little to ease the pressure on the Queensland goal, where 21-year-old Ross Kelly, despite conceding seven, had an outstanding game, brilliantly stopping at least six other attempts. United went on to add a further two goals before the end, from Aston and Best.

4 June 1967	Queensland at Brisbane.

Attendance: 23,000.

Won: 7–0.

Scorers: Aston 2, Charlton 2, Best 2, Cantwell.

Team: Stepney, Brennan, Dunne, Crerand, Sadler, Stiles, Best, Charlton, Cantwell, Kidd, Aston.

Three days later the United party, a man short as defender Francis Burns was forced to return to England for a cartilage operation, were in Sydney, where they were subjected to a rather hectic opening period as their opponents, a Representative XI, kept Stepney's goal under siege. Experience soon prevailed, however, as did the shock of almost going a goal behind when Reynolds shunned a golden opportunity after the ball rebounded from the crossbar. It was not long before the tourists were dictating the play.

Denis Law, returning to the United line up after having aggravated an injury he had picked up playing for Scotland against Russia, opened the scoring in the 14th minute with a header from a Kidd cross from close range.

Soon afterwards both Kidd and Best were guilty of missing open goals. The former blasted over from close range, while the latter ran the ball into the goalkeeper's open arms. Best, however, made amends in the 25th minute, when he took the ball along the goalline before scoring from a seemingly impossible angle. He had soon added a third, leaving two defenders in his wake before beating the 'keeper.

The change in United's play in the second half was very noticeable, as they eased up considerably, especially after losing Crerand with an injury. Although Charlton split open the Select XI's defence with numerous passes, no further goals materialised. The home side, who brought on the former Bolton forward Doug Holden as a second-half substitute, played extremely well and were certainly unlucky not to score.

Although the match was a friendly and played for the most part as such, there was one rather out of character incident. In the dying minutes Law was involved in a clash with the Sydney inside-right Giles, who was taken to hospital with a fractured cheekbone.

7 June 1967	Representative XI at Sydney.

Attendance: 25,000.

Won: 3–0.

Scorers: Best 2, Law.

Team: Stepney, Brennan, Dunne, Crerand, Sadler, Stiles, Best, Charlton, Cantwell, Law, Aston.

Substitute: Fitzpatrick for Crerand.

The performances of the Sydney players in the previous fixture must have been noted by their Victoria counterparts, who managed to secure a notable 1–1 draw in Melbourne.

However, even without Law, Crerand and Foulkes, United were still strong enough to ensure a comfortable victory, but they played well below their true form. Perhaps the tour was at last beginning to tire some of the players out, although they certainly never looked like losing.

Having strolled through a goalless first half, Bobby Charlton gave United the lead with a left-footed drive 12 minutes into the second half, but to the delight of the home crowd David Sadler, while attempting to deliver the ball back to Stepney, headed into his own net.

The former Czechoslovakian international goalkeeper Schroif had an inspired game, while Dunne, with his notable speed and ball control, Fitzpatrick, who was never far from the thick of the battle, and George Best were United's top players. The latter, in particular, entertained the appreciative crowd with his wide array of skills.

11 June 1967	Victoria XI at Olympic Park, Melbourne.

Attendance: 33,000.

Drew: 1–1.

Scorer: Charlton.

Team: Stepney, Brennan, Dunne, Fitzpatrick, Sadler, Stiles, Best, Ryan, Cantwell, Charlton, Aston.

Substitute: Kidd for Ryan.

United put up a sluggish performance against a Northern New South Wales team made up mainly of English and Scottish immigrants, although they managed to win 3–0. This lethargy was perhaps due to the fact that they had travelled some 700 miles, arriving in Newcastle just before midnight. Trainer Jack Crompton went on to describe the scene on their arrival 'as like taking part in some wartime secret mission.'

Writing in the *Manchester Evening News*, Jack continued: 'our arrival from Melbourne was a little weird. We had a pleasant flight and an excellent landing. But when we got out of the plane, it was pitch black, not a light anywhere, just a cluster of Nissan huts.

'Fortunately our coach arrived to pick us up for the 25 mile journey to Newcastle. We unloaded our baggage by the light of two torches and found out afterwards that they had forgotten we were coming and had closed down the airfield.'

The muddy Newcastle pitch prevented any classic football from being played, but it proved to be no deterrent to George Best, who once again gave the crowd a glimpse of his wide array of talents. Charlton had something of an off day, while the newest member of the United squad, Brian Kidd, gave further notice to manager Matt Busby that he would be pressing for a regular place in the starting 11 in the forthcoming season.

Taking it easy and shunning the countless scoring opportunities that they created as the game progressed, it nevertheless did look in the early stages like there could be

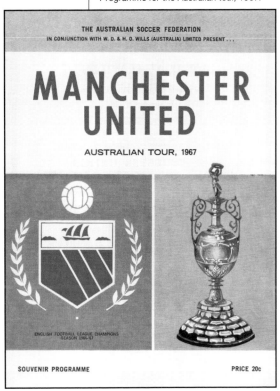

Programme for the Australian tour, 1967.

something of a goal glut, especially after Kidd gave United the lead in the eighth minute direct from a corner.

Both Kidd and Charlton had goals disallowed before the former gave United a 2–0 lead with 10 minutes remaining, beating a defender before hitting the ball high into the roof of the net. A third goal followed two minutes later when Best stirred the crowd, running through the opposition defence before beating Dorman with an unstoppable effort.

At the sounding of the referee's whistle for full-time, Charlton and Stiles moved quicker than they had done at any time during the previous 90 minutes, as they tried to evade the thousands of small boys who invaded the pitch.

---

12 June 1967　　　　　　　　　**Northern New South Wales at Newcastle.**

Attendance: 14,600.

Won: 3–0.

Scorers: Kidd 2, Best.

Team: Rimmer, Brennan, Dunne, Fitzpatrick, Foulkes, Stiles, Best, Sadler, Charlton, Kidd, Aston.

After a six-day break United had recharged their batteries and at the Sydney Showground they gave their best performance of the tour, with a 3–1 victory against New South Wales. However, they were given something of an early shock when the home side scored in the second minute, only to breathe a collective sigh of relief when the referee disallowed it for handball.

In the opening 20 minutes United had at least three scoring chances, but they were denied by goalkeeper Corry and it took them until eight minutes prior to the interval to open the scoring. John Aston got the better of the New South Wales defence as he took the ball along the goalline before pulling it back into the path of Bobby Charlton who scored with a first-time shot.

The second half got underway with goalkeeper Corry pushing a tremendous shot from Kidd against the crossbar, but the 'keeper was clearly at fault soon afterwards when he dropped a centre from Kidd, giving Foulkes the opportunity to score a rare goal. Five minutes later it was 3–0, Charlton beating three defenders before his angled shot gave Corry no chance. Kept on his toes throughout the game, with United hitting the bar or post on at least five occasions, Corry tipped a 15-yard drive from Charlton over the bar.

As the minutes ticked away, the New South Wales side gradually came more into the game and were rewarded with a goal from Hughes, their right-half and captain, who hit a rebound off Stiles past Stepney.

---

18 June 1967　　　　　　　**New South Wales at The Showground, Sydney.**

Attendance: 35,659.

Won: 3–1.

Scorers: Charlton 2, Foulkes.

Team: Stepney, Brennan, Dunne, Fitzpatrick, Foulkes, Stiles, Best, Sadler, Charlton, Kidd, Aston.

Denis Law, playing in only his second game of the tour, thrilled the Melbourne crowd with two goals as United avenged their 1–1 draw of the previous week against the Victoria State XI. However, it was another Scot, Billy Cook, who put United on their road to victory, lobbing the ball past his own goalkeeper as he attempted a pass back.

As in previous fixtures, George Best was the main entertainer, leading almost continuous onslaughts on the Victoria goal, and it was from his efforts that Law scored his two goals, with the Irishman himself scoring United's third. Picking the ball up midway inside the Victoria half, he ran round four defenders before smashing the ball past goalkeeper Schroif.

---

21 June 1967 — **Victoria State XI at Melbourne.**

Attendance: 20,000.

Won: 4–0.

Scorers: Law 2, Best, opp. own-goal.

Team: Stepney, Brennan, Dunne, Sadler, Foulkes, Stiles, Best, Law, Charlton, Kidd, Aston.

Once again it was Law, Best and Charlton who stole the limelight as United got back on the goal trail with an easy five-goal win against a South Australia side in Adelaide.

It was Law who opened the floodgates in the 12th minute, but he was overshadowed by Bobby Charlton, who scored with one of his trademark efforts from 15 yards and, had the 'keeper got his hand, or indeed his body, behind the ball, he would most probably have ended up in the net as well. Brian Kidd, however, bettered both, scoring a notable hat-trick, two goals of which were exceptional headers. The other cannoned in off Best, but the youngster had no hesitation in laying claim to it.

The consolation Adelaide goal came in the closing minutes through Lovell.

---

24 June 1967 — **South Australia at Adelaide.**

Attendance: 20,000.

Won: 5–1.

Scorers: Kidd 3, Law, Charlton.

Team: Rimmer, Edwards, Dunne, Fitzpatrick, Sadler, Stiles, Best, Law, Charlton, Kidd, Aston.

And so came the last game of a long and gruelling tour, with United bidding the southern hemisphere farewell with a dazzling seven-goal victory over Western Australia. The only low point of the 90 minutes in Perth was the sending off of Denis Law in the 33rd minute, when United were already 3–0 in front. It was a dismissal which cost him £20 when he was found guilty of having used 'bad' language, after being found not guilty of using 'abusive' language.

This was disappointing for the many who had travelled quite a distance to see the Scot in action, but they were compensated by the ongoing 'George Best Show', with the Irishman bringing down the curtain with yet another notable display, creating two of the goals and claiming a fine hat-trick for himself.

Never troubled by the opposition, United were able to play at half pace and still maintain a high level of play to go along with the seven goals.

---

27 June 1967 — **Western Australia at Perth.**

Attendance: 20,500.

Won: 7–0.

Scorers: Best 3, Kidd 2, Law, Charlton.

Team: Stepney, Brennan, Dunne, Sadler, Foulkes, Stiles, Best, Law, Charlton, Kidd, Aston.

And so the United players and directors flew back to Manchester, following what had been a rather gruelling few weeks. The W.D. & H.O. Wills sponsored tour had proved to be something of a money earner for the Australian Football Federation, and it was estimated that the organisers would pocket around £50,000 from what was described as 'the most successful soccer tour ever undertaken in Australia'.

Back on home soil it was soon back to the grindstone for pre-season training. Rather surprisingly, preparation for the months ahead differed completely from that of previous seasons, with the only warm-up friendly taking United no further than Trafford Park in Manchester, with the Italian Olympic XI providing the relatively easy opposition.

The Italians were in England in preparation for the Mediterranean Games, due to be held in Tunis during the following month, and the Olympic Games, to be held in Mexico next year. This was their fifth and final run-out, and they had lost three of the previous four and drawn the other, but, according to reports, the selectors could be pleased with the performances and their preparations in general.

United began rather haphazardly, but in the end were far more convincing winners than the score actually suggests. The Italian amateurs did apply themselves well to create an excellent impression on the somewhat sparse Old Trafford crowd.

Savoldi, already of interest to Inter Milan, added to his growing reputation with a rising drive that rattled the post, with the rebound forcing Stepney into making a fine save. The Italian outside-right's play was often to cause United embarrassment.

It took United 33 minutes to open the scoring through Brian Kidd, star of the recent Charity Shield 3–3 draw against Tottenham. Crerand's finely measured pass sent the youngster through and, despite the close attention of Cresci, he managed to put the ball beyond Vecchi in the Italian goal.

Undeterred by this setback, the young Italians almost equalised straight from the restart, Scala hitting the angle of the crossbar and post with a fierce shot. However, it was to prove something of a token gesture, as within two minutes Stiles had added a second for United. Following an interchanging of passes with Crerand, the diminutive half-back scored with a well-hit drive.

With a two-goal advantage United soon switched to entertainment mode, with Best at his most dazzling, accompanied by Charlton, who was quick to try his luck at goal from any distance. However, the best chance of the match fell to Anastasi, who failed to put the ball past Stepney as the United defence stood still looking for offside.

The programme for the match versus Italian Olympic XI, 15 August 1967.

15 August 1967	Italian Olympic XI at Old Trafford.

Attendance: 20,887.

Won: 2–0.

Scorers: Stiles, Kidd.

Team: Stepney, Brennan, Dunne, Crerand, Foulkes, Stiles, Best, Law, Charlton, Kidd, Aston.

Substitute: Sadler for Dunne.

As it turned out, season 1967–68 turned out to be as memorable as any in the history of Manchester United, with the team finally winning the European Cup, beating Benfica 4–1 at Wembley on a humid, tear-stained evening. So it was as European Champions that United began season 1968–69, against old foes Hamburg. They got off to an ideal start with a comfortable 2–0 victory. The game was not only the ideal start to the pre-season build-up, but also a welcome return to first-team football for Denis Law, proving his fitness after the disappointment of missing the European Cup Final with a knee injury.

By the end of the 90 minutes there was little doubt that 'the King' would return to his best, although there was one worrying moment in the 39th minute, when he was brought down in full flight by no-nonsense defender Kurt Kurbjuhn. He lay motionless for several seconds, much to the anxiety of the United bench. 'I got a heavy kick on the troublesome left knee, on which I had had the operation, but thankfully there was no ill effect,' he later reported.

Charlton looked fast and sharp, getting in some good defensive work along with Best and Law, while Stepney stood between United and defeat, bringing off some notable saves. He was only beaten once, when a Seiffert cross was deflected by Charlton onto the crossbar, with Tony Dunne alert to the danger and hooking the ball away.

John Aston was on hand to play a part in the opening goal, pushing the ball out to Charlton, who in turn passed it to Best to score with a first-time shot from around 18 yards out.

It was not until the 82nd minute that United managed to increase their lead, when a solo effort from Bobby Charlton put the result beyond any doubt. Latching on to the ball, he set off on a 30-yard dribble before firing a thunderbolt past the helpless Ozcan from well outside the area.

31 July 1968	Hamburg at Volkspark Stadium, Hamburg.

Attendance: 25,000.

Won: 2–0.

Scorers: Best, Charlton.

Team: Stepney, Brennan, Dunne, Crerand, Sadler, Stiles, Best, Kidd, Charlton, Law, Aston.

The second of the pre-season 1968–69 friendlies took United to Dublin to face Drumcondra, in what was a benefit match for John Whelan, brother of former Old Trafford favourite Liam, who had died in the Munich air disaster.

With a tough season in front of them, this particular fixture was never going to provide United with a serious test, but it was more than adequate to get to the standard of match fitness required.

Augmented by a couple of guest players from Waterford, the home side found themselves a goal behind after 15 minutes, Denis Law latching on to a loose ball after goalkeeper Smyth failed to hold a George Best centre.

As the first half progressed United were content to amble along, occasionally treating the match as little more than a training session, and it was not until well into the second 45 minutes that they were given something of a wake-up call from their hosts, who had slowly begun to threaten the United defence.

With 15 minutes remaining, and having been held hostage in their own half for long periods, the Select pushed forward and fine work between Hale and Matthews, two Waterford players, resulted in the former scoring with a well-taken goal.

Shaken by this equaliser and certainly not wanting to be disgraced by the part-timers, United stepped up a gear for the remainder of the game and, four minutes from time, Law seized on a pass from Charlton and scored the decisive goal, disappearing almost immediately under a crowd of schoolboys.

The programme for the match versus Hamburg, 31 July 1968.

Not prepared to give in, despite there only being a couple of minutes remaining, Drumcondra pushed forward in the hope of snatching an equaliser. However, they just did not have the experience to overcome the European champions.

---

4 August 1968   **Drumcondra Select at Dalymount Park.**

Attendance: 35,000.

Won: 2–1.

Scorer: Law 2.

Team: Stepney, Brennan, Dunne, Crerand, Sadler, Stiles, Best, Kidd, Charlton, Law, Aston.

Substitute: Gowling for Law.

Having begun season 1968–69 with high expectations of further glory at home and abroad, it was somewhat disappointing that the League campaign drew to a close with United finishing in 11th position, accumulating 42 points from their 42 games.

Perhaps even more disappointing was the failure to retain the European Cup, losing to AC Milan 2–1 on aggregate, with the Old Trafford second leg ending in controversy and disgrace, due to a disallowed 'goal' and the Milan goalkeeper being hit by an object thrown from the Stretford End.

Given the complaints that are made today about the scheduling of games and the number of fixtures played, it may come as something of a surprise that those ruling the roost at Old Trafford decided that Matt Busby's team would travel to the Republic of Ireland to play two meaningless friendlies. However, if an excuse is required, the games were arranged, not for any financial gain, but due to the fact that following the defeat in Milan on 23 April United would not have played again until the second leg at Old Trafford on 15 May. So in reality, match practice was something that would certainly not go amiss.

As it was, there were three notable omissions from the United side that ran out onto the Dalymount Park pitch to face Shamrock Rovers in the first match of the double-header. However, the reasons for the absence of Best, Law and Charlton had little to do with the need to rest the match-winning trio prior to the visit of Milan to Manchester, but was due to the fact that they were on international duty with their respective countries.

There were still plenty of star players on show to whet the appetite of the Irish football-loving public, but they almost failed to see a full 90 minutes of football, as the referee was forced to take both teams off the pitch with 10 minutes remaining after a pitch invasion.

As the second half moved towards the closing stages, the referee's attention was drawn to a large number of youths who had begun to congregate around Jimmy Rimmer's goal. At times, with play at the opposite end of the pitch, the United 'keeper was barely visible. Indeed, there had been a couple of occasions earlier on when two youths had appeared with a rubber ball and begun their own impromptu game in front of the bemused United custodian.

Repeated requests were made over the public address system for the youths to move back behind the barriers, but they were constantly ignored, giving Billy O'Neill, the match official, little option than to call a halt to the game, with both sets of players making a hasty exit into the tunnel.

Following a brief wait, the match official was told that the situation outside was 'hopeless', and there was little point in contemplating finishing the game. He was, however, keen to conclude the proceedings and with the stewards and the local gardai (Irish police force) succeeding in clearing the pitch of the unwelcome invaders, the referee summoned both sets of players back onto the pitch to play out the remaining minutes of the game. This produced a flurry of activity in the United dressing room, as a few of the players had actually begun to discard their playing attire and head for the showers.

As it was, the remaining 10 minutes made no difference to the outcome of the match. United had put the outcome beyond any doubt within the first 17 minutes, taking a two-goal lead, then scoring a third just after the half-hour mark and a fourth three minutes prior to the interval.

The first of the quartet of goals came as early as the second minute, when Crerand sent Sadler through for a simple effort, but it was the second and third goals which received much acclaim from the crowd, as they were scored by former Dublin schoolboy Don Givens, whose impressive display bolstered his claims for international recognition. Brian Kidd added the fourth.

The home side fought gamely, but even when United eased off a little in the second half they were no match for the European Champions. Pugh did come close to scoring from an O'Neill corner, however, and Kinsella was foiled twice by fine saves by Rimmer.

5 May 1969	Shamrock Rovers at Dalymount Park.

Attendance: 18,000.

Won: 4–0.

Scorers: Givens 2, Sadler, Kidd.

Team: Rimmer, Brennan, Burns, Crerand, Foulkes, Stiles, Ryan, Kidd, Givens, Sadler, Aston.

Substitute: Dunne for Brennan.

Three days later United concluded their whistle-stop tour in a relaxed fashion with a 3–0 victory over Waterford, and once again two early goals put the outcome beyond any doubt.

With eight minutes gone, Crerand headed down a Bryant clearance to Stiles, with the United wing-half immediately pushing the ball through to Givens. Despite being in a good scoring position, the young Irishman unselfishly flicked the ball to Kidd, who headed past the outstretched arm of Thomas.

Seven minutes later it was 2–0. Morgan's left-sided corner was deflected via the head of Givens to Kidd, who did little more than chest the ball over the line with the Waterford defence in disarray.

Sadler, Givens and Aston all scorned good opportunities to increase United's lead, and it was not until the 64th minute that Morgan snatched a third when he intercepted a pass from McGough and ran past the stranded Morrissey before hitting the ball firmly past the helpless Thomas.

The home side created few problems, although Buck and O'Neill had their moments, while centre-half Morley kept Givens under close control.

All in all the two games did provide the United players with much-needed match fitness, especially Dunne, Stiles and Morgan, who had all been receiving treatment for injuries, with Dunne not having played for five weeks.

The programme for the match versus Waterford, 8 May 1969.

Waterford at Kilcohan Park.

Attendance: 7,000.

Won: 3–0.

Scorers: Kidd 2, Morgan.

Team: Rimmer, Dunne, Burns, Crerand, Foulkes, Stiles, Morgan, Kidd, Givens, Sadler, Aston.

Substitute: Stepney for Rimmer, James for Foulkes.

On 9 April, with the season approaching a heady climax, United chairman Louis Edwards issued a statement proclaiming that, following Sir Matt Busby's decision to stand down as manager, Wilf McGuinness would be appointed as 'Chief Coach'. They were certainly difficult shoes to fill for the United assistant trainer and, as the future was to reveal, it was to be something of an impossible task.

McGuinness, whose United playing career was brought to a premature end through injury when he was only 22, began his new appointment on 1 June 1969 but, despite taking the club to two Football League Cup semi-finals and one FA Cup semi-final, he was demoted to trainer-coach of the reserve team in December 1970, as the overall form in the First Division was little more than average.

The career of Wilf McGuinness as United manager, however, did get off to a more promising start, with 17 goals for and only three against in his first three fixtures in charge. Admittedly they were only friendlies, but few would dismiss victories of 6–2 and 9–1 at any level.

The reign of the unfortunate McGuinness began in North Wales, at the home of Bangor City, where United took on a Welsh International XI as part of the investiture celebrations for His Royal Highness, the Prince of Wales. This was a match that was destined never to satisfy the packed ground in terms of physical endeavour, as many of the Welsh players were due to play again the following evening, when Wales took on a Rest of the United Kingdom side in Cardiff. Despite this knowledge, the ground was packed to overflowing, with those who could not obtain tickets watching the proceedings from the houses and trees on the steep hill overlooking the ground.

The early pre-season training had left many of United's seasoned campaigners commenting that they had 'never experienced anything so gruelling', but following the 2–0 victory they were quick to admit that 'they had never felt fitter by the end of a game', with the victory, according to *Manchester Evening News* reporter Matt D'Arcy, 'carved out of determination to run and to work slavishly for each other.'

With everyone bar Bill Foulkes joining in the attack and the defence augmented by everyone except Brian Kidd and Don Givens, who played 45 minutes each, the Welsh side, containing the likes of Gary Sprake, Terry Hennessey, Mike England and Wyn Davies, were always going to have their work cut out. Their task became harder when United took the lead after only five minutes.

Willie Morgan, who completely dominated full-back Rod Thomas of Swindon throughout the game, opened the scoring, with Brian Kidd adding a second in the 34th minute. The accurate work of Charlton and Best also made a contribution to the scoreline.

United's lead should have been increased to three in the 71st minute, but Denis Law blotted his copybook by missing a penalty, crashing the ball against the crossbar rather the back of the net. The Scot missed numerous other good scoring opportunities.

At the end of the day, the spot-kick miss mattered little, as the victory was immaterial, but it was an ideal start to the reign of Wilf McGuinness.

26 July 1969	Welsh XI at Bangor.

Attendance: 12,000.

Won: 2–0.

Scorers: Morgan, Kidd.

Team: Stepney, Dunne, Burns, Crerand, Foulkes, Sadler, Morgan, Kidd, Charlton, Law, Best.

Substitutes: Givens for Kidd, Brennan for Burns.

The programme for the match versus Welsh International XI, 26 July 1969.

Five days later United were in Denmark and facing a Copenhagen XI. They struggled against a team who had recently defeated the likes of Eire, Mexico and Hungary.

The evening kicked off as usual, with Best dribbling through the Copenhagen defence before scoring with a precise low drive in the third minute and then proceeding to entertain the crowd with his skill, impishness and guile.

If the visitors had any thoughts that this early goal would set a precedent for the remainder of the game then they were mistaken, as they fought back to equalise in the 20th minute when Andersen eluded Foulkes before setting up Praest to beat the reinstated Rimmer with ease.

Rimmer was then forced into making two fine saves, but within five minutes United had regained the lead as Kidd headed on a Crerand cross and Morgan drifted past Nielsen and Jensen to score. It was a lead that lasted until a minute prior to the interval, when Forsing, the only uncapped forward, equalised.

After the interval McGuninness brought on Alan Gowling, a relatively unknown 20-year-old Manchester University undergraduate, who had been a last minute call-up for the two-game tour due to an injury to Denis Law. Gowling wasted little time in making his mark on the proceedings, scoring twice as United stepped up a gear to overcome the Danish part-timers.

His first, in the 50th minute, saw him run through the defence to guide a pass from John Aston past Niels Jensen in the Copenhagen goal. His second, 15 minutes later, was more impressive, beating the 'keeper from all of 18 yards: a goal that was to put the outcome of the game beyond any doubt.

Further goals from the direct and ever-dangerous Brian Kidd and Willie Morgan completed the scoring, leaving the Danish side demoralised and Wilf McGuinness 'highly pleased with this performance.'

The programme for the match versus Copenhagen Select, 31 July 1969.

31 July 1969	Copenhagen Select at National Stadium.

Attendance: 20,400.

Won: 6–2.

Scorers: Gowling 2, Morgan 2, Best, Law, Kidd.

Team: Rimmer, Dunne, Burns, Crerand, Foulkes, Sadler, Morgan Kidd, Charlton, Givens, Best.

Substitutes: Gowling for Givens, Aston for Best, Brennan for Foulkes.

From Denmark the team travelled to Switzerland, and if the six goals against Copenhagen satisfied the new United manager, then the nine scored against FC Zurich would certainly have given him confidence on the eve of the new season.

The programme for the match versus FC Zurich, 2 August 1969.

Having endured a strenuous return to training at the Cliff, the United players must have been looking forward to a relaxing few days away, but they were to find things slightly different from life under Sir Matt, as Wilf McGuinness put his charges through a rigorous training session on the morning of the game. Once again, the manager's preparation proved correct, with the players showing a degree of freshness and zest in their play.

With only 90 seconds on the clock United were a goal in front. Willie Morgan, playing more in the inside-forward position than in his familiar place on the wing, scored the first of a hat-trick from a Kidd pass.

In the 14th minute Brian Kidd, occupying a rather deeper role than normal, flashed home a superb angled drive from 18 yards for United's second. A minute later it was 3–0, George Best scoring with a shot that took a slight deflection off Grunig's leg.

Despite the game being in its infancy, the Zurich defence were in complete disarray and it was no surprise that United went on to enjoy a free-scoring 90 minutes. They did, however, breathe something of a sigh of relief with the score at 4–0, Morgan having scored his second with a slick back-heeler from a Givens cross. George Best had to leave the field with a head injury, having collided with a television camera situated behind one of the goals.

The home support had something to shout about in the 26th minute when inside-right Quentin hit a low drive past Rimmer from 12 yards, but for most of the game they could only admire United's 'new look' quick-passing, free-flowing football, with Kidd sweeping home a fifth in the 33rd minute.

McGuinness left Charlton, Crerand and Rimmer in the dressing room for the second half, but the changes did little to stem United's attacking play. Bill Foulkes added a sixth, hammering the ball home from 30 yards in the 42nd minute. Morgan completed his hat-trick on the hour, with Gowling getting in on the act 15 minutes later with the eighth. John Aston rounded things up with the ninth five minutes from time.

The big question now was, could United transfer this form back to the domestic field?

2 August 1969	**FC Zurich at Letzigrund Stadium.**

Attendance: 17,000.

Won: 9–1.

Scorers: Morgan 3, Kidd 2, Best, Foulkes, Gowling, Aston.

Team: Stepney, Dunne, Burns, Crerand, Foulkes, Sadler, Morgan, Kidd, Gowling, Charlton, Best.

Substitute: Aston for Best.

The answer was, unfortunately, no. Despite some fine displays, for example 7–0 against West Bromwich Albion, there were also low points, such as a 5–1 defeat at Newcastle. This inconsistency brought a placing of eighth in the First Division and semi-final defeats in both the Football League Cup and the FA Cup.

The 1970s

Today footballers are more than happy to see the end of each season, more so if it has failed to produce any silverware, as they have a few weeks of rest to look forward before thinking about pre-season training. For the United players of this particular period, there was to be no rest, as for those not involved in the World Cup there was a tour of Bermuda and the United States to focus upon.

With Bobby Charlton, David Sadler, Brian Kidd, Alex Stepney and Nobby Stiles all in the England squad for the World Cup Finals in Mexico, there were spaces in the United party for a trio of youngsters – John Connaughton, Tony Young and Tony Whelan – as it set off on the first leg of the post-season tour.

Kicking-off amid perfect conditions, with temperatures of around 70 degrees Fahrenheit, the tour got under way against the Bermuda National side, with what was reportedly 'the most entertaining game seen there in years.' On a flat grassy pitch, United dominated the opening 45 minutes without exerting themselves too much and went in at the interval leading 2–0, with goals from Willie Morgan and John Fitzpatrick.

After the interval, with George Best on as substitute for the debutant Tony Whelan, United continued to hold the upper hand, but an own-goal by Francis Burns brought a distinct change to the flow of the game, with the physically stronger Bermuda beginning to put some pressure on the United goal. This was ultimately rewarded with an equaliser through Brangman, stirring the locals into something of a frenzy.

United now brought some urgency into their play and in the 65th minute Fitzpatrick restored their lead, which was increased shortly afterwards when Burns made amends for his earlier misdemeanour when he added a fourth.

To their credit, and in contrast to their first-half display, Bermuda did threaten on occasion with several promising attacks, but they were unable to penetrate the United defence. At the opposite end George Best, who had arrived in Hamilton only an hour before kick-off, repaid the warm applause he received when he came on after the interval with a fine display. Three shots produced excellent saves from the Bermuda goalkeeper, while one mesmerising run, in which he beat six defenders, ended with a thunderous drive that rebounded off the crossbar.

The itinerary booklet for the tour of Bermuda, Canada and the United States of America, 24 April to 19 May 1970.

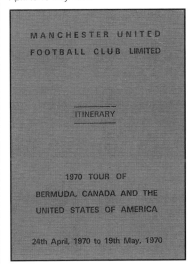

26 April 1970	Bermuda XI at National Stadium, Hamilton.

Attendance: 4,091.

Won: 4–2.

Scorers: Fitzpatrick 2, Morgan, Burns.

Team: Rimmer, Edwards, Dunne, Crerand, Ure, Burns, Morgan, Sartori, Fitzpatrick, Aston, Whelan.

Substitutes: Best for Whelan, Watson for Fitzpatrick, James for Crerand.

Although scheduled for the same venue, the second of the two Caribbean fixtures, this time against the Bermuda Football Union, had to be switched to a ground with floodlights, which unfortunately did not have the same playing surface as the first venue. This, however, did not deter United in any way, as they scored three times in the opening half, before adding a further three after the break. John Fitzpatrick, continuing in the unfamiliar centre-forward position, scored twice, as did George Best, with the others coming from Carlo Sartori and debutant Tony Young.

The Bermudan side had no answer to United's play, despite making four substitutions, but their undoubted determination was rewarded with a consolation goal in the 72nd minute through Lewis.

---

30 April 1970   **Bermuda Football Union at Hamilton.**

Attendance: 1,200.

Won: 6–1.

Scorers: Fitzpatrick 2, Best 2, Young, Sartori.

Team: Connaughton, Edwards, Dunne, Crerand, Ure, Watson, Young, Fitzpatrick, Best, Sartori, Morgan.

Substitutes: Burns for Crerand, Whelan for Morgan.

Leaving behind the sunshine of Bermuda, the United party moved on to Canada to take part in a three-club tournament for the Toronto Cup, against the Italian side Bari and Glasgow Celtic.

The first match of the tournament, against Bari, was a rather lacklustre game, although the Italians did try to spice it up a little with some rather dubious play, which earned them three bookings. With a close watch also being kept on Best, who was fortunate not to be sent off himself, neither team really looked like scoring, as the United defence was equally as tight with its marking.

At times it was feared that the game would get completely out of hand and, when the referee awarded a penalty to United in the 74th minute, after Sartori was rather unceremoniously brought down in the area, he was surrounded by a number of jostling, protesting Italians. So prolonged were their complaints, that it was some five minutes before Willie Morgan could take the spot-kick and score the goal that was to decide the outcome of the game.

---

2 May 1970   **Bari at Che Stadium, Toronto.**

Attendance: 10,000.

Won: 1–0.

Scorer: Morgan (pen.).

Team: Rimmer, Edwards, Dunne, Crerand, Ure, Burns, Morgan, Sartori, Fitzpatrick, Aston, Best.

An additional fixture had been arranged between United and Bari outside of the Toronto Cup and three days later the two teams moved to New York, where an even more sensational game took place.

With the kick-off delayed some 30 minutes due to a traffic jam around the stadium, and the temperature a mere three degrees above freezing, forcing many in the rather sparse crowd to light fires on the terracing, it was perhaps not surprising that the game itself was something of an anti-climax.

When the game eventually got underway it took United only four minutes to open the scoring against the Italian Second Division side, as Crerand crossed to Best to give goalkeeper Spalazzi no chance with a powerful shot from close range.

The behaviour of the Italian players showed a vast improvement from that of the previous fixture and, 10 minutes before half-time, they levelled the scoring through Dino Spadetto, their recent signing from Inter Milan. Collecting the ball in midfield, he proceeded to race through the United defence before scoring with a shot from 15 yards.

The programme for the match versus Bari, 2 May 1970.

Eighteen minutes into the second half United made it 2–1. Tony Dunne raced down the wing, playing a neat one-two with Willie Morgan before the winger crossed the ball into the Bari penalty area. With the Italian defence expecting an offside decision, Carlo Sartori superbly pulled the ball down before slipping it past the static 'keeper.

Although disappointed when the referee signalled the goal, the Bari players accepted the decision. However, as they prepared to restart the game, a large number of New York's Italian community invaded the pitch, making a beeline for the referee. Aware of the immediate danger, players from both teams surrounded the match official and a dash was made for the sanctuary of the dressing rooms. Bottles, cans and even dustbins crashed on to the pitch as things began to get totally out of hand, and it was some 20 minutes before order was restored.

5 May 1970	Bari at New York.

Attendance: 5,823.

Won: 2–1.

Scorers: Best, Sartori.

Team: Rimmer, Edwards, Dunne, Crerand, Ure, Watson, Morgan, Sartori, Fitzpatrick, Aston, Best.

Substitutes: Young for Best, James for Ure.

Returning to Toronto, United came face to face with Celtic, fresh from the European Cup Final defeat by Feyenoord, in the second of their Toronto Cup fixtures. For the Scottish side it was akin to a home fixture, such was the support they had in the Canadian city. The Scottish expats on the terracing were, however, quickly silenced, as after seven minutes of play Morgan nudged a corner to the feet of John Aston and the winger's cross was met by Best, who in turn sent a tremendous left-footed drive towards the Celtic goal. Billy McNeil managed to get his head to the ball, but only succeeded in helping it past his own goalkeeper.

Compared to the two previous fixtures, play was fast and furious, much to the enjoyment of the crowd, but it lacked what they had really paid to see – goals.

Celtic enjoyed most of the second-half play, but failed to produce a clear scoring opportunity and were subsequently punished for this 15 minutes from time, when a six-man move ended with Aston scoring United's second goal. Paul Edwards began the move in his own penalty area, pushing the ball to Crerand, who in turn exchanged passes with Sartori. The ginger-haired Italian-born player then passed to Best, who moved forward, leaving two defenders in his wake before sending Morgan scurrying down the wing. Upon reaching the byline the winger cut the ball back into the path of the oncoming Aston, who beat Williams from 15 yards.

The final 10 minutes of the game was all Celtic, but the defensive combination of James and Ure kept them at bay to ensure that the Toronto Cup was packed away for the journey back across the Atlantic to Manchester.

11 May 1970	Celtic at Varsity Stadium, Toronto.

Attendance: 24,466.

Won: 2–0.

Scorers: Aston, opp. own-goal.

Team: Rimmer, Edwards, Dunne, Crerand, Ure, James, Morgan, Sartori, Fitzpatrick, Aston, Best.

The programme for the match versus Glasgow Celtic, 11 May 1970.

Before United headed for home there were two further fixtures to fulfil, against the German side Eintracht Frankfurt in San Francisco and Los Angeles.

The first half of the first match was a rather featureless affair, with both teams quite happy to play defensive football, despite the game being nothing more than a friendly, but after the interval George Best turned on a sparkling display as he opened the scoring a minute after the restart. While lying on the ground Sartori managed to hook a long ball towards Best, who moved forward before sending a 20-yard shot past a helpless Kunter.

The goal seemed to unshackle the play of both sides, perhaps more so the Germans, but Eintracht's attempted fightback was repelled time and time again by Ian Ure in the heart of the United defence.

United went further ahead in the 65th minute, Best dribbling through the German defence on a 40-yard run before slipping the ball to Sartori, whose cross was headed home from close range by Fitzpatrick.

Nine minutes from time Eintracht pulled a goal back when Jusufi crossed from the right and Holzenbein pushed the ball past Connaughton, but by then it was too late for any attempt at a fightback.

---

13 May 1970   **Eintracht Frankfurt at Memorial Coliseum, San Francisco.**

Attendance: 9,485.

Won: 2–1.

Scorers: Best, Fitzpatrick.

Team: Connaughton, Edwards, Dunne, Crerand, Ure, Burns, Young, Sartori, Fitzpatrick, Best, Whelan.

It is perhaps ironic that it was in the final game of the tour that United had their first taste of defeat, losing to Eintracht 3–2 in a game that was to conjure up one of the most bizarre substitutions in the history of Manchester United Football Club.

United took an early two-goal lead, with strikes from Best and Fitzpatrick, the latter having had an immensely enjoyable tour after being placed in an attacking role. However, despite some fine saves by Jimmy Rimmer, the Germans not only levelled the scoring with goals from Nicket and Kalb before the interval, but also took a 3–2 lead with a second half penalty from Huberts.

As for the aforementioned substitution, it involved Francis Burns, who was replaced by Steve James in the 33rd minute. Burns then returned to the fray in the 46th minute, coming on for Paul Edwards. In the 70th minute he was again taken off and replaced by Willie Watson, but he only had time to sit down and have a quick drink before coming back onto the field to replace Pat Crerand in the 80th minute. Perhaps surprisingly, he managed to play out the remaining 10 minutes.

---

17 May 1970   **Eintracht Frankfurt at Los Angeles.**

Attendance: 12,733.

Lost: 3–2.

Scorers: Fitzpatrick, Best.

Team: Rimmer, Edwards, Dunne, Crerand, Ure, Burns, Morgan, Sartori, Fitzpatrick, Aston, Best.

Substitutes: James for Burns, Burns for Edwards, Young for Morgan, Watson for Burns, Burns for Crerand, Morgan for Young.

The United players had only a matter of weeks in which to enjoy a break away from the game before having to report back for pre-season training. Much to their relief, however, they were not required to repack their bags, as the warm-up games took on the format of the Watney Cup, a competition which saw the top-scoring sides in the Football League up against each other. Perhaps a trip abroad would have been of greater advantage, and certainly less embarrassing than the new Cup competition, as in their first game United struggled to defeat Reading 3–2.

Managed by former United amateur Jack Mansell, Reading often drew United out of position and at times the visitors leant heavily on Alex Stepney to survive.

Falling behind after a diving header from Paul Edwards, following a Dunne free-kick in the 12th minute, Reading immediately got back into the game, with Habbin squeezing the ball past Stepney at the second attempt two minutes later.

A challenge on Kidd saw the ball break to Charlton, whose shot cannoned off the bar before crossing the line. Charlton made it 3–1 soon afterwards with a low drive as United slowly gained the upper hand.

Death, in the Reading goal, kept the scoreline down and, although they pulled a goal back in the 61st minute, the Third Division side could not manage the extra that was required to draw level and snatch the advantage.

1 August 1970	**Reading at Elm Park, Reading.**

Attendance: 18,348.

Won: 3–2.

Scorers: Charlton 2, Edwards.

Team: Stepney, Edwards, Dunne, Crerand, Ure, Sadler, Morgan, Law, Charlton, Kidd, Best.

Substitute: Fitzpatrick for Law.

In what was effectively the semi-final, United were again pushed to their limit at Boothferry Park against Hull City, falling behind to an 11th-minute Chilton goal as Sadler only half-cleared a Butler cross.

Law equalised in the 78th minute with a goal that took the tie into extra-time and ultimately penalty-kicks. Spot-kicks by Best, Kidd and Charlton were matched by player-manager Neill, Butler and Houghton, but then Law saw his kick saved by McKechnie. Wagstaff failed to gain the advantage for Hull by shooting wide, with Morgan then making it 4–3 to United. Everything then depended on McKechnie converting his kick, but the 'keeper could only watch as his shot struck the bar and went over.

5 August 1970	**Hull City at Boothferry Park, Hull.**

Attendance: 34,007.

Drew: 1–1 (after extra-time). **Won:** 5–4 after penalties.

Scorers: Law (Best, Kidd, Charlton, Morgan).

Team: Stepney, Edwards, Dunne, Crerand, Ure, Sadler, Morgan, Law, Charlton, Kidd, Best.

Substitute: Stiles for Dunne.

In the final against Derby County United were left struggling after Law went off injured in the 22nd minute. An uncertain and unimaginative performance, particularly in defence and midfield, saw the trophy remain at the Baseball

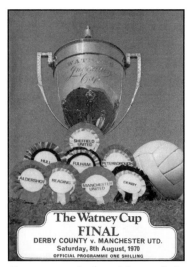

The programme for the match versus Derby County, 8 August 1970.

Ground as Derby won 4–1 and were the first team to have their name engraved upon it.

Derby opened the scoring in the 19th minute through McFarland and, after the departure of Law, added two more before the interval through Durban and Hinton in the 23rd and 35th minutes respectively. George Best pulled a goal back for United two minutes before Hinton's astute back-heeled goal, but it would prove to be little more than a consolation.

Crerand and Charlton were often caught in possession as Derby continued to dominate and, by the time Dave Mackay drove a free-kick through a non-existent defensive wall, it was all over as a contest.

8 August 1970	**Derby County at the Baseball Ground, Derby.**

Attendance: 32,049.

Lost: 4–1.

Scorer: Best.

Team: Stepney, Edwards, Dunne, Crerand, Ure, Sadler, Morgan, Law, Charlton, Kidd, Best.

Substitutes: Stiles for Morgan, Fitzpatrick for Law.

It was not until November 1970 that the first friendly of the season took place, a visit to Old Trafford by near neighbours Manchester City.

However, the first 'derby' of the season was not just some ordinary run-of-the-mill friendly, it was instead an opportunity for the United support to salute one of the club's most loyal servants, Bill Foulkes. The St Helens-born defender had seen 20 years of triumph and tragedy with the club. During that time he had earned one England international cap, helped United to the European Cup triumph in 1968 after scoring the all-important goal in the Madrid semi-final, while also being involved in the horrors of the Munich air disaster some 10 years earlier.

Sadly, the weather on the night of the game was what many expect of Manchester and the rain, unfortunately, had an affect on the crowd, with only 26,161 turning up, an attendance which generated a sum of around £10,000 for the stalwart defender.

Depleted by injury and international call-ups, which deprived them of the likes of Best, Law and Kidd, United had eight reserves in their line up and, against a determined City side, they were never able to give Foulkes the send-off he deserved.

City took the lead through Hill with only 60 seconds gone and it was a blow from which United never recovered. Crerand, missing from the first team since the end of August, did little to prove that he was worthy of a recall, while Sartori, a player of potential, was another who failed in his chance to regain a place in the starting line up on a regular basis.

Towers added a second for City prior to half-time and, in a second half which dragged, Mike Doyle took great pleasure in scoring a third from the penalty spot after Fitzpatrick brought down Bell.

10 November 1970	**Manchester City at Old Trafford.**

Attendance: 26,161.

Lost: 3–0.

Team: Stepney, Watson, Burns, Crerand, James, Fitzpatrick, Morgan, Sartori, Charlton, Gowling, Aston.

Substitutes: T. Young for Crerand, E. Young for Morgan.

Having lost to Aston Villa, then a Third Division side, 3–2 on aggregate in the semi-final of the Football League Cup, the knives were out for manager Wilf McGuinness, as United had failed to win any of their four First Division fixtures prior to the 1–1 first leg at Old Trafford. They fared little better in their next outing, a 3–1 home defeat by Arsenal, before the disastrous 2–1 defeat in the second leg at Villa Park.

Three days later a 4–4 Boxing Day thriller at the Baseball Ground, Derby, was not enough to keep the man who had been chief coach for 14 months and manager for only four months and 27 days in a job, as the *Manchester Evening News* of Tuesday 29 December proclaimed 'United Sack McGuinness'.

Back to the helm, rather reluctantly, came Sir Matt Busby and, as he had done many years previously, he realised that the team he had built up was getting past its best, and the way ahead was now once again in the hands of the younger players at the club.

A woeful display against Middlesbrough in an FA Cup third round replay at Ayresome Park saw United crash out of the competition 2–1 and, with the prospect of a blank Saturday on the horizon, Sir Matt decided that it would do little harm to organise a friendly, selecting Bohemians as the ideal opposition, where he could run his eye over some of the promising reserve-team players.

During lean times at Old Trafford, any victory was welcome and, against an Irish side who could offer nothing but enthusiasm, the two-goal victory was treated as more than satisfactory.

In the opening 45 minutes United plodded away with little reward and it was not until the 42nd minute that they managed to breach the resolute home defence. Brian Kidd headed home a Sartori cross as the latter made the most of a defensive error.

After the interval Busby made three substitutions, throwing teenagers Tony Young, Eric Young and Sammy McIlroy into the fray. The latter, a 16-year-old from Belfast, wasted little time in making an impression and pounced on a wayward pass by Martin in the 59th minute before running through a gap in the Bohemians defence, drawing goalkeeper Smyth off his line and slipping the ball neatly into the back of the net from 12 yards.

21 January 1971	**Bohemians at Dalymount Park, Dublin.**

Attendance: 30,000.

Won: 2–0.

Scorers: Kidd, McIlroy.

Team: Stepney, Fitzpatrick, Dunne, Crerand, Edwards, Sadler, Morgan, Sartori, Charlton, Kidd, Aston.

Substitutes: Burns for Dunne, T. Young for Sartori, E. Young for Morgan, McIlroy for Aston.

The performance of Sammy McIlroy against Bohemians warmed the heart of Sir Matt Busby and the United manager went as far as to say that his latest starlet was already showing the class and skill of a certain George Best, whose waywardness was already beginning to bring much unneeded attention to the Irishman and the club itself. However, the return of his mentor to the position of manager rekindled the old fire and crowds around the country were once again treated to those silky skills that mesmerised defenders.

One such fixture, against struggling Second Division side Blackburn Rovers towards the end of March, produced Ewood Park's biggest gate of the season, with

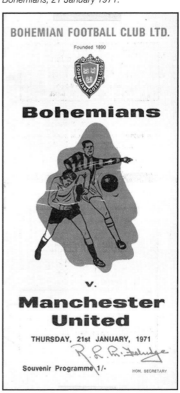

The programme for the match versus Bohemians, 21 January 1971.

The programme for the match versus Blackburn Rovers, which was originally arranged for 12 February 1971, but was postponed and played on 22 March 1971.

George Best the obvious draw. He did not disappoint, giving those present plenty to enjoy. The fixture had actually been postponed from earlier in the season and, with United not having played for a fortnight, it was an ideal opportunity to fulfil the fixture and get back into the swing of things.

The first half saw United well in command, but some rather inaccurate shooting, plus a number of fine saves from Blackburn goalkeeper Roger Jones, kept the home side in the game. Blackburn were rather unfortunate not to take the lead early on after Martin chipped a shot against the crossbar.

After the interval, however, it was a completely different game. The crowd came alive in the 59th minute when United opened the scoring in spectacular fashion with a goal that had George Best's trademark all over it. A centre from Carlo Sartori into the Blackburn penalty area was calmly plucked out of the air with one foot as the Irishman gave Jones no chance at all. The goal broke the ice for United and they settled down to run the game as they pleased, with 19-year-old debutant, Dublin-born Damien Ferguson, on in place of Bobby Charlton, making a major contribution to the game.

Jones pulled off an amazing double save from Best and Kidd as United pushed forward, but it was not long before they increased their lead, John Aston calmly dribbling round two defenders and the goalkeeper.

Rimmer, on as a substitute for Stepney, destroyed Blackburn's hopes of any comeback with several notable saves, sending the home support away with a painful reminder of the difference in class between the two sides.

22 March 1971	**Blackburn Rovers at Ewood Park.**

Attendance: 11,685.

Won: 2–0.

Scorers: Best, Aston.

Team: Stepney, Fitzpatrick, Burns, Crerand, Edwards, Sadler, Morgan, Kidd, Charlton, Givens, Best.

Substitutes: Stiles for Crerand, Ferguson for Charlton, Rimmer for Stepney.

Having finished the season in eighth position, 22 points behind Champions Arsenal, the United players headed off for a three-match tour of Austria and Switzerland. Sir Matt Busby had since bowed out following a memorable 4–3 victory at Maine Road in the final match of the campaign.

The first stop was Klagenfurt for a game against the local non-League side, who rather surprisingly kept their visitors well under control until the final 20 minutes. Perhaps out of politeness United did little more than go through the motions.

Five minutes after the interval United thought they had finally broken the deadlock when Brian Kidd forced the ball home after Bobby Charlton had seen his 20-yard drive saved by Medanhodzic, only for it to be disallowed for offside.

Twenty minutes later United eventually went in front, Best scoring from the penalty spot after he had been sent through by Charlton, only to be rather unceremoniously bundled off the ball by Stemberga, with Kidd also sent crashing to the ground in the goalmouth mêlée. Medanhodzic managed to save the spot-kick, but failed to hold it, with the Irishman making no mistake as he followed through.

Kidd scored a second from 25 yards in the 85th minute and three minutes later Denis Law completed the scoring from a Charlton pass.

25 May 1971	Klagenfurt.

Attendance: Unknown

Won: 3–0.

Scorers: Best (pen.), Kidd, Law.

Team: Stepney, Watson, Burns, Crerand, Edwards, Sadler, Law, Gowling, Charlton, Kidd, Best.

The programme for the match versus Styrian Provin, 28 May 1971.

Moving on to Graz, where they took on a Styrian Provin side, United repeated their 3–0 success, outclassing their willing opponents. Despite setting up a couple of early opportunities, the Austrians were always second best in a match which was organised to celebrate the 60th anniversary of the Styrian Football Association.

A defensive blunder in the 31st minute presented Sartori with the first goal, with the Italian-born player notching up the second in the 68th minute following a dazzling solo run by George Best. The third was scored by Charlton 10 minutes from time.

28 May 1971	Styrian Provin at Graz.

Attendance: 8,000.

Won: 3–0.

Scorers: Sartori 2, Charlton.

Team: Rimmer, Watson, Burns, Sartori, Ure, Sadler, Law, Morgan, Charlton, Best, Aston.

Three days later United wound up their whirlwind tour in Switzerland against Zurich Grasshoppers, a game that was played at exhibition pace with neither side breaking sweat.

Brian Kidd opened the scoring after only nine minutes and 16 minutes later George Best, having coaxed two defenders into making attempts to tackle him, outfoxed them both before shooting from the edge of the penalty area to make it 2–0.

Grahn, the home side's best player, gave the crowd plenty to shout about with two goals either side of half-time, but his efforts were soon cancelled out when Gowling scored United's third in the 56th minute.

An opportunity for the Swiss Champions elect to once again draw level was squandered when Clitherlet hit a penalty against the United crossbar, with another shot also rattling the woodwork as United hung on to preserve their unbeaten record.

The programme for the match versus Zurich Grasshoppers, 1 June 1971.

1 June 1971	Zurich Grasshoppers at Hardtrum Stadium, Zurich.

Attendance: 6,500.

Won: 3–2.

Scorers: Kidd, Best, Gowling.

Team: Stepney, Watson, Burns, Crerand, Edwards, Sadler, Law, Gowling, Charlton, Kidd, Best.

In their search for a replacement manager the Manchester United directors turned to Frank O'Farrell, a softly spoken Irishman, who had made a big impression during his two years at Leicester City, having learned the managerial trade at his two previous clubs, Torquay and Weymouth.

His Old Trafford career, however, did not get off to the best of starts, with a demoralising defeat at the hands of Halifax Town in the Watney Cup, the Third Division side winning 2–1.

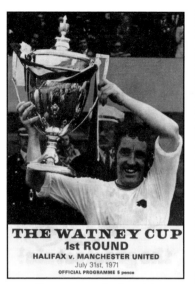

The programme for the match versus Halifax, 31 July 1971.

As in the previous season's competition, fingers were pointed at the mid field duo of Charlton and Crerand and after the Halifax centre-forward Dave Chadwick rose unchallenged to head home the opening goal as early as the third minute the home side never looked back. Even if Morgan had converted a 24th-minute penalty it is still unlikely that United would have secured a victory.

One minute after that penalty miss it was 2–0, Wallace showing Morgan how a penalty kick should be taken following Sadler's trip on Robertson.

Best converted the game's third penalty eight minutes from the end, but there was no way back for the shamefaced United.

31 July 1971	**Halifax Town at The Shay, Halifax.**

Attendance: 19,765.

Lost: 2–1.

Scorer: Best (pen.).

Team: Stepney, Fitzpatrick, Dunne, Crerand, James, Sadler, Morgan, Gowling, Charlton, Law, Best.

Substitutes: Burns for Crerand, Kidd for Gowling.

Four days later, however, O'Farrell got that important first victory under his belt with a 2–0 win against Luton Town.

With former United players Don Givens and Jimmy Ryan in their line up, Luton, well aware of what lowly Halifax had managed to achieve, were keen to add further turmoil to Frank O'Farrell's early days in the United hot seat. Much to their disappointment, however, United were not going to slip up twice in a row and gave Luton few scoring opportunities during the 90 minutes.

Taking command from the start, United did enough to ensure victory without overdoing things. Alan Gowling gave them the lead, stabbing the ball home after good work by Charlton, Best and Law.

In the 31st minute of a game completely devoid of any atmosphere Gowling almost made it 2–0, but his shot hit the post. His luck continued to run unkindly when another goal-bound header, from a Best corner, was prodded over the line by Denis Law.

4 August 1971	**Luton Town at Kenilworth Road.**

Attendance: 16,397.

Won: 2–0.

Scorers: Gowling, Law.

Team: Stepney, Fitzpatrick, Burns, Crerand, James, Sadler, Morgan, Gowling, Charlton, Law, Best.

Substitute: Aston for Morgan.

The programme for the match versus Luton Town, 4 August 1971.

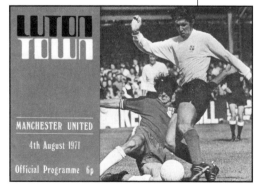

For reasons unknown, United's pre-season preparations were confined to home shores and, three days after the visit to Luton, they travelled to Craven Cottage to face Fulham. The overhead thunderstorms may well have been an early warning to the new United manager of what lay ahead.

Second Division newcomers Fulham added to O'Farrell's woes as they became the second lower grade opposition to defeat his new charges.

Even without their two main strikers, Earle and Conway, Fulham were always a threat to their guests. Playing 4–3–3, with Morgan in a midfield role rather than his more familiar position out on the wing, United struggled, with too many players having an off day.

Fulham's goals both came from winger Les Barrett, reportedly a one-time United target, with his first coming five minutes after the interval following an unchallenged run. His second, in the 73rd minute, followed a fine build-up and pass by Halom.

With the game not going their way, a number of United players let their frustration show, with Brian Kidd and the rather inconspicuous George Best the main culprits. The former became involved in a flare-up with Halom, while Best, had it been a League game, would probably have been sent off. Callaghan had continuously irritated Best by tugging on his shirt, but when Matthewson pushed the ball into the Irishman's face, there was a distinct threat of retaliation, resulting in the exchanging of punches amid a minor bout of pushing and shoving. The referee, however, decided to treat the incident in the same context as the match itself and, following a brief lecture, it was handshakes all round.

Best was later to get some recompense when he scored United's only goal, a well-taken effort from a Morgan cross.

The programme for the match versus Fulham, 7 August 1971.

7 August 1971	Fulham at Craven Cottage.

Attendance: 14,078.

Lost: 2−1.

Scorer: Best.

Team: Stepney, O'Neil, Burns, Morgan, James, Sadler, Law, Gowling, Charlton, Kidd, Best.

Substitute: Aston for Gowling.

The third of Frank O'Farrell's pre-season friendlies was something of a rarity, as it was played at Old Trafford. For those who did not follow United away from home it was their only opportunity to see their favourites before 4 September, as United had been ordered by the Football Association's Disciplinary Committee to play their first two First Division home fixtures away from Manchester following a knife-throwing incident during a game against Newcastle United the previous season.

The pre-season performances by O'Farrell's team were worrying enough, without the added problems of having to play six away games on the trot, but, it was hoped that the visit of Coventry City to Old Trafford would give the players the opportunity to improve on their form to date.

As it was, Coventry played a rather cautious game, allowing United to restore some of that lost confidence and offering their dubious support a little confidence for the rough road ahead.

The match was not without its moments of worry, however, as the visitors took the lead in the 19th minute, with a goal from Ernie Hunt. After that initial thrust their early enterprise faded and they appeared to lose all interest in the game, content to sit back and hope that they would manage to contain United. This was a rather misguided idea, as they were soon overrun in midfield, with Gowling excelling in an experimental role in that position.

Packing their defence, with seven men at times covering United's three strikers, did not help, as United fought back with a determination rarely seen in any of the earlier fixtures. Goals from Kidd, Law and Best secured a much-needed victory.

9 August 1971 Coventry City at Old Trafford.

Attendance: 14,589.

Won: 3–1.

Scorers: Law, Kidd, Best.

Team: Stepney, O'Neil, Dunne, Gowling, James, Sadler, Morgan, Law, Charlton, Kidd, Best.

A three-day break on the island of Jersey saw United take on local side St Ouens, who were supplemented by Jimmy Rimmer, Willie Watson, Ian Ure and Ian Donald, all United players, plus former Blackburn, Stoke and Everton favourite Roy Vernon and Romford's Dave Bickles.

The 11,000 crowd – the biggest attendance for a game on the island for 21 years – were kept on their toes with a couple of early attacks, but United settled quickly into a smooth passing unit, with Best an obvious favourite with the islanders, and it took them only 10 minutes to take the lead.

A free-kick near to the edge of the St Ouens penalty area saw Law casually flick the ball sideways to Kidd, who hit the ball low, just inside the post. Shortly afterwards a quick juggling act on the wing by the Irishman was followed by a cross into the centre for Law, but his shot was blazed just off target.

The blond head of Ure stood out in the home defence, with Rimmer foiling his United teammates on several occasions with smart saves, but United were happy to keep the pace at a relaxed level and to exhibit skill rather than showing any real finishing power.

The programme for the match versus Coventry City, 9 August 1971.

Six minutes prior to half-time the ground vibrated to the biggest cheer of the evening when George Best satisfied his admirers with a goal. From the left Kidd crossed to Charlton on the opposite side of the pitch, and he lofted the ball high into the goalmouth for Best to head in from close range with a neat flick.

At the interval the home side made numerous changes, but they were to no avail, despite United leaving Law and Best in the dressing room, much to the disappointment of the crowd. United simply picked up where they had left off and in the 61st minute they scored a third. Gowling drove the ball towards goal, where Rimmer could only parry it out and into the path of the alert Kidd. Before the 'keeper could react the ball was in the back of the net.

Charlton fired an effort narrowly past the post as United, rather surprisingly, stepped up the pace and, minutes after Rimmer was replaced in the home goal by Breuilly, United increased their lead to 4–0, Kidd completing his hat-trick.

30 November 1971	St Ouens at Springfield Stadium, Jersey.

Attendance: 11,112.

Won: 4–0.

Scorers: Kidd 3, Best.

Team: Stepney, O'Neil, Burns, Gowling, James, Sadler, Morgan, Kidd, Charlton, Law, Best.

Substitutes: Sartori for Law, Aston for Best.

At the end of yet another disappointing season for Manchester United, as they finished eighth in the First Division, 10 points behind champions Derby County, they managed to bring the curtain down at Maine Road, providing the opposition in a testimonial match for Manchester City's long-serving half-back, Alan Oakes.

On a cold, wet evening, just over 30,000 supporters paid £11,789, a fine reward for the loyal City man, who had made over 500 senior appearances during a 14-year career. However, it was those of the red persuasion who went home happy, with United winning 3–1.

In the opening minutes it was City who were in command, with Marsh and Bell celebrating their England call-ups with some neat touches and, truth be told, they should have gone in at the interval with more than their one-goal advantage.

The goal had come in the 32nd minute, when a Summerbee corner was headed on by Booth and was met on the volley by Marsh, the ball flying past a helpless Stepney.

The game was played at a rather sedate pace, although City continued to keep Stepney the busier of the two goalkeepers. United, however, eventually got the better of the home defence, with Moore pouncing on an attempted clearance by Towers to equalise in the 70th minute. Two minutes later, Best made a rare contribution to the evening, robbing Book of the ball before squaring it across goal for McIlroy to accept an easy scoring opportunity.

Doyle was moved forward by City in order to try to inject some life into their attack, while Marsh brought some joviality to the rather dismal evening when he surged forward towards the United goal while still in the process of changing his shorts. However, as the minutes ticked away, it was United who looked the most likely to score, with Storey-Moore coming close 10 minutes from time.

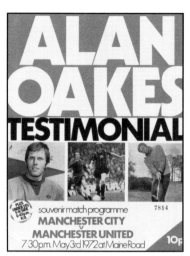

The programme for the match versus Manchester City, 3 May 1972.

3 May 1972 **Manchester City at Maine Road.**

Attendance: 30,429.

Won: 3–1.

Scorers: Storey-Moore 2, McIlroy.

Team: Stepney, O'Neil, Dunne, Buchan, James, Sadler, T. Young, Kidd, Law, Best, Storey-Moore.

Substitutes: E. Young for Morgan, McIlroy for Kidd.

If the United party who flew out of Manchester Airport thought that they were heading for a trio of leisurely paced games abroad then they were wrong, as the matches turned out to be the exact opposite of what friendly fixtures should be.

In the first of the three games, against Mallorca, the local newspaper described the 90 minutes as 'almost an all out battle', with three players sent off, one of them United's Tony Young, who received his marching orders as early as the 36th minute following an incident with Munoz, who was also sent to the dressing room. Referee Boras also sent off Mallorca's inside-right Reina.

There were many British holidaymakers in the 20,000 crowd who thought they were in for a United victory when Morgan opened the scoring in the second minute from the penalty spot. However, United could not make their vacation that little bit more enjoyable, as they were held to a 1–1 draw, Moya equalising seven minutes later.

18 May 1972 **Mallorca at Luis Si-Jar Stadium.**

Attendance: 20,000.

Drew: 1–1.

Scorer: Morgan (pen.).

Team: Stepney, O'Neil, Dunne, Gowling, James, Sadler, Morgan, Kidd, Charlton, T. Young, Storey-Moore.

Substitute: Morton for Storey-Moore.

Moving from one end of the Mediterranean to the other, the United party continued their tour in the sun with a game against Panathinaikos, managed by the former Real Madrid legend Ferenc Puskas.

Francis Burns had flown out with the United party simply to make up the numbers and any appearances he made in the course of the next two games would be his last for the club, as he had agreed to join Southampton upon his return for a fee of £40,000.

Despite no longer being one of the top teams back home, the visit of United caused a Greek Cup semi-final to be postponed. The game itself saw the visitors emerge with much credit, despite only managing to draw, as they played under immense provocation and intimidation from a home side eager to gain a prestige victory by any means possible.

Making six substitutions, the Greeks regularly kicked out at the United players, who received little protection from a referee with a complete lack of control of the game. John Aston even received a blow to the leg from one of the substitutes sitting on the bench.

If a poor referee was not bad enough, there was an equally poor linesman on one side of the pitch. 'The most biased match official I have ever seen,' proclaimed Matt D'Arcy of the *Manchester Evening News*, 'who persistently halted United attacks with outrageous offside decisions. One, when Ian Moore had four Greeks between him and the goal.'

The home side dominated the first half, although Sadler played well in the United defence, but they had to be content with a draw. United took the lead in the 52nd minute when Moore created the opening for Kidd. Centre-forward Antoniandis equalised in the 76th minute.

---

24 May 1972   **Panathinaikos at Apolstolos Nikolaidis Stadium, Athens.**

Attendance: 23,000.

Drew: 1—1.

Scorer: Kidd.

Team: Connaughton, O'Neil, Dunne, Sadler, James, T. Young, Morgan, Kidd, Charlton, Storey-Moore, Aston.

Substitute: Burns for Charlton.

The next stop was Israel and Hapoel, with Frank O'Farrell suffering a minor problem with his team selection when Sammy McIlroy failed to show up due to his father being ill.

Against the lesser opposition United won by the odd goal in three, although they enjoyed much more of the game than the scoreline suggests, with the match producing something of a boom in black market tickets, despite it being shown live on television and being broadcast on the radio.

Prior to kick-off the players ran to the touchline to hand out bouquets of flowers to the crowd and, as the game got underway, it took United only eight minutes to open the scoring. Brian Kidd collected the ball from Sadler with his back to goal and scored with an excellent overhead kick. Sadler himself notched United's second, driving home a powerful shot following good work by Kidd and Charlton.

Hazum hit the crossbar for the Select in the first half, but their chances were few and far between, although the same player did manage to pull a goal back in the 61st minute.

---

30 May 1972   **Maccabi-Hapoel XI at Bloomfield Stadium, Jaffa.**

Attendance: 22,000.

Won: 2—1.

Scorers: Sadler, Kidd.

Team: Stepney, O'Neil, Dunne, Buchan, James, Sadler, Morgan, Kidd, Charlton, Law, Storey-Moore.

Substitutes: Gowling for Charlton, Burns for Sadler.

For a second consecutive summer, United's pre-season preparations began at home, travelling down to the south coast for a couple of holiday resort fixtures, the first of the two coming at Torquay.

Frank O'Farrell's initial line up showed only a couple of changes to the one that had finished the previous campaign, with Tony Young taking over from David Sadler and Brian Kidd replacing George Best, but there was little difference in the overall play, with the 0–0 draw doing little to appease the United support.

Denis Law did have a couple of opportunities to gain United the victory, while Kidd brought the best out of Torquay goalkeeper Payne with a ferocious drive, although Ian Storey-Moore was the only United player who gave the travelling support anything to look forward to in the weeks and months ahead.

The programme for the match versus Torquay United, 29 July 1972.

29 July 1972   **Torquay United at Plainmoor.**

Attendance: 17,000.

Drew: 0–0.

Team: Stepney, O'Neil, Dunne, Buchan, James, T. Young, Morgan, Kidd, Charlton, Law, Storey-Moore.

Two days later, any hopes that the goalless draw at Torquay was something of a false start and that the season would get underway at Bournemouth were proved totally unfounded, as the Dean Court club stunned United with a 3–1 victory.

Neither was there any summer sun, as the day of the match brought torrential rain, but the heavy pitch proved to be a surface better suited to the Bournemouth pairing of MacDougall and Boyer, as the United defence were to struggle on the sodden pitch.

The double strike-force proved to be a real thorn in United's side, with MacDougall unfortunate not to have scored twice before he finally put Bournemouth in front in the 42nd minute. Sainty sent Chadwick away down the right and, after the winger had eluded two defenders, he put over a cross which the unmarked MacDougall had little trouble heading past Rimmer.

Within a minute United were back on level terms. As Charlton moved into the penalty area, he was nudged in the back by Powell and, to the surprise of the majority of the crowd and the Bournemouth players, the referee pointed to the spot, Charlton himself scoring the goal.

The disappointment of conceding the disputed penalty did not last for long, as five minutes into the second half Bournemouth regained the lead. Under pressure from Cave, Buchan tried to cut out a high ball into the United area, but he failed to make proper contact with the ball and it skimmed off his head and past Stepney, a half-time replacement for Rimmer, into the top right-hand corner.

Unselfish work by Morgan and some neat touches from Eric Young gave United some inspiration, but Bournemouth goalkeeper Davies was equal to anything that came his way. Two saves in particular brought warm applause, a block with his legs from a Kidd effort and a superb save from a curling shot-cum-cross from McIlroy.

Despite the attempted fightback, the result was put beyond any doubt nine minutes from time when Cave raced down the left, beating O'Neil, to watch as MacDougall slid in to steer his cross past Stepney.

The programme for the match versus Bournemouth, 31 July 1972.

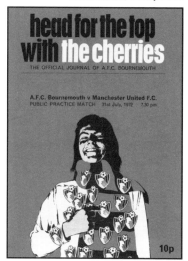

31 July 1972   **Bournemouth at Dean Court.**

Attendance: 16,934.

Lost: 3–1.

Scorer: Charlton (pen.).

Team: Rimmer, Donald, Dunne, Buchan, James, E. Young, Morgan, Kidd, Charlton, Law, McIlroy.

Substitutes: Stepney for Rimmer, O'Neil for Dunne, T. Young for Charlton.

Fortunately, Frank O'Farrell had a couple more friendlies arranged before the League programme got underway, allowing him the opportunity to decide on tactics and playing personnel for the coming season. This time he was away from the close scrutiny of the majority of the United support and the British press, with the games taking place on the Continent against a West Berlin XI and the Danish Olympic XI.

As it turned out, United finally put their woeful start behind them and recorded their first victory, although they certainly had to work hard for it. Morgan, again employed in midfield, had an inspiring game, but it was mainly due to the fine performance from goalkeeper Jimmy Rimmer that victory was achieved.

A Morgan-Kidd move in the second minute carved out the opening goal, with the former, in his more familiar position, accurately crossing for Kidd to sweep home. However, there was to be no building on this advantage, as United soon found themselves reeling from a double strike by Bertelsen and Simonsen.

Seven minutes from half-time the scores were level. Morgan, once again moving forward, found Buchan, another who had forsaken his position, who headed home.

The second half was 11 minutes old when United scored what was to turn out to be the winner. Morgan crossed the ball into the Danes' penalty area, where Law headed the ball down to Kidd to fire home the winner.

The programme for the match versus the Danish Olympic XI, 2 August 1972.

2 August 1972	**Danish Olympic XI at Copenhagen.**

Attendance: 20,000.

Won: 3–2.

Scorers: Kidd 2, Buchan.

Team: Rimmer, O'Neil, Dunne, Buchan, James, Sadler, Morgan, Kidd, Charlton, Law, McIlroy.

Substitutes: Sartori for Morgan, T. Young for Charlton, McIlroy for Law, Storey-Moore for McIlroy.

The final match of the tour produced a more polished performance than any of the previous three fixtures, with United opening strongly against the West Berlin XI.

In the ninth minute, United's efforts were finally rewarded when Tony Young pushed forward in a defence-splitting move which ended in the youngster scoring his first senior goal.

Morgan was once again a major threat to the opposition, although, at the opposite end, Stepney also had to be alert to save from Hermanduug. Horr hit the side netting as the Germans fought back with determination, while Walleitnet was also denied by the United goalkeeper.

After the interval, with Law off with an ankle injury and the Germans also making a couple of changes, United began to take control. Morgan's centre saw McIlroy create a chance for Storey-Moore, but Wolter saved brilliantly. Young shot wide, and the missed opportunities were soon regretted, as a breakaway in the 62nd minute saw Buchan clip the heels of Horr inside the penalty area, leaving the referee no alternative but to point to the spot. The German forward picked himself up and smashed the penalty past Stepney.

With 21 minutes left Dunne pulled the ball back into the path of the on-running Charlton, who met the ball to fire a tremendous shot past the replacement German 'keeper Grundenberg from the edge of the box.

The advantage was only to be held for three minutes, as once again the Germans drew level. Horr, who had tormented Buchan throughout the game, beat the United defender on the edge of the area before striking the ball just inside the post to earn a draw.

75 Jahre
Verband Berliner
Ballspiel-Vereine
e.V.

Internationale
Jubiläums-
Veranstaltung

AMATEUR-VORSPIEL

Manchester
United –
Berliner Stadt-
Auswahl

NIEDERBAYERN-BERLIN

5. August 1972
15.30 Uhr
Olympiastadion

The programme for the match versus West Berlin, 5 August 1972.

| 5 August 1972 | West Berlin at Olympic Stadium. |

Attendance: 10,000.

Drew: 2–2.

Scorers: T. Young, Charlton.

Team: Stepney, O'Neil, Dunne, Buchan, James, T. Young, Morgan, Kidd, Charlton, Law, Storey-Moore.

Substitutes: E. Young for Morgan, McIlroy for Law.

Bobby Charlton's playing career had begun back in 1956 and almost 16 years later a packed Old Trafford, setting a British record attendance for a testimonial match, acknowledged his contribution to not only Manchester United but also to England and football in general.

Testimonials can often be frivolous affairs, turning into pantomime at any given moment, but the visit of Celtic to Old Trafford saw a highly competitive 90 minutes, with goals the only thing lacking on the night.

Celtic had certainly not travelled south simply to make up the numbers and, backed by a considerable support, they were intent on victory. Deans, Dalglish and Macari were all regular threats to the United defence and all came close to opening the scoring.

Charlton was little more than an onlooker at times during the opening exchanges, but a trademark 40-yard pass in the 18th minute earned the applause of the crowd and found Kidd, who headed the ball forward to Young. The latter's shot, however, was blocked by Murdoch.

Law almost squirmed his way through in the 23rd minute, while new signing Wyn Davies just failed to get his head to a cross, with Charlton scraping the paint off the crossbar 10 minutes later.

Moments prior to the interval, Charlton should have marked his evening with a goal when he ran onto a pass from Davies but, with only the goalkeeper to beat, he crashed the ball into the crowd.

The second half saw Celtic pressing forward with a little more regularity, Macari sneaking through the United defence only to rush his shot. The United 'keeper had to be equally alert to save from Deans in the 57th minute.

With only three minutes remaining, a shot from second-half Celtic substitute Harry Hood looked goal-bound, but Stepney flung himself to pull off a magnificent save and keep the score level.

With the referee's whistle signalling the end of an emotional evening, a handful of schoolboys ran onto the pitch to salute their hero. They scurried along behind Charlton as the United hero lapped the ground to the warm applause of the crowd.

With the crowd gone, Bobby Charlton stood and looked out over an empty Old Trafford and said to journalist James Lawton, 'I felt so moved that I was glad when the game started and it was exactly the sort of game I had hoped it would be.

'It was like the old days in Europe. It was a real football match and this is what delighted me so much. I wanted all those generous people to see a real game and they got it.

'I didn't want there to be any gimmicks or anything like that and when I lapped the pitch at the end, it was a spontaneous gesture.'

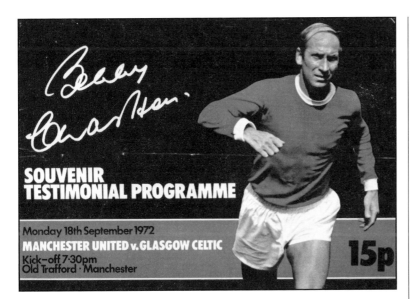

18 September 1972	Celtic at Old Trafford.

Attendance: 60,538.

Drew: 0—0.

Team: Stepney, Donald, Dunne, T. Young, James, Buchan, Morgan, Law, Charlton, Davies, Kidd.

Substitutes: Sartori for Law, McIlroy for Kidd.

The goalless draw ensured that United had still to win a game since season 1972–73 had got underway, and by the time their next friendly came along, with a long haul north to Aberdeen, they had managed only one solitary victory, against Birmingham City at home. They had even been unceremoniously dumped out of the League Cup by Bristol Rovers after losing 2–1 at Old Trafford.

Why manager Frank O'Farrell wanted to play so many friendlies so early in the season was a mystery, especially with League form so poor and any injuries received adding to the already mounting pressure that he was finding himself under.

In the north-east of Scotland nothing changed, with centre-half Dick Edwards, on trial from Torquay United, having a difficult time and showing little to persuade O'Farrell that he was worth a further outing, never mind a contract.

Despite a goal from recent £200,000 signing Ted MacDougall from Bournemouth in the 15th minute, United went in at the interval 3–1 behind. Harper, Taylor and Mitchell scored for Aberdeen.

A second goal for MacDougall in the 70th minute reduced the deficit, but the Dons quickly regained control and taught the United side a lesson in teamwork and individual skill, emphasising their superiority with further goals from Harper in the 80th minute and Jarvie two minutes later.

23 October 1972	Aberdeen at Pittodrie.

Attendance: 34,000.

Lost: 5—2.

Scorer: MacDougall.

Team: Stepney, Watson, Dunne, T. Young, D. Edwards, Buchan, Morgan, MacDougall, Davies, E. Young, Best.

Substitutes: McIlroy for E. Young.

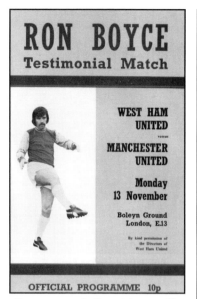

The programme for the match versus West Ham, 13 November 1972.

Another month brought another friendly and more despair for the bedraggled United side as they conceded a further five goals against West Ham United, in a testimonial for their 1964 FA Cup Final hero Ron Boyce.

Very little can be read into the results of friendly or testimonial matches, but victories of any kind inspire confidence and at this particular time, this was something that United certainly lacked. The 5–2 defeat at Upton Park did little to maintain faith in O'Farrell.

The evening produced an entertaining match, with a sparkling display from George Best. However, had it not been for a superb display of goalkeeping, the scoreline could quite easily have been 5–5.

The goals began to flow in the 25th minute, when Tyler sidestepped Paul Edwards to collect Brooking's pass and score from 20 yards. Ten minutes later, Taylor deflected a McIlroy shot past his own goalkeeper for the equaliser. Five minutes before the interval West Ham again took the lead, Robson putting Tyler through for his second.

There was no scoring in the second half until the 61st minute when the Hammers increased their lead through Robson, after Brooking's cross-field pass split the United defence. Nine minutes later Brooking was again in the thick of things, robbing George Best before interchanging passes with Robson and scoring.

United had no answer to the slick passing of the West Ham side and went further behind in the 81st minute. Tyler split the United defence to send Lampard clear on the left, with his cross giving Robson the opportunity to score.

Three minutes from time Kidd, with a glancing header, added a second for United to round off the evening.

13 November 1972	West Ham United at Upton Park.

Attendance: 19,000.

Lost: 5–2.

Scorers: McIlroy, Kidd.

Team: Stepney, O'Neil, P. Edwards, T. Young, James, Sadler, Best, MacDougall, Charlton, McIlroy, Storey-Moore.

Substitutes: Rimmer for Stepney, Kidd for Storey-Moore, E. Young for T. Young.

Conceding five goals in two consecutive friendlies was all very well, but a 5–0 defeat at Crystal Palace on 16 December, leaving United one place from bottom in the First Division, signalled the end of Frank O'Farrell's reign as manager.

It came as no surprise that a new manager was installed in the Old Trafford hot seat almost immediately, with the wise-cracking Tommy Docherty walking out on the Scottish national side to take over the reins.

The controversial Scot wasted little time in bringing in players with whom he was familiar and, needless to say, shared the same nationality, two of whom were in place when the United team ran out at Old Trafford for a hastily arranged fixture against one of Docherty's former clubs, Hull City. Into the side came Alex Forsyth, a full-back signed from Partick Thistle, and midfielder George Graham, with two of O'Farrell's signings, Wyn Davies and Ted MacDougall, nowhere to be seen.

United survived an early scare when Pearson, with only Stepney between him and the goal, managed to run the ball out of play, but they soon settled down although they failed to show much in the way of inspiration.

Despite the relaxed pace, Hull always looked dangerous, but it was United who took the lead on the half-hour mark. McKechnie in the Hull goal had managed to keep a Storey-Moore effort out, but he could not prevent Law from opening the scoring, following a move involving Graham and Kidd. Four minutes later it was 2–0, Morgan working his way to the goalline before pulling the ball back to Charlton to score with a hard, low shot after Law had missed the ball.

Hull, to their credit, managed to pull a goal back just before the interval, Wagstaff deflecting a free-kick by player-manager Terry Neill into the net.

In the second half there were opportunities at both ends. Law went close for United and Forsyth cleared off the line from Greenwood, while substitute McIlroy missed a trio of chances, one with only the 'keeper to beat.

As United lost interest, Hull pressed for the equaliser and the minutes and spectators drifted away together.

The programme for the match versus Hull City, 30 December 1972.

30 December 1972	**Hull City at Old Trafford.**

Attendance: 24,103.

Won: 2–1.

Scorers: Charlton, Law.

Team: Stepney, T. Young, Forsyth, Graham, Sadler, Buchan, Morgan, Kidd, Charlton, Law, Storey-Moore.

Substitutes: McIlroy for Storey-Moore.

Although he took over in December 1972, it was not until 1 February 1973 that the Doc managed to record his first victory, and even then it was little more than a 3–1 success against Bohemians in Dublin.

The home side hustled United into early mistakes, but slowly the superior fitness and depth of experience began to tell and the Bohemians side were soon penned back in their own half. Morgan threatened down the flanks, with Mick Martin, back on home territory, toiling away in midfield. A goal by Macari chasing Holton's long ball gave United the lead in the 13th minute but, despite the wealth of talent within the United ranks, it was the little-known Peter Fletcher who grabbed the headlines.

Brought on as a half-time replacement for MacDougall, Fletcher required only three minutes in which to make his mark, scoring with a perfectly placed shot from 20 yards. With the home side beginning to crumble under the almost constant pressure he scored a second in the 57th minute after Davis could only parry a shot from Law.

Gerry Daly managed to pull a goal back for Bohemians with a well-taken effort, but any thoughts of a fightback were laid to rest in the 85th minute, when the referee took both sides off the field following a pitch invasion by over-enthusiastic youngsters, thereby bringing a premature end to the game.

The programme for the match versus Bohemians, 1 February 1973.

1 February 1973	**Bohemians at Dalymount Park, Dublin.**

Attendance: 38,000.

Won: 3–1.

Scorers: Fletcher 2, Macari. (Abandoned after 85 minutes).

Team: Stepney, T. Young, Forsyth, Law, Holton, Buchan, Morgan, MacDougall, Charlton, Macari, Martin.

Substitutes: Rimmer for Stepney, Sadler for Buchan, Fletcher for MacDougall, Anderson for Charlton, Kidd for Macari.

With so many new players in the ranks, an away friendly was an ideal opportunity for the players to get to know each other a bit better on and off the pitch, so it was not surprising that whenever the opportunity arose United were on the move to play friendlies.

Next stop on the tour circuit was Portugal and a visit to FC Porto, where the biggest crowd of their season saw United involved in more than they had bargained for.

The match itself was a dreary goalless draw, with little to whet the appetite, apart from a second half flare-up, which at least gave the supporters some action for their money.

A tackle by Jim Holton, described as 'fair' by the United man, on Porto forward Abel prompted retaliation and, after the pushing and shoving had died down, the referee decided to send both players off.

After that, play returned to the lacklustre standard it had been previously and the crowd were more than happy to hear the referee's whistle at the end.

---

4 February 1973   **FC Oporto at Portugal.**

Attendance: 45,000.

Drew: 0–0.

Team: Stepney, T. Young, Forsyth, Graham, Holton, Buchan, Morgan, MacDougall, Charlton, Macari, Martin.

Substitutes: Law for Martin, Kidd for MacDougall, Fletcher for Macari.

Tommy Docherty had managed to save United from relegation, but there was clearly much work to be done. With Law, Charlton and Dunne all leaving the club at the end of the campaign, and the manager never knowing whether George Best would turn up or not, there was clearly a lot of work to be done in order to get Manchester United back to where it belonged.

For managers today there is much debate about the number of fixtures played during the course of the domestic season. For clubs with a successful run in the two domestic Cup competitions and the Champions League the total number of games played can stretch even the largest of squads, but in the mid-1970s, when Tommy Docherty might have been better employed channelling his efforts into prolonging United's stay in the top flight, the number of friendlies played bordered on the ridiculous.

European football was only for the select few and in the 1970s Manchester United certainly did not fall into that particular category. There was, however, one avenue open to them and that was in the Anglo-Italian Cup, but even then they did not have the strength to win even this minor trophy.

A game played against Fiorentina at Old Trafford on 21 February in front of a meagre 23,951 resulted in a 1–1 draw thanks to a Jim Holton goal, with another draw, goalless, against Lazio in Rome.

The Italians set out their stall from the first blast of the referee's whistle, relying on their undoubted defensive ability and skill on the break. Despite going behind to that early goal, they stuck to the task in hand, snatching a deserved equaliser on the hour mark through Saltutti, who volleyed past a helpless Stepney after Macchi had flicked on a corner from Antognoni.

---

21 February 1973 **Fiorentina at Old Trafford.**

Attendance: 23,951.

Drew: 1—1.

Scorer: Holton.

Team: Stepney, Young, Forsyth, Graham, Holton, Buchan, Morgan, Kidd, Charlton, Macari, Martin.

Substitutes: Jones for Holton, Fletcher for Kidd.

Two months later, the second fixture of the tournament took United to Rome where they faced Lazio, with the 0–0 draw looked upon as a creditable performance. Despite the negative scoreline, there was considerable on-field action, with two players and the referee injured as the match simmered just below boiling point.

It was one of numerous confrontations which led to the match official's injury. Football League referee Gordon Hill had attempted to prevent one or two of the home players from taking revenge on Brian Kidd following a collision with Facco, which resulted in the Italian suffering a broken jaw. As Hill tried to restore some sort of order he received an arm injury and had to be carried off on a stretcher.

United should have taken the lead in the 50th minute, when Macari was through on goal, but the diminutive Scot missed an easy opportunity. At the opposite end Chinaglia, having outfoxed Holton and Buchan, shot timidly at Stepney.

Prior to the game, the United party had enjoyed the privilege of a private audience with the Pope at the Vatican, where they were told, 'Never cease to be conscious of the influence for the good that you can exercise. Always seek to live up to the finest ideals both of sport and right living.' Few could have been listening.

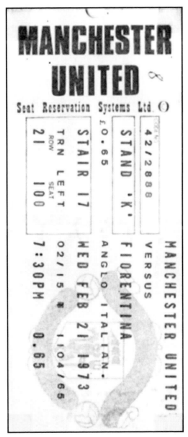

Ticket for the game versus Fiorentina, 21 February 1973.

---

21 March 1973 **Lazio at Stadio Olimpico.**

Attendance: 52,834.

Drew: 0—0.

Team: Rimmer, Young, Buchan, Graham, Holton, James, Morgan, Kidd, Charlton, Macari, Martin.

Substitutes: Fletcher for Kidd, Anderson for Macari.

With the domestic season careering towards its climax, Bari arrived at Old Trafford to be brushed aside by an on-form United, who had eased the threat of relegation with two wins and a draw in their previous three League fixtures. Despite this, the game failed to generate much in the way of interest, with only 15,000 paying at the turnstiles.

The Italians found themselves a goal behind after 15 minutes. Goalkeeper Merciai dropped a centre from Tony Young and Law did what came naturally to him. This should actually have been the second goal of the night, but Daly, perhaps suffering from nerves on his home debut, shot wide of an open goal.

Moore scored a second from close range before limping off, as Martini pulled a goal back in the 70th minute. Four minutes later, however, United's two-goal advantage was restored when Martin scored their third.

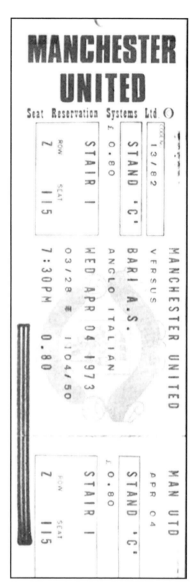

Ticket for the game versus Bari, 4 April 1973.

*Ticket for the match versus Hamburg SV,
3 August 1973.*

---

4 April 1973   **Bari at Old Trafford.**

Attendance: 15,000.

Won: 3–1.

Scorers: Law, Moore, Martin.

Team: Stepney, Young, Forsyth, Martin, James, Sadler, Morgan, Daly, Anderson, Law, Moore.

Substitutes: McGiven for Moore, Fletcher for Anderson.

In the fourth and final game of the competition United faced Verona, having managed to avoid relegation. Despite having failed to win in their previous three outings, they put four past the Italians. Perhaps the relaxed mood dictated the scoreline.

It was perhaps fitting that two of United's quartet of goals came from Bobby Charlton, playing his final game in the famous red shirt. The other goals came from the substitutes, unknowns Olney and Fletcher, who managed a couple of League outings the following season.

Unfortunately, the 4–1 victory was not enough to see United progress into the semi-final stage of the competition, as they failed to win either of the two opening fixtures.

---

2 May 1973   **Verona at Marc Antonio Bentegodi.**

Attendance: 8,168.

Won: 4–1.

Scorers: Charlton 2, Olney, Fletcher.

Team: Rimmer, Young, Sidebottom, Graham, Holton, Buchan, Morgan, Anderson, Charlton, Macari, Daly.

Substitutes: Olney for Morgan, Fletcher for Macari.

Pre-season 1973–74 began in Germany with a visit to old foes Hamburg SV and, despite the goalless draw, due mainly to the failure of the attack to create any scoring opportunities, it was considered a useful workout.

Hamburg, on the other hand, could easily have claimed victory, missing three glorious chances and being denied by a couple of fine saves by Stepney, while also monopolising the second half.

New signing Gerry Daly from Bohemians gave a creditable display in Charlton's old position, showing promise for the future, but all in all it was one of those nondescript pre-season fixtures that fail to linger for long in the memory.

---

3 August 1973   **Hamburg SV at Volksparkstadion.**

Attendance: Unknown.

Drew: 0–0.

Team: Stepney, T. Young, James, Daly, Holton, Buchan, Morgan, Kidd, Graham, Macari, Martin.

Substitute: McIlroy for Martin.

Today, as the song goes, *If the Reds will play in Rome or Mandalay, we'll be there*, a sizeable following will take in every 90 minutes played by United, no matter where it may be. In the early 1970s, however, it was an entirely different story, particularly for overseas fixtures. There was one member of the Red Army who did not miss a single first-team game in Britain between August 1971 and November 1980.

'It was a challenge in those days to find out what friendly matches were being played and when,' recalls Peter Molyneux. 'Nowadays, the games would be advertised well in advance and probably shown live on Sky Sports or MUTV. In the early 1970s, however, the communication industry around United, while still bigger than any other club, was very limited for friendly games. You had to seek out any bit of info from papers and magazines and keep a note of dates and times.

'Sometimes I'd write to Les Olive, the United secretary, to ask if any games were planned or to confirm rumours of arranged games. He was really good and I always got a reply.'

One such friendly that Peter found out about in advance was against Ross County. 'All I knew was that they were a Highland League side and that I had to be there. But where? I couldn't find a town called Ross on the map! A quick check with a mate at work confirmed that Ross County played at Victoria Park, Dingwall, just north of Inverness.

'For many friendlies, there was the normal van-load of travelling Reds, but for this one, none of the usual lot were interested and with a week to go, no firm plans had been made. However, on a night out I was introduced to a lad called Rik who was over from Australia. With the conversation drifting to football, he said that he longed to see a United game, having missed the Australian tour of 1967. I told him they were playing in Scotland and as he was keen to see Scotland, he promised to drive the pair of us up in his dad's Volvo.

'Sleeping in the car, we awoke to bright sunshine. As the game did not kick-off till 6.45pm we went to the Golf View Hotel and had a drink, only to stumble across Tommy Docherty, Tommy Cavanagh, George Graham and Jim Holton.

'Once we were at the match we found around 300 other travelling Reds, who created an excellent atmosphere on a balmy Saturday evening.'

As for the match itself, despite there having been some 13,000 tickets printed, the attendance was just under 5,000. Many had complained about the overly high admission charges, with £1 and 75p for children and OAPs considered profiteering.

Stepney was again in brilliant form, stopping two net-bound shots, while Tommy Docherty's frustration must have gone into overdrive, as time and again his forwards failed to cash in on the immaculate build-up play.

Both of United's goals came in the first half, with Daly continuing to show his potential with a goal in the fourth minute from a 20-yard drive that went in via the right-hand post. The second came 10 minutes before half-time, with Daly again involved. This time he gained possession on the right and shot low towards goal. County 'keeper Baines could only parry the ball into the path of Kidd, who scored easily from three yards out.

The goalless second half produced little in the way of excitement, providing the United manager with much to think about as he contemplated the lack of fire power up front.

11 August 1973	**Ross County at Victoria Park, Dingwall.**

Attendance: 4,970.

Won: 2–0.

Scorers: Daly, Kidd.

Team: Stepney, Forsyth, James, Daly, Holton, Buchan, Morgan, Kidd, Macari, Graham, Greenhoff.

Substitutes: McIlroy for Daly, Storey-Moore for Morgan, Anderson for Macari.

Ticket for the game versus Ross County FC, 11 August 1973.

The memories of the rather heated confrontations against Estudiantes in the World Club Championship were rekindled when United journeyed to Murcia in Spain to compete in the Cities Tournament. Prior to the game with South American side Penarol, Juan Faccio, their manager, spoke of peace between the two sides, in the hope that it would defuse any lingering threats. Tommy Docherty, on the other hand, was unfazed by the whole event, saying that it would be a good experience for his players.

Tony Young was booked as early as the fifth minute, but in the early stages, rather surprisingly, it was United who dictated play, with Morgan, along with Anderson, Daly and McIlroy, keeping the South American defence under pressure. The skilful play and superb ball control of the South Americans was easily absorbed by the United defence, as they crowded their opponents out of space while giving them little time on the ball.

In the 16th minute, a little against the run of play, Young gave away a penalty for handball, wrongly thinking he was outside the area and from the spot-kick Gonzales scored. It was a lead that Penarol manage to maintain until three minutes after the interval, when a long ball by Morgan found Anderson, who headed home the United equaliser.

As the game continued, neither side managed to gain any advantage and the lack of any further goals left the winners to be decided by penalty-kicks. Of the initial five kicks, only Penarol missed one and, with the score standing at 5–5, it was down to Alex Stepney to take the final kick for United, with the United custodian calmly slotting the ball home past his opposite number Corobo.

17 August 1973	Penarol at Murcia, Spain.

Attendance: 21,300.
Won: 6–5 (on penalties).
Scorers: Anderson; Graham, Fletcher, T. Young, McIlroy, Stepney.
Team: Stepney, T. Young, James, Daly, Holton, Buchan, Morgan, Anderson, Macari, Graham, Martin.
Substitutes: Fletcher for McIlroy.

In the second game of the competition United faced the host side Real Murcia and, in a closely fought encounter, they lost by a first-half goal, much to the disappointment of Tommy Docherty. 'It wasn't Murcia who beat us, it was Lou Macari. We were a goal down when he was sent off and it left an impossible task for 10 men to pull back,' said the United manager.

Macari had been booked in the 16th minute for talking back to the referee and received his marching orders four minutes later for throwing a punch at a Murcia defender who had gone in hard and was also holding him back.

The game produced little of note, with Docherty's plans for the season ahead still not entirely clear.

18 August 1973	Real Murcia.

Attendance: Unknown
Lost: 0–1.
Team: Stepney, Forsyth, James, Daly, Holton, Buchan, Morgan, Anderson, Macari, Graham, Martin.
Substitutes: Greenhoff for Forsyth, McIlroy for James, Fletcher for Morgan.

October turned out to be a hectic month for the United playing staff and supporters alike. There were four Football League fixtures against Wolves, Derby County, Birmingham City and Burnley, a Football League Cup tie against Middlesbrough and three friendlies. Of the eight fixtures, five were at Old Trafford.

The first of the three friendlies was a testimonial match for Denis Law, with European champions Ajax providing the opposition. Law was now plying his trade at neighbours City, having crossed Manchester on a free transfer during the summer.

While the 45,000 crowd that packed Old Trafford were there to salute their former hero, they were also more than happy to welcome back the prodigal son, George Best, who was making his first appearance in a United shirt for 10 months. The wayward Irishman had announced that he would never play for United again, but had since approached the board and asked to return, with the six directors agreeing to forgive and forget his indiscretions.

A groin injury prevented Law from making an emotional comeback to the scene of many of his most memorable moments, but he strode onto the Old Trafford turf prior to the kick-off to receive the acclaim of the fans. If those same supporters thought that even with Law missing they would be entertained by the likes of Krol, Neeskens, Rep and Muhern, they were to be disappointed, as the Dutch side treated the game for what it was, earning their £18,000 guarantee easily.

If Ajax were not going to go out of their way to entertain, then all eyes were on George Best to deliver the goods, but it took the Irishman most of the first half to get back into the swing of things, looking a little uncertain and considerably overweight. One move prior to the interval saw him beat three players, but his final shot was pushed past the post for a corner.

In the second half United, realising that the opposition were not going to cause them any problems, attacked with a little more fluency. Morgan came close twice in a matter of minutes, while a 30-yard shot from Best kept the Dutch defence on their toes.

The deadlock was finally broken in the 72nd minute when Forsyth latched onto an indirect free-kick, hammering the ball into the top corner of the net and catching the Ajax defence and the crowd unawares.

Ajax only now decided to push for a goal, but could find no way past a solid-looking United defence.

The programme for the match versus Ajax, 3 October 1973.

3 October 1973	Ajax at Old Trafford.

Attendance: 45,156.

Won: 1—0.

Scorer: Forsyth.

Team: Stepney, Buchan, T. Young, Greenhoff, Sidebottom, James, Morgan, Anderson, Macari, Kidd, Best.

Substitutes: Rimmer for Stepney, Forsyth for Young, McIlroy for Macari, G. Buchan for Anderson.

While the United first-team found themselves playing countless, sometimes unnecessary friendlies, the second string were also involved in non-competitive fixtures, with one in particular creating back-page headlines.

A testimonial match at Mossley for Kevin Burke was an ideal opportunity for manager Tommy Docherty to cast his eyes over his reserve-team players in a different environment. To give the relatively young side a hint of experience, the Doc had included Lou Macari.

Arriving at the ground of the Northern Premier League side half an hour before kick-off, the United manager, who had travelled to the ground separately from the team, told Macari: 'Don't bother to strip. You won't be playing.' After the match, Docherty dropped an even bigger bombshell, announcing: 'In consultation with the club directors, it has been decided to transfer-list Lou Macari and fine him two weeks wages (£400). Apart from that I have no comment to make at this stage.'

Macari, in response to the statement, said: 'I've a fair idea what this is all about but it's not true that I refused to play in this match – even though it would have been my fourth game in seven days.

'It is possible that there might have been a misunderstanding about my attitude to this match, but even if I gave the wrong impression I think the club could have waited to see what happened before reacting so hastily this way.'

Adding more fuel to the fire, the United manager told the press: 'Macari was selected to play for the reserves at Mossley on Wednesday because he has been having an indifferent time lately and a goal or two at lower level would help his confidence.

'But Macari then told me that he did not want to train with the reserves or play at Mossley and it didn't seem that he had changed his mind even after Cliff Lloyd, the PFA secretary, had spoken to him.

'I was surprised when he turned up at Mossley, but it was then too late. He had been given several chances to change his attitude, and had left me with no alternative but to take action.'

By the end of the month Macari was back in the first team, everything forgotten. However, he was missing from the United squad that travelled to Dublin to face Shamrock Rovers in the next friendly, as 20,000 people flocked to Dalymount Park, attracted by the prospect of seeing United, with George Best, fitter than he had been against Ajax, receiving top billing.

The Irish side had been struggling domestically, but United failed to dominate the game. Buchan, Graham and to a lesser extent Daly were prominent in the early stages, with Best, whose every move was cheered, showing some vintage touches on the left, but it was from the right that both of United's first-half goals came.

In the 32nd minute the home defence were confused by a whistle from the crowd as Greenhoff timed his jump superbly to head home a cross from Martin Buchan. Seven minutes later, however, they were beaten fair and square when Anderson measured his cross perfectly for Graham to head home.

With the second half only seven minutes old, United were left stunned when Shamrock Rovers pulled a goal back. Steve James brought down Leech just inside the area and for a few seconds it looked as though Paddy Roche had marked his United debut with a penalty save, but he could only parry the spot-kick back to O'Neill's feet and the Irishman made no mistake with the rebound.

Even at half pace, United continued to dominate, but as the game moved into its final 20 minutes there were a few doubts that the entire 90 minutes would be played out, as a considerable number of spectators began to encroach on the field. With nine minutes remaining, hundreds of youngsters raced onto the pitch, leaving the referee with little alternative but to abandon the game.

15 October 1973	**Shamrock Rovers at Dalymount Park, Dublin.**

Attendance: 20,000.

Won: 2–1.

Scorers: Greenhoff, Graham. (Abandoned with nine minutes remaining).

Team: Stepney, Buchan, O'Brien, Greenhoff, James, Sadler, Daly, Anderson, Kidd, Graham, Best.

Substitutes: Roche for Stepney, Forsyth for Anderson, Martin for Graham, Young for Greenhoff, G. Buchan for Kidd.

The programme for the match versus Shamrock Rovers, 15 October 1973.

Tony Dunne had left Manchester United on a free transfer in the close season, joining near neighbours Bolton Wanderers after 12 trophy-laden seasons at Old Trafford. Having rarely hit the headlines, although a consummate professional with a high level of consistency, it was fitting that his service was rewarded with a testimonial match.

Had it not been for the bedrock of United support at the Stretford End, then the attendance for Dunne's night might have been rather embarrassing, as the 17,000 crowd was a far cry from the attendances attracted to the testimonials for Denis Law and Bobby Charlton. Commenting on this in his *Manchester Evening News* match report, David Meek wrote: '..but that's life for full-backs compared with goalscoring heroes, of course.'

Although a local 'derby' match, there was little of the needle that is normally evident in such fixtures, with neither team exerting themselves. The game began well, with Kidd coming close and Stepney having to be alert to save at the feet of Lee, but the tempo slowly dropped to a level of boredom. Surprisingly, the atmosphere was rekindled at half-time, thanks to an 'old-timers' match between United and an International side, with the players of yesteryear putting more endeavour into their 10 minutes of play than many of the modern-day players were putting into their 90.

Tony Dunne, back in the red and white shirt again, was accompanied by the likes of Charlton, Quixall, Setters and Herd, with Gordon Banks and Roger Hunt in the England line up. Even Tommy Docherty and trainer Tommy Cavanagh tried to get in on the act.

Back in the 'real' game, the crowd were roused from their state of inertia when Tommy Booth opened the scoring for City in the 75th minute, switching their cries of abuse to cheers 60 seconds later when George Best equalised, slotting the ball home from a narrow angle.

Any hopes of a moral victory, however, were soon dispersed when Lee scored City's second with a 25-yard free-kick.

The programme for the match versus Manchester City, 24 October 1973.

24 October 1973	**Manchester City at Old Trafford.**

Attendance: 17,800.

Lost: 2–1.

Scorer: Best.

Team: Stepney, Buchan, Dunne, Greenhoff, James, Sadler, Anderson, Young, Kidd, Graham, Best.

Substitutes: Albiston for Dunne, Roche for Stepney, McIlroy for Kidd, Martin for Graham, Daly for Martin.

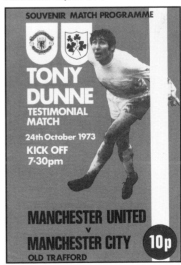

United made a trip to Scotland in early November, this time to Glasgow, where they faced Partick Thistle in a testimonial for defender Donnie McKinnon. United

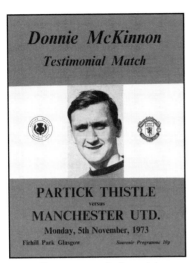

The programme for the match versus Partick Thistle, 5 November 1973.

needed only four minutes to breach the home defence and were 2–0 in front eight minutes later. George Graham notched up the first, side-footing a Best corner into the net, while Lou Macari made it two after Buchan had moved forward, beating three defenders and scoring from a tight angle. The diminutive forward had actually come close to opening the scoring a couple of minutes into the game, his header being cleared off the line by Ralston.

Despite Craig having a goal-bound shot blocked by a defender, Thistle had no answer to United's play, with Best, although not the player he once was, trying his hardest to take over the fixture, which was soon to drift into exhibition mode.

There were odd flourishes at either end, but it was not until the 82nd minute that there was any further scoring. A ball into the Thistle penalty area was handled by Campbell, although many were uncertain about why the spot-kick had been awarded and former Firhill favourite Alex Forsyth scored from the spot.

5 November 1973	**Partick Thistle at Firhill, Glasgow.**
Attendance: 10,000.	
Won: 3–0.	
Scorers: Graham, Macari, Forsyth (pen.).	
Team: Stepney, Buchan, Forsyth, Greenhoff, Holton, Griffiths, Young, Anderson, Macari, Graham, Best.	
Substitutes: Roche for Stepney, G. Buchan for Best.	

A 0–0 draw against Norwich City at Old Trafford on 24 November dragged United into the relegation dogfight, but the friendlies continued with a mid week trip to the south coast to face Portsmouth.

United made use of five substitutes in a game that rarely sprung into life and ended all square at 1–1. The playing of so many meaningless fixtures finally caught up with United as Kidd had to limp off in the 22nd minute, with Holton following him on a stretcher three minutes later.

Portsmouth took the lead through a Piper header early on and it was to take United until the 63rd minute to grab an equaliser, Anderson scoring following good work by Morgan and Young.

The programme for the match versus Portsmouth, 4 December 1973.

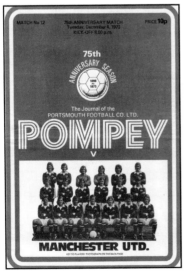

4 December 1973	**Portsmouth at Fratton Park.**
Attendance: 17,226.	
Drew: 1–1.	
Scorer: Anderson.	
Team: Stepney, Buchan, Forsyth, Greenhoff, Holton, James, Morgan, Young, Kidd, Macari, Best.	
Substitutes: Roche for Stepney, Anderson for Macari, Griffiths for Holton, Martin for Greenhoff, McIlroy for Kidd.	

12 December saw a testimonial against Stoke City for their former goalkeeper and England hero, Gordon Banks, whose career was cut short when he damaged his right eye in a car accident.

Despite the incessant rain, a crowd of over 21,000 earned Banks, who returned to the Stoke goal for the night, an estimated £15,000. With his old rival Eusebio also playing, as was Bobby Charlton, the evening was eagerly anticipated.

Banks was called into action as early as the first minute, when he had to punch out a cross from Best, Greenhoff failing to find the target as the ball fell his way.

Stoke opened the scoring in the 26th minute through Eusebio, following a neat move with Pejic, and as the first half drew towards a close, Forsyth did well to clear off the line from the Portuguese guest. Hurst also came close to increasing the Stoke advantage.

As the second half got underway, United came more into the game and snatched the equaliser in the 51st minute, Best creating the goal for Tony Young. Three minutes later it was 2–1 to United, Macari, one of five substitutes, beating Banks from 30 yards, again from a Best pass.

The programme for the match versus Stoke City, 12 December 1973.

12 December 1973	Stoke City XI at Victoria Ground.

Attendance: 21,308.

Won: 2–1.

Scorers: Young, Macari.

Team: Stepney, Buchan, Forsyth, Greenhoff, James, Griffiths, Morgan, Anderson, McIlroy, Young, Best.

Substitutes: Roche for Stepney, Graham for Greenhoff, Sidebottom for James, Martin for Morgan, Macari for Anderson.

With the fight for First Division survival reaching a rather precarious state, a blank Saturday saw another friendly appear on the fixture list. Not only could the players have done without it, the Manchester public could have done without it too, as off-field events were to cause numerous problems.

The game itself developed into a typical 'Auld Enemy' clash, in a no-holds-barred confrontation. Brian Greenhoff, playing in an unfamiliar forward position, hammered home the first goal in the seventh minute after Morgan had dribbled round McDonald on the right flank. It was a lead that United managed to hold onto for the remainder of the first half.

One minute after the interval John Greig equalised with a thunderous shot from 15 yards, following a fine passing movement between O'Hara and Parlane. Within 10 minutes, however, they were behind again.

A through ball into the Rangers half saw Derek Johstone miskick and, as Greenhoff ran through, he was brought down just outside the area. As the Rangers defence lined up, Forsyth blasted the ball high into the net from 20 yards.

Greenhoff hit the post a minute later and then Johnstone cleared a Morgan effort off the line, as the tempo began to rise. Holton became the second United player to be booked after a foul on Jardine, Houston having found his way into the referee's notebook earlier for striking the same Rangers player.

Rangers lost their rhythm temporarily, but were soon back in the game, when a McLean free-kick, following a lunge by Holton on Parlane 25 yards from goal, found the head of Johnstone.

With 10 minutes remaining Nicholl, who had been on the field for less than a minute, brought down Young inside the area and, despite numerous protests, the referee pointed to the spot. Parlane, unnerved, placed the ball confidently past Roche.

However, the game was to be overshadowed by events off the pitch. 'Riot Ruins Friendly Meeting' read the headline above the report of Douglas Peacock in the *Daily Telegraph*, with the correspondent writing: 'The football interest in this "friendly" was largely overshadowed by disgraceful scenes before kick-off, when about 500 spectators, mostly Scottish, rampaged across the pitch, and fights broke out all over the terraces.

'There were many arrests at the ground, and others before and after the match. Dozens were treated for injuries, and, but for the intervention of Rangers' manager Jock Wallace, the chaos could have been much worse.'

Noel Wild of the *Sunday Express* echoed these views, saying: 'It is certainly the unfriendliest "friendly" I have ever seen, both on and off the terraces. But, to be fair, it was also highly entertaining.'

An estimated 7,000 Scots had descended upon Manchester, with United officials saying that they had never anticipated this number, although they were well aware of the Rangers supporters' record of trouble. Pubs, shops and cafes counted the costs following the invasion, which also saw 77 arrests. Court appearances afterwards revealed tales of criminal damage, drunkenness and police assault, with one supporter from Greenock being accused of having a fireman's axe in his possession on the terracing.

9 March 1974	Glasgow Rangers at Old Trafford.

Attendance: 22,215.

Lost: 3–2.

Scorers: Greenhoff, Forsyth.

Team: Roche, Forsyth, Houston, Martin, Holton, Buchan, Morgan, McIlroy, Greenhoff, Daly, Beilby.

Substitutes: Fletcher for McIlroy, Wardrop for Daly, Nicholl for Buchan.

The Official Programme of Manchester United Football Club Ltd.

9th MARCH, 1974
KICK-OFF 3 p.m.

PROGRAMME NUMBER 20

6p

MANCHESTER UNITED VERSUS **GLASGOW RANGERS**

The programme for the match versus Glasgow Rangers, 9 March 1974.

By the time the final friendly of season 1973–74 came around, Manchester United were a Second Division club, their fight for survival brought to an end by three consecutive 1–0 defeats within a six-day period. It was therefore unsurprising that Eddie McCreadie's testimonial against Chelsea at Stamford Bridge was largely ignored by the United support, producing a small crowd of just over 6,000.

United manager Docherty had brought McCreadie to Stamford Bridge while in charge of the south London club and it was rather ironic that his current side would spoil the Chelsea defender's big night by winning 2–1.

First half goals from George Buchan and Lou Macari for United and Hollins for Chelsea entertained the fans scattered around the ground and the night could have come to something of a fitting end had McCreadie himself not shunned the opportunity of scoring an equaliser from the penalty spot, 15 minutes from the end.

The programme for the match versus Chelsea, 1 May 1974.

1 May 1974 — Chelsea at Stamford Bridge.

Attendance: 6,437.

Won: 2–1.

Scorers: Macari, G. Buchan.

Team: Stepney, M. Buchan, Forsyth, Greenhoff, Holton, Sidebottom, Morgan, Macari, Young, McCalliog, G. Buchan.

Substitutes: Roche for Stepney, Nicholl for McCalliog.

Despite the fall in status, there were still friendlies to be played, with four in the pre-season warm-up programme taking the players and supporters to Belgium, Denmark, Jutland and Hull.

The first of the four games brought a short jaunt across the English Channel to the ferry port of Ostend, in a game that was to set an unwanted precedent for the majority of away fixtures throughout the season ahead. A 2–1 victory was favourably received by the press, who reported that, judged on this performance, life in the lower tier of the Football League might not be long term.

Making his United debut was Stuart Pearson, a £200,000 signing from Hull City, who got off to the ideal start by scoring both goals. Apart from a few uncomfortable minutes in the second half when the home side drew level, United enjoyed a favourable workout.

Pearson's first, on the half-hour, came from a Macari cross, against an Ostend side who were at times slow to exert any pressure on the United defence, with Stepney having only one first-half save.

However, Ostend did manage to draw level in the 55th minute through ex-international forward Carteus, and they should also have added a second through Fogh, but he blasted the ball high and wide.

It was a miss that they were to rue, as Pearson added a second in the 75th minute and was unfortunate not to claim a debut hat-trick, but a lobbed effort, three minutes from time, was disallowed for offside.

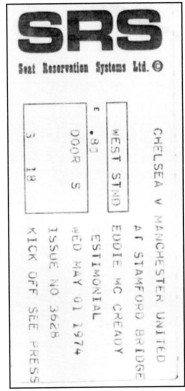

Ticket for the game versus Chelsea, 1 May 1974.

3 August 1974 — Ostend in Belgium.

Attendance: 8,000.

Won: 2–1.

Scorer: Pearson 2.

Team: Stepney, Young, Houston, Greenhoff, Sidebottom, Buchan, McIlroy, Daly, Pearson, Macari, McCalliog.

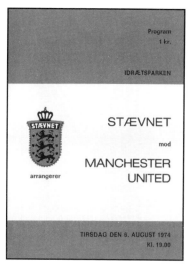

The programme for the match versus Stævnet, 6 August 1974.

Pearson continued to impress as United maintained their build-up with a narrowly won match against Stævnet in Denmark. His goal, halfway through the first half, was enough to give United victory.

Against a team made up from the nine League clubs in Copenhagen, United were always the stronger of the two sides, but they often lacked sparkle in what was a rather uninspired 90 minutes.

The Danes did have a few moments when they threatened the United defence, Fogh blasting high and wide, but it was during a period when they were playing against 10 men, Pearson lying dazed on the touchline.

---

6 August 1974   **Stævnet at Denmark.**

Attendance: 2,900.

Won: 1—0.

Scorer: Pearson.

Team: Stepney, Forsyth, Houston, Greenhoff, Holton, Buchan, McIlroy, Daly, Pearson, McCalliog, Anderson.

Substitute: Martin for Greenhoff.

In the second game of the tour United, according to the local press, 'showed great strength and determination' and the local reporter was very impressed by the overall play of Docherty's team, especially their tendency to defend and attack in numbers.

Play in the opening 45 minutes was even, but the fitness of the visitors came to the fore in the second half, although the locals, made up of six Holstebro players and five guests from other Jutland First Division clubs, did have a couple of chances, which they failed to take.

Goals from Anderson, a McCalliog penalty and a McIlroy double were enough to grab United victory in what Tommy Docherty described as 'the best game of the tour.'

---

8 August 1974   **Holstebro at Idraetspark.**

Attendance: 4,000.

Won: 4—0.

Scorers: McIlroy 2, Anderson, McCalliog (pen.).

Team: Stepney, Forsyth, Houston, Greenhoff, Holton, Buchan, McIlroy, Macari, Pearson, McCalliog, Daly.

Substitute: Anderson for Pearson.

As part of Stuart Pearson's transfer, United had agreed to play a friendly against Hull City, a club who would be visited on League business in the coming months. However, without the sparkle of Best, Law and Charlton, and perhaps the impeding danger from what was becoming a rather notorious support, the locals stayed away, with around 3,000 of the 8,303 attendance (less than 300 above Hull's average attendance of the previous season) United supporters.

The home side thought they had taken the lead in the 20th minute, when Deere beat Stepney from 12 yards after Greenwood had hit the bar with a header, but the referee disallowed it for offside. Ten minutes prior to the interval, however, they did gain the advantage, Hemmerman shooting past Stepney after good work by Hawley.

Four minutes after the interval it was all square. Pearson, back on his old stomping ground, headed down a McCalliog corner before firing a left-footed shot past Wealands.

As the second half wore on both sides missed chances. Macari headed over after Pearson had drawn Wealands out of his goal, while at the opposite end Stepney had to stop a Hawley header at point-blank range. From the resulting corner, Hemmerman saw his header glance the crossbar before going over.

10 August 1974	**Hull City at Boothferry Park.**

Attendance: 8,303.

Drew: 1—1.

Scorer: Pearson.

Team: Stepney, Forsyth, Houston, Greenhoff, Holton, Buchan, Morgan, Macari, Pearson, McCalliog, Daly.

Substitutes: Young for Houston, McIlroy for Morgan.

The visit of Portsmouth to Old Trafford on Wednesday 28 August attracted a crowd of 42,547, not bad for a mid week Second Division fixture, but seven days later a meagre 8,065 clicked through the turnstiles for a friendly against a Republic of Ireland side.

Former United player Johnny Giles, now in charge of the Republic side, used the game as a chance to run his eye over his charges in preparation for the forthcoming European Nations' Cup ties. It gave Tommy Docherty, the opportunity to give some of the players a run out, with two apprentices, 17-year-old Peter Sutcliffe and 16-year-old David McCreery, making their first-team debuts.

It was rather ironic that the Republic's two goals should come from a former United player, with Mick Martin scoring two opportunist efforts in what was little more than a full-scale practice match, which saw a total of 11 second-half substitutions.

The Republic side took the lead in the 23rd minute. Player-manager Giles slipped the ball to Mulligan, whose clip through the hesitant United defence allowed Martin to lob the ball over the head of the advancing Stepney.

McCreery showed some nice touches, while Greenhoff put in some hard work trying to prompt his forwards into action. The nearest they came to scoring, however, was through Anderson, but his shot, from a useful position, went high and wide.

Conroy set up Martin for his second, Stepney stopping his initial effort, but was unable to prevent his former teammate from scoring with the rebound.

4 September 1974	**Republic of Ireland at Old Trafford.**

Attendance: 8,065.

Lost: 2—0.

Team: Stepney, Forsyth, Houston, Greenhoff, Sidebottom, Buchan, Morgan, Anderson, McCreery, Young, Sutcliffe.

Substitutes: Roche for Stepney, Botham for Anderson, Kelly for Morgan, Nicholl for Buchan.

Once again United found a visit to the Emerald Isle not without its problems. This time, their match against Shelbourne had to be stopped for 15 minutes, after the throwing of missiles at the Shelbourne goal.

Shelbourne had taken a 13-minute lead when a Cervi cross was put beyond Roche by Swan. United struggled to get back into the game, but two second-half crowd disturbances did not help their concentration or the flow of the game.

The programme for the match versus Republic of Ireland, 4 September 1974.

WELCOME TO OLD TRAFFORD

UNITED REVIEW — The official programme of Manchester United Football Club Ltd

4th SEPTEMBER 1974 Kick-off 7.30 p.m.

INTERNATIONAL FRIENDLY MATCH

UNITED

V

REPUBLIC OF IRELAND XI

No. 3   4p

The programme for the match versus Shelbourne, 6 November 1974.

The first hint of potential trouble, in a game which saw three Shelbourne players booked and McCalliog carried off injured, came when young supporters began climbing the fences at the start of the second half, with the second, more serious incident leaving the pitch littered with missiles.

With only two minutes remaining, United's blushes were spared by Gerry Daly, who pounced when Shelbourne 'keeper Byrne failed to hold a shot from Houston, crashing the ball high into the roof of the net.

6 November 1974	**Shelbourne at Dalymount Park, Dublin.**

Attendance: 20,000.

Drew: 1–1.

Scorer: Daly.

Team: Roche, Forsyth, Houston, Greenhoff, Sidebottom, Buchan, Macari, McIlroy, Pearson, McCalliog, Daly.

Substitutes: Morgan for Pearson, Young for McCalliog, Martin for Greenhoff.

With the Second Division Championship won in style, the United squad went on a pre-season tour which took them from West Germany to Iran and on to Australia. The tour also brings a number of unfamiliar names in the United line ups.

The first fixture of the marathon tour saw Tony Grimshaw and Peter Loughnane both earning praise from Docherty for their performances against Swiss Cup winners Basel, the latter scoring United's only goal three minutes from the end of the 3–1 defeat.

Hizfield gave Basel the lead on the half-hour, but United were unlucky not to equalise just before the break when Odermatt headed off the line. The game, however, went beyond United's grasp in the second half when Schoenenberger notched a double in the 53rd and 70th minutes.

8 May 1975	**FC Basel at Lorrach, West Germany.**

Attendance: Unknown.

Lost: 3–1.

Scorer: Loughnane.

Team: Stepney, Forsyth, Houston, Greenhoff, James, Buchan, Loughnane, McIlroy, Pearson, Macari, Grimshaw.

Substitutes: Ryan for Stepney, G. Coyne for an unknown player.

The programme for the match versus FC Basel, 8 May 1975.

Four goals in a 15-minute second-half spell were enough to grab United victory against the Swiss First Division part-time side Lausanne.

Lou Macari opened the scoring for United in the 12th minute, with a 35-yard shot into the roof of the net from a Loughnane pass, and it was only down to some fine goalkeeping from Veillard that the score remained at 1–0 at the interval. Loughnane, McIlroy and Pearson were all denied by the 'keeper.

Three minutes after the break, Loughnane moved past a defender on the right before cutting the ball back for McIlroy to score a second, with the same player adding a third five minutes later, hitting the ball into an empty net after Pearson and Loughnane had done all the leg-work.

Brian Greenhoff made it 4–0 a minute later following an interchange of passes between McIlroy and Houston, the fifth coming from Macari, who scored from 15 yards after a neat one-two with Pearson.

10 May 1975   **Lausanne at Stade Olympique, Lausanne.**

Attendance: 4,000.

Won: 5–0.

Scorers: Macari 2, McIlroy 2, Greenhoff.

Team: Stepney, Forsyth, Houston, Greenhoff, James, Buchan, Loughnane, McIlroy, Pearson, Macari, Grimshaw.

Substitutes: Ashworth for an unknown player.

The programme for the match versus Lausanne, 10 May 1975.

The United players made a brief return to Manchester before setting off on the second leg of their world tour. The party for this jaunt was depleted by the loss of Martin Buchan, Lou Macari, Alex Forsyth and Stewart Houston, who were all required for Scottish international duty, while Steve Coppell was also a late arrival due to exams at Liverpool University.

With the squad assembling at Manchester Airport for the month-long tour, Tony Young failed to appear. A telephone call to the midfielder's mother brought the reply that she had been told not to pack his bags for the trip and the player himself was later to tell *Manchester Evening News* reporter Matt D'Arcy: 'This was not a sudden decision. I have been unhappy at United for some time. I played only seven League games last season and came on eight times as substitute and this is not good enough.

'I asked for a move last Tuesday and the manager rang me on Wednesday to tell me it had been granted.

'I realised then there would be no point in me going on the tour. I rang the manager on Friday to tell him I wouldn't be going, but he had gone to London and I wasn't able to get hold of him.'

An impromptu board meeting in an airport lounge before the outward flight resulted in Young being transfer-listed and fined a fortnight's wages.

The first stop was Tehran for a game against Persepolis, where a rather doubtful penalty decision saw United having to be content with a 1–1 draw.

United opened the scoring in the 10th minute when Jim Holton, returning to the side following a broken leg against Sheffield Wednesday, headed the ball down to the feet of Sammy McIlroy to blast into the roof of the net. Three minutes later Daly missed a golden opportunity to make it 2–0, lobbing the ball over the bar with Mavedat in the home goal badly placed.

It was then United's turn to breathe a sigh of relief as Adibi sent a perfect cross into the penalty area, but there was no one there to take advantage. Neither could Persepolis's numerous attacks produce a goal.

After the interval Persepolis failed to exert a similar amount of pressure on a United side who were beginning to feel the effects of the heat and altitude. One of their few sojourns into the visitors' penalty area produced a rather dubious penalty award, when the referee decided a Persepolis player had been pushed. Ali Parven scored from the spot.

27 May 1975   **Persepolis at Tehran.**

Attendance: 20,000.

Drew: 1–1.

Scorer: McIlroy.

Team: Stepney, Nicholl, Albiston, Greenhoff, Holton, James, Loughnane, McIlroy, Pearson, Grimshaw, Daly.

Substitutes: McCreery for Loughnane, Roche for Stepney, Loughnane for Greenhoff.

Next stop was Indonesia, where a crowd of 65,000 for a game against PSSI Tamtama demonstrated United's pulling power even in the 1970s, around three decades before the club were recognised as a worldwide phenomenon.

Sadly, those who paid their admission money were left disappointed by a goalless draw, and resorted to boos, especially during the slow first half. United did manage to put the ball in the net in the 24th minute, but referee Kartadireja disallowed it for offside.

Perhaps the only notable incident came five minutes prior to the interval when United made a substitution, with a certain Tommy Docherty replacing the injured Gerry Daly.

Such was the standard of the game that a local reporter wrote: 'PSSI players, who performed a fast play and battled with full spirit, made Manchester United look terrible. In the second half, both teams performed rather rough play and some times appeared to show bad ways. Peter Loughnane (outside-right) and Tommy Docherty (right-half) who substituted Gerry Molly [sic] in the 39th minute were given warnings of yellow cards.'

1 June 1975	**PSSI Tamtama at Senayan Stadium, Jakarta.**

Attendance: 65,000.

Drew: 0–0.

Team: Stepney, Nicholl, Albiston, Daly, Holton, James, Loughnane, McIlroy, Pearson, McCreery, Grimshaw.

Substitutes: Docherty for Daly.

Remaining in Jakarta, United played more familiar opposition, in front of a large crowd of 110,000, as they took on Ajax.

The actual attendance for this particular game, kicked-off by Foreign Minister Adam Malik in a stadium which was capable of holding 130,000, varies from report to report. The *Daily Mirror* states 'a crowd of 100,000', while the *Manchester Evening News* report mentions 'a crowd of 80,000 watched the Reds'. A local reporter, probably more in the know, wrote: 'A crowd of 125,000 jam-packed the 130,000 thousand capacity [sic] main stadium.'

David McCreery opened the scoring for United in the eighth minute, beating Schrijvers from around 15 yards. It was a lead that they managed to hold on to for only 20 minutes before Johnny Rep 'booted a good passing from Jan Mulder. Jan Mulder was breaking through the defence line of Manchester United while Johnny Rep also broke open into defenders of his opponent to majestically head his first goal.'

Ajax went further in front seven minutes later through Brokamp and extended their lead eight minutes into the second half when Geels, a substitute for Rep, added a third, Mulder again the supplier.

In the 62nd minute United did manage to pull a goal back through Sammy McIlroy but, despite further attacks, they could not get the better of a strong Ajax defence. The local correspondent, perhaps letting the excitement get too much for him, wrote: 'Tommy Doucherty [sic] headed the ball into goalmouth of Piers Schrijvers. He lessened his team defeat to 3–2.'

---

3 June 1975 **Ajax at Senayan Stadium, Jakarta.**

Attendance: 110,000.

Lost: 3–2.

Scorers: McIlroy, McCreery.

Team: Roche, James, Albiston, Daly, Holton, Nicholl, Loughnane, Grimshaw, McIlroy, Pearson, McCreery.

Substitute: Docherty for an unknown player.

Moving on to Hong Kong, United recorded their first victory of their tour with a last-gasp winner against a lively Hong Kong Rangers side.

It was the local side who took the lead when forward Chung Chor-Wai made no mistake with a firm header in the 27th minute from a perfectly flighted Lai Wing-fu cross, as the United defence stood surprisingly still. The goal shocked United and they were fortunate not to go further behind when another effort from the Hong Kong striker went just over the bar.

Their lead was short-lived, however, as four minutes later Lou Macari made his way down the right before passing to Sammy McIlroy to fire home from 18 yards. Another United effort hit the post, while a poor goal-kick from goalkeeper Liddell almost cost his side a goal.

A double save by Liddell from Macari and Pearson at one end and a spectacular dive by Stepney got the second half off to a lively start. United, however, continued to waste opportunities and the game looked as though it was heading for a draw.

However, with seconds remaining Macari smashed a 20-yard shot towards the Hong Kong goal, which the full-stretched Liddell could only block. Reacting immediately, Pearson pounced and placed the rebound into the net for the winner.

---

8 June 1975 **Hong Kong Rangers at Hong Kong Stadium.**

Attendance: 12,759.

Won: 2–1.

Scorers: McIlroy, Pearson.

Team: Roche, Forsyth, Houston, Grimshaw, Holton, Buchan, Macari, Loughnane, McIlroy, Pearson, Daly.

Substitutes: Stepney for Roche, Albiston for Houston, McCreery for Grimshaw.

United were not to come up against any difficulties during their three games in Australia, although they were certainly to make hard work of their opening fixture against a Western Australia side.

Cheered on by a 15,000 crowd, the home side launched a series of early attacks, forcing Stepney into making a point-blank save as early as the third minute. United, however, weathered this early storm and went on to take an eighth-minute lead when a perfect through pass from Pearson allowed Coppell to fire past goalkeeper Witschge.

Continuing to stretch their visitors, Western Australia missed a penalty which would have put them level and paid the price four minutes after the interval as United scored a second. A Coppell cross found McIlroy at the near post, with the Irishman making no mistake with a back-header.

Ticket for the match versus HK Rangers, 8 June 1975.

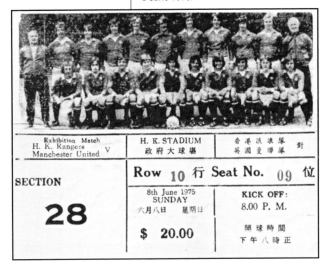

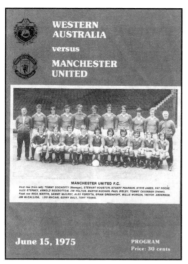

The programme for the match versus Western Australia, 15 June 1975.

SOCCER FEDERATION OF W.A. (Inc.)
INTERNATIONAL SOCCER
PERRY LAKES STADIUM
SUNDAY, 15th JUNE, 1975
1.00 p.m. — S.F.W.A. AMATEUR TEAM
v.
WESTRALIAN AMATEUR SOCCER ASS.
3.00 p.m.—
MANCHESTER UNITED
v.
WESTERN AUSTRALIA
ADMIT ONE $4.30

Ticket for the game versus Western Australia, 15 June 1975.

The home side reduced United's advantage in the 55th minute when McMillan accepted a 40-yard pass from Elliott before wrong-footing Buchan and beating Stepney from 12 yards.

15 June 1975   Western Australia at Perry Lakes Stadium, Perth.

Attendance: 15,000.

Won: 2–1.

Scorers: Coppell, McIlroy.

Team: Stepney, Forsyth, Houston, Buchan, Holton, Daly, Grimshaw, Macari, McIlroy, Pearson, Coppell.

Substitutes: Albiston for Houston, Loughnane for Coppell, McCreery for Pearson.

There was no touch and go about United's second victory in the southern hemisphere as they defeated New South Wales 4–0.

Much to the relief of spectators and players alike, the three-day rainstorm that had deluged Sydney stopped on the afternoon of the game. It was the home side who were to start the strongest, going close to scoring twice in the opening five minutes. One of the efforts saw Stepney fumble a shot from Harding, but Richards shot into the side netting when a goal looked certain.

Almost on the half-hour Macari seized upon a defensive error to open the scoring and, with four minutes to go before the interval, McIlroy made it 2–0.

After the break United continued to dominate, with Macari by far United's most effective player, and they increased their lead in the 59th minute when Wilson and Williams hesitated, allowing Loughnane to present Daly with an easy opportunity. With the game now more or less over, Pearson added a fourth.

18 June 1975   New South Wales at Sydney.

Attendance: 20,000.

Won: 4–0.

Scorers: Macari, McIlroy, Pearson, Daly.

Team: Stepney, Nicholl, Houston, Greenhoff, Holton, Buchan, Coppell, McIlroy, Pearson, Macari, Daly.

Substitutes: Loughnane for Greenhoff, Grimshaw for McIlroy, Forsyth for Nicholl.

The fixture against Queensland would see a name in the United line up that you will not find in any history of the club, nor indeed find mentioned elsewhere in this book.

Had it not been for the immigration employment laws, however, the name of Atti Abonyi might well have featured at some point in the months to come. The 28-year-old was Hungarian-born and an Australian international and Tommy Docherty was indeed keen to sign him, but Abonyi would have had to live in England for two years before he could turn out for the club.

He did manage to pull on a red shirt, however, but only as a substitute, although he marked his appearance with a goal, scoring United's third in a 4–0 victory. The headlines back in the UK, however, were taken over by Jim Holton, highlighting his comeback from a broken leg with a scorching goal and a fine defensive display in the heart of the United defence.

United began well, but lost their rhythm in the first half and it was not until midway through the second half that they began to move smoothly into top gear.

A close-range Gerry Daly shot gave them the lead in the 60th minute, with Holton adding the second five minutes later before Abonyi rounded things off with the third.

---

22 June 1975	**Queensland at Lang Park, Brisbane.**

Attendance: Unknown

Won: 3–0.

Scorers: Daly, Holton, Abonyi.

Team: Roche, Nicholl, Houston, Greenhoff, Holton, Buchan, Coppell, McIlroy, McCreery, Macari, Daly.

Substitutes: Forsyth for Greenhoff, Cosgrave for McCreery, Abonyi for McIlroy.

The programme for the match versus Queensland, 22 June 1975.

The tour came to an end in New Zealand with a 2–0 victory over Auckland, but it took two late goals to round things off with a victory and things might have turned out a little different had referee Coffman not disallowed a 29th-minute goal by Turner. The effort from the edge of the area looked legitimate until a linesman's flag suggested otherwise.

If the first half belonged to the home side, then the second 45 minutes were United's, with Auckland finally buckling under the pressure.

The first of the two goals came when Holton headed the ball down to Grimshaw, who scored with the outside of his left foot. The second, scored by Loughnane, was the result of goalkeeper Curtin dropping a cross from McIlroy.

Twice in the closing minutes Auckland came close to scoring, Roche being in the right place at the right time to stop a Taylor effort, while Elrick hurried a shot wide.

---

24 June 1975	**Auckland at Newmarket Park.**

Attendance: 8,000.

Won: 2–0.

Scorers: Loughnane, Grimshaw.

Team: Roche, Forsyth, Albiston, Daly, Holton, Buchan, Loughnane, McCreery, Coppell, Macari, McIlroy.

Substitute: Grimshaw for McCreery.

The programme for the match versus Auckland, 24 June 1975.

Following one season in the lower regions, United were back where they belonged, having won the Second Division in front of full houses.

In preparation for their return to the First Division United returned to Denmark for a trio of fixtures which produced three straight victories. However, these games against relatively nondescript opposition were not without their problems.

Prior to kick-off for the opening fixture against Halskov, a naval band entertained the crowd at the tiny parkland pitch, with the additional back-up of around 250 boisterous chanting United supporters.

When the game got underway it took United 12 minutes to breach the Halskov defence, Lou Macari turning quickly to volley home. Two minutes later it was 2–0, Gerry Daly tucking away a rebound after Coppell's shot had hit the woodwork. Just before the interval Macari scored to make it 3–0.

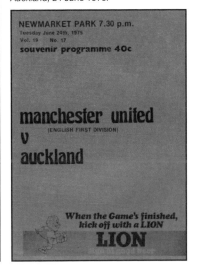

Five minutes into the second half United's workout went pear-shaped. Jim Holton, who had not played a League match since the previous December, moved forward for a corner and, 'bumped into' Halskov defender Hansen, who fell to the ground, leaving the referee reaching for his red card.

Despite this minor hiccup, the game was played out without any further incident, although it left Tommy Docherty with the worry that he would be starting the season without his Scottish international centre-half.

---

3 August 1975   **Halskov Select XI at Korskor, Copenhagen.**

Attendance: 3,000.

Won: 3–0.

Scorers: Macari 2, Daly.

Team: Stepney, Forsyth, Houston, Greenhoff, Holton, Buchan, Loughnane, Coppell, Pearson, Macari, Daly.

Substitute: McCreery for Loughnane.

As things turned out, the Danish FA did not report the sending off, with a spokesman saying: 'We see this as a private match played on for fun. Jim Holton will hear nothing more about it.' FIFA had other thoughts on the matter, but there was to be no ban for the cult hero.

Two days later, United continued their tour with a 3–1 victory over Hvidovre. This time the added entertainment came from an exuberant United supporter, who celebrated Stuart Pearson's two first-half goals with an impromptu strip-cum-streak during the half-time interval, which began with the shedding of his red and white scarf and finished in the centre circle with the abandonment of his Union Jack underpants.

United had gone ahead in the 17th minute, McIlroy dummying a defender on the right before crossing for Pearson to glance a header into the top corner. His second followed a misjudged clearance by Neilsen two minutes prior to the interval, as sun blurred the defender's vision and the ball dropped from Roche's kick. The United number nine quickly snatched the chance and rounded the 'keeper to score.

The home side pulled one back 10 minutes into the second half when Ziegler centred for Larsen to head home, but it was a short-lived revival as Pearson added a third in the 74th minute, putting away a McIlroy cross.

---

5 August 1975   **Hvidovre at Hvidovre Stadium.**

Attendance: 7,932.

Won: 3–1.

Scorer: Pearson 3.

Team: Roche, Forsyth, Houston, Greenhoff, Holton, Buchan, Coppell, McIlroy, Pearson, Macari, Daly.

Substitutes: Loughnane for McIlroy, Jackson for Daly.

A narrow 3–2 win over Holstebro saw United return home unbeaten, but once again they had to finish the 90 minutes with only 10 men. This time it was Lou Macari who saw red, being dismissed for pulling down a Danish player. The United man attempted to go back and punch his opponent after being sent off by the referee.

'The player had been pulling my shirt,' said the Scot, 'and I only pushed him. When I realised that I was being sent off for such a trifling offence I thought I might as well earn it with a proper punch.'

Houston gave United the lead in the 11th minute, but by half-time they were 2–1 behind. Coppell equalised from Loughnane's centre in the 50th minute, with Macari's sending off coming seven minutes later. Determined not to lose their unbeaten record, United stepped up a gear and, with 10 minutes remaining, a short corner from Jackson provided Daly with the opportunity to score the winner.

One supporter who made the journey to Denmark for those fixtures was Jim Thomas, who recalled: 'The grounds were very small with little or no policing and before one game I and hundreds of others ran on to the pitch in a friendly invasion. Steve Coppell, rather surprisingly, agreed to me taking his photo but Martin Buchan, true to form and rightly so, told me in no uncertain terms that I shouldn't be on the pitch anyway! That perhaps is being polite about it, as he really only used two words, with the second one being "off".

'Strangely, I can't really remember much of the games. We won all three and there were a couple of sendings off. I watched one match lying down on the grass next to the United substitutes bench. Imagine doing that now! I do remember one United fan doing a streak, then making a lot of money by taking a collection from the crowd for his troubles.'

The programme for the match versus Holstebro, 7 August 1975.

7 August 1975	Holstebro at Idraetspark.

Attendance: 4,000.

Won: 3–2.

Scorers: Houston, Coppell, Daly.

Team: Roche, Forsyth, Houston, Greenhoff, Holton, Buchan, Coppell, McIlroy, Pearson, Macari, Daly.

Substitutes: Albiston for Houston, Jackson for Holton, Loughnane for Pearson.

The return to First Division football was a mere four days away, with a trip to the Midlands to face Wolves, but there was still one more warm-up fixture to fulfil, as United were visited by a team whose name will forever be etched in the history of Manchester United: Red Star Belgrade.

Determined to wind up their preparations with a victory, Tommy Docherty's plans were dealt a cruel blow minutes before kick-off when Jim Holton had to leave the pitch with concussion and twisted knee ligaments. A loose ball from Alex Forsyth had hit the big centre-half in the face and he had twisted his knee as he slumped to the ground.

Minutes after the kick-off the United manager was reeling again as the Yugoslav side took the lead. A superbly measured pass from Suchic beat Buchan and found Savic, who drew Roche from his goal before firing the ball low past the 'keeper.

Red Star made it 2–0 in the 26th minute with another well-worked goal. Baralic moved through the middle as Acimovic drew Houston wide, allowing Filipovic to slip the ball through to the now unmarked Baralic to drive the ball home.

Stunned, but certainly not downhearted, United slowly clawed their way back into the game and six minutes later Gerry Daly reduced the advantage from three yards out after McIlroy had hit the crossbar. Five minutes later it was all square, McIlroy scoring from 18 yards after Novokovic had headed out a Pearson effort from underneath the bar.

The programme for the match versus Red Star Belgrade, 12 August 1975.

The game was even for only 60 seconds, before Petrovic put the visitors back in the lead, his effort going in off the post.

Four minutes into the second half it was 3–3. Summer signing from Nottingham Forest Tommy Jackson shot into the bottom corner after passing with Lou Macari.

Substitute Jovanovic restored Red Star's advantage in the 69th minute with a neat individual effort, but with 12 minutes remaining United once again drew level. Coppell, put through by Greenhoff, scored the best goal of the night.

12 August 1975	Red Star Belgrade at Old Trafford.

Attendance: 27,138.

Drew: 4–4.

Scorers: Daly, McIlroy, Jackson, Coppell.

Team: Roche, Forsyth, Houston, Greenhoff, Jackson, Buchan, Coppell, McIlroy, Pearson, Macari, Daly.

Substitutes: Albiston for Forsyth, Loughnane for McIlroy, Lowey for Pearson.

Seven years on from the memorable humid May evening, United's European Cup-winning heroes made a nostalgic reappearance in their all-blue kit for Pat Crerand's testimonial match in front of a 36,646 crowd. Only Bill Foulkes and John Aston were missing from that victorious line up. Their places were taken by Francis Burns and Denis Law, with George Best making his Old Trafford return after 22 months away.

Against the current United side, it was perhaps no surprise that the players from 1968 would be up against it, and the tone was set as early as the first minute when Crerand, with his first touch of the ball, passed it across the face of his own goal, where United's latest addition, Gordon Hill, accepted the easy scoring opportunity.

However, 10 minutes later the Old Trafford crowd rose as one to salute the equaliser. Bobby Charlton sent a 30-yard defence-splitting pass towards the on-running George Best and, with a shimmy of the hips, he sent the 'keeper the wrong way before slipping the ball into the net.

The evening, however, was set to belong to another Belfast-born youngster, David McCreery, with the 18-year-old stealing the show with four goals, his first, an overhead kick which went in off the crossbar, restoring the 1975 side's lead.

After the interval, refreshed with five substitutes, the current side turned the screws on the players of yesteryear. Coppell made it 3–1 with a curling 25-yard effort. Eleven minutes later McCreery scored his second from close range and an ironic cheer greeted a fifth in the 65th minute when Stiles put through an own-goal while under pressure from McCreery and Paterson.

In the 70th minute Nobby atoned for his earlier mishap with a fine pass which allowed Law to scrape a goal back, but it was to mean little, as seven minutes later McCreery completed his hat-trick, adding a fourth with three minutes remaining.

26 November 1975	Manchester United XI at Old Trafford.

Attendance: 36,646.

Won: 7–2.

Scorers: McCreery 4, Coppell, Hill.

Team: Roche, Forsyth, Houston, Daly, Nicholl, Buchan, Coppell, McCreery, Lowey, Macari, Hill.

Substitutes: Mountford for Roche, Albiston for Forsyth, Storey for Daly, Grimshaw for Macari, D. Jackson for Lowey.

There was only one other friendly played during this particular season, with Tommy Docherty taking his players to the south coast, where they played a testimonial match against Plymouth Argyle.

A road accident three years earlier had forced Peter Middleton out of the game and the visit of the crowd-pulling United was a touching gesture and earned the unknown individual a nice little sum. Rather ironically, Middleton was unable to attend as he was at home suffering from appendicitis!

Plymouth took the lead in the 22nd minute when Mariner scored from close range following a McAuley free-kick. United, however, hit back promptly, equalising 10 minutes later when a 30-yard effort from Nicholl was deflected into the net. Coppell put the visitors in front with an angled drive in the 36th minute.

McIlroy and Daly were denied by Furnell in the Plymouth goal, who made a number of fine saves to keep the score down as United piled on the pressure during the second half. Meanwhile, at the opposite end, Mariner thought he had scored an equaliser with 13 minutes remaining, but his header was disallowed for offside.

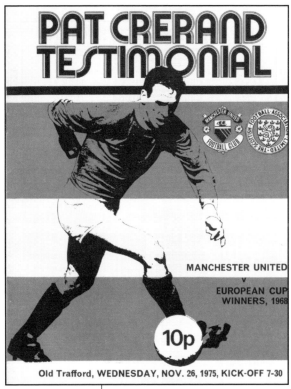

The programme for the match versus the European Cup Winners 1968, 26 November 1975.

9 December 1975	Plymouth Argyle at Home Park.

Attendance: 16,023.

Won: 2–1.

Scorers: Nicholl, Coppell.

Team: Roche, Nicholl, Albiston, Daly, Greenhoff, Buchan, Coppell, McIlroy, Pearson, Macari, Jackson.

Substitutes: McKeown for Nicholl, Grimshaw for Daly, Paterson for Greenhoff, Lowey for McIlroy, McCreery for Pearson.

Having lost the 1976 FA Cup Final to underdogs Southampton 16 days previously, United travelled north to Glasgow to face Celtic in a testimonial for Bobby Lennox and Jimmy Johnstone. This was to be a match that was to set something of a precedent of testimonials between the two clubs.

The night certainly belonged to Lennox and Johnstone, with United, weakened by the absence of several first-team regulars, having no answer to the Johnstone-inspired Glasgow side.

Celtic, however, with manager Jock Stein back in charge for the first time since his car crash the previous July, had to wait until the 32nd minute before opening the scoring, Bobby Lennox rising to head home a Hay cross.

Five minutes after the interval it was 2–0. Kenny Dalglish, the Celtic captain, swivelled past Buchan before hitting a shot that squirmed underneath the body of Stepney and into the net. In the 69th minute it was Dalglish again, working a 1–2 with Johnstone on the right before slipping the ball into the roof of the net, making it 3–0.

Ten minutes from the end Dalglish chalked up his hat-trick as he scored Celtic's fourth. McGrain, with a typical run down the right, passed the ball inside to his captain, who then wrong-footed Buchan before beating Stepney from 15 yards.

The programme for the match versus Plymouth Argyle, 9 December 1975.

The programme for the match versus Celtic, 17 May 1976.

JIMMY JOHNSTONE & BOBBY LENNOX TESTIMONIAL GAME

CELTIC PARK GLASGOW

MONDAY 17th MAY 1976 at 8 p.m.

OFFICIAL SOUVENIR PROGRAMME 25p

CELTIC·MANCHESTER UNITED

17 May 1976   **Celtic at Celtic Park.**

Attendance: 48,000.

Lost: 4–0.

Team: Stepney, Forsyth, Houston, Jackson, Waldron, Buchan, Coppell, McIlroy, McCreery, Loughnane, Storey.

Substitutes: Albiston for Buchan, Nicholl for Forsyth, Coyne for Loughnane.

The programme for the match versus Vancouver Whitecaps, 24 May 1976.

Seven days later, United were in Canada for the first fixture of a three-match American mini-tour. The first game saw them take on Vancouver Whitecaps, with the host side more concerned about the $30,000 lost revenue, due to a driving rainstorm, than the goalless draw that was played out on the soggy artificial pitch. A crowd of over 20,000 had been expected, but rain forced many to remain indoors, with Tommy Docherty proclaiming, 'Every fan out there deserves a gold medal for turning up to watch.' He added, 'I thought it was a great game in horrible conditions.'

As the rain pelted down, mistakes were inevitable and Peter Coyne almost cashed in on one by Lenarduzzi when he robbed the Whitecap defender and raced through to the goal, only to have his shot blocked by Wilson. At the opposite end, Stepney almost paid the price for dashing from his goalline, becoming stranded in no-man's-land with Robinson closing in. Much to the United 'keeper's relief the forward elected for power and Stepney was able to smother the ball.

Phil Parkes, better known as goalkeeper with Wolves, was kept on his toes by numerous crosses from Alex Forsyth, possibly United's best player. The big 'keeper, however, was fortunate not to be picking the ball out of his net in the 65th minute when Storey gathered Waldron's pass on the edge of the area and splashed towards goal before hitting the ball wide of the post from 14 yards.

With only two minutes remaining, McCreery should have won the game for United. Escaping the close attention of Wilson for the first time, he hit a point-blank shot to the right of Parkes, but the 'keeper managed to save it.

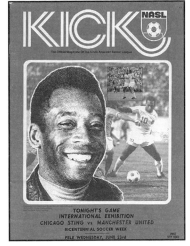

The programme for the match versus Chicago Sting, 26 May 1976.

24 May 1976	Vancouver Whitecaps at Empire Stadium, Vancouver.

Attendance: 16,091.

Drew: 0–0.

Team: Stepney, Forsyth, Houston, Daly, Waldron, Buchan, McIlroy, Jackson, Coyne, Storey, McCreery.

Two days later United had to be content with another draw, this time against Chicago Sting, managed by former United defender Bill Foulkes. If the result was pleasing to the European Cup-winning defender, then it was even more so for John Lowey, the United youth-team forward, who was spending the summer on loan with the American club, as he scored both of the home side's goals.

Lou Macari, playing his first game since the FA Cup Final, gave United the lead two minutes prior to the interval with a 25-yard drive. However, straight from the restart the Americans attacked, with Lowey beating Stepney from 15 yards.

In the 62nd minute the home crowd were on their feet as Lowey again proved to be a thorn in United's side. Collecting a loose pass back about 30 yards out, he was faced with a one-on-one with Alex Stepney, but kept his head and coolly put the ball beyond the United 'keeper.

There was to be no fairy-tale ending, however, as three minutes later Sammy McIlroy scored from a direct free-kick, a goal that was to give United a draw.

Pennant for the match versus Chicago Sting, 26 May 1976.

26 May 1976	Chicago Sting at Soldier Field, Chicago.

Attendance: 8,213.

Drew: 2–2.

Scorers: Macari, McIlroy.

Team: Stepney, Forsyth, Albiston, Daly, Waldron, Buchan, McIlroy, Jackson, Coyne, Macari, McCreery.

Substitutes: Nicholl, Storey, Patterson for unknown players.

United's tour reached an unbelievable climax in Texas, against Dallas Tornado, with the pre-match build up something that could only happen in America.

When a Texan announced to the United players prior to the match 'you ain't seen nothing yet' he certainly was not kidding, as entry onto the pitch was made on board two stagecoaches, with the players wearing their kit complete with 10-gallon hats.

After the Dallas side had made their entrance the visitors were introduced to the crowd. All the players were given a 'middle' name: 'Ladies and gentlemen, Stewart "Paleface" Houston, Alex "Longhorn" Forsyth, Lou "Quick Draw" Macari…' With the introductions over, three men then parachuted out of the pitch-black sky 7,000 feet up, dropping onto the centre circle.

It was also announced that if the home side scored between the 30th and 45th minute then there would be a free suit for some lucky fans. The half-time interval

Poster for the match versus Chicago Sting, 26 May 1976.

DALLAS TORNADO vs. MANCHESTER UNITED
May 29, 1976
International Game. $1.00

The programme for the match versus Dallas Tornado, 29 May 1976.

continued along the same theme, with a penalty shoot-out earning any of the six takers $1,000 if they scored, with the 'keeper earning the same for any that he saved.

The entertainment did not end with the final whistle, as there was a little matter of $40,000 up for grabs. Two armoured cars appeared and spread the dollar bills over the pitch, with two lucky programme holders invited to grab as much as they could in a minute.

As for the match? It was yet another draw.

Arthur Albiston set up David McCreery for United's first in the 14th minute, but they could not add to their total until 15 minutes before the end, when Jimmy Nicholl scored with a right-footed drive from 25 yards.

With the game looking over and only nine minutes remaining, Dallas pulled a goal back. Kewley picked up Garcia as he ran through the middle of the United defence to score from 10 yards.

Three minutes later it was all square, as former West Brom forward Bobby Hope passed to Stremlau, whose shot dipped under the crossbar and into the net from 22 yards.

29 May 1976   **Dallas Tornado at Ownby Stadium, Dallas.**

Attendance: 15,234.

Drew: 2–2.

Scorers: McCreery, Nicholl.

Team: Stepney, Forsyth, Houston, Daly, Waldron, Buchan, McIlroy, Storey, McCreery, Macari, Albiston.

Substitutes: Nicholl, Jackson and Patterson for unknown players.

Preparations for the new campaign got underway with Tommy Docherty taking his players to Germany to face Nuremberg and Hamburg. They got off to the perfect start, with a 2–1 win over the former.

Against the German Second Division side, who had already enjoyed the benefit of playing a handful of pre-season games, Docherty's team wasted little time in showing their intent.

With 13 minutes gone Forsyth swept over an inviting cross and his full-back partner Houston scooped the ball home. Three minutes later Forsyth was again scurrying down the flank, with Hill this time snatching the opportunity to put United two up.

The Germans, although shaken by United's frantic start, pulled a goal back in the 20th minute through a Malkowski header. However, despite threatening Stepney's goal on numerous occasions, and forcing the United 'keeper into making several outstanding saves, they could not force an equaliser.

Victory for United was always on a knife-edge and certainly not guaranteed until the full-time whistle.

30 July 1976   **Nuremberg at Stadtisches Stadion.**

Attendance: 6,000.

Won: 2–1.

Scorers: Houston, Hill.

Team: Stepney, Forsyth, Houston, Daly, Greenhoff, Buchan, Coppell, McIlroy, Pearson, Macari, Hill.

Substitutes: McCreery for Pearson, Storey for Hill.

A much sterner test awaited United in Hamburg against the West German Cup winners and Bundesliga runners-up. They were a team described by Bob Russell, the *Daily Mirror*'s man on the spot, as 'the richest club in Europe, with a profit of over £1 million to show over the last two years'. Such things mattered little to Docherty's players as they brushed the Germans aside, backed by a volatile and vocal support, which was estimated at around 5,000.

United went ahead in the 20th minute as Daly and Macari enjoyed the best of the mid field exchanges and Coppell stretched the home defence down the right. It was from one of the winger's attacking thrusts that United opened the scoring, his cross finding McIlroy, who scored from eight yards out.

It was a lead, however, that they held for only seven minutes, as rather surprisingly they relaxed slightly. From one Hamburg attack Nogly went down rather feebly under a challenge from Buchan and Volkert was able to score from the penalty spot.

With only minutes remaining before the interval all hell broke loose, as beer cans and bottles were showered across the terracing. Police moved in with their dogs and a number of German fans were arrested before order was restored.

Five minutes into the second half Stuart Pearson restored United's lead as he headed home a Gerry Daly cross, and 13 minutes later the outcome was put beyond any doubt when Daly scored from the penalty spot, after Kaltz had pushed McIlroy off the ball. 'It might have been six, we were that good,' exclaimed the Doc.

The programme for the match versus Nuremberg, 30 July 1976.

---

2 August 1976 **SV Hamburg at Volkspark Stadion.**

Attendance: 35,000.

Won: 3–1.

Scorers: McIlroy, Pearson, Daly (pen.).

Team: Stepney, Nicholl, Houston, Daly, Greenhoff, Buchan, Coppell, McIlroy, Pearson, Macari, Hill.

'ANOTHER RED RIOT' proclaimed the headlines in the *Daily Mirror*, above Bob Russell's match report for the match against AZ Alkmaar. The behaviour of a section of the travelling United support was once again overshadowing the performance on the pitch.

'Bottles and beer cans rained from the red-dominated area behind a goal as Alkmaar, the country cousins of United's UEFA Cup opponents Ajax, paraded a Japanese-sponsored trophy at the end of this hard, but hardly inflammatory friendly' wrote Russell. 'Suddenly Alkmaar, seconds earlier in a team of dancing, prancing though ungainly giants, were the fleeing Dutchmen – dashing away from the danger zone as dog handlers moved in only to make a similarly rapid retreat as a hundred and more rebels against the true Old Trafford cause went wild.'

On the pitch, despite United being far superior to the Dutch side, they just could not put the ball in the net, with the game fading out to a goalless draw.

The programme for the match versus SV Hamburg, 2 August 1976.

> **4 August 1976** **AZ Alkmaar at Alkmaarder Hout.**
>
> **Attendance:** 18,000.
>
> **Drew:** 0–0.
>
> **Team:** Stepney, Nicholl, Albiston, Storey, Waldron, Buchan, Jackson, McCreery, Pearson, Macari, Hill.
>
> **Substitutes:** Daly for Storey, Greenhoff for Buchan, Houston for Greenhoff.

It was to be Lou Macari who was to grab the headlines next, as, seeking a new pay deal, things were to come to a head when he was substituted against Red Star Belgrade. The Scot claimed that it was unclear whether or not he was wanted by the club and that all he was seeking was a fair deal: 'A few problems have been building up for me and the substitution in Belgrade seemed like the last straw.'

Tommy Docherty viewed things a little differently, saying, 'all players with Manchester United are treated alike. There is neither favouritism nor victimisation when it comes to making a substitution in any games. Lou has not been playing as well as he can play on our tour and when I took him off it was because I felt I had to do something about it.'

As for the game, United took the lead in the 15th minute when Hill beat Fisk on the left wing and crossed for Pearson to score with a glancing header. However, rather surprisingly they proceeded to concede two goals. The first came in the 24th minute when Fillpovic got past Waldron while the second came a minute after the interval when Lukic shot between Hill and Houston with the ball going through Stepney's legs.

> **8 August 1976** **Red Star Belgrade at Stadion Crvena Zvezda.**
>
> **Attendance:** 35,000.
>
> **Lost:** 2–1.
>
> **Scorer:** Pearson.
>
> **Team:** Stepney, Nicholl, Houston, Daly, Waldron, Buchan, Coppell, McIlroy, Pearson, Macari, Hill.
>
> **Substitutes:** Albiston for Houston, McCreery for Macari.

With the first League fixture of the 1976–77 season a mere 10 days away, United's final warm-up game was a little nearer to home at Lansdowne Road, Dublin, where a Home Farm Select side provided the opposition. Tougher opponents might have given the manager a better idea of how his charges were shaping up, but after the defeat in Belgrade a victory would boost confidence for the start of the new campaign.

Despite the Home Farm side being augmented by the likes of Latchford and Dobson of Everton and Daly of Wolves, United tore the opposition apart in the opening 20 minutes.

Defending from the outset, the Select's good fortune held out until only the 11th minute, when a neat interchange of passes between Daly and McCreery created a huge gap in their defence and Hill fired home from 15 yards. Five minutes later it was 2–0, as Bourke's attempted interception of a Houston pass presented Macari with an easy opportunity.

In midfield Home Farm were unable to cope with the effervescent Macari and Daly, while the direct running of McCreery up front kept their defence on their toes. It was rather surprising that they did not go further in front until five minutes into the second half, when Coppell made it 3–0, scoring from six yards following an in-swinging McIlroy corner.

---

11 August 1976 Home Farm Select at Lansdowne Road, Dublin.

Attendance: 15,000.

Won: 3–0.

Scorers: Hill, Macari, Coppell.

Team: Stepney, Forsyth, Houston, Daly, Greenhoff, Buchan, Coppell, McIlroy, McCreery, Macari, Hill.

Substitutes: Roche for Stepney, Albiston for Hill, Nicholl for Forsyth, Waldron for Greenhoff.

The programme for the match versus Home Farm Select, 11 August 1976.

A trip to Ninian Park in Cardiff would normally mean 90 minutes against Cardiff City, but on this particular occasion the opposition was a South Wales XI in a match arranged to help save Newport County, a team whose £100,000 debts threatened to put them out of existence. The crowd of 13,000 brought in receipts of £7,848, leaving them with around £6,000 after expenses (United playing for nothing), which would keep the struggling Fourth Division club in business until the end of the season at least.

With no game the previous Saturday, Tommy Docherty welcomed the run-out, but there was little to bring a smile to his face as the Select XI won by the only goal of the game.

Despite enjoying plenty of attacking possession, Pearson and Jimmy Greenhoff failed to get on the end of Coppell's numerous crosses.

This game saw the return of Martin Buchan in defence after missing 10 games through injury. His return, however, did not keep things watertight, as the hosts scored just before the interval when a centre from James on the left was converted by the unmarked Dwyer, who leapt above the United defence to head home.

Hill should have equalised early in the second half when Macari put him through, while the Welsh side could quite as easily have increased their lead when Evans foiled Roche, only for Curtis to smash his close-range shot against the post.

---

8 December 1976 South Wales XI at Ninian Park.

Attendance: 13,033.

Lost: 1–0.

Team: Stepney, Forsyth, Houston, McIlroy, B. Greenhoff, Buchan, Coppell, J.Greenhoff, Pearson, Macari, Hill.

Substitutes: Roche for Stepney, Daly for McIlroy, McCreery for Hill, Albiston for B. Greenhoff, McGrath for Pearson.

The programme for the match versus South Wales XI, 8 December 1976.

The turning point of the 1968 European Cup Final had probably been Alex Stepney's point-blank save from Portuguese legend Eusebio, so it was fitting that the United 'keeper was rewarded with a testimonial match to acknowledge his 10 years at Old Trafford, with Benfica providing the opposition.

The 38,000 crowd and the £40,000 receipts were a further thank-you to the United custodian and he was given a thunderous reception prior to the kick-off when he made his way on to the Old Trafford pitch, before proceeding to make a series of superb saves.

The programme for the match versus Benfica, 9 February 1977.

A two-goal burst in a 12-minute first-half period was enough to win the game for United. Coppell opened the scoring after seven minutes when Bento had failed to hold Hill's centre, with the second, scored by Macari, coming in a move which swung from one end of the pitch to the other. Stepney's long throw picked out Macari, who in turn found McCreery and, after beating Alberto, he crossed to the Scot to head home.

The announcement that England were losing 2–0 against Holland prompted chants of 'Stepney for England' and the United 'keeper had to be alert to save from Chalana and Jose Luis as Benfica pressed forward.

Bento did well to prevent Macari and McGrath from increasing the score, but with 16 minutes remaining it was Benfica who found the net, Chalana pushing the ball home in a goalmouth scramble for Nene's centre.

9 February 1977	**Benfica at Old Trafford.**

Attendance: 37,988.

Won: 2–1.

Scorers: Coppell, Macari.

Team: Stepney, Nicholl, Houston, McIlroy, Waldron, Buchan, Coppell, J. Greenhoff, McCreery, Macari, Hill.

Substitutes: Forsyth for Waldron, McGrath for McCreery, Jackson for Hill, Rogers for Nicholl.

Another testimonial match rounded off the friendly fixtures for season 1976–77. This time the game was held across Manchester at Maine Road in a match against Manchester City for Glyn Pardoe, whose career was tragically cut short by a complicated leg fracture. In a keenly fought confrontation in front of a rather poor crowd for a 'derby' match, two second-half City goals were enough to send the blue half of Manchester home happy.

It was United, however, who made the brighter start, with Macari heading home Jackson's corner in the 25th minute, a lead that they managed to hold on to until a minute before half-time when Hartford equalised.

After the interval Palmer, who had replaced injured former United hero Brian Kidd, put Roche under pressure, with the United 'keeper making a succession of notable saves before finally being beaten by a Bennett drive in the 64th minute. Seventeen minutes later Palmer made it 3–1, scoring from close range following good work from Barnes and Donachie.

With nine minutes remaining United pulled a goal back when Jimmy Greenhoff rammed home Coppell's pass, but Palmer wrapped things up two minutes from time, scoring his second of the evening from the penalty spot after being fouled by Forsyth.

United's former players, led by Bobby Charlton, could not even get the better of a Francis Lee side in a half-time five-a-side contest which City won 3–2.

25 March 1977	**Manchester City at Maine Road.**

Attendance: 7,564.

Lost: 4–2.

Scorers: Macari, J. Greenhoff.

Team: Roche, Forsyth, Albiston, Jackson, Nicholl, Buchan, Coppell, J. Greenhoff, McCreery, Macari, McGrath.

Substitutes: Grimes for Macari, Bradley for Buchan.

Having succumbed to underdogs Southampton in the 1976 FA Cup Final, the United players retraced their steps 12 months on, only to find themselves classed as the underdogs. They also found themselves standing between opponents Liverpool and an unprecedented treble. Tommy Docherty, in what was to be his last match at the helm, guided his team to a notable victory, but that elusive dream of Championship success was to remain just that, as his private misdemeanour was considered by the board of directors a sackable offence. Into the manager's office came Dave Sexton, an entirely different type of personality, but the former boss of Queen's Park Rangers was viewed by most as a suitable replacement.

Sexton had the luxury of a couple of weeks and a quartet of friendlies in which to get to know his players before the season began properly. This gave him time to decide which positions required strengthening and the best formation to use with those players he had available.

In his initial 90 minutes against Werder Bremen everything looked rosy as United stormed into a two-goal lead in the opening quarter of an hour. Macari knocked a low, probing cross into the Bremen penalty area, Jimmy Greenhoff dummied and McIlroy slotted the ball home from eight yards after six minutes. Eight minutes later it was 2–0, Pearson climbing to an in-swinging corner from Hill to back-head the ball into the net.

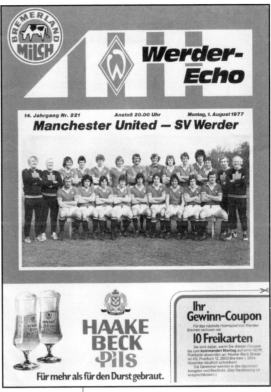

The programme for the match versus Werder Bremen, 1 August 1977.

There was more trouble among the United supporters as, rather surprisingly, this was the cue for around 20 being ejected after police with guard dogs moved in.

On the half-hour the home side pulled a goal back when Albiston grounded Konschal in the area and Rober hammered home the spot-kick. Seconds before the interval United's lead had disappeared. Dressel had cut in from the wing, but clipped his shot against the post. His second attempt was blocked by Nicholl, but he managed to beat Stepney with his third attempt.

United's slick, inventive play of the opening period had by now disappeared and it was not a surprise when, on the hour mark, Rober scored a third for Bremen with a 20-yard drive.

---

1 August 1977   **Werder Bremen at Wasar Stadium.**

Attendance: 20,000.

Lost: 3–2.

Scorers: McIlroy, Pearson.

Team: Stepney, Nicholl, Albiston, McIlroy, B. Greenhoff, Buchan, Coppell, J. Greenhoff, Pearson, Macari, Hill.

Substitutes: McCreery for McIlroy, Forsyth for B. Greenhoff.

Dave Sexton got his first win as manager of Manchester United against the bottom club in the Norwegian First Division, Rosenborg, in a contest where the opposition were poor.

Four goals in each half kept the crowd entertained, but the match raised the question of whether such fixtures were really productive. Stronger opposition might perhaps provide a better warm-up for the rigours of First Division football.

3 August 1977	**Rosenborg Ballklub at Trondheim.**

Attendance:

Won: 8–0.

Scorers: Hill 2, Forsyth, McIlroy, McCreery, J. Greenhoff, Buchan, opp. own-goal

Team: Roche, Forsyth, Albiston, Grimes, Nicholl, Buchan, McGrath, J. Greenhoff, Pearson, McCreery, Hill.

Substitutes: McIlroy for Grimes, Macari for Pearson.

The 8–0 victory five days previously gained United new supporters in Norway and a further four goals against the unambitious, defensively minded amateurs Hamarkameratene (HamKam) earned them a few more, although the slow-motion win laboured along in the opening minutes, with United failing to put together a solitary move to satisfy their new admirers.

Indeed, it was not until two minutes before half-time that United breached the Norwegian defence. A long clearance by Stepney was latched on to by Jimmy Greenhoff, who scored with an awkward angled drive which went in off the far post.

The second half saw United step up a gear, with substitute McCreery bringing the game to life when he got on to the end of a flying header from Pearson, two yards from goal, to make it 2–0 in the 61st minute.

In the 75th minute Pearson made it 3–0 with a shot that went in off the post after Macari had penetrated the defence. A fourth followed five minutes later when McCreery claimed his second after Coppell had left a trail of unsuccessful tackles in his wake.

8 August 1977	**Hamarkameratene at Briskeby.**

Attendance: 7,000.

Won: 4–0.

Scorers: McCreery 2, J. Greenhoff, Pearson.

Team: Stepney, Forsyth, Albiston, McIlroy, Nicholl, Buchan, Coppell, J. Greenhoff, Pearson, Macari, Hill.

Substitute: McCreery for J. Greenhoff.

The programme for the match versus HamKam, 8 August 1977.

In the fourth and final game of the Norwegian tour Second Division leaders Strømsgodset collapsed as United turned on the style with an uncharitable nine-goal display.

The goal-fest began in the fourth minute when Macari sent Hill clear and, after a mind-boggling piece of ball-juggling, the winger crossed for Pearson to head home. Jimmy Greenhoff tucked home the first of his five-goal haul after Hill's initial shot was half blocked. A 52nd-minute header, a prod in a minute later and another header at the near post in the 58th minute gave him the easiest hat-trick of his career.

McGrath dummied the defence for a solo goal in the 63rd minute, while McCreery set up two for Macari in the 69th and 73rd minutes. To the surprise of the crowd, the Norwegians managed to notch up two goals before Greenhoff rounded off the scoring by steering home a Macari free-kick.

10 August 1977   **Strømsgodset at Drammen.**

Attendance: Unknown

Won: 9–2.

Scorers: J. Greenhoff 5, Macari 2, Pearson, McGrath.

Team: Stepney, Nicholl, Albiston, McIlroy, B. Greenhoff, Buchan, Coppell, J. Greenhoff, Pearson, Macari, Hill.

Substitutes: Roche for Stepney, Forsyth for Albiston, Grimes for McIlroy, McCreery for Pearson, McGrath for Hill.

The programme for the match versus Strømsgodset, 10 August 1977.

United had agreed to play the Iran B side at the request of the British Government, as part of the British Trade Week export drive in the Middle East.

It was a game that manager Dave Sexton could certainly have done without, coming on the back of two successive 4–0 defeats, against FC Porto in the European Cup-Winners' Cup and West Bromwich Albion in the League. The latter, perhaps, had more to do with the injections for cholera and smallpox, which had laid low Arthur Albiston and Jimmy Greenhoff, than the performance of the Midlands club.

Watched by Crown Prince Reza and the British Ambassador, United went straight on to the attack and goalkeeper Nadar Faryad-Shirai did well to keep out an effort from Jimmy Nicholl as early as the fifth minute. Coppell squandered another opportunity soon afterwards, while Macari, who was clean through on goal, was denied by the Iranian 'keeper.

A chance fell to the home side in the 15th minute, but Hussein Fedaker fumbled his shot past the post, a miss which was to prove costly as Coppell was soon to pounce amid a goalmouth mêlée to probe the ball home.

Another fine save from the Iranian 'keeper kept out a Buchan header following a corner and after the interval the United defence found themselves stretched as the equaliser was sought in a flurry of promising attacks by the Iran side.

As it turned out, there was to be no equaliser as the confident United side took everything in their stride, with McGrath adding a second and the club pocketing a cheque for £10,000 before heading home at 2am in the morning.

24 October 1977   **Iran B at Amjadieh Stadium, Tehran.**

Attendance: 20,000.

Won: 2–0.

Scorers: Coppell, McGrath.

Team: Roche, Forsyth, Grimes, McIlroy, Nicholl, Buchan, McGrath, Coppell, Pearson, McCreery, Hill.

Substitutes: T. Jackson for McIlroy, Clark for Pearson, Ashworth for Hill.

With United's European Cup-Winners' Cup fixture against St Etienne causing much unwanted publicity due to crowd disturbances, it was perhaps strange that the French cancer research organisation should invite United back across the English Channel for a friendly.

Compared to the previous fixture between the two clubs, the 90 minutes in the French capital were played in an atmosphere of almost total serenity, although the final whistle brought derisive jeers from the crowd, as well as welcome relief following the 0–0 draw.

Ticket for the match versus St Etienne, 6 December 1977.

Stuart Pearson missed a golden opportunity in the opening minutes after Hill left three defenders sprawled in his wake, the normally clinical finisher perhaps having too much time to pick his spot.

Revelli should have put the French ahead five minutes before the interval, but fired over from eight yards. He was also to scorn two other scoring opportunities in the opening minutes of the second half, firstly with a header smothered by Roche and then when the United 'keeper dived at his feet.

Sarramagna, Farison and Rocheteau headed and shot over the United bar when they could have been expected to score, while at the opposite end Jimmy Greenhoff saw his 14-yard volley go narrowly past the post.

The game proceeded to fizzle out, although there were odd signs of an aftermath from the previous encounters between the two teams.

---

6 December 1977 **St Etienne at Parc des Princes Stadium, Paris.**

Attendance: 19,500.

Drew: 0—0.

Team: Roche, Nicholl, Albiston, McIlroy, B. Greenhoff, Houston, McGrath, J. Greenhoff, Pearson, Grimes, Hill.

Substitutes: Ritchie for Pearson, Clark for McIlroy.

Manager Dave Sexton took his time bringing in new faces to spruce up a United side that often struggled and displayed uncharacteristic flaws. Joe Jordan became his first signing, in a club record £350,000 deal from Leeds United, and was closely followed by former Elland Road teammate Gordon McQueen, whose protracted transfer cost United £500,000.

A clause in McQueen's transfer contract prevented him from making his United debut against his former teammates and it looked as if his first appearance in a red shirt would be on 15 February in the unfamiliar surroundings of Barrow-in-Furness, when Dave Sexton took a team to face North West League side Greengate United. This was a match arranged to pay for the medical expenses of local three-and-a-half-year-old Alison Miners.

Greengate Secretary David Ball said that he had written to United asking for a signed ball and, rather tongue in cheek, for a game, expecting only the former. He was astonished when a reply came to the club, which had a regular attendance of around 25 to 30 supporters, agreeing to both.

As it was, McQueen did not make his debut at the footballing outpost of Holker Street, but a crowd of 6,100 did turn up, raising £1,800 for the appeal fund, a figure that United said they would add to due to the non-appearance of their latest signing. Manager Dave Sexton had decided that the bumpy, straw-strewn pitch was not the ideal setting for his big-money signing to make his debut. However, any disappointment about his non-appearance was soon forgotten in what turned out to be a bustling 90 minutes. United won 2–0 with goals from Chris McGrath in the 17th minute and Jonathan Clark two minutes later.

On Tuesday 11 April United took time out from a busy First Division schedule in order to acknowledge one of their former players, as Dave Sexton took his first-team squad to Preston North End to play a testimonial for 1968 European Cup winner David Sadler.

Against the promotion-seeking Deepdale side, United struggled and were 3–0 down to a Mike Elwiss hat-trick in just over half an hour, the Preston front man giving United's international defenders a difficult time.

The home side's confidence was so high that they sent out seven reserves as substitutes for the second half and, conceding the game, United did likewise, making nine changes as the game faded.

11 April 1978	Preston North End at Deepdale.

Attendance: 10,380.

Lost: 3–0.

Team: Stepney, B. Greenhoff, Houston, McIlroy, McQueen, Buchan, Coppell, Jordan, Pearson, Macari, McCreery.

Substitutes: Roche for Stepney, Forsyth for B. Greenhoff, Albiston for Houston, T. Jackson for McIlroy, Duxbury for McQueen, Nicholl for Buchan, Ashworth for Jordan, Paterson for Pearson, McGrath for Macari.

The programme for the match versus Preston North End, 11 April 1978.

United brought the curtain down on the home front with a testimonial match for Queen's Park Rangers defender Dave Clement, in a match played under farcical conditions on a puddle pitch.

The conditions altered Dave Sexton's team selection, but did give Lou Macari his first 90-minute run out after missing five games with a foot injury. It also gave Jimmy Greenhoff an opportunity, after he had spent a number of weeks on the sidelines.

Goals from Joe Jordan and substitute Alex Forsyth were not enough to give United victory, as two goals from Paul Goddard and two others from former United player Don Givens and Paul McGhee propelled the Londoners to victory.

5 May 1978	Queen's Park Rangers at Loftus Road.

Attendance: 6,000.

Lost: 4–2.

Scorers: Jordan, Forsyth.

Team: Stepney, B. Greenhoff, Albiston, McIlroy, Nicholl, Houston, Coppell, Jordan, Pearson, Macari, Grimes.

Substitutes: Roche for Stepney, McCreery for McIlroy, Forsyth for Nicholl, McGrath for Coppell, J. Greenhoff for Pearson.

The programme for the match versus Queen's Park Rangers, 5 May 1978.

As Lou Macari, Martin Buchan and Joe Jordan headed to Argentina on Scotland's ill-fated World Cup campaign, their United teammates had an end-of-season tournament in Norway and two games in the United States before they could enjoy a well-earned rest in the sun.

In their opening game of the triangular tournament, organised to celebrate the 75th anniversary of Bergen club Brann, United lost 3–0 to Dutch side Ajax, whose 29-year-old striker Rudi Geels blasted a hat-trick.

Geels had scored five of his team's 12 goals against the host club the previous Thursday and his teammates kept United under constant pressure throughout the 90 minutes, with the nearest United could come to scoring being a 25-yard effort from McCreery which hit the bar.

Playing in his last game for the Dutch side before joining Anderlecht, Geels scored the first of his treble from 15 yards out, with his second and third both coming from passes by Arnesen.

The match, played in a highly competitive manner, saw three players booked, including Lou Macari, who had been given special permission by Scotland to play before setting off on World Cup duty. The Scot, like his fellow United travellers to Argentina, would have probably opted to spend the next couple of weeks on club rather than international duty, had they known what lay ahead.

21 May 1978	Ajax at Brann Stadium, Bergen.

Attendance: 10,700.

Lost: 3–0.

Team: Roche, Forsyth, Rogers, McCreery, Houston, Nicholl, McGrath, J. Greenhoff, Ritchie, Macari, McIlroy.

Substitutes: Clark for McCreery, Ashworth for McIlroy.

In the second fixture, against the host club Brann, United performed much better, notching up a 3–1 victory, although neither this nor the previous fixture conjured up any interest in the local or national press.

It was certainly of little importance: even within Manchester, many supporters cared little whether Sexton's team had won or lost. Perhaps the only person who was actualy concerned about the outcome of the game was goalkeeper Gary Bailey, who had lined up for Brann against his United

The programme for the match versus Brann, 24 May 1978.

teammates as the Norwegians did not have a fit custodian within their ranks. Unfortunately he could not keep his colleagues at bay, conceding three.

---

24 May 1978   **Brann at Brann Stadium, Bergen.**

Attendance: Unknown

Won: 3–1.

Scorers: J. Greenhoff (pen.), McGrath, McIlroy.

Team: Roche, Forsyth, Houston, McIlroy, Paterson, Nicholl, McGrath, J. Greenhoff, Ritchie, Macari, Ashworth.

Substitutes: Moran for McIlroy, Duxbury for Nicholl, Clark for Ritchie, Rogers for Ashworth.

Following the 3–1 victory in Norway, Dave Sexton took his troops to the United States, where they were scheduled to play two fixtures, the first in Florida against Tampa Bay Rowdies. Football in America was still finding its feet and was awash with so many side attractions that the whole thing was, at times, more akin to a circus.

The whole 90 minutes were punctuated with advertising jingles, bursts of music and the booming voice of the PA announcer urging on the local heroes, who had all been given their own colourful nicknames.

Despite all the distractions, it was United who took the lead in the 16th minute through Stuart Pearson, after Houston had sent Coppell's cross back across the Tampa goal.

Augmented by a host of familiar names, including Hammond, ex-Crystal Palace, Paddon and McGuire, both ex-Norwich City and Rodney Marsh, ex-City, the home side resiliently fought back and just before the interval they equalised through Connell, following good work from Brazilian Miradinha.

Despite the commentator asking the fans if they 'would like one more goal?' and the club song blasting out from the speakers as the cheerleaders danced along the touchline, it was not until the 71st minute that United fell behind. David Robb, former Aberdeen colleague of Martin Buchan, accepted the opportunity after Grimes had collided with Roche, a substitute for Stepney, who had to leave the field with a cracked rib.

The heat also claimed a few casualties, with the game played in a clammy temperature of 87 degrees Fahrenheit.

The programme for the match versus Tampa Bay, 28 May 1978.

---

28 May 1978   **Tampa Bay Rowdies at Tampa Stadium.**

Attendance: 15,000.

Lost: 2–1.

Scorer: Pearson.

Team: Stepney, Forsyth, Albiston, McIlroy, Houston, B. Greenhoff, Coppell, J. Greenhoff, Pearson, McCreery, Grimes.

Substitutes: Roche for Stepney, Clark for J. Greenhoff, McGrath for Pearson, Ashworth for Grimes.

Moving on to Tulsa, United fared slightly better against the local Roughnecks, salvaging some pride with a 2–1 victory, although it was not until the final half-hour that the match swung their way.

The Tulsa team, managed by former United defender Bill Foulkes, included four Englishmen, one Yugoslav, one Irishman and one veteran American. They

The programme for the match versus Tulsa, 30 May 1978.

gave United a good game and deservingly took the lead just on the hour through Caskey, although their goal had survived one or two narrow escapes earlier on.

Coppell went close on two occasions, while two minutes before the break Houston, having got his head to a Forsyth free-kick, was disappointed to see it coming back off the underside of the bar.

Tempers began to fray slightly after the interval, with Houston and Sautter both being spoken to by the referee, the latter being replaced shortly afterwards by goalscorer Caskey.

United took only 10 minutes to equalise, McIlroy setting up Brian Greenhoff, who fired home from 20 yards. It was Greenhoff, with a low shot from 25 yards, who won the game for United five minutes from time.

After the match Bill Foulkes thought that his side should have won, saying: 'I knew I would spoil our balance when I made all those substitutions. I probably blew the game. But winning the game wasn't the objective of our playing Manchester United. The object was to let everyone play against a great team.'

30 May 1978	**Tulsa Roughnecks at Skelly Stadium.**

Attendance: 5,872.

Won: 2–1.

Scorer: B. Greenhoff 2.

Team: Roche, Forsyth, Albiston, B. Greenhoff, Houston, Nicholl, McGrath, J. Greenhoff, McCreery, McIlroy, Coppell.

Substitutes: Ashworth for McGrath, Ritchie for J. Greenhoff, Clark for McCreery, Grimes for McIlroy, McIlroy for Grimes.

Pre-season preparations for 1978–79 got underway with two matches in Germany, as Dave Sexton set out in search of that elusive League Championship. There were to be few crumbs of comfort for the United boss, however, as both fixtures were to end in draws.

United's travelling support, forever a thorn in the side of the authorities and opposing clubs, had been given a pre-season warning that all away fixtures would be 'all-ticket', with no admission on the day. This did little to quell the crowd trouble which marred the club's opening pre-season fixture against FC Cologne.

At half-time Dave Sexton made an appeal over the public address system to the fans, asking: 'I would appreciate it if United supporters would behave. Apparently 10 people have been injured. Please just enjoy the game and support us as well as you can. We don't want trouble.' Rather surprisingly, his words seemed to have some effect, as the second half was played out without any further incidents.

As for the match itself, it was contract rebel Jimmy Greenhoff, looking for a deal that would put him in line with fellow teammates, who earned United the 1–1 draw, putting them in front in the 22nd minute with a low left-footed shot which beat Schumacher with its pace.

Cologne, the reigning German League and Cup holders, equalised six minutes later after a period of sustained pressure, during which they might have had a penalty when Houston knocked Konopka to the ground. The German full-back, however, had his revenge, when he crossed from the right for Glwacz to volley home.

The second half saw the pace of the game slow as temperatures touched the nineties and both teams happily played out the 90 minutes in a relaxed manner.

29 July 1978	**FC Cologne at Mungersdorfer Stadium.**

Attendance: 11,000.

Drew: 1—1.

Scorer: J. Greenhoff.

Team: Roche, Albiston, Houston, B. Greenhoff, McQueen, Buchan, Coppell, J. Greenhoff, Jordan, Macari, McIlroy.

Substitutes: Grimes for B. Greenhoff, McCreery for McIlroy, McGrath for J. Greenhoff, Ritchie for Coppell.

Following the match in Cologne, United Supporters' Club Chairman, David Smith, said: 'I believe we have reached the stage where United must consider planning these games in secret and playing them further afield. Somewhere like Denmark, for example, where it would be much more expensive and difficult for the wrong sort of people to get to. I appreciate the club's desire to play against the best opposition but there is also a duty to protect people.'

It was thus with some trepidation that United moved on to Gelsenskirchen for the second fixture against FC Shalke, a team who were reputed to have supporters even more violent than those of Cologne. 'Unless the local police turn out in strength and with a definite plan to keep the two sets of fans apart, I shudder to think what the consequences might be,' said David Smith.

Much to the relief of Shalke officials and the local police, heavy rain dampened the spirits of those who turned up to watch the game, with scenes from the previous match nowhere to be seen.

The match marked a return to action for Gordon McQueen, who had been missing for 10 weeks with a damaged knee, and he marked it with a goal, heading McCreery's shot out of the reach of goalkeeper Grob after Grimes's cross had been punched clear.

Despite not playing too well, United managed to hold on to their lead until seven minutes from the end when Fischer scored from 25 yards, after having seen previous efforts hit the crossbar and round the wrong side of the post.

The programme for the match versus Schalke, 1 August 1978.

1 August 1978	**FC Shalke 04 at Park Stadium, Gelsenkirchen.**

Attendance: 3,500.

Drew: 1—1.

Scorer: McQueen.

Team: Stepney, Albiston, Houston, B. Greenhoff, McQueen, Buchan, Coppell, J. Greenhoff, Jordan, Macari, McIlroy.

Substitutes: Grimes for B. Greenhoff, McCreery for McIlroy.

Although exact details of the club's formation as Newton Heath have never been accurately pinpointed, 1878 is widely given as the formative year, making 1978 the club's centenary year. While deciding on suitable celebrations, it was thought that Real Madrid were the club most worthy of marking the occasion.

When details of the fixture were revealed, the directors also announced that because of the occasion, they would reward the club's loyal and regular supporters by admitting those who had a complete set, or near complete set, of programme tokens from the previous season free of charge.

Manchester United Centenary Souvenir, 1878–1978.

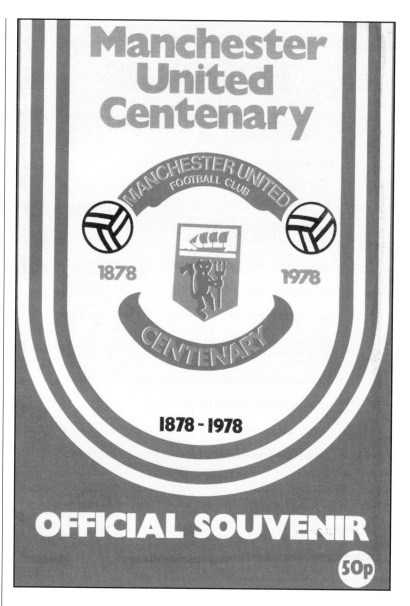

This was indeed a magnificent gesture, as the cost of the centenary match and celebrations was estimated at around £50,000, with the cost of bringing Real Madrid to Manchester alone being £34,000 of that sum. The other £16,000 was earmarked for a special banquet and other necessary expenses.

However, everything did not go to plan, as former goalkeeper Harry Gregg pulled out of the proposed 'parade of honour' of former United stars after the club did not invite seven of the Munich heroes to the celebration dinner. Wives of staff, League officials and managers of other clubs had been invited, but there were no places for the seven survivors.

As it was, the likes of Stan Pearson, Johnny Carey, Jack Crompton and Jimmy Delaney took the applause of the crowd prior to kick-off, as representatives of all the supporters' club branches paraded around the pitch.

The Real Madrid side provided ideal opposition for the occasion and as the game proceeded the friendly tag was quickly cast aside with the fixture taking on a truly competitive edge.

McCreery tested the Madrid goal with a couple of early shots, while McQueen also caused problems for their defence with his appearances in the penalty area, but it was the nimble footwork of McIlroy that engineered United's initial breakthrough.

In the 22nd minute the Irishman combined with Jimmy Greenhoff on the right, drawing the Madrid defence out of position before slipping the ball through to McIlroy. Despite still having Pirri and Stielika in front of him, a shuffle of the feet and a swerve created the necessary space he required to curl the ball out of Angel's reach at the far post.

Eleven minutes later it was 2–0, McIlroy again volleying home from 18 yards as Jordan back-headed a centre from Macari on the left. Jimmy Greenhoff added a third in the 35th minute, heading home a free-kick from his brother Brian.

Stepney, the sole survivor of the 1968 European Cup victory, replaced Roche at half-time and within five minutes was facing a penalty-kick after McQueen had brought down Jensen. Keeping his cool, he dived to his right to save Pirri's spot-kick.

Jimmy Greenhoff added a fourth in the 75th minute, curling a right-footed shot past substitute 'keeper Ramos, but the referee had to restore order before restarting the game, as players pushed and shoved each other following a foul on McQueen in the build-up to the goal.

7 August 1978	Real Madrid at Old Trafford.

Attendance: 49,397.

Won: 4–0.

Scorers: McIlroy 2, J. Greenhoff 2.

Team: Roche, B. Greenhoff, Albiston, McIlroy, McQueen, Buchan, Coppell, J. Greenhoff, Jordan, Macari, McCreery.

Substitutes: Stepney for Roche, Nicholl for B. Greenhoff, Ritchie for J. Greenhoff, Grimes for McCreery.

Three days later it was back to the airport for a flight to Denmark, to face Holstebro before yet another season got underway. The game itself was a rather uninteresting 90 minutes, brought to life following the dismissal of Joe Jordan. A solitary Lou Macari goal was all that separated the two teams.

10 August 1978	Holstebro Ballklub at Idraespark.

Attendance: 5,000.

Won: 1–0.

Scorer: Macari.

Team: Roche, Nicholl, Houston, McIlroy, McQueen, Buchan, Coppell, J. Greenhoff, Jordan, Macari, B. Greenhoff.

Substitutes: McCreery for Macari, Grimes for B. Greenhoff, Stepney for Roche, McGrath for Coppell, Albiston for Houston.

Only three friendlies during season 1978–79 made the campaign seem rather incomplete, more so because these were played prior to the start of the season, with nothing at all during or after the rigours of the League and FA Cup. Season 1979–80 was only slightly different, as following the ritual pre-season friendlies there were to be only a further two during and one after. Changed days indeed!

There could very well have been an additional match among the friendlies played during this particular season, as early June brought an announcement that United were likely to play hosts to World Champions Argentina in a star-studded friendly at Old

The programme for the match versus VfB Stuttgart, 28 July 1979.

Trafford in September. Club Secretary Les Olive said: 'Argentina are committed to a European tour later this year and a match against United would be a tremendous attraction for our fans. The World Champions are considering the invitation and we can accommodate them at Old Trafford if we get permission from the League and FA. We have a suitable date in September and there should be no problems.'

It turned out, however, to be little more than a dream, with red tape preventing the game from taking place.

It was still July when Dave Sexton began his warm-up preparations, taking United back to Germany, where only 12 months previously crowd trouble had captured the headlines.

Stuttgart, last season's runners-up in the German League, gave United a more than useful run-out in the first of their pre-season friendlies, holding them to a 0–0 draw. Much of the post-match analysis centred around United's need to step up their offer for the England international Ray Wilkins, as there was a distinct lack of sparkle in this particular department.

Under intense heat, United battled for an honourable draw as Stuttgart enjoyed most of the play and had the edge over their opponents, with goalkeeper Gary Bailey playing a major part in keeping the score sheet blank. He did well to save a free-kick from Mueller, while dealing capably with the hard-shooting of centre-forward Beck.

United ran out of steam in the final 20 minutes, but Dave Sexton was pleased with the workout, saying: 'It was a good performance after only a week back in training. We were about 70 per cent of our full potential which is reasonable for our first game.'

28 July 1979	VfB Stuttgart at Neckarstadion.

Attendance: 12,000.

Drew: 0–0.

Team: Bailey, Nicholl, Albiston, McIlroy, McQueen, Buchan, Coppell, Thomas, Pearson, Macari, Jordan.

Substitutes: Grimes for Pearson, B. Greenhoff for McIlroy.

United encountered a few problems on the park when they came up against Bochum in their second tour friendly, a game which marked the opening of their new super-stadium. Brian Greenhoff was stretchered off and Mickey Thomas sent off, while three others were booked in a match that bubbled over towards the end.

Mid-table in last season's German League, the host side played with a hard, competitive edge, which saw Joe Jordan take more flack than any of his teammates. Although a little overloaded in midfield, United stood up well against a Bochum side who worked hard and attacked in numbers.

Gordon McQueen put United in front in the 26th minute when he lost his marker to score with a diving header from Coppell's free-kick. This was a lead that they managed to hold onto until the final 20 minutes, when Eggeling broke through to steer a low shot wide of Bailey. Minutes later the game disintegrated, with Duisburg referee Hans Hennig losing control with a series of erratic decisions.

Houston was cautioned in the 72nd minute in a case of mistaken identity, after McQueen had scythed down goalscorer Eggeling, with Coppell and Nicholl's names also finding their way into the referee's notebook for failing to retreat 10 yards at a free-kick and for hitting out at Tenhagen in a scuffle for the ball.

Tenhagen was also on the receiving end of a kick from Mickey Thomas as the United player lay on the ground, leading to his dismissal. It later emerged that the two players had got their studs and laces caught and were merely trying to free themselves.

After the game United officials were told that they would probably hear no more about the sending off and indeed they forgot all about it until mid-September, when they received notice that the Welsh winger was suspended for one game.

1 August 1979	**VfI Bochum at Ruhrstadion.**

Attendance: 10,000.

Drew: 1—1.

Scorer: McQueen.

Team: Bailey, Nicholl, Houston, McIlroy, McQueen, B. Greenhoff, Coppell, Thomas, Grimes, Macari, Jordan.

Substitutes: Buchan for B. Greenhoff.

From Germany, United moved to Denmark for a further two warm-up games, with the first against a Danish Select in a match to celebrate the Danish FA's 75th anniversary. Although they won 2–0, there was only a half-filled stadium there to witness the rather poor performance.

The programme for the match versus Stævnet, 7 August 1979.

The first-half performance was so lacklustre that Danish international manager Sepp Piontek commented: 'So far that must be the worst performance I have ever seen from a so-called top English team. There was no imagination, no inventiveness. I'm not surprised that the spectators are so restless. They enjoy their English football on television, but nobody will want to know Manchester United over here if this is all they have to offer.'

Things did improve in the second half, but only after Sexton had juggled his side around after having lost Jimmy Greenhoff through injury. McCreery joined Jordan up front, with Coppell moving back to the wing. In the 65th minute, from a second McIlroy corner in the space of a minute, Gordon McQueen soared above everyone else to glance a header past Poulsen. The closest United had previously come to scoring was when Nicholl had hit the bar from 30 yards.

Chances, however, were few and far between and it took a penalty in the 82nd minute to put the game beyond any doubt, after Mickey Thomas picked himself up after being floored by Andersen to score from the spot.

7 August 1979	Stævnet at Idraespark Stadium.

Attendance: 2,800.

Won: 2—0.

Scorers: McQueen, Thomas (pen.).

Team: Bailey, Nicholl, Albiston, McIlroy, McQueen, Buchan, Coppell, Thomas, Jordan, Macari, Grimes.

Substitutes: B. Greenhoff for Nicholl, J. Greenhoff for Grimes, McCreery for J. Greenhoff.

The second of the two Danish fixtures produced a much better display from United, although FA Aalborg gave as good as they got. The goal deadlock was only broken when Martin Buchan scored a rare goal five minutes before the interval with a 35-yard drive from a Coppell cross.

After the break United took command of the game and, with the Danes tiring, Ritchie added a second in the 71st minute, heading home after a close-range Jordan effort had been deflected. McIlroy claimed the third with an angled shot from 10 yards eight minutes later, with substitute Houston completing the scoring in the 80th minute.

The programme for the match versus FA Aalborg, 9 August 1979.

9 August 1979	FA Aalborg.

Attendance: 2,855.

Won: 4—0.

Scorers: Buchan, Ritchie, McIlroy, Houston.

Team: Bailey, Nicholl, Albiston, B. Greenhoff, McQueen, Buchan, Coppell, Ritchie, Jordan, Macari, Thomas.

Substitutes: McIlroy for B. Greenhoff, Houston for Coppell, McCreery for Macari, Grimes for Thomas.

Having played over 700 games for Chelsea, long-serving goalkeeper Peter Bonetti certainly deserved a testimonial, and just over 10,000 turned up to watch a rather under-strength United side lose 5–3.

Langley put Chelsea in front in the ninth minute, but an own-goal by Droy gave United the equaliser after 22 minutes. Eleven minutes later Johnson regained Chelsea's lead, but within seconds Ashley Grimes equalised with a 30-yard effort.

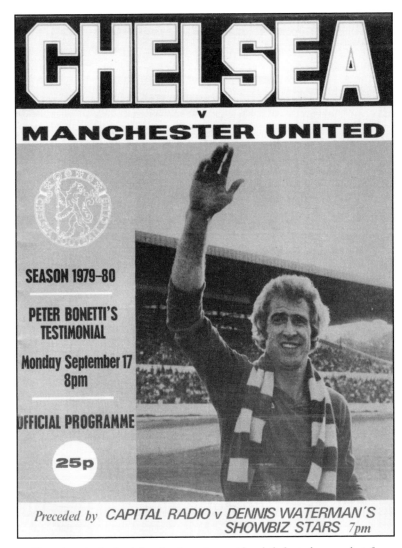

United took the lead for the first time with a left-footed cross shot from Albiston, his first ever senior goal, two minutes after the restart, but Chelsea soon took command of the game, scoring a further three times through Walker, Langley and Droy.

17 September 1979	**Chelsea at Stamford Bridge.**

Attendance: 10,652.

Lost: 5–3.

Scorers: Coppell, Grimes, Albiston.

Team: Bailey, Nicholl, Albiston, McIlroy, McQueen, Buchan, Grimes, Wilkins, Coppell, Macari, Thomas.

Substitutes: Roche for Bailey, Moran for Buchan, Ritchie for Coppell, Paterson for Macari, Worrall for McIlroy.

The 1980s

Absent from European competition and with a blank Saturday on the domestic fixture list, manager Dave Sexton was eager for his team to maintain their match fitness. The search was on to find suitable opponents and they could not have come up with more testing opponents than European Cup quarter-finalists Hadjuk Split.

Included in the United side, for his first-team debut, was Yugoslavian international Nikola Jovanovic, a recent £300,000 signing from Red Star Belgrade. Initially, there had been some doubt about whether Jovanovic would be able to play, as there was civil unrest in the country at this time and it was feared that a restriction might be put on nationals from moving within the country.

As it turned out, Jovanovic did make his debut, playing the second 45 minutes, but he surely would have wished that he had been excluded from the side as United were simply hit for six. Although, to be fair, the new signing did make an impressive debut.

Long before the final whistle, the Yugoslavs were cheering in a state of disbelief as United struggled hopelessly against a side which included nine internationals, with the local journalists, unfamiliar with the United players, asking whether they had sent a weakened team.

Split took the lead in the 23rd minute after Buchan pulled down Vujovic and Primorac made no mistake from the penalty spot. Ten minutes later it was 2–0 when Kestulovic guided home a high centre.

Five minutes prior to the interval Gary Bailey was at fault for the third after he allowed a high ball from Muzinic to slip under the crossbar.

After the restart, instead of easing off due to their three-goal advantage, the Slavs stepped up a gear and continued to attack the United goal, scoring a fourth in the 57th minute when Vujovic ran half the length of the pitch before firing home a low shot.

A minute later Martin Buchan repeated his first half misdemeanour when he again brought down the speedy Vujovic. Primorac once again beat Bailey from the spot-kick.

Eight minutes from the end the Slavs added a sixth, Bogdannovic providing the finishing touch to a move which saw an interchange of passing between no fewer than nine Split players.

Chances for United were few and far between, with Grimes failing to score from a mere 10 yards and McIlroy having a shot cleared off the line. Jovanovic almost snatched a late goal in a game that he and his teammates would want to forget.

27 January 1980	Hadjuk Split at the Gradski Stadium.

Attendance: 30,000.

Lost: 6–0.

Team: Bailey, Nicholl, Houston, McIlroy, McQueen, Buchan, Coppell, Wilkins, Jordan, Macari, Thomas.

Substitutes: Grimes for Thomas, Jovanovic for Houston.

United were close, but not close enough, as they finished second in the First Division, a mere two points behind Liverpool. It had been a long, hard season, but there was still one remaining fixture, against Portland Timbers in Oregon. The non-England internationals in the United squad knew that at the end of the 90 minutes they would be heading to Hawaii for a well-earned break.

So, less than 24 hours after the final whistle at Elland Road, the squad were heading stateside to a venue shared by the NASL side and the Portland Beavers Baseball team, greeted on to the pitch by a Dixieland jazz band, a seven foot-tall racoon and a chainsaw-swinging lumberjack.

Lou Macari put United in front after nine minutes, against a side with a number of familiar names in their line up, players such as Willie Donnachie (ex-City) and Clyde Best (ex-West Ham). This was a game that also saw a running commentary from the PA announcer. His crisp tones filled the stadium with the likes of 'Free-kick to United', 'Goal for Manchester United, scored by Lou Macari, assisted by Arthur Albiston and Steve Coppell.'

During the interval a member of the public had the opportunity to win a car if he could shoot a football through one of the three openings on a sheet hanging from the crossbar: he missed.

The second half passed without any further scoring or either team coming close to doing so.

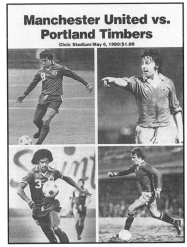

The programme for the match versus Portland Timbers, 6 May 1980.

6 May 1980	Portland Timbers at Civic Stadium.

Attendance: 7,976.

Won: 1–0.

Scorer: Macari.

Team: Bailey, Jovanovic, Albiston, McIlroy, McQueen, Moran, Coppell, Wilkins, Jordan, Macari, J.Greenhoff.

Substitutes: Ritchie for J.Greenhoff, Grimes for Macari, Houston for Albiston, Sloan for Wilkins.

The 1980–81 pre-season build-up was dominated by the push to sign Arsenal's Liam Brady (Chairman Martin Edwards claiming that £2 million was too much for the player) and Sir Matt Busby collapsing with a stroke. The latter made a complete recovery, while Brady turned his back on a move to Manchester.

United decided once again to venture to Germany for a pre-season fixture, ignoring the recent problems created by crowd trouble in similar circumstances. It was therefore not too surprising that the 90 minutes of football was once again overshadowed by events off the pitch.

Perhaps the United directors were naïve in thinking that the visit to Nuremburg would pass calmly, as headlines such as 'Soccer thugs run riot in a night of shame' and 'Germans sling Red Army into the cells for a night' reveal another story.

On the pitch United were held to a 1–1 draw in a sometimes volatile match, but their first-half performance in the hot and sultry conditions left a lot to be desired. They rarely penetrated the German defence, and in the 15th minute, on a rare occasion when they did, Moran headed Albiston's free-kick over the bar.

At the opposite end Bailey endured a far from comfortable evening. He scrambled across his goal when a Tauber shot hit the foot of the post and later moved off his line and missed a curling centre, which left him stranded as the ball moved menacingly around his area.

The 'keeper's confidence recovered slightly in the second half, along with his teammates performance in general, and the deadlock was almost broken when Sloan pulled the ball back for Thomas, but the latter's effort rebounded off the crossbar.

In the 67th minute the elusive goal finally materialised. Jordan challenged the Nuremburg goalkeeper to a high Thomas cross and the ball broke loose for Ritchie to accept a simple scoring opportunity.

Bailey redeemed his earlier mishaps with a couple of fine saves, but there was little he could do to prevent the equaliser when a deflected free-kick bounced in front of him and Frank headed past the helpless 'keeper.

Off the field there was trouble before, during and after the game, with a pregnant woman being hit on the head and thrown off a train and an 85-year-old pensioner also caught up in the trouble. German police had to break up fighting between rival supporters during the 90 minutes, with many German supporters leaving the ground to try and gain re-entry in the United section, while after the final whistle fighting continued in the streets and parks throughout the night.

26 July 1980	**IFC Nuremburg, Stadtisches Stadion.**

Attendance: 6,000.

Draw: 1—1.

Scorer: Ritchie.

Team: Bailey, Nicholl, Albiston, McIlroy, Moran, Buchan, Grimes, J. Greenhoff, Jordan, Macari, Thomas.

Substitutes: Sloan for Macari, Ritchie for Greenhoff, McGrath for McIlroy.

The programme for the match versus Nuremburg, 26 July 1980.

From Germany United travelled to Vienna to play 90 minutes against FK Austria. The news of the Red Army's reputation preceded them and the local police were warned about what to expect. The Austrian's vice-president even voiced the opinion that United should be banned from playing European friendlies if there were any repeat of the trouble that occurred in Nuremburg. It was fortunate, therefore, that the game against the Austrian League and Cup holders passed without incident off the pitch.

The fixture itself provided United with a tough test and they were fortunate not to find themselves a goal behind in the 11th minute when Schachner sneaked in between Buchan and Albiston, with the latter tripping him to concede a penalty. Fortunately, Schachner blasted the spot-kick over.

Two minutes later United took the lead, Grimes finding McIlroy with an accurate centre and the Irishman evading a couple of defenders before firing home. However, the Austrians drew level in the 23rd minute through the ever-alert Schachner, later taking the lead in the 77th minute when Steinkoger hit a low shot past Bailey.

With only three minutes remaining and the game looking lost, Jordan smashed home a powerful shot after breaking clear of the home defence.

30 July 1980	FK Austria at Prater Stadium.

Attendance: 10,000.

Draw: 2–2.

Scorers: McIlroy, Jordan.

Team: Bailey, Jovanovic, Albiston, McIlroy, Moran, Buchan, Coppell, Ritchie, Jordan, Thomas, Grimes.

Substitutes: Nicholl for Jovanovic, Sloan for McIlroy, J. Greenhoff for Ritchie.

Ticket for the game versus FK Austria, 29 July 1980.

Returning to Britain, United headed to Glasgow to face Celtic in a testimonial match for Danny McGrain, one of Scotland's finest-ever full-backs. Any supporters leaving the ground prior to the final whistle missed the only goals of the evening, as the 90 minutes ended 0–0, leaving the result to be decided on penalty kicks.

Applauded onto the pitch by both teams, McGrain proceeded to do a lap of honour with the Scottish Cup before the action got underway. It was United who stirred the crowd in the third minute when Coppell, creating space for himself, tested Bonner from eight yards. A second opportunity came United's way in the 17th minute when Jordan headed down a Coppell cross to the unmarked Greenhoff, but Bonnar was again alert to the danger.

It was not until the 21st minute that Celtic produced a worthwhile attack, with McCluskey trying his luck with a right-footed drive. Provan also came close early in the second half, deceiving Bailey with a curling cross, but there were no teammates on hand to take advantage.

Bonnar denied United a breakthrough on the hour, stopping an 18-yard effort from Macari, while minutes later he punched clear a Nicholl cross. He also did well to stop a Grimes free-kick and an angled drive from Jordan.

The spot-kicks saw Celtic scoring only once through MacLeod, with McCluskey and McAdam both missing and Bailey saving from Provan. United on the other hand scored three, through Thomas, Grimes and Greenhoff, with Man of the Match Bonnar saving from Coppell.

4 August 1980	Celtic at Celtic Park.

Attendance: 45,000.

Draw: 0–0 (**Won:** 3–1 on penalties).

Scorers: Thomas, Grimes, J. Greenhoff.

Team: Bailey, Nicholl, Albiston, McIlroy, Moran, Buchan, Coppell, J. Greenhoff, Jordan, Macari, Grimes.

Substitutes: Thomas for McIlroy.

The programme for the match versus Celtic, 4 August 1980.

Dave Sexton's preparations continued in Sweden, where United recorded their first pre-season victory against Vasteras. However, his plans were somewhat derailed following injuries to Andy Ritchie and Paddy Roche, who joined Gordon McQueen and Ray Wilkins on the treatment table.

Ritchie was forced to leave the field after only 25 minutes, injuring his ankle after chasing a ball down the touchline, a run that saw him end up sprawled on the cinder track surrounding the pitch, while Roche damaged his thigh as he grappled for a loose ball 10 minutes from time.

In the packed compact stadium, United struggled against the part-timers, with Coppell scoring what was to be the only goal of the game after 36 minutes following a corner from Grimes.

Sloan came close when he hit the post, while Macari, Greenhoff and Jovanovic all narrowly missed the target, but the Swedes, who were a mid-table Second Division side, were relieved to find United unable to raise their game and turn the opportunities into goals.

6 August 1980	IFK Vasteras, Arosvallen Stadium.

Attendance: 8,042.

Won: 1—0.

Scorer: Coppell.

Team: Roche, Nicholl, Jovanovic, Sloan, Moran, Buchan, Coppell, J. Greenhoff, Ritchie, Macari, Thomas.

Substitutes: Grimes for Ritchie, Bailey for Roche.

Two days later United faced another Swedish Second Division side, Gefle. Again they struggled, eventually winning a closely fought encounter 2–1, thanks mainly to the attacking play of Joe Jordan. The big Scot opened the scoring with a header in the 35th minute and five minutes into the second half nodded the ball down to the feet of Coppell for the winger to put United two in front.

There should have been more goals for the visitors, with both Mickey Thomas and stand-in captain Sammy McIlroy producing some neat touches, but the only other goal came from the hosts, who claimed a consolation effort in the 73rd minute when Per Erikson netted with a fine drive.

8 August 1980	Gefle IF – Brynas at Stromvallen Stadium.

Attendance: 2,409.

Won: 2—1.

Scorers: Jordan, Coppell.

Team: Bailey, Nicholl, Albiston, McIlroy, Moran, Jovanovic, Sloan, Coppell, Jordan, Thomas, Grimes,

Substitutes: J. Greenhoff for Jordan, Macari for Grimes, Buchan for Moran.

League form in the opening half of the season was nothing to write home about, with twice as many games drawn as were won. Any victory was worth celebrating, whether it was a competitive or a friendly fixture.

So it was a content United party who returned from Dublin following a 3–0 victory over the noted amateur side Home Farm. Played at a leisurely pace, the game marked a return to first-team action for Jimmy Greenhoff, making his first senior start since September, and Martin Buchan, who had missed a similar number of games due to a thigh injury.

Under the new Tolka Park floodlights, United went in front in the 20th minute when Coppell intercepted a pass from McAlle of Wolves, which was intended for Ryan, and hammered the ball past Finnerty.

Augmented by several 'guest' players, the Irish side were still no match for United and went further behind a minute before the interval when Jimmy Greenhoff marked his return to the senior side with a goal. Timing his run perfectly, he collected Coppell's cross before scoring with a fine effort.

Dave Sexton made several changes at half-time, but United maintained their momentum and Chris McGrath, on for Jordan, headed home an Albiston cross in the 73rd minute to round off the scoring.

KICK OFF

Matchtidning utgiven av Gefle IF/Brynäs fotboll.

Vi hälsar Manchester United välkomna till Strömvallen

Gefle IF/Brynäs 1980

HYR-KÖP TRUCK MED SERVICE
AB BYGG- och TRANSPORTEKONOMI
GÄVLE - Tel. 026/11 62 44, 18 16 19

80-talets CLARK utvecklad genom erfarenhet

The programme for the match versus Gefle, 8 August 1980.

---

1 December 1980	Home Farm at Tolka Park, Dublin.

Attendance: 12,000.

Won: 3—0.

Scorers: Coppell, J. Greenhoff, McGrath.

Team: Bailey, Duxbury, Albiston, McIlroy, Jovanovic, Buchan, Coppell, J. Greenhoff, Jordan, Macari, Grimes.

Substitutes: McGrath for Jordan, Pears for Bailey, Sloan for Macari, Whelan for McIlroy.

United returned to Ireland a couple of months later, this time to the city of Belfast, where they took on Linfield amid a high level of security. It was a game, however, that almost never took place, as several of the United players threw the plans for this particular fixture into disarray when they told Dave Sexton that they considered the game unnecessary in a country where tensions were running high.

Sexton eventually managed to talk his players round. Had he not managed to do so, there could well have been a serious situation, as all reserved seats had been sold. A Belfast football correspondent stated: 'If United had pulled out, it would

The programme for the match versus Home Farm, 1 December 1980.

have been the biggest let-down in Northern Ireland for years. The Irish following for United in Ulster is fantastic. I've not seen anything like it for a long time. The club will get an incredible welcome.'

After it was decided to go ahead with the game, one unnamed player said: 'We have all agreed to go, but at first we were alarmed. It seems unnecessary to choose Belfast for a friendly. The least they could have done would have been to consult us before committing us.'

Played in front of a bigger crowd than many Northern Ireland international fixtures at the same venue, the game did not live up to its expectations. There was little to whet the appetite, with a rare Gary Birtles goal after 22 minutes, his second in 16 outings, the only goal of the game. The bearded forward had latched on to an error by goalkeeper George Dunlop, who allowed a McIlroy corner to slip through his fingers, giving the United striker the opportunity to touch the ball over the goalline.

Captained on the night by Sammy McIlroy, United only created another two chances, a drive from Coppell just before the interval which was deflected wide, and a shot by defender Jimmy Nicholl. Their hosts fared little better, testing Bailey on a similar number of occasions.

Macari, McIlroy and Wilkins worked hard in midfield but, with the play failing to flow, few scoring opportunities were created. It was disappointing that United could not match the reception that they were given by their strong Irish fanbase, but, having picked up a cheque for around £10,000, Dave Sexton's men had more important matters on their minds than a mere friendly.

---

10 February 1981 **Linfield at Windsor Park, Belfast.**

Attendance: 35,000.

Won: 1—0.

Scorer: Birtles.

Team: Bailey, Nicholl, Albiston, Wilkins, Duxbury, Buchan, Coppell, Birtles, Jordan, Macari, McIlroy.

Substitute: Thomas for Macari.

Despite his team finishing the season with a run of seven successive victories, Dave Sexton found himself sacked, along with his assistant Tommy Cavanagh, for failing to bring out the style expected from Manchester United teams. Many felt that the supporters had played a major part in the directors' decision, as they often voiced their displeasure at the football they watched.

It was thus a managerless United side who flew out to Tel Aviv to play the Israeli national side, a team that contained nine of the players who had recently played against Scotland in a World Cup qualifying tie at Hampden Park.

Before a capacity 18,000 crowd, a Lou Macari goal gave United a draw in what was often an overly physical encounter. However, the visit to Israel enabled the players to wind down after a long season, come to terms with having lost their manager and debate who their new boss would be.

There was also the opportunity to take in some sightseeing, with the Wailing Wall in Jerusalem, Bethlehem and the site of the crucifixion all visited by the players.

7 May 1981	**Israel Select XI at Tel Aviv.**

Attendance: 20,000.

Drew: 1—1.

Scorer: Macari.

Team: Bailey, Duxbury, Albiston, Moran, McQueen, Buchan, Coppell, Birtles, Jordan, Macari, Wilkins.

Substitutes: Nicholl for Buchan, Thomas for Birtles.

Numerous names were bandied about as a successor for Dave Sexton was sought and as the shortlist slowly melted away, only one name remained prominent: Ron Atkinson, the current manager of West Bromwich Albion. With the advances made and Atkinson's signature obtained, Manchester United had a new man in the hot seat.

Despite his summer appointment, Atkinson did not have an opportunity to get to know his inherited squad of players, as it was reserve-team coach Jack Crompton who took charge of things for the match against the Malaysian Select. His managerial qualities, however, were soon to be tested, as Sammy McIlroy, Jimmy Nicholl and Mickey Thomas all went AWOL as the squad prepared to fly out.

The former failed to make the shuttle flight from Manchester to Heathrow, later explaining that he was 'jaded after playing for Northern Ireland in Sweden and my little boy was ill with asthma. As I sat down I realised my family needed me and I would be no good to anyone. So I got off and went home and phoned the chairman with my reasons.'

As for his two teammates, Northern Ireland's World Cup tie was also considered to be behind Nicholl's disappearance from Heathrow, with Thomas also leaving the squad as it waited for its London flight. Domestic problems were originally thought to be the reason behind his disappearance and, in later years, Mickey readily admitted that playing for United became too much for him and at that this particular time everything simply came to a head and he could not take any more.

With McQueen already out through injury and Wilkins given permission to remain at home to look after his sick wife, United were down to the bare bones, with only 11 players, including two youth-team youngsters, flying from Heathrow to play in the three arranged fixtures.

The mini-tour kicked off against a Malaysian Select XI with the 0–0 draw perhaps a disappointment to the hosts, who felt that they deserved to win. Stand-in manager Jack Crompton described United's performance as 'disappointing', but what the Malaysians lacked in skill, they more than made up for in determination, showing much enthusiasm in the tackle.

United's best scoring opportunity came in the 51st minute, when a low shot from Birtles caught goalkeeper Rajah wrong-footed, but he managed to recover and grab the ball as it rebounded back off the post.

Substitute Din had a couple of chances to run with the ball but failed to make the most of them, while Ibrahim faced Roche one-on-one a couple of times, but was dispossessed on each occasion.

7 June 1981	**Malaysian Select at Merdeka Stadium.**

Attendance: 25,000.

Draw: 0—0.

Team: Roche, Lane, Albiston, Buchan, Moran, Grimes, McGarvey, Birtles, Jordan, Macari, Worrall.

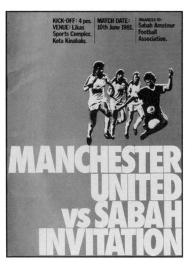

The programme for the match versus Sabah Invitation, 10 June 1981.

A free-kick from just outside the penalty area by Ashley Grimes, a minute before half-time, was enough to give United victory in their second tour fixture against a Sabah Invitation. In a packed stadium, United could have scored more goals, but a resolute Sabah defence, held together by James Wong and Soh Chin Aun, did well to contain the raids on their goal.

The home side almost took the lead in the 12th minute, but Hassan Sani's shot went straight at Gary Bailey, the forward proving to be a constant menace to the United defence. Along with Salleh, Wong and Aun, he pushed the visitors to the limit.

Despite winning numerous corners, none caused the Sabah side too much trouble, while Macari should probably have done better in front of goal before Grimes finally broke the deadlock.

The second half again produced numerous opportunities at either end. In the 59th minute Sani provided Wong with a perfect pass, but the shot that followed went narrowly past the post. In the 67th and 69th minutes United again came close, but Aun headed one of those efforts clear while the other went just wide. Further opportunities for the home side were also squandered as the game moved towards full-time.

10 June 1981	Sabah Invitation at Likas Stadium.

Attendance: 10,000.

Won: 1–0.

Scorer: Grimes.

Team: Roche, Lane, Albiston, Moran, Buchan, Duxbury, Coppell, Macari, Jordan, Grimes, Worrall.

Substitutes: McGarvey for Jordan.

The trio of Malaysian tour fixtures was rounded off with a 4–1 victory over a Selangor Invitation side, a result described by local reporter P'ng Hong Kwang as 'a flattering farewell'.

Despite the distinct differences between the two teams, it was not until the 20th minute that United went in front. Ashley Grimes took the ball off Abdullah and his pass into the area found Coppell, whose low, powerful shot was fumbled by goalkeeper Yu Tiang and the ball rolled into the net.

In the centre of the Selangor defence, axed national skipper Soh Chin Aun was not enjoying the best of games and his vulnerability led to United increasing their lead with two goals in seven minutes. Both efforts came from headers via Joe Jordan and Gary Birtles in the 24th and 31st minutes respectively.

The home side, driven on by Mokhtar Dahari, were not to be outdone, scrambling one back nine minutes after the interval. A corner by Khan Hung Meng found Too Sen Fee, who quickly passed the ball across the face of the United goal. Muin missed the ball and it fell to Kanagaraja, who beat Bailey from close range.

This brought the rather subdued crowd to life, but their joy was short-lived as Coppell restored United's three-goal advantage two minutes later, squeezing the ball past the Selangor 'keeper.

14 June 1981	Selangor Select at Merdeka Stadium.

Attendance: 25,000.

Won: 4–1.

Scorers: Coppell 2, Birtles, Jordan.

Team: Bailey, Lane, Albiston, Moran, Buchan, Duxbury, Coppell, Macari, Jordan, Birtles, Grimes.

Substitutes: McGarvey for Jordan, Worrall for Birtles.

There was plenty of activity at Old Trafford during the summer of 1981, with Joe Jordan departing for Italian giants AC Milan and United receiving £350,000 from the Italians. Mickey Thomas moved to Everton in a deal that was reportedly worth around £600,000 or £800,000, depending which newspaper you read, with John Gidman joining United.

Gidman was to pull on the red shirt of United for the first time in the Aberdeen Tournament, where Ron Atkinson's side, having endured only five days' pre-season training, joined the host club and the more familiar Southampton and West Ham United.

Paired with Southampton in the opening tie, the lack of fitness was obvious as United stumbled to a 3–1 defeat.

Steve Moran almost opened the scoring for the Saints in the 20th minute, Bailey palming his shot over the bar. Holmes also came close minutes later, but Buchan blocked his shot on the line. This was only a minor let-off for Atkinson's team, as Keegan struck in the 26th minute to give Southampton the lead, diving knee high to head a Williams cross past Bailey.

When McQueen left the field with an injury and was replaced by Duxbury, the United defence were left looking even more vulnerable. Southampton continued to surge forward, Moran hitting the post as they sought to increase their lead.

Ten minutes before the interval the second goal did indeed come; Keegan's superbly flighted cross was headed past Bailey by the unmarked Charlie George.

In a dull second half, Southampton continued to dominate, although it was not until the 75th minute that they increased their lead, Holmes crashing a cross from Williams high into the net. By the time Coppell scored a consolation goal for United, many of the crowd had left the stadium.

1 August 1981	Southampton at Pittodrie Stadium, Aberdeen.

Attendance: 8,800.

Lost: 3–1.

Scorer: Coppell.

Team: Bailey, Gidman, Albiston, Moran, McQueen, Buchan, Coppell, Wilkins, Birtles, Macari, McIlroy.

Substitutes: Grimes for McIlroy, Duxbury for McQueen.

If United's performance against Southampton was considered poor, then their 90 minutes the following day against West Ham United was even more so. It was descibed in the press as 'dreadful' and 'a lethargic match'. The 1–0 defeat earned them the wooden spoon, while the David Cross goal was considered the sole highlight of a dire afternoon.

2 August 1981   West Ham United at Pittodrie Stadium, Aberdeen.

Attendance: 10,000.

Lost: 1—0.

Team: Bailey, Nicholl, Albiston, Duxbury, Moran, Buchan, Grimes, Wilkins, Birtles, Macari, McIlroy.

Substitutes: McGarvey for Macari.

With the newspapers full of transfer speculation, United journeyed to Dublin to face Bohemians, where they at last got their pre-season preparations on track, although they were to suffer an early scare from old boy Gerry Daly. The home side also included current United players Ashley Grimes and Tony Whelan in their line up, both of whom were former Bohemians players.

A bad mistake by Wilkins after only four minutes presented Eviston with an opportunity, but he rushed his shot from 20 yards out and the ball went weakly wide. Ten minutes later, at the opposite end of the pitch, United almost gained the advantage when Birtles fired a shot just wide. Minutes later he had another chance, beating O'Brian in the Bohemians goal, but this was disallowed for offside.

Macari, McGarvey and Birtles all came close to scoring, but it was former United favourite Gerry Daly, guesting for Bohemians, who opened the scoring in the 33rd minute.

Having been fortunate not to go further behind just prior to the half-time whistle when Eviston had headed inches over, United began the second half strongly, but could only manage one worthwhile effort from McIlroy and it was not until the 63rd minute that they finally managed to equalise. Birtles found Albiston, who controlled the ball well before shooting into the corner of the net.

Two minutes later came a second, substitute Worral sending McIlroy away, who in turn found Birtles, with the move being rounded off by McGarvey. Birtles added a third in the 73rd minute with a superb header.

With five minutes remaining Daly had the opportunity to pull a goal back from the penalty spot, but saw his kick rebound off the crossbar.

8 August 1981   Bohemians at Dalymount Park, Dublin.

Attendance: 10,000.

Won: 3—1.

Scorers: Albiston, Birtles, McGarvey.

Team: Bailey, Nicholl, Albiston, Duxbury, Moran, Buchan, McIlroy, Wilkins, Birtles, Macari, McGarvey.

Substitutes: Worral for Macari, Gidman for Nicholl.

Staying close to home for the next pre-season fixture, Ron Atkinson took his players to Port Vale, where a solitary goal was enough to give United victory.

It was the home side who enjoyed most of the first-half play, with their new signing, Ernie Moss, coming close on a couple of occasions. However, it was United who should have taken the lead in the 25th minute, but Duxbury mis-timed his shot from 10 yards as Port Vale goalkeeper Harrison lay stranded on the ground after the ball flew across the goalmouth.

The opening goal did materialise, just over 10 minutes later, when Gary Birtles notched up his second in two games, confounding his critics as he moved onto a McGarvey pass before beating the advancing 'keeper with ease.

The programme for the game versus Bohemians, 8 August 1981.

DALYMOUNT PARK

DEVELOPMENT FUND

Bohemians F.C.
v
Manchester United

Saturday,
8th August, 1981
3.00 pm.

Official Programme 50p

Despite keeping up the pressure in the second half, Port Vale failed to breach the United defence and the crowd had to be content with just one goal.

---

11 August 1981   **Port Vale at Vale Park.**

Attendance: 8,000.

Won: 1–0.

Scorer: Birtles.

Team: Bailey, Gidman, Albiston, Duxbury, Moran, Buchan, McIlroy, Wilkins, Birtles, Macari, McGarvey.

Substitutes: Roche for Bailey, Grimes for Albiston, Nicholl for Buchan.

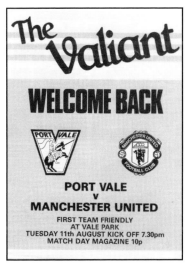

The programme for the match versus Port Vale, 11 August 1981.

Pre-season just would not be the same without a game abroad and as Ron Atkinson tried to tempt his former club West Bromwich Albion with a bid of £1.8 million for Bryan Robson, United travelled to Norway to face Second Division side EIK Tonsberg.

The fixture did little to relax the United manager or his squad for the season ahead and once again, despite the opposition being little more than part-timers, United only won the game by a solitary goal. The Scandinavians should have been seen off in the first half, following Scott McGarvey's 10th-minute strike, but many of the United players failed to break sweat and play stuttered along for the remainder of the game.

McGarvey, who was filling in following the departure of Jordan and the imminent arrival of Frank Stapleton, looked a capable substitute, coming close on two occasions before scoring. His first effort, a thundering header, clipped the crossbar, while a second was saved by the goalkeeper. His goal eventually came when he rose at the far post to meet an Albiston cross.

Sandberg clipped a chance wide in the 72nd minute after McIlroy and Nicholl got in a tangle, but the home side's threats were few and far between, as were those of the visitors, who lost much of their urge and direction following the substitution of Macari.

---

18 August 1981   **EIK Tonsberg, Norway.**

Attendance: 7,000.

Won: 1–0.

Scorer: McGarvey.

Team: Bailey, Gidman, Albiston, Duxbury, Moran, Nicholl, McGarvey, Wilkins, Birtles, Macari, McIlroy.

Substitutes: Coppell for Duxbury, Jovanovic for Nicholl, Grimes for Macari.

Moving from Norway to Finland, the pre-season build-up continued and, much to Ron Atkinson's relief, the goals finally appeared, although little could be read into the 4–0 victory against Third Division standard Hanko Select.

It was once again the back-in-form Gary Birtles who inspired the victory. He set up the first, in the 34th minute, for Kevin Moran to head home at the far post. Birtles then made a decoy run to allow Albiston to find Coppell with a low cross for a second goal one minute before the interval. Seconds later it was Birtles himself who made it three, hammering home from close range after being set up by McIlroy.

The programme for the match versus VND Hanko, 20 August 1981.

After the break play was more relaxed and there was only one further goal. Again Birtles supplied, the striker sending Macari through to score the fourth in the 70th minute with his first touch, having come on as a substitute.

20 August 1981	VND Hanko.

Attendance: 3,200.

Won: 4–0.

Scorers: Moran, Birtles, Coppell, Macari.

Team: Bailey, Gidman, Albiston, Duxbury, Moran, Nicholl, Coppell, Wilkins, Birtles, McGarvey, McIlroy.

Subtitutes: Roche for Bailey, Jovanovic for Wilkins, Macari for McGarvey, Grimes for McIlroy.

On the day of the above fixture, Ron Atkinson was relieved to hear that a tribunal had at last fixed a transfer fee for Frank Stapleton's move from Arsenal, with United having to pay £1,080,000, considered at the time to be a bargain. The player could actually have cost United nothing had they not rejected him following a trial as a 16-year-old some nine years previously.

So, following a lengthy dispute, which saw Arsenal asking for a fee of £2 million, Stapleton finally pulled on the red shirt of United against Blackpool at Bloomfield Road in the last of the pre-season outings. However, it was a fixture tinged with some sadness, as at a training session prior to the fixture physiotherapist Jim Headridge collapsed and died from a massive heart attack.

If those who had made the trip to the seaside expected to be thrilled by the new addition to the United ranks, then they were in for something of a surprise, as it was Blackpool youngster Colin Greenall who caught the eye as he kept the Republic of Ireland international under close control.

It was also the home side, who had cost a mere £60,000 to put together, who opened the scoring. Stan McEwen netted from the penalty spot after Albiston had brought down Morris. Within six minutes, however, United were level, after Macari met a McIlroy cross to head home.

United increased their lead in the 70th minute, when McIlroy smashed the ball home from 35 yards, but, to their credit, Blackpool drew level 10 minutes later through Morris, after Bailey had been penalised for having his foot up as he challenged for the ball. Three minutes from time the Seasiders almost snatched a late winner, with only a fingertip save from Bailey preventing Harrison's drive from going in just below the crossbar.

The programme for the match versus Blackpool, 24 August 1981.

24 August 1981	Blackpool at Bloomfield Road.

Attendance: 12,442.

Drew: 2–2.

Scorers: Macari, McIlroy.

Team: Bailey, Gidman, Albiston, Macari, Moran, Jovanovic, Coppell, Wilkins, Stapleton, Birtles, McIlroy.

Subtitutes: McQueen for Moran, Nicholl for McQueen.

With the First Division title race off the starting blocks and United showing their counterparts a clean pair of heels, November brought a trio of friendly fixtures, two of which can be classed as 'first-team' outings, while the other, worthy of a mention here, was a reserve-team fixture.

The first of the three, on 4 November, saw Australian touring side Sydney Olympic visit Old Trafford, with Ron Atkinson fielding a reserve side as Macari, McIlroy and McQueen were all carrying injuries. With the fixture, an afternoon 2pm kick-off, not exactly one to grab the attention of many supporters, certainly not those in the far-lying corners of the country, the United directors decided to admit supporters free of charge. Unsure of how many would actually turn up, they decided that the best option was to leave the gates open. How many bothered to turn up? Just over 3,000.

Jimmy Nicholl and Scott McGarvey were the only real names of note in the United line up for a game that the home side won 2–1, with a youngster by the name of Mark Hughes, having recently made the breakthrough into the A team, coming on as one of the substitutes.

Seven days later the first team were called into action as they faced Poole Town, but had everything gone to plan then the United players would have been enjoying a rather more exotic location.

Plans had been made for United to make a 6,500-mile round trip to the Sudan to play two fixtures on 10 and 12 November in Khartoum. However, with the team not due back in England until one day before vital World Cup qualifying games, the Football Association were severely critical of the proposed trip, despite having suspended First Division football that weekend.

Both Chairman Martin Edwards and manager Ron Atkinson hit back at the criticism from the FA regarding the trip, with Edwards saying: 'We are certainly not trying to upset anybody and we don't see that this trip will put any undue strain on international players. Our second game in Khartoum is on 12 November, but the night before, there will be several World Cup players involved in League Cup games'.

Atkinson was also quick to point out that he had always planned to send the international trio of Robson, Coppell and McIlroy back home 24 hours prior to the rest of the party and that England manager Ron Greenwood was well aware of United's plans.

In the end the trip was cancelled, but it was at the request of the Sudanese authorities, who asked United if they would postpone their visit until a later date.

So it was to Dorset that United went, with Poole putting up a spirited performance against their much more experienced visitors, and it was not until the final 15 minutes of the game that they finally succumbed and the goals came.

The first came from Sammy McIlroy, returning from a five-week lay-off with a ligament injury, beating the 'keeper from just inside the area, with Scott McGarvey adding a double towards the end.

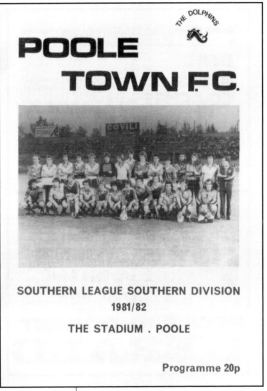

SOUTHERN LEAGUE SOUTHERN DIVISION
1981/82

THE STADIUM . POOLE

Programme 20p

The programme for the match versus Poole Town, 11 November 1981.

11 November 1981 Poole Town at Poole Stadium.

Attendance: 6,200.

Won: 3–0.

Scorers: McGarvey 2, McIlroy.

Team: Roche, Nicholl, Albiston, Macari, Moran, Jovanovic, Robson, Birtles, McGarvey, Moses, McIlroy.

Substitutes: Worrall for Moses, Duxbury for Robson.

FRIENDLY FIXTURE

UNITED	V	SYDNEY OLYMPIC
STEVE PEARS	1	GARY MAILE
JIMMY NICHOLL	2	GEORGE AKOUTASS
TOM CONNELL	3	ANDY SCOTT
ALAN DAVIES	4	PETER RESKOPOLAS
DAVID JEFFREY	5	JIMMY ZEROS
MARTIN LANE	6	KENNY WILSON
CHRIS LYNAM	7	JIMMY REDFERN
TOM SLOAN	8	JIMMY CAMPBELL
SCOTT McGARVEY	9	MARK KOUSAS
DAVID WYNN	10	PETER KATHOLAS
GARRY WORRALL	11	GRAHAM JENNINGS
DANNY KEOUGH	12	IAN RODEN
MARK HUGHES	13	DEREK LAING
TONY WHELAN	14	ALEC JAMESON

REFEREE - J. Worrall
Linesman (Red Flag) - D. M. Charnley
Linesman (Yellow Flag) - G. Howarth

The programme for the match versus Sydney Olympic, 4 November 1981.

The programme for the match on 23 November 1981.

TESTIMONIAL MATCH
23 NOVEMBER 1981

The third of the trio of friendlies brought a modest crowd of just over 15,000 to Old Trafford, for a fixture that would have produced the unusual circumstances of the crowd cheering both teams with equal enthusiasm, as it was United versus United in a testimonial match for Sammy McIlroy, with the current side facing the United FA Cup-winning side of 1977.

Braving a bitterly cold night, the crowd were treated to the first-ever ladies' match to be played at Old Trafford prior to the main event, between the United Supporters Club and a Manchester Division Select, with the former winning 3–0. The two more familiar United teams proceeded to add their own entertainment to the evening in the form of an eight-goal thriller.

The 1977 Cup Final side showed only a couple of alterations to its original line up, with Jim Holton, making a nostalgic return to Old Trafford, wearing the number-five shirt, replacing Buchan, and McCreery, forsaking the substitute's jersey, replacing Coppell.

It was the Cup winners who dictated the early play and they were soon two goals in front through Jimmy Greenhoff. Frank Stapleton pulled one back prior to the interval and shortly after the break Bryan Robson levelled the scoring.

Gerry Daly, guesting for the 1977 side, put them 3–2 in front, but, in a matter of minutes, Robson once again equalised and Wilkins put the current side in front for the first time. Before the end the crowd were treated to an eighth goal when Jimmy Greenhoff, once again set up by Jimmy Nicholl, notched up his hat-trick.

23 November 1981	Manchester United 1977 FA Cup winners at Old Trafford.

Attendance: 15,947.
Drew: 4–4.
Scorers: Robson 2, Wilkins, Stapleton.
Team: Roche, Lane, Connell, Wilkins, McQueen, Moran, Robson, Sloan, Stapleton, McGarvey, Charlton (guest).
Substitutes: Pears for Roche, Wynn for Sloan.

Two days after a 3–2 defeat at Southampton on 5 December, United remained in the south of England to play Torquay, where they supplied the opposition for a testimonial match for one of Ron Atkinson's former West Bromwich Albion players, Tony Brown.

Despite the defeat at the Dell, United were still sitting at the top of the First Division. However, if there was concern about conceding three goals in each of their two previous away fixtures, then there was even more when they found themselves four goals behind at Plainmoor after only 29 minutes.

Free-transfer signing from Wolves, 19-year-old David Butler, who had made his debut only a couple of days earlier, gave Torquay the lead after five minutes. Young added a second with a shot from 25 yards in the 17th minute and three minutes later Cooper made it 3–0.

United came close to clawing one back shortly afterwards, but O'Keefe brought off a great save from Macari. Most of the action, however, was focused at the opposite end of the pitch and Torquay increased their lead even further when Butler headed past Roche after Cooper had headed against the crossbar.

After the interval United came more into the game, Wilkins reducing arrears within three minutes of the restart and Macari adding a second seven minutes later. That, however, was as far as the comeback went, with United paying the price for perhaps underestimating their opponents.

---

7 December 1981   **Torquay United at Plainmoor.**

Attendance: 7,200.

Lost: 4–2.

Scorer: Wilkins, Macari.

Team: Roche, Gidman, Albiston, Wilkins, McQueen, Buchan, Robson, Macari, Stapleton, Moran, McIlroy.

Substitute: Coppell for Robson.

What was unknown to everyone at Old Trafford, as well as the supporters, was how far off the next competitive fixture actually was. The winter's first big freeze had created havoc across the country and Old Trafford soon found itself under six inches of snow, with a backlog of fixtures soon developing. One postponement suddenly became two and so it continued, with United being unable to play either a League or FA Cup fixture for the best part of a month.

So, with match fitness something of a worry, the search was on for clubs whose grounds were playable and who, due to postponements of their own, were able to host friendlies.

The first friendly was played north of the border on Boxing Day, against Hibs at Easter Road, which had been a regular stomping ground of the United sides of the 1950s. Hibs were worthy opposition and Ron Atkinson was glad of the fixture to keep his players ticking over.

As this was a hastily arranged fixture, and with transport over the festive period being somewhat limited, the travelling support was certainly not what it might have been.

Had it been anything but a friendly the game would not have gone ahead, as not only was the pitch rather firm, but the terracing along the touchline was also little more than an ice rink in places.

The fixture itself ended all square, with Hibs treating the game as a full-scale 'Battle of Britain'. Indeed, they thought that they had taken the lead in the 17th minute, when Rae jumped with Bailey and the ball rolled off the 'keeper's arm and trickled towards the line. Bailey managed to turn and grasp the ball, but as the Hibs players celebrated a goal, the referee refused to agree and waved play on.

Duncan came close to opening the scoring, as did Wilkins at the opposite end with a 30-yard drive, but it was not until the 60th minute that the deadlock was broken. Duncan put a cross into the United area and Callaghan headed towards goal. Bailey managed to parry the ball, which came back out towards Callaghan, who put in a second header. This time the ball eluded Bailey and Jamieson ran through to push it over the line.

It was, however, to be a short-lived lead, as within seven minutes United were level. Albiston combined with McIlroy, with the latter's cross being headed past McArthur in the Hibs goal by Stapleton.

26 December 1981	Hibs at Easter Road, Edinburgh.

Attendance: 12,017.

Drew: 1–1.

Scorer: Stapleton.

Team: Bailey, Gidman, Albiston, Wilkins, McQueen, Buchan, Robson, Birtles, Stapleton, McIlroy, Coppell.

Substitutes: Macari for Robson, Moses for McIlroy, Moran for McQueen.

Four days later came a journey to Portsmouth and, with an FA Cup tie against Watford scheduled for a few days later, fitness, especially that of talisman skipper Bryan Robson, was an important factor. Robson, who had injured a rib in the Hibs

The programme for the match versus Portsmouth, 30 December 1981.

friendly, showed no ill effects, pushing Portsmouth aside and delighting the biggest Fratton Park crowd of the season with a hat-trick.

The snow had given way to rain and, on a saturated pitch, Ray Wilkins ran the show, setting up two of Robson's goals. The first came in the 27th minute, the second on the hour, with the United captain leaving the Portsmouth defence stranded as he ran through to score. His third, in the 68th minute, was an individual effort, as he turned sharply on the edge of the area before hitting the ball past the helpless goalkeeper.

30 December 1981	**Portsmouth at Fratton Park.**

Attendance: 13,917.

Won: 3–0.

Scorer: Robson 3.

Team: Bailey, Gidman, Albiston, Wilkins, Moran, Buchan, Robson, Birtles, Stapleton, Moses, Coppell.

Substitutes: McIlroy for Wilkins, Macari for Robson, McGarvey for Birtles, Roche for Bailey.

Robson's hat-trick and Ron Atkinson's friendly arrangements were not sufficient preparation, however, as the journey to Watford in the FA Cup was to prove fruitless, with the Second Division side springing something of a Cup shock with a 1–0 victory. However, it was the inclement weather that was to bring about yet another friendly, rather than the premature cup exit.

With the home fixture against Coventry City postponed, United journeyed a few miles north to the under-soil heated Boundary Park to face Oldham Athletic.

It took United only two minutes to open the scoring, Coppell sending over an inviting cross for Birtles to beat McDonnell with a header. Oldham, however, were not put off their game in any way by this early setback and pushed forward at every opportunity. Their resilience was rewarded 15 minutes later, when Heaton finished off Palmer's through ball.

Twelve minutes after the interval Palmer should have given Oldham the lead, but he dwelt too long on the ball, allowing Bailey to make a fine save. It was a miss that was to prove costly, as 10 minutes later United were in front, a Wilkins effort rebounding off the underside of the crossbar and allowing Scott McGarvey to nudge the ball home with his first touch after coming on as a substitute for Birtles.

With a minute remaining, Bryan Robson made it three, scoring from 18 yards to round off an entertaining afternoon.

16 January 1982	**Oldham Athletic at Boundary Park.**

Attendance: 12,762.

Won: 3–1.

Scorers: Robson, Birtles, McGarvey.

Team: Bailey, Duxbury, Albiston, Wilkins, Moran, Robson, Coppell, Birtles, Stapleton, Macari, McIlroy.

Substitutes: McQueen for McIlroy, McGarvey for Birtles.

Windsor Park, Belfast, was the next destination for Ron Atkinson's squad, a fixture arranged primarily to push through the transfer of Tommy Sloan from United back to his native Northern Ireland. It also gave the natives of Belfast an all too rare glimpse of the famous red shirts on their own turf.

The programme and ticket for the match versus Oldham, 16 January 1982.

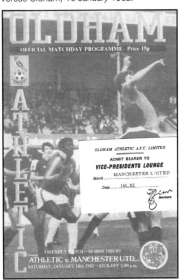

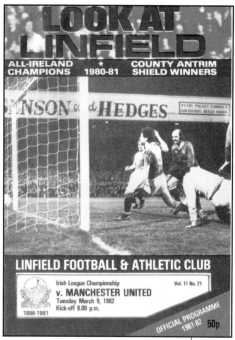

The programme for the game versus Linfield, 9 March 1982.

With the Irish side chasing their domestic League and Cup double, it had been hoped that the game would have provided a good workout, but at the end of the 90 minutes their confidence had taken a severe knock, with a 5–1 defeat.

United took a sixth-minute lead through Steve Coppell, as a three-man move ended with the winger hammering the ball home after Stapleton's shot had rebounded off goalkeeper Dunlop.

Coppell made it two in the 37th minute, moving on to a Stapleton pass before shrugging off a challenge from Gibson and beating the 'keeper. This effectively ended the match as a contest and United strolled through the remainder, treating it as little more than a limbering-up exercise.

With the home side disputing a free-kick with the referee, Moses quickly passed to Stapleton, who made it 3–0, with Moses himself adding a fourth from Gidman's corner in the 67th minute.

Linfield did pull a goal back through Crawford, but it was nothing more than a consolation, and Coppell went on to increase United's lead in the dying minutes, claiming his hat-trick from the penalty spot after he had been brought down.

9 March 1982	**Linfield at Windsor Park, Belfast.**

Attendance: 8,257.

Won: 5–1.

Scorers: Coppell 3, Stapleton, Moses.

Team: Bailey, Nicholl, Albiston, Wilkins, McQueen, Buchan, Moses, Birtles, Stapleton, Duxbury, Coppell.

Substitutes: McGarvey for Birtles, Roche for Bailey, Gidman for Duxbury, Sloan for Wilkins, Connell for Albiston.

The trek around the countryside continued with a journey south to Alliance Premier League outfit Barnet, with the game a testimonial for their manager, the former United junior player Barry Fry. Despite the standard of the opposition, Atkinson took a strong side to the rather spartan ground.

For those in attendance, the announcement of the United line up raised more than a few eyebrows, as there was a totally unfamiliar figure in the red shirt lining up alongside the familiar faces of Robson, Wilkins and Stapleton. His name was Barry Keough, a 19-year-old Irishman, on trial from Dundalk. Twenty-four hours earlier he had played in an Irish League fixture for his club against Home Farm, but here he showed no tiredness nor lack of sharpness in an impressive 90 minutes.

Having recently been made redundant from his job as a welder, Keogh made it a dream night on the infamous sloping pitch, scoring United's first goal in the 58th minute, slamming home after a shot from Wilkins had been blocked. Stapleton added a second from the penalty spot in the 66th minute after Robson had been brought down by Tuffs.

Keough flew home to Ireland the following day to play for Dundalk against Bohemians, but his starring role for United and favourable write-ups in the press failed to see him further his playing career with the Reds.

29 March 1982   **Barnet at Underhill.**

Attendance: 25,000.

Won: 2–0.

Scorers: Stapleton, Keough.

Team: Bailey, Gidman, Albiston, Wilkins, Whelan, Buchan, Robson, Birtles, Stapleton, Keough, Coppell.

Substitutes: Lane for Albiston, Roche for Bailey.

The programme for the match versus Barnet, 29 March 1982.

Two days after bringing down the curtain on their First Division campaign with a 2–0 victory over Stoke City at Old Trafford, Ron Atkinson and his players headed off to the US for three fixtures over a five-day period in the Vancouver Europac Tournament.

End-of-season tours are often regarded as rather pointless and mean little to anyone except those supporters in far-flung destinations who have only rare opportunities to see their heroes in the flesh. Sometimes, however, you can be let down when your dream becomes a reality, and those Canadians who had been looking forward to United's visit were certainly let down by the display of those in the famous red shirts against the Vancouver Whitecaps.

Two goals from former Carlisle United starlet Peter Beardsley and another by Ray Hankin were enough to see off United, who never really recovered from going two behind as early as the ninth minute. 'Very sloppy and untidy,' was how manager Ron Atkinson described his charges' performance in the opening 45 minutes.

Frank Stapleton managed to pull one back for United, but there was never any possibility of them clawing their way back into the game.

17 May 1982   **Vancouver Whitecaps at Empire Stadium, Vancouver.**

Attendance: 12,875.

Lost: 3–1.

Scorer: Stapleton.

Team: Bailey, Duxbury, Albiston, Sloan, Moran, McQueen, Davies, Whiteside, Stapleton, Macari, Grimes.

Substitutes: McGarvey for Sloan.

The programme for the match versus Vancouver, 17 May 1982.

One person who did gain something from the 3–1 defeat was Peter Beardsley. Having been brought to United's attention prior to his departure for Canada, he returned to Old Trafford for a trial period. Surprisingly, Ron Atkinson failed to make the most of the opportunity and the talented youngster was allowed to leave and go on to prove his worth and ability elsewhere.

In the second game of the tournament United once again slumped to a disappointing defeat, in what the American press described as 'an energetic and exciting game', which saw the sides quite evenly matched, each having nine shots at goal, although it was the Sounders who gained the upper hand.

A solo effort from Peterson in the seventh minute opened the scoring, but United immediately set about looking for the equaliser. Pushing forward at every opportunity left them vulnerable to a counter-attack and, sure enough, they were eventually caught out, good work by Daley and Evans setting up Greaves in the 31st minute.

Grimes, Stapleton and Whiteside all came close, but failed to cause the Sounders 'keeper too many problems and, with seconds ticking away prior to the interval, Peterson added a third.

The second half saw United well on top, with almost three times the number of shots as the home side, but, sadly, none ended up in the back of the Seattle net.

Ticket and programme for the game versus Seattle, 20 May 1982.

20 May 1982   **Seattle Sounders at Kingdome, Seattle.**

Attendance: 12,639.

Lost: 3–0.

Team: Bailey, Gidman, Albiston, Duxbury, Moran, McQueen, Sloan, Whiteside, Stapleton, Grimes, Birtles.

Having lost the previous two fixtures, United regained some dignity in the third and final fixture, against Hajduk Split, with a 2–1 victory. Finishing third in the three-club tournament, although something of an embarrassment, was not too much of a concern for the club.

Mick Duxbury opened the scoring for United in the 41st minute, but the Yugoslavs drew level four minutes prior to the interval through Rumac. Fourteen minutes from time Gordon McQueen scored what turned out to be the winner and the United party headed for home.

22 May 1982   **Hajduk Split.**

Attendance: 12,488.

Won: 2–1.

Scorers: McQueen, Duxbury.

Team: Bailey, Gidman, Albiston, Duxbury, Moran, McQueen, Sloan, Whiteside, Stapleton, Grimes, Birtles.

Substitutes: Macari for Birtles, Davies for Sloan.

The build-up for season 1982–83 began with a fixture at Aldershot in aid of the South Atlantic Fund, with the proceeds of around £20,000 going to the Parachute Regiment based in the town. They had played a major part in winning back the Falklands during the recent conflict with Argentina.

United were dealt a blow during the warm-up when Gary Bailey pulled a hamstring and was replaced by debutant Stephen Pears, but it was Ron Atkinson's two free-transfer summer signings, Peter Bodak from Coventry City and Arnold Muhern from Ipswich Town, who caught the eye, with the Dutchman opening the scoring in the 10th minute.

Two minutes later Bodak sent over an inch-perfect cross for Stapleton to head home a second, and Mike Duxbury slipped the ball into the Aldershot net for a third in the 34th minute. The hosts managed to pull one back five minutes before the interval through Sanford.

A spate of substitutions followed in the second half and it was no surprise that the tempo of the first 45 minutes dropped and there were no further goals, although Norman Whiteside, fresh from his World Cup exploits, came close with one effort that rebounded off the crossbar.

2 August 1982   **Aldershot at Recreation Ground.**

Attendance: 7,152.

Won: 3–1.

Scorers: Muhren, Stapleton, Duxbury.

Team: Pears, Duxbury, Grimes, Wilkins, McQueen, McGrath, Robson, Muhren, Stapleton, Macari, Bodak.

Substitutes: Buchan for Duxbury, Moran for McGrath, Whiteside for Robson, Albiston for Muhren, McGarvey for Stapleton, Davies for Macari.

The countdown to the forthcoming season continued in Finland against amateur side Valur, who included a familiar name in their line up – George Best. However, it was another Irishman, Norman Whiteside, displaying touches that the Belfast legend would have approved of, who stole the limelight with two goals in United's 5–1 victory.

United, who never really moved out of second gear, took the lead in the sixth minute through Bryan Robson, who scored from close range, but, despite the difference in playing personnel between the two teams, that lead was not increased until the 63rd minute, when Wilkins made it 2–0.

Valur, surprisingly, pulled a goal back, but further goals from Whiteside and a Scott McGarvey double saw United coast to an easy victory.

4 August 1982	**Valur at Reykjavik, Iceland.**

Attendance: 9,300.

Won: 5–1.

Scorers: McGarvey 2, Robson, Wilkins, Whiteside.

Team: Pears, Duxbury, Albiston, Wilkins, Moran, Buchan, Robson, Muhren, Stapleton, Whiteside, Bodak.

Substitute: McGarvey for Stapleton.

A second fixture in Iceland, against AK Akureyri, who were also strengthened by the presence of George Best, brought a further avalanche of goals as the local First Division side were hammered 7–1.

Scott McGarvey staked his claim for a place in Ron Atkinson's starting 11 with four goals, in a game which saw United three up at half-time. Further strikes from Macari, Moran and Robson rounded off the scoring.

There was a brief flicker of the old Best magic in the 16th minute, but his effort was well saved by Steve Pears, who continued to deputise for the injured Gary Bailey.

5 August 1982	**KA Akureyri – Iceland.**

Attendance: 5,000.

Won: 7–1.

Scorers: McGarvey 4, Macari, Moran, Robson.

Team: Pears, Buchan, Albiston, Wilkins, McQueen, McGrath, Robson, Davies, Whiteside, McGarvey, Macari.

Substitutes: Moran for Wilkins, Duxbury for Buchan.

The programme for the match versus KA, 5 August 1982.

Preparations for the forthcoming season continued closer to home, with a testimonial match in Dublin for former United player Don Givens, against an Ireland XI.

Givens, who had scored 19 goals in 55 appearances for the Republic of Ireland, was given a warm reception prior to the kick-off and United proceeded to treat the fans to some excellent football, which unfortunately did not seem to be appreciated by sections of the crowd, as stones and bottles were thrown. However, on the field it was Norman Whiteside who once again stole the show, scoring twice.

The rather makeshift Irish side always struggled, although Liam Brady and Gary Waddock caught the eye with some impressive play, but they were never going to be a match for the visitors, who went in front in the 20th minute through Wilkins with a close range effort. Paul McGrath added a second seven minutes later, before going off injured.

Inspired by Liam Brady, the Irish side pulled a goal back when Waddock, with a dipping 25-yard effort, caught Bailey off his line, but a Whiteside double early in the second half killed off any hopes that they had of winning the game, although Houghton did pull one back after 73 minutes.

10 August 1982	**Ireland XI at Dalymount Park, Dublin.**

Attendance: 20,000.

Won: 4–2.

Scorers: Whiteside 2, Wilkins, McGrath.

Team: Bailey, Duxbury, Moran, McGrath, Albiston, Wilkins, Robson, Muhren, Bodak, Birtles, Whiteside.

Substitutes: Buchan for McGrath, Grimes for Albiston, McGarvey for Birtles.

An inquiry held after the match by the FA of Ireland cleared the match organisers of responsibility for the crowd disturbances which had marred the 4–2 victory. Around 20 people, most of whom were teenagers, were injured and police reinforcements had to be called to the ground. A FAI spokesman said that they had laid down stringent security plans for the game, which had been observed, but a tiny minority of those present had got involved in hooliganism.

Continuing their pre-season build-up across the Irish Sea, in a testimonial match for Pat Nolan, FAI Cup holders Limerick offered little resistance to a United side who were more than happy to dictate the pace of the game throughout the 90 minutes.

Gary Birtles, whose career at Old Trafford continued to have a question mark hovering above it, made the opening for United's first goal in the 16th minute, threading the ball through to Macari, who in turn found Kevin Moran, with the defender making no mistake from four yards out. Three minutes later Limerick found themselves further behind, after Bryan Robson swept past three defenders before beating goalkeeper Power.

It was mainly due to numerous fine saves from Power that the scoreline did not alter until 15 minutes from the end when Robson scored his second, chipping the stranded 'keeper from 30 yards out.

With the referee looking at his watch, Limerick managed a consolation goal from the penalty spot following a handball by Moran. O'Mahoney beat Bailey from the spot.

12 August 1982	**Limerick at Markets Field, Limerick.**

Attendance: 5,000.

Won: 3–1.

Scorers: Robson 2, Moran.

Team: Bailey, Duxbury, Albiston, Wilkins, Moran, Buchan, Robson, Grimes, Birtles, Macari, Davies.

Substitutes: McQueen for Duxbury, Bodak for Wilkins, McGarvey for Birtles, Whiteside for Robson.

Norman Whiteside returned to his native Belfast to a hero's welcome following his World Cup exploits for his country. However, he was rather subdued and certainly upstaged in this particular game by an even bigger name in Northern Ireland who was making a guest appearance for Glentoran.

Not for the first time during this pre-season, George Best lined up against his old club, but while he still managed to stand out, despite being far from the player he once was, the 36-year-old could do little to inspire his part-time teammates.

The 'Belfast Boy' began the game quietly, but slowly the old confidence began to reappear and he took on the United defence with relish. On one occasion he nutmegged Birtles, while on another his foot work became too much for McGarvey, who unceremoniously upended the local hero, only to have Best pick up the ball and offer it to him.

However, it was United who won the game, scoring twice without reply. A one-two between Grimes and Wilkins on the half-hour saw the former open the scoring. The second came in the 72nd minute, when Wilkins finished off another one-two with McGarvey.

---

14 August 1982   **Glentoran at The Oval, Belfast.**

Attendance: 19,000.

Won: 2—0.

Scorers: Grimes, Wilkins.

Team: Bailey, Buchan, Albiston, Wilkins, Moran, McQueen, Robson, Grimes, Birtles, Whiteside, Bodak.

Substitutes: Pears for Bailey, Macari for Grimes, McGarvey for Birtles, Davies for Bodak.

From cloudy Belfast to sunny Spain, the build-up to the new season gathered pace. Manager Ron Atkinson was hot on the trail of Kevin Keegan, although the wage demands of the Southampton player were soon to push United out of the reckoning.

The first match in the Zaragoza tournament paired United with Honved, a side who were a far cry from their once mighty status in the 1950s. Despite something of an uneasy start, a goal from Norman Whiteside in the 13th minute, converting a Birtles cross, gave United the lead.

It was the much-maligned Birtles who increased United's lead with a header, Whiteside reciprocating 11 minutes into the second half, adding a third in the 62nd minute when he rifled home a Duxbury cross.

The Hungarians restored something of their reputation 10 minutes from time, when Varga converted a penalty after Duxbury had handled Detari's header on the line, but there was never any doubt that it would be United who would claim a place in the tournament's final.

The programme for the match versus Glentoran, 14 August 1982.

19 August 1982 **Honved at La Romareda, Zaragoza, Spain.**

Attendance: 1,000.

Won: 3–1.

Scorers: Birtles 2, Whiteside.

Team: Bailey, Duxbury, Albiston, Wilkins, Moran, McQueen, Robson, Muhren, Birtles, Whiteside, Bodak.

Substitutes: Grimes for Robson, Macari for Bodak, McGarvey for Whiteside.

Up against the host club Real Zaragoza in the final, United gave a watching delegation from UEFA Cup opponents Valencia plenty to think about, as they not only stood up to the provocation of the hosts, but also showed that they were more than capable of defending strongly with their backs to the wall.

A 30-yard volley from Ray Wilkins, eight minutes from the end, looked to have given Ron Atkinson's men their eighth successive pre-season victory, but with only two minutes remaining, substitute Toto scrambled home an equaliser.

Having clawed themselves back from the jaws of defeat, the Zaragoza players felt confident that they could now go on to win the game, but soon discovered that the United players, although disappointed at losing a goal so near to the end, were certainly not there for the taking.

Gary Birtles hammered United in front again two minutes into extra-time, only for Herrera to equalise eight minutes later. Robson headed home a Wilkins corner to restore the lead, but Herrera once again found the net to make it 3–3.

The second period of extra-time saw United tear the Spaniards apart with some superb football. Robson, playing with two stitches in a cut eyebrow, showed little care for his wellbeing as he headed home soon after the restart, before blasting a free-kick at Vitaller in the Zaragoza goal, which the 'keeper failed to hold, allowing substitute Alan Davies to nip in to score a fifth two minutes from the end of the extra half-hour.

20 August 1982 **Real Zaragoza at La Romareda, Spain.**

Attendance: 20,000.

Won: 5–3. (After extra-time).

Scorers: Wilkins, Birtles, Robson 2, Davies.

Team: Bailey, Duxbury, Albiston, Wilkins, Moran, McQueen, Robson, Muhren, Birtles, Whiteside, Macari.

Substitutes: Grimes for Muhren, Davies for Birtles.

There was one final warm-up game before the 1982–83 season got underway proper, with Bolton Wanderers visiting Old Trafford. This, however, was no normal 90 minutes, as it was tinged with sadness due to the fixture being a benefit match for the late Jim Headridge, the former United and Bolton physiotherapist, who had collapsed and died the previous year.

With only a matter of days before the opening fixtures of a new season, there were places to play for, with 17-year-old Norman Whiteside making a strong claim with a notable couple of goals.

On the half-hour he cracked home United's first from all of 20 yards, which gave the surprised McDonagh in the Bolton goal no chance. His second came in the 64th minute, when he coolly picked his spot just inside the post, tucking home an inch-perfect pass from Ray Wilkins.

Coppell, Wilkins and Birtles all came close to adding to those two goals, but their failure to score enabled Bolton to rally, impressing their new manager John McGovern with two goals in a three-minute spell. Their first came in the 64th minute, when Rudge robbed Moran before beating Bailey, while the second saw Berry heading on a corner for Moores to score.

Disappointingly, the game only attracted a crowd of 5,648, which resulted in around £7,500 for the Headridge family.

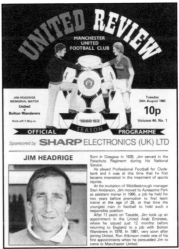

The programme for the match versus Bolton Wanderers, 24 August 1982.

---

24 August 1982   **Bolton Wanderers at Old Trafford.**

Attendance: 5,638.

Drew: 2–2.

Scorers: Whiteside 2.

Team: Bailey, Duxbury, Albiston, Wilkins, Moran, Buchan, Robson, Muhren, Stapleton, Whiteside, Coppell.

Substitutes: Birtles for Whiteside, Grimes for Robson.

Despite the League programme having more or less just got underway, with the season having the added attraction of European football after a long spell in the wilderness, United still found time to squeeze an additional 90 minutes into their fixture list. The game against Oldham Athletic, played on 21 September, was a testimonial for their former long-serving manager Jimmy Frizzell.

This was not really a United first-team friendly, more of a United XI, as the squad for the game read: Grobbelaar, Herd, Bond, Albiston, Macari, Buchan, Reid Johnston, Beardsley, Whiteside, Tueart, Bodak.

An attendance of 6,041 saw the home side record a 3–2 victory, with Roger Wylde scoring two goals in a minute and a Martin Buchan own-goal. Tueart and Macari both scored for United. The game also saw Peter Beardsley make his first appearance in a red shirt, but it did little to convince United manager Ron Atkinson to give him a regular contract.

Three months later, another mid week journey took United slightly further afield to Tranmere Rovers, but it meant a double journey for many as the game, originally arranged for 24 hours previously, was postponed due to fog.

When the game, which not only marked the centenary of Rovers, but also provided some much-needed extra income (this match brought in around £8,000), did get underway, the Fourth Division side showed that they were more than able to battle for survival, with a 2–0 victory.

The mudded midfield suited the home side more than their talented visitors and their two-goal victory, with Kerr and Brown as the scorers, could have been more had Buchan not cleared off his line. A couple of other efforts hit the woodwork, while Bailey pulled off one or two top-class saves.

Returning to his former club, Coppell captained the side and hit the bar with a shot-cum-cross, but there was always only going to be the one winner and it was not United.

The programme for the match versus Tranmere Rovers, which was originally planned for 6 December 1982 but was not played until 18 December 1982.

18 December 1982   **Tranmere Rovers at Prenton Park.**

Attendance: 5,164.

Lost: 2–0.

Team: Bailey, Gidman, Albiston, Macari, Buchan, McQueen, Grimes, Muhren, Stapleton, Beardsley, Coppell.

Substitutes: Moses for Muhren, Whiteside for Stapleton, Bodak for Coppell.

There was a space on the pre-Christmas fixture list that had been earmarked for a much higher profile friendly, with a proposed visit of Barcelona to Old Trafford, but this was subsequently shelved. 'We toyed with the idea because we haven't a match in Christmas week,' said manager Ron Atkinson, 'but the fact that we have three home games out of four over the holiday period made us decide to abandon the offer.'

Two other proposed friendlies failed to get past the planning stages. One was to have taken place in either February or March to mark the 25th anniversary of the Munich air disaster, with United travelling to Belgrade to face Red Star. The match, sponsored by a local newspaper, was to have had a special cup up for grabs, but in the end a suitable date could not be found and the plans were scrapped.

Another friendly suggestion was given the thumbs-down by manager Ron Atkinson, when he blocked a move by the United Arab Emirates, who wanted 14 top British players to play a series of end-of-season games in Dubai, with each player reportedly being offered £15,000.

It was well into the new year, however, before what was to be the final friendly played during the 1982–83 season took place, with a short flight to Dublin to face St Patrick's Athletic. The fixture had been agreed as part of the previous season's transfer of Paul McGrath from the Irish club and was played with a Milk Cup Final on the horizon.

Manager Ron Atkinson opted not to cross the Irish Sea with his players, but instead watched FA Cup semi-final opponents Arsenal slump to a 2–1 defeat against Birmingham City. In his absence, a relatively full-strength United side had little problem defeating the Dubliners 2–0.

Throughout the game United seldom moved into top gear, giving St Patrick's, and Cervi in particular, the opportunity to cause the visiting defence the odd problem or two. One effort from Brandish from 20 yards went just wide, while a header from Buckley was well saved by Wealands. Cervi, however, came the closest to opening the scoring, as, dispossessing McGrath in midfield, he set off on a 40-yard run that finished with a powerful 16-yard shot that was tipped over the bar by Wealands.

United almost went in front on the half-hour, when a Wilkins, McGrath, Gidman and McQueen move ended with Henderson depriving the latter. However, it was not until the 75th minute that the visitors managed to break the deadlock after dominating the second half. Macari scored from 16 yards after playing a one-two with Wilkins.

Five minutes later it was 2–0, Muhren curling home a left-footed free-kick from 22 yards after Malone had fouled Macari.

The programme for the match versus St Patrick's Athletic, 15 March 1983.

15 March 1983   **St Patrick's Athletic at Dalymount Park, Dublin.**

Attendance: 16,000.

Won: 2–0.

Scorers: Macari, Muhren.

Team: Wealands, Gidman, Albiston, Moses, McGrath, McQueen, Wilkins, Muhren, Stapleton, Macari, Grimes.

Substitutes: Duxbury for McQueen, Whiteside for Moses.

With the domestic season ending beneath Wembley's twin towers and an FA Cup Final replay victory over Brighton on 26 May, 12 days after the final League fixture of a long drawn out campaign, the players still had two fixtures to fulfil.

With much being made today of unnecessary fixtures, taken on for purely financial reasons, United's two games against Division One rivals Tottenham Hotspur in Swaziland certainly fell into a similar category, with the club earning £50,000 from the trip.

The organisers and sponsors, the Holiday Inn Hotel group, had originally earmarked Liverpool as United's opponents, with the games taking place in South Africa and a figure of around £250,000 each being mentioned. The proposal was put to the FA from both clubs, but when it was passed further along the line to FIFA permission was refused, as South Africa were not members of the world football organisation.

'The venture would have been worth a fortune,' said Atkinson. 'We would have earned more money than if either of us had reached the Cup Final. But neither of us wanted to risk the criticism that inevitably would have come our way.'

Liverpool opted to go to Egypt instead, while United were given the option of playing in Swaziland in a bid to get round the FIFA red tape, although the cash on the table was considerably less than previously bandied about. The South African businessmen behind the trip felt that the switch to the neighbouring country would still pull in the crowds.

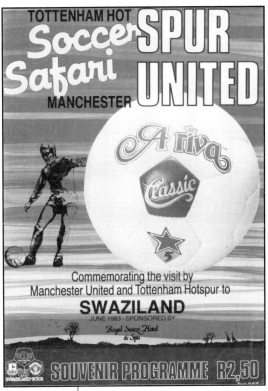

The programme for the games versus Tottenham Hotspur, 4 June and 11 June 1983.

The first of the two fixtures for the Swazispa International Challenge Cup took place less than 24 hours after the two teams had flown in from Heathrow on a 12-hour flight and, despite the hints of tiredness, the 90 minutes produced some good football.

Archibald gave Tottenham the lead on the half-hour after United target Alan Brazil had created the opening, but the second 45 minutes belonged completely to United. Muhren equalised from the penalty spot in the 52nd minute after Perryman had fouled Wilkins and Stapleton made it 2–1 16 minutes from the end.

---

4 June 1983 **Tottenham Hotspur at Somhlolo Stadium, Lobamba.**

Attendance: 8,000.

Won: 2–1.

Scorers: Muhren (pen.), Stapleton.

Team: Bailey, Duxbury, Albiston, Wilkins, Moran, McQueen, Moses, Muhren, Stapleton, Whiteside, Grimes.

Substitutes: McGrath for McQueen, Macari for Whiteside.

Although there was a week before the second of the fixtures, 24 hours after the opening encounter a combined United/Tottenham XI – 'Tottman' – took on a Swaziland XI. Bailey, Gidman, Grimes, McGrath, Macari and McGarvey all started, with Pears and Duxbury coming on as substitutes in the 6–1 victory. Macari and McGarvey scored two of the goals.

After seven days of relaxation, the second fixture against Tottenham saw United somewhat depleted, with Whiteside, Muhren and McQueen all out through injury.

Rather surprisingly, admission to the game was quite expensive, the terracing costing an equivalent of £6, with the stand up to £28. This was more than the FA Cup Final itself!

Mabbutt gave Tottenham the lead in the 29th minute and three minutes later Perryman made it 2–0, which was enough to give Tottenham a 3–2 aggregate win, or so many of those present thought. It was, however, not to be, as it turned out that the Tottenham victory simply made it one victory each and a penalty shoot-out was needed to decide the ultimate winners.

Grimes and McGarvey gave United a 2–0 lead, but these two spot-kicks were the only ones to beat Clemence, with Price and Brazil scoring to make it 2–2 after five kicks each. So it was down to sudden death.

Moses stepped up for United's sixth kick, only to see his effort saved by Clemence. Perryman did not make the same mistake and minutes later he was lifting the trophy.

---

11 June 1983   **Tottenham Hotspur at Somhlolo Stadium, Lobamba.**

Attendance: 5,000.

Lost: 2–0 (**Lost:** 3–2 on penalties).

Scorers: Grimes, McGarvey.

Team: Bailey, Duxbury, Albiston, Moses, Moran, McGrath, Gidman, Wilkins, Stapleton, McGarvey, Grimes.

Substitute: Macari for Gidman.

The tournament was not without its mishaps. One day, a few of the United players decided to go on a day trip to neighbouring South Africa. 'Gordon McQueen, Kevin Moran and myself decided to hire a car, having been told that we could make the trip in four hours,' recalled Arthur Albiston. Kevin unfortunately left his passport on the coach, so we had to telephone ahead and ask the lads to leave it at the border post when they passed through.

'Having negotiated various forms of wildlife lying on or wandering across the road, we eventually reached the border, only for none of the gun-toting guards to understand a word that Kevin was saying. His passport photograph was also not a good resemblance due to his hair being a different length. Eventually, we managed to get things sorted out'.

Prior to the normal FA Charity Shield curtain-raiser at Wembley, United faced the reigning League champions Liverpool at Windsor Park, Belfast, in a testimonial match for the retiring IFA secretary Bill Drennan, showing their Merseyside rivals that they intended to do their utmost to knock them off their perch in the months ahead.

Liverpool pressed forward straight from the kick-off, with Gary Bailey tipping over a teasing chip from Sammy Lee as early as the third minute. Two minutes later the United 'keeper was helpless as Souness gave the Merseysiders the lead, finishing off a Dalglish and Hodgson move.

With an extra week's training under their belt, Liverpool enjoyed the midfield advantage as United sought to get a foothold in the game, only to find themselves two behind after 24 minutes. Dalglish hit the bar, while Rush latched onto the rebound only to see his effort blocked by Bailey, but followed through to prod the ball over the line with the United 'keeper stranded.

After a rather uncertain half-hour, United slowly began to claw their way into the game and in the 37th minute Whiteside pulled a goal back, beating Grobbelaar after the erratic 'keeper failed to cut out a Stapleton pass. Liverpool, however, restored their two-goal lead straight from the kick-off, as Rush volleyed past Bailey.

Atkinson reshuffled his midfield at half-time, bringing on Grimes and Moses, and United were soon in search of a goal that would get them back into the game.

Stapleton hit the post with a shot from the edge of the penalty area on the hour mark, but six minutes later they managed to pull a goal back, Moran hooking a Graham corner into the net.

With further substitutions taking United's tally of players used to 17, they continued to put the Liverpool defence under pressure. Their persistence paid off in the 84th minute, when Stapleton equalised from a Grimes cross which eluded the entire defence.

With only a minute remaining, it was Grimes again who caused the Liverpool defence problems, sending over a perfect cross which was steered home by Macari to claim a remarkable victory for United.

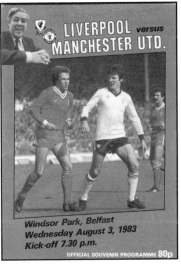

The programme for the match versus Liverpool, 3 August 1983.

3 August 1983	**Liverpool at Windsor Park, Belfast.**

Attendance: 30,000.

Won: 4–3.

Scorers: Whiteside, Moran, Macari 2.

Team: Bailey, Duxbury, Albiston, Wilkins, Moran, McQueen, Robson, Muhren, Stapleton, Whiteside, Graham.

Substitutes: Gidman for Duxbury, Moses for Wilkins, McGrath for McQueen, Grimes for Muhren, Macari for Whiteside, Davies for Graham.

It had taken a replay to separate United and Brighton back in May when the two sides contested the FA Cup Final. With the two teams coming face to face once again, this time for the Townsend Thoresen Cup, 90 minutes was once again not enough to settle the outcome.

Brighton were clearly out to avenge their Cup Final defeat, as their supporters bayed for blood every time Norman Whiteside warmed up down the touchline; his tackle on Ramsey in the first match under the twin towers still clear in their minds. Such was the hostile reaction to the Northern Ireland international's presence, that Ron Atkinson kept him away from the action on the pitch. Ramsey, on the other hand, was clearly after revenge of some sort and was perhaps fortunate to remain on the pitch following a lunging first-half challenge on Grimes and a scything tackle on Wilkins later in the game.

The south-coast club raised the game, particularly in the second half, but they failed to breach the United defence, although they came close on more than one occasion in the dying minutes. Bailey had to be alert to save from Smillie, before O'Reagan shot wide and Grealish had a shot cleared off the line. Minutes before this flurry of activity Wilkins had an opportunity to secure victory, but missed from close range.

So, with no score at the end of the 90 minutes, it was down to penalties to decide the winner. Grimes missed United's first spot-kick, but Stapleton, Graham and McGrath all converted. Howlett and O'Reagan both shot wide for Brighton, making it 3–3 as Gidman stepped up to take the final kick of the evening. His shot gave Digweed no chance.

The programme for the match versus Brighton and Hove Albion, 9 August 1983.

9 August 1983   **Brighton and Hove Albion at Goldstone Ground.**

Attendance: 6,853.

Drew: 0—0 (**Won:** 4—3 on penalties).

Scorers: Stapleton, Graham, McGrath, Gidman.

Team: Bailey, Gidman, Albiston, Moses, Moran, McQueen, Robson, Grimes, Stapleton, Macari, Graham.

Substitutes: Wilkins for Robson, McGrath for Moran.

The next stop for United was the Netherlands, for the Amsterdam 708 Tournament, where Feyenoord provided the opposition in the opening fixture of the four-club competition. Although a rather ordinary side, the Dutch did have the masterful Johan Cruyff within their ranks and his presence was clearly the difference between the two teams.

Feyenoord took the lead as early as the sixth minute, when Wejstekers caught Bailey out with an acute angled dipping drive from 30 yards out. However, United's continual aerial threat provided results when Stapleton rose to head home a Graham free-kick on the stroke of half-time.

The second half saw United struggle to gain any sort of momentum and their shortcomings were punished in the 76th minute when Cruyff set up Jeliazkov for what proved to be the winner. Four minutes from time Moses had an opportunity to net an equaliser, but he squandered the pass from Wilkins.

12 August 1983   **Feyenoord at Olympic Stadium, Amsterdam.**

Attendance: 40,000.

Lost: 2—1.

Scorer: Stapleton.

Team: Bailey, Duxbury, Albiston, Moses, Moran, McQueen, Robson, Grimes, Stapleton, Whiteside, Graham.

Substitutes: Wilkins for Robson, Macari for Graham.

Against host club Ajax things once again did not quite go according to plan, with Ron Atkinson describing the game, which saw United lose 1–0 and Gordon McQueen sent off, as 'our worst performance in my two years here'.

Despite the scoreline only showing a single goal separating the two sides, United were quite simply outplayed by a young and certainly talented Ajax side. If it had not been for Gary Bailey making at least seven outstanding saves, then there would have been more goals than just Olsen's 50th-minute strike. According to Atkinson, 'Ajax should have scored 10'.

'Bailey and Duxbury both had good games, but after that you were searching for another outstanding player,' bemoaned the United manager, who had also plenty to say regarding McQueen's sending off.

With the third place play-off game meandering towards a close, and with only five minutes remaining, Moby nutmegged the Scottish defender, only to have his legs suddenly swept from underneath him by a totally unprofessional and impetuous tackle. The referee had no option other than to send the United player off.

After the game, Atkinson was quick to voice his opinion of the incident, saying, 'It was a stupid reaction. There was no need for it. He should be

Ticket for the match versus Feyenoord, 12 August 1983.

suspended for two years, not two matches, for what he did. There is every chance that the club will discipline him as well.'

14 August 1983	Ajax at Olympic Stadium, Amsterdam.

Attendance: 37,000.

Lost: 1—0.

Team: Bailey, Duxbury, Albiston, Macari, Moran, McQueen, Wilkins, Grimes, Stapleton, Whiteside, Graham.

Substitutes: Gidman for Moran, McGarvey for Whiteside.

Old Trafford friendlies are few and far between and quite often those that do take place are testimonial matches for a long-serving stalwart. The recipient on this occasion was former club captain Martin Buchan, with his former club Aberdeen travelling south to provide the opposition.

Buchan had joined United some 11 and a half years previously for a fee of £130,000. He had been Aberdeen's youngest-ever captain, leading them to Scottish Cup success against Celtic in 1970, and became the only player to complete a similar feat south of the border with United seven years later.

The game would be rather more than a basic testimonial, as Alex Ferguson's Aberdeen were also European Cup-Winners' Cup holders and the fixture would provide United with a good pre-season workout.

United, playing in a one-off red strip supplied by Puma, were overshadowed for long periods by the Gordon Strachan-inspired visitors, who only lacked penalty area penetration. They managed only one shot at goal in the opening 45 minutes.

United were able to slowly gain the advantage, taking the lead in the 33rd minute. Former Aberdeen winger Arthur Graham found Stapleton with a probing cross and the Republic of Ireland striker beat Leighton with a glancing header.

Three minutes later it was 2–0, Stapleton once again the scorer, this time from close range after Robson turned a Muhren cross into his path.

The two-goal advantage persuaded Atkinson to make a few changes to his line up, but the reshuffle enabled Aberdeen to get back into the game as United struggled to regain their momentum.

Two minutes after the restart Strachan's cross was headed past Bailey by Weir and suddenly the game took on a completely different look. Ferguson brought on Eric Black, who gave the United defence another body to think about, and it was a move that was to pay dividends. Combining with McMaster, he created the opening for Weir to ram home the equaliser at the far post to give the Dons a creditable draw.

An ovation, second only to that afforded to Buchan, was given to Strachan as he left the pitch with minutes to go. Little did those watching realise that he, and his manager, would be regular Old Trafford features in the not too distant future.

The programme for the match versus Aberdeen, 17 August 1983.

MARTIN BUCHAN TESTIMONIAL

Manchester United v. **Aberdeen**

F.A. Cup Winners 1983 — European Cup Winners' Cup and Scottish F.A. Cup Winners 1983

17 August 1983   **Aberdeen at Old Trafford.**

Attendance: 18,042.

Drew: 2–2.

Scorer: Stapleton 2.

Team: Bailey, Gidman, Albiston, Wilkins, Moran, Buchan, Robson, Muhren, Stapleton, Macari, Graham.

Substitutes: Moses for Robson, McGrath for Buchan, Hughes for Macari.

The falling temperatures of an English winter were left behind as United headed to the sun to take on the national sides of Algeria and Libya.

In the first of two trips into the unknown United had to be content with a no score draw. The Algerians had rocketed to prominence due to their performances in the 1982 World Cup finals in Spain and, for the latter half-hour of this friendly, they took advantage of some poor United play, although their breakaway attacks failed to pay dividends.

Attendances for the game differ by about 20,000, with one giving 15,000, while another mentions 35,000. The report with the former also goes on to say that the game was shown live on television and if it had not been then there would undoubtedly have been a 70,000 sell-out.

United did improve on their first-half performance as the game went on and, 20 minutes from time, Kevin Moran headed home a Muhren free-kick, although, not for the first time in the game, the referee did not impress with his neutrality and disallowed the goal.

On the return journey to England, there was some mid-air drama, as United's Air Algeria Boeing 737 developed a minor fault 15 minutes after take-off.

25 January 1984   **Algeria XI at Algiers.**

Attendance: 35,000.

Drew: 0–0.

Team: Bailey, Moses, Albiston, Wilkins, Moran, Duxbury, Robson, Muhren, Stapleton, Hughes, Graham.

Substitutes: Hogg for Albiston, Whiteside for Hughes.

Having pocketed £15,000 from their trip to Algeria, United doubled their money a month later, flying to North Africa to face the Libyan national side, another fixture encouraged by the early FA Cup and Milk Cup exits.

Many newspapers failed to even print the score, never mind give you a report of the action. Even the *Manchester Evening News* was not up to printing a kick-by-kick account.

United won 2–0, with goals from Stapleton and Hughes.

21 February 1984   **Libya XI at Tripoli.**

Attendance: 45,000.

Won: 2–0.

Scorers: Stapleton, Hughes.

Team: Bailey, Gidman, McGrath, Moses, Moran, Hogg, Robson, Muhren, Stapleton, Hughes, Graham.

Substitute: Macari for Robson.

The scoreboard end of Old Trafford was awash with banners and the anthems rolled down the terraces, as the away support joined the United faithful to salute Lou Macari, who was saying his farewell at the ground where he first pulled on a United shirt some 11 years previously.

This, however, was no ordinary testimonial match, as United took the game to Celtic in the opening half, only to be denied on more than one occasion by goalkeeper Bonnar. The visitors were so subdued that it was not until the 35th minute that they managed a shot at goal, Bailey turning the effort from Burns round the post.

Five minutes into the second half United took the lead. Graham cleverly lobbed the ball over the head of Aitken, raced past Reid and slammed the ball past Bonner. It was a goal which seemed to jolt the visitors into action and they should have equalised a minute later, but MacLeod shot wildly over from only five yards out. Burns came closer in the 65th minute when he hit the crossbar, but it was not until Celtic made a surprising change in personnel 14 minutes later that they finally managed to score.

To a rousing reception, Macari disappeared up the tunnel, only to reappear to even louder acclaim wearing the green and white hoops of Celtic. This gesture seemed to lift the game and inside a minute, with his first touch of the ball, he helped set up the equaliser for Tommy Burns.

There was to be no magical ending, but on the final whistle a number of Celtic supporters invaded the pitch and carried off Macari shoulder high.

The gate receipts created a record for such a match and were some £25,000 more than the previous highest – £60,000, for Bobby Charlton's testimonial, also set at Old Trafford against Celtic.

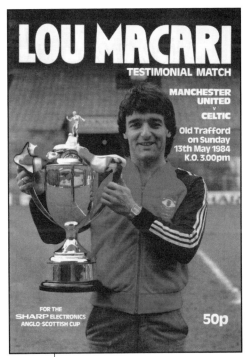

The programme for the match versus Celtic, 13 May 1984.

13 May 1984	**Celtic at Old Trafford.**

Attendance: 40,140.

Drew: 1–1.

Scorer: Graham.

Team: Bailey, Duxbury, Albiston, Wilkins, McGrath, McQueen, Blackmore, Moses, Robson, Macari, Graham.

Substitutes: Pears for Bailey, Garton for Duxbury, McGarvey for Robson, Dempsey for Wilkins, Moran for Macari.

The 1983–84 domestic season came to an end on 16 May and a dismal 2–0 defeat at Nottingham Forest knocked United into third place in the First Division. Five days later, with many still asking how the expensively assembled team had failed on all fronts, Ron Atkinson and his players were as far away from the criticism as possible in Hong Kong, where they played the first match of a Far East–Australian tour against local First Division side Bulova.

It took United only six minutes to go in front, Robson heading home, and seven minutes later, it was 2–0 thanks to Macari.

Despite maintaining the upper hand, the home side pulled a goal back in the 28th minute with a penalty after Albiston handled and shocked their visitors by drawing level on the hour through Parlane.

Hopes of a historic result were soon dismissed, with further United goals from Moran, a header in the 65th minute, and Macari with his second in the 74th, giving United a comfortable advantage to play out the game.

21 May 1984	Bulova at Hong Kong.

Attendance: 28,485.

Won: 4—2.

Scorers: Macari 2, Robson, Moran.

Team: Bailey, Duxbury, Albiston, Wilkins, Moran, McGrath, Robson, Graham, McGarvey, Macari, Barnes.

Substitutes: McQueen for McGrath, Dempsey for Wilkins, Blackmore for Robson.

Moving on to Australia, where the first fixture saw them take on the national XI, a rather nondescript United side failed to make much of an impression.

If you glance at the United team line up you may well scratch your head in wonder with the appearance of the names Hutchison and Worthington. A local Australian journalist, Gino De la Scerri, wrote in his report: 'Facing the Socceroos were Manchester United, five regular players, five guest players, plus Frank Worthington, who is expected to sign for the Red Devils.' The guest players, according to the man with the pen, were Pears, Davies, Blackmore, Dempsey and Hutchison. The latter three, according to Ron Atkinson, 'always wanted to play for Manchester United.'

The leggy Hutchison was perhaps better known from his career with the likes of Blackpool and Manchester City, while the more outlandish and flamboyant Worthington enjoyed his best days with Huddersfield Town and United's near-neighbours Bolton. The latter would certainly have been a big favourite at Old Trafford.

Despite the scoreline, United never looked like losing and in reality should have won. Worthington nearly did his quest for a permanent deal the world of good in the 15th minute, but fired over from 20 yards. The home side could well have taken the lead in the fourth minute, but Kosmina flashed his header wide of the goal.

United were simply content not to lose and it was not until the final 15 minutes that they really settled, with Arthur Graham shooting just wide, and also having another shot saved by the 'keeper.

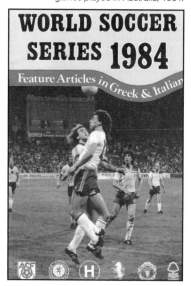

The programme which covered all the games played in Australia, 1984.

WORLD SOCCER SERIES 1984

Feature Articles in Greek & Italian

26 May 1984	Australia at the Sydney Cricket Ground.

Attendance: 16,047.

Drew: 0—0.

Team: Pears, McGrath, Blackmore, Dempsey, Moran, McQueen, Hutchison, Davies, Worthington, Hughes, Graham.

Moving on to Melbourne, the next opponents, Nottingham Forest, were a bit more familiar to the United players. The closely fought encounter saw the two teams separated by a solitary Mark Hughes ninth-minute goal.

Having been deprived of the runners'-up spot in the First Division by Forest, there was much to play for in a game that United controlled from start to finish. Moses commanded in midfield, with Hutchison and Barnes (another guest) outstanding upfront along with Mark Hughes.

Forest had little bite upfront and never really threatened after United took a ninth-minute lead. A direct through ball from Moses found Hughes, with the robust striker shrugging off a challenge before slipping the ball past Sutton in the Forest goal.

Swain, Forest's most prominent player, almost created an opening minutes before the interval, but his pass to Walsh and the cross that followed was missed by everyone.

Five minutes into the second half, Moses almost made it 2–0. Fairclough allowed Hutchison to break down the right. The chip forward by the United guest found Moses, but Fairclough made amends by knocking the midfielder's effort over the bar. Four minutes later it was McQueen who caused the problems in the Forest defence. Charging forward, the big central-defender collected a ball from Barnes but put his final shot wide of the goal.

Perhaps an Australian press report summed the game up best: 'Lots of good, clean fun and entertainment and some fine individual performances, but it really was only an exhibition match.'

---

3 June 1984　　　**Nottingham Forest at Melbourne Cricket Ground.**

Attendance: 21,099.

Won: 1–0.

Scorer: Hughes.

Team: Bailey, Garton, McGrath, Moses, Moran, McQueen, Hutchison, Davies, Worthington, Hughes, Barnes.

Next it was back to the Sydney Cricket Ground, where the friendly took on a real European feel as United lined up against Juventus, who had just won the Italian League and the European Cup-Winners' Cup.

Despite playing without the likes of Stapleton, Muhren, Robson and Whiteside, United managed to hold their own, but the goalless confrontation disappointed the crowd, who showed their feelings with slow handclapping.

The game could well have ended up 2–2, but for excellent saves by Bailey and Tacconi. The former punched over a pile-driver from Vignola before whipping the ball off the feet of Cabrini. At the opposite end Tacconi pulled a dangerous Garton cross out of the air before pushing the ball round the post from Man of the Match Worthington.

Play moved from end to end, and as the second half progressed it was not played at the same pace as the first. Due to this lack of commitment, not to mention goals, it was announced five minutes from time that the result would be determined by penalty-kicks. All of the Italian team's spot-kicks were converted, but Tacconi stopped Blackmore's to give Juventus a 5–4 victory.

Once again, the Australian press was not impressed by what they saw. 'Juventus win SCG farce on shootout,' wrote one, continuing, 'It was a sad indictment that a player like Frank Worthington, who confesses to be more than 35, should be one of the stars'.

---

6 June 1984　　　**Juventus at Sydney Cricket Ground.**

Attendance: 24,286.

Drew: 0–0 (**Lost:** 5–4 on penalties).

Scorers: Worthington, Hutchison, Barnes, McGarvey.

Team: Bailey, Garton, McGrath, Moses, Moran, McQueen, Hutchison, Davies, Worthington, Graham, Barnes.

Substitutes: Hughes for Graham, McGarvey for Hughes, Blackmore for Garton.

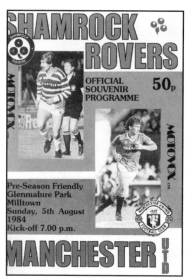

The programme for the match versus Shamrock Rovers, 5 August 1984.

Manager Ron Atkinson made three major signings during the summer of 1984: Alan Brazil, Jesper Olsen and Gorden Strachan, in an attempt to get his hands on some silverware. Only two of the three, however, lined up against Shamrock Rovers in the first of the 1984–85 pre-season warm up fixtures.

The League of Ireland champions and Cup finalists were no match for the well-supported visitors, with many of the fanatical crowd managing to get closer to Jesper Olsen than the Shamrock defenders as the game progressed.

It was a comfortable, rather than convincing, performance from United, with Brazil being outshone by his fellow debutant Olsen, who after something of a subdued 60 minutes suddenly sprang to life. Knocked to the ground by Byrne, he immediately robbed the Irishman before taking a couple of paces and curling the ball into the corner of the net.

With Mark Hughes having opened the scoring earlier on, slotting the ball home from 10 yards, this second goal put the game well beyond the reach of the part-timers, who had a Campbell effort cleared off the line by McQueen seven minutes from time.

---

5 August 1984   **Shamrock Rovers at Glenmalure Park, Dublin.**

Attendance: 10,000.

Won: 2–0.

Scorers: Hughes, Olsen.

Team: Bailey, Duxbury, Albiston, Moses, Moran, McQueen, Robson, Muhren, Hughes, Brazil, Olsen.

Substitutes: Graham for Muhren, Pears for Bailey, Gidman for Duxbury, Hogg for Moran.

The build-up continued in Spain, where the Teresa Herrera Trophy was contested, against European Cup finalists Roma, Spanish Champions Athletico Bilbao and Vasco da Gama.

In the opening fixture against Roma the third of Atkinson's summer signings, Gordon Strachan, was included among the substitutes. However, the Italians proved to be too strong for United, with early goals from Falcao and Graziani putting them well in control before a late goal from Hughes eight minutes from time.

With 60 seconds remaining, however, it looked as if a Robson header was going to level the score, but 'keeper Malgioglio pulled off a magnificent save on the line to put the Italians into the Final.

---

11 August 1984   **AS Roma at Riazor Stadium, La Coruna, Spain.**

Attendance: 22,000.

Lost: 2–1.

Scorer: Hughes.

Team: Bailey, Duxbury, Albiston, Moses, Moran, McQueen, Robson, Muhren, Hughes, Brazil, Olsen.

Substitutes: Strachan for Muhren, Gidman for Albiston.

With Vasco da Gama having beaten Athletico Bilbao on penalties the previous day, the game against the Spaniards mattered little, and match fitness was the main priority, although finishing third did have more appeal to it than last place.

During the opening half-hour it looked as though United would be returning to Manchester with the wooden spoon, as the Spaniards controlled the game.

However, a Moses–Brazil move created an opening for Norman Whiteside to score what turned out to be the only goal of the game.

Once in the lead United, with their trio of new signings starting together for the first time, played some excellent football. Olsen in particular caught the eye in a rather uneventful 90 minutes.

12 August 1984	**Athletico Bilbao at Riazor Stadium, La Coruna.**

Attendance: 26,000.

Won: 1–0.

Scorer: Whiteside.

Team: Bailey, Duxbury, Hogg, Moses, Moran, McQueen, Robson, Strachan, Whiteside, Brazil, Olsen.

Substitutes: Graham for Olsen, Hughes for Brazil.

From sunny Spain it was back to Old Trafford for a visit from Ajax. It was the turn of the smallest players on the pitch to make the biggest impact, with Strachan shrugging off his transfer wrangle from Aberdeen and Olsen, according to Bob Russell in the *Mirror,* showing 'something of George Best, Gordon Hill and Denis Law'.

The programme for the match versus Ajax, 14 August 1984.

After a bright opening the visitors began to slowly take control and United could consider themselves rather fortunate to go in at the interval on level terms. Boeve and De Wit both squandered scoring opportunities, while Bailey denied Koeman as half-time approached.

At the opposite end of the pitch, Brazil was a rather anonymous figure and it was unsurprising that he failed to reappear after the break. His place was taken by Hughes and it took the young Welshman four minutes to make his mark, cottoning on to a Whiteside pass before scoring from 15 yards.

Ajax's play gave the crowd an insight into the work that had yet to be done by their hosts and it came as little surprise when substitute Gasselich beat Bailey from close range for the equaliser, although there was a suspicion of handball about it.

As the game petered out, the crowd's disappointment was obvious, as they realised that the future was not as rosy as had first been thought.

14 August 1984 — **Ajax at Old Trafford.**

Attendance: 22,682.

Drew: 1—1.

Scorer: Hughes.

Team: Bailey, Duxbury, Hogg, Strachan, Moran, McQueen, Robson, Muhren, Whiteside, Brazil, Olsen.

Substitutes: Hughes for Brazil.

The United players were soon on their travels again, heading to Holland for another four-club event. Their opening fixture in the Rotterdam Tournament paired them with German Bundesliga champions Stuttgart, with the promising Mark Hughes and Jesper Olsen scoring the goals that ensured United a place in the final.

A goalless first half gave way to a much livelier second period, but the deadlock was not broken until the 71st minute when Hughes, who had come on seven minutes earlier in place of Whiteside, finished off a fine run by Olsen.

Stuttgart equalised five minutes later through Claessen, who headed past Bailey after Allgower's free-kick had rattled off the crossbar.

However, it was United who snatched the winning goal, Olsen latching on to a loose clearance before weaving his way through the German defence and planting his final shot wide of the 'keeper.

17 August 1984 — **VFB Stuttgart at Feyenoord Stadium, Rotterdam.**

Attendance: 34,261.

Won: 2—1.

Scorers: Hughes, Olsen.

Team: Bailey, Duxbury, Albiston, Moses, Moran, McQueen, Robson, Strachan, Whiteside, Brazil, Olsen.

Substitutes: Hughes for Whiteside.

With the host club having beaten Anderlecht 2–0 in the other fixture, it was Feyenoord who stood between United and some silverware. However, a solitary goal from Ruud Gullit was enough to see the trophy remain on Dutch soil.

United's hopes of getting the better of the Dutch side were dealt a severe blow with an injury to Gordon McQueen in the ninth minute. The Scottish defender fell awkwardly on his shoulder as he tackled the ever dangerous Gullit. His departure unsettled United and 12 minutes later the Dutch side went in front, Gullit scoring with a fierce drive following a Houseman corner. Without McQueen, many thought that United were going to be on the end of a serious beating, but, to their credit, they managed to get their act together. They were denied two penalty claims, and unfortunately could not manage to score.

---

19 August 1984   **SC Feyenoord at Feyenoord Stadium.**

Attendance: 33,000.

Lost: 1–0.

Team: Bailey, Duxbury, Albiston, Moses, Moran, McQueen, Robson, Strachan, Hughes, Brazil, Olsen.

Substitutes: Hogg for McQueen, Whiteside for Brazil.

Ian Botham is better known as a cricketer, but his talent as a sportsman also saw him turn out for Scunthorpe United. As part of his testimonial activities, United sent a team over to the Old Show Ground, for a game that attracted a crowd of just over 4,000.

Had it been a League or Cup match, the headlines would have proclaimed 'Ten Goal Thriller', but this particular 5–5 draw attracted hardly any attention at all from the media, despite Scunthorpe going 3–0 in front within 10 minutes. 'It was certainly not the sort of farcical, half-pace game some testimonials become. There may have been an absence of robust tackles, but what entertainment the sides provided for a useful crowd,' wrote Nigel Fisher of the *Scunthorpe Evening Telegraph*.

United almost took a first-minute lead, but Strachan's right-wing chip went narrowly over. After action in both goalmouths, the home side scored the opening goal of the night in the sixth minute as Botham headed a Brodie corner past Wealands.

A minute later it was 2–0 when Lees set up Cowling to score from 10 yards.

A McQueen header from an Albiston cross almost pulled a goal back, but United found themselves three goals behind in the 10th minute when Graham scored with a first-time effort, with Lees again the supplier.

A Hughes effort from 20 yards went narrowly past the post before the visitors finally managed to find the net in the 16th minute. Strachan fed Stapleton, whose cut-back from the by-line was prodded home by Olsen at the near post.

Many felt that United would now up the tempo and claw their way back into the game, but it was not until they found themselves 4–1 behind in the 21st minute that they took something of a different approach to the game.

A hard, low Stapleton cross was turned in by Hughes in the 28th minute and Stapleton should have reduced the scoreline further within three minutes, but Olsen's good work was wasted when Stapleton blazed the ball over.

McQueen did make it 4–3 in the 32nd minute, heading home a free-kick from Muhren, and four minutes later it was all square. Olsen glided past a handful of defenders before curling a 20-yard effort into the far corner.

It was certainly value for money and with United now in full flight, Neenan had to be at his best to keep both Hughes and McQueen at bay.

The second half was played at a slightly slower pace, although United continued where they had left off. Olsen claimed his hat-trick within three minutes of the restart, side-stepping the 'keeper following another solo run.

The programme for the match versus Scunthorpe United, 17 December 1984.

Brodie ran through on goal as the United defence shouted for offside, but his shot cannoned off the legs of Wealands, rebounding to Botham. From some 25 yards out, his effort went just over.

Scunthorpe did not have too long to wait to pull level, however, as Duxbury, handling a Brodie centre in the area, allowed Botham to try his luck from the spot, the Test star driving the ball into the roof of the net.

Despite there being further scoring opportunities for both sides, there were no further goals and the game fizzled out.

17 December 1984	Scunthorpe United at the Old Show Ground.

Attendance: 4,039.

Drew: 5–5.

Scorers: Olsen 3, McQueen, Hughes.

Team: Wealands, Blackmore, Albiston, Moses, McQueen, Duxbury, Strachan, Muhren, Stapleton, Hughes, Olsen.

Substitutes: Russell for Hughes, Kelch for Blackmore.

The first friendly of 1985 saw United make the short journey to Oldham Athletic. The game saw the re-emergence of defender Kevin Moran following a 10-week lay-off, with the Irishman proving his fitness for the important weeks ahead. He had formed an impressive partnership with Graeme Hogg, who had also recently returned from injury.

United took the lead in what was a rather scrappy affair, as Frank Stapleton accepted Whiteside's pinpoint cross to head home. Paul McGrath, playing in midfield, added a second with a fine solo effort.

Oldham's solitary goal came from 17-year-old Wayne Harrison.

The programme for the match versus Oldham Athletic, 20 January 1985.

20 January 1985	**Oldham Athletic at Boundary Park.**

Attendance: 8,849.

Won: 2–1.

Scorers: Stapleton, McGrath.

Team: Pears, Gidman, Albiston, Moses, Moran, Hogg, McGrath, Strachan, Stapleton, Hughes, Whiteside.

Substitutes: Brazil for Hughes, Davies for Strachan.

Having lifted the FA Cup with a 1–0 victory over Everton, United headed off to the sunshine five days later for a couple of end-of-season money-making fixtures.

While flying over the Atlantic Ocean on their way to Trinidad, there was a special moment for Kevin Moran, who had suffered the ignominy of becoming the first player to be sent off in an FA Cup Final, when he was dismissed for a mistimed tackle on Peter Reid. The Irishman was summoned to the cockpit where he received a telephone call telling him that the medal he was not given after the Final would be his after all.

The first destination was Port of Spain in Trinidad, where they faced the familiar opposition of Southampton in the national stadium.

For the locals it was not much of a spectacle, with neither set of players really too concerned about the outcome. One goal was all that separated the two sides, coming from Southampton's George Lawrence in the second half.

24 May 1985	**Southampton at the National Stadium, Port of Spain, Trinidad.**

Attendance: 19,000.

Lost: 1–0.

Team: Pears, Duxbury, Garton, Whiteside, McGrath, Moran, Blackmore, Muhren, Hughes, Brazil, Olsen.

Substitute: Graham for Whiteside.

Two days later the action moved to Jamaica, where the national team provided the opposition.

Having played the first fixture at night, this game was played under the blazing sun. The scorching temperatures meant that United were always going to attempt to play the game at their own pace, but they were shocked in the second minute when Jamaica took the lead through Plummer.

Despite the heat, it was experience that won the day, with goals from Blackmore and a Mark Hughes double enough to give United victory without too much exertion.

26 May 1985	Jamaica XI at the National Stadium, Kingston, Jamaica.

Attendance: 15,000.

Won: 3–1.

Scorers: Hughes 2, Blackmore.

Team: Pears, Duxbury, Garton, Whiteside, McGrath, Moran, Blackmore, Muhren, Brazil, Olsen.

Substitute: Graham for Olsen.

It is around this time that the documenting of United's friendlies begins to become slightly more complicated. Fixtures would be advertised in the media, on programme covers and in statistical records as either 'Manchester United' or 'Manchester United XI'. Either line up could include a mixture of first-team and reserve-team personnel, making it debatable whether the match was regarded as a first-team fixture or not.

As I mentioned at the start of this book, I will differentiate between first team or otherwise by following what the official club publications state. However, I will now include, from time to time, 'United XI' fixtures, but without the full statistical detail of the 'first-team friendlies'.

The build-up for season 1985–86 saw United remain in England due to a UEFA ban on English club sides playing abroad, following the events which had preceded the Liverpool–Juventus European Cup Final in Brussels the previous May.

First stop was Cambridge United where Peter Barnes, having played as a guest for United in Australia a year ago, made his debut as a second-half substitute, in a game that should have seen the re appearance of George Best, although he was reportedly unable to get away from an engagement in London.

The game, a double testimonial for Steve Spriggs and Steve Fallon, both of whom had been signed by Ron Atkinson during his time at the Abbey Stadium, certainly gave the fans value for money, with United storming into a two-goal lead.

Andy Sinton gave Cambridge the lead, but just before the interval Mark Hughes equalised with an excellent solo effort. He was to blot his copybook just after the restart, however, when he missed a sitter from only a few yards out after Barnes had left three defenders chasing shadows.

A back-header from a Robson cross minutes later saw Hughes give United the lead, but once again Cambridge fought back to equalise, Bailey shovelling a Keith Osgood 40-yard effort into his own net.

However, it was Barnes who had the final say, making a strong run down the wing before delivering a teasing cross, which was helped over his own line by Scott to clinch victory for United.

The programme for the match versus Cambridge United, 30 July 1985.

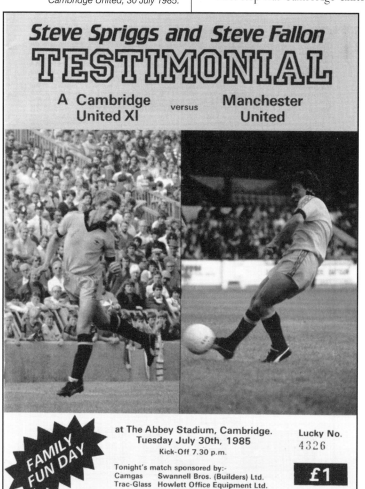

---

30 July 1985   **Cambridge United at Abbey Stadium.**

Attendance: 5,637.

Won: 3—2.

Scorers: Hughes 2, opp. own-goal.

Team: Bailey, Gidman, Albiston, Duxbury, McGrath, Moran, Robson, Blackmore, Hughes, Stapleton, Olsen.

Substitutes: Sinai for Albiston, Barnes for Olsen.

Glancing through the United line up, there is one name that will have the vast majority of supporters scratching their heads in puzzlement.

The name of (Moshe) Sinai does not appear in any United books, as the 24-year-old Israeli international was at Old Trafford on loan from Hapoel, having previously impressed Ron Atkinson. How much he was regarded in his native country could be measured by the fact that Radio Tel Aviv did a live commentary on the Cambridge match. He was actually expected to return home following the game at Cambridge, but saw his trial extended for the remainder of the pre-season period following some nice touches during his appearance.

Sinai made his second United appearance, again as substitute, in the second pre-season friendly against Hereford United, a game that should never actually have taken place.

The game, a testimonial for Colin Addison, manager of Newport County, should have been played at Newport, but the ban on English clubs playing outside England prevented United from travelling to Wales. Hereford had therefore agreed to stage the fixture due to Addison's connections with the Edgar Street club.

In an evenly matched contest it took United until 12 minutes from time to break the deadlock with the only goal of the game. Had the service to Olsen and Barnes been better, then there might well have been more goals.

United lost Moran through injury in the 55th minute, while Hughes was closely watched by Cegielski, so much so that both players were spoken to by the referee.

With 12 minutes remaining Barnes, having switched wings, surged forward, leaving four Hereford players in his wake before stroking the ball inside to Brazil. His centre was met by the on-running Olsen, whose shot flew into the net from 20 yards.

The programme for the match versus Hereford, 1 August 1985.

---

1 August 1985   **Hereford United at Edgar Street.**

Attendance: 6,996.

Won: 1—0.

Scorer: Olsen.

Team: Turner, Gidman, Albiston, Duxbury, McGrath, Moran, Barnes, Blackmore, Hughes, Stapleton, Olsen.

Substitutes: Garton for McGrath, Sinai for Blackmore, Brazil for Stapleton.

A sunny afternoon in the West Country saw United visit Bristol City as Mark Hughes once again stamped his name on the game at a venue that had once boasted First Division football.

Having found themselves well out of pocket following their years at the top, City were more than pleased to have United as their guests again, to bring in some much-needed funds. During the 90 minutes they were certainly not disgraced.

THURSDAY, AUGUST 1st, 1985

COLIN ADDISON

HEREFORD UNITED
v
MANCHESTER UNITED
MATCH SPONSORED BY
RAVENHILL'S
FORD MAIN DEALERS

50p

Ford

The programme for the game versus Bristol City, 3 August 1985.

Kick-off was delayed so that John Gidman, who was having a problem with his vision, could receive attention from United physio Jim McGregor. After treatment he declared himself fit to start the game, which also saw Sinai make his first start. The Israeli, however, failed to make much of an impression and was replaced by Whiteside 15 minutes into the second half. He subsequently disappeared into the wilderness, never to be heard of again.

Hughes was involved in the game from the start, shooting over, hitting the post and being upended for what seemed to be, to everyone except the referee, a certain penalty. Robson half-volleyed over the bar, while Olsen discovered it was a friendly in name only after leaving the field for almost 10 minutes to receive treatment for a knock.

Bristol did well to keep United at bay in the opening 45 minutes and they came close to opening the scoring just after the interval, but a double save from Bailey not only kept the scoreline blank, but also brought about the only goal of the game.

His clearance upfield led to a throw-in and, quickly taken by Barnes, it gave Hughes possession. Despite having his back to the goal, the Welshman turned quickly, unleashing a powerful left-footed volley which flew into the Bristol net and was warmly applauded by all present. Olsen rammed the ball home from a Stapleton cross in the 64th minute, but was disappointed to see it chalked off for offside against Stapleton.

3 August 1985	**Bristol City at Ashton Gate.**
Attendance: 6,707.	
Won: 1—0.	
Scorer: Hughes.	
Team: Bailey, Gidman, Blackmore, Sinai, McGrath, Duxbury, Robson, Barnes, Hughes, Stapleton, Olsen.	
Substitutes: Whiteside for Sinai.	

Three days later United travelled across the Pennines to play Bradford City in aid of the 56 supporters who had lost their lives on that ill-fated May afternoon, when fire had swept through the stand at the Valley Parade ground.

Due to the damage at the ground, this particular fixture took place at Huddersfield's Leeds Road ground, with the crowd standing in silence prior to kick-off. However, with the sound of the referee's whistle it soon became business as usual, the players of both sides treating the game as if the result really mattered.

United enjoyed most of the play, but could not turn their superiority into goals and eventually found themselves on the end of their first pre-season defeat, despite taking the lead through Olsen.

Three goals in 16 minutes from City, from Hendrie, Singleton and Campbell, altered the course of the game, with United unable to claw their way back into the match.

The programme for the game versus Bradford, 6 August 1985.

6 August 1985	**Bradford City at Leeds Road, Huddersfield.**
Attendance: 5,719.	
Lost: 3—1.	
Scorer: Olsen.	
Team: Turner, Gidman, Albiston, Whiteside, McGrath, Hogg, Robson, Blackmore, Stapleton, Brazil, Olsen.	
Substitutes: Duxbury for Gidman, Barnes for Olsen, Garton for Hogg.	

For the purposes of this book I have decided to include the Screen Sport Super Cup fixtures. Technically they were friendlies, but they were also played as part of an organised competition.

It was a one-off competition, launched in the aftermath of the Heysel Stadium disaster, for the English sides who, having qualified for the three European competitions, found themselves banned from taking part through no fault of their own.

Liverpool was one of the clubs invited to take part and, along with United, they were joined by Everton, Tottenham, Norwich City and Southampton. Split into two groups of three, United were paired with Everton and Norwich City.

In the opening fixture against League Champions Everton at Old Trafford on 18 September, a crowd of 33,859 saw the Toffees win 4–2. United had begun well enough, but although unbeaten in the League they were soon under pressure and found themselves two goals behind. Sheedy scored the opener in the 25th minute, the first goal that United had conceded at home that season, with Lineker heading the second past Bailey three minutes before the interval.

Bryan Robson missed a golden opportunity to give United the lead in the 11th minute and, despite Hughes gaining the advantage over Marshall and Stapleton hitting the woodwork, United could not get that vital finishing touch until the stroke of half-time, when Robson pulled one back from the penalty spot. It was an award considered by many to be debatable, with Harper booked for his prolonged protest to the referee.

United's hopes of a second half fightback were dashed, as eight minutes after the break it was 3–1, Sheedy notching up his second of the night. The game came alive in the 61st minute when United scored a second. Robson found Barnes with an excellent cross-field pass and the winger's cross was headed home by Stapleton.

There was, however, to be no grand finale, as Sharp scored a fourth for the visitors 10 minutes from time.

18 September 1985	Everton at Old Trafford.

Attendance: 33,059.

Lost: 4–2.

Scorers: Robson (pen.), Stapleton.

Team: Bailey, Duxbury, Albiston, Whiteside, McGrath, Moran, Robson, Strachan, Hughes, Stapleton, Barnes.

On 23 October a United team travelled to the home of Notts County to play in a testimonial match for Iain McCullough, who had been forced to retire due to an injury received, ironically, against United in April 1984, when he broke his leg in a collision with Gary Bailey.

This particular fixture falls under the banner of a United XI, but it was certainly a strong visiting side, which managed to upstage County 2–1.

23 October 1985	Notts County.

Attendance: 3,022

Won: 2–1.

Team: Bailey, Duxbury, Garton, Murphy, McGrath, Hogg, Olsen, Bowyer (Nottingham Forest), Hughes, Brazil, Barnes.

Substitutes: Wood for Hughes, Turner for Bailey, McGuinness for Hogg, Russell for Murphy.

The programme for the match versus Notts County, 23 October 1985.

The second Screen Sport match, on 6 November, saw 20,130 fans scattered around Old Trafford to witness a 1–1 draw against Norwich City in a game which marked the debut of goalkeeper Chris Turner, a £275,000 signing from Sunderland.

It was to be a Turner error that saw the Second Division side, who would have been in Europe due to their Milk Cup triumph, take the lead after only six minutes. Having already misjudged a Biggins shot which had rattled his crossbar, he was caught out when the same player opened the scoring. A further fumble in the 26th minute saw the ball break for Norwich centre-half Phelan, but he lashed the ball wildly over.

Driven forward by McGrath, United once again struggled to convert the chances into goals until a combined Culverhouse and Watson challenge in the 54th minute brought down Strachan, allowing captain Norman Whiteside to earn United a point.

Despite enjoying the best of the second half, United failed to find any way through the resolute Norwich defence.

6 November 1985	Norwich City at Old Trafford.

Attendance: 20,130.

Drew: 1–1.

Scorer: Whiteside (pen.).

Team: Turner, Gidman, Albiston, Whiteside, McGrath, Hogg, Blackmore, Olsen, Hughes, Brazil, Barnes.

Substitute: Strachan for Barnes.

Moving on a month, United ventured over the Pennines to Elland Road, a venue that few today would expect to extend a welcome to Manchester United for a friendly.

This fixture against Leeds United, a testimonial for their former Scottish international forward Peter Lorimer, comes under the United XI umbrella, with some classing it as a first-team fixture, and others considering it a reserve-team one. The fixture is also unusual because its duration was only one hour, 30 minutes each way.

The United support was considerably smaller than that which normally visited the Yorkshire stadium. However, they raised their voices as Frank Stapleton gave United the lead from the penalty spot in the 10th minute.

George McCluskey levelled the scoring in the 22nd minute, but within 60 seconds United were back in front through Mark Hughes. It was a lead that they held until a minute from the end, when Sheridan made it 2–2.

20 November 1985	Leeds United at Elland Road.

Attendance: 8,167.

Drew: 2–2.

Scorers: Stapleton (pen.), Hughes.

Team: Bailey, Robinson, Garton, Dempsey, McGrath, Moran, Russell, Olsen, Hughes, Stapleton, Murphy.

Substitute: Hanrahan for Hughes.

December saw the second-leg fixtures of the Screen Sports Super Cup, with United visiting Goodison Park to take on Everton.

Manager Ron Atkinson suffered something of a setback prior to the game, when he was told that he was not allowed to field Mark Higgins. The former Everton player had been out of action due to a pelvic injury since he last featured for the Toffees in December 1983. He had actually quit the game after a testimonial match and an insurance pay-out. A three-month trial with United, playing in the reserves, led to Atkinson believing that he could play Higgins in the Screen Sport fixture as a non-contract professional. However, his plans were shattered by a Football League ruling maintaining that Higgins had collected compensation and was not registered.

A bizarre own-goal by Frank Stapleton turned out to be all that separated the two teams. Without six of the first-team players, it was always going to be a hard slog.

In the United goal Turner produced something of a one-man show to defy the home side, keeping out efforts from Van den Hauwe, Steven, Heath, Lineker and Wilkinson, while Gidman and Gibson both made goalline clearances.

United did have the odd break, but Hughes seemed more concerned about carrying out a one-man attack on anything in blue, although 10 minutes from time he was perhaps unfortunate to see a goal-bound shot hit the legs of Southall. Four minutes earlier Dempsey had taken too long in moving for a ball and the chance was gone.

The decisive goal came five minutes from time. A Lineker shot was blocked by Turner, but the ball flew into the air and, as stand-in central-defender Frank Stapleton moved in to clear, the ball went off his outstretched foot and into the empty net.

The programme for the match versus Norwich City, 11 December 1985.

---

4 December 1985   **Everton at Goodison Park.**

Attendance: 20,542.

Lost: 1–0.

Team: Turner, Gidman, C. Gibson, Whiteside, McGrath, Stapleton, Blackmore, Strachan, Hughes, Brazil, Olsen.

Substitutes: Dempsey for Whiteside.

Seven days later United, the current League leaders, travelled to Carrow Road, requiring a victory by at least two clear goals against Norwich City in order to progress into the semi-finals. Once again, however, despite their lofty League position, they failed to produce a victory, with the game ending in a 1–1 draw.

A ninth-minute goal from Williams caught United cold and, with the Milk Cup holders unbeaten in 14 games, Norwich were in no mood to relinquish their record, Drinkell and Biggins keeping the United defence on their toes.

United improved as the game went on, but Brazil squandered numerous opportunities, while at the opposite end Phelan could have put the game beyond any doubt seven minutes after the restart but shot into the side netting. Wood saved from Strachan, following a 20-yard run by the midfielder, but the Norwich 'keeper could not prevent Colin Gibson from grabbing a 71st-minute equaliser.

---

11 December 1985   **Norwich City at Carrow Road.**

Attendance: 15,449.

Drew: 1–1.

Scorer: C. Gibson

Team: Bailey, Gidman, C. Gibson, Whiteside, McGrath, Garton, Dempsey, Strachan, Stapleton, Brazil, Blackmore.

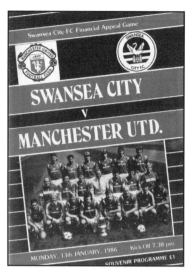

The programme for the match versus Swansea, 13 January 1986.

On 13 January 1986 United were in Swansea to play a much-needed fund-raising fixture for the impoverished Welsh side. Despite persistent rain the crowds did not stay away, with many of the turnstile operators giving their services for free and the crowd of almost 20,000 (more than had watched the First Division fixture between the two sides three years previously) paid more than £50,000 towards Swansea's survival.

13 January 1986	**Swansea at Vetch Field, Swansea.**

Won: 5–1.

Scorers: Brazil 3, Olsen (opp. own-goal).

Team: Bailey, Duxbury, McLaughlin, Blackmore, Ratcliffe, Moran, Dempsey, Olsen, Brazil, Russell, Barnes.

Substitutes: Hogg for Moran, Turner for Bailey, Worthington for Blackmore.

There was certainly no off-field drama when Ron Atkinson took his United side to Glasgow in a bid to keep his Championship-chasing squad on their toes, for what was, for a change, just an ordinary friendly.

With Celtic the Scottish Cup holders and United the FA Cup holders, the winner could proclaim themselves 'Cup Kings' of Britain and, along with national pride, a thrilling encounter was certainly hoped for by those who flocked to Glasgow. They were certainly not disappointed, with both sides playing fine, attacking football, giving the referee very little to do throughout the 90 minutes.

Celtic, however, lacked the organisation of their red-shirted visitors and their concentration was also suspect early on, as United took a fifth-minute lead. Olsen slipped a short free-kick to Colin Gibson, who crossed low into the goalmouth where Terry Gibson sneaked in before Aitken could react and slipped the ball past Latchford to open the scoring.

For the rest of the first half Celtic tried to make their mark on the game, coming close through Tommy Burns, but for all their endeavour Turner in the United goal was seldom troubled.

After the interval, during which the police had to go into the crowd to quell some trouble, the home side and their supporters were annoyed not to see a penalty given when Higgins appeared to handle an Archdeacon cross. Had it been awarded, the course of the game might well have changed, but United's defence stood firm and it came as no surprise when they increased their lead in the 61st minute. Terry Gibson beat White, before setting up Stapleton to head past substitute 'keeper Bonner.

United increased their lead 15 minutes from time when Strachan, who had been booed loudly throughout the night, was put through by Terry Gibson and clipped the ball past Bonner.

25 February 1986	**Celtic at Celtic Park, Glasgow.**

Attendance: 36,144.

Won: 3–0.

Scorers: Strachan, Stapleton, T. Gibson.

Team: Turner, Sivebaek, Albiston, Duxbury, McGrath, Higgins, Strachan, C. Gibson, Stapleton, T. Gibson, Olsen.

Substitutes: Barnes for Olsen, Walsh for Turner, Moran for McGrath, Hanrahan for Stapleton.

Early March saw United once again casting aside their hectic domestic schedule and agreeing to send a team to Grantham to play in a special fund-raising fixture for the Christopher Buckingham Appeal Fund, hoping to raise money for the five-year-old leukaemia sufferer.

The fixture had been arranged months previously, but on the afternoon of the game United reserve-team manager Brian Whitehouse received a telephone call from a man who claimed to be Barry Shaw, the Grantham manager. He said that the game would have to be called off due to one of the floodlight pylons having failed, which could not be fixed until a few days later. Whitehouse offered to play the game under the three remaining lights, but was told that Grantham had trained on the pitch the night before and two players had clashed heads. Whitehouse therefore took the players training instead.

As it turned out, the phone call proved to be a hoax and, as the United players were going through their paces on the training ground, a crowd of more than 2,000 were waiting, along with the young beneficiary who was to kick-off, for the team to arrive. Eventually the reason behind United's non-appearance was discovered and Grantham's reserves put together a team to give the crowd some football to watch. Ron Atkinson told viewers on *BBC Breakfast Time* the following morning what had happened and said that he would be sending a team to Grantham later in the season.

The game was eventually played on 1 May, and 2,600 saw a United side, with first-teamers Sivebaek, Moses Hogg, Moran and Barnes in the line up, win 3–0. Unfortunately, Christopher Buckingham was too ill to attend and actually died a week later.

Three days after crashing out of the FA Cup 2–0 against West Ham United at Old Trafford in a fifth-round replay, United were in Israel to face Maccabi Haifa.

The game was never going to be a spectacle, with the home side more involved than the rather subdued visitors. Gordon Strachan gave United the lead in the 58th minute, but Malmillian equalised for the home side two minutes later.

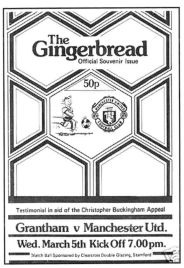

The programme for the match versus Grantham, 5 March 1986.

12 March 1986 Maccabi Haifa at the Municipal Stadium, Haifa, Israel.

Attendance: 15,000.

Drew: 1–1.

Scorer: Strachan.

Team: Bailey, Sivebaek, Albiston, Duxbury, McGrath, Higgins, C. Gibson, Strachan, Stapleton, T. Gibson, Barnes.

With fourth place in the League, FA Cup and League Cup defeats at the hands of West Ham and Liverpool, and with no good news in the Screen Sport Super Cup either, it was a season of disappointment for United which finally came to a close with a trio of fixtures in Singapore, Bangkok and Hong Kong.

The first of the three fixtures, which are further examples of United games where match reports are scarce, was against Singapore, and goals from Duxbury and Stapleton were enough to give United victory.

The programme for the match versus Singapore, 11 May 1986.

11 May 1986 Singapore National XI at the National Stadium, Bangkok.

Attendance: 11,000.

Won: 2–0.

Scorers: Duxbury, Stapleton.

Team: Turner, McGrath, C. Gibson, Duxbury, Moran, Hogg, Blackmore, Davenport, Hughes, Stapleton, Barnes.

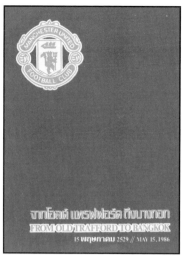

The programme for the match versus Rajpracha Club, 15 May 1986.

15 May 1986 **Rajpracha Club at the National Stadium, Bangkok.**

Attendance: 10,000.

Won: 2–0.

Scorers: Davenport, Barnes.

Team: Turner, McGrath, C. Gibson, Duxbury, Moran, Hogg, Blackmore, Davenport, Hughes, Stapleton, Barnes.

Substitutes: Dempsey for Blackmore, Digby for Turner, Hanrahan for Stapleton, Higgins for Hogg, Moses for Duxbury.

Ten minutes into the second half of the game against South China, Frank Stapleton passed to Mark Hughes, who in turn blasted the ball into the South China goal, for his last United goal before his transfer to Barcelona.

17 May 1986 **South China Athletic Association at the Hong Kong Stadium.**

Attendance: 4,575.

Drew: 2–2.

Scorers: Davenport, Hughes.

Team: Turner, McGrath, C. Gibson, Moses, Moran, Hogg, Blackmore, Davenport, Hughes, Stapleton, Barnes.

Substitute: Hanrahan for Barnes.

The plans to bring top Brazilian side Flamengo to Old Trafford to kick-start the 1986–87 pre-season warm-up, a fixture that was also being played in aid of the Prince Charles Trust, were thrown into disarray when the Brazilian FA ordered the proposed visitors to fulfil a domestic League fixture instead.

United officials did manage to find a replacement in the form of Fluminense, the current Brazilian champions. The fixture attracted over 32,000, but they were to be disappointed at the lack of goals, with the blank scoreline somewhat flattering to United.

Stapleton should have given United a first-half advantage, as the Fluminense goalkeeper, Victor, twice fumbled shots from the Irishman. Blackmore should also have done better, but after taking a pass from Davenport he shot wide. At the other end it was mainly due to Chris Turner that United's goal remained intact, with the 'keeper making several important saves, especially in the second half when he foiled Rene, Renato and Jandir.

In a much livelier second half two Fluminense counter-attacks should have brought goals; Souza chipped the ball into the box only for Washington to head over, while Romerito created an opportunity for Tato, who blasted over from 10 yards.

With no score at the end of the 90 minutes, it was down to penalties to decide the destination of the trophy. It was Turner, once again, who became a decisive factor in the outcome, saving two Fluminense penalties.

Peter Barnes, Colin Gibson, Gordon Strachan and Paul McGrath all converted their spot-kicks, while John Sivebaek saw his spot-kick turned round the post by Victor.

The programme for the match versus South China, 17 May 1986.

<table>
<tr><td colspan="2">6 August 1986</td><td align="right">Fluminense at Old Trafford.</td></tr>
</table>

6 August 1986   **Fluminense at Old Trafford.**

Attendance: 32,275.

Drew: 0–0 (**Won:** 4–3 on penalties.)

Scorers: Barnes, C. Gibson, Strachan, McGrath.

Team: Turner, Sivebaek, Albiston, Duxbury, McGrath, Hogg, Strachan, Blackmore, Stapleton, Davenport, Olsen.

Substitutes: Moran for Hogg, Hanrahan for Davenport, C. Gibson for Blackmore.

Once again United had accepted an invitation to play in a four-club tournament on the Continent, but these games were to be marred by violence between rival supporters.

United faced the Russian side Dynamo Kiev in their opening fixture and, once again, goalkeeper Chris Turner was the United hero, as the outcome of the game was decided on penalties.

With only 15 minutes gone Moran brought down Alexander Savaraov, one of seven Kiev players who had been members of the Russian squad in Mexico for the World Cup, but from the penalty spot Zavarov shot wide. It was, however, only a brief let-off for United, as three minutes later Belanov swept through the United defence before drawing Turner from his goal and slipping the ball past him.

Davenport, Stapleton, Olsen and Whiteside all went close for United, while Belanov had another opportunity to increase his side's advantage, but it was not until the second half that United managed to draw level.

Having replaced Sivebaek, Blackmore had only been on the pitch seven minutes when he latched on to the ball some 20 yards from goal and it flew past a helpless Russian 'keeper via an upright.

With no more scoring, it was again down to penalties and, with the Russians failing to score with two of their first three spot-kicks, United were able to make the most of their efforts from 12 yards out.

8 August 1986   **Dynamo Kiev at Olympic Stadium, Amsterdam.**

Attendance: 27,500.

Drew: 1–1. (**Won:** 4–1 on penalties.)

Scorers: Blackmore (C. Gibson, Davenport, Strachan, Blackmore).

Team: Turner, Sivebaek, Albiston, Whiteside, McGrath, Moran, Strachan, Duxbury, Stapleton, Davenport, Olsen.

Substitutes: C. Gibson for Olsen, Blackmore for Sivebaek, T. Gibson for Whiteside.

Coming face-to-face with the host club Ajax, United's pre-season goal drought continued, although they did have scoring opportunities which could easily have won them the tournament.

The only goal of the game came four minutes before the interval, Marco van Basten blasting a dipping shot past Turner from 30 yards. Both Stapleton and Strachan had come close for United and Hogg had headed off the line.

In the second half Sivebaek burst through the middle only to see his shot rattle the crossbar, with Stapleton blazing the rebound high over the bar. Frank Rijkaard had to head off the line from Blackmore, but United's play slowly deteriorated as the minutes ticked away.

10 August 1986   **Ajax at the Olympic Stadium, Amsterdam.**

Attendance: 23,000.

Lost: 1–0.

Team: Turner, Sivebaek, Albiston, Whiteside, Moran, Hogg, Strachan, McGrath, Stapleton, Davenport, C. Gibson.

Substitutes: Hanrahan for C. Gibson, T. Gibson for Whiteside, Blackmore for Moran.

Thankfully the next pre-season fixture, four days later, brought no further cause for concern off the field, as United visited Dublin to play Shamrock Rovers in a testimonial for former Old Trafford hero Shay Brennan. The popular Irishman, who had graced Old Trafford for 18 years and was a member of the 1968 European Cup-winning side, was a worthy benefactor of such a fixture.

Despite the opposition being nowhere near the same class as Ajax, Dynamo Kiev or Fluminense, United once again failed to end their goal famine, going down 2–0 to the Irish part-timers.

Bennett struck the ball against the United post in the 28th minute, with the pace-setting Irishmen deservedly going ahead four minutes later, when Bennett proved to be a little more accurate as he slid home a Doolin pass.

Eleven minutes after the interval United were further behind. McGrath conceded a free-kick outside the box, with Liam O'Brien blasting the ball at Turner and the United 'keeper allowing it to slip from his grasp and roll over the line. United tried to raise the tempo, bringing on Davenport and Hanrahan, but it proved to be too little too late.

14 August 1986   **Shamrock Rovers at Glenmalure Park, Dublin.**

Attendance: 10,200.

Lost: 2–0.

Team: Turner, Sivebaek, C. Gibson, Duxbury, McGrath, Moran, Strachan, Blackmore, Stapleton, T. Gibson, Olsen.

Substitutes: Davenport for Blackmore, Hogg for Moran, Hanrahan for Stapleton.

The programme for the match versus Shamrock Rovers, 14 August 1986.

Season 1986–87 proved to be one of testimonials, with United taking part in no fewer than five such fixtures

For Steve Coppell's testimonial match against Real Sociedad less than 13,000 saw United come through with a draw. Old Trafford Chairman Martin Edwards had decided to bring forward the kick-off time from 3pm to 2pm in an effort to reduce the chance of trouble erupting. Coppell would be lucky to collect £20,000 after expenses.

As they had in the previous fixtures, United failed to pose much of a scoring threat to their opponents, with their defence all over the place as Lopez Ufarte weaved his way through to give the Spanish side a 59th-minute lead.

With 20 minutes remaining, Blackmore headed home a Strachan cross to equalise, but the biggest cheer of the afternoon came 15 minutes from the end when Coppell made an appearance as a substitute for Olsen.

17 August 1986   Real Sociedad at Old Trafford.

Attendance: 12,826.

Drew: 1–1.

Scorer: Blackmore.

Team: Turner, Sivebaek, Albiston, Whiteside, McGrath, Moran, Strachan, Blackmore, Davenport, T. Gibson, Olsen.

Substitutes: Duxbury for Whiteside, Hanrahan for T. Gibson, Coppell for Olsen.

When Middlesbrough found themselves facing a financial crisis, they contacted United regarding the possibility of an early season visit to play in a fund-raising fixture. A visit to the North East was pencilled in for Wednesday 27 August. However, the game never materialised.

With the early-season form of the team far from satisfactory, Ron Atkinson was already walking the managerial tightrope and should perhaps have saved the energy of his players for their League fixtures. However, United headed to Edinburgh to face Heart of Midlothian on 2 September.

On a wet Edinburgh evening it looked as though United's poor start to the season, with three consecutive defeats, was going to continue when Hearts took a 2–0 lead.

Ian Jardine gave the home side the lead after six minutes, slipping the ball past Turner after Levein, taking a through ball from Sandison, had floated through the United defence before passing to Jardine on the right side of the United penalty area.

Turner kept out shots from Mackay and Robertson before the interval, but was helpless in preventing Hearts from going further in front in the 70th minute. Foster broke on the right, but his shot was blocked, rebounding to Watson, who fired the ball over the head of Turner.

Three minutes later, however, United were thrown something of a lifeline when Murray tripped Olsen inside the area, with the Dane getting up to stroke the ball low and wide of Smith from the spot-kick.

United mounted something of a fightback and were rewarded with an equaliser in the 75th minute when, following good work from Strachan, Terry Gibson prodded the ball home from close range.

2 September 1986   Heart of Midlothian at Tynecastle Park, Edinburgh.

Attendance: 10,438.

Drew: 2–2.

Scorers: Olsen (pen.), T. Gibson.

Team: Turner, Sivebaek, Albiston, Whiteside, McGrath, Hogg, Strachan, Duxbury, Stapleton, T. Gibson, Olsen.

Substitute: Davenport for Stapleton.

It was felt by many that one of the reasons United had stuttered along in the early weeks of the 1986–87 campaign was the absence of captain Bryan Robson due to a shoulder injury sustained during the summer's World Cup. Getting his captain back to match fitness was a major priority for Ron Atkinson and, having agreed to visit Linfield in order to help celebrate the Irish club's centenary, the match fell at an ideal time.

The programme for the match versus Linfield, 10 September 1986.

It certainly proved to be a worthwhile exercise, as not only did the United captain take another step on his comeback trail, he also scored twice in United's 3–0 victory. He gave United the lead in the 15th minute, gliding into the six-yard box to finish off a move which was started by Whiteside.

Davenport hit the bar as Robson followed through for the rebound, but his effort was tipped over by the alert Dunlop. Robson added a second 15 minutes from time, while Davenport himself scored the third six minutes from time.

10 September 1986	**Linfield at Windsor Park, Belfast.**

Attendance: 10,919.

Won: 3–0.

Scorers: Robson 2, Davenport.

Team: Turner, Gidman, Albiston, Whiteside, Garton, Hogg, Robson, Duxbury, Davenport, Wood, Barnes.

Substitutes: Moses for Duxbury, Hanrahan for Wood, Ratcliffe for Whiteside.

By the time the next friendly of season 1986–87 came around, the manager's seat at the club had changed hands.

Alex Ferguson arrived in Manchester with glowing credentials, but he had a major job on his hands. His first friendly as United's manager came just over a month after his arrival, when United flew to Bahrain to help celebrate their National Day with a game against a GCC Select XI.

United's performance over the 90 minutes certainly did not impress Santosh Shetty, a reporter for the *Gulf Daily News*, who wrote of the visitors' 1–0 victory: 'A disappointing performance from Manchester United. They came here with a reputation for playing bright attacking football, but they did nothing that lived up to that image last night.'

The game failed to grasp the attention of the locals, with fewer present than attended some local League fixtures, as United simply went through the motions. Even the referee's performance was questionable, as he refused to award three obvious penalties. The only goalmouth action of the first half came when Olsen set the ball up for Nicky Wood, but the youngster struck his shot straight at goalkeeper Sulman.

In the second half the action altered very little, but it did bring a goal, Norman Whiteside heading home five minutes after the restart. The Select side had the opportunity to draw level soon afterwards, when a shot from Saleh Hassawi was deflected off a United defender and eluded 'keeper Gary Walsh, but Moran was well positioned to clear off the line.

At full-time, captain Bryan Robson was presented with the National Day Cup by Crown Prince and Commander-in-Chief of the BDF, Shaikh Hamad bin Isa Al Khalifa.

Ticket for the match versus GCC All stars, 15 December 1986.

15 December 1986	**GCC All Stars at the Bahrain National Stadium.**

Attendance: 4,000.

Won: 1–0.

Scorer: Whiteside.

Team: Walsh, Sivebaek, C. Gibson, Moses, Moran, Whiteside, Robson, Strachan, Wood, T. Gibson, Olsen.

Substitutes: O'Brien for Olsen, Turner for Moses, Barnes for Wood.

Results were still somewhat erratic under the new regime, defeating Liverpool one day but losing to Norwich the next, but there was the odd glimmer of light. Friendlies were now seen as important fixtures, games where Ferguson could experiment with his squad.

January saw the manager decide to squeeze a friendly into his diary, and Red Star Belgrade flew over to Manchester. However, the game was given a miss by many of United's regular supporters. 'Fans Snub Euro Aces' proclaimed the *Manchester Evening News*, while the *Daily Mail* headline stated 'The Fans Boycott United'. Those who were present saw only one solitary goal and according to the *Evening News* correspondent David Meek those who did bother to turn up saw little in the way of entertainment, with the match little more than a 'damp squib'.

The game's solitary goal came from Milan Jankovic two minutes from the end, but, by then, many of the crowd were on their way home.

The programme for the match versus Red Star Belgrade, 21 January 1987.

21 January 1987	**Red Star Belgrade at Old Trafford.**

Attendance: 10,652.

Lost: 1–0.

Team: Turner, Sivebaek, C. Gibson, Whiteside, Garton, Moran, Duxbury, Strachan, T. Gibson, Wood, Olsen.

Substitutes: McGrath for Sivebaek, Hogg for Moran, Blackmore for C. Gibson, Stapleton for Wood.

One month later Alex Ferguson took his United side to Swansea City to play in a testimonial match for former United goalkeeper Jimmy Rimmer. As things turned out, Rimmer, who was understudy to Alex Stepney, pulled on the United shirt for one last time, as Ferguson did not want to risk Gary Bailey, who had a slight injury. The game earned the 39-year-old former United custodian around £10,000.

Terry Gibson opened the scoring after only four minutes, volleying home a Colin Gibson cross. Whiteside made it 2–0 in the 19th minute and 10 minutes later Davenport made the most of a lack of concentration by the Swansea defence.

Alan Kennedy pulled a goal back for Swansea, but United, although easing up during the second half, kept them at bay.

24 February 1987	**Swansea City at Vetch Field, Swansea.**

Attendance: 6,467.

Won: 3–1.

Scorers: T. Gibson, Whiteside, Davenport.

Team: Rimmer, Sivebaek, C. Gibson, Whiteside, McGrath, Moran, Moses, Duxbury, T. Gibson, Davenport, Wood.

Substitute: Bottomley for T. Gibson.

United made the trip across the Irish Sea to face Shramrock Rovers on 18 March. While prolonged snow showers made ball control difficult, the weather did not prevent the home side from taking the lead in the seventh minute, Brady's cross being deflected by Moran into the path of Larkin, whose header from 12 yards gave Bailey no chance.

The programme for the match versus Swansea City, 24 February 1987.

United managed to equalise in the 25th minute, when Garton headed a Strachan corner towards the near post, leaving Robson with the chance of scoring from practically underneath the crossbar.

Not many sides can boast of beating United twice in one season, but Byrne's volley, 19 minutes from the end, gave Shamrock Rovers that distinction, with the Irishman beating a stranded Turner.

18 March 1987   **Shamrock Rovers at Glenmalure Park, Dublin.**

Attendance: 8,000.

Lost: 2–1.

Scorer: Robson.

Team: Bailey, Garton, Duxbury, O'Brien, McGrath, Moran, Robson, Strachan, Stapleton, Hanrahan, C. Gibson.

Substitute: Sivebaek for Garton, Turner for Bailey, Davenport for Hanrahan.

Seven days later Alex Ferguson was back in his native Glasgow, taking his team to the East End of the city to take part in a testimonial for Celtic and Scotland captain Roy Aitken. This, however, was to be no friendly, as the sides slugged it out in a fast, vigorous and entertaining 90 minutes.

Many of the 36,000 crowd were still settling down for their evening's entertainment when Alan McInally put Celtic in front after only four minutes. Aitken won possession in midfield, moving forward quickly before releasing the ball to Brian McClair, who in turn threaded the perfect pass through to McInally to beat Walsh from just inside the area.

Bonner in the Celtic goal was in exceptional form, making numerous fine saves, but was fortunate that Robson did not make more of an ideal opportunity to equalise, when a cross from Wood was squared into the United captain's path by Stapleton, only to be harmlessly hit into the Celtic 'keeper's arms.

United were denied what many felt was a penalty when Robson was pulled down in the area by Whyte just before the interval. After the break they pushed forward on numerous occasions, but to no avail.

25 March 1987   **Celtic at Celtic Park, Glasgow.**

Attendance: 36,000.

Lost: 1–0.

Team: Walsh, Sivebaek, Albiston, Moses, McGrath, Duxbury, Robson, Strachan, Stapleton, Wood, C. Gibson.

Substitutes: O'Brien for Strachan, Turner for Walsh, T. Gibson for Wood.

On 7 April United supporters headed to the north-east of Scotland for a fixture against Aberdeen, which had been pending since Gordon Strachan's transfer. Little did they know, however, that while they were heading for the Granite City, the United players and staff were stranded at Manchester Airport as Aberdeen was under a blanket of fog.

Having lost out on the Aberdeen game, Ferguson arranged one of those late in the day games that few found out about until afterwards.

On Thursday 9 April, Norwegian club Rosenborg Trondheim visited Manchester and, in front of a sprinkling of spectators, conceded seven goals to a strong United side.

The programme for the match versus Aberdeen, 7 April 1987.

With only a couple of changes to the side that had defeated Oxford United 3–2 in their last game, United showed their visitors little mercy as Terry Gibson pressed for inclusion in the next starting line up with a three-minute hat-trick.

9 April 1987	Rosenborg Trondheim at The Cliff, Manchester.

Attendance: Very few.

Won: 7–0.

Scorers: T. Gibson 3, Robson 2, Sivebaek, Stapleton.

Team: Turner, Sivebaek, C. Gibson, Moses, McGrath, Duxbury, Robson, Wilson, Stapleton, T. Gibson, Davenport.

Substitute: Todd for Wilson.

Gary Bailey, the United and England goalkeeper, had a career blighted by injuries, forcing him to retire without actually reaching his peak. Before hanging up his gloves, he managed one final game between the Old Trafford goalposts, playing in his testimonial match against an England XI.

For many, testimonial fixtures have little appeal. There was, however, one added attraction for those considering attending Bailey's farewell and that was the reappearance in a red shirt of Mark Hughes. The Welshman was currently playing

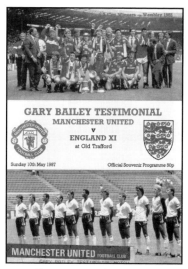

The programme for the match versus England, 10 May 1987.

Ticket for the match versus Naxxar Lions, 16 May 1987.

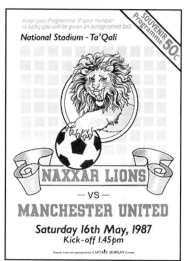

The programme for the match versus Naxxar Lions, 16 May 1987.

for Barcelona and his guest appearance showed the supporters what they were missing and the manager what he needed to invigorate his team.

Playing in a relaxed fashion, the hastily assembled England side found themselves unable to contain Hughes, who celebrated his return to Old Trafford with a first-half hat-trick. He scored goals in the fourth minute, breaking through the middle to beat Bailey, in the 17th, a header from Blackmore's cross, and in the 34th minute when he volleyed home in spectacular fashion from an Olsen centre.

A Bond own-goal in the 14th minute and two others from Lee Martin in the 39th minute and Terry Gibson five minutes before the break rounded off the scoring in a breathtaking first half.

After the interval, Marwood and Chapman pulled two goals back for the England side, but Hughes made it 7–2 in the 64th minute to complete the scoring, with Bailey now in the United goal.

10 May 1987	**England XI at Old Trafford.**

Attendance: 16,907.

Won: 7–2.

Scorers: Hughes 4 (1 pen.), Martin, T. Gibson, Bond (og).

Team: Walsh, Sivebaek, Albiston, Martin, McGrath, Moran, Blackmore, O'Brien, Hughes, T.Gibson, Olsen.

Substitutes: Stapleton for Martin, Bailey for Walsh, Todd for T. Gibson.

Alex Ferguson's first season in charge of Manchester United came to an end on the Mediterranean island of Malta, where they came up against the local Division Two champions Naxxar Lions. They could do little to prevent a landslide victory for United, who were playing on the island for the first time since their European Cup visit to play Hibernians in 1967–68. The playing surface on this occasion was certainly more suited to football, as United's first away fixture of that campaign had been played on a pitch of sand.

Rather surprisingly, despite the 9–0 scoreline, it was not until the 41st minute that the scoring began as Davenport converted a penalty. Whiteside and Blackmore made it 3–0 before the half-time whistle blew.

After the break the floodgates opened, with Whiteside scoring twice and O'Brien making it 6–0 within eight minutes of the restart. A further surge of goals within a six-minute period brought the scoring to an end; O'Brien netting his second for the seventh, Stapleton heading number eight and Duxbury netting the ninth.

16 May 1987	**Naxxar Lions at National Stadium, Ta'qali, Malta.**

Attendance: 4,000.

Won: 9–0.

Scorers: Whiteside 3, O'Brien 2, Blackmore, Davenport (pen.), Duxbury, Stapleton.

Team: Walsh, Duxbury, Albiston, O'Brien, McGrath, Moran, Robson, Blackmore, Whiteside, Davenport, C. Gibson.

Substitutes: Stapleton for Robson, T. Gibson for Blackmore, Garton for Whiteside.

Having put his players through pre-season training for the first time, Alex Ferguson then took them to Scandinavia, where new signings Viv Anderson and Brian McClair made their first appearances in the red shirt against Naestved. The former had been signed to add some experience and stability to the defence, while the former Celtic man was brought south to score goals.

Sadly, he failed to do so on this initial outing, although he did come close on a couple of occasions. At one point he ran from the halfway line, accompanied by two interloping United supporters. His final shot was saved, while the intruders were quietly escorted back into the crowd.

United opened the scoring against the part-timers in the 18th minute when Olsen floated a corner into the area, Whiteside headed the ball on and Moran smashed it home.

Goal number two came six minutes after the interval when Robson sent Anderson off down the wing. The leggy full-back's cross was headed down to the feet of the on-running captain by Whiteside, with the ball swiftly despatched into the net.

United tired as the second half progressed, but they maintained their momentum to win the game 2–0.

---

22 July 1987 **Naestved at Naestved Stadion, Denmark.**

Attendance: 6,500.

Won: 2–0.

Scorers: Moran, Robson.

Team: Turner, Anderson, Duxbury, Moses, McGrath, Moran, Robson, Strachan, McClair, Whiteside, Olsen.

Substitute: Albiston for Duxbury.

Moving on to Sweden for the second fixture, Brian McClair was once again overshadowed and was still searching for his first United goal when the final whistle blew. It was the Scot's front-line partner, Norman Whiteside, who stole the honours, with four goals in a rather undemanding friendly.

McClair was involved in the build-up to many of the United goals, the first of which came in the 11th minute when Whiteside headed home from Anderson, after Strachan had opened up the Swedish defence.

Strachan, rivalling Whiteside for Man of the Match, laid on the second goal for Davenport in the 25th minute, while minutes later McClair was unfortunate not to open his account when his centre hit the legs of a defender and crossed the line for an own-goal.

Whiteside made it 3–0 before half-time, but there were to be no further goals until the 61st minute when the same player made it 4–0. Ten minutes later the home side grabbed their only goal, as the floodgates opened with a further four United goals in a 10-minute spell.

Davenport notched up his second in the 74th minute. Whiteside made it 6–1 two minutes later, with Olsen netting the seventh in the 78th minute. Four minutes later Strachan got into the scoring act and two minutes later it was nine, Whiteside claiming his fourth.

---

24 July 1987 **I.S. Halmia at Orjans Vall, Halmstad.**

Attendance: 2,607.

Won: 9–1.

Scorers: Whiteside 4, Davenport 2, Strachan, Olsen, opp. own-goal.

Team: Turner, Anderson, Albiston, Moses, McGrath, Garton, O'Brien, Strachan, McClair, Whiteside, Davenport.

Substitutes: Olsen for Moses, Sivebaek for Anderson.

Brian McClair finally got his name on the score sheet when he slotted home a penalty in the 3–2 victory against B 1903.

Having coasted to a 9–1 victory in their previous fixture, the United players were taken aback when they found themselves two goals down to the Danish Cup holders in the opening seven minutes.

Garton brought down one of the home defenders to concede a penalty in the third minute, Jensen leaving Turner with no chance. Four minutes later United's defence were caught out, allowing Ramussen the opportunity to add a second with a powerful drive into the top corner of the net.

Slowly United clawed their way back into the game, with Robson leading by example as he finished off a Davenport–O'Brien move. Davenport himself was sent through by McClair to score the equaliser.

In the second half both teams had the chances to secure victory, but the game was decided by a rather dubious penalty award in the 56th minute, after Olsen had been brought down. McClair took on the mantle of penalty taker and drilled the ball home with a sigh of relief, having already missed an opportunity from six yards in the first minute.

26 July 1987 **B 1903 at Allinge, Denmark.**

Attendance: 2,500.

Won: 3–2.

Scorers: Robson, Davenport, McClair (pen.).

Team: Turner, Sivebaek, Albiston, Moses, Moran, Garton, Robson, O'Brien, McClair, Davenport, Olsen.

Substitute: McGrath for Moses.

In the final game of the Scandinavian tour United recorded a 4–1 victory against Vejle, John Sivebaek's previous club. New signing Viv Anderson stamped his name on the game with a solid defensive display, while also showing his attacking abilities in scoring one of the goals.

Davenport opened the scoring with a memorable overhead kick in the 36th minute, making it four in three games, with Jesper Olsen adding a second two minutes before half-time when he rocketed a Sivebaek cross into the roof of the net.

Anderson made it 3–0 in the 72nd minute following an Olsen corner, and substitute McClair made it 4–0 seven minutes from time. For the home side there was scant consolation as Christensen scored their only goal three minutes later.

28 July 1987 **Vejle Bk at Vejle Stadion.**

Attendance: 7,000.

Won: 4–1.

Scorers: Anderson, Davenport, Olsen, McClair.

Team: Turner, Anderson, Albiston, Sivebaek, McGrath, Moran, Robson, Strachan, Davenport, Whiteside, Olsen.

Substitute: Garton for Moran.

The pre-season of 1987–88 continued with the Manchester International Football Tournament, held at Maine Road, with City, Athletico Mineiro and PSV Eindhoven making up the quartet.

United found themselves up against neighbours Manchester City in the first semi-final. The game turned out to have plenty of action, as it was treated as a regular derby match and could well have ended amid unruly scenes.

United looked more polished than their neighbours, with Bryan Robson opening the scoring in the 12th minute after Nixon had made a mess of what should have been an easy save. Three minutes before the break McClair made it 2–0 with a far-post header from an Albiston cross.

Six minutes into the second half the match boiled over and had referee Neil Midgley not taken firm action then there was no telling what could have happened.

City striker Paul Stewart, being closely marked by Duxbury, elbowed the United defender in the face, which resulted in a gash under his eye requiring five stitches. After giving the City man a severe telling-off the official spoke to the City bench, telling manager Mel Machin, 'if you do not take him off, I will have to send him off'.

Brian McClair then proceeded to issue his own form of punishment, scoring United's third before Stewart was halfway down the tunnel.

Simpson scored for City in the 72nd minute, but it was too little too late as United eased their way into the Final.

Ticket for the match versus Manchester City, 4 August 1987.

4 August 1987	**Manchester City at Maine Road.**

Attendance: 20,250.

Won: 3–1.

Scorers: McClair 2, Robson.

Team: Walsh, Anderson, Albiston, Duxbury, McGrath, Moran, Robson, Strachan, McClair, Whiteside, Olsen.

Substitutes: C. Gibson for Olsen, O'Brien for Duxbury.

The following evening, in front of a rather sparsely populated Maine Road, United faced the Brazilian side Athletico Mineiro in the Final. They continued their excellent pre-season with a 3–1 victory to enjoy lifting a trophy at the home of their rivals.

This was no ordinary pre-season friendly, with the Brazilians, who had defeated PSV 3–1, wanting to win just as much as United did. The game turned out to be a hard, physical encounter, which saw three Mineiro players booked for violent tackles.

Having taken time to rediscover his scoring touch, Brian McClair was United's match-winner, notching up a hat-trick. His first goal, a minute before the interval, almost brought the game to a premature end.

Colin Gibson forced his way down the left flank for a corner, although the Mineiro players thought differently. From Strachan's corner, McClair steered the ball home amid a crowded goalmouth. Already upset at the referee for having awarded a corner instead of a goal-kick, the Mineiro players felt that there had been some pushing prior to the goal and followed the official back to the centre circle, looking as though they were about to leave the field.

Five minutes into the second half the former Celtic striker made it 2–0, but the Brazilians showed their ability by pulling a goal back in the 75th minute, setting up a frantic final quarter of an hour.

The programme for the Manchester International Football Tournament, 4 and 5 August 1987.

Manchester International Football Tournament at Maine Road, Manchester. Tuesday 4th and Wednesday 5th August 1987.

TOURNAMENT BROCHURE 60p

OFFICIAL CLUB SPONSORS. **brother** The future at your fingertips.

Ticket for the Manchester International Football Tournament, 5 August 1987.

With nine minutes remaining, McClair put the game beyond any doubt, completing his hat-trick after getting on the end of a McGrath header.

5 August 1987	Athletico Mineiro at Maine Road.

Attendance: 7,150.

Won: 3–1.

Scorer: McClair 3.

Team: Walsh, Anderson, C. Gibson, Duxbury, McGrath, Moran, Robson, Strachan, McClair, Whiteside, Olsen.

Substitutes: Sivebaek for Anderson, O'Brien for Whiteside, Davenport for Olsen.

United continued their pre-season programme against an Irish League select side in Belfast, in what was something of a make or break 90 minutes for midfielder Remi Moses. He was attempting to put 18 months of injuries behind him, having again suffered a problem with his ankle during the Scandinavian tour.

Against the Irish part-timers, for the first time in seven warm-up games United failed to score, which provided a reminder that there was still a lot of work to be done.

United could well have been half a dozen goals up in the opening 45 minutes, with former City 'keeper George Dunlop making outstanding saves from Moses, Davenport, Anderson, Olsen and McClair as his goal was besieged.

The Irish played it tight and at times rode their luck, but the United players were guilty of wasting numerous scoring opportunities.

10 August 1987	Irish League at Windsor Park, Belfast.

Attendance: 10,000.

Drew: 0–0.

Team: Walsh, Anderson, Albiston, Moses, Garton, Moran, Whiteside, Strachan, McClair, Davenport, Olsen.

Substitutes: C. Gibson for Albiston, Duxbury for Garton, O'Brien for Strachan.

The programme for the match versus Irish League, 10 August 1987.

It had been more than 37 years since United had faced Weymouth over 90 minutes, as they came up against the Dorset club in an FA Cup third-round tie at Old Trafford, which United won 4–0. The meeting had been to commemorate the official opening of the Wessex Stadium, which was carried out prior to kick-off by former England manager Ron Greenwood.

Revenge, they say, comes to those who wait and Weymouth had certainly waited a long time. On a cold night the visitors, although at full strength, but perhaps not playing to their full potential, found themselves on the end of a rather embarrassing defeat.

Without a name of note in their line up, Weymouth matched their illustrious visitors stride for stride and it was Manchester-born Peter Conning, a former Rochdale and Altrincham player, who scored the only goal of the game five minutes before the interval.

There was no second-half onslaught from the visitors and, cheered on by the near 5,000 crowd, the home side recorded a memorable and well-deserved victory.

---

21 October 1987   **Weymouth at Wessex Stadium.**

Attendance: 4,904.

Lost: 1–0.

Team: Turner, Anderson, Albiston, Moses, Garton, Moran, Blackmore, Davenport, McClair, O'Brien, C. Gibson.

Substitutes: Graham for Gibson, Martin for McClair.

With a blank weekend on the fixture list, Alex Ferguson took his squad for an eight-day break to Bermuda and a two-match schedule.

The first 90 minutes saw United face the Bermuda national side and, with their favourites taking a 17th-minute lead, the 4,200 plus crowd wondered if they were about to witness a historic victory.

With only two minutes gone, Musson nearly opened the scoring. Eluding Moran, he raced forward before hitting a powerful drive from some 15 yards out, which went narrowly over. United themselves pressed forward, with Robson close on a couple of occasions, shooting wide of the post and then forcing goalkeeper Darrell into making a fine save. The opening goal finally came after 17 minutes, Musson finishing off a neat move involving Swan and Russell to drive the ball under the body of Walsh.

It took United only three minutes to draw level. An Albiston cross to the far post was headed back across goal by Whiteside and Robson's goalward header was deflected over the line by a Bermudan defender.

The home side had scarcely got over the setback when United went 2–1 in front. McClair broke clear through, but was taken down by goalkeeper Darrell, with the Scot hitting the resulting spot-kick firmly past the 'keeper. Robson almost made it 3–1 eight minutes from the interval, but his shot smacked against the crossbar.

Any hopes of a fightback by the home side were finally dashed when Davenport made it 3–1 within two minutes of the second half getting underway. Whiteside finished off the scoring with a neat lob over the advancing 'keeper from a Blackmore through ball.

---

28 November 1987   **Bermuda at Somerset Cricket Ground.**

Attendance: 4,200.

Won: 4–1.

Scorers: Robson, McClair (pen.), Whiteside, Davenport.

Team: Walsh, Blackmore, Albiston, Whiteside, Moran, Duxbury, Robson, Strachan, McClair, Davenport, Olsen.

Substitute: Wilson for Moran.

The second of the two fixtures was against the Somerset Trojans, the island's League Champions, and the match was not without controversy.

Assistant manager Archie Knox lined up at right-back and turned back the years with a creditable display. McClair, Davenport and Robson all missed good chances before David Wilson gave United a 19th-minute lead and Olsen broke through to make it 2–0 just on half-time.

Twelve minutes into the second half the home side pulled a goal back, after Walsh had been penalised for pushing and Brown scored from the penalty spot. Any hopes of snatching a draw were dashed nine minutes later when Strachan chipped the ball across the penalty area for McClair to side-foot home.

The game was put further beyond the Trojans when, to the surprise of the players and crowd alike, Archie Knox scored a fourth with an incredible 35-yard drive four minutes from the end.

Despite only minutes remaining, the evening's drama was still not over. A through ball into the United penalty area saw Gary Walsh and Somerset striker Wellman race for possession and, as the United 'keeper dived on the ball, he was kicked on the head by the forward. Walsh and Wellman were both taken to hospital and Wilson took over in goal for the final two minutes. Following the incident, the match officials had to hold back the players of both teams, as things threatened to boil over.

A late substitution had also brought Alex Ferguson into the action. Having donned his boots and playing kit, the manager had decided that he wanted to be in the thick of the action. He wasted no time, after he had come on to replace Peter Davenport, in displaying the traits that had seen him stand out as a forward to be reckoned with two decades previously, leaving one or two of the home side wishing that he had indeed remained on the bench.

The tour reportedly made around $70,000, although the BFA did admit that several people had asked for their money back as it had been mentioned that George Best might turn out, but his agent later said that he was in Ireland trying to negotiate his testimonial match with the Irish Football Association.

1 December 1987	Somerset Trojans at Somerset Cricket Ground.

Attendance: 2,000.

Won: 4–1.

Scorers: Wilson, McClair, Knox, Olsen.

Team: Walsh, Knox, Albiston, Wilson, Moran, Duxbury, Robson, Strachan, McClair, Davenport, Olsen.

Substitutes: Ferguson for Davenport, Gardner for Moran.

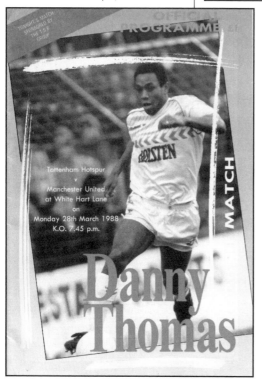

The programme for the match versus Tottenham Hotspur, 28 March 1988.

February 1988 marked the 30th anniversary of the Munich air disaster and there were plans afoot to create a Sports Medicine Centre in Dudley named after local hero Duncan Edwards. At the helm of the ambitious plans was former Wolves star Derek Dougan, who had planned to bring together former United and City players for a fixture at Altrincham's Moss Lane ground. Despite some media publicity, when people turned up on the night the floodlights were off and the doors locked.

That, however, was not the only piece of controversy surrounding the anniversary, with articles appearing in both *The Sun* and the *Daily Mirror* relating to the club snubbing a match organised between United and an England XI at West Bromwich Albion's ground in memory of Duncan Edwards. Tickets and programmes were printed, but on the night, with numerous clubs having offered to help out with players, things became farcical as no United or current England players were to be seen.

Derek Dougan said at the time: 'I'm bitterly disappointed. I was told a week ago by United to phone back a few days later and they would send me some players. Then on Saturday evening we were told we wouldn't even be getting a reserve player.'

Martin Edwards was quick to jump to the club's defence, saying: 'We warned all along of our difficulties regarding this game. It just wasn't feasible to send anybody. We play Spurs on Tuesday and we also have a lot of injuries.'

Supporters did get value for money the following month, when United travelled to White Hart Lane to face Tottenham Hotspur in a testimonial for Danny Thomas, whose playing career had been ravaged by injury.

On the night United turned on a superb display of football, winning 3–2 after going a goal behind in the 18th minute through Steve Hodge.

Gordon Strachan equalised for United six minutes later, before putting them in front with a second 10 minutes after the break. Davenport added a third, with former Tottenham favourite Steve Archibald scoring with practically the last kick of the ball.

---

28 March 1988   **Tottenham Hotspur at White Hart Lane.**

Attendance: 20,190.

Won: 3–2.

Scorers: Strachan 2, Davenport.

Team: Turner, Albiston, C. Gibson, Bruce, McGrath, Moses, Robson, Strachan, McClair, Davenport, Olsen.

Substitutes: Albiston for Gibson, Moran for McGrath, O'Brien for Robson, Blackmore for Moses.

April 1988 saw United head for Wembley for a two-day 'Festival of Football' to celebrate the centenary of the Football League. Billed as a once in a lifetime event, it is debatable whether it should be classed as a 'friendly' or not.

The games were to be played on a knockout basis, lasting 20 minutes each way, and kicking off at 10am. Each team, eight from the First Division, four from the Second and two each from the Third and Fourth, was able to select an 18-man squad, but could only use two substitutes. The participants qualified through gaining the most points in their League in their first 15 games played after 1 November last year. Goal difference and goals scored were used where necessary.

In their opening game, United came up against Luton Town, with the early exchanges fairly even. Black curled a fierce drive round the post as Turner scurried across his goal, while a United free-kick saw Robson square the ball to the on-running Gibson, but Luton 'keeper Dibble pulled off an excellent save. Whiteside also came close to scoring, but his header bounced off the top of the crossbar.

With the second half only a minute old, Brian McClair opened the scoring by slipping a pass from Strachan past the advancing Dibble for his 28th of the season, as the Luton defence looked for a non-existent offside decision.

An injury to Donaghy unsettled the Luton defence and 10 minutes later it was 2–0 to United, Peter Davenport running through the heart of the opposition defence before rounding the 'keeper. To their credit, Luton did try to get themselves back into the game, Wilson shooting directly at Turner and Hartford heading wide from good position, but it was United who progressed through to the quarter-finals.

16 April 1988   **Luton Town at Wembley.**

Attendance: 41,500

Won: 2–0.

Scorers: McClair, Davenport.

Team: Turner, Duxbury, Gibson, Bruce, McGrath, Whiteside, Robson, Strachan, McClair, Davenport, Olsen.

There was certainly not the mass exodus for the capital that you would normally get for an appearance beneath the twin towers, not only by the United support, but also by the followers of the other participating clubs, as only 41,500 were present on the opening day. How many were present when United played their quarter-final tie against Everton is unknown, but it was perhaps just as well, as a solitary Steve Bruce goal was all that separated the two teams.

16 April 1988   **Everton at Wembley.**

Attendance: Unknown.

Won: 1–0.

Scorer: Bruce.

Team: Turner, Duxbury, Gibson, Bruce, McGrath, Whiteside, Robson, Strachan, McClair, Davenport, Olsen.

Substitute: Blackmore for Duxbury.

One step from the Final the duration of the two games was stretched to 30 minutes each way, but it made little difference to United, as, despite being clear favourites to win, they failed to overcome Sheffield Wednesday. A controversial penalty robbed them of a place in the Final and the £60,000 prize money.

Peter Davenport, enjoying a new lease of life, gave United the lead from the penalty spot after Olsen had been brought down. Wednesday equalised with a Mel Sterland spot-kick after Robson was adjudged to have handled, a decision he reacted to furiously as he claimed he had used his chest, not his hand.

It was a decision which changed the game and Wednesday went on to win 2–1, thanks to an excellent Colin West drive from 25 yards, leaving a fuming United to depart for home earlier than expected.

17 April 1988   **Sheffield Wednesday at Wembley.**

Attendance: 17,000.

Lost: 2–1.

Scorer: Davenport (pen).

Team: Turner, Blackmore, Gibson, Bruce, McGrath, Whiteside, Robson, Strachan, McClair, Davenport, Olsen.

Substitutes: O'Brien for Olsen, Moses for Strachan.

With his United career on a downward slide, Paul McGrath showed his capabilities by turning in a polished display against Walsall in a match organised to celebrate the Midlands club's centenary year. The brawn of Bruce complemented the class of McGrath, as United were a cut above the Third Division side.

Norman Whiteside gave United the lead in the sixth minute and from then on they never looked back. Strachan, set clear by McClair, waltzed round the Walsall goalkeeper before slipping the ball into the net in the 53rd minute. An unstoppable 20-yard shot from Hawker raised the volume a little, but with 13 minutes still to go and the home side looking lively, the home goalkeeper fumbled the ball and McClair accepted the gift for United's third.

---

22 April 1988   **Walsall at Fellows Park.**

Attendance: 6,141.

Won: 3–1.

Scorers: Whiteside, Strachan, McClair.

Team: Turner, Anderson, Blackmore, Bruce, McGrath, Whiteside, Robson, Strachan, McClair, Davenport, Olsen.

Substitute: Martin for Anderson.

Having joined United as a Scottish Schoolboy international, Arthur Albiston made his debut against Portsmouth in October 1974, going on to make over 460 appearances for the club.

Due to injuries and a lack of first-team opportunities, he was given a free transfer as the 1987–88 season drew to a close, while also being awarded a testimonial against neighbours Manchester City.

Despite being augmented by a selection of notable guest players, Albiston's farewell ended in a 2–0 defeat, with both City goals coming in the first half-hour from Simpson and Morley. Albiston, on the other hand, could celebrate a notable career with United, a cheque for around £60,000 and the opportunity to extend his career elsewhere.

---

8 May 1988   **Manchester City at Old Trafford.**

Attendance: 14,898.

Lost: 2–0.

Team: Turner, Duxbury, Albiston, Bruce, Hogg, Moses, Robson, Strachan, McClair, Hughes, Wilkins.

Substitutes: Jordan for Strachan, Stapleton for Bruce, Macari for McClair, Pearson for Duxbury.

It is not often that a friendly fixture attracts enough attention for it to be televised live in 14 different countries, but the visit of Italian champions AC Milan to Old Trafford certainly did.

With hopes high for a reappearance in European competition the following season, Alex Ferguson was anxious to test his players against some of the Continent's best.

Ruud Gullit was soon in the thick of the action. A quick pass through to Evani saw the latter's shot go just wide, while a finely measured flighted pass to Borghi was wasted by a poor first touch. Just before the interval the man himself shot into the side netting.

The game always held a competitive edge, perhaps more so following a challenge by Bruce on Massaro after only 10 minutes, which saw the Italian having to leave the field.

Gullit failed to reappear for the second half and, with less than a minute gone, Bruce brought down Van Basten and substitute Virdis sent Turner the wrong way from the spot to give the Italians the lead.

Eight minutes later McClair should have equalised, running in with only the 'keeper to beat, but he shot wide. United paid the price for this and other misses when two goals from Borghi, in the 62nd and 67th minute, all but secured victory for AC Milan.

The programme for the match versus Manchester City, 8 May 1988.

To their credit, United kept plodding away and they managed to pull two goals back in the closing stages. Olsen broke through to score 10 minutes from time and McClair added a touch of respectability with a second almost right on time.

---

17 May 1988   **AC Milan at Old Trafford.**

Attendance: 37,392.

Lost: 3–2.

Scorers: McClair, Olsen.

Team: Turner, Anderson, Gibson, Bruce, McGrath, Duxbury, Robson, Strachan, McClair, Davenport, Olsen.

Substitutes: Blackmore for Anderson, Martin for Duxbury.

Pre-season 1988 had United planning to tour Greece, but following trouble during the European Championships, the Football League refused the club permission to play there in an international competition.

Plans to hold the second Manchester Football Tournament also hit the buffers, with United due to host the year's competition. However, having recently laid a new playing surface at Old Trafford, they decided that the pitch would not be ready for four games over a two-day period, with two other pre-season fixtures already pencilled in for the ground.

So it was off once again to the pre-season haunt of Scandinavia, with the first stop on the four-game itinerary at Laxa, where Alex Ferguson watched his charges ease their way back with a 4–0 victory against the Swedish Third Division team.

Robson and McClair both went close early on, but it was Mark Hughes who celebrated his return to the fold by putting United 1–0 in front after 11 minutes. Having shown that he had lost none of his old aggression, he took the ball from the feet of Johansson moments later, before pushing the ball past the 'keeper from a narrow angle.

United were struck with an injury blow 10 minutes before the interval, when Gibson went down after a challenge and had to be carried off on a stretcher. This did little to alter the flow of the game and, with only four minutes remaining before the interval, United increased their lead.

Rinne in the Laxa goal had been alert earlier on, preventing Robson and Hughes from adding to the scoreline, but he was helpless when McClair ran through to score from O'Brien's right wing cross.

After the interval United continued on the attack, with even Bruce joining in as the Laxa goal remained under siege. McClair sent Olsen through in the 65th minute to score a third, while Hughes and Olsen again came close before McClair put Karlsson under enough pressure to put through a goal to make it 4–0.

---

6 August 1988   **Laxa IF at Ramundervallen, Sweden.**

Attendance: 1,521.

Won: 4–0.

Scorers: McClair, Hughes, Olsen, opp. own-goal.

Team: Leighton, Blackmore, Gibson, Bruce, Garton, O'Brien, Robson, Strachan, McClair, Hughes, Olsen.

Substitutes: Davenport for Robson, Martin for Gibson, Rodlund for O'Brien.

If you cast your eyes over the statistical information for 1988–89 there are some unfamiliar names, as Alex Ferguson began introducing younger players into the first-team arena.

The first of those 'unknowns', Jonny Rodlund, appeared against Laxa, coming on as substitute for Liam O'Brien. Rodlund was a talented 16-year-old who had been with Anderlecht for six months, and had also attracted the attention of Roma and Gothenburg. He had spent the previous fortnight on trial with United and signed as an apprentice following the Laxa match.

Moving to Norway for their next game, against Valerengens, there was no sign of the Swedish youngster, but in the United line up came another new face, 21-year-old Paul Dalton. Hailing from Middlesbrough, Dalton had given up the game for 18 months after failing to get into his school side, but after pulling on his boots again at Sunday League level, he was signed by Brandon United and after a mere 25 appearances for the club he joined United.

There could well have been a further surprise in the United line up during the tour if goalkeeper Jim Leighton had picked up an injury. Reserve 'keeper Chris Turner had to return home due to the death of his mother-in-law and if a stand-in between the sticks had been required, the gloves would have been handed to Peter Davenport.

In Oslo United disappointed their local support, as because of injuries and experiments by the manager, the team was without any real pattern against the First Division side.

McClair and Hughes worked hard upfront but to no avail, and in an effort to inject some goals into the game, the manager brought on Strachan and Olsen for the last half-hour. Although things livened up slightly, the nearest United came to scoring was a scrambled effort from McClair and a header from Robson, which the 'keeper did well to save.

None of the youngsters let the team down, with Martin and Beardsmore, who had been flown out to strengthen the squad, both looking promising.

---

10 August 1988   **Valerengens IF at Bislet Stadium, Olso, Norway.**

Attendance: 6,296.

Drew: 0–0.

Team: Leighton, Blackmore, Martin, Bruce, Garton, O'Brien, Robson, Dalton, McClair, Hughes, Davenport.

Substitutes: Strachan for Dalton, Olsen for O'Brien, Beardsmore for Bruce.

Further depletion of the squad forced Ferguson to once again juggle with his team prior to the game against Karlstad, but with a patched-up XI, there was certainly no lack of goals as the Swedes were hit for six.

Two weeks after turning down a move to Lens, Gordon Strachan took over the United captaincy in place of the injured Robson and played an inspirational part in getting the tour back on track. Davenport opened the scoring in the seventh minute, putting away an Olsen cross, before Strachan set off on a dribble which took him past defenders and the goalkeeper for a second five minutes later.

Moving smoothly, United increased their lead through Hughes in the 28th minute, McClair in the 34th and O'Brien in the 44th. The pace of the second 45 minutes was, however, much slower than in the first, with only one further goal being scored, through substitute Dalton, who rounded off the scoring 12 minutes from time.

11 August 1988	**Karlstad BK at Tingvalla, Sweden.**

Attendance: 3,416.

Won: 6–0.

Scorers: Davenport, Strachan, Hughes, McClair, O'Brien, Dalton.

Team: Leighton, Beardsmore, Blackmore, McClair, Garton, Martin, O'Brien, Strachan, Davenport, Hughes, Olsen.

Substitutes: Dalton for O'Brien, Rodlund for Blackmore.

One of Alex Ferguson's earliest awards came in Gothenburg, when he was made a member of the Order of the Goets, becoming Sweden's first honorary Viking, in a ceremony prior to the final game of the Scandinavian tour.

That final 45 minutes of the tour brought the goals for total to 14 in two games, with Trollhattans unable to come to grips with their more experienced opponents.

Peter Davenport scored the first of a hat-trick after only six minutes, with United storming into a 4–0 half-time lead through further goals from Strachan (21st), O'Brien (33rd) and Olsen (40th). The home side came out strongly after the interval, hitting back with a goal from Jorfors three minutes after the restart, but United slipped up a gear and added a further four goals through Davenport (52nd and 85th), Hughes (61st) and McClair (75th).

14 August 1988	**Trollhattans IF at Edsborg, Sweden.**

Attendance: 3,018.

Won: 8–1.

Scorers: Davenport 3, O'Brien, Strachan, McClair, Hughes, Olsen.

Team: Leighton, Blackmore, Martin, Bruce, Rodlund, O'Brien, Davenport, Strachan, McClair, Hughes, Olsen.

Substitute: Beardsmore for Rodlund.

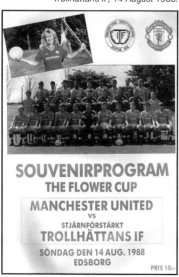

The programme for the match versus Trollhattans IF, 14 August 1988.

Back on home ground, Hamburg, regular opponents from the late 1950s and early 1960s, visited Old Trafford, where a rather sparse crowd endured a goalless draw, mainly due to the fine performances of the two goalkeepers. United were forced to rely heavily on £750,000-signing Jim Leighton, with the former Aberdeen 'keeper making a string of excellent saves. The first came as early as the fourth minute when he denied Jussufi. Ten minutes later he dived to push a shot from Labbadia round the post. Another outstanding block prevented Kaltz from scoring. At the opposite end Golz also enjoyed a brilliant game, doing particularly well to foil Strachan and Hughes.

As well as Leighton, 19-year-old Russell Beardsmore was also making his debut and he also turned in a fine performance, earning a standing ovation when he went off near the end.

A diving header from McClair was the nearest either side came to a goal, but a raised linesman's flag saw the effort from the forward-cum-midfielder disallowed for offside.

Looking over the team line up for this match, the name Buttigeig stands out. Maltese defender John Buttigeig had arrived at Old Trafford following a two-week trial at Brentford. The 24-year-old Sliema Wanderers player was making something of an impression. However, the Maltese Footballer of the Year failed to make the most of his trial with United and was not given a contract.

16 August 1988	Hamburg SV at Old Trafford.

Attendance: 14,348.

Drew: 0—0.

Team: Leighton, Beardsmore, Blackmore, Bruce, Martin, McClair, Robson, Strachan, Davenport, Hughes, Olsen.

Substitutes: Buttigeig for Beardsmore, Dalton for Strachan.

With less than 15,000 spectators present for the visit of Hamburg, Kevin Moran must have wondered how many supporters were going to click through the turnstiles for his testimonial match against Manchester City. Speculation was rife that a cameo appearance by a certain George Best was going to happen. However, true to form, the Irishman's first appearance at Old Trafford since Pat Crerand's testimonial in 1975 failed to materialise, with a phone call shortly before kick-off telling Moran that his guest would not be turning up.

A pre-match newspaper article revealed that Alex Ferguson was only giving Best 20 minutes on the Old Trafford pitch, as he wanted to give his strongest side a run out. This could well have had something to do with the former player's non-appearance.

Although disappointed, the crowd were treated to a thrilling seven-goal encounter. City, then a Second Division side, gave United a testing workout and opened the scoring through Morley after 18 minutes, heading home Gleghorn's cross from six yards. However, it was a lead that they held for only five minutes, as Brian McClair equalised from the penalty spot after Gleghorn had been rather harshly adjudged to have handled the ball.

A Bruce cross, deflected on by McNab, was driven home by Olsen to give United an interval lead, but Morley levelled for the visitors in the 67th minute, only for United to step up the pressure.

Hughes scored a characteristic goal in the 75th minute, finishing off good work by Strachan, with the same player setting up Olsen only for the winger's shot to be blocked by Dibble in the City goal, leaving McClair to net the rebound for United's fourth. Martin capped a fine performance with the fifth, running on to a Garton long ball before chipping it over Dibble.

Moran, who had joined United in January 1978, left the field to a rousing reception 12 minutes into the second half and stood to make around £60,000 from his testimonial.

The programme for the match versus Manchester City, 21 August 1988.

21 August 1988	Manchester City at Old Trafford.

Attendance: 25,432.

Won: 5—2.

Scorers: McClair 2 (1 pen.), Olsen, Hughes, Martin.

Team: Leighton, Blackmore, Martin, Bruce, Moran, McClair, Robson, Strachan, Davenport, Hughes, Olsen.

Substitutes: Garton for Moran, Sharpe for Davenport.

Three days after the 5—2 victory over City in Kevin Moran's testimonial match, what was classed as a 'reserve'-team friendly took place in the North East against Hartlepool United. Despite its classification, the names of Turner, Anderson, Duxbury, McGrath and Whiteside all appeared on the team sheet, but with the new season only a few days away, the outcome of this particular fixture led to the manager not only reading the Riot Act, but cancelling the players' day off, furious at them for allowing themselves to be overrun by such lowly opposition.

The United XI were not simply beaten, but trounced 6–0 by the Fourth Division side. Centre-forward Kevin Dixon ran riot, scoring a hat-trick, and giving Alex Ferguson much to think about for the weeks ahead.

Another competition that ranks among those that are difficult to categorise as a friendly or not was the Mercantile Credit Centenary Trophy. Featuring the top eight teams from the previous season's First Division, United were paired with Everton in their opening fixture on 29 August at Old Trafford. The home support were not taken with the competition, however, as a mere 16,439 decided to spend their Bank Holiday Monday in the vicinity of Trafford Park.

Those who stayed away were proved correct in their decision as it was a dull and uninspiring 90 minutes. Anderson livened things up with a reckless challenge on Wilson, for which he was booked, while an off the ball skirmish between Hughes and Snodin saw them follow suit.

A rare Gordon Strachan header in the 66th minute was enough to win the game and give United a boost in confidence as well as an Old Trafford semi-final tie against Newcastle United.

---

29 August 1988   **Everton at Old Trafford.**

Attendance: 16,439.

Won: 1–0.

Scorer: Strachan.

Team: Leighton, Anderson, Blackmore, Bruce, Garton, Duxbury, Robson, Strachan, McClair, Hughes, Olsen.

Substitutes: Martin for Anderson, Davenport for Olsen.

For the fixture against Newcastle the supporters once again stayed away, only 14,968 turning up this time around, but at least they got value for money, with the game running into extra-time.

'An uninspired, laboured performance,' was how *Manchester Evening News* correspondent David Meek viewed the game, as United struggled to see off 'an ordinary Newcastle team'.

Steve Bruce finally broke the deadlock in the first minute of extra-time after McClair had headed Olsen's cross against the post. Nine minutes later McClair was on target with another header to give United a 2–0 lead. Two other goals were disallowed; Hughes for offside and Robson for an alleged handball.

The game also marked the debut of a 17-year-old Lee Sharpe, who, after a shaky start, turned in a creditable performance at full-back.

---

21 September 1988   **Newcastle United at Old Trafford.**

Attendance: 14,968.

Won: 2–0.

Scorers: Bruce, McClair.

Team: Leighton, Blackmore, Sharpe, Bruce, Garton, Duxbury, Robson, Davenport, McClair, Hughes, Olsen.

Substitutes: O'Brien for Davenport, Beardsmore for Olsen.

It was October before the next friendly, with United travelling north to Edinburgh to face Hibs in a testimonial for defender Gordon Rae. Despite the experience on show, it was 19-year-old reserve-team player David Wilson who stole the headlines in his senior debut. Taking over Robson's midfield role he turned in a good all-round performance, rounding it off with a memorable goal.

The game was somewhat reduced as a spectacle after only six minutes when Hibs were reduced to 10 men. A sending off in a friendly is something of a rare event, but referee George Smith was left with little option after Joe Tortolano sent Gordon Strachan crashing on to the running track with a recklessly late tackle down near the corner flag.

From then on, Hibs struggled to get into the game and could well have found themselves two behind had Hughes been slightly more accurate, but they did well to keep the visitors at bay until five minutes before the interval. Anderson and Strachan combined well to allow David Wilson to stride past the Hibs defence before firing a 12-yard shot past Goram, with the 'keeper just a bit too slow in getting down for the ball.

Hughes again wasted a good opportunity as the second half got underway, while Hibs only looked threatening at set pieces, although their defence managed to keep the score down to that solitary goal until the final 20 minutes.

Alex Ferguson brought Beardsmore and Robins into the action and, soon after the substitutions, Mark Hughes made up for his earlier misses. After Goram had failed to punch the ball completely clear and it had been returned to the area by Anderson, Hughes grasped the opportunity to score from close range.

Within eight minutes of coming on, Robins, another player making his senior debut, scored United's third goal of the night, heading an Anderson cross past Goram.

---

3 October 1988   **Hibs at Easter Road, Edinburgh.**

Attendance: 14,236.

Won: 3–0.

Scorers: Wilson, Hughes, Robins.

Team: Leighton, Anderson, Sharpe, Bruce, Wilson, Olsen, Robson, Strachan, McClair, Hughes, Davenport.

Substitutes: Beardsmore for Sharpe, Dalton for Strachan, Robins for Wilson.

The Final of the Mercantile Credit Centenary Trophy was scheduled to be played at Villa Park, so United travelled to the Midlands to face Arsenal.

The Londoners dominated the first half as torrential rain fell, restricting United to one solitary McClair effort, which Lukic saved with his feet.

Two goals in the space of four minutes stunned United and they never really recovered. In the 36th minute Davis dispossessed Duxbury and exchanged a one-two with Marwood before volleying past Leighton. Four minutes later it was 2–0. Davis split the United defence with a pass to Thomas and as Leighton moved off his line, the Arsenal forward coolly chipped the 'keeper.

The game was played at a brisk pace and continued to flow from end to end, but by the time Blackmore pulled a goal back for United in the 85th minute it was too late to make a miraculous comeback.

The programme for the match versus Arsenal, 9 October 1988.

9 October 1988	Arsenal at Villa Park.

Attendance: 22,182.

Lost: 2–1.

Scorer: Blackmore.

Team: Leighton, Blackmore, Sharpe, Bruce, Garton, Duxbury, Robson, Davenport, McClair, Hughes, Olsen.

Substitutes: Strachan for Olsen, Beardsmore for Davenport.

United's drawing potential was called upon again at the end of November, when Birmingham City managed to secure them to play in a benefit match for Ian Handysides, who had been forced out of the game due to a pre-season accidental kick to the head, which saw him remain seriously ill in hospital.

Listening to the pre-match team announcements, there were more than a few puzzled looks, not just from the Birmingham City support, when the name Maiorana was read out.

The 19-year-old from Cambridge, who had been playing part-time with Histon, had been sought after by the likes of Chelsea, Tottenham and Watford, but Alex Ferguson had put him through his paces in a secret practice match 24 hours previously, before throwing him into the fray of a full-scale fixture. His 45 minutes at St Andrews were enough for the manager to offer the boutique assistant a permanent contract.

Despite the torrential rain, the game attracted a good 2,000 more than Birmingham's average gate and those who braved the weather were rewarded with seven goals. In a friendly atmosphere United treated the crowd to some excellent football.

Brian McClair claimed the first goal of the evening from the penalty spot in the 10th minute after Maiorana had been tripped by Langley. Mark Hughes quickly added a second, with Bryan Robson increasing United's lead before the interval.

Easing off as the second half got underway, United allowed the home side to get back into the game with goals from Sturridge and a Steve Bruce own-goal. However, United simply upped the tempo again and there was to be no fightback as the visitors increased their lead with goals from Clayton Blackmore and Mark Robins, the latter coming off the bench to score his 35th of the season.

IAN HANDYSIDES
Benefit

Birmingham City
v
Manchester United

Played at St Andrews - Tuesday November 29th 1988 - Kick Off 7.30 p.m.
Programme 50p

The programme for the match versus Birmingham, 29 November 1988.

29 November 1988	Birmingham City at St Andrews.

Attendance: 8,993.

Won: 5–2.

Scorers: Hughes, McClair (pen.), Robson, Blackmore, Robins.

Team: Leighton, Garton, Martin, Bruce, Blackmore, Donaghy, Robson, Milne, McClair, Hughes, Maiorana.

Substitutes: Robins for Hughes, Wilson for Maiorana, Sharpe for Martin, Gill for Robson.

Less than a month after that friendly against Birmingham City, on the evening of Wednesday 21 December, a Boeing 747 crashed on to the town of Lockerbie. In the wake of the disaster a fund was set up to help those affected and when the then chairman of Queen of the South, Willie Harkness, approached Alex Ferguson about sending a team up to Dumfries, the United manager had no hesitation in complying.

If a similar fixture between the two teams were to take place today, there is no way that Palmerston Park could handle it, but in 1989 United did not have the same charisma and just under 4,000 fans contributed to the Lockerbie Disaster Fund.

The Queens team was in fact a Select XI, boosted by the likes of Roy Aitken and Mark McGhee from Celtic, while United fielded a smattering of first-team and reserve players, with every one of the 32 players giving their all on the night.

There was an eerie silence around the ground as players and spectators respected a minute's silence, broken only by a lone piper's lament, before the teams were introduced to Sir Matt Busby, but the noise of the crowd soon took over as the match got underway, with the first of the evening's nine goals coming in the 13th minute.

A long ball forward by McGrath deceived Hetherington and McClair quickly read the situation and ran through to beat Holland for the opener. Queens had a chance to draw level three minutes later when Aitken was brought down in the area by Bruce. The Celtic man took the kick himself, but blasted the ball over.

The equaliser came in the 18th minute. McGuire crossed from the left, but Sloan's shot was blocked by Leighton, only for the Queens man to react quickest and send the ball across goal for Cook to prod home.

Blackmore rattled the post in the 29th minute before Donaghy regained United's lead four minutes later with a shot from the edge of the penalty area. Four minutes from the break McClair made it 3–1 from a Gill cross.

The players were given an enthusiastic reception as they left the pitch and the crowd were in full voice again within four minutes of the restart when Aitken made amends for his earlier miss by narrowing the gap. This was only temporary, as the ever-dependable Mark Robins notched up two in six minutes, with Gill adding a sixth eight minutes from time from the penalty spot.

Wishart, another guest player, scored a third for Queens in the 85th minute, to send the crowd home more than satisfied.

---

1 March 1989   **Queen of the South at Palmerston Park, Dumfries.**

Attendance: 3,776.

Won: 6–3.

Scorers: McClair 2, Robins 2, Donaghy, Gill (pen.).

Team: Leighton, Martin, Donaghy, Bruce, McGrath, Blackmore, Beardsmore, Strachan, McClair, Milne, Gill.

Substitutes: Robins for McClair, Goater for Milne, Maiorana for Strachan, Dalton for Blackmore, Brazil for McGrath, Heseltine for Donaghy.

As part of the deal that took winger Giuliano Maiorana to United, Alex Ferguson had agreed to a friendly against his former club Histon at the Abbey Stadium, Cambridge. Although having to pay their neighbours £2,000 for the use of their ground, Histon still stood to make around £4,000 from the game.

On a warm evening United strolled through the game, with Alex Ferguson not even bothering to stay for the whole 90 minutes, heading back to Manchester after a first half which saw United score three times.

Maiorana used the opening 45 minutes to show his undoubted ability, certainly not wishing to be outshone by his brother Salvatore in the Histon side.

Histon scored the only goal of the second half through Warner, who blasted a fine shot past a helpless Leighton.

---

19 May 1989   **Histon at Abbey Stadium, Cambridge.**

Attendance: 3,981.

Won: 3–1.

Scorers: Toal, Blackmore, Hughes.

Team: Leighton, Martin, Sharpe, Bruce, Duxbury, Donaghy, Blackmore, Beardsmore, Toal, Hughes, Maiorana.

Substitutes: Tonge for Martin, McAuley for Toal, Sixsmith for Sharpe, Lydiate for Bruce, D. Ferguson for Blackmore, Bullimore for Maiorana, Andrews for Duxbury.

Preparations got underway for season 1989–90 in the unlikely destination of Bangkok, where the Thailand National XI provided the opposition, with a penalty shoot-out required to separate the two sides at the end of the 90 minutes.

Despite having new midfield signings Neil Webb and Mike Phelan on show, United looked a bit rusty, especially in the opening 45 minutes. The Thai side, on the other hand, proved to be tricky and were certainly more suited to the heat and humidity.

The first half saw a Blackmore shot rattle against the crossbar, with Robson hitting the rebound against the 'keeper and Hughes volleying a Phelan cross over the top. Robson again came close with a Webb chip. At the opposite end, Leighton made a couple of excellent saves as the host side pushed forward.

Seven minutes into the second half the National side went in front. Phas shot against the post and, with Leighton helpless, Vitoon blasted home the rebound. It was a lead that lasted only two minutes. United attacked down the left, Sharpe crossed towards the Thailand goal, and McClair set up Robson to equalise. The United captain, however, paid the price for scoring when he collided with goalkeeper Virat, taking the full impact of a lunging boot, and as a result was forced to leave the field with a badly bruised thigh.

With no further scoring, it was down to penalties to decide the winner and Jim Leighton proved to be United's match-winner, saving two spot-kicks, while teammates McClair, Webb, Bruce and Martin made no mistake with their penalties.

30 July 1989	**Thailand National XI at Bangkok.**

Attendance: 12,000.

Drew: 1–1 (**Won:** 4–2 on penalties).

Scorers: Robson (McClair, Webb, Bruce, Martin).

Team: Leighton, Duxbury, Sharpe, Bruce, Blackmore, Donaghy, Robson, Webb, McClair, Hughes, Phelan.

Substitutes: Beardsmore for Blackmore, Martin for Robson.

The second fixture of the pre-season had a certain edge to it. Not just because it brought United up against First Division rivals Everton, but because there was a new addition to the Goodison Park club's playing squad in the shape of former United hero Norman Whiteside.

United began promisingly, with full-backs Martin and Sharpe supporting the forwards. However, two Everton goals in three minutes completely changed the course of the game.

A Cottee cross was diverted past Leighton by Sheedy for the first in the 17th minute, then two minutes later Whiteside beat Duxbury to the ball and opened up the United defence for Pointon to crash the ball into the roof of the net for the second. Whiteside exchanged passes with Cottee before brushing aside two defenders in the 33rd minute for Everton's third.

Ferguson tried to rearrange his side after the interval, bringing on Beardsmore for Duxbury and pushing Sharpe forward, and it did seem to have some effect, but it was Everton who always looked the more likely to score, with Leighton pulling off two notable stops from Newell.

United were finally rewarded for their efforts when Robson sent McClair away, with the Scot crossing for Webb to beat Southall from close range in the 74th minute.

2 August 1989	**Everton at Kobe.**

Attendance: 8,000.

Lost: 3–1.

Scorer: Webb.

Team: Leighton, Martin, Duxbury, Bruce, Phelan, Donaghy, Robson, Webb, McClair, Hughes, Sharpe.

Substitutes: Beardsmore for Duxbury, Blackmore for Martin, Milne for Sharpe.

Moving to Japan for the third and final game of the tour, against the Japanese National XI on a plastic pitch, it was the boy with the 'goalden' touch, Mark Robins, who once again found the back of the net, his solitary strike giving United victory.

Robins got his chance in the starting line up following a pre-match training accident to Brian McClair and turned in a creditable performance, his goal coming seven minutes before the interval.

Milne could have given United the lead in the 16th minute, but he just failed to get on the end of Blackmore's cross, as Robins had a strong shot well saved and Hughes hit the side netting as United pushed forward.

The Japanese proved to be a fast and skilful side, but they were no real match for United. They too had an opportunity to open the scoring following a quick 19th-minute breakaway, but Maeda shot wide.

The second half was mainly United, who by now had come to terms with the pitch. Phelan came close with a chip which the 'keeper did well to push over the bar. Hughes also came close after a fine run by Milne. However, much to the disappointment of the large crowd, there was to be no further scoring.

7 August 1989	**Japan National XI at Jingu Baseball Stadium, Tokyo.**

Attendance: 40,000.

Won: 1—0.

Scorer: Robins.

Team: Leighton, Blackmore, Duxbury, Bruce, Phelan, Donaghy, Robson, Webb, Robins, Hughes, Milne.

Substitutes: Beardsmore for Robins.

The victory over former Red Joe Jordan's Bristol City was not as clear-cut as many expected and, with the new season on the horizon, there were still a few doubts hanging over both the team and the manager.

With neither of United's main strike force of Hughes and McClair finding the net on the tour, it was something of a relief when the latter gave United a fifth-minute lead. Neil Webb once again shone in midfield and added a second in the 16th minute with help from Hughes.

Pender pulled a goal back for the home side 10 minutes after the interval, but Beardsmore restored United's two-goal advantage 14 minutes from time. Rennie did score a second for Bristol City in the 87th minute, but by then the outcome of the game was ensured.

11 August 1989	**Bristol City at Ashton Gate.**

Attendance: 9,799.

Won: 3—2.

Scorers: McClair, Webb, Beardsmore.

Team: Leighton, Duxbury, Gibson, Bruce, Phelan, Donaghy, Blackmore, Webb, McClair, Hughes, Milne.

Substitutes: Carey for Duxbury, Graham for McClair, Beardsmore for Gibson.

The final fixture of the pre-season build-up was an Old Trafford testimonial match for long-serving Mike Duxbury, with local rivals Manchester City providing the opposition. Once again, however, it was obvious that Old Trafford friendlies failed to stoke the imagination and even a player with 13 years service could only attract a crowd of 20,000.

It was the City fans that went home happy, having seen their team score twice without reply, giving Alex Ferguson even more to think about for the season ahead.

Newly promoted City controlled the opening 45 minutes with ease, playing some excellent football and scoring twice in the opening 17 minutes. A cross from Allen was headed home by Gleghorn at the far post in the eighth minute and Allen was again the provider in the 17th minute, when he sent a long ball from within his own half straight through the United defence to Oldfield, who raced in to score.

The midfield of Robson, Webb and Phelan toiled away to no avail, leaving everyone present wondering what the season ahead was going to bring.

---

13 August 1989　　　　　　　　**Manchester City at Old Trafford.**

Attendance: 19,958.

Lost: 2–0.

Team: Leighton, Duxbury, Donaghy, Bruce, Phelan, Carey, Robson, Webb, McClair, Hughes, Blackmore.

Substitute: Robins for Carey.

Originally scheduled for 15 August, but postponed due to United's travel weariness, the final part of Lee Sharpe's transfer to United, a match against his former club Torquay United, finally took place almost a month late.

Action was confined to one end of the pitch, with Jim Leighton more or less a spectator, while his opposite number Veysey pulled off a string of fine saves and was beaten only once. Mike Duxbury scored the only goal of the game in the 52nd minute from a Mark Hughes pass which saw the United veteran chip the 'keeper from just inside the penalty area.

Efforts from McClair and Hughes came to nothing, but it was mainly due to the agility of Veysey that United failed to add to the scoreline.

---

12 September 1989　　　　　　　**Torquay United at Plainmoor.**

Attendance: 4,108.

Won: 1–0.

Scorer: Duxbury.

Team: Leighton, Anderson, Donaghy, Bruce, Phelan, Pallister, Beardsmore, Duxbury, McClair, Hughes, Sharpe.

Substitutes: Blackmore for Hughes, Martin for Sharpe.

Although it was only September, United had gone through a proposed takeover, there were new additions in the form of Pallister, Wallace and Ince, and the team had suffered an absolutely mind-blowing 5–1 defeat at Maine Road.

Three days after the disastrous defeat at the hands of their neighbours, the United squad travelled north to Edinburgh to play in a testimonial match for Eamonn Bannon, and it was unfortunate that it was Hearts who were first to bear the brunt of that embarrassing derby day defeat.

The match opened briskly, with McClair hitting a 20-yard drive just wide of the post and Colquhoun sending an inviting ball across the face of the United goal to be missed by everyone in the opening minutes.

United had the first real chance of the game in the 10th minute, when a cross from Beardsmore found Hughes, whose volley was blocked by 'keeper Smith before being hastily cleared by a defender for a corner.

Six minutes later the visitors were in front. McPherson fouled Hughes 20 yards out and, from the resulting free-kick, Wallace blasted the ball high into the roof of the net past the helpless Smith. Within 60 seconds, however, Hearts were level, Pallister allowing Crabbe to win the ball and score from close in.

Hughes came close in the 20th minute, but it was Hearts who went in front 17 minutes later. Blackmore brought down Mackay inside the area and Bannon made no mistake from the spot. Two minutes after the restart United were level, as a long clearance from Leighton found Blackmore, who slotted the ball past substitute 'keeper Smith.

With 16 minutes to go, Blackmore claimed his second of the night to restore United's lead when he turned a Sharpe cross past Smith. Ten minutes later it was 4–2, McClair completing the scoring with a close-range header.

---

26 September 1989   **Heart of Midlothian at Tynecastle Park, Edinburgh.**

Attendance: 9,001.

Won: 4–2.

Scorers: Blackmore 2, Wallace, McClair.

Team: Leighton, Anderson, Donaghy, Duxbury, Phelan, Pallister, Beardsmore, Blackmore, McClair, Hughes, Wallace.

Substitutes: Martin for Hughes, Sharpe for Anderson.

With more serious matters to concentrate on, Alex Ferguson's side took part in only one other friendly during the 1989–90 season, with United travelling north to the unfamiliar surroundings of Perth. This was a game to mark the official opening of McDiarmid Park, the new home of St Johnstone, one of the United manager's former clubs.

After spending £5 million on a brand-new stadium you would have thought that there would be a few teething problems and, sure enough, with 32 minutes played the floodlights flickered and the 10,000-capacity, all-seater stadium was plunged into complete darkness for 23 minutes. The crowd remained calm as the referee took both teams off the park until emergency repair work was carried out at a nearby electricity sub-station.

Leighton was by far the busiest of the two 'keepers, with the home side producing much of the early goalmouth action. Cherry and Moore both missed uncharacteristic scoring opportunities and although Grant did have the ball in the United net it was disallowed for offside.

United's best efforts came when a cross from Sharpe was pushed against the bar by Balavage, with the 'keeper saving a second attempt, and a Hughes run ending with a shot from McClair. Once again, however, the 'keeper was able to keep the ball out.

The Scottish First Division club continued to command much of the game, but they were to rue their missed opportunities when McClair scored what was to be a face-saving winner with an angled drive from Phelan's pass in the 62nd minute.

---

17 October 1989   **St Johnstone at McDiarmid Park, Perth.**

Attendance: 9,788.

Won: 1–0.

Scorer: McClair.

Team: Leighton, Martin, Donaghy, Bruce, Phelan, Pallister, Robson, Ince, McClair, Hughes, Sharpe.

Substitutes: Gibson for Donaghy, Blackmore for Robson, Duxbury for Martin, Maiorana for Hughes.

The 1990s

New seasons are always looked forward to with eager anticipation, but the 1990–91 campaign was that little bit more special, as European soccer chiefs lifted the five-year ban on English clubs participating in the UEFA competitions, with United, having won the FA Cup, being allowed to enter the European Cup-Winners' Cup.

There were still, however, friendlies to be played, with trips to the Continent still very much on the agenda.

The first pre-season friendly of 1990–91 did not involve much travelling, with near neighbours Bury welcoming the FA Cup holders for former United manager Wilf McGuinness's testimonial match.

McGuinness had joined United from school in 1953, making his debut two years later, and within three years had progressed to the full England international side. His playing career came to an end after breaking a leg against Stoke reserves, although he attempted to make a spirited fightback during 1966–67, being named as substitute for the first team. However, in the end he was forced to call it a day and reverted to coaching, progressing through the ranks once again before being named as United's manager upon Sir Matt Busby's retirement. This did not go according to plan and he was soon demoted to reserve-team coach.

His testimonial was arranged due to his 10 years of sterling service as something of a utility man, and now physio, to the Gigg Lane side. He was afforded a warm reception as, along with two young mascots, he carried the FA Cup around the ground prior to kick-off. It was a toss-up as to which was the more popular, the FA Cup or Wembley hero Les Sealey, who was also greeted warmly by the away support.

Alex Ferguson set his team up with a new look formation, introducing a sweeper system, making Mike Phelan the 'spare man', as well as giving new signing Denis Irwin his United debut. It was certainly enough to blot out any Bury threats, restricting them to long-range efforts which were comfortably dealt with between the posts by Les Sealey.

Sadly, United's front men also failed to find the back of the net, though Pallister saw a header hit the post. Much of that failure was due to the fine form of the Third Division side's goalkeeper Gary Kelly, who made acrobatic saves from Irwin, Webb and twice from Mark Hughes. Another save denied the benefactor's son Paul McGuinness from making the evening that little bit more memorable with a goal.

1 August 1990	Bury at Gigg Lane.

Attendance: 7,162.

Drew: 0–0.

Team: Sealey, Irwin, Martin, Bruce, Phelan, Pallister, Ince, Webb, McClair, Hughes, Wallace.

Substitutes: Gibson for Martin, McGuinness for McClair.

It was only the second pre-season run out, but there were already alarm bells ringing as United failed to find the back of the net for the second game running. This time it was the Irish part-timers of Cork City who kept their illustrious opponents at bay.

The programme for the match versus Bury, 1 August 1990.

WILF McGUINNESS TESTIMONIAL

SOUVENIR BROCHURE

The magnetism of United drew a crowd of 8,000 supporters to the ground, but many left disappointed with their display. They certainly expected more than they got, as only a few days previously Everton had defeated Cork 3–0.

Irwin received a rapturous welcome on his return home and was only denied a goal by a desperate tackle inside the area as he bore down on the goal.

Donegan in the Cork goal set his standards for the evening as early as the seventh minute when he saved from Gibson, but was beaten by both Wallace and Ince soon afterwards. The former's shot, however, went narrowly over, while the latter's header rebounded off the crossbar.

Cork also had their opportunities and certainly created the better openings. Freyne released Cotter, whose cross saw Thompson head straight at Leighton. A minute later Barry was through one-on-one with the United 'keeper, but his low hard shot inched past the United post. On the stroke of half-time Bruce fouled Morley just outside the area, but Crainie's free-kick was touched over the bar by Leighton.

The second half failed to produce the same amount of action as the first and, although United enjoyed most of the play, Pallister going close with a header and Beardsmore having a shot cleared off the line by Cotter, they just could not put the ball into the back of the net.

---

3 August 1990	**Cork City at Musgrave Park, Cork.**

Attendance: 8,000.

Drew: 0–0.

Team: Leighton, Irwin, Donaghy, Bruce, Phelan, Pallister, Gibson, Ince, McClair, Hughes, Wallace.

Substitutes: Robins for Hughes, Sharpe for Wallace, Beardsmore for Gibson, Blackmore for Phelan.

Following the 0–0 draw at Cork manager Alex Ferguson admitted: 'We've got to get our forwards back in the habit of scoring', while he warned his Hughes–McClair strike force, 'You've got to pull your fingers out and start scoring'. His words were certainly adhered to in the second game of the mini-tour of Ireland against Waterford United.

Ferguson actually decided to split up his strike force, with McClair being 'rested' and Mark Robins being brought in in his stead.

It was Mark Hughes who ended United's goal drought, breaking free from Barry to latch on to the ball as it rebounded off the crossbar following a shot from Blackmore five minutes before the interval. The relief on the United bench was patently obvious.

In the opening five minutes of the second half United almost went three up. Pallister headed a Beardsmore free-kick against a post, while Quinlivan saved brilliantly from Anderson following an Irwin cross. The 'keeper, however, was finally beaten when Anderson saw him off his line and cleverly chipped the ball over his head for United's second.

Seven minutes later it was indeed 3–0, Robins scoring an excellent individual effort as he forced his way past the Waterford central-defenders before hitting an unstoppable shot from just inside the area.

With four minutes remaining Hughes created the opening for Sharpe to add a fourth.

| **5 August 1990** | **Waterford United at Kilcohan Park.** |

Attendance: 4,750.

Won: 4–0.

Scorers: Hughes, Anderson, Robins, Sharpe.

Team: Sealey, Anderson, Martin, Donaghy, Phelan, Pallister, Beardsmore, Blackmore, Robins, Hughes, Sharpe.

Substitute: Irwin for Martin.

The programme for the match versus Waterford United, 5 August 1990.

Lee Martin and Colin Gibson had been sent home with injuries, forcing them to miss the game against Derry City, as United's third game across the water induced the correspondent from the *Irish Independent* to open his match report with: 'Don't put too much money on Manchester United ending their 23-year-long spell without winning the English First Division title next season. Based on their performance in a 1–1 draw, the wilderness of the middle table or possibly another relegation struggle awaits them when the new season begins in three weeks time'.

Danny Wallace almost opened the scoring against the Irish part-timers in the second minute, after Sharpe dispossessed Carlyle inside the Derry half and his pass found the unmarked United winger, whose drive from 15 yards went narrowly wide. Four minutes later it was a 30-yard speculative effort from Ince that came close to opening the scoring, but the ball bounced on the penalty spot and went over the bar.

The closest Derry came to scoring in the opening exchanges was when Healy's 15th-minute free-kick from 20 yards out curled around the defensive wall, but Leighton managed to get his body behind the ball.

United took the lead on the half-hour. Sharpe set off on a dazzling 30-yard run down the left wing and, although Dalton managed to save the winger's acute angled shot, he was helpless in preventing Robins from netting the rebound.

Play in the second half was uninspiring, with few scoring opportunities from either team, and just as United felt that they had done enough to secure victory, former United youngster Joe Hanrahan intercepted a loose ball deep in the United half and went on to beat Leighton with a fierce left-footed drive, for what many regarded as a well-deserved draw.

The programme for the match versus Derry City, 8 August 1990.

| **8 August 1990** | **Derry City at Brandywell Stadium.** |

Attendance: 9,710.

Drew: 1–1.

Scorer: Robins.

Team: Leighton, Irwin, Donaghy, Bruce, Phelan, Pallister, Sharpe, Ince, McClair, Robins, Wallace.

Substitutes: Anderson for Irwin, Blackmore for Sharpe, Beardsmore for Wallace.

Arranged to celebrate the centenary of the Irish League, United came up against an Irish League side made up of £20-a-week part-timers, who lacked pace, skill and class, making the 90 minutes a completely one-sided affair. Even the loss of Gary Pallister in the 25th minute, with a badly cut head, failed to give the home side any advantage.

Not for the first time on this mini-tour, the home goalkeeper turned in an excellent performance, with Portadown's Mickey Keenan pulling off a string of breathtaking saves, including tipping scorching drives from McClair and Blackmore over the bar. Despite his heroics, he could do little to prevent United's victory, but it was not until the 32nd minute that they took the lead, neat exchanges between Wallace and Ince creating the opportunity for McClair to open the scoring. A second goal arrived two minutes prior to the interval, when Ince sent Webb clear down the left, with a cross picking out Hughes, who scored with a low shot inside the post.

Rather surprisingly, there was no further scoring until the 77th minute, when Wallace, on the halfway line, evaded the offside trap and took off on a solo run, which ended with the ball being slipped past substitute 'keeper Smith.

If you purchased the famous *Pink* on the Saturday evening of the Irish League match you were led to believe that United had beaten the Irish side 4–0. There was a small column of the goalscorers from the game which listed: Brian McClair (32 mins), Mark Hughes (43 mins), Danny Wallace (77 mins) and Clayton Blackmore (89 mins).

So, what happened to this mysterious fourth goal? The answer was revealed in the Monday edition of the *Manchester Evening News* when David Meek wrote: 'Blackmore looked to have scored a few seconds from the final whistle but the referee later ruled no-goal.'

---

11 August 1990   **Irish League at Windsor Park, Belfast.**

Attendance: 10,037.

Won: 3–0.

Scorers: McClair, Hughes, Wallace.

Team: Sealey, Irwin, Donaghy, Blackmore, Phelan, Pallister, Webb, Ince, McClair, Hughes, Wallace.

Substitute: Anderson for Pallister.

The final match in Ireland took United to Dublin, where they came up against Bohemians. The kick-off was delayed for 11 minutes due to congestion at the turnstiles, as those eager to see United attempted to gain entry to the ground.

With another friendly in Glasgow scheduled for 24 hours later, United rarely slipped into top gear as Bohemians never gave them any trouble.

The scoring was opened within 10 minutes of kick-off. Irwin's precise cross allowed Robins the opportunity to power his way into the six-yard box and head past the helpless 'keeper.

Blackmore, Sharpe and Beardsmore all came close to increasing the lead, but once again it was the 'keeper rather than poor finishing that prevented the score from increasing.

To their credit, the Irish side did come into the game briefly at the start of the second half, Walsh and Carroll both coming close, but United increased their lead in the 58th minute when Blackmore found Wallace and, cutting in from the left, the winger made no mistake as he took advantage of a defensive mix-up.

King replied with a 25-yard drive which struck the reinstated Leighton's post with the 'keeper well beaten. Two minutes later, however, it was game over when Wallace found Sharpe on the left and, as the cross came over, Robins was on the spot to head home his second of the night.

---

13 August 1990   **Bohemians at Dalymount Park, Dublin.**

Attendance: 13,878.

Won: 3–0.

Scorers: Robins 2, Wallace.

Team: Leighton, Irwin, Donaghy, Blackmore, Beardsmore, Anderson, Webb, Ince, Robins, Hughes, Sharpe.

Substitutes: McClair for Ince, Wallace for Hughes, Phelan for Anderson.

Ticket for the match versus Bohemians, 13 August 1990.

Concerned about the prospect of crowd trouble, the FA wanted travelling supporters banned from the game against Rangers at Glasgow, with a blackout on news of the fixture actually taking place also requested. However, with an expected 50,000 crowd and given the standing of both clubs, this was never going to be a possibility and United were eventually given an allocation of tickets.

A heavy downpour of rain on the night subdued the pre-match fears of crowd trouble, while also taking much away from the game as a spectacle.

Jim Leighton, continuing his search for confidence following his omission from the FA Cup Final replay a couple of months previously, must have wondered when his luck would improve, as he conceded a penalty after only six minutes. Phelan hesitated on the ball just outside his penalty area and was dispossessed by Walters. Swiftly the Rangers winger moved forward with the goal at his mercy, only to be brought down by Leighton. Walters himself took the kick, but screwed it wide of the left-hand post. Prior to this, Hateley had already fired well over the United bar when in a good position. Following the penalty miss, Rangers continued to press forward, with Steven prominent. However, as the first half wore on, United slowly came more into the game, with McClair influencing the proceedings.

The weather certainly dampened the atmosphere as well as the play, and it was obvious to those present that there were not going to be many goals to excite them.

A Blackmore shot was held by Woods, but the substitution of the former on the hour, with Sharpe coming on, almost created the opportunity for United to open the scoring. The substitute was only on the pitch a few minutes when he found himself slithering across the Rangers penalty area, having been clumsily challenged by Walters. From the resulting kick Bruce could only watch Woods dive to his right and palm the ball round the post.

With nine minutes remaining the only goal of the game was scored, with substitutions once again a telling factor. After Beardsmore and Robins had replaced Ince and Wallace, the latter pushed the ball into the path of Beardsmore, who slipped the ball past Woods for the only goal of the night.

---

15 August 1990   **Rangers at Ibrox Park, Glasgow.**

Attendance: 31,818.

Won: 1–0.

Scorer: Beardsmore.

Team: Leighton, Irwin, Donaghy, Bruce, Phelan, Blackmore, Webb, Ince, McClair, Hughes, Wallace.

Substitutes: Sharpe for Blackmore, Beardsmore for Ince, Robins for Wallace, Anderson for Webb.

Ticket for the match versus Rangers, 15 August 1990.

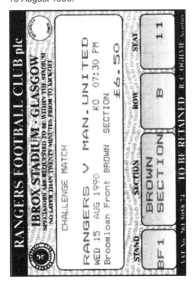

Not all United players receive thousands of pounds from sell-out testimonials. However, those who have worn the red shirt for the 10 years or more required to

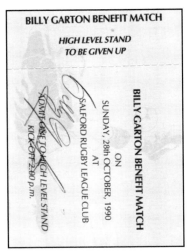

Ticket for the Billy Garton benefit match, 28 October 1990.

earn such a reward, or those, like Billy Garton, who have been unfortunate enough to have their careers at the club cut short through injury and illness, deserve to receive a little help from the club.

Billy Garton, forced to quit the game due to myalgic encephalomyelitis, was told by the club that a testimonial arranged on his behalf would not be staged at Old Trafford, as they felt the game would not attract a big enough crowd to justify taking over the Old Trafford stadium. Instead, the game was moved down the road to Salford Rugby Club's Willows Ground.

On 28 October around 1,600 turned up on a Sunday afternoon to see a United XI, made up of the likes of Bosnich, Beardsmore, Wallace, Ferguson, Robins, Maiorana and a youngster by the name of Giggs coming on as substitute, take on a former United XI, with old boys such as Stapleton, Albiston, Nicholl, Strachan and Macari.

The present XI stormed into a 5–0 lead, but a late rally by the former Reds reduced the leeway to 5–3 by the end of a relaxed 90 minutes. Chris Turner, goalkeeper for the former Reds, spent only 45 minutes between the posts before moving into an outfield position for the second half, a 45 minutes that they completed with 12 men, United youngster Jim Shields adding to their number.

The only other friendly in season 1990–91 saw United entertain the other half of the Glasgow 'Old Firm', as Celtic and around 15,000 of their supporters visited Old Trafford for Bryan Robson's testimonial match.

Robson was determined to play an active part at some point in the 90 minutes and took a place on the bench, following a rapturous reception from the two teams and the 41,658 crowd as, along with his two daughters and the FA Cup, he walked on to the Old Trafford pitch.

United opened the sharper of the two sides, with Brian McClair setting up Hughes three times in the first 10 minutes to no avail. Celtic's reply was a 30-yard drive from Galloway which went just over Sealey's bar. Ince brought down Nicholas in the area, but the referee waved the protests away.

United photographed with the Mazda team prior to kick-off, 1991.

The atmosphere matched the occasion and at times threatened to overshadow the actual football, as United took a 15-minute lead. Blackmore's through pass found Webb unmarked in a central position and, as Bonner advanced from his goal, the United midfielder stroked the ball to his left for Hughes to score with ease.

Six minutes from the interval Celtic were level, Collins finishing off a Nicholas–Hayes move. Three minutes later they were in front, Wdowdzyk crossing a long ball from the left for Nicholas to bundle the ball over the line.

Substitute 'keeper Leighton did well to block an effort from Dziekanowski, but few had seen it, as all eyes were on the touchline, where Bryan Robson was warming up. The United 'keeper made a further two excellent stops, parrying Fulton's drive and diving to his left to stop Coyne's rebound, before he was beaten for Celtic's third goal.

Robson had only been on the pitch two minutes before Dziekanowski and Grant combined on the right, with the latter's low cross being turned beyond Leighton by Coyne. With 17 minutes remaining, even 'Captain Marvel' could not inspire his troops to pull two or even three goals back.

Ticket for the match versus Celtic, 20 November 1990.

20 November 1990   **Celtic at Old Trafford.**

Attendance: 41,658.

Lost: 3–1.

Scorer: Hughes.

Team: Sealey, Irwin, Blackmore, Bruce, Phelan, Pallister, Webb, Ince, McClair, Hughes, Wallace.

Substitutes: Donaghy for Webb, Leighton for Sealey, Beardsmore for Hughes, Sharpe for Ince, Robson for Wallace.

The opening friendly of season 1991–92 for the European Cup-Winners' Cup holders conjured up a fixture that appears in the *Manchester United Official Yearbook* under the 'first team' heading, but it is a game that very few people actually knew about at the time.

Due to the lack of information regarding the fixture, there were only around three dozen or so people at the Littleton Road training ground to watch United go through their paces against a Japanese touring side who were coached by former Red Bill Foulkes.

The game marked the first-team debut of Peter Schmeichel, who was to go on and play a major part in United's history. He could not, however, prevent the visitors from recording a surprise 2–1 win.

Unfortunately, with the lack of coverage in the newspapers there is little to write about the 90 minutes of football.

24 July 1991   **Mazda at Littleton Road, Salford.**

Attendance: Unknown.

Lost: 2–1.

Scorer: Ferguson.

Team: Schmeichel, Webb, Blackmore, Bruce, Phelan, Donaghy, Kanchelskis, Ince, McClair, Hughes, Ferguson.

Substitutes: Wratten for Kanchelskis, Whitworth for Bruce, Martin for Blackmore, Robins for McClair.

As United prepared to set off on their pre-season tour of Norway, there were some doubts cast over the forthcoming testimonial for Sir Matt Busby, due to around 10 withdrawals from the Republic of Ireland side who were providing the opposition. Committee chairman Colin Barlow, however, was quick to confirm that the match would go ahead.

First stop on the tour took United to Drammen, where they faced Strømsgodset, with manger Alex Ferguson more than happy with the 3–1 victory, although an injury to Mike Phelan saw the midfielder return home for treatment.

Surprisingly, the home side, who were second bottom of the Norwegian Premier League, took an eighth minute lead through Erlandsen, but Ince put United back on level terms in the 26th minute.

With seven minutes to the interval, Beardsmore gave United the lead from a Webb pass and Danny Wallace wrapped it up 10 minutes from time with a third.

---

29 July 1991　　**Strømsgodset at Marienlyst Stadium, Drammen, Norway.**

Attendance: 7,809.

Won: 3–1.

Scorers: Ince, Beardsmore, Wallace.

Team: Schmeichel, Beardsmore, Blackmore, Bruce, Phelan, Donaghy, Webb, Ince, McClair, Hughes, Ferguson.

Substitutes: Irwin for Martin, Wallace for Ferguson, Martin for Phelan.

'The Norwegians were the beater team and we were lucky to win,' proclaimed Alex Ferguson following the 1–0 victory over Viking Stavanger, 90 minutes which once again showcased the potential of Peter Schmeichel, who pulled off a string of first-class saves.

The Norwegians plodded away admirably and held United for just over an hour, before Mark Robins popped up to score the only goal of the game.

---

30 July 1991　　　　　　　　　**Viking Stavanger in Norway.**

Attendance: 6,025.

Won: 1–0.

Scorer: Robins.

Team: Schmeichel, Irwin, Blackmore, Bruce, Wallace, Donaghy, Ince, Webb, McClair, Hughes, Sharpe.

Substitutes: Robins for Hughes, Ferguson for Wallace, Whitworth for Irwin, Beardsmore for Sharpe.

After touring the fjords, the United party set off for the final match of the tour against Molde, with the game played amid an unexpected heatwave.

Molde, like their fellow countrymen in the opening fixture, took the lead, with Jan Erlend Kruse beating Schmeichel in the 13th minute. This was a lead that they were to hold onto until substitute Clayton Blackmore equalised in the 63rd minute.

Hughes made it 2–1 in the 75th minute, scoring another four minutes later to make it 3–1.

Having fielded something of a second-string side, Alex Ferguson was hit with further injury problems when his son Darren, having replaced Webb in the 12th minute, was himself replaced a mere four minutes later.

---

1 August 1991　　　　**Molde at Privatkamp Stadium, Norway.**

Attendance: 3,468.

Won: 3–1.

Scorers: Hughes 2, Blackmore.

Team: Schmeichel, Whitworth, Martin, Bruce, Robins, Donaghy, Ince, Webb, McClair, Hughes, Ferguson.

Substitutes: Blackmore for Whitworth, Beardsmore for Robins, Wallace for Ferguson, Ferguson for Webb.

Boghead Park played host to what must be one of the smallest crowds ever to witness a United friendly (except for the Mazda game), when the Reds visited to face Dumbarton in the Alex Wright testimonial match.

If there had been any visible cobwebs as the team struggled in Norway, the journey back over the North Sea had blown them away, as the home side were swept aside by a five-star performance.

Treating the game very seriously, the full strength United side showed little mercy, although it did take them 22 minutes to open the scoring. A 50-yard downfield throw from Schmeichel found McClair out wide on the right and his cross was bravely headed home by Robins. The goal could well have been an equaliser, as McQuade had missed a good opportunity to score from a Gibson pass as early as the fifth minute.

Although not overawed by their visitors, Dumbarton were always chasing the game and, four minutes after the first goal, Hughes added a second, tapping the ball into an empty net following good work from Robins.

That United strike force had doubled the score to 4–0 by the 63rd minute, with Robins notching up his second nine minutes earlier with an angular shot, while Hughes added the fourth.

A McCracken foul on Hughes inside the area presented Bruce with the opportunity to make it five, but his spot-kick hit the bar. Schmeichel, at the opposite end, was to save a McNair penalty 10 minutes later, after Bruce had fouled McGarvey.

McClair added a fifth in the 79th minute with a simple tap-in.

---

4 August 1991　　　　**Dumbarton at Boghead Park.**

Attendance: 1,570.

Won: 5–0.

Scorers: Robins 2, Hughes 2, McClair.

Team: Schmeichel, Martin, Blackmore, Bruce, Whitworth, Robins, Webb, Ince, McClair, Hughes, Wallace.

Substitutes: Beardsmore for Ince, Ferguson for Wallace, Irwin for Martin.

From the outskirts of Glasgow, the United party headed north to the manager's old stomping ground of Aberdeen, to face his former club in the Cutty Sark Tall Ships Challenge Match.

Both sides provided the near capacity crowd with an exciting evening's entertainment and it was the home side who made the early running. Irwin had to bring down Gillhaus to halt a threatening attack, with the same Aberdeen player trying to dribble round Schmeichel in the 13th minute, his shot hitting the side netting. United were soon producing openings of their own and a Bruce

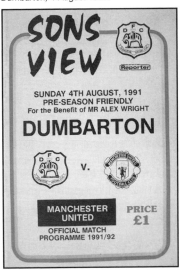

The programme for the match versus Dumbarton, 4 August 1991.

header was held confidently by Snelders, while Darren Ferguson was not too far away with a 30-yard drive in the 16th minute.

Two minutes later United were in front against the run of play. A long ball from McClair found Blackmore, who laid it down to Ferguson. The ball was rolled forward to Hughes, who blasted the ball past Snelders.

Schmeichel saved well from Jess and McKimmie, but United should have put the outcome of the game beyond any doubt before the interval, when they missed a handful of chances within a minute. Snelders pulled off two first-class saves and Bett cleared off the line.

In the second half Aberdeen once again upped the ante and drew level within five minutes of the restart. Grant squared the ball to Dutchman Caat, whose 50-yard shot left Schmeichel helpless. A flurry of substitutions, however, took some of the wind out of the second half and in the dying seconds Blackmore should have won the match for United, but his shot went wide.

So, with the result all square at the end of the 90 minutes, it was down to penalties to determine the winners of the Cutty Sark trophy. Bett and Connor scored from the spot, as did Blackmore and Ince. Booth's effort was saved by Schmeichel and McClair gave United the edge. Gillhaus hit the post with Aberdeen's fourth, leaving Webb with the opportunity to wrap up the shoot-out by scoring United's fourth spot-kick.

5 August 1991	**Aberdeen at Pittodrie.**

Attendance: 20,300.
Drew: 1–1 (**Won:** 4–3 on penalties).
Scorers: Hughes (Blackmore, McClair, Ince, Webb).
Team: Schmeichel, Irwin, Blackmore, Bruce, Whitworth, Robins, Webb, Ince, McClair, Hughes, Ferguson.
Substitute: Beardsmore for Irwin.

Having already played six games in a 13-day period, United's hectic pre-season schedule continued with a match in Vienna against Austria Memphis, where they were given something of a run around in a 5–1 defeat. Debutant Paul Parker had a difficult game, with fingers being pointed in his direction for two of the goals, as well as finding his way into the referee's notebook.

Completely outplayed, United were three goals down by the 39th minute through goals from Ivanauskas, Narbekovas and Kern. McClair pulled one back just on half-time, but that was about the only time that United looked like scoring.

The Austrians' superiority was further underlined in the second half, although it was not until the 89th minute that they increased their lead further through Schmidt, Prosenik making it 5–1 in injury time.

7 August 1991	**Austria Memphis in Vienna.**

Attendance: 12,000.
Lost: 5–1.
Scorer: McClair.
Team: Schmeichel, Beardsmore, Blackmore, Bruce, Ferguson, Parker, Webb, Ince, McClair, Hughes, Wallace.
Substitutes: Whitworth for Webb, Wratten for Ferguson.

The next testimonial that was arranged was no ordinary match, organised for no ordinary benefactor, with Jackie Charlton's Republic of Ireland side providing the Old Trafford opposition to honour Sir Matt Busby, the man who had sowed the initial seeds to make Manchester United the team that it is today.

The depleted Irish side, as always, set out to give little away at the back and United struggled to make any sort of headway in the opening 45 minutes. Goalkeeper Gerry Peyton did not have one save to make in that opening period. In fact it was the 66th minute before he was called into action, as he saved from Mark Hughes.

Having not had the best of debuts against Austria Memphis, Paul Parker was hoping that his first Old Trafford appearance would win over the home support, but four minutes before the break he tried desperately to beat John Aldridge to a Sheridan through ball, only to watch aghast as the ball came off his toe and rolled past Schmeichel into the net to give the Republic the lead.

The big 'keeper, also making his initial home appearance, certainly endeared himself to the supporters with a number of fine saves, the best of them being an excellent double stop from McLaughlin and Sheedy and tipping a 30-yard drive from Brady over the bar.

The introduction of Bryan Robson at half-time lifted United and the club captain scored the equalising goal 15 minutes from time. Beardsmore found him with a cross, which he headed home.

The programme for the match versus Republic of Ireland, 11 August 1991.

Unfortunately, the game itself did not match the occasion, but the seven-a-side curtain-raiser at the sunlit stadium made sure that the majority of the crowd were in their places earlier than normal, as the opportunity to see George Best in the flesh was not to be missed.

Alongside the likes of Bill Foulkes, Pat Crerand and Nobby Stiles, the bearded Irishman lined up against a team of former City players, including Book, Tueart, Summerbee and Barnes, to entertain the crowd with some vintage skills in a 3–3 draw.

11 August 1991	Republic of Ireland at Old Trafford.

Attendance: 33,412.

Drew: 1–1.

Scorer: Robson.

Team: Schmeichel, Donaghy, Parker, Bruce, Blackmore, Pallister, Webb, Ince, McClair, Hughes, Wallace.

Substitutes: Robson for Wallace, Ferguson for Webb, Beardsmore for Pallister, Pallister for Bruce.

Old Trafford was again the venue for the penultimate friendly of the 1991–92 season, with Everton supplying the opposition for Norman Whiteside's testimonial. Despite the popularity of the Northern Ireland international star, the match was a low-key affair, with many staying away, still disappointed by United's failure to defeat Liverpool a few days earlier to keep alive the slender hopes of snatching the Championship from the grasp of another rival, Leeds United.

Whiteside, the goal-scoring hero of the 1985 FA Cup Final, ironically against Everton, had joined the Goodison Park side in 1989, but a persistent knee injury forced him out of the game after only 29 games for his new club.

The programme for the match versus Everton, 3 May 1992.

With United having faced Tottenham Hotspur and Everton having played Chelsea only 24 hours earlier, the game was always going to be a modest affair. United, however, took a 2–0 lead with goals from Ince and Hughes, but the second half saw Everton mount a fightback, scoring four times through Esin, Ward (2) and Beardsley, without reply.

The game, which would earn Whiteside around £35,000, will be remembered not for the Irishman's farewell, but as the last time supporters would be able to stand on the Stretford End and cheer on their team. Within a matter of weeks, the area which housed the hotbed of the United support would be reduced to rubble in preparation for the new stand that was to take its place.

3 May 1992   **Everton at Old Trafford.**

Attendance: 7,434.

Lost: 4–2.

Scorers: Ince, Hughes.

Team: Schmeichel, Webb, Irwin, Bruce, Phelan, Donaghy, Kanchelskis, Ince, McClair, Hughes, Sharpe.

Substitutes: Carey for Donaghy, Butt for Kanchelskis, Giggs for Hughes, Toal for Ince, Whitworth for Irwin.

The final fixture of the season meant only a short journey across Manchester to Maine Road to face neighbours City in a testimonial for retiring chief scout Ken Barnes, who was celebrating 40 years of service with the Blues.

A crowd of just under 5,000 saw United get one over on their rivals, with Steve Bruce opening the scoring from the penalty spot in the 13th minute. Quinn came close on a couple of occasions for City, but United strengthened their grip on the game after just an hour, when Kieron Toal chipped Bibby for an excellent goal.

This seemed to jolt City into action, but, despite the late fightback, with Hughes blasting a close range effort past Schmeichel, victory on the night went to United.

8 May 1992	**Manchester City at Maine Road.**

Attendance: 4,696.

Won: 2–1.

Scorers: Bruce (pen.), Toal.

Team: Schmeichel, Sharpe, Irwin, Bruce, Phelan, Carey, Toal, Ince, McClair, Blackmore, Ferguson.

United returned to Norway for their 1992–93 pre-season preparations, kicking off with a 3–0 victory over IK Start.

It was a slightly weakened United squad due to Webb, McClair and Kanchelskis all being given additional time off following the European Championships, while Mark Hughes was hit by food poisoning. The star of the European Championships, Peter Schmeichel, was included in the travelling party by public demand.

A brilliant save from Frode Olsen prevented Ince from opening the scoring in the 15th minute, but it was only a matter of time before United went in front and, true to the run of play, Giggs crossed for Blackmore to open the scoring five minutes later. It was also a Welsh double act that produced a second goal two minutes before the interval, with Giggs again the provider, setting up Mark Hughes, who fired home.

Danny Wallace scored a third for United four minutes after half-time, after which the tempo of the game dropped a few gears, with the visitors more than happy just to see the 90 minutes out.

28 July 1992	**IK Start at Kristiansand, Norway.**

Attendance: 4,118.

Won: 3–0.

Scorers: Blackmore, Hughes, Wallace.

Team: Walsh, Parker, Irwin, Bruce, Blackmore, Pallister, Robson, Ince, Wallace, Hughes, Giggs.

Substitutes: Phelan for Robson, Martin for Parker, Ferguson for Ince, Robins for Wallace.

The tour of Norway was abruptly interrupted as United headed back to the UK to face Celtic in Glasgow, for a match to celebrate their 25th anniversary of becoming the first Scottish and British clubs to win the European Cup.

Although having only managed a few hours sleep after the match against Start, and requiring further rest before facing the Scottish side, there was a lively start to the game, which was delayed some 20 minutes to allow supporters into the ground.

The programme for the match versus Celtic, 29 July 1992.

There was no holding back in the tackle, despite the 'friendly' tag, and it was the home side that looked the most dangerous in the opening exchanges, with Creaney wasting a good opportunity as Schmeichel saved well.

Continuing to push forward, Celtic eventually made the initial breakthrough in the 28th minute. Boyd gained possession on the left, found Creaney on the opposite side of the area and the striker controlled the ball before veering around Schmeichel to score.

However, within four minutes United were level. Ince latched on to the ball after Irwin drove it deep into the area and, as the Celtic defence hesitated, he thumped the ball high into the roof of the net.

Robson was forced to leave the field just before the interval and minutes later Nicholas wasted a good chance to regain the lead for Celtic, but his shot, straight at the 'keeper, was held at the second attempt by Schmeichel.

Despite retaining something of a competitive edge, a flurry of substitutions blotted the second half, which saw McClair almost putting United in front on two occasions, but both opportunities were thwarted by Marshall. At the opposite end, Creaney cracked a shot against the post. Peter Schmeichel also came close to scoring, with one clearance forcing his opposite number to make a frantic dive to grab the ball.

29 July 1992	**Celtic at Celtic Park, Glasgow.**

Attendance: 34,368.

Drew: 1–1.

Scorer: Ince.

Team: Schmeichel, Martin, Irwin, Bruce, Kanchelskis, Pallister, Robson, Ince, McClair, Hughes, Giggs.

Substitutes: Phelan for Irwin, Ferguson for Robson, Wallace for Ferguson, Blackmore for Kanchelskis.

United returned to Norway to face Lillestrom, where they had to come from behind to earn a draw in their third game in four days.

With the Norwegian season well under way, Lillestrom were always going to be capable of causing United problems and they should have taken the lead on more than one occasion, but the opportunities were squandered.

It was not, however, until the 54th minute that the deadlock was eventually broken, when Kenneth Nysather, Norway's leading scorer, shot past Schmeichel. Two minutes later it was nearly 2–0 when Kallstad rattled the United crossbar.

A Kanchelskis run created the equaliser for Brian McClair in the second half, and United could have gone on to win the match, but both Blackmore and Webb shot over the bar in the closing minutes.

31 July 1992	**Lillestrom in Arasen, Norway.**

Attendance: 5, 569.

Drew: 1–1.

Scorer: McClair.

Team: Schmeichel, Irwin, Blackmore, Bruce, Phelan, Pallister, Kanchelskis, Webb, McClair, Robins, Wallace.

Substitutes: Ferguson for Bruce, Giggs for Robins.

United completed their three-match tour of Norway with a closely fought 3–2 victory over Rosenborg, which could be considered something of a moral victory by the locals, as some 15 years previously they had conceded eight to their illustrious visitors.

This time around the home side could well have opened the scoring in the opening minutes, when Tore-Andre Dahlum hit the post and Skammelsrad shot wide. However, it was United who took the lead in the ninth minute, McClair sending Ince through to beat Seinaes. One minute before the interval a reversal of roles made it 2–0.

Unbeaten on their own ground for some 18 months, Rosenborg were certainly not going to relinquish their record without a fight and staged an impressive fightback, with goals from Skammelsrad and Loken levelling the scores.

The Norwegians, however, were only level for a minute. Hughes was wrestled to the ground just outside the area and Denis Irwin blasted the ball home from 20 yards out.

---

2 August 1992   **Rosenborg at Lerkendal Stadium, Tronheim, Norway.**

Attendance: 9,379.

Won: 3–2.

Scorers: Ince, McClair, Irwin.

Team: Schmeichel, Martin, Blackmore, Bruce, Ferguson, Pallister, Kanchelskis, Ince, McClair, Hughes, Giggs.

Substitutes: Irwin for Martin, Phelan for Ince, Webb for McClair, Wallace for Kanchelskis.

To complete their Scandinavian tour United flew to Sweden to face Elfsborg, with the five games in eight days schedule clearly showing as the 90 minutes stuttered to a 0–0 draw.

There was a distinct lack of atmosphere, with the home side more than happy to keep six men at the back throughout the 90 minutes. Substitute Ryan Giggs had the best opportunity to give United the lead, but 'keeper Verdin did well to smother the shot. Wallace also came close, but headed past the post, while the same player was also active at the opposite end, running back to clear when it looked like Andreasson was about to score.

One interesting aspect of this particular fixture was the naming of Brian Kidd as a substitute. Unfortunately for the record books, the recently appointed United assistant manager was not called upon.

---

4 August 1992   **Elfsborg at Ryavallen, Boraas, Sweden.**

Attendance: 4,491.

Drew: 0–0.

Team: Schmeichel, Irwin, Blackmore, Webb, Phelan, Pallister, Kanchelskis, Ince, Robins, Hughes, Wallace.

Substitutes: Ferguson for Ince, Giggs for Robins.

Having returned to home shores, the bulk of the pre-season work was now complete, with only a couple of nearer to home fixtures left to play. The first of these took United to Dublin to face a Republic of Ireland side and, despite their hosts once again being vastly under strength, United could only stumble to their

Ticket for the match versus Republic of Ireland, 9 August 1992.

2–0 victory. The only real winner at the end of the day was the Athletic Union League complex at Clonshaugh, where the profits of the game were going.

In the United side for the first time was Dion Dublin, a recent £1 million signing from Cambridge United, and the gangling forward laid on the opening goal for Brian McClair, who gave former teammate Pat Bonner no chance from 12 yards as early as the 10th minute.

According to *The Irish Times*, 'that this effectively ended the match became apparent as the Irish midfield struggled to cope with the opposition, let alone to create the sort of chances which the novel pairing of Coyne and Slaven could convert'.

Bonner did well to turn a Giggs shot round the post, and a few minutes later his defenders were all over the place when Bruce sent a long ball forward towards McClair, but Kanchelskis failed when the Scot's pass set him up in an ideal position to score. Ince was only just off target with a 20-yard drive, while Bonner almost blotted his copybook when a clearance landed at the feet of Dublin, but the debutant's chip went just over.

The game was definitely over in the 63rd minute, when substitute Mark Hughes headed home from close range after McClair had created the opening following a pinpoint pass from Ince.

Such was the lack of incident and atmosphere throughout the game, that the reporter for *The Irish Times* wrote that the most interesting feature of the game was how both sides coped with the new FIFA regulation on the back pass to the goalkeeper!

9 August 1992   **Republic of Ireland at Landsdown Road, Dublin.**

Attendance: 30,069.

Won: 2–0.

Scorers: McClair, Hughes.

Team: Schmeichel, Parker, Irwin, Bruce, Ferguson, Pallister, Kanchelskis, Ince, McClair, Dublin, Giggs.

Substitutes: Hughes for Kanchelskis, Blackmore for Parker.

There was more than a hint of sadness surrounding United's visit to Swansea on the eve of the new season, as the fixture was played in aid of the family of former United player Alan Davies, who had tragically died during the previous season.

The Welsh youngster had joined United in September 1977 and, after making his first-team debut against Southampton in May 1981, made only eight appearances (plus two as substitute), scoring one goal, before joining Newcastle in July 1985. He was with Swansea City at the time of his death.

Dion Dublin had a couple of opportunities to open the scoring in the first half, but Freestone, who forgot about the back pass ruling in the opening minute, pulled off some notable saves. Brian McClair hit the bar from 30 yards, with another effort being cleared off the line by James.

Freestone was soon in action again, pushing a Giggs effort round the post, but was finally beaten in the second half when Hughes once again came off the bench to score in the 59th minute.

United were now more fluent in their play, with both Robins and Webb coming close to increasing the tally, with Freestone once again the saviour.

With 10 minutes remaining Swansea hit back, as new signing Andy McFarlane from Portsmouth headed past Schmeichel.

The match raised around £60,000 for the Davies family.

Swansea City at Vetch Field, Swansea.

Attendance: 9,744.

Drew: 1–1.

Scorer: Hughes.

Team: Schmeichel, Irwin, Blackmore, Bruce, Webb, Pallister, Kanchelskis, Ince, McClair, Dublin, Giggs.

Substitutes: Beardsmore for Irwin, Phelan for Ince, Hughes for McClair, Robins for Dublin, Wallace for Giggs.

The programme for the match versus Brondby, 11 November 1992.

The next friendly, against Peter Schmeichel's old club Brondby, organised as part of his transfer, drew a meagre 5,102 crowd, the smallest at a senior game at Old Trafford for 50 years.

Those who braved the inclement weather were rewarded with their first glimpse of two 17-year-old debutants, Keith Gillespie and Nicky Butt. Both the youngsters showed potential, with Gillespie eager to get up and down the wing as United pushed the Danish defence.

Brian McClair ended his two-month goal famine when he powered home from close range in a goalmouth scramble. Danny Wallace surprised everyone by out-jumping a defender to head home a second just before the interval.

Brondby showed a dramatic improvement in the second half, catching United on the hop with some good free-flowing football, and they were rewarded for their endurance with a goal from Hogh's penalty following a Phelan foul.

The United midfielder, however, made amends for his error of judgement when he side-footed home a Sharpe corner to regain the two-goal advantage. Brondby, to their credit, reduced the leeway in the final minute when Larsen scored their second.

11 November 1992 **Brondby at Old Trafford.**

Attendance: 5,102.

Won: 3–2.

Scorers: McClair, Wallace, Phelan.

Team: Schmeichel, Parker, Martin, Bruce, Phelan, Butt, Robson, Gillespie, McClair, Wallace, Sharpe.

Substitute: G. Neville for Gillespie.

At the beginning of this book I stated that I had used the *Manchester United Official Yearbook* as the definitive source for deciding if a particular fixture was first team or not. There are occasions when I disagree slightly with the 'official' view, for one reason or another, with such a disagreement occurring on Sunday 15 November, when Alex Ferguson sent a selection of his United squad north to his old familiar territory of Aberdeen to face Cove Rangers.

It is slightly unclear why this particular fixture appears under the 'Reserves Other Matches' in the *Yearbook*, as there were eight first-team players in the starting line up, five of whom were in the line up or on the bench for the match against Oldham Athletic seven days later.

This match was arranged to commemorate the switching on of the Aberdeen club's new floodlighting system, and the visitors certainly did it in style, winning comfortably with a 6–2 scoreline.

Watched by a full house of 2,000, Lee Sharpe was the undoubted Man of the Match, scoring four, his first coming as early as the second minute, to be followed by a second soon afterwards.

Much to the delight of the home support, Cove pulled a goal back just before the interval, but they soon found themselves two goals behind again minutes after the restart, when Sharpe claimed his hat-trick. A second Cove goal kept the game alive, but Bruce stretched United's lead from the penalty spot after Sharpe had been brought down by the goalkeeper and in the closing minutes the same two United goalscorers rounded off the scoring.

15 November 1992 **Cove Rangers at Allan Park, Aberdeen.**

Attendance: 2,000.

Won: 6–2.

Scorers: Sharpe 4, Bruce 2 (1 pen.).

Team: Digby, O'Kane, Martin, Bruce, Carey, Phelan, Robson, Kanchelskis, McClair, Wallace, Sharpe.

Substitutes: Switzer for O'Kane, Gillespie for Wallace, Beardsmore for Kanchelskis.

The next match was not simply another United friendly, but marks the first appearance in the United line up of an individual who would claim a major place in the United history books. His name? Eric Cantona.

Signed the previous week from Leeds United, Cantona carried a certain amount of baggage, but it certainly did not worry Alex Ferguson, who reckoned the Frenchman was a steal at £1.2 million.

In the opening 45 minutes of the game against Benfica Cantona treated the crowd to some nice touches and was the only player who seemed to take the game seriously. In the 12th minute he sent McClair clear, but the Scot shot narrowly wide and with one deft touch in the 43rd minute set up Kanchelskis, but the Ukrainian was soon surrounded by five defenders and his shot was blocked. The United winger also had a couple of opportunities to get the ball over towards the Frenchman in a good position at the far post, but failed to notice him, much to the new signing's annoyance.

Yuran missed an opportunity for Benfica early on and a couple of efforts from Mostovoi kept Schmeichel on his toes.

After the break Parker's cross was just inches too high for Cantona to connect with, while at the opposite end Pacheco's shot beat Schmeichel but skimmed the angle of the post and crossbar.

With nine minutes remaining, the debutant's entrance into United folklore was dimmed somewhat when Costa scored the only goal of the game, after Kennedy's shot had been blocked by Schmeichel. Aguas hit the bar for the home side moments later.

Pre-match, the crowd were treated to a Portugal veterans' side, led by Eusebio, who defeated an international select 4–2, with the likes of Bobby Charlton, Mario Kempes, Johnny Rep and Franz Beckenbauer on view.

1 December 1992 **Benfica at the Stadium of Light, Lisbon.**

Attendance: 40,000.

Lost: 1–0.

Team: Schmeichel, Parker, Irwin, Bruce, Phelan, Pallister, Robson, Kanchelskis, McClair, Cantona, Giggs.

Substitutes: Hughes for Giggs, Martin for Robson, Wallace for Kanchelskis, McKee for McClair.

Having claimed their first League Championship for 26 long years, there were still three fixtures to fulfil in six days before the players could revel in their triumph.

The first came on 12 May when United travelled to Belfast to face Aston Villa, the team who had pushed them all the way in the title race only to falter at the final hurdle. The game was a memorial match for Melvyn Brown, the former Irish League secretary, who had also scouted for United. Sadly, safety regulations restricted the crowd to 22,000, but with track advertising, sponsorship and programme sales, a figure of around £200,000 was expected to be raised from the game.

With the squads for next season's European competition being limited to three foreign players, Alex Ferguson experimented slightly, playing Lee Sharpe at full-back in place of Denis Irwin, with the youngster showed his capacity to play in both a defensive and an attacking role.

United took the lead in the 32nd minute through Mike Phelan, who steered a short Ince pass beyond Bosnich. The former Reds reserve 'keeper was fortunate not to concede a further two goals, as Dublin hit both posts with one effort and was denied by the woodwork again on another occasion.

Villa equalised in the 78th minute, when Yorke scored from close range.

Ticket for the match versus Aston Villa, 12 May 1993.

12 May 1993	**Aston Villa at Windsor Park, Belfast.**

Attendance: 22,000.

Drew: 1–1.

Scorer: Phelan.

Team: Sealey, Parker, Sharpe, Carey, Phelan, Pallister, Robson, Ince, McClair, Dublin, Giggs.

Substitute: McKee for McClair.

Two days later United travelled to Ashton Gate to face Bristol City in a testimonial match for City legend Chris Garland, who was suffering from Parkinson's Disease.

United's visit raised over £100,000 for the player and they were quick to make an impression on the game, as Hughes controlled a McKee pass before firing past Welch from the edge of the area in the 10th minute.

Ten minutes later it was 2–0, as Dublin headed a rebound into the path of Hughes for him to net his second. Blackmore made it 3–0 on the half-hour, with a 25-yard drive.

Despite everything pointing towards an United victory, an influx of City youngsters at half-time revitalised the home side, with Harrison, and then Wyatt, pulling two goals back in the first 20 minutes of the second half. Rosenoir headed home the equaliser in the closing minutes.

Ticket for the match versus Bristol City, 14 May 1993.

14 May 1993	**Bristol City at Ashton Gate.**

Attendance: 21,716.

Drew: 3–3.

Scorers: Hughes 2, Blackmore.

Team: Schmeichel, Phelan, Blackmore, Bruce, Carey, McKee, Robson, Ince, Dublin, Hughes, Sharpe.

Substitute: McClair for McKee.

The final fixture of the 1992–93 campaign took United to Arsenal for yet another testimonial. There was, of course, little love lost between the two sides back in the early 1990s, but with United's pulling power they were welcome visitors for any club or individual when there was money to be raised.

The testimonial marked 20 years of service for central-defender David O'Leary, with his final Highbury appearance producing an eight-goal evening of entertainment. The home side played their FA Cup 11, despite a replay looming a few days later, but there was never any fear of serious injury, as there was practically no tackling by either side.

Substitute United goalkeeper Les Sealey kept the crowd amused with a 'virtuoso performance', while Peter Schmeichel, having been replaced by the Londoner, soon took up an outfield role and would surely have scored near the end had Giggs only passed to him.

The star of the show, however, was United's Steve Bruce, who not only had one of the linesmen take United's throw-ins, but also ran to the dugout when Robson missed an open goal and held up the number seven to have his co-captain substituted.

When play was kept serious, Dublin and Sharpe both netted twice for United, but Arsenal, trailing 4–3 following goals from Campbell, Merson and Dickov, drew level 10 minutes from time when O'Leary fittingly scored the equaliser.

---

17 May 1993   **Arsenal at Highbury.**

Attendance: 22,117.

Drew: 4–4.

Scorers: Dublin 2, Sharpe 2.

Team: Schmeichel, Parker, Blackmore, Bruce, Sharpe, Pallister, Robson, Phelan, Dublin, Hughes, Giggs.

Substitutes: Carey for Pallister, Sealey for Schmeichel, Schmeichel for Dublin.

Rarely have United begun a new season by playing the club they faced in the final game of the previous campaign, but it happened in 1993, when they began their preparations for the defence of their title against Arsenal. This game happened thousands of miles from the usual venues of Highbury, Old Trafford or Wembley, instead taking place in Johannesburg, South Africa.

United, complete with new signing Roy Keane, arrived at Jan Smuts airport to a rousing reception, with the local supporters' club out in force. The following day saw the team travel to Tembisa, a settlement described in the *Manchester Evening News* as made up of 'matchbox houses and corrugated iron huts', where they conducted a coaching clinic.

With half an hour gone in the game against Arsenal, United were 2–0 behind, with Alex Ferguson on the touchline shaking his head in disbelief. Not at his players' performance, but at the decisions which led to his side losing two goals, both of which were penalties.

Ten minutes into the game Bruce seemed to stumble in front of Campbell, an offence which, at worst, should have brought an indirect free-kick. The referee, however, thought differently and pointed to the spot. Ian Wright sent the kick wide of Schmeichel's right hand and into the net.

After 27 minutes Bruce ducked to allow a Merson centre to reach his 'keeper (if you read the *Mail*) or the United defender mistimed his jump for the Merson centre, while also being pushed by Campbell, only for the ball to hit the back of his arm as he looked the other way (if you read the *Times*). Either way, the referee judged it as handball and pointed to the spot. Wright once again stepped forward and this time sent the United 'keeper the wrong way.

There was more drama to come, with referee Sweeney once again in the thick of things. In the 69th minute Irwin saw a shot handled inside the Arsenal area by Lee Dixon, but the match official simply waved play on. Irwin ran towards the referee, manhandling him, but as Arsenal cleared the ball upfield play was stopped and the referee sent off Bryan Robson for 'foul and abusive language'.

The decision did not only upset the United players, but also the vast number of United supporters in the crowd, with some of them coming on to the pitch and attempting to present the referee with a red shirt to match the Arsenal colours. After the match Sweeney said: 'There was no problem with the penalties, if I had to do it again, I would do so without hesitation'.

This was actually the second United penalty claim turned down by the referee. The first came as early as the fourth minute, when Hughes nutmegged Linighan just outside the area and, as he moved forward, was bundled to the ground by Adams.

Brian McClair also found his way into the official's notebook, again for dissent, while Keane had an undistinguished debut, but he showed a glimpse of what was in store when he had an ugly tussle with Martin Keown.

---

25 July 1993 | **Arsenal at Ellis Park, Johannesburg.**

Attendance: 65,000.

Lost: 2—0.

Team: Schmeichel, Parker, Irwin, Bruce, Phelan, Keane, Robson, Blackmore, McClair, Hughes, Giggs.

Substitute: Ferguson for Blackmore.

In the second match of the United Bank International Soccer Festival against local champions Kaizer Chiefs, United did not play at the same pace as they had against Arsenal and might even have gone a goal down as early as the seventh minute, when Mthimkulu managed to push the ball through to Khuse, who sliced the ball narrowly wide of the goal with only Schmeichel to beat.

However, it was United who opened the scoring in the 12th minute of the second half, when McClair laid the ball back to Robson just outside the penalty area and the captain's first-time volley deflected off the leg of Dublin and past goalkeeper Eshele.

The goal lifted United a little, but the Chiefs bravely held out, before midfielder Moshoeu worked his way into the area, his low cross being finished off by substitute Leseyane.

---

29 July 1993 | **Kaizer Chiefs at Fnb Stadium, Johannesburg.**

Attendance: 65,000.

Drew: 1—1.

Scorer: Dublin.

Team: Schmeichel, Parker, Irwin, Bruce, Phelan, Keane, Robson, Blackmore, McClair, Dublin, Ferguson.

Substitutes: Beckham for Blackmore, O'Kane for McClair

The Old Trafford curtain came up for the new season with the visit of old rivals Benfica, in a follow-up fixture to that played in Portugal during the previous campaign. The game also marked the 25th anniversary of the two clubs meeting in the 1968 European Cup Final at Wembley.

Ticket for the match versus Benfica,
31 July 1993.

Prior to kick-off, the United heroes of that memorable evening under the twin towers, with the exception of Law, Best and Benfica's Eusebio, were paraded out on the pitch. This appeared to bring the biggest cheer of the afternoon from the rather disappointing crowd of just over 20,000.

Without Cantona, Ince and Sharpe, United always looked second best and even the visitors shuffling their team around failed to allow United to get a toe-hold in the action.

Perhaps the 18-hour flight from South Africa had something to do with it, but if Schmeichel had not been in top form, the scoreline would have been dramatically different.

The opening 45 minutes failed to produce any goals, although just on half-time Keane, following a 50-yard run, drove a low shot just past the post. It was to prove a costly miss, as 11 minutes into the second half Benfica took the lead, substitute Mostovoi sending a 20-yard drive past a helpless Schmeichel.

Keane should have done better in the 71st minute when he headed an easy chance over the bar from a Parker cross, but he was not the only culprit who squandered an opportunity, as Ryan Giggs put a shot wide with four minutes to go. Two minutes later Dublin saw a superb effort hit the underside of the bar. The ball bounced invitingly to Giggs, but Silvino in the Benfica goal pounced on it.

For Benfica's visit, United turned out in their away kit of yellow and green for a game at home.

31 July 1993	Benfica at Old Trafford.

Attendance: 21,859.

Lost: 1–0.

Team: Schmeichel, Parker, Irwin, Bruce, Kanchelskis, Pallister, Robson, Keane, McClair, Hughes, Giggs.

Substitutes: Thornley for Robson, Ferguson for Hughes, Dublin for McClair.

Yellow and green colours were again predominant three days later, as Celtic were in Manchester for a fixture that had been arranged to mark the official opening of the new-look Stretford End. The Manchester police lifted a ban on match-day ticket sales, even though the visitors had sold their 7,000 allocation and were likely to bring more than that. As it was, over 31,000 were in Old Trafford to see United win, courtesy of a freak goal in the eighth minute, scored by Andrei Kanchelskis. His 25-yard drive was hopeful more than anything else, but it took a deflection off Wdowcyk and the ball moved slowly goalwards, bounced off the post and went over the line.

Following an Ince foul on Nicholas, Wdowcyk had visions of redemption seven minutes later when his free-kick beat Schmeichel, but it clipped the post and bounced to safety, and Celtic began to take the game to United.

Ince should have done better following a Giggs–Kanchelskis move. Pallister did well to thwart Nicholas before Kanchelskis, always looking to be involved, fired wide from a McClair pass.

Schmeichel was called into action when he managed to claw away a rising drive from McStay in the 38th minute, but was fortunate 60 seconds later when a Nicholas header bounced off the bar and into his hands.

Eight minutes after the restart Nicholas, the main Celtic threat, missed an easy opportunity to equalise, as did Creaney in the 62nd minute when his shot went through Schmeichel's legs but wide of the post.

Despite the seemingly never-ending goalmouth action, there was no further scoring and United held on to their slender advantage.

United again played this home game in their away kit. This time, however, it was all black.

3 August 1993	Celtic at Old Trafford.

Attendance: 31,727.

Won: 1–0.

Scorer: Kanchelskis.

Team: Schmeichel, Parker, Blackmore, Bruce, Kanchelskis, Pallister, Robson, Ince, McClair, Hughes, Giggs.

Substitutes: Keane for Robson, Sharpe for Giggs, Irwin for Blackmore.

Having gained revenge in the FA Charity Shield against Arsenal with a 5–4 penalty shoot-out win, United travelled to Denmark, where they rounded off their pre-season workout with a 2–0 victory against Brondby.

Ryan Giggs practically ran the show, as Alex Ferguson experimented with a three-man midfield of Robson, Ince and Keane, although it was not until Hughes came on for the injured Cantona in the 35th minute that United began to settle.

Giggs hit the woodwork shortly after the interval, but Brondby could quite easily have had a penalty when Parker brought down Bjur. Soon afterwards, Schmeichel saved from Risager as the game began to move from end to end. It was not, however, until five minutes from the end that the first goal materialised.

Ince found his way into the Brondby area, but was brought down by the 'keeper as he tried to force his way past; Bruce scored from the spot. With the clock ticking away, Keane moved in from the left before pulling the ball back to Hughes, who made no mistake from just inside the area to give United a 2–0 victory.

10 August 1993	Brondby at Copenhagen, Denmark.

Attendance: 11,372.

Won: 2–0.

Scorers: Bruce (pen.), Hughes.

Team: Schmeichel, Parker, Irwin, Bruce, Keane, Pallister, Robson, Ince, McClair, Cantona, Giggs.

Substitute: Hughes for Cantona.

The programme for the match versus Brondby, 10 August 1993.

Revenge was sweet for the Lou Macari-managed Celtic as they returned to Old Trafford for the Mark Hughes testimonial. Such was the attraction of the game, with over 42,000 inside the ground, that there were hundreds more outside, still queuing to get in when the half-time whistle blew.

Giggs created the first goal threat in the third minute, setting up Lee Sharpe, but Muggleton turned the shot round the post, with the Welshman himself coming close with a drive which went just over.

Donnelly then found himself one-on-one with the daunting figure of Schmeichel, following a cross from Byrne, but the 'keeper managed to block the shot. The Dane was not so fortunate two minutes after the interval when Donnelly, having dispossessed Keane, outwitted Bruce before firing the opener.

Within four minutes though, United were level, Phil Neville sending a deep cross into the Celtic area, which Dublin headed home.

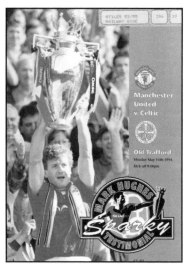

The programme for the match versus Celtic, 16 May 1994.

The game swung back in Celtic's favour in the 54th minute when their guest forward, Chic Charnley, lobbed the ball in front of Donnelly, who ran on to beat substitute 'keeper Walsh with ease. The Celtic forward almost claimed a third 20 minutes from time, but his shot hit the bar.

Victory, however, was secured in the 74th minute when Charnley, doing his prospects of a contract no harm, set up the chance for Falconer to notch up a third, with chants of 'Fergie, Fergie, what's the score?' soon to echo around the ground.

16 May 1994	Celtic at Old Trafford.

Attendance: 42,709.

Lost: 3–1.

Scorer: Dublin.

Team: Schmeichel, P. Neville, Blackmore, Bruce, Keane, Butt, McClair, Sharpe, Dublin, Hughes, Giggs.

Substitutes: Walsh for Schmeichel, Sealey for Walsh, Cantona for Dublin, Phelan for Butt, Whitworth for Bruce.

Having successfully defended their Premier League title, as well as winning the FA Cup, United began their quest to make it a hat-trick of Championship successes by easing their way back into action against Dundalk, in a testimonial match for Gino Lawless. If, however, United were to be judged on their performance in the opening 20 minutes or so, there would certainly not be any celebrations in Manchester in 10 months time.

Much to Alex Ferguson's annoyance, poor defensive play allowed the home side to take a 2–0 lead. Loughlin opened the scoring after only a quarter of an hour, chipping the ball confidently over Peter Schmeichel after Patmore had headed the ball forward. Three minutes later the provider became the goalscorer as he steered the ball past the United 'keeper.

On the half-hour United pulled a goal back, Mark Hughes getting on to the end of a Kanchelskis cross.

United sprang into action immediately after the break and within a minute Ince had been brought down in the area by Lawlor. Cantona for once failed from the spot, Van Boxtel saving his kick. This, however, was only a brief reprieve for the Irish National League side, as within four minutes Ince took a reverse pass from Sharpe before scoring with a fierce drive.

It was only a matter of time before United went in front. Hughes notched up the third in the 63rd minute from a Cantona pass, before setting up Giggs, who shot under the 'keeper for a fourth five minutes later.

As a footnote to this game, the *Manchester United Official Yearbook* gives the attendance as 4,500. However, the *Irish Sunday World* report mentions that United were cheered on by 'a 12,000 strong crowd', while the *Sunday Press* correspondent wrote: 'A disappointing 7,000 watched the game.'

30 July 1994	Dundalk at Oriel Park, Dundalk.

Attendance: 4,500.

Won: 4–2.

Scorers: Hughes 2, Ince, Giggs.

Team: Schmeichel, Parker, Kanchelskis, Bruce, Sharpe, Pallister, Cantona, Ince, McClair, Hughes, Giggs.

Substitutes: May for Bruce, Dublin for Giggs, Casper for Kanchelskis.

The second game of the three-match mini-tour saw United treat the Dublin public to some first-class entertainment as they defeated a gallant Shelbourne side 3–0. However, despite the visitors' obvious supremacy, they were kept at bay until four minutes before the interval. Two goals in that four-minute spell were enough to ensure victory.

The first came when Giggs, who kept the crowd on their toes throughout the match, swung over a corner into a crowded penalty area for Ince to head home. Two minutes later Cantona scored from the spot, after Broughan was adjudged to have fouled Hughes inside the area, although many felt it was a harsh decision.

Both Hughes and McClair hit the bar before United notched up their third eight minutes from time. Ince swept the ball to Cantona, who channeled a pinpoint cross into the area for McClair to send a diving header into the roof of the net.

Shelbourne, although well beaten, did have a couple of opportunities in the closing stages. Rutherford shot weakly at Schmeichel, while substitute Howlett chipped the ball narrowly over.

---

1 August 1994   **Shelbourne at Tolka Park, Dublin.**

Attendance: 12,500.

Won: 3–0.

Scorers: Cantona, Ince, McClair.

Team: Schmeichel, May, Dublin, Bruce, Sharpe, Pallister, Cantona, Ince, McClair, Hughes, Giggs.

Substitutes: Casper for Bruce, Gillespie for Dublin.

Back on home soil, United played what used to be a regular date on the First Division calendar, a game against Wolverhampton Wanderers at Molineux. The match was arranged as part of the deal that took Darren Ferguson to the Midlands.

United's 2–1 victory was, not for the first time, mainly due to the goalkeeping heroics of Peter Schmeichel, who made a string of notable saves, but he could do little to prevent Steve Bull from putting the home side in front after nine minutes. He out-jumped Steve Bruce before running round the static defender and lifting the ball over the advancing 'keeper's head.

Hughes and Cantona both scorned good chances to equalise towards the end of the first half, and it was not until eight minutes after the break that they eventually drew level. Giggs floated a corner into the Wolves area and Ince dived forward to head past Stowell.

United continued to press forward and gained the advantage in the 63rd minute after Giggs broke down the left, before cutting inside and firing a low shot towards the Wolves goal. Stowell managed to stop the ball, but failed to hold it and as it bounced out, the oncoming Blades, in an effort to clear, diverted the ball into his own net.

The action soon reverted to the opposite end, with Schmeichel preventing Froggatt, Thomas and Ken from scoring, but in the final four minutes, with Wolves tiring, it was their substitute 'keeper Jones who kept the scoreline down, saving brilliantly from Cantona, Dublin and Butt.

| **3 August 1994** | **Wolverhampton Wanderers at Molineux.** |

Attendance: 28,500.

Won: 2–1.

Scorers: Ince, opp. own-goal.

Team: Schmeichel, May, Sharpe, Bruce, Gillespie, Pallister, Cantona, Ince, McClair, Hughes, Giggs.

Substitutes: Butt for Gillespie, Dublin for Hughes, Davies for Bruce, Casper for Sharpe.

Alex Ferguson returned to the familiar corridors of Ibrox for a four-club tournament which saw the Reds face Newcastle United in their opening fixture, with the hosts entertaining Italian side Sampdoria.

Once again it was Peter Schmeichel who grabbed the headlines, making a handful of super saves, the first from Fox after only five minutes. Within two minutes it could well have been United who were in front, but Cantona chipped the ball against the crossbar after Ince had headed Srnicek's attempted clearance back into the area.

Newcastle went in front after 19 minutes when Fox took the ball forward before firing it past Schmeichel, but it was a lead that they would only hold until a minute before the interval. Srnicek failed to get his hand to a David May cross, which Cantona easily headed home as the 'keeper pounded the turf in disgust.

Both sides had opportunities to snatch the game within the normal 90 minutes. Peacock, who was booked along with Hughes, saw a header saved by Schmeichel, while Ince hit the bar with a venomous effort. An equally powerful shot by Beardsley left Bruce lying stunned on the ground.

The match was still level when the final whistle blew, so it was down to penalties to decide who would face Sampdoria in the Final. Bruce, Ince, Giggs, Sharpe and Davies all converted their kicks, but McClair, much to the delight of the home support, Cantona and Gillespie all missed, allowing recent Newcastle signing Hottiger to score the decider.

| **5 August 1994** | **Newcastle United at Ibrox Park, Glasgow.** |

Attendance: 27,282.

Drew: 1–1. (**Lost:** 5–6 on penalties).

Scorers: Cantona. (Bruce, Ince, Giggs, Sharpe, Davies).

Team: Schmeichel, May, Sharpe, Bruce, Gillespie, Pallister, Cantona, Ince, McClair, Hughes, Giggs.

Substitute: Davies for Hughes.

Fielding something of an under-strength side, the headlines following a 'Battle of Britain' clash against Rangers proclaimed: 'Eric Sees Red Again', 'Cantona Off In Ibrox Bust-up', 'Cantona's Off In Rage' and 'Ferguson Blasts Ibrox Fans'. Few column inches were given over to the actual match action.

With Rangers also fielding a weakened 11 due to their forthcoming European Cup qualifying match four days later, the game was never going to have much of a sparkle, but it was not until after David May had diverted Gordon Durie's low cross past Schmeichel in the 42nd minute, for what was to be the only goal of the game, that things began to liven up. Prior to this, United had managed only one shot on goal when Beckham, left in the clear, hit the ball feebly at Maxwell.

Determined to try and obtain something from the game, Ferguson introduced Giggs and Cantona into the fray and suddenly Rangers had a game on their hands.

Maxwell did well to stop a Butt volley from 10 yards, while twice Hughes failed to get the necessary touch in front of goal and Butt, again pushing forward from midfield, looked to have been obstructed by Moore inside the box. The referee thought otherwise.

Ten minutes from time, the headline writers got their copy. Cantona fouled Steven Pressley and was given a yellow card for ignoring the referee. Two minutes later the red mist came down, as the Frenchman lunged two-footed at the same player. Although he failed to actually make contact, the referee had no hesitation in sending him off. This left United to play out the game with only nine men, as Pallister had limped off injured and both substitutes had been used.

Alex Ferguson, while aggrieved at Cantona's sending off, felt that his player should have received more protection from referee Waddell, with Pressley's challenges from behind the reason for the Frenchman's reactions. The United manager also criticised the Ibrox crowd for the 'loutish hatred' that was shown towards his team in his native city.

6 August 1994	**Rangers at Ibrox Park, Glasgow.**

Attendance: 29,500.

Lost: 1—0.

Team: Schmeichel, Casper, Sharpe, Butt, May, Pallister, Beckham, Ince, Dublin, Hughes, Davies.

Substitutes: Cantona for Dublin, Giggs for Beckham.

Not for the first time a transfer between United and another club had the added clause of a friendly fixture to be arranged between the two, and for most clubs it was a welcome source of additional income. The latest benefactors were Cambridge United, who had already received £1 million from the sale of Dion Dublin and who stood to make a further few thousand from United's visit.

The Second Division side almost managed more than a boost to their bank balance, as they took the game to United and were only 12 minutes away from a notable victory, only to be denied by Lee Sharpe's late goal.

Slow in its initial build-up, the game progressed to a whirlwind of goalmouth activity as United sought to rectify Carlo Corazzin's 48th-minute goal. He had the opportunity to wrap things up 11 minutes from time, but passed instead of having a shot when through on goal.

Kanchelskis was a constant threat and it was one of his runs into the area that brought the penalty, awarded after he was shouldered of the ball. Sharpe converted the spot-kick after the 'keeper had blocked his initial shot.

After this United pushed forward, with Butt and Tomlinson in the thick of the action and Dublin coming close in the dying minutes, but the game was to end in a moral victory for Cambridge.

9 August 1994	**Cambridge United at Abbey Stadium.**

Attendance: 30,186.

Drew: 1—1.

Scorer: Sharpe (pen.).

Team: Schmeichel, G. Neville, P. Neville, Casper, May, Sharpe, Cantona, Dublin, McClair, Hughes, Kanchelskis.

Substitutes: Butt for McClair, Davies for Hughes, Scholes for Davies.

Ayresome Park was the venue for the testimonial of former United utility man Clayton Blackmore.

Blackmore, who had joined United as a Welsh international schoolboy in 1978 and holds the unique distinction of wearing every United shirt from number 2 to 11, plus 12 and 14, joined the North East club on a free transfer in May 1994. A near 20,000 crowd gave Clayton a pay-day of around £150,000 and United treated the crowd to an exhibition of football which earned them a 3–0 victory.

It was perhaps fitting that it was a fellow Welshman, Mark Hughes, who scored two of United's goals, both of which were neatly weighted chips over the head of 'keeper Miller. The first, in the 25th minute, came from a Phil Neville cross and was nudged on by Butt.

Middlesbrough tested United's stand-in 'keeper Pilkington, who produced fine saves from Mustoe and Wright. In the final 15 minutes United increased their lead with two more goals. A McClair cross was headed past Miller by Sharpe, before Hughes again chipped the ball over Miller from the corner of the penalty area.

---

16 August 1994   **Middlesbrough at Ayresome Park.**

Attendance: 19,658.

Won: 3–0.

Scorers: Hughes 2, Sharpe.

Team: Pilkington, Parker, P. Neville, Butt, May, Pallister, Kanchelskis, Scholes, McClair, Hughes, Sharpe.

Substitutes: Gillespie for Kanchelskis, Beckham for Butt.

On 31 July United played a friendly against a Selangor Select XI after they had travelled halfway around the world to Kuala Lumpur. Brian Kidd was in charge of the squad, due to the absence of manager Alex Ferguson with an ear infection.

Against the Malaysian champions, United got their pre-season off to an excellent start with a comfortable 4–1 victory. Steve Bruce opened the goal account for the new campaign three minutes after the interval and Nicky Butt added a second four minutes later, racing clear before slipping the ball past the oncoming goalkeeper.

Pallister made it three in the 64th minute with an identical header to that of his defensive partner Bruce. Then, to the delight of the crowd, Lee Sharpe, the number one visiting attraction due to Cantona and Giggs being back in Manchester, ran down the left wing before scoring a spectacular fourth in the 64th minute.

An equally loud cheer, 12 minutes later, greeted a consolation goal for the home side, scored by Ollerenshaw.

---

31 July 1995   **Selangor at Shah Alam Stadium, Kuala Lumpur.**

Attendance: 50,000.

Won: 4–1.

Scorers: Bruce, Butt, Pallister, Sharpe.

Team: Schmeichel, Parker, Irwin, Bruce, G.Neville, Pallister, Scholes, Butt, McClair, Keane, Sharpe.

Substitutes: Beckham for Scholes, P. Neville for Parker.

In the 'second leg' of the Glamoir Invitational Cup United once again got the better of the Selangor side, although on this occasion they only managed to score two goals, despite enjoying more of the play. There was a much smaller crowd than a couple of days previously, with the 20,000 spectators failing to make much of an impression in the vast 80,000-capacity stadium.

Steve Bruce once again opened the scoring for United, throwing himself at Denis Irwin's free-kick, despite a defender's raised boot, to head past the home side's Iraqi 'keeper. Paul Scholes added a second in the 29th minute.

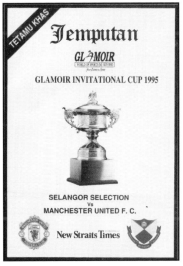

Menu from a dinner for the match versus Selangor, 2 August 1995.

---

2 August 1995   **Selangor at Shah Alam Stadium, Kuala Lumpur.**

Attendance: 20,000.

Won: 2–0.

Scorers: Bruce, Scholes.

Team: Schmeichel, Parker, Irwin, Bruce, P. Neville, Pallister, Scholes, Butt, McClair, Keane, Thornley.

Substitutes: Pilkington for Schmeichel, Cooke for Scholes, G. Neville for Parker, Beckham for Parker.

Back on home soil, the pre-season preparations continued with a trip to face Birmingham City, but it was to be a disappointing evening for United as they failed to find the net, although this was mainly due to the heroics of Birmingham 'keeper Ian Bennett. In the 17th minute he blocked a shot from Scholes as the United player ran onto a McClair pass and Butt scooped the rebound over the bar. A point-blank stop from Roy Keane in the 54th minute was the pick of the bunch.

United went a goal behind in the 44th minute when substitute Chris Whyte, unmarked at the far post and having been on the field for only six minutes, headed home a quickly taken free-kick from Hunt.

Strangely, United had adopted a five-man defence, but the experiment was soon abandoned when they went behind, with Parker going off in favour of the promising Ben Thornley. However, the change failed to alter the course of the game, with the home side managing to hold onto their solitary goal advantage.

---

7 August 1995   **Birmingham City at St Andrews.**

Attendance: 13,330.

Lost: 1–0.

Team: Schmeichel, Parker, Irwin, Bruce, Sharpe, Pallister, Butt, Keane, McClair, Scholes, G. Neville.

Substitute: Thornley for Parker.

The friendly against Bradford City at Valley Parade was never going to be a high-profile affair, but it was completely overshadowed by the news that Eric Cantona had announced that he wanted to leave the club. Much to the relief of all concerned, Cantona was persuaded to remain at Old Trafford, for the time being at least.

At Bradford, the United support made their feelings relating to Cantona known by unfurling a giant flag which announced that ''66 was a great year for English football, Eric was born', but they had to endure something of a drab 90 minutes.

Bradford's Ian Ormondroyd gave the visitors a scare in the sixth minute, when he should have scored with a gaping goalmouth at his mercy, and it was a miss which was to prove costly as the evening wore on.

With Keane and Butt running the show from midfield, United were always in command, although they had only one goal to show for their superiority at the end of the night.

That solitary goal came in the 38th minute, when Butt crossed the ball to Bruce with the defender laying the ball off to Keane, who picked his spot before shooting past Ward in the Bradford goal.

Less than 60 seconds later Keane became needlessly involved in a tussle with Younds, following a rather robust challenge from behind by the Bradford midfielder. The referee stepped in and booked both players, although Nicky Butt continued the 'feud' with Younds before the latter was substituted by manager Lenny Lawrence.

Keane cleared off the line from Mitchell early in the second half, but neither side showed much of an inclination for turning the game into a goal-scoring spectacle and the game faded as the minutes ticked away.

---

9 August 1995   **Bradford City at Pulse Valley Parade.**

Attendance: 13,457.

Won: 1–0.

Scorer: Keane.

Team: Schmeichel, Parker, Irwin, Bruce, Sharpe, G. Neville, Butt, Keane, McClair, Tomlinson, Beckham.

Substitutes: Cooke for Beckham, Scholes for Tomlinson.

The next friendly was in Dublin against Shelbourne, a team that features regularly among the list of friendly fixtures. Ferguson was keen to find a solution to the problems surrounding his team selection for the season ahead. Having lost Kanchelskis, and with the possibility of losing Cantona, the manager had much to think about, more so perhaps following the 2–2 draw against the Irish National League side.

A replacement for the Ukrainian was the immediate priority, with both Young Player of the Year Terry Cooke and substitute David Beckham showing up well as United fought back from going behind twice.

With 12 minutes gone Arkins opened the scoring, but Butt levelled. Geoghegan dispossessed Gary Neville before restoring the Irishmen's lead in the 52nd minute, but Beckham did his chances of a first-team place the world of good when he controlled a through ball from Keane in the 66th minute, before rounding the 'keeper for the equaliser.

---

11 August 1995   **Shelbourne at Tolka Park, Dublin.**

Attendance: 12,500.

Drew: 2–2.

Scorers: Butt, Beckham.

Team: Pilkington, Parker, Irwin, Bruce, Sharpe, G. Neville, Butt, Keane, McClair, Scholes, Cooke.

Substitutes: P. Neville for Bruce, Beckham for Butt, Thornley for Cooke, O'Kane for Irwin.

United have graced most, if not all, of the world's greatest stadia, but every now and again they venture to some of the more down-to-earth venues around the country. One such ground was the quaintly named Bayview, home of Scottish Second Division side East Fife, for the testimonial of Jimmy Bonthrone, the club's commercial manager and an old friend of United manager Alex Ferguson. The Fifers manager Steve Archibald was another individual who was familiar to the United manager, having played for him at Aberdeen.

Although the Fifers had played their opening League fixture only 24 hours previously, there was no way that they were going to pass up the opportunity of playing against Manchester United.

Despite the United line up having something of a young look about it, the 5,385 crowd were still entertained by an enjoyable afternoon's football, with David Beckham once again showing his worth with two goals in the 4–0 victory.

The youngster blasted home the first on the hour from a Sharpe pass and Brian McClair celebrated his return to his native country with a second five minutes before the interval. Lee Sharpe put United further in front in the 58th minute, as the visitors were now cruising.

Balmain almost pulled a goal back, but Pilkington managed to stick a foot out and divert it past, although the novice 'keeper was nowhere near an Allan shot-cum-cross which skimmed the top of the crossbar.

The best, however, was kept until last, with Beckham again on the score sheet after firing home a blistering 30-yard rocket for United's fourth in the 72nd minute.

---

13 August 1995   **East Fife at Bayview.**

Attendance: 5,385.

Won: 4–0.

Scorers: Beckham 2, McClair, Sharpe.

Team: Pilkington, Parker, Irwin, Bruce, Sharpe, G. Neville, Beckham, Keane, McClair, Scholes, Thornley.

Substitutes: Cooke for Scholes, P. Neville for Irwin, O'Kane for Parker.

The pre-season fixtures were wound up much nearer to home, with a short journey north of Manchester to face Oldham Athletic, a game arranged as part of the Boundary Park side's centenary celebrations.

The game itself was something of a dull affair, with United never really stretching themselves, especially after they took the lead in the 26th minute through Lee Sharpe. The winger, running on to a Brian McClair pass, hit the ball past Gerrard without breaking stride.

Nine minutes into the second half Jobson had the unfortunate experience of putting through an own-goal, but the Oldham substitute defender could do little about it, with Hallworth's clearance rebounding off his legs and into the net.

The home side had the odd scoring opportunities, with Banger perhaps missing the best of those prior to Sharpe's opener. The Oldham forward shot into the side netting after getting the better of Gary Pallister. But they were never going to pose a threat to a United side who, despite the introduction of a handful of young substitutes, never looked liked losing.

---

15 August 1995   **Oldham Athletic at Boundary Park.**

Attendance: 8,766.

Won: 2–0.

Scorers: Sharpe, opp. own-goal.

Team: Pilkington, P. Neville, Irwin, G.Neville, Sharpe, Pallister, Butt, Keane, McClair, Davies, Beckham.

Substitutes: Tomlinson for Butt, McGibbon for Davies, Thornley for Sharpe, O'Kane for Irwin.

Having been held to a 1–1 draw at home by Chelsea a few days earlier, United stumbled to a 2–1 defeat against an International Select XI in Belfast. United's visit to the province was on behalf of Co-operation North, a non-political, non-sectarian organisation, set up to promote mutual understanding and respect in the communities in the trouble-torn country, with their visit raising more than £160,000, thanks to their vast following across the water.

Despite the array of talent on show, there was no edge to the game, with no hard tackles, little aggression and a minimum of actual physical contact.

The 'Select' opened the scoring in the 37th minute through Leeds striker Masinga, but Paul Scholes equalised for United nine minutes after half-time, popping home a Beckham pass.

Scholes, along with Cantona, came close to giving United the lead, but a minute from the end Jimmy Quinn scored what proved to be the winner from 12 yards.

---

5 December 1995 | **International Select at Windsor Park, Belfast.**

Attendance: 22,000.

Lost: 2–1.

Scorer: Scholes.

Team: Pilkington, Parker, Irwin, G. Neville, Sharpe, May, Cantona, Beckham, McClair, Cole, Scholes.

Substitutes: McGibbon for Irwin, Davies for G. Neville, Appleton for McClair, Cooke for Beckham, Mulryne for Sharpe.

Seven days later United were involved in what was certainly a more physical and emotional encounter when they took part in the Paul McStay testimonial match against Celtic in Glasgow. The Scotland midfielder earned around £400,000 from the fixture, although he had not forgotten his roots, sending around 600 tickets for the game to his old school in Hamilton.

On a freezing cold night a Celtic Park full house saluted McStay, with the volume of noise inspiring the home side to a notable victory over their old rivals from south of the border.

Visibility was poor, but the supporters could see enough to send them home happy and they were almost treated to the perfect start when, after eight minutes, McStay burst forward to try his luck from 25 yards. However, Pilkington was equal to the shot and pulled off a fine save.

Five minutes later, the noise around the ground rose as Celtic took the lead. Donnelly moved forward from the halfway line and released Walker on the left side of the area and his pass across the face of the United goal was diverted into the net by Van Hooijdonk.

United should have drawn level in the 19th minute when MacKay gave the ball away to Scholes, who quickly found Cole, but the United striker was adjudged to be in an offside position as he slipped the ball into the net. On another occasion he shot at least 15 yards wide of the goal, much to the amusement of the crowd.

Kerr saved well from Sharpe, pushing the winger's shot round the post for a corner in the build-up to United's goal. From the resulting corner Bruce knocked the ball down to Scholes, who then fired a low right-footed shot through the crowded goalmouth and into the net.

As United began to take control, Cole came close to giving them the lead in the 25th minute, but his shot was blocked by a defender. After the break, however, it was Celtic who grabbed the initiative and took the lead when Van Hooydonk scored with a spectacular effort from 22 yards out.

Five minutes from time Celtic added a third, substitute Hay applying the finishing touch.

---

12 December 1995　　　　　**Celtic at Celtic Park, Glasgow.**

Attendance: 37,306.

Lost: 3–1.

Scorer: Scholes.

Team: Pilkington, Parker, O'Kane, Bruce, P. Neville, May, Davies, Sharpe, McClair, Cole, Scholes.

Substitutes: Tomlinson for Cole, Appleton for O'Kane.

Amid frantic transfer activity in the summer of 1996, which saw Johnsen, Cruyff, Van der Gouw and Poborsky all arrive at Old Trafford, United's pre-season build-up began in Ireland against Irish League champions Portadown. It was an ideal opening fixture for Alex Ferguson's squad, with a chance to notch up a few goals for a quick confidence boost.

Any cobwebs that had gathered during the summer lay-off were soon blown away as, despite being without eight first-team players, United still managed to brush the opposition aside, with Paul Scholes causing most of the problems.

United took the lead in the 17th minute. Ronny Johnsen, playing in a rather unfamiliar full-back role, sent a neat pass down the wing to Cantona, who in turn floated the ball into the penalty area for Scholes to head home at the back post.

Within two minutes it was 2–0. Cantona sent yet another ball over the heads of the Portadown defence from the halfway line and Scholes was again on the end of it to beat the 'keeper.

Van der Gouw showed his capabilities with a fine double stop from Haylock and Kennedy in the 27th minute, but a minute later Portadown were to find themselves 3–0 down. Keane moved past Byrne, but his initial shot at goal was blocked by 'keeper Dalton, only to rebound to the midfielder, who made no mistake with his second effort.

Five minutes later it was 4–0. A Johnsen run down the wing was brought to a premature end by Davidson, but justice was carried out by Beckham, with the winger curling the free-kick into the net from 20 yards.

One minute from the interval Scholes completed his hat-trick, side-footing a Keane drive past the helpless goalkeeper.

As far as the scoring went that was it, as United were simply content to pass the ball around and play out the game without incurring any injuries.

---

27 July 1996　　　　　**Portadown at Shamrock Park.**

Attendance: 6,100.

Won: 5–0.

Scorers: Scholes 3, Keane, Beckham.

Team: Van der Gouw, Johnsen, Irwin, McGibbon, Keane, Pallister, Cantona, Butt, Scholes, Beckham, Sharpe.

Substitutes: McClair for Pallister, Pilkington for Van der Gouw, May for Johnsen, Appleton for Keane, Davies for Sharpe, Casper for Irwin, Clegg for Beckham.

Twenty-four hours later the action moved to Tolka Park, Dublin, where United came up against an Irish National League XI.

Without the likes of Giggs, Schmeichel, Cole, the Nevilles, Cruyff and Poborsky, Cantona was, more than ever, the centre of attention and it was the enigmatic Frenchman who set up United's first goal in the 23rd minute. He played a perfect pass through the Irish defence and Lee Sharpe ran on to round the 'keeper to score.

United held the lead for a mere three minutes as Gormley chipped Van der Gouw from the edge of the area to equalise.

Play moved frantically from end to end and within a further two minutes United were again in front, Pallister rising unchallenged to head home a Sharpe corner. Sharpe was also the provider of United's third goal, two minutes before the interval, setting up the easiest of chances for Paul Scholes.

On the stroke of half-time good work by McClair was finished off by Cantona for United's fourth.

Torrential rain marred the second half, with perhaps the only bright spot coming when one of the linesmen, having raised his flag to deny United a third 'offside' goal, was approached by Cantona, but there was to be nothing more than a finger pointed to his own eye from the Frenchman.

There was no further scoring and the game slowly dissolved into little more than a training exercise.

---

28 July 1996	**National League XI at Tolka Park, Dublin.**

Attendance: 7,720.

Won: 4–1.

Scorers: Sharpe, Pallister, Scholes, Cantona.

Team: Van der Gouw, Clegg, Irwin, May, Keane, Pallister, Cantona, Butt, McClair, Scholes, Sharpe.

Substitutes: Beckham for Butt, Pilkington for Van der Gouw, Davies for Clegg, Appleton for Scholes, McGibbon for May, Johnsen for Pallister, Casper for Sharpe.

From Ireland United travelled to Italy for the next warm-up fixture, where there was a distinct difference in the class of opposition compared to the previous two fixtures. Having crashed out of Europe 10 months previously to the somewhat unknown Rotor Volgograd, the fixture against Inter Milan would be an ideal opportunity to judge themselves against top Continental opposition and see how far away they were as a team to challenging for silverware on foreign fields.

With ex-Red Paul Ince in the opposition line up, there was always going to be an edge to the battle in midfield.

For much of the opening half United looked comfortable, coming close through both Cantona with a cheeky lob and Beckham, with something of a trademark drive, but United were to go in at the interval a goal behind. Benito Carbone beat a helpless Schmeichel from all of 25 yards in the 43rd minute.

Nine minutes into the second half a United move broke down and their defence was caught out of position, thereby providing Branca with the opportunity to make it 2–0.

Debutant Djorkaeff saw an effort ruled out for offside, before Branca scored his second just before the hour mark.

| **31 July 1996** | **Inter Milan at San Siro Stadium.** |

Attendance: 33,578.

Lost: 3–0.

Team: Schmeichel, Irwin, P. Neville, May, Keane, Pallister, Cantona, Butt, McClair, Scholes, Beckham.

Substitutes: Thornley for Butt, Davies for Scholes, G. Neville for P. Neville.

Four-club pre-season tournaments are usually something to be found on the Continent, but United were invited to take part in one in the unlikely surroundings of Nottingham.

Competing for the Umbro Trophy, United found themselves paired with the Dutch champions Ajax in their opening fixture and, having faced Inter Milan just a few days previously, they were certainly having a testing pre-season.

With five Dutch stars from Euro '96, Ajax were always going to be a handful and United survived a few early scares. Ronald De Boer sent a dipping effort just over the bar in the 14th minute and a couple of minutes later Wooter's corner had to be palmed to safety by Schmeichel.

It was 20 minutes before United came close to scoring, McClair heading a Keane cross just wide. The Irishman also came close as United enjoyed a period of pressure around Van der Sar's goal, but his 35-yard effort went narrowly wide.

United should have taken the lead just before the half hour, but as Cantona steadied himself to head Sharpe's cross goalward, Marcio Santos sneaked in to head the ball away. A goal then might have altered the course of the game, but as it was Ajax took the lead three minutes later, Frank De Boer scoring from a free-kick after May had pulled Musampa to the ground.

Keane was fortunate not to be booked by referee David Elleray for a trip on Wooter and was certainly riding his luck when he fouled the same player again. Alex Ferguson, sensing that Keane's next offence would attract a booking at the least, removed his midfielder from the action.

McClair raised United's hopes with an equaliser 13 minutes from the end, but Ajax clinched victory in the 86th minute when Louhenapessy supplied the pass which enabled Musampa to score.

| **3 August 1996** | **Ajax at City Ground, Nottingham.** |

Attendance: 27,427.

Lost: 2–1.

Scorer: McClair.

Team: Schmeichel, G. Neville, Irwin, May, Keane, Johnsen, Cantona, Beckham, McClair, Scholes, Sharpe.

Substitutes: P. Neville for May, Butt for Keane.

With Chelsea having defeated the host club, it was a battle between United and Nottingham Forest to avoid being left with the wooden spoon and, although the 3–1 victory gave United some credibility, they were left with some injury problems with the start of the new campaign on the near horizon.

In the early exchanges it looked as though United were going to finish in fourth place, even more so when a long ball from Pearce caught the United defence flat-footed, allowing Campbell to beat Schmeichel.

Crossley denied United an equaliser, but could do little when United hit the hosts with three goals in a late six-minute spell. Beckham finished a five-man move by curving the ball into the net with the outside of his right boot for the first. He set up McClair three minutes later for the second and then two minutes from time Phil Neville added a third.

4 August 1996 **Nottingham Forest at City Ground, Nottingham.**

Attendance: 21,760.

Won: 3–1.

Scorers: Beckham, McClair, P. Neville.

Team: Schmeichel, G. Neville, P. Neville, May, Keane, Johnsen, Cantona, Beckham, Butt, Scholes, Sharpe.

Substitutes: Van der Gouw for Schmeichel, McClair for Sharpe, Davies for Keane, McGibbon for Johnsen, Casper for G.Neville.

It is difficult to imagine United taking on such a tough pre-season fixture list as they did in the summer of 1996, with a return match against Inter Milan just two days after the Wembley FA Charity Shield showpiece against Newcastle United.

Against the Italians, the second of a quartet of fixtures arranged around the transfer of Paul Ince, the double winners once again failed to record a victory. Having lost the first fixture in Milan 3–0, there was just a solitary goal separating the two teams on this occasion.

With seven changes to the side which won the Charity Shield, United only created one real scoring opportunity, Cruyff's sweeping volley being turned over by Pagliuca.

Poborsky shone in midfield, but it was the visitors who claimed victory when Zamorano headed past Van der Gouw in the 63rd minute.

13 August 1996 **Inter Milan at Old Trafford.**

Attendance: 30,266.

Lost: 1–0.

Team: Van der Gouw, G. Neville, O'Kane, May, Johnsen, McClair, Cantona, Poborsky, Scholes, Beckham, Cruyff.

Substitutes: Solskjaer for Scholes, Davies for Poborsky, Casper for O'Kane.

Celtic were invited to Old Trafford to mark the testimonial match for Brian McClair. He had served both clubs with distinction over a 14-year period and deserved nothing less than a full house at Old Trafford on his big night.

As he walked out of the Old Trafford tunnel prior to the game he was greeted with an explosion of applause, which he was later to say left him 'humbled and privileged'. Sadly, though, his big night was not to end in a victory for his current pay-masters, as his former club stole the honours with a 2–1 victory.

Kick-off had to be delayed some 20 minutes to allow the majority of the crowd through the turnstiles. The 7,000-strong support from Glasgow wasted little time in making themselves heard, as the green and white hoops stormed the United goal in the opening minutes. Cadete and Thom both powered their way through the United defence to try their luck, while Grant was just off target with a long-range effort.

McClair squandered a good opportunity to make it more of a night to remember after Cantona had managed to lose Mackay inside the area before sending in an inch-perfect pass across goal. Shortly afterwards Gary Neville found McClair with a cross from the right, but his header was easily held by Marshall.

Cadete, finding himself clear in the United area, shot weakly at goal, Gary Neville clearing. Di Canio then robbed the United defender on the edge of the box, before slipping the ball through to Johnsen, but the forward wasted his second opportunity to open the scoring. The first had seen him being dispossessed by Keane, while on this occasion Van der Gouw was equal to his effort.

Poborsky tried his luck from 15 yards, only for McKinlay to clear off the line, and as half-time loomed the Celtic support called for a penalty when Johnsen upended Cadete, but the referee waved play on.

However, with seconds remaining before the break it was the home side who took the lead. McClair flicked the ball across goal to the waiting Cruyff, but as Donnelly intercepted it only went as far as Keane, who headed home.

After the interval there was the customary flock of substitutions and United should have increased their lead when McClair, again in the thick of things, set up Cruyff, but the Dutchman wasted the opportunity. Mulryne also came close, but a fingertip save from Marshall denied him.

With 12 minutes remaining, Celtic equalised. Donnelly's long ball into the United area found Hay and from 12 yards out, he swept the ball home. Two minutes later, with the Celtic fans still celebrating the goal, Hay struck again after Di Canio's pass was touched on by Weighorst to spoil McClair's evening.

15 April 1997	**Celtic at Old Trafford.**

Attendance: 43,743.

Lost: 2–1.

Scorer: Keane.

Team: Van der Gouw, G. Neville, P. Neville, Keane, Johnsen, Scholes, Cantona, Butt, McClair, Cruyff, Poborsky.

Substitutes: Curtis for P. Neville, Wallwork for Keane, Casper for Johnsen, Mulryne for Scholes, Tomlinson for Butt, Beckham for Cantona.

It was perhaps only fitting that, having had his career come to a end in a game against United, it was Alex Ferguson's side who would travel to Coventry to play in a benefit match for David Busst, keeping the manager's promise to the unfortunate player.

So, with the Championship trophy newly installed in the Old Trafford museum, it was a strong United side that travelled to the Midlands and in front of Coventry City's biggest crowd of the season, with the home side strengthened by Les Ferdinand and Paul Gascoigne, they help supply a carnival atmosphere for the game and swell Busst's bank balance by some £250,000.

Gazza, who entertained the crowd at every opportunity, put Coventry in front in the 26th minute, heading home Telfer's cross, but two second-half goals from Eric Cantona, determined not to be outshone by the Geordie, gave United the lead. His first goal came from a penalty in the 69th minute after Gary Neville had been fouled, the second four minutes from time from Thornley's centre.

With the game heading towards the final minute, the ball found its way into the United penalty area and, for the first and only time in Alex Ferguson's tenure as

The programme for the match versus
Coventry City XI, 16 May 1997.

United manager, there was no hint of a protest when the referee pointed to the spot to award a penalty that even 'dubious' would not describe after Gary Neville's tackle on Speedie.

Leaving his place on the bench to a loud roar, David Busst placed the ball past Van der Gouw with the last kick of the game.

16 May 1997	**Coventry City XI at Highfield Road.**

Attendance: 23,325.

Drew: 2–2.

Scorer: Cantona 2 (1 pen.).

Team: Schmeichel, G. Neville, P. Neville, May, Clegg, McClair, Cantona, Butt, Solskjaer, Beckham, Cruyff.

Substitutes: Thornley for Butt, Van der Gouw for Schmeichel, Cooke for Beckham, Davies for McClair, Appleton for May, McClair for Solskjaer.

The United team now headed to the Far East, where they faced the Thailand national side in the opening fixture. New signing Teddy Sheringham had something of an anonymous debut, while Roy Keane captained the side for the first time.

Due to the intense heat, the game was played at a slow pace, with United dominating possession. However, they could well have been three goals behind at the interval, due to some sloppy defending that the Thais failed to capitalise on.

Having failed to see any goals in the first half, United eventually took the lead in the 57th minute through Nicky Butt, whose 25-yard drive left Kamplian in the Thailand goal helpless.

Although having broken the deadlock, United still failed to capitalise on their play and it was not until a Poborsky cross, intended for Sheringham, was headed past his own 'keeper by Tongsukkaew three minutes from the end that the victory was assured.

Ticket for the match versus Thailand, 17 July 1997.

17 July 1997	**Thailand at National Stadium, Bangkok.**

Attendance: 38,000.

Won: 2–0.

Scorer: Butt, opp. own-goal.

Team: Schmeichel, P. Neville, Irwin, May, Keane, Pallister, Scholes, Butt, Cole, Sheringham, Cruyff.

Substitutes: Van der Gouw for Schmeichel, Poborsky for Cruyff.

United's popularity on the other side of the world waned a little when furious supporters in Hong Kong demanded their money back on tickets bought for the game against South China, due to the non-appearance of three of the club's big names: Ryan Giggs, David Beckham and Gary Neville.

The Hong Kong Consumer Council, who had received a handful of formal complaints plus countless inquiries relating to refunds, decided to look into the matter to see if the local public had been misled, as advertising for the game had featured all three players, as well as the now retired Eric Cantona.

Martin Edwards, the United Chairman, made it clear that the signed contract was with United as a club and carried no guarantees about the appearance of certain individuals: 'We've got 15 internationals here, out of a squad of 20, with the players in question unable to travel due to medical advice'.

This second match of the tour once again saw United fail to make the most of the opportunities that they created and it was not until the 76th minute that the only goal of the game materialised.

Keane hit the bar in the 13th minute and a minute later Phil Neville also failed to find the net when in a good position. A further opportunity was scorned on the half-hour mark, when Solskjaer had a header saved by the 'keeper. Sheringham, with another header, could only watch as it went narrowly wide and a couple of minutes later Schmeichel had to pull off a fine save to prevent Song Lianyong from giving the home side the lead.

Cruyff seemed to bring something extra to United's play after coming on as substitute, but it still took him three chances to find the net. Rising above the China defence, he headed Irwin's cross into the left-hand corner for what was the only goal of the game.

Ticket for the match versus South China, 20 July 1997.

20 July 1997	**South China at Hong Kong Stadium.**

Attendance: 36,611.

Won: 1—0.

Scorer: Cruyff.

Team: Schmeichel, P. Neville, Irwin, May, Johnsen, Keane, Scholes, Poborsky, Solskjaer, Sheringham, McClair.

Substitutes: Cruyff for Solskjaer, Mulryne for Sheringham, Cooke for Scholes, Clegg for Irwin, Thornley for Poborsky.

Two first-half goals from Solskjaer in the third and final tour game were enough to defeat Urawa Red Diamonds in Tokyo and win the Sharp Cup, a further addition to the already bulging trophy cabinet, with the Toyota Invitation Cup and the Marlboro Cup having been won in Bangkok and Hong Kong respectively.

The Norwegian's opener came in the 14th minute when he climbed above two defenders to head home a Mulryne cross, scoring a second five minutes before the interval with a rising shot into the top right-hand corner after Cole and Butt had created the opening.

Had it not been for an injury to the double-scoring forward, forcing him out of the second half, then there would surely have been more goals.

22 July 1997	**Urawa Red Diamonds at Urawa Komamba Stadium, Tokyo.**

Attendance: 17,642.

Won: 2—1.

Scorer: Solskjaer 2.

Team: Schmeichel, Clegg, P. Neville, Johnsen, Keane, Pallister, Cruyff, Butt, Cole, Solskjaer, Mulryne.

Substitutes: Irwin for Clegg, Van der Gouw for Schmeichel, McClair for Johnsen, Scholes for Mulryne, Poborsky for Solskjaer.

For once United were not the main attraction, as they were overshadowed against Inter Milan by the Italians' new £18 million signing Ronaldo in the Final of the Pirelli Cup. A similar friendly fixture between the two sides last season had attracted a crowd of around 20,000, but this time, with the new star signing, there were certainly fewer empty seats.

The home support were out of their seats within two minutes of the start, as Ronaldo evaded David May to move on to a superb pass from Djorkaeff, but he just failed to bring the ball under control. Another run towards goal was thwarted by Irwin and that was as far as the Ronaldo show went, as he was substituted after just 17 minutes and 15 seconds.

Despite being the mere support act, United took the lead in the 15th minute. Scholes picked out Butt on the edge of the area with a first-time ball, which saw the United midfielder skip past an attempted tackle from Sartor before scoring.

Keane was flattened by Simeone just after the half-hour mark, but remained cool despite some overly robust tackles and off the ball incidents from Zamarano, Ze Elias and the aforementioned Simeone. However, it was Djorkaeff who became the victim of the United captain's revenge, and Keane received his first yellow card as a United player.

United more than held their own as the match progressed, but the Italians had a little bit of luck in the 70th minute when Gary Neville headed the ball past his own 'keeper for the Milan equaliser.

With the scores still level at full-time, it was down to penalties to decide the winners of the Cup and the visitors could only manage to find the net with one effort from Sheringham, as both Cruyff and Butt missed their kicks. Recoba, Berti, Mezzano and Cauet all scored for Milan.

---

27 July 1997   **Inter Milan at San Siro Stadium.**

Attendance: 49,718.

Drew: 1–1 (**Lost:** 4–1 on penalties).

Scorer: Butt (Sheringham pen.).

Team: Schmeichel, Irwin, P. Neville, May, Johnsen, Keane, Scholes, Butt, Solskjaer, Sheringham, Giggs.

Substitutes: Cole for Solksjaer, Cruyff for Giggs, McClair for Irwin, G. Neville for May.

Inter Milan flew into Manchester a couple of days later for the second leg of the double header. United had brought in Dante Poli, a Chilean international, to play against the Italians as they were lacking defensive cover, Pallister, Irwin and May all carrying injuries. The Club Deportivo Universiatad Catolica player had only been seen on video by Alex Ferguson.

Once again United surprised their fans by running out in their away strip of all blue. They had the best of the opening half but could not match their effort with goals. Giggs saw a header go wide in the eighth minute and Sheringham missed a couple of easy chances. But as luck would have it, against the run of play, Milan took the lead four minutes before the interval. A hopeful Recoba cross should have been cleared by Neville or Johnsen, but Simeone got the better of the two defenders before setting up the unmarked Ganz.

Neville suffered a dead leg and was replaced by Clegg, with the substitute, the smallest player on the pitch, rising above everyone to head home a Poborsky corner in the 67th minute, after Cruyff's shot had been blocked by Pagliuca.

Solskjaer was also taken off injured, having been on the pitch as a substitute for only 16 minutes. With the United manager having used all his outfield substitutes, he sent on young goalkeeper Kevin Pilkington as his replacement and he almost became the hero of the night, very nearly scoring with an overhead kick during his nine minutes as an outfield player.

30 July 1997	Inter Milan at Old Trafford.

Attendance: 48,579.

Drew: 1–1.

Scorer: Clegg.

Team: Schmeichel, Irwin, P. Neville, Butt, Johnsen, G.Neville, Scholes, Poborsky, Cole, Sheringham, Giggs.

Substitutes: Clegg for G. Neville, Cruyff for Sheringham, McClair for Poborsky, Solskjaer for Cole, Poli for Johnsen, Beckham for Scholes, Pilkington for Solskjaer.

Ticket for the match versus Inter Milan, 30 July 1997.

David Beckham showed everyone what he was capable of in a rather nondescript friendly against Slavia Prague at Old Trafford. Such was his determination to prove his worth to both the manager and the supporters that he ran his socks off for the 70 minutes he was on the pitch, but still could not guide United to a morale-boosting eve-of-season victory.

United went in front as many were still making their way to their seats, Poborsky finding the net from a low left-wing cross from Giggs after only 34 seconds.

Three minutes into the second half Horvarth for Slavia equalised from the penalty spot after the referee adjudged Johnsen to have handled.

Substitute Terry Cooke reclaimed United's advantage in the 78th minute, shooting through a crowd of players, but once again the visitors drew level. Asanin, cutting in from the right eight minutes from time, fired a ferocious drive past a helpless Van der Gouw.

Trialist Poli played for the full 90 minutes, but his performance was not enough to earn a full-time contract with the club and he returned home just as anonymously as he had arrived.

5 August 1997	Slavia Prague at Old Trafford.

Attendance: 22,075.

Drew: 2–2.

Scorers: Poborsky, Cooke.

Team: Van der Gouw, G. Neville, P. Neville, Poli, McClair, Pallister, Beckham, Poborsky, Cole, Cruyff, Giggs.

Substitutes: Johnsen for Pallister, Cooke for Cole, Thornley for Giggs, Curtis for P. Neville, Mulryne for Beckham.

Having beaten Crystal Palace 2–0 at Old Trafford 24 hours previously, Alex Ferguson led his team across Manchester to Maine Road to take part in a testimonial for Paul Lake, whose career had been ended prematurely through injury. The City player, although unable to play in the match, took the applause of the crowd prior to kicking off.

City themselves had also played the previous day, losing 1–0 at Ipswich, but the local rivals both fielded full-strength sides, although those with international commitments were only supposed to feature in the opening 20 minutes.

Paul Scholes opened the scoring for United in the eighth minute with a notable volley from a Beckham cross, but both were soon to depart the stage as City drew level through Kinkladze with a 17th-minute strike, which Schmeichel could not stop from spinning over his head into the net.

With the international players substituted by a few unfamiliar faces, the game took on a more physical and serious nature. Dickov came close for City, with teammate Scully missing an easy chance, but they did take the lead when Rosler scored in the 76th minute.

With seven minutes remaining United drew level, as young forward Alex Notman, on in place of Scholes, prodded the ball home.

---

5 October 1997   **Manchester City at Maine Road.**

Attendance: 22,062.

Drew: 2–2.

Scorers: Scholes, Johnsen.

Team: Schmeichel, G. Neville, P. Neville, May, Johnsen, McClair, Beckham, Butt, Poborsky, Scholes, Giggs.

Substitutes: Irwin for Johnsen, Van der Gouw for Schmeichel, Curtis for P. Neville, Clegg for G. Neville, Thornley for Beckham, Notman for Scholes, Twiss for Clegg, Mulryne for Butt.

Losing 4–3 to Birmingham was certainly not the best of starts for a new season, but there was little likelihood of the United manager selecting the side that turned out at St Andrews in a competitive match during the months ahead.

According to Tom Watt of *The Observer*, the afternoon 'proved on the watchable side, thanks to a sharp performance from Cole and some laughable defending by the odd assortment in front of United's third-choice 'keeper, Culkin'.

Adebola, Birmingham's new signing from Crewe, caused the United defence all sorts of problems, getting the better of Curtis and May on three separate occasions. His crosses were converted into goals by Ndlovu in the eighth minute, when he tricked Denis Irwin playing in an unfamiliar role of sweeper, in the 25th minute by the same player, and finally by Furlong four minutes before the interval.

The young United side replied to Birmingham's first two goals through Mulryne. Set up by Andy Cole, the Irishman scored his first in the 20th minute as he drove the ball home with his right foot, and his second in the 38th minute with a low shot into the bottom corner.

Ndlovu completed his hat-trick nine minutes into the second half, but Mulryne, snatching at this rare first-team opportunity, was not going to be outdone by the City forward and claimed his own hat-trick with a 56th-minute penalty kick after he had been brought down by Charlton.

It was certainly a frustrating afternoon for the United manager, but with his big guns yet to pull on their boots, he was not unduly worried about the Midlands reversal.

---

25 July 1998   **Birmingham City at St Andrews.**

Attendance: 20,708.

Lost: 4–3.

Scorer: Mulryne 3 (1 pen.).

Team: Culkin, Curtis, P. Neville, Wallwork, May, Irwin, Mulryne, Butt, Cole, Cruyff, Giggs.

Substitutes: Twiss for Irwin, Wilson for Cruyff, Ford for Mulryne, Notman for Cole.

It was a completely different United 11 that took part in the second pre-season fixture against Norwegian side Vålerenga in Oslo, although they fared little better than the second-string side who had lost in Birmingham two days previously.

Cheered on by around 1,000 travelling fans and a much larger contingent of locally based followers, United failed to live up to their expectations against the part-time side and went behind in the seventh minute when Carew, allowed to run unchallenged through the United defence, put the ball past Schmeichel from close range.

It took United only five minutes to draw level. Ryan Giggs found Solskjaer, whose cross beat Tore Krogstad and allowed Scholes to tap the ball in with ease. Another 10 minutes saw United take the lead, a through ball from Phil Neville finding Solskjaer, who rounded the 'keeper to score.

Two minutes before the interval Keane was booked for a foul on Walltin, his last act before being substituted at half-time. Within two minutes of the restart the Norwegians were level, Viljugrein squeezing the ball past Schmeichel from a tight angle.

As in many similar fixtures, the players were more than happy to simply go through the motions for the remainder of the half.

---

27 July 1998 **Vålerenga IF at Bislett Stadium, Oslo.**

Attendance: 19,700.

Drew: 2–2.

Scorers: Solskjaer, Scholes.

Team: Schmeichel, G. Neville, P. Neville, Berg, Johnsen, Keane, Beckham, Butt, Solskjaer, Scholes, Giggs.

Substitutes: Irwin for Butt, Sheringham for Scholes, Cole for Keane, Cruyff for Giggs, Curtis for Beckham.

The Scandinavian tour continued in Denmark against Peter Schmeichel's old club Brondby, and United literally hit them for six.

This game marked the debut of £10.75 million Jaap Stam, the world's most expensive defender, who could not have asked for a better first game in the red shirt, making the first goal for Sheringham with a lob over the Danish defence in the 33rd minute.

Schmeichel was put under some early pressure by both Sand and Hansen, as Brondby kept United on their toes in the opening 20 minutes. However, the tables were quickly turned and the Danes were on the receiving end of a morale-crushing defeat.

Four minutes before the break United doubled their lead when Sheringham and Solskjaer combined to create an opening for Scholes. They went 3–0 in front in the 64th minute, when Cole scored with a volley after having missed a much easier opportunity.

Johnsen and Cole combined to give Sheringham his second from the edge of the area with 19 minutes remaining, while Cole notched up his second of the game 12 minutes later. The rout was completed as Giggs laid on a pass for Cruyff to get his name on the scoresheet.

The programme for the match versus Brondby IF, 31 July 1998.

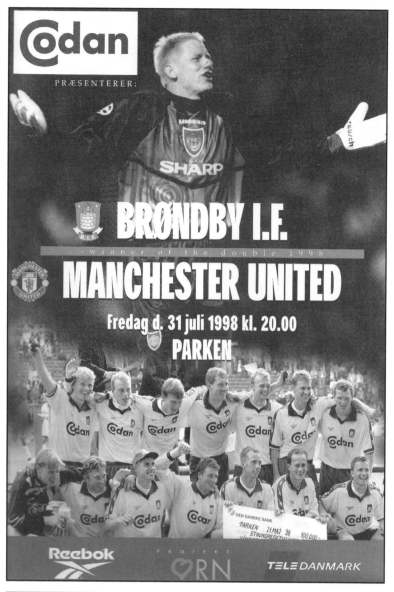

---

31 July 1998	Brondby IF at Parken Stadium, Denmark.

Attendance: 27,022.

Won: 6–0.

Scorers: Sheringham 2, Cole 2, Scholes, Cruyff.

Team: Schmeichel, G. Neville, Irwin, Keane, Johnsen, Stam, Beckham, Scholes, Solskjaer, Sheringham, Giggs.

Substitutes: Berg for Stam, Butt for Beckham, Cole for Solskjaer, Cruyff for Sheringham, Curtis for Johnsen.

The third and final game of the tour took United to Bergen, where they came up against local side Brann, and it was to take a hat-trick from a most unlikely source for United to claim victory.

It was not until a minute before the interval that United managed to take the lead from a deflected free-kick. Nicky Butt was brought down on the edge of the area and from the resulting kick Denis Irwin curled the ball towards the defensive wall where it hit the head of Samuelson before swerving past Westad in the Brann goal.

Within seconds of the restart Solskjaer was bearing down on the Brann goal, but before he managed to get a shot in two defenders combined to bring him down. From the penalty spot Irwin made it 2–0 with his second of the night.

Seven minutes later Irwin was stepping up to take another spot-kick, this time after Scholes had been pulled down by the goalkeeper. Having blasted his first kick straight into the middle of the goal he changed tactics this time, hitting the ball firmly into the bottom right-hand corner.

The Norwegians had given up by the time Andy Cole added a fourth seven minutes from time, as he controlled Butt's cross from the right and took two touches before volleying the ball into the roof of the net.

---

4 August 1998   **SK Brann at Homespark Stadium, Bergen.**

Attendance: 16,100.

Won: 4–0.

Scorers: Irwin 3 (2 pens), Cole.

Team: Schmeichel, Curtis, Irwin, Keane, Berg, Stam, P. Neville, Butt, Cole, Scholes, Solskjaer.

Substitutes: Culkin for Schmeichel, May for Berg, Sheringham for Scholes, Beckham for Solskjaer, Cruyff for Keane.

The game against an Eric Cantona European XI, which was organised as a tribute to those players who had lost their lives at Munich and those who had survived, was snubbed by many who considered it to be more of an Eric Cantona showcase.

The Guardian carried a double heading of, 'Cantona Steps out For One Last Hurrah', with 'Vivek Chaudhary at Old Trafford sees a ball-playing French actor bid a belated adieu'. The 13-paragraph article mentioned Munich only once.

There was little in the way of physical contact when the actual football got underway, as the 12-goal scoreline certainly confirms.

Cantona began the night in the black and white striped shirt of the guest XI alongside Mark Hughes, but it was United who took the lead, David Beckham setting up Ryan Giggs in the 11th minute, the latter having come close a couple of minutes previously with a chip that went narrowly over.

The evening's star act, Pascal Olmeta, a Corsican goalkeeper, almost gifted United a second goal when he was robbed of the ball as he tried to dribble downfield, but Beckham's 40-yard effort bounced off the bar.

The goals came thick and fast, as did the substitutions, but there was only one player that the crowd wanted to see score. His moment finally came 10 minutes from the end, while wearing the red of United. Dribbling, as if in slow motion, past three defenders, he casually lifted the ball over Olmeta as the crowd rose as one.

The programme for the match versus Eric Cantona European XI, 18 August 1998.

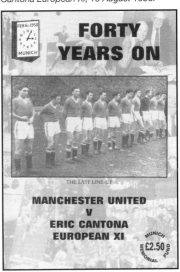

---

18 August 1998   **Eric Cantona European XI at Old Trafford.**

Attendance: 55,210.

Won: 8–4.

Scorers: Notman 2, P. Neville, Butt, Cantona, Cruyff, Scholes, Giggs.

Team: Culkin, G. Neville, P. Neville, May, Brown, Keane, Beckham, Butt, Sheringham, Scholes, Giggs.

Substitutes: Cantona for Scholes, Gibson for Culkin, Casper for May, Cruyff for Giggs, Notman for Sheringham, Greening for Beckham, Higginbottom for Keane, Clegg for G. Neville.

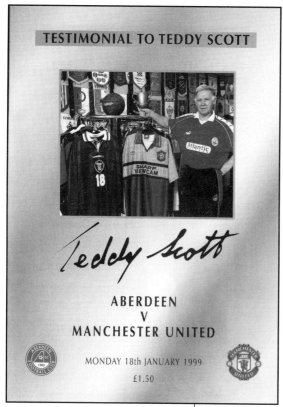

TESTIMONIAL TO TEDDY SCOTT

Teddy Scott

ABERDEEN V MANCHESTER UNITED

MONDAY 18th JANUARY 1999
£1.50

The programme for the match versus Aberdeen, 18 January 1999.

During what was to become a momentous season in the history of Manchester United, Alex Ferguson interrupted the domestic campaign halfway through to send a team north to Aberdeen. The fixture was a testimonial match for Teddy Scott, a member of the Aberdeen back-room staff for some 44 years.

Scott was rewarded with a standing ovation from the crowd as he emerged from the tunnel prior to the kick-off to be introduced to both teams, as United fielded a full-strength side.

Around 500 United supporters made the journey north, but it was the Aberdeen fans who were in full voice as their favourites took the game to the visitors. Robbie Winters had Schmeichel diving at his feet early on, while also heading against the United bar. Trialist Mayer forced an excellent save from the big Dane with a 20-yard effort. The United 'keeper was soon performing similar heroics to keep a curling 20-yard free-kick from Jess from going in.

Andy Cole should have given United the lead in the 36th minute, but headed a Beckham corner over the bar when he was completely unmarked.

Jess saw another effort parried by Schmeichel and just before the interval found himself one-on-one with the United 'keeper, although just as he prepared to round the Dane, a giant gloved hand grabbed the ball off his feet.

Six minutes into the second half the deadlock was finally broken when Johnsen fired home from 15 yards out, after Yorke had hit the crossbar. A lapse in concentration by Smith allowed Blomqvist to claim possession, before slipping the ball inside to Solskjaer. The Norwegian's shot, however, was blocked by Stillie in the Aberdeen goal.

With around an hour gone Winters had a shot deflected over by Schmeichel and minutes later Aberdeen eventually claimed the equaliser, Newell heading home Hart's cross.

Solskjaer should have put the result beyond doubt with the minutes ticking away. His initial shot beat Stillie, but it hit the inside of the post and rebounded back towards him. With the ball at his feet and the goal gaping, the Norwegian shot past from a mere four feet out.

Aberdeen then wasted a similar chance when Jess put Kiriakov through, but with Newell in a better position the Bulgarian put the ball wide.

It went to penalties to decide a winner and it was to take 13 kicks before the outcome finally reached a conclusion, John Curtis seeing his spot-kick saved by Stillie.

---

18 January 1999   **Aberdeen at Pittodrie.**

Attendance: 20,391.

Drew: 1–1 (**Lost:** 7–6).

Scorers: Johnsen (P. Neville, Butt, Scholes, Solskjaer, Yorke, Greening).

Team: Schmeichel, P. Neville, Irwin, May, Johnsen, Butt, Beckham, Scholes, Cole, Solskjaer, Giggs.

Substitutes: Yorke for Cole, Greening for Beckham, Blomqvist for Giggs, Curtis for Irwin, Brown for May.

The events of May 1999 will always be etched into the memory, as the unprecedented treble was won in an unbelievable 11 days, taking the Red Army from Old Trafford to Barcelona via Wembley.

With the Premier League trophy, FA Cup and the European Cup sitting safely in the United Museum, the first fixtures as treble winners were on the opposite side of the world in Australia.

The tour opened with a game against Australia in Melbourne, on a pitch that was criticised by both sides as being rock hard and in poor overall condition. It did not, however, prevent United from kicking-off the new campaign with a victory.

Jesper Blomqvist opened the scoring with 'a rasping volley' in stoppage time at the end of the first half, but, despite the hosts being without nine of their regular squad, United could not capitalise on their overall supremacy and it was not until the final quarter of an hour that they made it 2–0, Nicky Butt scoring with a half-volley from 25 yards.

---

15 July 1999   **Australia at Melbourne Cricket Ground.**

Attendance: 70,000.

Won: 2–0.

Scorers: Butt, Blomqvist.

Team: Bosnich, P. Neville, Irwin, May, Berg, Wilson, Greening, Butt, Yorke, Sheringham, Blomqvist.

Substitutes: Stam for May, Cruyff for Blomqvist, Giggs for Greening, Brown for Berg, Curtis for Irwin, Clegg for Wilson.

The second game against Australia was again a closely fought encounter, with tempers simmering away throughout the 90 minutes. One particular tackle by Cole on Colosimo added to the ill-feeling.

The Australians struggled to make an impact and it was a 25th-minute Dwight Yorke goal that was the difference between the two teams, Giggs picking out the striker's run to perfection.

Back on home soil, Mark Bosnich was rarely tested, although a poor clearance fell to Wehrman, whose long-range shot was caught easily by the 'keeper. Manchester City's Tiatto also came close. However, at the end of the day, the Sharp Challenge Trophy found its way back to England.

---

18 July 1999   **Australia at Stadium Australia, Sydney.**

Attendance: 78,032.

Won: 1–0.

Scorer: Yorke.

Team: Bosnich, P. Neville, Irwin, Wilson, Berg, Stam, Cruyff, Butt, Cole, Yorke, Giggs.

Substitutes: Solskjaer for Wilson, Van der Gouw for Bosnich, Greening for Cruyff, Sheringham for Cole, Clegg for P. Neville.

As the United party moved from Australia to China interest in the game against Shenhua was huge, with tickets changing hands on the black market for more than four times face value. Those who were lucky enough to have tickets were treated to a more interesting 90 minutes than the paying public in Australia had witnessed.

United always looked threatening, but it took them until after the interval to break the deadlock. Wes Brown was booked five minutes into the second half and six minutes later Blomqvist flighted a perfect ball through to Solskjaer, who controlled the ball on his chest before scoring with a left-footed shot just inside the far post.

In the 69th minute Solskjaer turned provider, as, taking a back-heel from Blomqvist, the Norwegian pushed the ball across the area for Sheringham to score a second.

The Chinese League leaders had no answer to United and goalkeeper Chuliang did well to prevent a Sheringham free-kick from making it three, while later May shot wide from another set piece. Even the humidity could not slow down the visitors, who played out the game in a relaxed fashion to maintain their unbeaten tour record.

---

21 July 1999   **Shenhua at Shanghai, China.**

Attendance: 80,000.

Won: 2–0.

Scorers: Solskjaer, Sheringham.

Team: Van der Gouw, Curtis, Irwin, Wilson, Brown, Stam, Greening, Butt, Cole, Solskjaer, Blomqvist.

Substitutes: Sheringham for Cole, P. Neville for Butt, Bosnich for Van der Gouw, Yorke for Wilson, Clegg for Irwin, May for Stam, Cruyff for Greening.

Faced with temperatures of 96 degrees against Asian Cup holders South China, United, wearing their new dark blue strip, once again tackled both heat and opponents admirably, rounding off their tour in style with two goals in four first-half minutes giving them victory.

Teddy Sheringham opened the scoring in the 22nd minute after Cole pulled the ball back into his path, and four minutes later the roles were reversed as Sheringham squared the ball to Cole, who gave Leonard in the South China goal no chance.

The home side had little answer to United's play and their only real first-half chance fell to Leung Chi Wing, but his effort was tipped over by Bosnich. At the opposite end Leonard did well to prevent United going 3–0 in front, stopping a fine effort from Cruyff.

South China came more into the game after the interval, Bosnich having to dive at the feet of Nigerian striker Aggbo, but it was still United who carved out the best opportunities. Yorke sent a 20-yard effort just wide in the 65th minute and Leonard once again foiled Cruyff, but it was the heat that provided United with their biggest test.

---

24 July 1999   **South China at Hong Kong National Stadium.**

Attendance: 40,000.

Won: 2–0.

Scorers: Cole, Sheringham.

Team: Bosnich, Brown, Irwin, P. Neville, Berg, Stam, Cruyff, Yorke, Cole, Sheringham, Blomqvist.

Substitutes: May for Stam, Greening for Blomqvist, Curtis for Irwin, Clegg for Berg.

The tiny St Julian's Road ground, home of Irish First Division Omagh Town, resembled Old Trafford in miniature as the treble winners added a few thousand pounds to the Omagh Bomb appeal, almost a year after the tragedy had hit the town.

Against a team made up of plumbers, students and teachers, United strolled to a 9–0 victory, with Teddy Sheringham opening the floodgates after only 27 seconds. Debutant winger Luke Chadwick left the Irish defence stranded before crossing for Sheringham to finish in style.

Andy Cole made it 2–0 in the sixth minute, diverting an Irwin cross past the luckless Callaghan, but there was a lull until the 27th minute, when Clegg scored with a powerful header from a corner kick.

By half-time it was 6–0, with the three goals coming in six minutes from the same three scorers. Sheringham made it 4–0 with a diving header from Cole's left-wing cross, Cole scored his second of the game from a Keane corner, while Clegg made it six just on the half-time whistle with a low shot.

Play slowed in the second half, but it was still all United. A Chadwick cross was diverted past his own goalkeeper by Nixon to make it 7–0, with the romp rounded up by another two goals from Sheringham in the final 18 minutes.

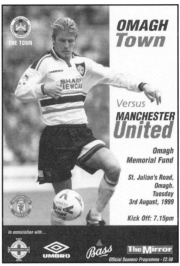

The programme for the match versus Omagh Town, 3 August 1999.

3 August 1999	Omagh Town at St Julian's Road.

Attendance: 7,000.

Won: 9–0.

Scorers: Sheringham 4, Cole 2, Clegg 2, opp. own-goal.

Team: Culkin, Clegg, Irwin, May, G. Neville, Keane, Greening, Wilson, Cole, Sheringham, Chadwick.

Substitutes: Notman for Wilson, Healy for Cole, Stewart for Chadwick, Wellens for Greening, Ford for G. Neville, O'Shea for May.

Twenty-four hours later, Sir Alex Ferguson had an almost entirely different line up ready for action at the JJB Stadium, the new home of Wigan Athletic, for the official opening of the £30 million ground.

Jordi Cruyff returned to the United side following his loan spell at Celta Vigo and turned in an impressive performance, as Wigan battled to keep their illustrious opponents at bay. However, late goals from Scholes and Solskjaer were enough to secure United victory.

4 August 1999	Wigan Athletic at the JJB Stadium.

Attendance: 15,000.

Won: 2–0.

Scorers: Solskjaer, Scholes.

Team: Van der Gouw, P. Neville, Curtis, May, Berg, Scholes, Beckham, Butt, Solskjaer, Cruyff.

Substitutes: Clegg for P. Neville, Healy for Butt, O'Shea for May.

Testimonials are not just for long-serving players, as the 54,842 who filled Old Trafford to salute Sir Alex Ferguson proved.

Having taken on the rest of the world, and beaten them, it was fitting that the opposition on this special evening was a Rest of the World XI, managed by Ottmar

Hitzfeld, with his team consisting of names such as Larsson, Vialli, Cafu, Gascoigne, Weah, Schmeichel and Cantona.

The game, beamed live on Sky TV, was never going to live up to its billing, but those watching at home and at Old Trafford were certainly not disappointed, despite the scoreline favouring the World XI.

Gianluca Vialli opened the scoring in the 11th minute following good work between Weah and Cafu, but Sheringham equalised just before the interval from a Phil Neville cross.

Careca made it 2–1 for the World XI early in the second half, but with 20 minutes to go there was a mass substitution of their players, who were replaced by a former United XI; Schmeichel, Parker, Blackmore, Bruce, Pallister, Darren Ferguson, Hughes, Sharpe and three number sevens: Robson, Beckham and Cantona.

Two goals from Mark Hughes, one a typical 20-yard stunner, made it 4–1 for the United Old Boys before Paul Scholes rounded off the scoring for the night.

The game was seldom a serious affair, mad-cap goalkeeper Pascal Olmeta, who had captured the crowd's admiration during the previous season's Munich Memorial Match, once again did his best to add to the evening's entertainment, leaving his net unattended whenever the opportunity arose to venture downfield in search of a goal.

11 October 1999	**Rest of the World at Old Trafford.**

Attendance: 54,842.

Lost: 5–1.

Scorer: Sheringham.

Team: Van der Gouw, P. Neville, Silvestre, Solskjaer, Berg, Stam, Yorke, Butt, Cole, Sheringham, Giggs.

Substitutes: Scholes for Solskjaer, Cruyff for Giggs, Greening for Cruyff, Irwin for Berg, Curtis for Stam, Clegg for P. Neville

The New Millennium

United opened their friendly fixtures for the new millennium with a rare visit to Bootham Crescent to face York City, a game set up as part of the transfer of goalkeeper Nick Culkin. The Third Division side picked up record gate receipts of almost £100,000 as their opponents strolled through the afternoon, treating it as little more than a workout.

David Beckham, widely rumoured to be on his way out of Old Trafford, seemed to have more on his mind than 90 minutes of football. The England midfielder did have his moments, with one 70-yard pass finding Giggs, but his teammate was unable to make the most of the opportunity and his lob was easily saved by Fettis. Another move involving Beckham and Giggs set up Paul Scholes, but his shot came back off the base of the post.

Roy Keane also came close to scoring, having been set up by Paul Scholes, but his 25-yard shot was saved by Fettis.

York also had their moments in the opening 45 minutes and indeed nearly went ahead in the ninth minute when Potter, moving down the left, produced a deep cross which eluded the United defence before falling for Edmondson. His shot, however, was well stopped by Van der Gouw.

The home side resumed the second half with a vengeance and almost scored within minutes of the restart when substitute Conlon produced a fine save from Van der Gouw. A further effort from the same player, from 25 yards, went inches over.

Having at times trudged through the opening 45 minutes, United began the second half more positively as they broke the deadlock in the 51st minute when Keane fired home Gary Neville's right-sided cross after the York 'keeper had blocked his first attempt.

Eleven minutes later Keane drove home Yorke's cross, which went in via the post. The Irishman lost his chance of completing his hat-trick when, moving forward unchallenged on goal, he lifted the ball over both goalkeeper and crossbar.

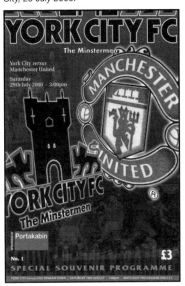

The programme for the match versus York City, 29 July 2000.

29 July 2000	York City at Bootham Crescent, York.

Attendance: 9,003.

Won: 2—0.

Scorer: Keane 2.

Team: Van der Gouw, G. Neville, Irwin, Wallwork, Silvestre, Keane, Beckham, Scholes, Notman, Yorke, Giggs.

Substitutes: Teather for G. Neville, Djordjic for Giggs, Notman for Webber.

Twenty-four hours later United returned to action against Shrewsbury Town. The Gay Meadow side had only escaped relegation to the Conference on the final day of the previous season and were never going to be any real match for an experienced United side, who showed little mercy by hitting eight past their opponents.

United were in front within three minutes, Nicky Butt scoring with a thunderous 25-yard left-footed shot which gave Edwards no chance. It was a lead which Solskjaer doubled soon afterwards, thanks to a Fortune pass.

Much to the visitors' surprise, Shrewsbury pulled a goal back in the 35th minute when Freestone's header left Bosnich helpless, but it was the only opportunity that the home crowd had to cheer, as Solskjaer restored United's two-goal advantage just before the interval.

Teddy Sheringham made it 4–1 with a stooping header five minutes into the second half, with Clegg in the 58th minute, a double from Fortune in the 62nd and 68th minute and Healy in the 79th minute rounding off the scoring.

Although embarrassed by the scoreline, Shrewsbury received around £40,000 from the game, as United played for expenses only.

---

30 July 2000   **Shrewsbury Town at Gay Meadow, Shrewsbury.**

Attendance: 8,000.

Won: 8–1.

Scorers: Solskjaer 2, Fortune 2 (1 pen.), Butt, Sheringham, Clegg, Healy.

Team: Bosnich, Clegg, P. Neville, Johnsen, Berg, Fortune, Healy, Butt, Solskjaer, Sheringham, Blomqvist.

Substitutes: Teather for Johnsen, Berg for Brown, Lynch for P. Neville, Webber for Butt, Wallwork for Blomqvist, Notman for Solskjaer.

The latest encounter against Real Madrid, played in Munich to celebrate the German club's centenary, was not a classic meeting, and there were certainly not the goals that some of the previous meetings between the two clubs had produced.

Despite having the likes of Figo and Roberto Carlos on the bench, Madrid still enjoyed the best of the first half, coming close to opening the scoring in the 10th minute, but Van der Gouw saved well from Morientes. Soon afterwards Keane managed to nudge Savio off the ball just as he was about to shoot.

As the half moved towards a close, Scholes came close with two efforts in the 38th minute and again two minutes later, following a quickly taken Beckham free-kick, which saw his shot go inches wide.

For the Germans in the crowd, who had stayed behind after watching the host club defeat Galatasaray 3–1, the half-time whistle could not come soon enough, and they booed both sides off the pitch.

Early in the second half Morientes escaped the clutches of Johnsen and Silvestre, but headed Savio's cross over the bar. As the action switched ends, both Beckham and Solskjaer saw efforts blocked and Keane hit a better scoring opportunity over the top.

As the game progressed United had the best of the chances to secure victory. Sheringham produced the space for Beckham, but the winger was denied by Sanchez. A cross by Silvestre, following the full-back's run down the flank, saw Solskjaer's volley go narrowly wide. Giggs, having done the difficult part by dribbling through the Madrid defence, prodded the ball weakly into the 'keeper's arms and Solskjaer, again, had a shot blocked by Cesar.

With penalty-kicks looming with a minute remaining, Teddy Sheringham headed a long clearance forward and Solskjaer pounced to shoot beyond Cesar for the deciding goal.

---

4 August 2000 — **Real Madrid at Olympic Stadium, Munich.**

Attendance: 39,000.

Won: 1—0.

Scorer: Solskjaer.

Team: Van der Gouw, G. Neville, Irwin, Keane, Johnsen, Silvestre, Beckham, Scholes, Solskjaer, Sheringham, Giggs.

Substitute: Yorke for Giggs.

Replacing Van der Gouw in goal, Fabien Barthez made his United debut, following his £7.8 million transfer from Monaco, in the stadium where he had collected a Champions League-winners' medal seven years previously, when he helped his Marseille teammates defeat AC Milan. This time around he was to finish on the losing side, as Bayern Munich secured revenge for the defeat in Barcelona 17 months previously by capturing the Opal Supercup.

For Barthez it was no easy baptism, as with only 13 minutes gone he came out to intercept a Scholl through ball, only to allow it to bounce over his arm and past him towards the unmarked Santa Cruz. The Paraguayan, much to the 'keeper's relief, failed to connect with the ball and it rolled wide. Ten minutes later he was to redeem himself with a reflex save from Zickler.

A clumsy shove by Silvestre on Santa Cruz in the penalty area, a minute before the interval, saw the referee point to the spot and Scholl did not waste the opportunity. Neither did Keane, who voiced his thoughts at the defender.

Five minutes into the second half the ball was once again placed on the penalty spot after Khan brought down Fortune, but the 'keeper guessed correctly and dived to save Beckham's kick.

Zickler was a constant thorn in the side of the United defence, with both Berg and Silvestre brushed aside on separate occasions to allow the German to increase the home side's lead.

Khan saved well from Cole before Fortune, who had been on the end of some rough treatment from the German defenders, grabbed a consolation goal five minutes from the end, sending a rising shot into the roof of the net.

---

5 August 2000 — **Bayern Munich at the Olympic Stadium, Munich.**

Attendance: 43,000.

Lost: 3—1.

Scorer: Fortune.

Team: Barthez, G. Neville, P. Neville, Berg, Silvestre, Keane, Beckham, Butt, Cole, Yorke, Fortune.

Substitutes: Wallwork for Silvestre, Giggs for Beckham, Scholes for Keane, Sheringham for Cole.

The next game was little more than a whistle-stop visit for United, as they flew to Malta to face the local champions Birkikara. There had been a possibility that Sir Alex Ferguson's players would come up against Diego Maradona, but the former Argentina star had asked for £150,000 to play.

United were much too strong for the islanders, who were on par with a Third Division side in England. However, to be fair, they deserved credit for keeping the score down to 1–0 at the interval.

The only goal of that first half came when David Beckham took a long ball from Silvestre in his stride before rounding the Birkikara 'keeper to open the scoring.

Blomqvist came close to making it two, with a shot which skimmed the crossbar, while a 30-yard effort from Beckham rebounded off the bar.

With nine changes for the second period it took United only two minutes to score their second, Yorke diving forward to head home a Gary Neville cross. Seven minutes later it was 3–0, Yorke cutting the ball back for Solskjaer to slam home.

Scholes, with something of a trademark strike, made it 4–0 in the 70th minute with a thunderous shot from Fortune's back heel. Solskjaer notched up his second from another cut back from Yorke three minutes later.

With 10 minutes remaining, the Maltese side celebrated their 50th anniversary with a goal, Brincat sending the ball past Van der Gouw from 30 yards.

---

9 August 2000 **Birkikara at the TA Qali Stadium, Valetta.**

Attendance: 10,000.

Won: 5–1.

Scorers: Solskjaer 2, Beckham, Yorke, Scholes.

Team: Barthez, P. Neville, Silvestre, Berg, Johnsen, Wallwork, Beckham, Keane, Cole, Sheringham, Blomqvist.

Substitutes: Van der Gouw for Barthez, G. Neville for Berg, Stam for Johnsen, Irwin for Silvestre, Scholes for Beckham, Giggs for Keane, Yorke for Sheringham, Solskjaer for Cole, Giggs for Blomqvist.

Having lost the FA Charity Shield 2–0 against Chelsea two days earlier, a local derby against Manchester City was manager Sir Alex Ferguson's last opportunity to size up his squad before the new season got underway. The outcome of a friendly against the neighbours did not matter too much, nor did it have any real effect on the months ahead. However, for one United player the evening was something special.

Denis Irwin had joined United from Oldham Athletic in the summer of 1990 for a fee of £650,000, having been rescued from the footballing scrapheap by the Boundary Park manager Joe Royle after being given a free transfer by Leeds United in 1986. This match was to be his testimonial, a thank you to one of football's nice guys.

It turned out to be a night to remember, but, sadly, for all the wrong reasons.

With the game only eight minutes old, Denis was sent crashing to the turf, the victim of a clumsy challenge from George Weah, the former World Player of the Year. The tackle left the United full-back sprawled on the turf and clutching his left ankle. Following treatment Denis limped on for a further half-hour, but eventually he had to call it a day.

This seemed to set the tone for the afternoon, with tackles being slightly more obvious than in other testimonials and a few individual head-to-heads taking place across the park. Haaland locked horns with Butt, Gary Neville clashed with Dickov, and there was none more obvious than that between Beckham and Tiatto. Had it been a League fixture or a Cup tie it would have been difficult to imagine either side finishing with 11 men.

Despite Irwin's disappearance down the Old Trafford tunnel, his record of never having lost to City was kept intact, thanks to goals from Sheringham and Cole.

It was a left-footed shot from Sheringham on the edge of the City area in the 36th minute that broke the deadlock, but the outcome was not ensured until the final minute, when Andy Cole accepted a pass from Fortune before beating Weaver.

Irwin pocketed around £500,000 from his testimonial.

16 August 2000   **Manchester City at Old Trafford.**

Attendance: 45,158.

Won: 2—0.

Scorers: Sheringham, Cole.

Team: Van der Gouw, G. Neville, Irwin, P. Neville, Johnsen, Scholes, Beckham, Butt, Sheringham, Cole, Fortune.

Substitutes: Brown for Johnsen, Wallwork for Irwin, Stewart for Beckham, Greening for Scholes.

The visit to Glasgow to face Celtic was to be the first leg of a double header, with this particular fixture organised to pay tribute to Tom Boyd. The second leg in Manchester, at the start of the following season, would pay a similar tribute to Ryan Giggs.

Celtic were still a far cry from being a match for United and with Sir Alex Ferguson happy to offer odds of 4–1 against 52-goal Henrik Larsson scoring against the visitors, he could have departed south with an even bigger smile on his face.

Larsson almost scored when he rattled the bar with a header in the 24th minute, but play quickly switched to the opposite end, where Beckham floated over a cross and Silvestre headed home from point-blank range.

Sheringham tested Douglas with a half-volley from 25 yards, but the Celtic 'keeper managed to palm it over the bar. Phil Neville blocked a goal-bound Larsson shot, as play quickly switched from end to end and Thompson's effort was cleared after Van der Gouw failed to hold the ball.

It was certainly value for money for the crowd, who had, prior to kick-off, paid a silent tribute to Lisbon Lion Bobby Murdoch, who had died the previous day, but they had little problem in finding their voices in the 65th minute when Sir Alex Ferguson brought on Andy Goram as a replacement for Van der Gouw. The former Rangers player grinned widely as he took his place between the posts.

The countless changes on either side tempered the flow of the game, but Agathe almost prised the ball through for a rare Celtic opening, as did McNamara, while more should have been made of a free-kick won by Maloney.

However, with two minutes remaining Vega failed to close down United substitute Djordjic and the boy from Brommapojkarna coolly chipped the ball over the head of Gould as he came off his line.

15 May 2001   **Celtic at Celtic Park, Glasgow.**

Attendance: 57,268.

Won: 2—0.

Scorers: Silvestre, Djordjic.

Team: Van der Gouw, P. Neville, Irwin, Butt, May, Stam, Beckham, Scholes, Silvestre, Sheringham, Giggs.

Substitutes: Fortune for Irwin, Goram for Van der Gouw, Stewart for Beckham, Stam for Johnsen, Djordjic for Giggs.

Arriving in Kuala Lumpur, Sir Alex Ferguson was addressed as 'Your Excellency' and few would deny the United manager his new title.

United's presence in the country was big news and although at times the players looked less than happy to be there, they quickly settled into the old routine and hit the first opponents of their tour, a Malaysia XI, for six.

Van Nistelrooy crashed the ball against the crossbar in the opening minute, but had to wait just a further five before he found the net to open the scoring, adding a second in the 36th minute, a goal which gave United a 3–0 lead, as David Beckham had scored in the 26th minute.

Andy Cole, having spent the first 45 minutes on the bench, took only 25 seconds to make his mark on the game after coming on as one of a number of half-time substitutes. Cole made it 5–0 in the 70th minute, with Luke Chadwick rounding off the scoring with a sixth in the 84th minute.

New signing Juan Sebastian Veron had something of a quiet debut, while David Beckham blotted his copybook with a show of petulance following a tackle by Chow Chee Weng.

---

22 July 2001 **Malaysia XI at Bukit Jalil Stadium, Kuala Lumpur.**

Attendance: 68,000 (or 100,000).

Won: 6–0.

Scorers: Van Nistelrooy 2, Cole 2, Beckham, Chadwick.

Team: Barthez, G. Neville, Irwin, Veron, Johnsen, Stam, Beckham, Keane, Yorke, Van Nistelrooy, Giggs.

Substitutes: P. Neville for Irwin, Brown for Johnsen, Chadwick for Beckham, Butt for Keane, Cole for Yorke, Scholes for Veron, Fortune for Giggs, Solskjaer for Van Nistelrooy.

If his debut was considered rather low-key, then Juan Veron certainly made up for it when United moved on to the Kallang Stadium to face a Singapore XI. The Argentinean turned on a dazzling display, as United improved on the impressive 6–0 victory in the previous match with an 8–1 triumph in front of yet another stadium full of fervent supporters.

Veron was always one move in front of the opposition, running the show from midfield, but it still took United half an hour to open the scoring, Solskjaer heading home Keane's knock-on from a Beckham free-kick.

This, however, was not the start of the rout, as Indra Sahdran caught the United defence napping and beat Barthez with a right-footed shot. However, Phil Neville restored United's lead four minutes before the break with a right-footed volley from yet another Beckham cross. Just on the stroke of half-time Solskjaer made it 3–1, as goalkeeper Rezal Hassan let the ball squirm through his hands.

Despite the 90 degree heat and the energy-sapping humidity, it was the home side who struggled to cope. Beckham scored the fourth, his free-kick taking a wicked deflection off the defensive wall. Yorke, having come off the bench at half-time, played a one-two with Fortune to make it 5–1 in the 65th minute

Yorke notched up his second three minutes later and Van Nistlerooy made it 7–1, latching onto Fortune's pass in the 71st minute. Ryan Giggs rounded off the scoring with United's eighth two minutes from time.

Despite the eight-goal scoreline, there was one particular incident that stood out and that was a United substitution 10 minutes from time as Fabien Barthez replaced Van Nistelrooy. Having pleaded with his manager for the best part of 25 minutes, the flamboyant Frenchman at first tried to take the field wearing David Beckham's number-seven shirt, but had to change into a number-14 jersey. Once on the pitch, after having received the biggest cheer of the night, he played on the left wing, showing that he was more than capable of doing a job in an outfield position should the occasion ever arise.

---

24 July 2001   **Singapore XI at Kallang Stadium, Singapore.**

Attendance: 44,000.

Won: 8–1.

Scorers: Solskjaer 2, Yorke 2, P. Neville, Beckham, Van Nistelrooy, Giggs.

Team: Van der Gouw, G. Neville, P. Neville, Veron, Brown, Stam, Beckham, Keane, Solskjaer, Van Nistelrooy, Scholes.

Substitutes: Silvestre for P. Neville, Barthez for Van Nistelrooy, Irwin for Stam, Yorke for Solskjaer, Fortune for Beckham, Chadwick for Veron, Giggs for Keane.

When you find yourself being offered £1,700 if you can simply score against United, you realise what you are actually up against. Such was the reward for the players of Thailand who were to face United in the third and final game of the Far East tour, as a Bangkok businessman offered £1,550 to any player who managed to find the net, with team manager Virat Charnparich throwing in £150 of his own money to raise the stake.

It was Veron who once again stood out for United, in a game where the Thais were more than happy to soak up the United pressure. He was the first to test goalkeeper Meesajtham in the 17th minute with a 25-yard volley. Twelve minutes later United were in front, the goalkeeper flapping at a left-footed shot from Giggs from an Irwin through pass.

Within four minutes, however, Sirapan earned himself the £1,700, when he got the better of Johnsen, Butt and Brown with a neat dummy before hitting the ball firmly past Barthez.

A Veron pass set up Cole, but the 'keeper did well to save and a minute before half-time Van Nistelrooy missed a header after a magical piece of play by Veron, who swivelled before playing the ball across goal with his right leg behind his left.

In the second half United squandered numerous chances before Fortune's cross was headed home by Yorke in the 77th minute.

---

29 July 2001   **Thailand at Rajamangala Stadium, Bangkok.**

Attendance: 65,000.

Won: 2–1.

Scorers: Giggs, Yorke.

Team: Barthez, Brown, Irwin, Veron, Johnsen, Silvestre, Beckham, Butt, Cole, Van Nistelrooy, Giggs.

Substitutes: P. Neville for Irwin, Van der Gouw for Barthez, G. Neville for Cole, Keane for Veron, Fortune for Giggs, Scholes for Butt, Yorke for Van Nistelrooy, Chadwick for Beckham.

Few players in the history of the game can have represented one team and won as many honours as Ryan Giggs and it was unfortunate that his big Old Trafford evening did not end in victory. However, the game itself was everything 90 minutes of football should be: a packed house, end-to-end action, the odd physical confrontation and no shortage of goals.

Backed by a large following, the Scottish treble winners, already into their domestic campaign, caught United cold. With only a minute gone Didier Agathe moved down the right, past two red shirts, before sending a low ball towards

MANCHESTER
UNITED
v.
CELTIC

Wednesday
1st August 2001
Kick-off 7.45pm

OLD TRAFFORD

Official Programme £2

The programme for the match versus Celtic,
1 August 2001.

Larsson. The Swede dummied the ball, wrong-footing two defenders, and allowed Sutton to beat Barthez with a left-footed shot from eight yards.

Three minutes later it was 2–0, Larsson setting up Lennon with a perfectly timed pass, which enabled him to beat Barthez.

Beckham was involved in a number of confrontations, with the referee on one occasion having to intervene when he became involved in a head-to-head with McNamara, a scuffle which also saw Barthez joining in.

Van Nistelrooy pulled a goal back in the 26th minute, turning quickly on a Scholes pass and sending a low shot past Kharine from 10 yards. However, within four minutes Celtic's two-goal advantage was restored, Lambert's right-footed shot beating Barthez from 18 yards.

Substitutions strengthened the United side, but Martin O'Neill's changes gave Celtic something of a reserve-team look and they were punished in the 64th minute with the pick of the evening's goals, Veron's right-footed drive flying past Gould from 30 yards.

However, Celtic once again drew on their inner strength and within two minutes Moravcik had scored their fourth of the evening, with an effort that almost eclipsed the previous goal, as he fired a 25-yard free-kick past Barthez.

With 17 minutes remaining, the crowd rose to its feet as the United manager made yet another substitution, this time bringing on Eric Cantona, a guest for the evening.

Van Nistelrooy scored a third for United seven minutes from the end, while in injury time the game almost reached a fitting climax. Giggs, however, volleyed over the bar.

---

1 August 2001   **Celtic at Old Trafford.**

Attendance: 66,967.

Lost: 4–3.

Scorers: Van Nistelrooy 2, Veron.

Team: Barthez, G. Neville, Irwin, Veron, P. Neville, Stam, Beckham, Scholes, Keane, Van Nistelrooy, Giggs.

Substitutes: Brown for Irwin, Silvestre for P. Neville, Johnsen for G. Neville, Yorke for Beckham, Butt for Keane, Chadwick for Veron, Cantona for Scholes.

With two fixtures on the same day, supporters were in a quandary as to which game they should attend. Should they go to Hereford United or should they head for North Wales and watch their favourites take on Wrexham?

In hindsight the best option would have been the former, where United hit Conference side Hereford for six. The scoreline mattered little to Graham Turner's side, but the £35,000 gate money was a more important matter for the cash-strapped side.

Nicky Butt opened the scoring in the 23rd minute, with Quinton Fortune netting the first of his double right on half-time, the second coming in the 69th minute.

Dwight Yorke got into the act four minutes later and Andy Cole also notched up a double in the 78th and 87th minutes to round off the scoring.

This particular fixture is classed in the *Manchester United Official Yearbook* as a reserve-team fixture. It is difficult to understand how the authors came to this conclusion, as if one looks at the teams below it is hard to say which side would have won if the two United XI's that faced Hereford and Wrexham went head-to-head.

At Wrexham, the game being played as a joint testimonial for Bryan Flynn and Kevin Reeves, Veron was once again United's best player. His pinpoint 30-yard pass allowed Solskjaer to open the scoring in the 31st minute with a neat chip over Roggers. Thirteen minutes into the second period, after Scholes had been brought down from 20 yards out by former United player Brian Carey, the Argentinean curled the ball into the top right-hand corner for United's second, despite the presence of a large defensive wall.

Substitutions weakened United's hold on the game and the Welsh side came to the fore, drawing level with goals from Thomas and Morrell in the final eight minutes.

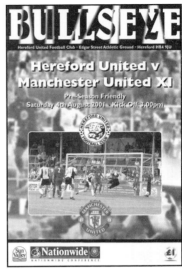

The programme for the match versus Hereford United, 4 August 2001.

4 August 2001 — Hereford United at Edgar Street, Hereford.

Attendance: 4,625.

Won: 6–0.

Scorers: Cole 2, Fortune 2, Yorke, Butt.

Team: Van der Gouw, Irwin, P. Neville, Brown, Johnsen, Keane, Fortune, Butt, Cole, Yorke, Djordjic.

Substitutes: Stewart for Djordjic, Tate for Johnsen.

4 August 2001 — Wrexham at the Racecourse Ground, Wrexham.

Attendance: 7,614.

Drew: 2–2.

Scorers: Solskjaer, Veron.

Team: Carroll, G. Neville, Silvestre, Veron, May, Stam, Chadwick, Scholes, Solskjaer, Van Nistelrooy, Giggs.

Substitutes: Wallwork for G. Neville, Rachubka for Carroll, O'Shea for Stam, Nardiello for Van Nistelrooy, Davis for Scholes, Rankin for Solskjaer, M. Williams for Chadwick, Muirhead for Giggs.

The pre-season warm up next moved to Gigg Lane, Bury, for the final game before the 2001–02 campaign got underway, with the headlines heaping praise on the heroics of Paddy Kenny in the home goal and scorn on United's Andy Cole for missing a hatful of chances against the Division Two side.

On at least eight occasions, the Bury 'keeper denied United with crucial saves and it was not until three minutes after the interval that he was beaten, Phil Neville getting the better of the home defence to score. By then Bury could well have been a goal in front, when the diminutive Bhutia snatched upon a poor Brown clearance in the 17th minute, but his effort hit the underside of the crossbar.

United's second goal of the night came from Yorke on the hour mark after the Bury defence failed to clear the ball, while Solskjaer made it 3–0 nine minutes later. The Norwegian was then denied a second in the 75th minute, after Kenny saved his spot-kick.

The programme for the match versus Wrexham, 4 August 2001.

The programme for the match versus Bury, 8 August 2001.

8 August 2001   **Bury at Gigg Lane, Bury.**

Attendance: 9,929.

Won: 3–0.

Scorers: P. Neville, Yorke, Solskjaer.

Team: Van der Gouw, G. Neville, P. Neville, Brown, Silvestre, Yorke, Chadwick, Butt, Cole, Solskjaer, Fortune.

Substitutes: May for G. Neville, Carroll for Van der Gouw, Roche for P. Neville, O'Shea for Silvestre, Djordjic for Fortune, Stewart for Chadwick, Wallwork for Butt.

Long-haul trips for pre-season friendlies are now considered normal for the travelling supporter. The summer of 2002, however, brought no such luxurious surroundings.

The game against Shelbourne at Tolka Park marked captain Roy Keane's return to action on home soil for the first time since his World Cup expulsion. If the Republican people were of a divided opinion regarding the affair, then it was quite clear which side of that divide the 8,000 supporters inside the Tolka Park ground were on, as cries of 'Keano' vibrated through the afternoon air.

Keane challenged, foraged and berated his teammates when necessary as United scored five without reply, but it took them until the 17th minute to open their account following several near misses.

A chip down the right from Keane sent Phil Neville clear and the full-back, spotting the advancing Giggs, pulled the ball back with the Welshman's shot being deflected into the net via Van Nistelrooy.

Within three minutes they had scored two more. Poor Shelbourne defending following a United corner presented Van Nistelrooy with more than enough room in the six-yard box to simply pick his spot for the second and the Dutchman was involved again for the third. Turning the ball out to Phil Neville, Van Nistelrooy accepted the return pass before sending Forlan clear to beat the 'keeper.

Veron, Forlan and Blanc all went close, but it was not until the 59th minute that a fourth goal materialised, Yorke playing a one-two with Giggs, with the former slipping the ball under goalkeeper Bennion.

A pass from Giggs three minutes later helped Van Nistelrooy complete his hat-trick, but he could quite easily have had four as, after rounding the 'keeper, his goal-bound shot was cleared off the line by Morgan.

The afternoon's biggest cheer, however, was reserved for the substitution of Keane 20 minutes from the end, the United captain going off to a standing ovation.

The programme for the match versus Shelbourne, 20 July 2002.

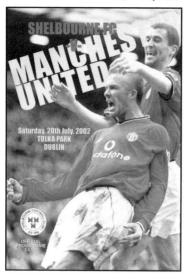

20 July 2002   **Shelbourne at Tolka Park, Dublin.**

Attendance: 8,000.

Won: 5–0.

Scorers: Van Nistelrooy 3, Yorke, Forlan.

Team: Carroll, P. Neville, Blanc, O'Shea, Silvestre, Forlan, Veron, Keane, Giggs, Solskjaer, Van Nistelrooy.

Substitutes: Yorke for Solskjaer, Stewart for Keane, Djordjic for Giggs, Solskjaer for Van Nistelrooy, Roche for Silvestre, Tierney for P. Neville, Williams for Carroll.

With Rio Ferdinand now a Manchester United player, Alex Ferguson had the option of where to give the central-defender his debut in the famous red shirt, as two fixtures had once again been arranged for the same afternoon. One squad of players were headed for the south coast and Bournemouth, while a second squad made the much shorter journey to Chesterfield.

Ferdinand found himself included in the party that journeyed south to Bournemouth. It was familiar ground for the world's most expensive defender, as he had played 10 games for the Cherries in 1996 as a 17-year-old loan player from West Ham. However, there were certainly going to be more eyes on him as he made his initial outing as a United player, with MUTV beaming the game live to China and an estimated 60 million viewers. It was, however, to be only a fleeting 18-minute appearance, as he came off the bench to replace Bojan Djordjic.

Bournemouth surprised their illustrious visitors by taking the lead in the 25th minute, Warren Feeney taking the ball off Stewart before setting up an easy scoring opportunity for trialist Caceres. It was a relatively short-lived lead, as it took United only seven minutes to draw level through Veron, the midfielder prodding the ball home with his right foot following a back-heel from Solskjaer.

However, United were to find themselves behind for a second time within two minutes of the restart, as their makeshift defence failed to prevent Fletcher moving onto Connell's pass before he beat Carroll with a right-footed shot from 15 yards.

United did have their opportunities, with Solskjaer twice being denied by the brilliance of both Bournemouth goalkeepers, Evans in the first half and his second-half substitute Stewart. Another of the Norwegian's efforts was cleared off the line by Tindall.

As the Third Division side began to tire, United came more into the game and snatched an equaliser in the 61st minute when Giggs created the opening for Ben Muirhead to score. Five minutes later they were in front, Veron and Solskjaer combining on the edge of the area for Michael Stewart to score what was to prove to be the winner.

The programme for the match versus Bournemouth, 27 July 2002.

27 July 2002	**Bournemouth at Dean Court, Bournemouth.**

Attendance: 8,104

Won: 3–2.

Scorers: Veron, Muirhead, Stewart.

Team: Carroll, Lynch, Silvestre, O'Shea, Pugh, Muirhead, Stewart, Veron, Djordjic, Giggs, Solskjaer.

Substitutes: Ferdinand for Djordjic, Nardiello for Giggs.

At Chesterfield the outcome was slightly more clear-cut, as United strolled to a 5–0 victory in a match arranged as a testimonial for the former Spireites manager John Duncan.

A goal from the unusual source of Lauren Blanc opened the scoring in the 19th minute, following a one-two with Diego Forlan. The veteran central-defender drew goalkeeper Muggleton from his line before slipping the ball home for what was to be the only goal of the opening half.

Van Nistlerooy hammered home the second nine minutes after the break, while Forlan received the biggest cheer of the afternoon when he scored with a spectacular 25-yard free-kick in the 80th minute, his first goal for the club on English soil since his transfer the previous season.

Three minutes later Roy Keane scored the fourth and a few minutes after that, the impressive teenage winger Kieran Richardson made it five.

The programme for the match versus Chesterfield, 27 July 2002.

---

27 July 2002   **Chesterfield at Saltergate, Chesterfield.**

Attendance: 6,583.

Won: 5–0.

Scorers: Blanc, Van Nistelrooy, Forlan, Keane, Richardson.

Team: Barthez, Roche, Blanc, Tate, Tierney, P. Neville, Davis, Keane, Richardson, Forlan, Van Nistelrooy.

Substitutes: Webber for Blanc, M. Williams for Van Nistelrooy.

Although encouraged from the terracing by countless members of the United Scandinavian Supporters' Club, there was to be no repeat of the goal glut of the previous fixture, as Vålerenga produced a notable performance, despite losing by the odd goal in three to their more illustrious opponents.

Pugh missed an inviting early opportunity in the eighth minute, but it was to take a 26th-minute penalty kick from Solskjaer, wearing a totally unfamiliar number-nine shirt, to open the scoring after he had been fouled by Knut Henry Haraldsen. The Norwegian should have made it 2–0 soon afterwards, but after gathering Forlan's pass he shot over from 12 yards out.

The home side, who had created few first-half opportunities, kept plodding away and came close to scoring through Freddy dos Santos, but he was denied by Barthez. They were, however, eventually rewarded for their endeavours 14 minutes from time when Pa-Modou Kah played a one-two with Tobias Grahn, who himself had come close earlier on, before blasting an unstoppable shot past a helpless Barthez.

Giggs and Forlan were both denied goals by 'keeper Bolthof as United suddenly shook themselves into action and, as they maintained their pressure, Roy Keane scored what was to prove to be the winner six minutes from time, latching onto a Forlan pass.

---

30 July 2002   **Vålerenga at Ulevaal Stadium, Oslo, Norway.**

Attendance: 25,572

Won: 2–1.

Scorers: Solskjaer (pen.), Keane.

Team: Barthez, P. Neville, O'Shea, Blanc, Silvestre, Forlan, Veron, Keane, Pugh, Solskjaer, Giggs.

Substitutes: Stewart for Giggs, Djordjic for Solskjaer.

Ticket for the match versus Vålerenga, 30 July 2002.

The programme for the match versus Vålerenga, 30 July 2002.

Along with Barcelona and Parma, United took to the Amsterdam Arena for a four-club tournament, with host club Ajax providing their opening-night opponents. With points awarded for 'goals scored', United had some ground to make up even before the game kicked off, as Barcelona had beaten Parma 4–2 in the opening fixture. By the end of the 90 minutes United were even further behind, having suffered a 2–1 defeat against the Dutch side.

With the game watched by some 175 million worldwide, United looked somewhat rusty, putting in a rather lacklustre performance.

Despite this poor display, United should actually have taken the lead, but Van Nistelrooy had pushed the ball too far in front of himself in the 29th minute, allowing Ajax 'keeper Stekelenburg to block the ball. Ryan Giggs was also a culprit, missing two good opportunities with headers. Ten minutes after Van Nistelrooy's miss, Ajax took the lead, having already squandered two opportunities themselves through Van der Meyde and Van der Vaart.

The Dutch were happy to add a more physical side to their play and it was following one incident, when Zlatan Ibrahimovic attempted to headbutt Phil Neville, only for the United player to be penalised for a foul, that the goal came. Galasek's free-kick hit the United wall, allowing new signing Sikora to beat United debutant Rio Ferdinand to the ball, before pushing it behind Barthez from seven yards. Chivu also made two crunching tackles on Scholes, for which the referee took no action.

Ibrahimovic increased Ajax's lead in the 75th minute, when he outran the United defence before beating Barthez from 15 yards. Two minutes later Scholes reduced arrears after Keane had lifted the ball over the heads of the Dutch defence, allowing him to volley home.

The defeat left United six points behind Barcelona, with little hope of lifting the trophy.

Ticket for the match versus Ajax, 2 August 2002.

2 August 2002	**Ajax at the Amsterdam Arena.**

Attendance: 48,000.

Lost: 2–1.

Scorer: Scholes.

Team: Barthez, P. Neville, Ferdinand, Blanc, Silvestre, Beckham, Veron, Keane, Giggs, Forlan, Van Nistelrooy.

Substitutes: Butt for Beckham, Scholes for Veron, Brown for Ferdinand, Pugh for Van Nistelrooy, Carroll for Barthez.

Rather surprisingly, United shrugged off their defeat by Ajax and came back with a bang against Parma in the battle to avoid the Amsterdam Tournament wooden spoon. They were certainly more creative in midfield and showed more bite up front. Had they performed to a similar standard in their opening fixture they would most certainly have been facing Barcelona in the Final.

Ryan Giggs opened the scoring in the 23rd minute, side-footing a Wes Brown cross home from just in front of goal, but, despite having most of the play, it was not until after the interval that they increased their lead. Veron scored five minutes after the restart, running onto a long kick out from Roy Carroll, before beating the 'keeper.

Solskjaer, having missed the first game with a neck injury, added a third five minutes later, which really wrapped up the game for United.

Ticket for day two of the Amsterdam Tournament, 4 August 2002.

4 August 2002	**Parma at the Amsterdam Arena.**

Attendance: 48,000.

Won: 3–0.

Scorers: Giggs, Veron, Solskjaer.

Team: Carroll, Brown, Ferdinand, O'Shea, Silvestre, Beckham, Veron, Butt, Giggs, Forlan, Solskjaer.

Substitutes: P. Neville for Silvestre, Stewart for Butt, Keane for Veron, Pugh for Forlan, Djordjic for Beckham.

From Holland it was off to Denmark, where the goals continued to flow, with five against an Aarhus XI, the semi-professional side augmenting their ranks with players from the Danish top flight. The scoreline, however, could be considered a little flattering, as three of the five came in the final eight minutes of the game, when the opposition were clearly flagging.

The programme for the Amsterdam Tournament 2002.

The programme for the match versus
Aarhus, 6 August 2002.

It was two minutes prior to half-time before United took the lead, Van Nistelrooy running across the area before scoring from a Solskjaer through ball. In the 61st minute they added a second, as Solskjaer nudged a low cross from Keane over the line.

Roy Carroll made the most of his rare opportunity in goal, producing some fine saves to keep the Danes out, but as the game progressed he began to see less of the ball, with the final 10 minutes played out at the opposite end of the pitch.

Giggs, having previously hit the post, provided Van Nistelrooy with the third in the 82nd minute, his precise cross being hammered high into the roof of the net by the Dutchman. Two minutes later the compliment was returned for the fourth and, with the Danes now having completely given up, Forlan made it five when he converted a Silvestre cross.

6 August 2002	Aarhus XI at Idraetspark, Denmark.

Attendance: 20,500.

Won: 5–0.

Scorers: Van Nistelrooy 2, Giggs, Solskjaer, Forlan.

Team: Carroll, Brown, O'Shea, Blanc, P. Neville, Beckham, Veron, Keane, Pugh, Solskjaer, Van Nistelrooy.

Substitutes: Forlan for Pugh, Giggs for Solskjaer, Silvestre for Brown, Williams for Carroll, Butt for Beckham, Djordjic for Veron, Stewart for Keane.

It was a friendly that rounded off the 2002–03 pre-season warm-ups, with the Argentinean side Boca Juniors in Manchester to play in a charity match in aid of Unicef. The current Argentinean League leaders, who could boast of Maradona, Batistuta and Veron as former players, were expected to provide United with a final test before the real action kicked off.

Despite the friendly tag, there was a distinct England-Argentina tinge to the proceedings, especially following the introduction of Paul Scholes early in the second half, but by then United were 2–0 in front and looking unlikely to loose their advantage.

Schiavi blasted over Roy Carroll's crossbar early on, but Van Nistelrooy was more relaxed and lethal in his finishing in the 17th minute when he ran on to a Veron chip. Despite his shot being rather scuffed, it still managed to beat Abbondacieri.

United lost the services of home debutant Rio Ferdinand 11 minutes later after the central-defender fell awkwardly, but five minutes before the interval Van Nistelrooy increased United's lead when he accepted Solskjaer's through ball, hitting the ball past the helpless 'keeper.

Blanc came close to making it three, while Solskjaer thought that he had, quickly moving in after the 'keeper had fumbled a shot from Scholes, only for his effort to be disallowed for offside.

The emergence of Scholes, however, lit the blue touch paper and following a couple of rather over enthusiastic challenges, Carlos Tevez, the 18-year-old Boca forward, decided to take revenge upon the midfielder with a swinging elbow catching the United man in the face. Referee Mike Riley had little option but to show the Boca player the red card, friendly or not.

Ticket for the match versus Aarhus, 6
August 2002.

10 August 2002   **Boca Juniors at Old Trafford.**

Attendance: 56,724.

Won: 2–0.

Scorer: Van Nistelrooy 2.

Team: Carroll, P. Neville, Blanc, Ferdinand, Silvestre, Beckham, Veron, Keane, Giggs, Solskjaer, Van Nistelrooy.

Substitutes: O'Shea for Ferdinand, Brown for P. Neville, Forlan for Van Nistelrooy, Butt for Veron, Scholes for Keane, Richardson for Giggs, Williams for Carroll.

2003 USA Tour Media Guide.

The sports section of the *Seattle Post* proclaimed: 'Europe's biggest soccer team hits US', with Tim Korte continuing: 'Imagine a team with the tradition and finances of the New York Yankees, the Hollywood flash of the Los Angeles Lakers and the love-hate following of the Dallas Cowboys during their "America's Team" heyday. That's Manchester United, the champion of England's Premier League. The boys in red, playing their first game since England captain David Beckham was sent to Real Madrid, are hoping to win the hearts – and wallets – of American sports fans'.

So United rode into town, and their performance against Celtic would certainly have won them a new army of supporters on the opposite side of the Atlantic, as they swept the floor with the Scottish side, who already had four pre-season games under their belt, in a 4–0 victory.

Ruud Van Nistelrooy got United's pre-season off to the best possible start with a goal after only seven minutes, picking up where he had left off a couple of months previously. The Dutchman took a pass from Solskjaer and fended off a challenge from Varga before beating Hedman with a left-footed shot.

Twice in relatively quick succession Keane fouled Petrov, with the second earning Celtic a penalty in the 18th minute. Thompson, however, failed to grasp the opportunity and shot wide of Carroll's post.

It was a miss that Celtic were to rue, as 10 minutes later Ryan Giggs made it 2–0. A finely placed ball from Gary Neville, over the head of Laursen, presented Solskjaer with the opportunity to make it 3–0 in the 39th minute.

The gap between the two teams was quite apparent long before the Norwegian's strike and Celtic were fortunate that United took the foot off the pedal in the second half, adding only once to their total through new signing David Bellion in the 72nd minute.

The former Sunderland youngster, on as a substitute for Giggs, accepted a pass from Scholes, kept his cool and slipped the ball past Douglas to round off the scoring.

Ticket for the game versus Celtic, 22 July 2003.

22 July 2003   **Celtic at Seahawks Stadium, Seattle.**

Attendance: 66,722.

Won: 4–0.

Scorers: Van Nistelrooy, Giggs, Solskjaer, Bellion.

Team: Carroll, G. Neville, P. Neville, Ferdinand, O'Shea, Fortune, Keane, Butt, Giggs, Solskjaer, Van Nistelrooy.

Substitutes: Veron for Keane, Bellion for Giggs, Forlan for Van Nistelrooy, Scholes for Fortune, Richardson for Butt, Fletcher for Solskjaer.

After a five-day break, United took centre stage in Hollywood, brushing aside the Mexican side Club America 3–1.

Although not as easy a 90 minutes as the previous encounter against Celtic, United always had the better of the Mexicans, despite the fact that it took them until a minute after the restart before they notched up the opening goal. Once again it was Van Nistelrooy who opened the scoring, this time heading home a Forlan cross. Three minutes later Forlan himself made it 2–0, again with a header, rising above two defenders on the edge of the six-yard box to power the ball home.

The Mexicans thought that they had pulled a goal back in the 54th minute, but Ortiz's free-kick was disallowed due to Bianco's involvement with the United defensive wall.

With Van Nistelrooy substituted, Forlan was now the main striker and he took advantage of his opportunity when a long ball up-field from Ricardo was headed on by Solskjaer, with the Uruguayan's shot on the run looping over the 'keepers head.

Three minutes from time Patino took advantage of some slack United defending and notched up a consolation goal.

27 July 2003	**Club America at the LA Coliseum, Los Angeles.**

Attendance: 57,365.

Won: 3–1.

Scorers: Forlan 2, Van Nistelrooy.

Team: Ricardo, P. Neville, O'Shea, Ferdinand, Bellion, Butt, Veron, Fortune, Richardson, Forlan, Van Nistelrooy.

Substitutes: Lynch for P. Neville, Pugh for Richardson, Giggs for Fortune, Fletcher for Bellion, Solskjaer for Van Nistelrooy.

Next stop was New Jersey, where United had, on paper at least, the sternest test of their pre-season preparations so far, a game against Italian giants Juventus.

Much was being made at the time about the future of Seba Veron, with Chelsea sniffing around the player, but his performance against Juventus should have cemented his future at Old Trafford.

In the 24th minute, with the Italians waiting on Veron to take a free-kick, Giggs quietly stepped forward and stroked the ball past Buffon to open the scoring. Although not directly involved with that particular effort, Veron was at the fulcrum of United's second in the 57th minute, threading the ball through the Juventus defence to Solskjaer, who in turn passed to Scholes to finish the job off.

Three minutes later it was Veron again, this time lifting the ball onto the chest of Van Nistelrooy, who turned and beat Buffon with a classic volley.

With United strolling to a comfortable victory, Juventus substituted nine players, but to no avail, as United continued to command the proceedings, with Tim Howard performing well on his debut, although he could do little about Nedved's 69th-minute strike. This was to be little more than a consolation effort and soon afterwards he was carried off, much to the annoyance of his teammates, following a crunching tackle by Keane.

Solskjaer made it 4–1 10 minutes later, with a typical finish to Forlan's cross-field ball, while the blond-headed Uruguayan should have made it five near the end.

Ticket for the game versus Club America, 27 July 2003.

31 July 2003   **Juventus at Giants Stadium, New Jersey.**

Attendance: 79,005.

Won: 4–1.

Scorers: Giggs, Scholes, Van Nistelrooy, Solskjaer.

Team: Howard, P. Neville, Ferdinand, O'Shea, Fortune, Solkjaer, Veron, Keane, Giggs, Scholes, Van Nistelrooy.

Substitutes: Fletcher for Veron, Bellion for Scholes, Forlan for Van Nistelrooy, Butt for P. Neville, Richardson for Solskjaer, Pugh for Fortune.

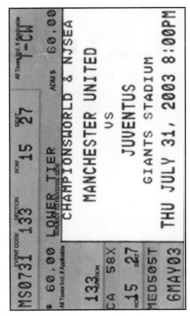

Ticket for the game versus Juventus, 31 July 2003.

The newest landmark in Philadelphia, the Lincoln Financial Field, built at a cost of a cool $512 million, opened its doors with United's final match of their American tour, against another familiar opponent: the Catalonians of Barcelona.

According to the *Philadelphia Metro*: 'Team officials called last night's 3–1 exhibition win by Manchester United over FC Barcelona a test run, a chance to see how well the stadium's engine ran, from the security to the escalators to the turf.

'The 68,396 fans in attendance got to enjoy a real 21st-century sports experience, complete with "not a bad seat in the house" design, concourses twice as wide as those at Veterans Stadium, and a lounge that boasts suede sofas and hundreds of plasma-screen televisions.'

As for the game itself, United found themselves up against one of manager Sir Alex Ferguson's summer targets, Ronaldinho, with the Brazilian placing a cross onto the head of teammate Kluivert for the Dutchman to open the scoring in the 10th minute.

With the Spaniards enjoying most of the opening play, it took United until the 26th minute to draw level, Forlan launching himself at a Giggs cross to divert the ball past Valdes. Eleven minutes later United were in front, Forlan again the scorer, this time side-footing a deflected Butt cross into the net.

Van Nistelrooy replaced Forlan after 53 minutes and, with five minutes remaining, it was the big Dutchman who scored United's third. Brushing past a Barcelona defender, he rounded substitute 'keeper Lopez before sliding the ball into the empty net.

Even the Americans were impressed, with the headlines of *The Philadelphia Inquirer* proclaiming: 'Oh, Man, What A Night', with Mike Jensen writing: 'Manchester United finished off its marketing tour in style, pleasing most of the people in the Eagles' new home and probably even the wannabe streaker who was tripped and carried off with his pants around his ankles right after the game'.

Ticket for the game versus Barcelona, 3 August 2003.

3 August 2003   **Barcelona at Lincoln Financial Field, Philadelphia.**

Attendance: 68,396.

Won: 3–1.

Scorers: Forlan 2, Van Nistelrooy.

Team: Howard, P. Neville, Ferdinand, O'Shea, Fortune, Fletcher, Butt, Keane, Giggs, Scholes, Forlan.

Substitutes: Bellion for Fletcher, Van Nistelrooy for Forlan, Solskjaer for Giggs.

On 6 August 2003 what on paper was nothing more than another pre-season fixture, organised to commemorate the opening of Sporting Lisbon's new home, turned out to be one of the most significant 90 minutes of non-competitive football that Manchester United have ever taken part in.

Although the record books will show that it marked the United debut of Eric Djemba-Djemba, signed for £4.2 million by from Nantes a few weeks earlier, it was the hugely impressive 90 minutes of play by an 18-year-old from Madeira, who went by the name of Cristiano Ronaldo Dos Santos Aveiro, who captured the imagination.

'The Portuguese were spearheaded by 18-year-old wonder kid Cristiano Ronaldo', wrote the *Manchester Evening News* correspondent Stuart Mathieson. 'Juventus are rumoured to have first option on him but one can only hope that United's new alliance with Sporting might give them a fighting chance of landing this gem of the future.'

Having won their three American tour games, it was back to earth with a bump for United. However, Djemba-Djemba began his career on bright note, making a few forceful challenges as well as supporting his forwards, with a 24th-minute foray seeing his 25-yard shot going narrowly wide.

Two minutes later United were behind, Luis Filipe converting a Joao Pinto cross at the far post. Ronaldo had been prevented from opening the scoring in the 20th minute by Barthez, who did well to stop his powerful drive, and the youngster, once again getting behind the United defence, found himself denied by the French 'keeper, who had also done well to save Beto's 30-yard drive in the 33rd minute.

Scholes should have levelled for United in the 57th minute, but his poor first touch resulted in his shot going well over the bar. It was a miss which would be regretted, as the Portuguese increased their lead five minutes later when Pinto escaped his marker before sending a powerful header past Barthez.

Ronaldo again tested the United 'keeper, and it was almost inevitable that the home side would score again. With nine minutes remaining United conceded a third, Pinto again the scorer.

With two minutes remaining United scored a consolation goal, when Hugo turned the ball into his own net.

---

6 August 2003   **Sporting Lisbon at Alvalade Stadium, Lisbon.**

Attendance: 55,000.

Lost: 3–1.

Scorer: Opp. own-goal.

Team: Barthez, O'Shea, Ferdinand, Silvestre, Fortune, Richardson, Butt, Djemba-Djemba, Solskjaer, Scholes, Bellion.

Substitutes: Lynch for O'Shea, Fletcher for Scholes, Pugh for Richardson, P. Neville for Butt, Van Nistelrooy for Fortune.

United, in their final warm-up fixture before setting off in earnest on the hunt for silverware, were given something of a rude awakening, tumbling to a 3–1 defeat at the hands of Stoke City.

For Fabien Barthez it was a night to forget, with the Frenchman at his erratic best. A mis-hit pass to full-back Mark Lynch early on got the young defender into trouble, but the 'keeper redeemed himself when he pulled off a notable one-handed save from an Asaba header.

Goodfellow opened the scoring for the home side, while Forlan equalised with a classic 25-yard strike. The Stoke midfielder struck again: this time his long-range effort hit the crossbar but rebounded against the back of the diving Barthez to give Stoke a 2–1 advantage.

A further Stoke goal, scored by Iwelumo, led to Barthez being substituted, while an injury to Silvestre did little to help the manager's preparations for the forthcoming season

---

13 August 2003   **Stoke City at the Britannia Stadium.**

Attendance: 21,438.

Lost: 3–1.

Scorer: Forlan.

Team: Barthez, Lynch, O'Shea, Pugh, Silvestre, Djemba-Djemba, Butt, Fletcher, Richardson, Forlan, Bellion.

Substitutes: Ricardo for Barthez, Nardiello for Butt, Jones for Djemba-Djemba, Tate for Silvestre, Wood for Forlan.

Previous tours of the United States had proved something of a success for United, but this visit across the pond turned out to be the opposite, with the Chicago crowd booing the team off the pitch after their dull 0–0 draw with Bayern Munich. Having paid up to $100 (around £60) for a ticket, they probably thought that they deserved considerably more for their money, with a team that included the likes of Van Nistelrooy, Ronaldo and Scholes. Not Eagles, Richardson, McShane and Djordjic.

Euro 2004 was used as the excuse for the non-appearance of the United star names, but with Liverpool and Chelsea both in the States fielding players who had taken part in the competition, it was an excuse that did not go down well with spectators and sponsors.

'Bayern, Man U put on sorry spectacle' proclaimed the *Chicago Sun-Times*, following on with: 'Chicago's first experience with the Champions World Series wasn't a good one. Sunday's game between two club power-houses – Manchester United and Bayern Munich – was more about pageantry and financial profitability for the participants than it was about quality soccer. Sloppy passing was commonplace and there were only five shots on goal the entire game.'

It was a young United side, made up of five teenagers and three debutants, which faced the Germans, with only Roy Keane bringing more experience to the side. For United it was a successful result, holding the more experienced Germans to a 0–0 draw over 90 minutes, but for the paying public it was anything but.

Local youngster Jonathan Spector looked good at left-back, with Keane alongside him in central defence, while upfront Alan Smith plodded away in his usual aggressive style.

It was the former Leeds man who set up Djordjic for what should have been United's opener in the 38th minute, but the youngster failed to convert. Smith himself might have scored had Bellion's pass been better directed.

So, with only a handful of shots on goal throughout the entirety of the game, it was little surprise that it was all level at the end of the 90 minutes, with penalties required to find a winner.

Alan Smith took the first for United, but failed to give them the advantage, while Frings made no mistake for Bayern Munich. Bellion put United back in the frame, but Scholl regained the advantage for the Germans. Keane then netted to level things at 2–2.

The programme for the match versus Bayern Munich, 25 July 2004.

Ticket for the game versus Celtic, 28 July 2004.

Ballack kept the Germans in front by netting their third kick, but O'Shea missed, to leave Santa Cruz with the opportunity of winning the game with his penalty, one that he did not turn down.

25 July 2004	**Bayern Munich at Soldier Field, Chicago.**

Attendance: 58,121.

Drew: 0–0 (**Lost:** 4–2 on penalties).

Scorers: Bellion, Keane.

Team: Carroll, Bardsley, McShane, Spector, Eagles, Djemba-Djemba, Keane, Richardson, Djordjic, Bellion, Smith.

Substitutes: O'Shea for Eagles, Jones for Djordjic, Chadwick for Richardson.

Moving onto Philadelphia, where Celtic were the next opponents, and despite the 2–1 defeat, there was an improvement on the previous fixture, with both sides putting in a more competitive 90 minutes.

Gary Neville was on the receiving end of a couple of challenges from Sutton and Hartson, while an Eagles challenge on Sutton in the second minute saw the Celtic man carried off, much to the annoyance of the Hoops' bench.

It was Celtic who took the lead in the eighth minute after Spector gave away a penalty when he fouled Petrov, Sutton converting from the spot. United, however, battled away to force the equaliser and from six yards out a glancing header from Richardson in the 19th minute went narrowly wide.

A Smith effort in the 34th minute was blocked by the Celtic defence, but a minute later he scored his first goal for United when he rose above McNamara to head home an Eagles corner for the equaliser.

Six minutes after the interval, Smith almost gave United the lead but shot over. Celtic regained their advantage in the 71st minute, Beattie getting the better of Keane before beating Howard from a tight angle for what proved to be the winning goal.

Forlan found himself through with the 'keeper to beat, but his poor first touch enabled Hedman to gather the ball with ease. With a minute remaining Bardsley could have snatched an equaliser, but the 19-year-old blasted over.

28 July 2004	**Celtic at Lincoln Financial Fields, Philadelphia.**

Attendance: 55,421.

Lost: 2–1.

Scorer: Smith.

Team: Howard, G. Neville, Keane, Spector, P. Neville, Eagles, Djemba-Djemba, O'Shea, Richardson, Bellion, Smith.

Substitutes: Bardsley for P. Neville, Jones for G. Neville, Forlan for Eagles, McShane for Richardson, Giggs for Bellion.

The final game in the United States took United to New York, where they came face to face with a familiar foe: AC Milan. Despite it being the first pre-season kick-about for the Italians, United's first victory of the tour still failed to materialise.

Paul Scholes had been flown out two days earlier to boost the United squad, after complaints from public and promoters alike, and he was the only real stand-out player among the red shirts.

Scholes darted into the Milan penalty area in the seventh minute, and cries went up for a penalty when he was floored by an Italian defender, but the referee waved away the appeals. However, revenge came in the 33rd minute when a Bellion cross was not cleared properly by Nesta and, as the ball fell to Scholes, the midfielder made no mistake.

Another Scholes effort was drilled into the side netting, while Giggs failed to make the most of a mistake by Maldini when only eight yards out.

Playing much better than in their two previous fixtures, United looked to be heading for victory but, with only seconds remaining, the United defence allowed Shevchenko the opportunity to snatch an equaliser, thereby pushing the game into penalties.

If any supporter had felt short-changed by the 90 minutes, then they certainly got their money's worth from the penalty shoot-out.

Still on a high from converting from the spot minutes earlier, Shevchenko stepped up to take the first kick and again converted. Forlan made it 1–1 and it looked as though Tim Howard might become the hero of the hour when he saved Crespo's spot-kick, but Roy Keane went on to hit the post.

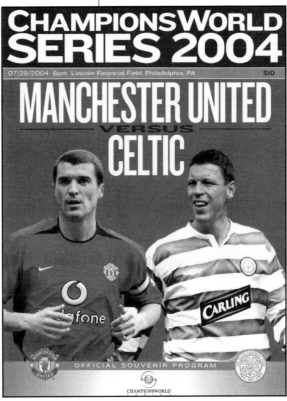

The programme for the match versus Celtic, 28 July 2004.

Ticket for the match versus AC Milan, 31 July 2004.

US Tour Media Guide 2004.

Serginho gave the Italians a 2–1 advantage, but Alan Smith pulled it back, making it 2–2. Kaka converted his kick to restore Milan's lead, but Gary Neville, not someone readily associated with goals, again pulled United level. Milan scored courtesy of Costacurta, but up stepped Chris Eagles to make it 4–4 and take it to sudden death.

Brocchi's spot-kick hit the post, but bounced over the line via Howard's back and it was 5–4. Wes Brown made it 5–5, but Cafu once again put the pressure on by converting penalty number 13. Richardson netted the 14th and Dida did likewise with the 15th. Bardsley took responsibility for the next United kick, confidently scoring to make it 7–7.

With the crowd on the edge of their seats, Kaladze beat Howard for the eighth time. Djemba-Djemba scored to make it 8–8, while Maldini stepped forward to score Milan's ninth. Then, with the 20th kick beckoning, up stepped Tim Howard, only for the United 'keeper to miss and seal the victory for Milan.

---

31 July 2004 AC Milan at the Giants Stadium, East Rutherford, New York.

Attendance: 74,511.

Drew: 1–1. **(Lost:** 9–8 on penalties).

Scorer: Scholes (Forlan, Smith, G. Neville, Eagles, Brown, Richardson, Bardsley, Djemba-Djemba).

Team: Howard, Bardsley, G. Neville, Brown, Silvestre, Bellion, Djemba-Djemba, Keane, Giggs, Scholes, Smith.

Substitutes: P. Neville for Bardsley, Eagles for Bellion, Forlan for Scholes, Spector for Silvestre, Richardson for Giggs.

So, with no victories and only two goals from open play, the 12-day tour came to an end, leaving only the Vodafone tournament at Old Trafford as preparation for the new season.

The Vodafone Cup was scheduled to become an annual tournament at Old Trafford, with this inaugural 'tournament of champions' pitting United against Boca Juniors, Urawa Red Diamonds and their opponents in the second game on the opening night, PSV Eindhoven.

A nine o'clock kick-off was a late start against the Dutch, with less than 30,000 choosing to turn up and watch, but they were soon to realise that the game was to be a bit more than just a fitness-finding fixture, as both Saha and Van Nistelrooy were on the receiving end of strong tackles from Bouma and Ooijer.

Alan Smith, making his home debut following his transfer from Leeds United, was eager to win over the United support and was soon accepted into the fold following his no-holds-barred challenges on Bogelund, Smit and Jan Vennegoor of Hesselink, which had the crowd up on their feet.

However, it was goals that the spectators had paid their money to see and, as on the American tour, they were not forthcoming, with a Mikel Silvestre effort in the 25th minute all that separated the two teams.

PSV had their opportunities, with a fierce free-kick from Alex and another firmly hit shot from Bakkal being well saved by Ricardo in the United goal. At the opposite end Gomes had second-half saves from Saha and Forlan. In the end, however, it was not exactly the start to the tournament that the sponsors wanted.

3 August 2004   PSV Eindhoven at Old Trafford.

Attendance: 29,479.

Won: 1–0.

Scorer: Silvestre.

Team: Ricardo, G. Neville, O'Shea, Brown, Silvestre, Eagles, P. Neville, Giggs, Saha, Smith, Van Nistelrooy.

Substitutes: Smith for Van Nistelrooy, Djemba-Djemba for Saha, Richardson for Brown, Bellion for Giggs.

The programme for the Vodaphone Cup Tournament, 2004.

With Boca Juniors having defeated the Japanese side Urawa Red Diamonds 5–2 in the opening fixture, giving them eight points – three for the victory and one for each of the goals scored – they were already a step ahead of United.

However, it turned out to be the game that never was, as during a torrential storm bolts of lightning reportedly struck the Old Trafford stands, forcing referee Mark Halsey to abandon the opening fixture between Boca Juniors and PSV Eindhoven after 76 minutes.

Due to the thunderstorm the organisers, having consulted with the Met Office, decided to call off the United game against the Red Diamonds. The crowd of around 15,000 showed their displeasure at the announcement by booing. United, however, immediately announced that they would be giving a full refund to those with tickets for the game.

The sound of booing, from both sets of supporters, filled the air again in Cumbernauld, at the three-sides Broadway ground that was home to Clyde. This time the booing was directed at one particular individual – Rio Ferdinand – for delaying signing a new contract, and having been seen in a London restaurant in the company of Chelsea's chief executive Peter Kenyon.

It had been some five decades since Clyde and United went head-to-head at their old Shawfield home, with the Scottish side a far cry now from the days when they were capable of challenging and beating the best.

This time around, cash-strapped Clyde were no match for the Reds and the visitors took a mere 54 seconds to show that they were not going to treat this particular fixture lightly, Kleberson curling the ball goalward from just outside the area. Much to the relief of Clyde 'keeper Cherrie, it clipped the top of the bar.

O'Donnell shot wide of Van der Sar's right post after Ferdinand sliced a clearance, something he repeated a minute later, but he was again spared his blushes. Rossi, at the opposite end, shot just wide as United began to up the tempo.

Kleberson's thunderbolt was pushed past by Cherrie for a corner and the 'keeper had to be alert again to keep out a Jones header.

McGregor and Hunter both came close for Clyde, before United eventually took the lead on the half-hour mark. Fletcher's pass to Saha was pushed on to debutant Ji-Sung Park, but the Korean's shot was blocked by the 'keeper, only to rebound to Kleberson to steer home.

Ferguson changed his entire team in the half-time break, with the outcome producing a further four goals. One, to the delight of the crowd, was for the home side.

A McKeown tackle on Van Nistelrooy saw the ball break to Scholes, who side-footed into the net for United's second, and it almost became three when Rooney released Van Nistelrooy, but Cherrie denied the Dutchman with a fine save. The Clyde 'keeper was, however, beaten by Van Nistelrooy from the penalty spot soon afterwards, having pulled the United front-man down as he raced in on goal.

Clyde pulled a goal back through McGregor when the United defence failed to clear a corner, but it was to be little more than a consolation, as Miller scored a fourth for United in the 79th minute and Van Nistelrooy scored a fifth with five minutes remaining.

16 July 2005	**Clyde at Broadwood Stadium, Cumbernauld.**

Attendance: 8,000.

Won: 5—1.

Scorers: Van Nistelrooy 2, Kleberson, Scholes, Miller.

Team: Van der Sar, McShane, Richardson, Pique, Ferdinand, Fletcher, Jones, Kleberson, Rossi, Saha, Park.

Second-half team: Howard, Bardsley, O'Shea, Silvestre, Eckersley, Miller, Smith, Scholes, Giggs, Rooney, Van Nistelrooy.

The programme for the match versus Peterborough United, 19 July 2005.

Ticket for the game versus Hong Kong, 23 July 2005.

'There's only two United's' was once again the chant from the stands, as the United manager fielded a completely different 11 players for the second 45 minutes of the friendly against Peterborough United, in what was a testimonial match for former United reserve-team player Barry Fry.

It was United's first-ever visit to London Road and they were certainly not given the best of welcomes, as the home side chased and harried for every ball.

The visitors thought that they had made the initial breakthrough when St Ledger headed Richardson's cross past his own 'keeper, but a linesman's flag cancelled the goal out.

After a goalless first 45 minutes and a complete change in United personnel, Peterborough soon found themselves under pressure. Van Nistelrooy headed an Eckersley cross onto the post, but with nine minutes gone in the second period the Dutchman took a pass from Rossi and shot into the bottom corner to give United the lead.

Peterborough enjoyed a brief spell of pressure on the United goal, but could not find an equaliser and were soon to pay for their inadequacy in front of goal.

A Ronaldo one-two with Van Nistelrooy created the opening, with Ronaldo putting United two up in the 69th minute. The Dutchman scored his second eight minutes later and his third in the 84th minute, after Rossi had made it 4–0 in the 81st minute with his first senior goal.

With Peterborough now tiring and the final whistle beckoning, Ronaldo made it 6–0 with his second of the night.

19 July 2005	**Peterborough United at London Road, Peterborough.**

Attendance: 15,460.

Won: 6–0.

Scorers: Van Nistelrooy 3, Ronaldo 2, Rossi.

Team: Van der Sar, Bardsley, Richardson, Park, Ferdinand, Pique, Fletcher, Rooney, Saha, Kleberson, Jones.

Second-half team: Howard, P. Neville, McShane, O'Shea, Eckersley, Ronaldo, Smith, Scholes, Giggs, Rossi, Van Nistelrooy.

The ING Cup was up for grabs as United lined up alongside a Hong Kong XI in the first fixture of the Far East tour, having just confirmed a £1 million sponsorship deal with Air Asia.

Situated in a valley carved into the cliffs and providing an eye-catching backdrop, United, at times, struggled against their less experienced opponents.

Van Nistelrooy had the ball slipped through to him by Rooney, but as Chun Yip Fan narrowed the angle, the Dutchman's shot went well wide. Saha, Park and even Rooney all shunned opportunities in front of goal, the former swinging his leg at thin air rather than the ball, and it was not until the 69th minute that the ball finally rested in the Hong Kong net, Rossi tapping home a Giggs cross.

Substitutions do not normally cause much in the way of excitement, but the introduction of the 20-year-old Chinese forward Dong Fangzhou created a buzz around the ground and he certainly did not disappoint. A mis-kick by substitute goalkeeper Ka Ki Chan went straight to the youngster and from some 40 yards out he set off for goal, past two defenders and, as the 'keeper committed himself, Dong lifted the ball over him and into the net.

23 July 2005	**Hong Kong XI at the Hong Kong Stadium.**

Attendance: 33,971.

Won: 2–0.

Scorers: Rossi, Dong.

Team: Van der Sar, P. Neville, Ferdinand, Pique, Richardson, Fletcher, D. Jones, Scholes, Park, Rooney, Van Nistelrooy.

Second-half team: Howard, Bardsley, G. Neville, Silvestre, O'Shea, Smith, Kleberson, Dong, Giggs, Saha, Rossi.

One name missing from the above line ups, and indeed all the others on this tour, was that of Roy Keane. Although the official reason behind the Irishman's omission was a hamstring strain, it was common knowledge that there had been a fall-out between player and manager. His omission from the tour cast a doubt over the long-term future of the United captain, especially as he had trained for a mere 24 hours prior to the party leaving for the Far East.

The second of the fixtures against Beijing Hyundai was, at times, as far from a friendly as you could get, with Wayne Rooney and Ruud Van Nistelrooy fortunate that they did not get sent off, and Alan Smith also walking the tightrope between red and yellow cards.

The first 45 minutes went more or less according to the script, with United taking a two-goal advantage. However, they should have perhaps taken the lead much earlier than five minutes before the break, as Fletcher just failed to find Rooney with a header and Van Nistelrooy, having seen a 25-yard effort palmed around the post by Yu, blazed well over when sent clean through. The home side also had their opportunities, with Van der Sar saving from both Jelic and Gao Lei. But it was to be United who broke the deadlock, Paul Scholes jumping above the Beijing defence to head home a Fletcher cross at the near post in the 40th minute, adding a second three minutes later after Van Nistelrooy mis-hit the ball.

A third United goal from Park, three minutes after the restart, put the game beyond the Beijing side, but there was still plenty of action to come.

The programme for the match versus Hong Kong, 23 July 2005.

Ticket for the game versus Kashima Antlers, 28 July 2005.

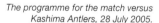

The programme for the match versus Kashima Antlers, 28 July 2005.

A late and somewhat clumsy challenge by Yang Pu on Rooney in the 54th minute saw the United player retaliate with a well-directed kick to the backside and, not long afterwards, Van Nistelrooy took exception to a tackle from Zhang Shuai, pushing him in the chest after chasing the player across the pitch. The Dutchman was substituted soon afterwards.

Had his rather overzealous tackle on Tao Wei taken place in the Premiership, Smith might also have seen red rather than yellow.

United's presence in Beijing did not attract the crowds that the organisers had hoped for, with a rather poor attendance of just over 24,000 scattered around the 70,000-capacity stadium, which three days earlier had seen around 45,000 watch Real Madrid in action. Tickets for the game were selling for as little as £1 outside the ground prior to kick-off.

26 July 2005 Beijing Hyundai at Workers Stadium, Beijing.

Attendance: 24,223.

Won: 3–0.

Scorers: Scholes 2, Park.

Team: Van der Sar, G. Neville, Ferdinand, Silvestre, O'Shea, Fletcher, Smith, Scholes, Park, Rooney, Van Nistelrooy.

Substitutes: Ronaldo for Scholes, P. Neville for G. Neville, Richardson for O'Shea, Giggs for Park, Dong for Van Nistelrooy, Steele for Van der Sar.

Moving on to Tokyo, United were brought down to earth with a bump, with a 2–1 defeat against Kashima Antlers, a club who had only turned professional in 1991.

United went a goal behind in the fifth minute, when midfield player Motoyama gave Howard no chance with a left-footed volley, but Ryan Giggs pulled United level two minutes later after good work by Ronaldo. Motoyama was on hand yet again to restore the Antler's advantage with another fine strike from an intelligent reverse pass from Ogasawara.

Ronaldo's skills had the stadium on its feet, but he could not inspire his teammates to victory and they went on to miss countless scoring opportunities.

Motoyama, however, was unfortunate not to claim a memorable hat-trick, with only the brilliance of Tim Howard denying him the match ball.

As the players left the pitch at full-time, the patience of Rio Ferdinand finally snapped, with the United central-defender reportedly flicking the V-sign at a section of the crowd who had baited him during the game.

The incident with the fans was not the only confrontation involving Ferdinand, as he was seen to argue with Van Nistelrooy after he had dallied on the ball instead of passing it to his teammate. Words were also exchanged at the final whistle.

28 July 2005 Kashima Antlers at the Tokyo National Stadium.

Attendance: 40,000.

Lost: 2–1.

Scorer: Giggs.

Team: Howard, P. Neville, G. Neville, Ferdinand, O'Shea, Kleberson, Jones, Miller, Ronaldo, Giggs, Saha.

Substitutes: Silvestre for G. Neville, Rooney for Jones, Smith for Miller, Van Nistelrooy for Saha, Park for Ronaldo, Bardsley for O'Shea.

The final fixture of the tour, against Urawa Red Diamonds, saw a United victory, but even a defeat could not have taken away a moment of sheer brilliance, a flash of genius and one of the greatest-ever United goals.

United were already 1–0 in front as Rooney, having accepted a pass from Scholes, brushed past two defenders before squeezing the ball past Tsuzuki from a narrow angle with six minutes of the second half played. It was just after the hour mark that the 19-year-old displayed the skill that sets him apart from others.

Picking up a poor clearance by an Urawa defender, Paul Scholes passed the ball forward to Rooney, who was faced with a wall of red-shirted Japanese players. With no one to pass to, Rooney went it alone, fending off one defender before threading his way past two more and finding himself on the edge of the 18-yard box. He carefully lifted the ball over the advancing 'keeper and watched as it drifted into the yawning goal.

As the United players rushed towards him, the backroom staff applauded from the touchline, while the substitutes sought out the television monitors to watch in disbelief as the goal was replayed.

The referee might as well have blown his whistle there and then, as nothing would surpass that goal.

30 July 2005	Urawa Red Diamonds at Saitama Stadium, Saitama.

Attendance: 58,000.

Won: 2–0.

Scorer: Rooney 2.

Team: Van der Sar, G. Neville, Silvestre, Pique, Richardson, Fletcher, Smith, Scholes, Rooney, Rossi, Saha.

Substitutes: Ronaldo for Saha, Dong for Rossi, Giggs for Fletcher, Miller for Scholes, P. Neville for Richardson.

Belgium is not one of the more familiar United destinations, but, with United and Royal Antwerp signing a partnership in November 1998, such a fixture was always going to happen. This season marked the 125th anniversary of the Belgian club and there was no time like the present to make the long-awaited return.

The agreement between the two sides saw United send some of their younger players, John O'Shea and Phil Bardsley, to play in the Belgian League, where they would not just be of assistance to Antwerp, but also gain some experience of playing football at a higher level.

There was only ever going to be one winner of this mismatched fixture, and it did not take United long to open their scoring account. Nor did it take many of the 200 or so travelling United supporters long to continue venting their anger at Rio Ferdinand, with the defender jeered with every touch as well coming in for a more vicious verbal attack as he left the field at half-time.

Van Nistelrooy opened the scoring in the 12th minute, having missed a couple of earlier opportunities, when he tapped home a low Ronaldo cross. Paul Scholes added a second three minutes later with a shot from just outside the area, which took a slight deflection.

A 27th-minute penalty kick from Van Nistelrooy, who had been brought down by 'keeper Willockx, made it 3–0, with the Dutchman completing his hat-trick on the stroke of half-time with a 20-yard free-kick. In between those two efforts Ronaldo had added a fourth with a powerful drive.

So it was 5–0 at the interval. It was a case of how many more would there be, or would United ease off a little and let their hosts back into the game?

It looked as though it might be the latter, as Severeyns, a guest player, pulled a goal back in the 51st minute with a penalty, sending Van der Sar the wrong way after Gunter Verjans had gone down in a challenge with Rio Ferdinand. The decision was considered rather soft.

On the hour mark Darren Fletcher made it 6–1 with a close-range tap-in, which to the relief of the Antwerp side rounded off the scoring, following some good work from Rooney.

---

3 August 2005 | **Royal Antwerp at Bosuil Stadium, Antwerp.**

Attendance: 17,500.

Won: 6–1.

Scorers: Van Nistelrooy 3 (1 pen.), Scholes, Ronaldo, Fletcher.

Team: Van der Sar, G. Neville, Ferdinand, O'Shea, Silvestre, Keane, Fletcher, Scholes, Ronaldo, Van Nistelrooy, Rooney.

Substitutes: Smith for Fletcher, Rossi for Ronaldo, Richardson for O'Shea, Bardsley for G. Neville.

With the packed domestic and European fixture list, mid-season friendlies are now far and few between, so it was of little surprise that there were no friendlies to be found between the visit to Antwerp in August 2005 and Celtic's visit to Manchester in May 2006.

The game was a testimonial match for Roy Keane, a fixture which brought the former United captain back to his old stomping ground following his somewhat acrimonious departure from Old Trafford in November 2005. In his 12 years with United, Keane was revered by most of the Old Trafford support, despite his career sometimes being blighted by controversy, and it was unsurprising that almost 70,000 filled the ground to salute their hero, who had been previously quoted as saying that he would never have a testimonial match. It was thought, however, that the majority of the money raised from this particular fixture would be given to charities in Manchester, Dublin and Cork.

Keane took to the field with his children beside him in the green and white of the visitors, as the chant of 'Keano, There's Only One Keano' echoed around the stadium.

Friendly it might well have been, but with the visiting support of over 25,000 not simply confined to their designated area of the North Stand, there was the need for the stewards to become involved when fighting broke out in the East Stand as the Celtic following belted out their *You'll Never Walk Alone* anthem.

Keane almost created an opening goal for Zurawski in the 27th minute, forcing Howard to dash to the edge of his area to clear. At the opposite end he was ideally placed to clear the ball after Boruc had dropped a Ronaldo free-kick.

The second half saw Keane pull on the red shirt for the last time and, after Dublin's header had been touched onto the bar by Van der Sar, the Irishman fed Solskjaer, but Boruc did well to push the ball behind for a corner.

With the game in its dying moments, there was almost a fitting ending as a Giggs corner floated towards Keane, but the ball slid off his chest.

The game ended in a 1–0 victory for United, Ronaldo scoring after running on to a Giggs pass 10 minutes after the interval.

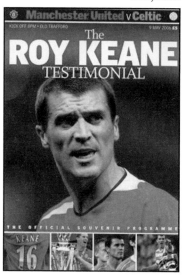

The programme for the match versus Celtic, 9 May 2006.

---

9 May 2006   **Celtic at Old Trafford.**

Attendance: 69,591.

Won: 1—0.

Scorer: Ronaldo.

Team: Howard, Pique, Brown, Vidic, Ferdinand, Evra, Ronaldo, Giggs, Richardson, Rossi, Saha.

Substitutes: Van der Sar for Howard, Neville for Pique, Silvestre for Evra, Keane for Ferdinand, Scholes for Rossi, Solskjaer for Saha, Lee for Brown, Campbell for Richardson, O'Shea for Ronaldo.

South Africa was the destination for the first couple of fixtures of the 2006–07 pre-season campaign, with the opening fixture in Durban, against Orlando Pirates.

The United manager was pleased to get his preparations off to a winning start, with the ever-dependable Solskjaer netting twice, backed by Paul Scholes in midfield.

Up front, the new talent Giuseppe Rossi showed his undoubted potential and was involved in United's opening goal, flicking a 60-yard cross-field pass from Scholes on to Giggs, who in turn fed Solskjaer to score with a half-volley.

Rossi was involved again for United's second, with a Pirates defender showing hesitancy in front of his own goal, allowing Solskjaer to double his tally.

David Jones also caught the eye and the young midfielder set up Richardson for the third. As he pushed forward in support of his forwards, he panicked Seema into sending what should have been an easy clearance into his own net via the head of goalkeeper Chansa.

---

15 July 2006   **Orlando Pirates at Durban, South Africa.**

Attendance: 40,000.

Won: 4—0.

Scorers: Solskjaer 2, Richardson, opp. own-goal.

Team: Foster, Bardsley, Brown, O'Shea, Evra, Fletcher, Scholes, Giggs, Richardson, Solskjaer, Rossi.

Substitutes: Evans for O'Shea, D. Jones for Giggs, Dong for Solskjaer, Eagles for Richardson, Miller for Scholes.

In the second of the South African tour fixtures against the Kaizer Chiefs the Red team bore little resemblance to the United of the previous fixture, with neither Solskjaer nor Rossi looking threatening. Evra was another who failed to shine, while the usually accurate Scholes slid the ball wide of an open goal with the game still poised at 0–0.

With six minutes remaining and the game looking as if it was going to finish goalless, Darren Fletcher took the ball to the byline before crossing into the opposition area, where the waiting Dong made no mistake from eight yards out to give United victory.

---

18 July 2006   **Kaizer Chiefs at Newlands Stadium, Cape Town.**

Attendance: 45,000.

Won: 1—0.

Scorer: Dong.

Team: Foster, Simpson, Brown, O'Shea, Evra, Fletcher, Scholes, Giggs, Richardson, Rossi, Solskjaer.

Substitutes: Dong for Solskjaer, Eagles for Giggs, Gibson for Rossi, D. Jones for Scholes.

Once again, there was little to get excited about in South Africa, as the 'play-off' fixture against the Kaizer Chiefs finished 0–0 after 90 minutes.

Had Dong been more capable in front of goal, the outcome of the game could well have been decided within the opening half-hour, but the former Dalian Shide front-man shunned four good scoring opportunities.

The first saw a long clearance from Steele drop into the Chiefs penalty area, but 'keeper Fernandez did well to block Dong's shot. Moments later an Evra cross found its way to the player, but instead of taking his time and pushing the ball on to a better-placed Fletcher, he hurried a shot, which was blocked by Spencer. His further failure to score when supplied by Bardsley and then by Scholes was to prove costly.

In the second half the Kaizer Chiefs could well have snatched victory, had it not been for a fine second-half save from Luke Steele, but the minutes ticked away without any scoring and it was down to penalties to decide the destination of the Vodacom Challenge Trophy.

From the penalty spot Jones and Evra placed the ball confidently to the right, while Richardson despatched his to the opposite side with his spot-kick. The other two penalties from Eagles, with a casually hit effort, and Foster, who blasted his kick against the bar, ensured that the trophy remained in South Africa.

---

22 July 2006   **Kaizer Chiefs at Loftus Versfeld Stadium, Cape Town.**

Attendance: 35,000.

Drew: 0–0 (**Lost:** 4–3 on penalties).

Scorers: Jones, Evra, Richardson.

Team: Steele, Bardsley, Brown, Evans, Evra, Fletcher, Scholes, Giggs, Richardson, Rossi, Dong.

Substitutes: D. Jones for Rossi, Eagles for Dong, Miller for Fletcher, Foster for Steele.

One of the most regular friendly fixtures of recent seasons is that of United against Celtic, with both clubs in demand for testimonials. This time around, however, it was little more than a pre-season warm-up meeting.

If Sir Alex Ferguson's second string had struggled in South Africa, they were quick to show their manager that it was little more than summer rustiness, as Gordon Strachan's side found themselves on the end of a 3–0 defeat. Who knows what the score would have been had United fielded a full strength side?

With only eight minutes played, United were a goal in front. Boruc in the Celtic goal had managed to stop Rossi from opening the scoring a minute earlier, but he could do little about the right-footed volley from Evans from a Richardson corner.

The Celtic 'keeper was then tested by an Eagles drive from the edge of the box, while Martin should have made it 2–0 instead of firing wide from 12 yards out. Fletcher also came close to scoring with a header at the far post.

It was not all United, however, as Thompson and Miller both tested Foster, with McGeady also causing a few problems for the United defence.

United went into a 2–0 lead on the hour when a Richardson free-kick, following a foul on the ever-troublesome Martin, saw Scholes nip in to score from three yards out. The same player made it 3–0 four minutes from the end, when Boruc failed to hold a rather weak header, allowing the midfielder to score with ease. By then, however, most of the home support were heading home, with their favourites having managed only one win and two goals in seven pre-season fixtures.

26 July 2006   Celtic at Celtic Park.

Attendance: 25,000.

Won: 3–0.

Scorers: Scholes 2, Evans.

Team: Foster, Bardsley, Brown, Evans, Evra, Eagles, Scholes, Fletcher, Martin, Rossi, Richardson.

Substitutes: Miller for Eagles, Gibson for Fletcher, Simpson for Bardsley, McShane for Brown, D. Jones for Richardson.

United's youngsters continued their footballing education at Preston North End. However, without much in the way of experience to guide them through the 90 minutes, their opponents took full advantage of the situation and recorded a 2–1 victory.

It took the home side a mere three minutes to get the better of the United defence, with former United reserve player Danny Pugh scoring from a Nugent cross. Dichio then rattled the crossbar as the visitors struggled to make any headway and they went further behind in the 58th minute when Pugh, finding Whaley, slammed the ball past Steele.

United did enjoy a brief flourish, pushing forward as Preston struggled to regain their momentum following a handful of substitutions, but it was not until six minutes from time that Solskjaer scored for the visitors, firing home a penalty after Fletcher had been brought down.

29 July 2006   Preston North End at Deepdale, Preston.

Attendance: 12,541.

Lost: 2–1.

Scorer: Solskjaer.

Team: Steele, Bardsley, McShane, Evans, Simpson, Martin, Gibson, Miller, Richardson, Solskjaer, Rossi.

Substitutes: Fletcher for Rossi, Eagles for Gibson, Lee for Bardsley, R. Jones for Richardson.

Wayne Rooney returned to the fray wearing the captain's armband against Macclesfield Town, in a game which saw the kick-off delayed some 15 minutes due to crowd congestion. The Moss Rose side were happy to squeeze as many as possible into their compact little stadium, pushing the gate receipts up to almost £25,000.

With Van der Sar and Ferdinand also in the United line up, they were always going to be too strong for Macclesfield, but in the opening 45 minutes former United goalkeeper Tommy Lee kept the visitors at bay with a string of fine saves. Rooney was denied on two separate occasions, the first, in the 13th minute, a point-blank save and then a header grasped underneath the crossbar. Chris Eagles and defender Paul McShane were also denied goals, the former by the busy Lee, the latter due to a well-positioned Macclesfield defender on the goalline.

Although the game was goalless at the interval, Wayne Rooney broke the deadlock within 60 seconds of the restart. Some were still in the queue and missed Town's equaliser two minutes later, when Swailes shot home through a crowd of players following a corner-kick.

With Rooney, Van der Sar and Ferdinand all substituted, it was left up to a young, inexperienced United side to fight for a victory, and with 17 minutes remaining Fraizer Campbell turned in mid-air to head home what was to prove to be the winning goal.

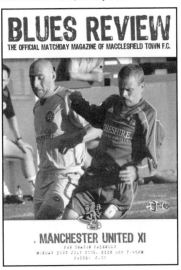

The programme for the match versus Macclesfield Town, 31 July 2006.

31 July 2006 Macclesfield Town at Moss Rose, Macclesfield.

Attendance: 5,500.

Won: 2–1.

Scorers: Rooney, Campbell.

Team: Van der Sar, Simpson, McShane, Ferdinand, Lee, D. Jones, Eagles, Gibson, Martin, Rossi, Rooney.

Substitutes: Heaton for Van der Sar, Gray for Gibson, Campbell for Rooney, Rose for Eagles, Shawcross for Ferdinand, R. Jones for D. Jones.

It had been a mere 34 days since Wayne Rooney had seen red playing for England against Portugal in the quarter-finals of the World Cup, and within 41 minutes of United's opening fixture in the LG Amsterdam Tournament against FC Porto he was being dismissed for the third time on foreign soil within 12 months.

Rooney clearly had his eyes on the ball as he jumped alongside Portuguese defender Pepe, but his hand brushed against his opponent's face. Referee Bossen showed little hesitation in reaching for his red card and United were reduced to 10 men.

Midway through the second half, with United leading 2–0, the referee was once again fumbling in his pocket for his red card, this time to brandish in front of Paul Scholes. The United midfielder had been booked earlier for a handball, but 46 seconds after being handed the captain's arm band by Ryan Giggs he foolishly tackled Quaresma from behind, leaving the referee with little choice but to send him off.

United, with Michael Carrick making his debut, had opened the scoring after 20 minutes through Paul Scholes with a typical strike, latching on to a Giggs corner some 25 yards out. Initially lining up to shoot with his right foot, he quickly switched to his left, giving the 'keeper little hope of stopping the ball.

Rooney added a second nine minutes later, blocking an attempted clearance by Bosingwa before beating the 'keeper. Despite being reduced to nine men, United increased their lead when Richardson found Solskjaer on the Porto byline and, from an improbable angle, the Norwegian managed to squeeze the ball past the 'keeper and into the net.

With 14 minutes remaining Pepe beat Foster from 25 yards, but there was to be no fightback by Porto.

4 August 2006 FC Porto at the Amsterdam Arena.

Attendance: 25,000.

Won: 3–1.

Scorers: Scholes, Rooney, Solskjaer.

Team: Van der Sar, Bardsley, O'Shea, Brown, Evra, Park, Carrick, Scholes, Giggs, Rooney, Solskjaer.

Substitutes: Simpson for O'Shea, Foster for Van der Sar, Richardson for Giggs, Fletcher for Park, Martin for Carrick.

The events of the second Amsterdam friendly were to cause more concern, as £18.6 million signing Michael Carrick suffered ankle ligament damage 12 minutes into the second half of the game against host club Ajax.

Ticket for the game versus FC Porto, 4 August 2006.

The United manager would certainly have been happier to have lost the tournament and returned home with a fully fit squad than to see his side blighted by injuries and possible suspensions, but that is one of the risks that you have to take when you play pre-season friendlies.

Another is dubious refereeing decisions, with the referee furious at the tackle from behind by Perez which left Carrick sprawled on the turf, while a similar challenge by Heitinga, the last Ajax defender, on Rossi, resulted in nothing more than a booking.

The latter challenge, 14 minutes from time, infuriated the United manager and he was in the process of venting his feelings at the fourth official when the free-kick from Ryan Giggs was adjudged to have crossed the line.

Heitinga had seen a first half-headed goal disallowed for offside and Van der Sar had made a superb penalty save from Huntelaar as the host side pressed forward. Giggs could also have found the back of the net earlier, after coming close on a couple of occasions, but his free-kick was to be the only goal of the game and enough to give United yet another piece of silverware to display in their already overflowing museum.

The programme for the Amsterdam Tournament, 2006.

5 August 2006	**Ajax at the Amsterdam Arena.**

Attendance: 45,000.

Won: 1–0.

Scorer: Giggs.

Team: Van der Sar, Simpson, Evans, Brown, Richardson, Miller, Fletcher, Carrick, Park, Rossi, Giggs.

Substitutes: Martin for Carrick, D. Jones for Miller, Bardsley for Giggs.

It took Ronaldo only six minutes to make his mark on the game against Oxford United. He chested the ball down to Solskjaer, with the Norwegian wasting little time in blasting the ball high into the roof of Oxford's net. Eight minutes later Ronaldo was claiming a goal for himself with a curling volley.

Darren Fletcher added a third with a rare goal in the 15th minute, but Duffy reduced that lead shortly before half-time with a far-post header.

A short Jones pass saw Ronaldo make it 4–1 with a shot into the bottom corner 13 minutes into the second half and, as far as the scoring went, that was that.

The programme for the match versus Oxford United, 8 August 2006.

8 August 2006	**Oxford United at Kassam Stadium, Oxford.**

Attendance: 11,463.

Won: 4–1.

Scorers: Ronaldo 2, Solskjaer, Fletcher.

Team: Foster, Bardsley, O'Shea, Silvestre, Heinze, Ronaldo, Fletcher, D. Jones, Richardson, Solskjaer, Saha.

Substitutes: Martin for Richardson, Simpson for Heinze, Evans for O'Shea, Miller for Solskjaer, Rossi for Ronaldo, Heaton for Foster.

The final warm-up game of the 2006–07 pre-season saw the previous seasons UEFA Cup winners Sevilla come face to face with a United depleted by injury, in a game organised to mark the official opening of the new quadrant sections of the Old Trafford stadium. Even without the likes of Gary Neville, Michael Carrick, Alan Smith, Nemanja Vidic and Rio Ferdinand, the Spaniards still found their hosts too strong for them. The visitors had been third choice for what was considered a showpiece friendly, as both Real Madrid and Barcelona were unavailable.

Back on familiar turf, Cristiano Ronaldo found himself playing up front alongside Louis Saha instead of in his more familiar wide role, although he still looked a little rusty following his extended summer break.

Had either of the original choices of opposition been available then the Old Trafford crowd might have enjoyed a more eventful opening 45 minutes, but as it was there was little to get excited about, with United's only real chance coming on the half-hour mark, when Giggs got the better of Alves before crossing into the area, and Park really should have done much better in front of goal.

The second half began as the first had ended, but with less than half an hour remaining the game sprang into life when Ronaldo's low right-sided cross was driven underneath goalkeeper Palop by Saha from 15 yards.

With two minutes remaining, Ronaldo sent a right-footed free-kick goalwards and, taking a deflection off midfielder Renato, it sneaked between goalkeeper Palop and the post. A through ball from Richardson with seconds remaining allowed David Jones to score his initial first-team goal with a firmly struck left-footed drive, which the 'keeper should have stopped.

12 August 2006 — **Sevilla at Old Trafford.**

Attendance: 40,134.

Won: 3–0.

Scorers: Saha, Ronaldo, D. Jones.

Team: Van der Sar, Bardsley, Brown, Silvestre, Heinze, Park, O'Shea, Scholes, Giggs, Ronaldo, Saha.

Substitutes: Kuszczak for Van der Sar, Evra for Bardsley, Solskjaer for Heinze, Miller for Saha, D. Jones for Giggs, Richardson for Scholes.

There was to be a double celebration at Old Trafford and a diversion from the rigours of domestic and European fixtures when United took on a European XI, in a match organised to celebrate the 50th anniversary of United's first venture into Europe and the Treaty of Rome, signed on 25 March 1957. It also saw £1.25 million raised for charity, with the crowd of 74,343 a record for a friendly at Old Trafford.

Big screens flashed up images of the Busby Babes, the 1968 European Cup Final and the more recent kick of Solskjaer's boot at the ball in the Nou Camp goalmouth, prior to the latter walking onto the pitch with the famous trophy in his hands.

Marcello Lippi's European side did not contain the stars who were originally billed, as numerous withdrawals meant that it was more of a 'reserve' side, but the crowd were still treated to an enjoyable evening's entertainment.

Scholes split the opposition defence to allow Rooney the privilege of opening the scoring in the sixth minute, rounding Canizares before slipping the ball into the empty net. Three minutes later the 'keeper was beaten again; this time Wes Brown got onto a Giggs cross at the far post.

Lyon's Malouda pulled a goal back with a stunning left-footed drive from 25 yards out, but this was bettered by a Ronaldo free-kick from all of 35 yards, 10 minutes before the break, which fitted the evening perfectly.

The select XI should have pulled it back to 3–2 in the 39th minute, but Ibrahimovic hit the crossbar with a penalty and the team were to soon find themselves 4–1 behind, as Rooney got his second of the night, converting a Ji-Sung Park cross.

Half-time entertainment was provided in the form of David Beckham, unable to play on the night, who received a rapturous reception before addressing the crowd. After that, it was all downhill.

Numerous substitutions took the edge off the game, especially as no one wanted to pick up injuries at such a crucial stage of the season. There were only two further goals, both coming from the European XI, with the familiar figure of Bolton's Diouf scoring both; a header seven minutes after the restart and a penalty after Heinze handled three minutes from the end.

13 March 2007	European XI at Old Trafford.

Attendance: 74,343.

Won: 4–3.

Scorers: Rooney 2, Brown, Ronaldo.

Team: Kuszczak, Neville, Brown, Heinze, Richardson, Ronaldo, Scholes, Giggs, Park, Rooney, Smith.

Substitutes: Heaton for Kuszczak, O'Shea for Neville, Eagles for Ronaldo, Carrick for Giggs, Andy Cole for Rooney, Dong for Smith.

United's pre-season tour of the Far East ran into problems from the start, as their proposed fixture in Kuala Lumpur on 27 July, arranged by the Malaysian government to celebrate the country's 50th anniversary, had to be postponed due to the Asia Cup still being played and the Asian Football Confederation unwilling for Manchester United to be a distraction from their competition. Without the permission of the AFC, United could not play in Malaysia. However, despite the shortage of time, alternative opposition was found in China.

There was also considerable bad press, with the media insisting that United were simply travelling the several thousand miles for financial reasons, something that Sir Alex Ferguson refused to admit, saying: 'Nowadays, people watch games on television and tours like this give them an opportunity to see some of their favourite players in the flesh and that is exciting for them.' The tour, however, was expected to firmly cement United as the number one club in the Far East and was expected to net the club around £5 million for their four-game, two-week jaunt. Their popularity was confirmed in the opening fixture against the J-League champions Urawa Red Diamonds, when just under 60,000 spectators turned up on a wet evening.

The home side gave their illustrious visitors, who were still suffering from jet lag, not to mention the 85 per cent humidity, something of a jolt when they opened the scoring in the 26th minute. Hideki Uchidate scored with a swerving shot past Van der Sar from some 20 yards out, with many suggesting that the Dutchman should have stopped the shot.

Two minutes after the interval Darren Fletcher equalised with one of his irregular strikes, with Ronaldo putting United in front five minutes later, cutting in from the left before beating Yamagishi. They failed, however, to hold on to this lead, as the defence allowed their opponents too much room and Ono gratefully took advantage of the situation to equalise in the 78th minute.

The programme for the match versus Urawa Red Diamonds, 17 July 2007.

17 July 2007	Urawa Red Diamonds at Saitama Stadium, Japan.

Attendance: 58,716.

Drew: 2–2.

Scorers: Fletcher, Ronaldo.

Team: Van der Sar, Brown, Ferdinand, Vidic, Evra, Ronaldo, Fletcher, Carrick, Giggs, Scholes, Rooney.

Substitutes: Evans for Ferdinand, Simpson for Vidic, Silvestre for Evra, O'Shea for Carrick, Smith for Giggs.

With the jet lag shrugged off, United made short work of FC Seoul, with Ronaldo once again turning on the style, while also scoring the opening goal after six minutes. A throw-in from Evra to Rooney to Ronaldo found the Portuguese star with too much room and an easy shot past the 'keeper opened the scoring.

A Ronaldo back-flick not only brought approval from the crowd, but also set up the second goal for Eagles in the 21st minute. Two minutes later he was once again the provider, combining with Evra to create the opening for Rooney to score the third.

With an estimated 750,000 South Koreans said to have a United credit card, and 50 per cent of the 49 million population reportedly being United supporters, there was little sympathy going to be shown to the home side and, with the game over as a contest, the visitors were simply content to work towards their match fitness.

Evra, beginning to show his capabilities as a first-class full-back, got in on the scoring act 14 minutes after the interval with United's fourth, as a reshuffled United side continued to run the show.

The only worrying aspect for Sir Alex Ferguson was the rather needless first-half retaliation from Wayne Rooney and the yellow card for Paul Scholes in the 74th minute, followed by a further lecture from the referee two minutes from time that could well have seen him dismissed.

20 July 2007	FC Seoul at Seoul World Cup Stadium.

Attendance: 64,000.

Won: 4–0.

Scorers: Ronaldo, Eagles, Rooney, Evra.

Team: Van der Sar, Bardsley, Ferdinand, Vidic, Silvestre, Eagles, Carrick, O'Shea, Evra, Rooney, Ronaldo.

Substitutes: Giggs for Ronaldo, Smith for Rooney, Scholes for Carrick, Simpson for Bardsley, Kuszczak for Van der Sar, Evans for Vidic.

Paul Scholes was sent home with a knee injury following the 4–0 victory over Seoul, but he was certainly not missed, as United continued their pre-season warm-up by hitting Chinese side Shenzhen FC for six without reply.

It took United 11 minutes to register their first goal, Ryan Giggs tapping home an unselfish Rooney pass. The Welshman returned the compliment nine minutes later, with Rooney beating the 'keeper with a delightful chip from the edge of the area.

It was Giggs again who set up goal number three for Nani. After scoring with a first-time effort from 20 yards on his debut, the former Sporting Lisbon player proceeded to perform a back-flip somersault, much to his manager's apparent anguish.

As in the previous encounter, the opposition simply gave up a lost cause and, despite United taking their foot off the pedal, they proceeded to score a further three goals. O'Shea made it 4–0 from a Ronaldo pass 10 minutes after the break, while Ronaldo added a fifth two minutes later and Eagles rounded off the scoring with a spectacular 30-yard dipping volley in the 64th minute.

---

23 July 2007   **Shenzhen FC at Macau Stadium, Macau.**

Attendance: 15,000.

Won: 6–0.

Scorers: Giggs, Rooney, Nani, O'Shea, Ronaldo, Eagles.

Team: Van der Sar, Brown, Evans, Vidic, Evra, Ronaldo, Fletcher, Gibson, Nani, Rooney, Giggs.

Substitutes: Kuszczak for Van der Sar, Ferdinand for Vidic, O'Shea for Gibson, Smith for Giggs, Silvestre for Evra, Eagles for Ronaldo, Carrick for Nani, Dong for Rooney.

It is very unlikely that United will ever play against such an oddly named side as Guangzhou Pharmaceutical, a Chinese side who were included in the tour itinerary as a last-minute replacement for the planned Malaysian leg of the tour. Like Shenzhen FC, they could do little to prevent United from returning home unbeaten.

Again, it was little more than a public training session, although it did take United longer than it should have to break the deadlock. In the 19th minute Carrick drifted into the penalty area, but was brought down by Oliveira. At first it appeared that the referee was going to play safe and award a free-kick outside the box, but to the annoyance of the Chinese he pointed to the spot. Wayne Rooney made no mistake with the kick to give United the lead.

Both Rooney and Nani came close to increasing the lead before the latter finally made it 2–0, two minutes before the interval, with a chip from the edge of the six-yard box.

The second half got underway with United having only 10 men on the pitch, as substitute goalkeeper Tom Heaton was still making his way from the dressing rooms. His appearance on the touchline prompted the referee to restart the game, although the *Manchester Evening News* United correspondent Stuart Mathieson noted in his report that, 'Heaton could have stayed on the bench and his goal would still have been intact'.

The third goal of this particular fixture, and the 15th and final goal of United's four-match tour, came in the 52nd minute and marked the first senior goal for 20-year-old substitute Lee Martin, as he cut in from the left to score with a fine 20-yard drive.

The programme for the match versus Shenzhen FC, 23 July 2007.

27 July 2007 **Guangzhou Pharmaceutical at Olympic Stadium.**

Attendance: 50,000.

Won: 3–0.

Scorers: Rooney, Nani, Martin.

Team: Kuszczak, Bardsley, Ferdinand, Vidic, Simpson, Martin, Carrick, Gibson, Nani, Rooney, Dong.

Substitutes: Heaton for Kuszczak, O'Shea for Gibson, Silvestre for Ferdinand, Brown for Vidic, Eagles for Martin, Evra for Nani, Smith for Dong, Ronaldo for Rooney.

A confrontation with Inter Milan saw the Italians secure a 3–2 victory. The game found its way into the record books, with the attendance of 73,738 being a record for an Old Trafford pre-season friendly.

The game actually began promisingly for United, as they took a 17th-minute lead through Wayne Rooney. The former Everton player latched on to Evra's low centre, which was dummied by Giggs, to blast the ball past Julio Cesar. However, it was a lead that the Reds were to hold for only four minutes against a Milan side who were soon to step up a gear and leave United struggling.

Former Real Madrid star Figo sent a testing ball into the United area, which caught Evra in two minds, while also failing to clear his lines properly. Ferdinand was also caught out by Figo's pass and Suazo snatched on the opportunity to score. The United full-back was left looking shaky for a second time five minutes later, when, after losing possession to Stankovic in his own half, he saw the midfielder's cross diverted beyond Van der Sar by Ibrahimovic.

There was more anguish to follow for the United defence, when Ronaldo was robbed of the ball by Materazzi, who in turn fed Ibrahimovic. Quickly despatching the ball to Figo, a further pass left Vidic beaten and presented Honduran striker Suazo with his second goal of the night.

Surprisingly, the United manager did not involve any of his substitutes, but the team certainly played better in the second 45 minutes. When Adriano headed a Ronaldo free-kick into his own net in the 58th minute the crowd had hopes of a fightback, but it was not to be.

1 August 2007 **Inter Milan at Old Trafford.**

Attendance: 73,738.

Lost: 3–2.

Scorers: Rooney, opp. own-goal.

Team: Van der Sar, Brown, Ferdinand, Vidic, Evra, Carrick, Eagles, O'Shea, Giggs, Ronaldo, Rooney.

Fresh from helping Brazil win the Copa America, £17-million signing Anderson ran out for his United debut against Doncaster Rovers at their Keepmoat Stadium. Despite only participating in the opening 45 minutes against the League One side, the young Brazilian certainly gave the impression that he was going to be a useful addition to the United squad.

While United fielded something of a second-string side due to the looming FA Charity Shield against Chelsea, Doncaster were at full strength, with a line up that included former United players Mark Wilson and Richie Wellens. Rovers were first to create a real opening, with Woods testing Kuszczak from around 20 yards out in the 10th minute.

Eight minutes later the United 'keeper was almost punished for his failure to grasp a Doncaster corner, but, much to his relief, Hayter's effort from only four yards out was blocked on the line by Sean Evans. Kuszczak did, however, redeem himself as the first half drew to a close, turning a header from Lockwood over the bar.

It was not all Doncaster though, as Sullivan's crossbar was rattled by a ferocious 25-yard, left-footed drive from Gibson in the 12th minute, while Martin should have followed up his goal on the Asian tour with another, but after being sent through by Campbell he hit his effort straight at Sullivan.

As in the opening half it was Doncaster who came closest to opening the scoring, Griffith blasting over with an open goal at his mercy after Kuszczak had come out to challenge McCammon. Dong then set up Campbell with a neat one-two, but he put the ball wide of the post. As it was, the crowd had to wait until just after the 70th minute for the first goal to come. A Ritchie Jones corner was only partly cleared, falling to Gibson, and he fired an unstoppable left-footed drive past Smith.

To their credit, the home side continued to press forward and almost equalised through Dyer, but his shot went narrowly past. In the end, the young United side proved just a little too strong for Rovers and, with a minute remaining, Dong and Campbell combined to set up Sean Evans to blast the ball past Smith for United's second.

---

3 August 2007 — **Doncaster Rovers at Keepmoat Stadium.**

Attendance: 13,080.

Won: 2–0.

Scorers: Gibson, S. Evans.

Team: Kuszczak, Bardsley, Pique, J. Evans, Silvestre, Martin, Fletcher, Gibson, S. Evans, Anderson, Campbell.

Substitutes: Shawcross for Pique, Dong for Anderson, Simpson for J. Evans, Lea for Fletcher, Eckersley for Silvestre, Jones for Martin.

Twenty-four hours later the United bandwagon rolled into Peterborough, where a similar 11 to that which had defeated Doncaster recorded a 3–1 victory against Darren Ferguson's side.

For many United supporters it was worth making a slight detour on their journey to Wembley for the Charity Shield, just to witness the debut of another of Sir Alex Ferguson's new additions, Owen Hargreaves. The former Bayern Munich player came on at half-time, but blended into the game rather than making a direct impression.

Full-back Adam Eckersley gave United the lead in the 23rd minute, with an angled drive, but the home side drew level four minutes after the interval through Howe.

Jones made it 2–1 after a Dong effort was blocked by the 'keeper and the Chinaman himself rounded off the scoring in the 77th minute following some neat footwork inside the area.

---

4 August 2007 — **Peterborough United at London Road, Peterborough.**

Attendance: 11,574.

Won: 3–1.

Scorers: Eckersley, Jones, Dong.

Team: Heaton, Simpson, Eckersley, Shawcross, J. Evans, Pique, Jones, Gibson, Campbell, Dong, Martin.

Substitutes: Bardsley for Shawcross, Hargreaves for Gibson, Lea for Pique, S. Evans for J. Evans.

Team Sheet for the match versus Dunfermline Athletic, 8 August 2007.

Two first-team friendlies on the same day conjured up something of a problem for the United supporters, with games against Dunfermline Athletic, scheduled as a testimonial match for Scott Thomson, and Glentoran.

United were to travel to Fife with Mike Phelan in charge of a United side that included Paul Scholes, returning to action a mere two weeks after a knee operation, and Owen Hargreaves, fresh from his 45-minute debut in a reserve-team friendly against Peterborough four days previously.

There was an impressive performance by Ryan Giggs, with the United veteran receiving a bigger round of applause than Thomson when he left the field 10 minutes from the end, with United treating the crowd to some vintage football in a 4–0 victory.

Dunfermline had already opened their Scottish League campaign and were fielding something of a weakened side, but it would have mattered little as they were no match for the visitors, despite creating a couple of early opportunities that could easily have broken the deadlock. Phinn had a shot deflected over, while Morrison volleyed into the crowd from a good position.

United soon grasped the initiative, however, and Chris Eagles opened the scoring in the 23rd minute, Giggs providing the final pass. Twelve minutes later a perfectly judged through ball from Rooney left the Welshman with just the 'keeper to beat and he did so with a neat flick.

A Rooney double in the second half, the first from the penalty spot after Fletcher was fouled by the 'keeper and the second from a fine solo effort, wrapped up the scoring and, despite the defeat, the Dunfermline support would certainly not have gone home disappointed following a memorable United display.

8 August 2007	**Dunfermline Athletic at East End Park, Dunfermline.**

Attendance: 11,500.

Won: 4–0.

Scorers: Rooney 2, Eagles, Giggs.

Team: Kuszczak, Brown, Pique, Silvestre, Fletcher, Scholes, Hargreaves, Eagles, Giggs, Rooney, Bardsley.

Substitutes: A. Eckersley for Brown, S. Evans for Hargreaves, Eikrem for Giggs.

Despite United being in action at Dunfermline the same night, it was still a very strong line up that entertained the strong Irish fan base, with the Glentoran side more than simply outclassed.

In the opening minutes, despite the likes of Nani and Anderson being the central attraction, it was the relatively unknown Lee Martin who caught the eye and created the opening strike. Having lost the ball to Nixon, he showed his eagerness for the fight by regaining possession before crossing to Campbell, who acrobatically volleyed past Dougherty from close range.

Nine minutes later it was 2–0, with the ball swiftly moving from one end to the other as an Anderson–Nani–Campbell move ended with Evra scoring with a low shot into the bottom right-hand corner.

Nani was now the major threat to the Irish and came close to scoring in the 16th minute before setting up an opportunity for Campbell, but the promising young forward scorned the chance. The Portuguese winger, however, did claim the third goal in the 36th minute, with a rising drive from 25 yards.

The second half failed to produce any further goals, despite the home side fielding an almost fresh 11. Evra, Martin, Anderson and Nani could all have added to United's tally. Glentoran, to their credit, never gave up and Martin did well to clear off his own goalline with 15 minutes remaining, while McManamin failed to make contact with a Halliday cross when ideally placed in front of goal.

8 August 2007	Glentoran at The Oval, Belfast.

Attendance: 14,000.

Won: 3–0.

Scorers: Campbell, Evra, Nani.

Team: Heaton, Simpson, Evra, Vidic, Ferdinand, O'Shea, Nani, Carrick, Campbell, Anderson, Martin.

Substitutes: Gibson for Simpson, Dong for Campbell, Lea for Vidic.

When the announcement was made that Sir Alex Ferguson would be taking his first-team squad to Saudi Arabia to play in a testimonial for Sami Al-Jaber, against Al-Hilal in Riyadh, more than a few eyebrows were raised. Most, however, were lowered when the figure of £1 million was mentioned as being the visitors 'fee'.

Sami had the distinction of having represented Saudi Arabia no fewer than 160 times and he was a veteran of five World Cup Finals, scoring in three of those: a notable feat in itself.

Ronaldo was happy to play to the crowd at every opportunity, delving deep into his box of tricks, and he put United 2–1 in front with a header from a Nani corner in the 32nd minute. This was after recent Manchester City trialist Yasser Al-Qahtani had given the Saudis a shock lead in the 19th minute, followed by a 25th-minute equaliser from Tevez.

Six minutes prior to the interval the crowd within the Bedouin tent-style structure were on their feet. Much to his displeasure, Rio Ferdinand was adjudged to have brought down Al-Jaber and a penalty-kick was awarded, a decision which brought laughter from the United manager seated along the touchline. Had it been given back home in a domestic fixture, it was more than possible that the United boss would not have remained on the correct side of the white line.

From the spot-kick the legendary Saudi made no mistake.

The referee again decided to award the home side a rather dubious penalty, a decision that Wayne Rooney failed to see in the same light as his manager had seen the first. He ran from the opposite end of the pitch to tell the referee about the error of his ways. Al-Jaber refused the opportunity to take the kick, instead handing the ball to teammate Mohammad Al-Shalhoub. To the delight of the crowd, the ball was again struck firmly into the United net, but surprisingly the referee, perhaps shaken by the irate Rooney, ordered a retake, which was blasted wide.

With just over 15 minutes remaining, Bader Al-Kharashi scored with a spectacular overhead kick, which United's third 'keeper of the game, Tom

2008 Tour Ticket.

Inside view of King Fahd Stadium

Heaton, could do little to stop. It was a goal which also proved to be the winner, as a last-minute penalty-kick from 17-year-old debutant substitute Danny Welbeck blazed over.

One of those who made the trip out to Saudi Arabia was Mick Groom and these are his memories of the match: 'Hargreaves, Ronnie and Tevez all looked up for it, but the rest of the squad were out for a stroll in the park. It's not often you see three goalkeepers being used.

'As for the game itself, "This is what football is all about" said one of the happy band of United followers when he found out that it was "males only" at the Al-Hilal fixture, although it was not a sentiment which the females of the Red Army agreed with.

'All in all, however, it was a fantastic trip and a great experience to see the Reds play in Saudi Arabia for the first time.'

21 January 2008	**Al-Hilal at King Fahd Stadium, Saudi Arabia.**

Attendance: 70,000.

Lost: 3–2.

Scorers: Tevez, Ronaldo.

Team: Van der Sar, Simpson, Ferdinand, O'Shea, Evra, Eagles, Fletcher, Anderson, Nani, Ronaldo, Giggs.

Substitutes: Vidic for Ferdinand, Park for Ronaldo, Kuszczak for Van der Sar, Hargreaves for Evra, Heaton for Kuszczak, Welbeck for Anderson, Rooney for Tevez.

Season 2008–09 got underway for the recently crowned European Champions back in the familiar surroundings of Aberdeen, in a match arranged to celebrate the 25th anniversary of the greatest night in the Pittodrie club's history, when they lifted the European Cup-Winners' Cup by defeating Real Madrid 2–1 in Gothenburg.

Outside view of King Fahd Stadium 2008.

United were much too strong for the Scottish side, and the 90 minutes was little more than a training session at times. This may have had something to do with it being their first outing of the summer and only 52 days since the Moscow triumph.

Despite United running the game, it was not until immediately before the half-time whistle that they eventually took the lead. An inch-perfect pass from Carrick split open the Aberdeen defence and, as Rooney attempted to take the ball round goalkeeper Langfield, he tumbled to the ground. The referee immediately pointed to the spot, although no United player had made any appeal for a penalty.

From the spot-kick Michael Carrick sent the goalkeeper the wrong way to give United a 1–0 lead.

Aberdeen had their moments in that opening half, having seen a Mackie close-range effort disallowed for offside and a 20-yard drive from de Visscher going narrowly wide, but they were always going to struggle against a strong United side, with Paul Scholes more than impressive in midfield.

Eagles should have put United further ahead two minutes after the restart, but volleyed an inviting opportunity over the bar from a mere seven yards out. Soon afterwards, Rooney curled a right-footed effort just wide of the Dons' left-hand post and substitute 'keeper Busso did well to fingertip a Giggs header on to the bar.

The closest Aberdeen came to scoring in the second half was in the opening minutes when a curling effort from Smith was pushed away by Amos in the United goal.

With 20 minutes remaining, the result was put beyond any doubt when Rooney scored United's second, Fletcher sending the ball into the Aberdeen area and the England forward rising to head home from seven yards.

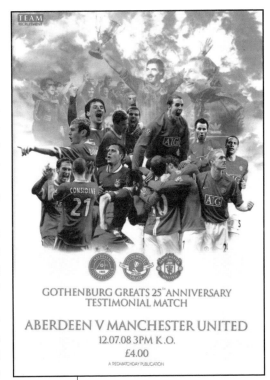

GOTHENBURG GREATS 25TH ANNIVERSARY TESTIMONIAL MATCH

ABERDEEN V MANCHESTER UNITED
12.07.08 3PM K.O.
£4.00
A REDMATCHDAY PUBLICATION

The programme for the match versus Aberdeen, 12 July 2008.

12 July 2008	Aberdeen at Pittodrie.

Attendance: 20,500.

Won: 2–0.

Scorers: Carrick, Rooney.

Team: Amos, Neville, Brown, Vidic, Silvestre, Fletcher, Carrick, Scholes, Martin, Rooney, Giggs.

Substitutes: Eagles for Martin, Simpson for Neville, O'Shea for Vidic, Gibson for Scholes, Evans for Brown, Campbell for Giggs, Woods for Amos, Hewson for Rooney.

Against Kaizer Chiefs, a team that had finished sixth in the South African League, United were far from convincing and it took a Chris Eagles equaliser in the 59th minute to rescue a draw in the Vodacom Challenge match.

The Chiefs had taken the lead in the 37th minute, when Tshabalala had been brought down by Neville, and from the penalty-kick Quartey sent Kuszczak the wrong way. Scholes perhaps should have equalised within minutes, but goalkeeper Khune was equal to the midfielder's effort.

Some slack defending by United could have seen them go behind early on, but they had Kuszczak to thank for keeping them in the game. Rooney came close for United with a free-kick from the edge of the area after Scholes had been brought down, and Vidic headed wide from an Eagles corner.

United were a different side after the break and, had Rooney kept his cool (he had been booked earlier in the game for wildly lashing out at defender after being dispossessed of the ball) and not forced the manager to substitute him, they might well have won.

---

19 July 2008   **Kaizer Chiefs at Newlands Stadium, Cape Town.**

Attendance: 40,000.

Drew: 1—1.

Scorer: Eagles.

Team: Kuszczak, Neville, Vidic, Brown, O'Shea, Fletcher, Scholes, Giggs, Eagles, Tevez, Rooney.

Substitutes: Simpson for Neville, Campbell for Eagles, Gibson for Rooney, Evans for Brown.

Having stuttered to a 1–1 draw in the opening South African fixture, a victory was required to boost the pre-season confidence and also to ensure a further encounter with the Kaizer Chiefs. However, with the opportunity to go head-to-head with their local rivals, the Orlando Pirates were certainly not going to give United an easy ride.

Played in front of a three-quarters full stadium, despite the local media proclaiming that the game would be near to a sell-out, there was certainly no lack of noise from the enthusiastic spectators, as the Pirates gave United a difficult time throughout the 90 minutes.

The visitors were certainly on top in the opening half-hour and could have been three goals in front by the interval. However, they had to be content with only one, with young winger Lee Martin, who had spent a fair amount of his United career out on loan to various clubs, scoring what was to be the only goal of the game in the 23rd minute. Campbell flicked on Wes Brown's header for the 21-year-old winger to shoot low past the 'keeper and into the far corner.

---

22 July 2008   **Orlando Pirates at Absa Stadium, Durban.**

Attendance: 55,000.

Won: 1—0.

Scorer: Martin.

Team: Foster, Brown, Ferdinand, Evans, Silvestre, Eagles, Carrick, Gibson, Martin, Tevez, Campbell.

Substitutes: O' Shea for Silvestre, Scholes for Carrick, Fletcher for Gibson, Simpson for Evans, Rooney for Tevez.

If the previous two fixtures of the South African tour were rather dull, uninspiring affairs, then spectators were certainly given their money's worth in the rematch against the Kaizer Chiefs in Pretoria.

Despite the close attention that he found himself given, the strong-tackling South Africans could not shackle the inspired Wayne Rooney, who scored one and made another in United's 4–0 victory. He was certainly driven close to breaking point and given little protection by the Madagascan referee throughout the game. One swing of the elbow in the 23rd minute almost caught Tinashe, and shortly afterwards Rooney was to find himself on the receiving end of a scything tackle by Valery.

It took a goalline clearance by Vidic to prevent United from going behind, after defender Craig Cathcart failed to clear with a header on the edge of the area.

However, it was United who went in at half-time a goal in front, Giggs scoring with a right-footed volley.

The second half opened with Rooney again on the end of a rash challenge, this time from Quartey, but he was to gain his revenge in the 57th minute when he collected a Simpson pass before slipping the ball past the advancing Khune. This could easily have been his second, as 10 minutes earlier he had hit the side netting after the 'keeper had blocked a shot from Giggs.

Five minutes later it was 3–0, a Rooney pass finding 18-year-old debutant Tom Cleverley, who stroked the ball home with ease.

Another substitute, Fraizer Campbell, added a fourth four minutes from the end.

---

26 July 2008   **Kaizer Chiefs at Loftus Versfeld Stadium, Johannesburg.**

Attendance: 50,000.

Won: 4–0.

Scorers: Giggs, Rooney, Cleverley, Campbell.

Team: Kuszczak, Simpson, Vidic, Cathcart, O'Shea, Fletcher, Carrick, Possebon, Giggs, Rooney, Martin.

Substitutes: Eagles for Martin, Cleverley for Possebon, Gibson for Fletcher, Evans for Vidic, Scholes for Carrick, Tevez for Rooney, Campbell for Giggs.

From South Africa the United party headed for Nigeria, where a dress rehearsal for the possibility of the Premier League's proposed '39th fixture' would be played against Portsmouth.

The first of three meetings with FA Cup winners Portsmouth saw United claim first blood with a 2–1 victory. Both managers made wholesale changes, as both sides had been in action 24 hours earlier and, given the humid conditions, the game was always going to be rather low-key.

With the game only six minutes old, Portsmouth almost found themselves a goal behind. Chasing a ball into the Pompey penalty area, Fraizer Campbell managed to avoid a challenge from goalkeeper James, but then found himself brought down by Johnson. Tevez sent James the wrong way from the spot-kick, but was immediately ordered to retake the kick, as Eagles was adjudged to have moved into the area. From the second attempt Tevez sent his kick crashing against the crossbar.

Eagles and Campbell both had further opportunities to open the scoring for United, the former failing to beat James from a one-on-one midway through the half, while the latter also failed in a similar situation five minutes before the interval.

Six minutes into the second half the United pressure finally paid off, as Eagles made up for his previous lapses when he latched on to a loose ball from 12 yards out that the Portsmouth defenders had failed to clear.

The programme for the Vodacom Challenge 19–26 July 2008.

The 14 United supporters who made the trip to Nigeria, including Mike Dobbin on the far right, to whom this book is dedicated.

Tevez was to make it 2–0 in the 65th minute, running down the right before firing the ball past an unsuspecting James from a tight angle.

It was goal from which Portsmouth were never going to recover, although they claimed a consolation effort in the final minute through Defoe.

Kevin Donald was one of the travelling Red Army who made the trip to Nigeria:

'For the regular supporters who attend these tour matches, the news that United would be playing in Nigeria was welcomed enthusiastically. It's always good to see United play in a new country and Nigeria was also a place that nobody had travelled to before.

'Tickets for these sort of games are hard to come by, so we asked Pat Crerand if he could get or organise 14 tickets for us. Pat is an absolute legend with the supporters and has time for everybody, a nicer man it would be hard to meet. Pat had also been instrumental in organising 17 tickets for us for the game in Saudi Arabia the previous January.

'Again Pat came through with the tickets and again United gave them to us, as they had done in Saudi Arabia, free of charge. I believe David Gill also had a hand in this, thanks David.

Ticket for the match versus Portsmouth, 27 July 2008.

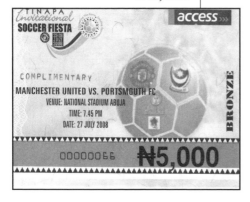

'The stadium at kick-off was barely a third full due to the pricing structure of the tickets, anything from between £20 to £200, which was double the price of the Kano Pillars v Portsmouth game the day before. This was in stark contrast to the Nigerian media reports that the United v Portsmouth match had had one million ticket applications and that 5,000 UK-based supporters would be travelling as well as an extra 5,000 from Ghana!

'I would like to dedicate this game to Michael Dobbin and the 14 Reds who made it to Nigeria and back: Michael Dobbin, Kevin Donald, Phil Holt, Mick Burgess, Paul Webb, Mark Bray, John Paul O'Neill, John Taylor, Erik Van den Polder, Charlie Samuels, Mick Groom, Steve Messer, Dave Chambers, Steve Tsichritzis.'

27 July 2008 — **Portsmouth at Abuja, Nigeria.**

Attendance: 30,000.

Won: 2—1.

Scorers: Eagles, Tevez.

Team: Kuszczak, Neville, Vidic, Evans, Silvestre, Gibson, Carrick, Scholes, Eagles, Tevez, Campbell.

Substitutes: Cathcart for Evans, Giggs for Tevez, O'Shea for Carrick, Possebon for Gibson, Amos for Kuszczak, Cleverley for Eagles.

Many football supporters share the belief that there is little need for testimonial matches in the modern game, as those for whom the fixture has been arranged often have little need for the money that they generate. However, many will donate the majority of the gate receipts to charities.

There are, however, exceptions to the rule, as the 70,000 who flocked to Old Trafford for the visit of Espanyol proved. For here they were celebrating a player who will forever be a United legend and whose flick of the foot, sending the ball into the roof of the net on a balmy Barcelona evening, will be forever etched in the minds of all who witnessed it.

Had his career not been brought to a premature end through injury, Ole Gunnar Solskjaer would have undoubtedly have produced the only thing missing from this particular fixture – goals – as United plodded along against a belligerent Spanish side. The Norwegian was only able to play a cameo role in the proceedings, coming on as a substitute for Tevez.

It was not until eight minutes from the end that the only goal of the game was scored, Ryan Giggs laying off the ball to Fraizer Campbell, who calmly put it past the Spanish 'keeper.

Scholes and Tevez both came close to scoring in the first half, which saw the visitors threaten with two early corners, but it was Nani who should have opened the scoring in the 19th minute, when a Scholes effort rebounded of the post and into his path. It left the Portuguese winger with little more to do than tap it past the 'keeper, but somehow he managed to place his shot wide of the right-hand post.

Solskjaer himself almost signed off with a goal, but the 35-year-old's half-volley was stopped by the Espanyol 'keeper.

One particular incident, a minute before the interval, certainly roused the crowd. A crude tackle from behind by Espanyol captain Jarque on Tevez saw the United man react with a shove and a push to the face. Rather surprisingly, Norwegian referee Hauge booked only the Spaniard.

After the break Vidic missed an inviting opportunity by heading wide, while Solskjaer himself almost signed off with a goal, the 35-year-old's half-volley testing the sometimes redundant Espanyol 'keeper.

The leaflet for the match versus Portsmouth, 27 July 2008.

2 August 2008 — **Rcd Espanyol at Old Trafford.**

Attendance: 68,868.

Won: 1—0.

Scorer: Campbell.

Team: Van der Sar, Simpson, Ferdinand, Vidic, Evra, Gibson, Fletcher, Scholes, Nani, Giggs, Tevez.

Substitutes: Kuszczak for Van der Sar, Brown for Ferdinand, Evans for Vidic, Silvestre for Evra, O'Shea for Gibson, Campbell for Nani, Solskjaer for Tevez.

The programme for the match versus Rcd Espanyol, 2 August 2008.

The programme for the match versus Peterborough, 4 August 2008.

For the second season in a row Sir Alex Ferguson sent a side to London Road in Peterborough, thereby allowing the players of the home side the opportunity to judge themselves against players of a higher calibre.

At the end of the 90 minutes there was a distinct buzz in the air, along with a feeling that something special had been witnessed. The game itself will be forgotten, but the debut performance of Brazilian youngster Rafael Da Silva would certainly stand out, with witnesses predicting a promising future for the fledgling full-back. Over the 90 minutes he showed both notable defensive and attacking flair, and in the second half the crowd were given something of a double helping when his identical twin brother Fabio was introduced into the fray.

Peterborough had competed favourably during the first 45 minutes and could perhaps consider themselves unfortunate to go in at half-time a goal behind, defender Russell Martin chesting a centre from David Gray past his own goalkeeper.

With a number of second-half substitutions the pace altered slightly, but United continued to maintain the early momentum set by the likes of Tevez, Evra and Nani, with Kuszczak having to be on his toes to keep the home side from scoring. However, the game was put beyond Peterborough's reach in the 68th minute, with a goal worthy of winning any game, never mind a pre-season friendly. On the field for a mere 60 seconds, Darron Gibson controlled a pass from Lee Martin, before sending an unstoppable drive past the helpless Posh 'keeper.

4 August 2008	**Peterborough at London Road, Peterborough.**

Attendance: 13,042.

Won: 2—0.

Scorers: Opp. own-goal, Gibson.

Team: Kuszczak, R. Da Silva, Brown, Ferdinand, Evra, Gray, Fletcher, O'Shea, Nani, Tevez, Campbell.

Substitutes: Cathcart for Brown, J. Evans for Ferdinand, F. Da Silva for Evra, Martin for Campbell, Cleverley for Tevez, Zieler for Kuszczak, Gibson for Fletcher, Possebon for Nani.

Seldom can two consecutive home fixtures at Old Trafford have produced such nondescript 90 minutes of football, as the visit of Juventus produced a goalless draw and showed the urgent need for some firepower to join the Red ranks.

Tevez toiled as a lone figure up front, while those in the crowd were treated to a view of the future through the young Brazilians Rafael and Possebon and the home-grown talents of Evans and Gibson.

Injuries made the manager's selection problems easier than normal, but the crowd still wanted to be entertained and there were cries for a United penalty during the early exchanges, when Martin was knocked over by Grygera.

There were few other moments of note, with perhaps only one other scoring effort from a United player coming when a Giggs shot was blocked by a defender. In the second half Tevez pushed a shot wide of the goal, having been prompted by Scholes, with the ball being snatched upon by substitute Rafael. The youngster's pinpoint cross was met by Scholes, but his downward header from six yards bounced over the bar.

The Italians had their moments, with Evra blocking a Del Piero close-range effort, but Van der Sar was little more than a spectator for most of the night and it was clear to the goal-hungry crowd that they were going to go home disappointed.

6 August 2008   **Juventus at Old Trafford.**

Attendance: 69,872.

Drew: 0—0.

Team: Van der Sar, Evra, Ferdinand, Vidic, Brown, Fletcher, Scholes, O'Shea, Martin, Giggs, Tevez.

Substitutes: Rafael for Brown, Gibson for Fletcher, Silvestre for Martin, Possebon for O'Shea, Campbell for Tevez, Evans for Vidic.

By the time you have finished reading this book a further number of friendly fixtures will have been played. Indeed, as I type these final few paragraphs, the pre-season itinerary for the summer of 2009 has just been released, with games in China, Indonesia and Malaysia.

These, and all the previously mentioned fixtures, are akin to a television soap opera, with the regular first-team players normally featuring on a regular basis, but with some lesser known characters making brief appearances. There are also the 'extras', who flit briefly across the screen; those unknown individuals who have enjoyed their 15 minutes of fame and are able to say that they have been part of the biggest club in the world, but who will never be remembered.